# AN INTRODUCTION TO
# MOTIVATION

# THE UNIVERSITY SERIES IN PSYCHOLOGY

*Editor*

DAVID C. MCCLELLAND
*Harvard University*

# AN INTRODUCTION TO
# MOTIVATION

*by*

## JOHN W. ATKINSON

*Professor of Psychology*
*University of Michigan*

# D. VAN NOSTRAND COMPANY, INC.

PRINCETON, NEW JERSEY

TORONTO                    LONDON

NEW YORK

159.4
at 5i

D. VAN NOSTRAND COMPANY, INC.
120 Alexander St., Princeton, New Jersey (*Principal office*)
24 West 40 Street, New York 18, New York

D. VAN NOSTRAND COMPANY, LTD.
358, Kensington High Street, London, W.14, England

D. VAN NOSTRAND COMPANY (Canada), LTD.
25 Hollinger Road, Toronto 16, Canada

Library of Congress Catalog Card No. 64-23961

TO MY PARENTS
MINNIE AND FRANK G. ATKINSON

# Preface

In this book, I attempt to identify the basic concepts of the psychology of motivation. My aim is to present an outline of the central plot and some of the best lines of the central characters in a story that began, as I see it, about seventy-five years ago.

My viewpoint, in telling this story of the study of motivation, is that of a participant observer in the current experimental analysis of human motivation. I believe that teaching a course in the subject is an integral part of the quest for a more adequate conceptual scheme (or theory) than our present knowledge provides. It is an important part of the scientific quest because the initial orientation and attitudes of a generation of students toward the subject matter may serve to help or to hinder the subsequent development of the field.

The book is called "an introduction" because it makes no claim of being exhaustive in its coverage. Many topics in addition to those listed in the table of contents might have been included if the book were an eclectic survey. That it is not. Yet it does cover quite a lot of ground. I have attempted to emphasize what I have found it important to know about the history of the problem of motivation, as it has been studied in the several disparate subfields of psychology, in order to understand the implications of contemporary research on human motivation and to get on with that task.

In writing this introduction to motivation, I have constantly tried to keep in mind two students. One is approaching the study of motivation for the first time. For him, the book is a beginning. The other is a more advanced student who, perhaps, has already taken a course in motivation or several courses in the various subfields having a share of interest in the topic. But this student does not, for whatever reason, have enough organized historical perspective concerning the evolution of thought about the topic to identify the basic issues and to separate the wheat from the chaff in what is currently popular. He does not yet understand why it is so extremely difficult to integrate all or very much of the contemporary literature called motivation in a sensible manner. Or he is skeptical about the topic and doubts (as do some of his mentors) that there is really anything of scientific importance in the psychology of motivation. For him, hopefully, this book provides a new beginning.

The needs of these two students are essentially the same. I have seen one of them in my undergraduate course, the other in my first-year graduate course. Today, they both require guidelines to help them identify the fundamental problems, the basic concepts, the important methods of study, i.e., the central threads which define a field of inquiry and an evolving body of empirical knowledge and theory. The student just beginning his study of motivation may have no professional scientific interest, as does the other fellow, but he does have the capacity for intellectual involvement as he begins to develop an understanding of science in the context of this intrinsically interesting problem.

Perhaps I am sensitive to the general need for identification and clarification of the basic concepts because it was my own need when I began, about eight years ago, to plan this book. I feel it is no less a need today for any psychologist who would hope to make a contribution to the basic knowledge of the subject. The book is designed to stir up thought about the basic concepts of motivation. If it does that, I shall be satisfied.

What are some of the special emphases of the book? First, several critical transitions in thought about the problem of motivation are reviewed. These begin with James' introspective analysis of conscious volition in 1890 and include the subsequent contributions of Freud, Lewin, and Tolman which culminate in a definition of the problem of motivation for an objective science. In order to understand and appreciate current developments, the student of motivation must work through the same transitions in thought about the problem and the method of study that it took psychology itself many years to accomplish.

Second, the book is designed to help the student appreciate how long a time it has taken some psychologists to recognize that the theoretical problem of motivation is separate and distinct from that of learning, the field in which many of them were trained. The focal point of interest in the study of motivation is the task of constructing a useful theoretical conception of how different factors *combine*, at a particular time, to influence the direction, vigor, and persistence of an individual's behavior in a given situation. It requires substantial emphasis of the basic ideas of Kurt Lewin to dispel the traditional misconception fostered by introductory textbooks, in particular, that the study of motivation is restricted to the influence of a certain class of psychological variables called needs, drives, interests, or whatnot. This book considers the question of traditional interest—"What causes behavior?"—and the complicated answers to that question which constitute the available theories of motivation. One of the central themes in the treatment of this important issue is the evolution in thought within the stimulus-response analysis of behavior from the time of Thorndike and Pavlov to the time of Hull and the most recent formulation of Spence.

Third, it is important for students to realize that despite the plethora of motivational language in the psychological literature (wants, interests, attitudes, needs, values, drives, etc.), only two different theories of motivation, i.e., conceptions of the contemporaneous determinants of action, have been spelled out with any degree of clarity. One is the familiar "Drive × Habit" theory which has dominated thought for a quarter of a century. The other, less familiar for that reason, was formulated even earlier by Tolman and Lewin and has been revived in the recent work of decision theorists among others. I refer to this other theory, which has been beclouded by the use of different terminology in different contexts, as the "Expectancy × Value" theory. It is a conception of motivation which emphasizes the determinative role of expectation (or expectancy) of the consequences of action.

Fourth, it is important for students to know about the traditional isolation of what Cronbach (1957) has called "the two disciplines of scientific psychology," viz., the study of individual differences and the study of basic behavioral processes. Even more important is to recognize that current theoretically oriented research on effects of individual differences in anxiety (the "Drive × Habit" theory) and achievement motivation (the "Expectancy × Value" theory) represents a substantial step toward conceptual integration of these two disciplines in the study of human motivation.

Finally, I have found it worthwhile to consider the fundamental difference in viewpoint among psychologists concerning the need to explain behavioral phenomena in terms of neurophysiological mechanism, on the one hand, or in terms of a mathematical conceptual scheme, on the other. These different orientations have produced fundamentally different disciplines for study of motivation. Because of the priority given the problem of human motivation and the obvious need today for substantial background in neurophysiology to pursue the *physiological* psychology of motivation with much profit, this introduction to motivation is aphysiological in its orientation. It does, however, trace the influence of physiological preconceptions on the development of the *psychology* of motivation.

In the treatment of contemporary approaches to motivation, I have been selective in order to develop the major themes established in earlier chapters of the book and in order to have an opportunity to present my own theoretical notions. When using the book in a more advanced course, I shall augment the text with lectures or readings dealing with current work on curiosity, frustration, incentive, and Mowrer's latest theorizing in the discussion of Chapter 7 on evolution of *S-R* Behavior Theory, and I shall find a place for cognitive dissonance somewhere near the end. These are the relatively new topics that I shall begin to develop more fully in my lectures now that the central threads of the old ones are available for reading.

In summary, the first eight chapters of this book represent an integration of what I have hoped my own students would get from my lectures and the list of core readings assigned in fifteen years of teaching. The last two chapters present the theoretical conception of motivation evolved in my own research during this period and some directives for future study which represent, I believe, a call for another important transition in thought about the problem which psychology must accomplish if it is to get on with its task of developing a really adequate theory of motivation. I hope that this survey of the historical evolution of basic concepts of motivation—the remembrance of things past—will enable the student to confront the vast contemporary literature on the topic with a greater degree of conceptual sophistication and perspective than he is likely to get from immediate contact with it.

## ACKNOWLEDGEMENTS
I want to express my gratitude to the John Simon Guggenheim Foundation for the award of a fellow-

ship during a sabbatical year, 1960–1961, to undertake this historical study of motivation. In addition to providing time for reading, thought, and the original draft of most of the book, their support made it possible for me to profit from sustained interaction with my Michigan colleague, Professor Dorwin Cartwright, then a Fellow at the Center for Advanced Study in the Behavioral Sciences, the locus of our collaborative work. In addition to improving my understanding and presentation of Lewin's Field Theory, these conversations considered the deficiencies of contemporary theories of motivation and bore the fruit of the basic ideas presented in the final section of Chapter 10, which is an expansion of an earlier collaborative summary statement (Atkinson and Cartwright, 1964).

Continuation of work on this book during the summers of 1961–1963 was supported in part by unrestricted grants in aid of my research from the Ford Foundation and the General Electric Foundation for which I am indeed grateful. A major part of the research reported in Chapter 9 was conducted during the period of a five-year project on personality dynamics supported by the Ford Foundation.

I want to express my appreciation of help offered by another Michigan colleague, Professor J. David Birch, from whom I have learned more in collaborative teaching and research than I can adequately document concerning the fundamental problems to be surmounted in the construction of an adequate theory of motivation.

The preparation of the manuscript and final stages of production of the book were made easier by the clerical and secretarial assistance at various times of Matina Horner, Patricia Porcello, Lucille Kroutel, Marianna Weiner, Georgia Mallon, and Frances Holland; and additional assistance in proof-reading by Philip Newman, Marvin Brown, and James Baerwaldt. The book could not have been finished without the friendly forbearance of my wife, Mary Jane. I greatly appreciate her help.

Permission to reprint selections from books or journals was kindly granted by authors and the following publishers: *American Journal of Psychology*, American Psychological Association, American Sociological Association, Annual Reviews, Inc., Appleton-Century-Crofts, Basic Books, Inc., Cambridge University Press, Charles Scribner's Sons, Clarendon Press, Columbia University Press, Duke University Press, George Allen & Unwin Ltd., Harper & Row, Publishers, Hogarth Press Ltd., Holt, Rinehart and Winston, Inc., John Wiley & Sons, Inc., *Journal of Conflict Resolution*, *Journal of Philosophy*, Liveright Publishing Corporation, McGraw-Hill Book Company, Inc., *Mental Hygiene*, Methuen & Co. Ltd., National Association of Mental Health, Oxford University Press, Psychoanalytic Quarterly, *Psychological Record*, Ronald Press Company, *Saturday Review*, University of California Press, University of Nebraska Press, W. W. Norton & Company, Inc., and Yale University Press.

J. W. A.

*Ann Arbor, Michigan*
*May, 1964*

# Contents

# CHAPTER 1

# Introduction:
# The Viewpoint
# of
# Common Sense

*". . . science must create its own language, its own concepts, for its own use. Scientific concepts often begin with those used in ordinary language for the affairs of everyday life, but they develop quite differently. They are transformed and lose the ambiguity associated with them in ordinary language, gaining in rigorousness so that they may be applied to scientific thought"* (Einstein and Infeld, 1951, p. 14).*

THE MEANING OF "MOTIVATION"

The study of motivation has to do with analysis of the various factors which incite and direct an individual's actions. A useful general description of the problem of motivation is offered by the editor of an annual symposium that was instituted ten years ago to keep workers in the field abreast of rapid developments in current research. This description of the problem will serve to introduce the topic of the book: "how behavior gets started, is energized, is sustained, is directed, is stopped, and what kind of subjective reaction is present in the organism while all this is going on" (Jones, 1955).

A more penetrating discussion of the meaning of the term "motivation" will be deferred. Only after the historical antecedents of contemporary ideas have been presented and some of the issues of current interest explored can we fully appreciate why the meaning of "motivation" has been a controversial subject among psychologists for some time. A premature acquaintance with the substance of contemporary discussion about this word might create the mistaken impression that some psychologists wish to abdicate responsibility for the solution of many vitally important questions having to do with the springs of action, the apparent goal-directedness of behavior, frustration, and the resolution of conflict. To avoid these misapprehensions, we shall refer to the description of the broad problem of motivation that has been stated as a "working definition" of the subject of this book.

A few further distinctions, however, will help to focus attention on the problem that we are investigating. In the history of experimental psychology,

* Reprinted from *The Evolution of Physics* by Albert Einstein and L. Infeld, by permission of the Estate of Albert Einstein.

the problem of motivation and the problem of learning—that is, how behavior changes as a result of training and practice—have been intimately linked. Many important motivational concepts have arisen originally as adjuncts of the analysis of how learning occurs in lower animals. As a result, some students of psychology now find it difficult to separate the two problems because the treatment of one so often involves reference to the other. This is an unfortunate stumbling block. The two problems must be distinguished at the outset if contributions to the study of motivation from outside the field of animal learning are to be fully understood and appreciated.

The study of learning is essentially *historical* in orientation. When the process of learning is examined, the primary consideration is to account for changes in an individual's tendency to behave in a certain way as a direct consequence of past experience. The study of motivation, in contrast, is essentially *ahistorical* in orientation. The primary interest in the study of motivation is to identify and to understand the effects of all of the important *contemporaneous influences* which determine the direction of action, its vigor, and its persistence. To be sure, dispositions to behave in certain ways which represent the *effects* of prior experience are factors to be taken into account when motivation is the subject of study. The effect of prior experience, however, is only one of a number of different kinds of factors to be considered when the main interest is to understand the *combined* effect of all the immediate influences which incite and direct behavior.

The study of motivation may also be distinguished from the study of perception and its primary emphasis. When perception is studied, the problem of central interest is to show how the characteristics of a physical stimulus together with other factors within the individual at the time influence what is seen, heard, or felt. *What* an individual perceives in a given situation is another of the factors to be considered in the study of motivation; but the study of motivation does not include analysis of the perceptual process *per se*.

In the division of labor and scientific interest which characterizes contemporary psychology, the study of motivation takes for granted *that* dispositions to behave in certain ways can be changed by practice, but it does not include as part of its subject matter an analysis of *how* learning occurs. The study of motivation also takes for granted *that* the individual is sensitive to cues in his immediate environment, but it does not include analysis of *how* perception occurs. Rather, the study of motivation is concerned with *how* what has been learned in the past and *how* what is momentarily perceived by the individual combine with still other factors to influence the direction, vigor, and persistence of his behavior on any particular occasion.

The treatment of the problem of motivation by specialists who have made some facet of it their special concern has changed quite dramatically since the end of the 19th century. The fairly rapid evolution of ideas and techniques of study is one source of present confusion surrounding the meaning of the term "motivation." Another source of confusion is the fact that the problem of motivation falls at the crossroads of so many different subfields within psychology, each of which has invented a technical language to treat its own problem. The student who undertakes the study of motivation must be prepared to encounter a number of different ways of thinking about the problem, advanced by psychologists who are primarily interested in very different phenomena. He must anticipate the further complication that sometimes different terms are introduced to designate essentially the same concept.

MAJOR THEMES OF THE BOOK

This book is organized to provide some guidelines for the development of historical perspective concerning the treatment of motivation since the end of the 19th century. Except for a few more general historical references, the introspective analysis of volition undertaken by William James (1890) will be taken as a point of departure in the next chapter. The subsequent chapters are designed to develop several major themes rather than to provide an exhaustive listing and summary of studies of motivation. First among these themes is the attempt to show how definition of the problem of motivation has changed as psychology, in its own evolution as an experimental science of behavior, has moved from the fund of prescientific, intuitive wisdom we call "common sense" through several stages of increased sophistication in method of study. Second is a study of the development of different conceptions of motivation in disparate fields of study and an attempt to show that, despite many differences in terminology, a convergence of basic concepts is the most evident trend in contemporary psychology. Third is an attempt to convey something of the spirit of science in the making, particularly the role of theoretical concepts, and the tentative nature of the conceptual schemes which guide the development of a science. Fourth is an emphasis, in later chapters, of the steps now being taken within the psychology of motivation to bring about an integration of knowledge about how individuals differ in personality and about the basic process of motivation.

Since our plan to study the evolution of ideas concerning motivation necessarily involves us almost immediately in the development of psychology as an experimental science of behavior, some introductory comments about the general function of science may serve as a useful foundation.

## THE TASK OF SCIENCE

Ordinarily a student who approaches concentrated study of some special topic like motivation has already learned a good deal about the nature of science—the importance of objectivity in observation and rigor in measurement to establish facts, the relationship of observation and experiment to the initial construction and later test of theory, etc. It is not uncommon, however, for the most obvious function of science in human affairs to escape notice as one begins to master the so-called "logic of science." The ultimate task of science, no matter what the subject of study, is to improve common sense. This is accomplished by creating new concepts, new ways of thinking about the subject of interest, whatever it is, that are more useful than the prescientific fund of wisdom man has developed through personal experience and intuition. The psychology of motivation is no exception. The goal of this field of scientific inquiry is to develop concepts which account for the direction, vigor, and persistence of an individual's behavior that are more useful than, for example, the vague concept of "motive" which is part of the fund of intuitive wisdom we so often refer to as "common sense."

Common sense regards a "motive" as the factor which explains the direction, vigor, and persistence of an individual's actions. This concept is defined in any standard dictionary. So are all the other concepts which people habitually use to explain their own actions to themselves and to each other. A motive, as defined by habitual usage, is "something (as a need or desire) that causes a person to act" (Webster's Seventh New Collegiate Dictionary, 1963). We may consider this the central concept in the prescientific (common sense) explanation of how action is instigated and directed.

To illustrate how the very technical concepts and schemes of science, after years of empirical exploration of the subject with repeated test and confirmation of theoretical ideas, gradually replace old, intuitive notions in "common sense," we need only consider an example from the mature natural sciences. Let us consider just one example from chemistry—the change in common sense concerning the nature of matter. Most of us have become so familiar with the way of thinking about the physical world (i.e., the conceptual scheme) which has grown out of several hundred years of scientific study in the natural sciences that it is difficult to realize the extent of change in common sense since ancient times concerning the ultimate constituents of all matter. We no longer hold that earth, air, fire, and water are the basic constituents of all the stuff which occupies the universe. It never occurs to us to think in these terms. The intelligent, ancient Greek, however, felt very knowledgeable thinking about the problem of matter in these terms. Today, any adult with at least high school education, when asked about the ultimate constituents of matter, will make some reference to a list of basic elements: oxygen, hydrogen, calcium, and so on. The youngster who has already been exposed to television presentations of models of the structure of the atom, which represent the most recent conceptual developments in nuclear physics, might be expected to give an even more sophisticated answer than his parents to the question, "What is matter?"

If we turn to the storehouse of conventional conceptions, a dictionary, we find ample testimony of the improvement of common sense regarding the basic constituents of matter. The initial definition of the term "element" is: "One of the four substances (as air, water, fire, or earth) *formerly believed* to compose the physical universe" (Webster's Seventh New Collegiate Dictionary, 1963). Then, the concept of modern chemistry is given: "Any of more than 100 fundamental substances that consist of atoms of only one kind and that singly or in combination constitute all matter." Following this definition of an element are listed the names, technical symbols, atomic numbers, and atomic weights of all known chemical elements. We hardly need to be reminded that the conceptual scheme of modern chemistry, that is, *the way of thinking about* the composition of substances and the transformations which they undergo, is vastly *more useful* than the way of thinking about the same phenomena which was "common sense" among the ancients. *It is the search for a more useful conceptual scheme which is the central characteristic of basic science in any field of study.*

Today, "common sense" concerning motivation is obviously more akin to the stage of earth, air, fire, and water than to the refined conceptual schemes of modern chemistry or physics. Even though much progress has been made in the empirical study of motivation, psychology still searches for a set of concepts which will win universal assent among research workers and then, ultimately, replace the old intuitive conception in common usage. Contemporary psychology is more accurately characterized by reference to its searching analysis of all aspects of the problem of motivation and by the variety of new insights and new concepts which have been proposed, which now guide empirical research, than by the attainment of any single conceptual scheme, or theory of motivation, about which there is universal agreement.

### THE TASK OF STUDENTS OF MOTIVATION

Our task as students of motivation is not simply to learn a new set of concepts and related principles and then to study their application to many different circumstances as we might, for example, in one of the well-developed subfields of natural science. Our task is more difficult than that and, consequently, intrinsically more interesting. In a very real sense, to study motivation at all we must become actively involved in the search for a more useful theory of motivation than the fund of wisdom that is part of our cultural heritage. The student of motivation must first develop some perspective concerning the contributions and advances that have been made in several different fields of study which have claimed an interest in the problem during the past 60 or 70 years. At the same time, he must begin to sharpen his wits to detect the not immediately obvious limitations in some apparently promising and exciting approaches to the problem and in some of the more pretentious concepts that have been advanced. To participate in science "on the move," he must quickly develop some useful criteria for evaluation of evidence. He must advance his understanding of the nature of the dialogue between experiment and theory which characterizes the initial stage of the search for more adequate concepts and the later stages of test and refinement of any promising conceptual scheme. But he must also learn to balance his critical judgment with an appreciation of the importance in science of creative speculative ideas—particularly in the formative years or when progress is clearly bogged down. At the same time, he must guard against becoming wedded to exciting speculative

ideas that show no promise of leading on to further empirical analysis of the problem and new factual discoveries. This is quite a tall order, and for that reason the study of motivation is an unusual challenge.

Throughout our consideration of the problem of motivation, let us not lose sight of the goal of the whole enterprise: to develop a conceptual scheme, or theory—*that is, a way of thinking about the problem of motivation*—which will explain, more adequately than conventional wisdom, what accounts for the direction, vigor, and persistence of an individual's actions. Perhaps a good way to begin is by taking stock of some conventional ideas about the immediate causes of behavior—the common sense of motivation.

## THE COMMON SENSE OF MOTIVATION

Suppose you are asked this simple question, "Why are you reading this book?" The question focuses on the direction of your behavior. You have obviously chosen to do this instead of something else. Why?

Your immediate answer will provide some insight concerning the common-sense theory of motivation, the one we all employ in everyday discourse. It will probably contain the words "want," "wish," or "desire." For example, you might say, "I want to complete the reading assignment." You are doing what you are doing because you *want to*. Or, you might say, "I wish to learn something about motivation." You are, in other words, reading because you wish to attain an objective (knowledge of motivation) and what you are doing is obviously the means to that end.

Let us stop to consider the meaning of these words: "want," "wish," "desire," and other related terms which refer to the conscious experience of motivation. We could explore the conventional wisdom about motivation by spending an hour or so following the interlocking definitions of these and closely related terms in any standard dictionary. We shall not, of course, give the problem that much time, although it is an interesting and recommended exercise. When we do this, we find, for example, that the word, *want*, means: "to be without, to lack, to suffer or feel the need of, to desire; wish; long for." *Desire* means: "a longing; a craving; an expressed wish; a request; to long for; covet; to express a wish for." *Wish* means: "to long for; to crave; to desire."

We are instructed that the three terms are ordinarily used somewhat differently. *Want* is most frequently used to suggest the lack of. *Desire* emphasizes the strength or ardor of feeling. (We recognize this as the term habitually employed by football coaches to characterize a good team: "They have *desire*.") A *wish* often refers to the unattainable ("When you wish upon a star").

Let us inquire further as to the meaning of "*to long for*" and "*crave*." We find a series of near equivalents: *long, yearn, hanker. Long* expresses strong desire or earnest wish. *Yearn* (chiefly elevated or poetical, we are told) implies eager or restless, often tender, longing. *Hanker* (chiefly colloquial or familiar) suggests the uneasiness; *craving*, the urgency, of *appetite. Appetite* is "an inherent or habitual desire or propensity for personal gratification, either of body or mind; craving." And *gratification*, we find, means "a source of satisfaction or pleasure."

Your answer to the initial question, "Why are you reading this book?" might have contained the words *like* or *dislike* instead of *want* or *wish* without, it turns out, much difference in meaning. For example, "I am reading this book because I *like* psychology." Or perhaps, "I *dislike* just sitting around doing nothing, so I picked up this book." *Like* means to choose; to feel inclined; to be attracted towards; to have a liking for; to wish for; to enjoy. *Dislike* means a feeling of aversion for something uncongenial or offensive; repugnance; distaste. *Offensive* means "causing displeasure or resentment." But what is the feeling of aversion? *Aversion* is the act of turning away; a state of mind in which attention to an object is coupled with dislike of it and the desire of turning from it; dislike; repugnance. So *like* means to be attracted towards, and *dislike* means to have a feeling of aversion and a desire of turning away.

Clearly suggested by this web of interlocking meanings is the following familiar conception: We like, want, or desire what is a personal gratification, that is, a source of satisfaction or pleasure. This we are attracted to, seek, choose, and enjoy. On the other hand, we dislike and want or desire to turn away from and avert what is offensive, causing displeasure and resentment. The origin of our impulses *to do* this or that, whether called a want, a wish, a desire (or even a longing, yearning, hankering, or craving) are all more generally considered motives— that is, that *within* an individual rather than *without* which incites him to action. In fact, the word "motivate" means "to provide with a motive; to impell;

incite," so we know we are dealing with the topic of interest.

We continue with our analysis of the common sense of motivation. An *action*, we know, is normally influenced by an *intention*. An *intention*, as commonly defined, is a determination to act in a certain way or to do a certain thing. The family of words closely tied to *intention* includes: *purpose, design, aim, object, end.* We find (still perusing our dictionary) that their meanings all have in common the notion that behavior is directed to the attainment of some conscious end, objective, or goal. This end is normally satisfaction or the aversion of some displeasure. But when we press for the meaning of a satisfaction, specifically, *to satisfy*, we find that we have completed a circle! *To satisfy* means to fill up the measure of a person's want, hence to gratify fully the desire of, to make content. Common sense begins its conception of motivation with a want and ends with satisfaction defined as the gratification of a want! It is not quite clear to us, nor was it to William James, who in 1890 pursued an introspective analysis of voluntary action much farther than we have (see Chapter II), whether our wants and desires are determined by the pleasantness of their objects, or whether the experience of pleasure is completely dependent upon the prior presence of an already urgent want which is then satisfied, yielding pleasure.

Perhaps we have gone far enough to catch the flavor of common sense concerning motivation and also some of its ambiguities. Were we to pursue our dictionary search farther, we could arrive at a more complete conception in which the words *want, decide,* and *act* might be the key terms. The individual experiences a *want*. He must then *decide* upon some course of action. Then he *acts*. Sometimes the decision is easy. For example, if a hungry man is confronted with choice between a plate of worms or a plate of spaghetti, it is a very simple matter for him to decide on the appropriate course of action. But sometimes choice is more difficult. Even now, you may be confronted with a friend's tempting invitation to join him for a movie. To go, or not to go, that is the question! Undoubtedly, if it promises to be a good movie, the anticipated satisfaction of an interesting two hours exceeds that of continued effort with these ponderously worded pages. But wait! There is, perhaps, a fleeting thought of being unprepared for tomorrow's class discussion of this material, perhaps even a quiz! The decision, now delayed by conflict, is not easy to make. Some kind of mental calculus is required to weigh the potential satisfactions and dissatisfactions, considering first one and then the other course of action. Or at least it would appear so. For some, at least, the movie may lose out. Our common-sense conception of motivation and related phenomena takes account of the feeling of frustration and irritation that usually accompanies the thwarting of desire. In this case, there may be irritation and regret at having to continue studying instead of going to the movie.

This is the stuff of which the conventional wisdom —the common sense of motivation—is made. The concepts of common sense have to do with satisfactions and dissatisfactions, with wants that lead to actions, with decisions that are arrived at concerning the appropriateness of alternative actions, with conflict of interest, with feelings of frustration and feelings of gratification—all of which constantly fill our daily conscious experience.

## SOME QUESTIONS FOR SCIENTIFIC STUDY OF MOTIVATION

Within the framework of conventional ideas concerning motivation, we may list, in a preliminary way, some of the questions that scientific study of motivation ought to deal with and even identify some of the factors that we should expect to find related to motivation. Let us consider some common everyday wants that most people, at one time or another, are likely to experience. We might list a few: want to eat; want to drink; want to succeed; want to get away by myself for a while; want people to like me; want people to do what I say; want to kiss someone. We can easily substitute the word *like* in place of the word *want* in these examples with no distortion: like to eat; like to drink; like to succeed; etc.

There are also many different wants that have to do with averting unpleasantness: want the headache to go away; want to avoid having an automobile accident; want to get inside when it rains; want the dust to settle; want the humidity to drop; want to avoid disapproval of friends; want to avoid making a fool of myself; want to avoid failing a test; and so forth. In these examples, we can substitute the term *dislike* and not distort the meaning: dislike headaches; dislike having an automobile accident; dislike getting wet in the rain; dislike the reproaches of friends; etc.

It is clear that there are many different potential objects of desire. Many different kinds of things are liked for the satisfaction they apparently provide; and many different kinds of things are disliked for their apparent inherent unpleasantness. One task for a psychology of motivation might be to provide *a useful scheme for classification* of specific wants that appear to have much in common.

Let us, for the sake of further analysis, consider the desire to eat and the desire to succeed, two important "motives" which every individual may have experienced at one time or another. We note that each of these is sometimes very urgent and sometimes hardly present at all. The desire to eat, which we call hunger, is usually much stronger a number of hours after the last meal than immediately after eating. The desire to succeed is certainly heightened when one finds himself challenged by some competitive activity like an examination or a tennis match.

Why is the desire to eat stronger after one has gone without food for some time? It is now part of common knowledge (because of advances in physiology) that food provides energy for bodily activity. After a period of time in which organic functions have continued and more or less activity has been undertaken, the fuel is used up and the tissues of the body are in need of renewed supply. Common sense acknowledges that the strength of certain desires, for example, for food or for water, are related to changes in *internal physiological conditions*.

Why should the desire to succeed be stronger when an individual finds himself in the midst of some competitive activity? Or why should the desire to eat be stronger after one has entered a restaurant and sniffed the aroma of well-cooked steaks at another table than a moment before while still on the street? In both cases, factors in the immediate environment influence the strength of motivation. We need a conceptual scheme which clarifies *the nature of immediate environmental influences on motivation*.

Why are some foods preferred to others? Why are some very attractive, others only moderately so, and still others hardly attractive at all, even though eating any of them will ultimately still the craving for food which we call hunger? Similarly, why should the competitive urge be sharpened by a good opponent in a tennis or golf match? Why should there be a stronger desire to win and greater satisfaction in the victory than when playing with someone—a child, for example—who is easily defeated? Different goals and activities seem capable of satisfying the same general desire (e.g., to eat or to succeed), but some are obviously more preferred than others. Some provide more of an incentive to the individual. Certainly the psychology of motivation should concern itself with the *relative attractiveness of specific goals* which might satisfy the same general desire. It should treat *the matter of incentives*.

Finally, why do some persons seem to have a greater appetite than others? Why do they seem to enjoy eating more than other people? It is a common observation that even when the number of hours since the last meal has been the same for two individuals and attractive food is presented, one will eat with great relish and lip-smacking enjoyment, the other will pick at his meal and hardly show any sign of enjoyment. Or in a competitive game, some individuals seem particularly desirous of winning; they seem to take great pride in their accomplishments. Others seem only moderately interested, even though the two seem equally skillful and should be equally challenged by the same opponent. There can be little question that individuals differ greatly in the kinds of things they become motivated for and in the strength of particular motives. There are, in other words, important *individual differences in motivation* to be considered and understood.

Given this brief excursion into the common sense of motivation, we may list some of the various topics we expect a study of motivation to include: (a) consideration of the conscious experience of desire, or want; (b) analysis of a person's behavior which is directed towards things he apparently likes or wants and away from things he apparently dislikes or wants to avoid; (c) consideration of those factors, both internal and external, that influence the strength of desire and subsequently the behavior of a person with respect to the liked or disliked object; (d) the fact that individuals seem to differ in the strength of their desire and their tendency to seek certain things and to avoid others.

Common sense identifies in a very general way the interrelated questions which have captured the attention of one or another group of psychologists. For example, psychologists who are mainly concerned with measurement of individual differences have developed techniques for assessing the strength of desire and preference for many different kinds of things. Experimental psychologists have been concerned with controlling the internal and external factors that influence what common sense considers the strength of desire in order to investigate the effect of variations in these motivating influences on behavior. Much of their research has been accomplished with lower animals. Clinical psychologists, on the other hand, have been mainly concerned with the task of trying to understand why individuals differ in the kind and strength of their motives through retrospective analysis of their past experiences. And a number of theorists have proposed conceptual schemes to explain how these various factors are interrelated.

Although we have stayed pretty much within the framework of conventional wisdom and language in our introductory consideration of factors which should influence the strength of conscious desire, we have obviously made some use of the knowledge that has already been gained through empirical study of motivation to guide the preliminary discussion. We have used the knowledge gained in various approaches to motivation to phrase questions that can be given, at best, ambiguous answers in the common-sense language. We have in this way identified some of the problems to be dealt with more thoroughly in later chapters, and in the process, we have outlined what common sense leads us to expect the study of motivation to be about.

## SOME HISTORICAL BACKGROUND

### THE GAP BETWEEN COMMON SENSE AND SCIENTIFIC ORIENTATION

Even without prior knowledge of the current status of the psychology of motivation, the reader will guess that there is a very substantial gap between the type of analysis we have just undertaken in terms of the conventional categories of thought concerning the experience of motivation and the type of analysis which characterizes contemporary scientific study of essentially the same questions. To begin to bridge this gap, we must appreciate the change in attitude concerning the legitimacy of making human motivation and behavior the subject of empirical scientific study. The attitude of the modern era is certainly different from the attitude of earlier periods of human history. We may call to mind how the important changes in attitude and orientation regarding questions of human behavior reflect the impact of the theory of evolution of species advanced by Charles Darwin in 1859. Subsequent chapters will treat the several stages of increased scientific sophistication regarding questions of motivation within psychology more thoroughly; here, we merely recall the important turning point—Darwin's theory of evolution.

### THE IMPORTANCE OF DARWIN

When scientific study of human motivation was receiving its first important impetus late in the 19th century in Sigmund Freud's pioneering investigations, the common-sense conception of motivation was undoubtedly less sophisticated than our introductory analysis has made it seem. For many centuries before Darwin, it had been held that men and animals were qualitatively different. Men were considered rational; animals were believed to be guided by instinct and other irrational forces. Man was obviously capable of thought; but animals, it was believed, were not. Man was capable of conscious deliberation and voluntary, free choice. The behavior of animals, on the other hand, was considered automatic, machine-like, and involuntary. Above all, man's will, unlike that of animals, was not commonly believed to be caught up in the causal nexus of natural events. Man was considered both mind (or spirit) and body, and his distinctive mental characteristic—reason—was what enabled him to transcend and control the irrational emotional tendencies which clearly reigned unchecked in the qualitatively different domain of animal behavior.

For many centuries (see, for example, Plato's *Protagoras*), thoughtful consideration of the basis of human choice had advanced the popular doctrine of hedonism, the doctrine that voluntary behavior is guided by the pursuit of pleasure and the avoidance of pain. Even economic theorists of the 19th century had taken the view that *rational* decisions in the market place were those which carefully considered the potential satisfactions (utility) and dissatisfactions (disutility) in alternative courses of action and which did, in fact, maximize utility. In later chapters we shall discover a rebirth of interest in the concept of utility.

In the middle of the 19th century, Darwin presented a convincing explanation of how man had evolved from lower forms of animal life and substantial evidence to support his view. The theory of evolution shattered the qualitative distinction between man and animal that had been accepted by common sense for centuries. It stands as one of the great achievements of science and as the prelude to scientific study of the behavior of organisms.

Darwin argued that from the beginning of life on earth there has been a constant struggle for survival among living organisms. Within each species, there are great individual variations (i.e., individual differences) in genetic characteristics. By sheer accident of fortunate native endowment, some members of the species are much better prepared than others to face the survival problem which is posed for them by the particular environment into which they are born. The long-haired animal born during one of the great glacial periods has a much greater chance than a short-haired animal. Those favorably endowed are more likely to survive. The environment, by virtue of the survival problem it presents, *selects* from among the members of a particular species those which will be most healthy and long-lived and hence more likely to reproduce themselves in greater numbers in the succeeding generation. This, in brief, is the principle of natural selection, which, operating for millions of years, has produced gradual changes in the dominant characteristics of particular species and an evolution from very simple to more complex forms of animal life.

THREE IMPLICATIONS OF DARWIN'S
THEORY OF EVOLUTION

Darwin's conception of the evolutionary process, sustained by the observations and experiments of biologists since his time, provides the impetus for scientific study of the adaptive behavior of both animals and men. Three important implications of Darwin's conception are reflected in the viewpoints taken in psychological investigations which began late in the 19th century. Each of these three courses of psychological inquiry, explicitly influenced by Darwin's ideas, has dealt with one or another aspect of the broad problem of motivation. We may summarize them:

1. If men and animals are not qualitatively different, if, instead, man is now to be viewed as the highest form of animal life, then it follows that qualities previously attributed only to man, like the capacity for intelligent behavior (reason), must also be present, but probably to a lesser extent, in lower animals. This hypothesis guided the initial empirical investigations of animal behavior, the beginning of comparative animal psychology (1890–1900). The earliest studies of animal behavior searched for evidence of intelligent behavior in animals. Their chief concern was the matter of comparative intelligence in different species. Very soon, however, the analysis of problem-solving behavior in animals gave way to a systematic experimental analysis of the broader problem of how animals learn to adjust to their environment. From the time of Edward L. Thorndike's classic experiments on how cats learn how to get out of puzzle boxes (1898), the study of animal intelligence, at least in American laboratories, has been virtually equated with the study of learning and adjustive behavior.

2. If men and animals are not qualitatively differ-

ent, but instead represent different points on a continuum of increasing complexity (the phylogenetic scale), then the instinctive, irrational, and automatic tendencies formally attributed to animals should also play a vital role in human behavior. Sigmund Freud's early discoveries (1890–1900) of the importance of irrational, unconscious influences on human behavior; the development of psychoanalytic theory, which argues the instinctive origins of these impulses; and the central importance of instinctive and emotional factors in the conceptions of human personality advanced by McDougall, Freud, and other theorists of the early 20th century represent an elaboration of this second implication of Darwin's theory.

3. The enthusiastic interest in the problem of individual differences and the development of tests of individual differences, which also began within psychology during the late 19th century and which soon yielded the practically useful intelligence test, follows naturally from another of Darwin's major assumptions: that there are individual variations in the characteristics which contribute to the survival. Only later, much later, did the "mental test movement," as this subfield of psychology has been called, turn from intelligence, abilities, and aptitude to the matter of measuring individual differences in interests and preferences which represent individual differences in motivation.

THE STUDY OF MOTIVATION WITHIN PSYCHOLOGY

Each of these three fields of interest, as well as some others not yet mentioned, has come upon some aspect of the broad problem of motivation, has developed methods for investigating it, and has advanced concepts considered appropriate for the particular issues that have arisen. Those psychologists whose special interest is to develop and refine suitable objective tests of individual differences for use in the solution of important, practical problems like vocational guidance or personnel selection in industry have directed their major attention to the task of constructing suitable tests of interests and attitudes. To them, the term "motivation" refers to what is measured by these tests. The conception of motivation seems essentially that of common sense. The measurement of individual differences in motivation is conceived as the discovery of how individuals differ in what they like and dislike.

On the other hand, for the clinical psychologist whose special concern is to help people who are in need of counseling or who are emotionally disturbed, the term "motivation" has come to refer—as it did

for Freud, whose lead they follow—to the whole complex of conflicted tendencies within the person, some of which may be entirely unconscious. Particular kinds of conflict are viewed as the major source of emotional distress, and neurotic symptoms are considered the manifestations or resolutions of unconscious conflict. Using techniques of study which have evolved out of Freud's early explorations and clinical practice since then, these workers emphasize the unconscious determinants of thought and action. Their conception of motivation is certainly a great departure from what we have referred to as the common sense of motivation.

Still another group of contemporary psychologists think about the problem of motivation differently. Among the experimental psychologists who have followed in the tradition of Thorndike, seeking the basic principles of behavior through systematic experimental study of the behavior of lower animals, the term "motivation" refers to various states of the animal such as hunger, which can be manipulated and controlled by depriving it of food, or fear, which can be induced by presenting a signal of a forthcoming noxious stimulus, and to anticipatory reactions to incentives such as the amount of food offered in the goal box of a maze, which influence the vigor of action and the direction it will take.

Still other psychologists are interested in the nature of the neurophysiological process which underlies all behavior. To them, the term "motivation" refers to specific neurophysiological events that are associated with eating, drinking, sexual activity, and other types of behavior which are known to contribute to the survival of the biological organism and the species.

THE SEVERAL LANGUAGES OF MOTIVATION

Our task is to review what has been learned about motivation in these and other fields of inquiry which together constitute contemporary psychology. Perhaps we have already seen enough of what the study of motivation is going to entail to anticipate that there will be not one, but rather several different languages of motivation, and within each language probably a number of dialects. There will be an *experiential language*, that is, the language with which we are already familiar which refers to the conscious experience of desire, emotion, feelings of determination, and the inclination to act. There will be a *neurophysiological language*, that is, a description of the process of motivation, and speculations about it when knowledge is incomplete, in the technical language of the neural and organic processes which are believed to accompany what is known in the other language as desire and emotion. There will be a *behavioral language*, that is, a language which considers motivation in terms of descriptions of the direction, vigor, and persistence of observable behavior in relation to observable environmental conditions. This language, for reasons that will become clear in the chapters which deal with the evolution of a method for study of motivation, has already been given a certain priority in our introduction to the meaning of motivation. And, in the interest of completeness, we must admit still another language to our list even though it has not been explicitly foreshadowed in these introductory comments, except perhaps in references to the construction of more useful conceptual schemes as the central task of the scientific enterprise. We can refer to this fourth language we shall encounter as the abstract language or perhaps, more appropriately, the *mathematical language* of motivation. This language describes motivation in terms of abstract mathematical concepts which are adapted or created to refer to the experiential, neurophysiological, and behavioral events called motivation, but with greater precision than can be accomplished with words and sentences. We shall confront several mathematical models of motivation in the course of our study.

A meaningful discussion of how the experiential event called motivation, the neurophysiological event called motivation, and the behavioral event called motivation are interrelated must obviously come after, not before, we have studied the problem of motivation. The several levels of discourse which may be found in the contemporary psychological literature are deliberately referred to as several "languages" in the present discussion in order to suggest the possibility of translation from one to the other. Recognition that there are, in fact, several different languages of motivation is the first step towards understanding why there is some confusion about the meaning of this term. The question, "Which of the several languages is preferable?" must be answered in terms of another question, "What use is the language to serve?" James B. Conant has answered this question in a general way in his book *Science and Common Sense* (1951), a book which identifies the scientific enterprise with the growth and development of conceptual schemes through observation and experiment. Here is what Conant said:

"One sometimes reads in current popular articles about science some such declaration as the following: 'Modern physics has shown that a wooden table is *really* composed of electrons, protons, and neutrons.' The word 'really' as used in this sentence is a word that has overtones which can be highly misleading. One is on safer ground if one says, 'The concept of a table is a useful one in a common-sense world and has been used without much difficulty by all but professional philosophers (when they are philosophizing); for many practical purposes the concept of "wood" is also useful and sufficiently defined in terms of the past history of the material. Some of the chemical transformations of wood can be usefully formulated in terms of two materials known as "cellulose" and "lignin," and still more profitably accounted for in terms of the conceptual scheme of atoms and a grouping of atoms in molecules. However, there is nothing that I am aware of that one can do with wood that makes it at all profitable to bring in electrons, protons, or neutrons. (If one were talking about uranium, that would be, of course, another story!)'

"In short, the question of the reality of many of the conceptual schemes of the scientist poses no more difficult problem than the question of the reality of the common sense concept of a table or the material we call wood. For scientists as for laymen, when they are not on their guard the degree of reality is largely a function of the degree of familiarity with the concept or conceptual scheme; this in turn is a function of the fruitfulness of the idea over a considerable period of time."*

## REVIEW OF THE PLAN OF THE BOOK

In this chapter we have presented a working definition of the problem of motivation. It will serve to move us into the subject matter. The prescientific meaning of "motivation" is indicated by the interlocking set of meanings of words like want, appetite, aversion, satisfaction, intention, and purpose to be found in any standard dictionary. Some of the factors that influence motivation can be identified in these common-sense terms. Our preliminary discussion has suggested in a general way what the scientific study of motivation ought to be about.

The gap between the common sense of motivation and the attitudes, methods, and concepts which characterize contemporary scientific analysis of the problem has been acknowledged. This book, an introduction to motivation, is designed primarily to bridge that gap. We begin by reminding ourselves that Darwin's theory of evolution is a turning point in human thought concerning the legitimacy of the assumption that man, after all, is part of the natural

* Reprinted from James B. Conant, *Science and Common Sense*, pp. 35–36, by permission of Yale University Press.

order and that both human and animal motivation can be studied empirically with some promise of improving common sense about the subject. The extent to which the implications of Darwin's theory are manifested in the disparate courses of psychological inquiry established in the late 19th century has been touched upon to suggest that the study of motivation will be largely an integrative task. We are forewarned to anticipate several different languages of motivation.

The next five chapters will consider the evolution of ideas and methods of study that marked psychology's transition from common-sense analysis to scientific study of motivation and behavior. The discussion will highlight the contributions of five men, William James, Sigmund Freud, Kurt Lewin, Edward Tolman, and Clark Hull, during the period 1890–1940. The discussion does not attempt an exposition of the complete theoretical systems of these men. That is not the intention. The works of these men are considered mainly because they were the spokesmen for certain ideas which had to be advanced and assimilated before psychology could move ahead in its analysis of the problem of motivation. These chapters deal selectively with issues, arguments, and substantive contributions in the field of motivation which characterize a period of transition in orientation towards the subject matter. From the vantage point of contemporary theory and research on motivation, which is outlined in later chapters, we consider several of the most important threads from earlier contributions which today, interwoven in the thinking of most psychologists, constitute the underlying fabric of their basic orientation. Were these transitions in thought to be ignored or minimized, as so often they are, many of the endeavors of contemporary psychology might appear trivial or irrelevant to the problem of motivation. *The change in viewpoint has mainly to do with how the problem of motivation should be initially defined and with a growth in understanding of the tactics and strategy of scientific study.*

The final half of the book will introduce the issues and innovations of the contemporary period. It will survey the recent evolution of what is known as *S-R* Behavior Theory, particularly in reference to the problem of motivation as defined in earlier chapters. Chapter 6 includes a survey of Hull's formal theory, advanced in 1943. Chapters 7 and 8, dealing with subsequent developments of this theory, will convey something of the dialogue between experiment and theory in the development of science.

They will review the different kinds of experimental facts and arguments which have been advanced by critics of *S-R* Behavior Theory and will treat the most recent revisions and reformulations of that theory which clearly show the impact upon theory of critical experimental evidence.

Chapters 8 and 9 will consider the various strategies of research having to do with assessment of individual differences in human motivation and the reason that measurement of individual differences and experimental analysis of the process of motivation of behavior have been isolated in the history of psychology until very recently. Current developments in research on anxiety and motivation to achieve are given special emphasis, for these contemporary programs nicely illustrate the integration of the experimental approach and the study of individual differences, the convergence of what Cronbach (1957) has called "the two disciplines of scientific psychology."

Looking back over material covered in earlier parts of the book, the final chapter will call attention to the convergence of systematic concepts which have been advanced to explain motivation. It will also identify some new directions for research that are suggested by a more heuristic conception of what constitutes the problem of motivation than the common sense with which we begin our study.

## SOME SUMMARY STATEMENTS

1. The study of motivation has to do with the contemporary (immediate) influences on the direction, vigor, and persistence of action.

2. The study of motivation, while historically linked to the study of how behavior changes as the consequence of training (learning), can be distinguished from this field of interest and from the study of perception.

3. The object of scientific study of the problem of motivation is to provide, as in all sciences, a more useful conception than the conventional intuitive wisdom usually referred to as "common sense."

4. The common-sense theory of motivation as described in any standard dictionary conceives behavior as appetitive and aversive; that is, as directed towards sources of satisfaction and away from sources of dissatisfaction, and as instigated by conscious desires or wants.

5. Some of the factors to be considered in the study of motivation are: the conscious experience of

desire or want; analysis of behavior directed towards potential satisfactions and away from potential dissatisfactions; internal and external conditions that influence appetitive and aversive behavior; individual differences in motivation.

6. Three implications of Darwin's theory of evolution have influenced the course of psychological investigations which are pertinent to the study of motivation: (a) the idea that animals may be capable of intelligent behavior or reason; (b) the idea that human behavior may be influenced by instinct; (c) the importance of individual differences.

7. The conceptions of motivation which have arisen through clinical study of human behavior, experimental investigation of human and animal behavior, and assessment of individual differences in human preference differ in certain important respects.

8. The psychology of motivation, as a distinct field of study, is a relatively recent development. Its task is to attempt an integration of what has been learned about the problem of motivation in previously disparate fields of inquiry.

9. The gap between common sense and contemporary scientific orientation concerning motivation has mainly to do with how the problem of motivation should be initially defined and with a growth in understanding of the tactics and strategy of scientific study.

# CHAPTER 2

# Introspective
# Analysis
# of Conscious
# Volition

"*A string of raw facts; a little gossip and wrangle about opinions; a little classification and generalization on the mere descriptive level; a strong prejudice that we have states of mind, and that our brain conditions them: but not a single law in the sense in which physics shows us laws, not a single proposition from which any consequence can be causally deduced. We don't even know the terms between which the elementary laws would obtain if we had them. This is no science, it is only the hope of a science*" (William James, 1892, p. 468).

We turn to the late 19th century "hope of a science" to begin our study of the evolution of the conception of motivation within psychology. Our intention in this and subsequent chapters is to acquire the historical background and perspective needed for an understanding and appropriate evaluation of contemporary developments in the study of motivation.

Following publication of Darwin's theory of evolution, the late 19th century became a period of heightened speculation concerning a problem which had interested philosophers for centuries: the relationship of "mind" to "body." Many of the insights which have had great influence on subsequent study of motivation have come from two men of this period, William James and Sigmund Freud. Both were trained in physiology and medicine and also greatly interested in this stubborn philosophical issue.

In this chapter, we shall consider James' analysis of instinct, habit, emotion, and "will" or conscious volition. We shall see the interrelatedness of a set of problems which together define the subject matter of the psychology of motivation. At the same time, our survey of what James had to say about these important problems will give us the flavor of the pre-experimental psychology of motivation in the period before the full impact of Freud's work was felt. James' speculative analysis is guided by anecdotal observations and introspective analysis of his own conscious states. This gives a picture of the method of study during the period. In addition, his analysis of the broad problem of motivation is guided by the conviction that the brain and nervous system must provide the physical mechanism of all "mental" phenomena. We glimpse the beginning of what is later to become an experimental physiological psychology.

Many of Freud's speculative ideas, which we shall consider in the next chapter, were likewise based on general observations and introspection. But Freud's most original concepts are based on extensive clinical observations of the action patterns and reported introspections of patients suffering neurotic disorders, observations that only a scientist who had begun to develop new concepts would even think of making.

The *experimental* psychology of the late 19th century had virtually nothing to say about motivation, or "will," as the problem was then commonly labeled. It was confined to the study of sensation, perception, and the beginnings of systematic study of memory. The writings of James and Freud provide the main fund of guiding hypotheses and initial observations about the problem of motivation to which later psychologists have often turned. In a very real sense, the work of James and Freud marks the beginning of the convergence of speculative thought about the springs of human action and relevant observations of behavior.

In an account of the rapid development of physical science in the 17th century, James Conant (1951) calls attention to the union of three streams of human thought and action that was essential to provide the impetus for science as we know it: *speculative thinking*, *deductive reasoning*, and *empirical experimentation*. In the transition from common sense to scientific study of motivation, we shall observe a similar convergence of these streams of thought and action. Both James and Freud engage in the kind of speculative thought which had long been characteristic of philosophy, but they do attempt to bring their ideas into closer contact with relevant empirical observations. The other two ingredients of contemporary behavioral science, an appreciation of the role of abstract (mathematical) concepts to guide scientific thought and of the vital importance of active experimentation, are added later and will be taken up in subsequent chapters.

## INTRODUCTION TO WILLIAM JAMES
(1842–1910)

The definitive history of experimental psychology has this to say about the two-volume *Principles of Psychology* by William James, which was published in 1890: "No other psychological treatise in the English language has in the modern period had such a wide and persistent influence" (Boring, 1929, p. 624). We turn to these volumes mainly to review James' treatment of "will" and "volition" and to catch the flavor of the late 19th century viewpoint about what now is considered the problem of motivation. We shall find the appeal to anecdotal evidence and the use of *introspection*, as a basic method of study, congenial to the common-sense orientation with which we begin our study. But we shall find, in addition, that James' interest in the *functions* of consciousness (the mind) and his effort to conceive plausible neural mechanisms in the brain corresponding to mental activities foreshadows the functional orientation of contemporary psychology.

PSYCHOLOGY: THE SCIENCE OF MENTAL LIFE

James defined psychology as "the Science of Mental Life, both of its phenomena and their conditions." The phenomena were considered "such things as we call feelings, desires, cognitions, reasonings, decisions, and the like . . ." (James, 1890, Vol. 1, p. 1). And it was clear to James that the conditions of all mental phenomena were the immediate physical processes of the brain: "*no mental modification ever occurs which is not accompanied or followed by a bodily change*" (James, 1890, Vol. 1, p. 5). James sought, at the outset, to delimit the subject matter of interest by describing "the manner in which the mental life seems to intervene between impressions made from without upon the body, and reactions of the body upon the outer world again" (James, 1890, Vol. 1, p. 6). He did this by comparing the behavior of inanimate objects and living things:

"If some iron filings be sprinkled on a table and a magnet brought near them, they will fly through the air for a certain distance and stick to its surface. A savage seeing the phenomenon explains it as the result of an attraction or love between the magnet and the filings. But let a card cover the poles of the magnet, and the filings will press forever against its surface without its ever occurring to them to pass around its sides and thus come into more direct contact with the object of their love. . . .
"If now we pass from such actions as these to those of living things, we notice a striking difference. Romeo wants Juliet as the filings want the magnet; and if no obstacles intervene he moves towards her by as straight a line as they. But Romeo and Juliet, if a wall be built between them, do not remain idiotically pressing their faces against its opposite sides like the magnet and the filings with the card. Romeo soon finds a circuitous way, by scaling the wall or otherwise, of touching Juliet's lips directly. With the filings the

path is fixed; whether it reaches the end depends on accidents. With the lover it is the end which is fixed, the path may be modified indefinitely. . . .

"Such contrasts between living and inanimate performances end by leading men to deny that in the physical world final purposes exist at all. Loves and desires are to-day no longer imputed to particles of iron or of air. No one supposes now that the end of any activity which they may display is an ideal purpose presiding over the activity from its outset and soliciting or drawing it into being by a sort of *vis a fronte*. The end, on the contrary, is deemed a mere passive result, pushed into being *a tergo*, having had, so to speak, no voice in its own production. Alter the pre-existing conditions, and with inorganic materials you bring forth each time a different apparent end. But with intelligent agents, altering the conditions changes the activity displayed, but not the end reached; for here the idea of the yet unrealized end co-operates with the conditions to determine what the activities shall be.

*"The pursuance of future ends and the choice of means for their attainment are thus the mark and criterion of the presence of mentality* in a phenomenon" (James, 1890, Vol. 1, pp. 6–8).

### THE FUNCTIONS OF CONSCIOUSNESS

James treated mentality, that is, consciousness, as if it were an organ added during evolution "for the sake of steering a nervous system grown too complex to regulate itself" (Boring, 1929, p. 501). We can see this clearly in statements he made after surveying what was then known of the neurophysiology of the brain centers:

"All the centres, in all animals, whilst they are in one aspect mechanisms, probably are, or at least once were, organs of consciousness in another, although the consciousness is doubtless much more developed in the hemispheres than it is anywhere else. The consciousness must everywhere *prefer* some of the sensations which it gets to others; and if it can remember these in their absence, however dimly, they must be its *ends* of desire. If, moreover, it can identify in memory any motor discharges which may have led to such ends, and associate the latter with them, then these motor discharges themselves may in turn become desired as *means*. This is the development of *will;* and its realization must of course be proportional to the possible complication of the consciousness" (James, 1890, Vol. 1, p. 78).

Thus, as James proceeded to write an introspective psychology in which the analysis of the functions of "the stream of thought" which is consciousness was the matter of central interest, he stopped as often as possible to consider what might be a plausible neural mechanism to explain what introspection revealed of the process intervening between sensory impressions and motor response. He anticipated the development of the behavioristic point of view of American psychology, which attempts to explain behavior in terms of stimulus ($S$) and response ($R$) and intervening neurophysiological mechanisms.

### THREE CLASSES OF BEHAVIOR

We shall review James' ideas about "the more important classes of movement consequent upon cerebro-mental change" which he listed as: "1) Instinctive or Impulsive Performances; 2) Expressions of Emotion; and 3) Voluntary Deeds . . ." (James, Vol. 2, pp. 381–382). James opens a chapter on "Will" in a way that helps us to see how he then conceived the relationship between conscious, voluntary behavior and more primitive, impulsive, and habitual behavior where consciousness plays a less determinate role:

"Desire, wish, will, are states of mind which everyone knows, and which no definition can make plainer. We desire to feel, to have, to do, all sorts of things which at the moment are not felt, had, or done. If with the desire there goes a sense that attainment is not possible, we simply *wish;* but if we believe that the end is in our power, we *will* that the desired feeling, having, or doing shall be real; and real it presently becomes, either immediately upon the willing or after certain preliminaries have been fulfilled.

"The only ends which follow *immediately* upon our willing seem to be movements of our own bodies. Whatever *feelings* and *havings* we may will to get, come in as results of preliminary movements which we make for the purpose. This fact is too familiar to need illustration; so that we may start with the proposition that the only *direct* outward effects of our will are bodily movements. The mechanism of production of these voluntary movements is what befalls us to study now. . . .

"The movements to the study of which we now address ourselves, being desired and intended beforehand, are of course done with full prevision of what they are to be. It follows from this that *voluntary movements must be secondary, not primary functions of our organism.* This is the first point to understand in the psychology of Volition. Reflex, instinctive, and emotional movements are all primary performances. The nerve-centres are so organized that certain stimuli pull the trigger of certain explosive parts; and a creature going through one of these explosions for the first time undergoes an entirely novel experience. . . . But if, in voluntary action properly so-called, the act must be foreseen, it follows that no creature not endowed with divinatory power can perform an act voluntarily for the first time. . . . We learn all our possibilities by the way of experience. When a particular movement, having once occurred in a random, reflex, or involuntary way, has left an image of itself in the memory, then the movement can be desired again, proposed as an end, and deliberately willed. But it is impossible to see how it could be willed before" (James, 1890, Vol. 2, pp. 486–488).

Obviously, to understand James' treatment of conscious motivation (i.e., "will" and "volition"), we must first grasp his conception of the "primary functions": instinct, reflex, emotion, and habit. These concepts are still very much intertwined in contemporary analyses of the motivation of behavior.

## INSTINCT

### DEFINITION OF INSTINCT

James defined instinct as *"the faculty of acting in such a way as to produce certain ends, without foresight of the ends, and without previous education in the performance"* (James, 1890, Vol. 2, p. 383). He took issue with the traditional way of talking about these tendencies. It did little more than name abstractly the purpose they appear to subserve, e.g., self-preservation, as if an animal were clairvoyant and prophetic concerning the ultimate consequences of its impulses. For James, the tendencies called instinctive were all reflexive actions. They were considered reactions called forth by determinate sensory stimuli in contact with the animal's body or at a distance in its environment. The nervous system was conceived as "a preorganized bundle of such reactions—they are as fatal as sneezing, and as exactly correlated to their special excitants as it is to its own" (James, 1890, Vol. 2, p. 384). The naturalist, James argued, may class these reactions under general headings for his own convenience, but "he must not forget that in the animal it is a particular sensation or perception or image which calls them forth" (James, 1890, Vol. 2, p. 384).

### CHARACTERISTICS OF INSTINCTIVE BEHAVIOR

James was less concerned that actions called forth by a stimulus without any prior experience be *called* instincts than that the blind, impulsive character of the action be clearly recognized as its central characteristic. To ask "why" an animal should act in a particular impulsive (instinctive) way he considered as meaningless as to ask a desperately hungry man who is devouring a tasty meal "why" he should want to eat more: "Not one man in a billion, when taking his dinner, ever thinks of utility. He eats because the food tastes good and makes him want more. If you ask him *why* he should want to eat more of what tastes like that, instead of revering you as a philosopher he will probably laugh at you for a fool" (James, 1890, Vol. 2, p. 386). The fundamental concept that different animals are so constructed that they are *impelled to like to do certain things and not others* is nowhere more clear than in his oft-quoted inference about the mother hen:

"To the broody hen the notion would probably seem monstrous that there should be a creature in the world to whom a nestful of eggs was not the utterly fascinating and precious and never-to-be-too-much-sat-upon object which it is to her" (James, 1890, Vol. 2, p. 387).

James concluded that to the animal which obeys it, "every impulse and every step of every instinct shines with its own sufficient light, and seems at the moment the only eternally right and proper thing to do. It is done for its own sake exclusively" (James, 1890, Vol. 2, p. 387).

It was fruitless, he felt, to enter a long discussion of the then common notion "that Man differs from lower creatures by the almost total absence of instincts, and the assumption of their work in him by 'reason'" (James, 1890, Vol. 2, p. 389). The issue would soon become, he felt, a quarrel about words if by "reason" one were to mean "the *tendency to obey impulses* of a certain lofty sort" and if the definition of instinct were extended to cover all impulses whatever, "even the impulse to act from the idea of a distant fact, as well as the impulse to act from a present sensation" (James, 1890, Vol. 2, p. 389). Restricting the meaning of instinct "to actions done with no prevision of an end," the facts of the case seemed more "tolerably plain" to James in 1890 than most contemporary psychologists admit them to be:

"Man has a far greater variety of *impulses* than any lower animal; and any one of these impulses, taken in itself, is as 'blind' as the lowest instinct can be; but, owing to man's memory, power of reflection, and power of inference, they come each one to be felt by him, after he has once yielded to them and experienced their results, in connection with a *foresight* of those results. In this condition an impulse acted out may be said to be acted out, in part at least, *for the sake* of its results. It is obvious that *every instinctive act, in an animal with memory, must cease to be 'blind' after being once repeated*, and must be accompanied with foresight of its 'end' just so far as that end may have fallen under the animal's cognizance. An insect that lays her eggs in a place where she never sees them hatched must always do so 'blindly;' but a hen who has already hatched a brood can hardly be assumed to sit with perfect 'blindness' on her second nest. *Some expectation of consequences must in every case like this be aroused; and this expectation, according as it is that of something desired or of something disliked, must necessarily either re-enforce or inhibit the mere impulse*" [italics added] (James, 1890, Vol. 2, p. 390).

## HUMAN INSTINCTS

What were the "motor reactions upon objects" that James counted as instincts among men? He embraced both actions aroused within the person that went no further than his own body and actions that take effect upon the outer world. In the former category, he considered such things as the "bristling of attention" when a novel object is perceived, or the "expression on the face or the breathing apparatus of an emotion it may excite" which merge into ordinary reflexes like laughing when tickled or making a wry face at a bad taste. In the latter category he included flight from a wild beast, imitation of what we see another do, and many other types of behavior which we shall merely list here to illustrate the scope of activities he included: sucking, biting, clasping, carrying to the mouth, crying, turning the head aside, holding head erect, sitting up, standing, locomotion, vocalization, imitation, emulation or rivalry, pugnacity (anger and resentment), sympathy, hunting, fear, acquisitiveness, kleptomania, constructiveness, play, curiosity, sociability and shyness, secretiveness, cleanliness, modesty, shame, love, jealousy, parental love.

The definition of the circumstances which "arouse" the instinct is relatively clear in the instances we today consider reflexive behavior: for example, "*clasping* an object which touches the fingers or toes." But many of the other tendencies listed as instincts seem no more than abstract names for kinds of behavior that are frequently observed. There is often little or no reference to the eliciting stimulus, which is the other half of a reflex arc. For example, here is all James says of one important "instinct":

"*Emulation or Rivalry*, a very intense instinct, especially rife with young children, or at least especially undisguised. Everyone knows it. Nine-tenths of the work of the world is done by it. We know that if we do not do the task someone else will do it and get the credit, so we do it. It has very little connection with sympathy, but rather more with pugnacity, which we proceed in turn to consider" (James, 1890, Vol. 2, p. 409).

## REFINEMENT OF THE ANCIENT DOCTRINE

The advance over ancient doctrine in the concept of instinct advanced by James lies in the specification that the term should refer to (a) actions that are elicited by particular stimulating conditions prior to any learning experience and therefore (b) without any prevision of consequences, because (c) the nervous system of the animal is constructed in a particular way. But James, like so many psychologists who followed him, could not resist advancing a quite arbitrary list of tendencies believed instinctive in man. In fact, it was once recorded that by 1924 no less than 14,046 different human activities had been labeled "instincts" in the psychological literature! This is a trivial statistic because it has since become abundantly clear that the mere naming and classification of behaviors as "instincts" without reference to the stimulating conditions which arouse them is a naïve, specious, and completely circular attempt to explain them. For example, the fallacy of circularity in explaining the tendency of animals to fight in terms of an "instinct of pugnacity" is immediately evident if one asks, "How do you know they have an instinct of pugnacity?" and the only answer forthcoming is, "Because they are observed to behave aggressively."

## THE SPECIOUS SIMPLICITY OF INSTINCT AS AN EXPLANATION

According to James, the difficulty in identifying instincts, particularly in the human case, is to be understood partly in terms of the influence of *habit*: "*no matter how well endowed an animal may originally be in the way of instincts, his resultant actions will be much modified if the instincts combine with experience . . .*" (James, 1890, Vol. 2, p. 390). If an object which elicits an instinctive impulse in an organism to react in a certain manner also, by virtue of past experience, is a *sign* of the nearness of another object which elicits an equally strong and incompatible instinctive impulse, the two impulses "struggle in his breast for the mastery":

"The fatality and uniformity said to be characteristic of instinctive actions will be so little manifest that one might be tempted to deny to him altogether the possession of any instinct about the object *O*. Yet how false this judgment would be! The instinct about *O* is there; only by the complication of the associative machinery it has come into conflict with another instinct about *P*" (James, 1890, Vol. 2, p. 391).

In other words, whether the reflex arc is organized at birth, "ripens spontaneously" later, or is due to acquired habit, "it must take its chances with all the other arcs, and sometimes succeed, and sometimes fail, in drafting off the currents through itself" (James, 1890, Vol. 2, p. 391).

We see that the attractive simplicity of explaining behavior as "instinctive" is immediately lost, even in this very early theory, when it is acknowledged that the animal is capable of responding to more remote stimuli which are merely "suggested" by the presented stimulus because they have been associated in its previous history. The task of identifying the stimulus to which the organism is responding is thus not an easy matter.

This is probably enough to convey in general what James and other late-19th-century writers meant by "instinct." It is important to note the importance of the concept to James. If an action must first be performed before there can be any conscious idea of it which would make it possible to "will" that action, so he argued, all actions must *initially* be blind, reflexive *reactions* to particular stimuli. Let us turn now to the complicating factor, *habit*.

## HABIT

### A NEURAL PATH BETWEEN STIMULUS AND RESPONSE

Experience gives rise to habitual action. Living creatures from an outward point of view seem to be "bundles of habits." To James, the habitual tendency to act in a certain way in a certain situation *because one has acted that way before in similar situations* is attributed to the plasticity of the organic material of which the body (the nervous system) is composed. James considered the habits of living things similar to the changes in the properties of inorganic matter which attend some fundamental structural change. Consider the ease with which a piece of paper which has already been creased can be folded the same way a second time:

"For the entire nervous system *is* nothing but a system of paths between a sensory *terminus a quo* and a muscular, glandular, or other *terminus ad quem*. A path once traversed by a nerve-current might be expected to follow the law of most of the paths we know, and to be scooped out and made more permeable than before; and this ought to be repeated with each new passage of the current" (James, 1890, Vol. 1, p. 108).

Thus, as a consequence of practice, the sequence of movements required to achieve a given result and the fatigue involved in the action should be diminished. The pattern of action should become "automatic." And, most important of all, "*habit diminishes the conscious attention with which our acts are performed*" (James, 1890, Vol. 1, p. 114).

### THE AUTOMATICITY OF HABITUAL ACTIONS

James described his conception of habit abstractly as follows:

"If an act require for its execution a chain, *A, B, C, D, E, F, G*, etc., of successive nervous events, then in the first performances of the action the conscious will must choose each of these events from a number of wrong alternatives that tend to present themselves; but habit soon brings it about that each event calls up its own appropriate successor without any alternative offering itself, and without any reference to the conscious will, until at last the whole chain, *A, B, C, D, E, F, G*, rattles itself off as soon as *A* occurs, just as if *A* and the rest of the chain were fused into a continuous stream. When we are learning to walk, to ride, to swim, skate, fence, write, play, or sing, we interrupt outselves at every step by unnecessary movements and false notes. When we are proficient, on the contrary, the results not only follow with the very minimum of muscular action requisite to bring them forth, they also follow from a single instantaneous 'cue.' The marksman sees the bird, and, before he knows it, he has aimed and shot. A gleam in his adversary's eye, a momentary pressure from his rapier, and the fencer finds that he has instantly made the right parry and return. A glance at the musical hieroglyphics, and the pianist's fingers have rippled through a cataract of notes. And not only is it the right thing at the right time that we thus involuntarily do, but the wrong thing also, if it be an habitual thing. Who is there that has never wound up his watch on taking off his waistcoat in the daytime, or taken his latchkey out on arriving at the door-step of a friend? Very absentminded persons in going to their bedroom to dress for dinner have been known to take off one garment after another and finally to get into bed, merely because that was the habitual issue of the first few movements when performed at a later hour. . . .

"In action grown habitual, what instigates each new muscular contraction to take place in its appointed order is not a thought or a perception, but the *sensation occasioned by the muscular contraction just finished*. A strictly voluntary act has to be guided by idea, perception, and volition, throughout its whole course. In an habitual action, mere sensation is a sufficient guide, and the upper regions of brain and mind are set comparatively free" (James, 1890, Vol. 1, pp. 114–116).

## IMPORTANCE OF RESPONSE-PRODUCED CUES

James' conception is presented diagramatically in Figure 2.1. The capital letters *A, B, C, D, E, F, G*

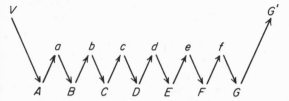

FIGURE 2.1    James' conception of habitual action. The capital letters, A to G, represent an habitual chain of muscular contractions, and the small letters, a to g, represent sensations produced by those contractions. Conscious volition, V, instigates the initial movement but is not needed after that; the whole sequence rattles off automatically. The "idea of the end" of the sequence is represented by G'. (From James, 1890, Vol. 1, p. 116)

represent the habitual chain of muscular contractions, and the small letters *a, b, c, d, e, f, g* represent what is today called the "sensory feedback" or "response-produced cues" which are central in James' theory of volition. He pointed out that such sensations are usually from the muscles, skin or joints of the parts moved, "but they may also be effects of the movement upon the eye or the ear" (James, 1890, Vol. 1, p. 116). In other words, we must consider also the changes in *external* stimulation which are immediate consequences of actions.

When such a series of movements is being learned, the sensations produced by each movement are separately perceived:

> "We hesitate, compare, choose, revoke, reject, etc., by intellectual means; and the order by which the next movement is discharged is an express order from the ideational centres after this deliberation has been gone through" (James, 1890, Vol. 1, p. 116).

In habitual action, however, the only impulse which is a matter of deliberate conscious choice is the initial impulse, the command to start which is labeled *V*, signifying volition, in the diagram. Though consciousness does not *will* all the later movements in the sequence, James preferred to think of the sensory consequences of each movement as "*sensations to which we are usually inattentive*" (James, 1890, Vol. 1, p. 118) unless something goes wrong rather than merely as nerve currents which are not sufficient to arouse any feeling whatever.

## SOCIETAL IMPLICATIONS OF HABIT

To James, *habit* was "the enormous fly-wheel of society, its most precious conservative agent." He waxed eloquent about the implications of habit:

> "It alone is what keeps us all within the bounds of ordinance, and saves the children of fortune from the envious uprisings of the poor. It alone prevents the hardest and most repulsive walks of life from being deserted by those brought up to tread therein. It keeps the fisherman and the deckhand at sea through the winter; it holds the miner in his darkness, and nails the countryman to his log-cabin and his lonely farm through all the months of snow; it protects us from invasion by the natives of the desert and the frozen zone. It dooms us all to fight out the battle of life upon the lines of our nurture or our early choice, and to make the best of a pursuit that disagrees, because there is no other for which we are fitted, and it is too late to begin again" (James, 1890, Vol. 1, p. 121).

> "The more of the details of our daily life we can hand over to the effortless custody of automatism, the more our higher powers of mind will be set free for their own proper work. There is no more miserable human being than one in whom nothing is habitual but indecision, and for whom the lighting of every cigar, the drinking of every cup, the time of rising and going to bed every day, and the beginning of every bit of work, are subjects of express volitional deliberation. Full half the time of such a man goes to the deciding, or regretting, of matters which ought to be so ingrained in him as practically not to exist for his consciousness at all" (James, 1890, Vol. 1, p. 122).

## SELECTIVE FUNCTION OF CONSCIOUSNESS

Having extolled the function and automatism of habit and having described the neural basis of both instinctive and habitual actions, James was forced to face the issue of what, then, could be the function of consciousness itself?

> "If neural action is as complicated as mind; and if in the sympathetic system and lower spinal cord we see what, so far as we know, is unconscious neural action executing deeds that to all outward intent may be called intelligent; what is there to hinder us from supposing that even where we know consciousness to be there, the still more complicated neural action which we believe to be its inseparable companion is alone and of itself the real agent of whatever intelligent deeds may appear?" (James, 1890, Vol. 1, p. 129).

He recalled that to Descartes (1637) belongs the credit of having been the first to boldly conceive of a completely self-sufficing nervous system capable of performing complicated and intelligent actions. But even Descartes had stopped short of man, restricting his view to animals and holding "that the higher acts of man were the result of the agency of his rational soul" (James, 1890, Vol. 1, p. 130). Now, late in the 19th century, James was confronted with new arguments from physiologists which considered consciousness as "an 'epiphenomenon,' an inert spectator, a sort of 'foam, aura, or melody'" (James, 1890, Vol. 1, p. 129) with no power over the neural occurrences themselves.

James' reply to these arguments, which sets the stage for his later analysis of will and volition, was: "The *particulars of the distribution of consciousness, so far as we know them, point to its being efficacious*" (James, 1890, Vol. 1, p. 138). First, he believed, though he admitted it would be difficult to prove, "that consciousness grows the more complex and intense the higher we rise in the animal kingdom. That of a man must exceed that of an oyster" (James, 1890, Vol. 1, p. 138). (We may wonder if such an assertion would be merely "difficult" or, indeed, impossible to prove.) Second, he argued that introspection reveals consciousness to be present "when nerve-processes are hesitant" (James, 1890, Vol. 1, p. 142), when, in other words, neither instinctive reaction nor rapid, automatic, habitual action is evident:

". . . Consciousness is at all times primarily *a selecting agency*. . . . We find it always doing one thing, choosing one out of several of the materials so presented to its notice, emphasizing and accentuating that and suppressing as far as possible all the rest. The item emphasized is always in close connection with some *interest* felt by consciousness to be paramount at the time. . . .
"Every actually existing consciousness seems to itself at any rate to be a *fighter for ends*, of which many, but for its presence, would not be ends at all. Its powers of cognition are mainly subservient to these ends, discerning which facts further them and which do not" (James, 1890, Vol. 1, pp. 139–141).

We perhaps learn most of James' disdain for further discussion of the philosophical subtleties of how *mind* can interact with *body* and of his conviction as to how psychology late in the 19th century should proceed from this passage, which concluded his review of the "automaton-theory":

". . . Psychology is a mere natural science, accepting certain terms uncritically as her data, and stopping short of metaphysical reconstruction. Like physics, she must be *naïve;* and if she finds that in her very peculiar field of study ideas *seem* to be causes, she had better continue to talk

of them as such. She gains absolutely nothing by a breach with common-sense in this matter, and she loses, to say the least, all naturalness of speech. If feelings are causes, of course their effects must be furtherances and checkings of internal cerebral motions, of which in themselves we are entirely without knowledge. *It is probable that for years to come we shall have to infer what happens in the brain either from our feelings or from motor effects which we observe* [italics added]. The organ will be for us a sort of vat in which feelings and motions somehow go on stewing together, and in which innumerable things happen of which we catch but the statistical result. Why, under these circumstances, we should be asked to forswear the language of our childhood I cannot well imagine, especially as it is perfectly compatible with the language of physiology. *The feelings can produce nothing absolutely new, they can only reinforce and inhibit reflex currents, and the original organization by physiological forces of these in paths must always be the ground-work of the psychological scheme* [italics added].
"My conclusion is that to urge the automaton-theory upon us, as it is now urged, on purely *a priori* and *quasi*-metaphysical grounds, is an *unwarrantable impertinence in the present state of psychology*" (James, 1890, Vol. 1, pp. 137–138).

## EMOTION

### RELATION OF EMOTION TO INSTINCT

One other involuntary process, *emotion*, deserves consideration before we turn to James' analysis of will and volition. James found it difficult to distinguish emotional excitement from instinctive reactions, for, as he argued, "*Every object that excites an instinct excites an emotion as well*" (James, 1890, Vol. 2, p. 442). If there is a meaningful distinction between them it is that "emotional reaction usually terminates in the subject's own body, whilst the instinctive reaction is apt to go farther and enter into practical relations with the exciting object" (James, 1890, Vol. 2, p. 442). The *object* of emotion may be something that is physically present which instigates an immediate reaction or, as also in the case of instinct, something which is merely thought of: "One may get angrier in thinking over one's insult than at the moment of receiving it . . ." (James, 1890, Vol. 2, p. 443).

### ATTITUDE TOWARDS CATALOGING EMOTIONS

James saw little value in the mere cataloging of emotions. He was overwhelmed at the infinite variety and subtleties of feeling already so well described in literature:

"But as far as 'scientific psychology' of the emotions goes, I may have been surfeited by too much reading of classic works on the subject, but I should as lief read verbal descriptions of the shapes of the rocks on a New Hampshire farm as toil through them again. They give one nowhere a central point of view, or a deductive or generative principle. They distinguish and refine and specify *in infinitum* without ever getting on to another logical level" (James, 1890, Vol. 2, p. 448).

James rejected the mere description and classification of contents of consciousness which interested so many other introspective psychologists of his period in favor of the search for the fundamental process or *function* of mental activities. If, he argued, we regard emotions "as products of more general causes . . . the mere distinguishing and cataloguing becomes of subsidiary importance. Having the goose which lays the golden eggs, the description of each egg already laid is a minor matter" (James, 1890, Vol. 2, p. 449).

JAMES-LANGE THEORY OF EMOTION

What is an emotion? Common sense holds that feelings like grief, fear, rage, and love arise in response to perception of some fact and that these states of mind then give rise to bodily expressions which are recognized by others as emotional reactions. The theory advanced by James (and also by a Danish physiologist, Lange, at about the same time) was that "*the bodily changes follow directly the perception of the exciting fact, and that our feeling of the same changes as they occur* IS *the emotion*" (James, 1890, Vol. 2, p. 449). This conception is now commonly called the James-Lange theory of emotion. It is the original contribution for which James is most explicitly credited in the subsequent literature of experimental psychology. His own elaboration of what the theory means defies improvement:

"Common-sense says, we lose our fortune, are sorry and weep; we meet a bear, are frightened and run; we are insulted by a rival, are angry and strike. The hypothesis here to be defended says that this order of sequence is incorrect, that the one mental state is not immediately induced by the other, that the bodily manifestations must first be interposed between, and that the more rational statement is that we feel sorry because we cry, angry because we strike, afraid because we tremble, and not that we cry, strike, or tremble, because we are sorry, angry, or fearful, as the case may be" (James, 1890, Vol. 2, pp. 449–450).

Again, James employs his notion of sensations produced by muscular movements and glandular contractions, this time to account for the conscious experience called emotion. In the case of habit, he employed this same concept to explain how long, habitual chains of action can "rattle off" without conscious deliberation and "will" at every step. In defense of the idea he scrutinized the subtle movements which provide the physical basis of emotional feelings:

"It is surprising what little items give accent to these complexes of sensibility. When worried by any slight trouble, one may find that the focus of one's bodily consciousness is the contraction, often quite inconsiderable, of the eyes and brows. When momentarily embarrassed, it is something in the pharynx that compels either a swallow, a clearing of the throat, or a slight cough; and so on for as many more instances as might be named. . . .
"*If we fancy some strong emotion, and then try to abstract from our consciousness of it all the feelings of its bodily symptons, we find we have nothing left behind*, no 'mind-stuff' out of which the emotion can be constituted, and that a cold and neutral state of intellectual perception is all that remains. . . .
"What kind of an emotion of fear would be left if the feeling neither of quickened heart-beats nor of shallow breathing, neither of trembling lips nor of weakened limbs, neither of goose-flesh nor of visceral stirrings, were present, it is quite impossible for me to think. Can one fancy the state of rage and picture no ebullition in the chest, no flushing of the face, no dilation of the nostrils, no clenching of the teeth, no impulse to vigorous action, but in their stead limp muscles, calm breathing, and a placid face? The present writer, for one, certainly cannot. . . . In like manner of grief: what would it be without its tears, its sobs, its suffocation of the heart, its pang in the breastbone? A feelingless cognition that certain circumstances are deplorable, and nothing more. Every passion in turn tells the same story. . . .
"If such a theory is true, then each emotion is the resultant of a sum of elements, and each element is caused by a physiological process of a sort already well known. The elements are all organic changes, and each of them is the reflex effect of the exciting object. . . .
"Now the moment the genesis of an emotion is accounted for, as the arousal by an object of a lot of reflex acts which are forthwith felt, *we immediately see why there is no limit to the number of possible different emotions which may exist, and why the emotions of different individuals may vary indefinitely*, both as to their constitution and as to objects which call them forth" (James, 1890, Vol. 2, pp. 451–454).
". . . The emotion both begins and ends with what we call its effects or manifestations. It has

no mental *status* except as either the vivid feeling of the manifestations, or the idea of them; and the latter thus constitute its entire material, and sum and substance" (James, 1890, Vol. 2, p. 458).

Anticipating the kind of problem that was to interest Freud so much, James called attention to certain pathological conditions of emotion when the person has no conscious awareness of the *object* of his emotion. He felt that these cases offered the best proof of his hypothesis that the immediate cause of emotion is the physical *effect* of movements and glandular reactions.

### THE MORE SUBTLE FEELINGS

The hypothesis as originally formulated was meant to apply primarily to what James called the "coarser" or stronger emotional reactions: grief, fear, anger, love. But he considered also what other writers of his time referred to as "the subtler emotions," that is, moral, intellectual, and aesthetic feelings:

"Concords of sounds, of colors, of lines, logical consistencies, teleological fitnesses, affect us with a pleasure that seems ingrained in the very form of the representation itself, and to borrow nothing from any reverberation surging up from the parts below the brain" (James, 1890, Vol. 2, p. 468).

Does not admission of these essentially "cerebral" forms of immediate pleasure and displeasure suggest that what James has considered the "coarser" emotions might also be immediate feelings instigated by the stimulating object? James begrudgingly admitted the possibility of aesthetic and other "cerebral" emotions which did not involve sensory effects of movements and glandular reactions, but then he proceeded to minimize their potency as feelings:

"In reply to this we must immediately insist that aesthetic emotion, *pure and simple*, the pleasure given us by certain lines and masses, and combinations of colors and sounds, is an absolutely sensational experience, an optical or auricular feeling that is primary, and not due to the repercussion backwards of other sensations elsewhere consecutively aroused. To this simple primary and immediate pleasure in certain pure sensations and harmonious combinations of them, there may, it is true, be *added* secondary pleasures; and in the practical enjoyment of works of art by the masses of mankind these secondary pleasures play a great part. The more *classic* one's taste is, however, the less relatively important are the secondary pleasures felt to be in comparison with those of the primary sensation as it comes in. . . .
"These secondary emotions themselves are assuredly for the most part constituted of other incoming sensations aroused by the diffusive wave of reflex effects which the beautiful object sets up. A glow, a pang in the breast, a shudder, a fulness of the breathing, a flutter of the heart, a shiver down the back, a moistening of the eyes, a stirring in the hypogastrium, and a thousand unnamable symptoms besides, may be felt the moment beauty *excites* us. And these symptons also result when we are excited by moral perceptions, as of pathos, magnanimity, or courage. The voice breaks and the sob rises in the struggling chest, or the nostril dilates and the fingers tighten, whilst the heart beats, etc., etc. . . .
"The bodily sounding-board is at work, as careful introspection will show, far more than we usually suppose" (James, 1890, Vol. 2, pp. 468–471).

In his own inimitable style, James considered what happens when prolonged familiarity with an aesthetic object blunts the more remote emotional reactions as taste and judgment are sharpened. He scrutinized the "pure and undefiled" feeling, "the intellectual emotion" as it may exist in the expert critic's mind, "the dryness of it, the paleness, the absence of all glow" (James, 1890, Vol. 2, p. 471). It is quite clear that the distinction between so-called "coarser" and "subtler" emotions resided almost completely, for James, "in the fact that the bodily sounding-board, vibrating in the one case, is in the other mute" (James, 1890, Vol. 2, p. 471).

The brain needed no special centers to account for emotion as James conceived it: "Sensational, associational, and motor elements are all that the organ need contain" (James, 1890, Vol. 2, p. 473). Emotions were concatenations of particular kinds of sensations, those resulting from the expressive movements and glandular reactions which produce for an observer the overt and visible signs of emotion in another person. Emotions can be revived by memory and imagination because the idea of the original object "produces the same organic irradiations, or almost the same, which were produced by its original, so that the emotion is again a reality" (James, 1890, Vol. 2, p. 474). James acknowledged that persons differ in emotional temperament, that is, in their susceptibility to the kinds of movements and glandular reactions which constitute the physical basis of emotion. Likewise, not all persons have equally "lively imagination," the second ingredient needed for what James called "an abundant emotional life." His final generalization about emotion was: *They blunt themselves by repetition more rapidly than any other sort of feeling*" (James, 1890, Vol. 2, p. 475). In modern technical language, we refer to this process as *adaptation.*

THE GENESIS OF EMOTIONS

In place of mere cataloging, James proposed that questions of the genesis of emotions were much more important:

"(1) *What special diffusive effects do the various special objective and subjective experiences excite?* and
"(2) *How come they to excite them?*" (James, 1890, Vol. 2, p. 477)

Returning to the difficulty of separating *instinct* and *emotion*, James concurred with the general hypothesis advanced by Darwin, Spencer, and other 19th-century naturalists that emotions are a revival in weakened, residual form of reactions that were at one time useful in more violent dealings with the object inspiring them:

"Some movements of expression can be accounted for as *weakened repetitions of movements which formerly* (when they were stronger) *were of utility to the subject*. Others are similarly weakened repetitions of movements which under other con-conditions were *physiologically necessary effects*. Of the latter reactions the respiratory disturbances in anger and fear might be taken as examples— organic reminiscences, as it were, reverberations in imagination of the blowings of the man making a series of combative efforts, of the pantings of one in precipitate flight" (James, 1890, Vol. 2, p. 478).

## SUMMARY: INVOLUNTARY BEHAVIOR

In preparation for our review of James' introspective analysis of "desire," "deliberation," and "will," which constitute his psychology of volition, we have considered what he viewed as more primitive or "primary" determinants of observable actions and reactions. Like others in the late 19th century, he emphasized the importance of instinctive reactions. However, he stripped the doctrine of instinct of the teleological overtone implying prevision of ends, which it so often still has in common-sense usage. The prime movers are stimuli which instigate blind impulses to respond in certain ways. These reflex arcs are completely explained by the structure of the nervous system. In man and other "higher" animals, the complexity and plasticity of the nervous system allows the neural path between sensation ($S$) and impulse to respond ($R$) to be deepened by repetition. Thus habitual neural chains of association—habits— are established, and the reactions to particular stimulus objects become more complicated. Impulses to

act in different ways are simultaneously aroused, one by the stimulus object that is physically present and others by different objects which are suggested because they are linked by neural association with the original object. The observed response to a given object is therefore not as uniform as in lower forms where the nervous system is less complex and plastic. The concept of habit refers also to the rapid running off of long sequences of movements which on the first occasion are performed hesitantly, gropingly, deliberately. The sensation produced by a movement becomes the effective "cue" for the performance of the next movement. Through repetition, action is smoothed and conscious attention to each element in the sequence is gradually reduced until finally the whole chain of complex movements can "rattle off" automatically without conscious attention or deliberation at each juncture. The concept of sensations produced by movements and glandular reactions also provides a link between impulses to respond in certain ways (instinct) and the conscious experience called emotion. The James-Lange theory states that the conscious feelings we call emotion are the sensations which occur as a consequence of the movements and glandular reactions constituting what common sense considers the overt expression of emotion. Thus, *instinct*, *habit*, and *emotion* are concepts which refer to the determination of actions and feelings prior to any consideration of more complicated instances of voluntary behavior. Volition, for James, most clearly typified the function of consciousness, as if it were an organ added to steer a nervous system which had become too complex to steer itself automatically.

## VOLITION

Voluntary movements, as conceived by James, are secondary, not primary functions of the organism, because being desired and intended beforehand, they must be performed with full prevision of what they are to be: "*A supply of ideas of the various movements that are possible left in the memory by experiences of their involuntary performance is thus the first prerequisite of the voluntary life*" (James, 1890, Vol. 2, p. 488).

RESIDENT AND REMOTE EFFECTS OF PAST ACTIONS

Our discussion of habit and emotion has drawn attention to the sensations produced internally by a movement itself. These *kinaesthetic* impressions constitute what James called the "*resident* effects of the motion" (James, 1890, Vol. 2, p. 488). In addition, the supply of "ideas" of movements already performed, and hence the repertoire of possibilities for voluntary action, is made up of *"remote effects"* of past actions:

> "Now the same movement involuntarily performed may leave many different kinds of ideas of itself in the memory. If performed by another person, we of course *see* it, or we *feel* it if the moving part strikes another part of our own body. Similarly we have an auditory image of its effects if it produces sounds, as for example when it is one of the movements made in vocalization, or in playing on a musical instrument. All these *remote* effects of the movement, as we may call them, are also produced by movements which we ourselves perform; and they leave innumerable ideas in our mind by which we distinguish each movement from the rest. It *looks* distinct; it *feels* distinct to some distant part of the body which it strikes; or it *sounds* distinct. These remote effects would then, rigorously speaking, suffice to furnish the mind with the supply of ideas required" (James, 1890, Vol. 2, p. 488).

THE CONTENT OF CONSCIOUSNESS IN VOLITION

The first conclusion in analysis of volition is that *"whether or no there be anything else in the mind at the moment when we consciously will a certain act, a mental conception made up of memory-images of these sensations, defining which special act it is, must be there"* (James, 1890, Vol. 2, p. 492).

Now comes a question to which James devoted a great deal of attention: *"Is there anything else in the mind when we will to do an act?"* His answer for the *simplest* cases of voluntary action was clearly, "No": *"in perfectly simple voluntary acts there is nothing else in the mind but the kinaesthetic idea, thus defined, of what the act is to be"* (James, 1890, Vol. 2, pp. 492–493). He rejected completely the notion advanced by other introspectionists of the period that there is also some "feeling of innervation." He disbelieved that there could be any sensation of the neural discharge in motor nerves which precipitates the movement:

> ". . . *All our ideas of movement*, including those of the effort which it requires, as well as those of its direction, its extent, its strength, and its velocity, *are images of peripheral sensations, either 'remote,' or resident in the moving parts, or in other parts which sympathetically act with them in consequence of the 'diffusive wave' "* (James, 1890, Vol. 2, pp. 493–494).

To support this conclusion, James advanced the principle that consciousness deserts any process

where it can no longer be of use: "We grow unconscious of every feeling which is useless as a sign to lead us to our ends, and where one sign will suffice others drop out, and that one remains, to work alone" (James, 1890, Vol. 2, p. 496).

Recalling his conception of habitual action, we can appreciate the point of his argument:

> "The marksman ends by thinking only of the exact position of the goal, the singer only of the perfect sound, the balancer only of the point of the pole whose oscillations he must counteract. The associated mechanism has become so perfect in all these persons that each variation in the thought of the end is functionally correlated with the one movement fitted to bring the latter about" (James, 1890, Vol. 2, p. 497).

IDEO-MOTOR THEORY OF VOLUNTARY BEHAVIOR

Urging the principle of parsimony upon his contemporaries who insisted that a "feeling of innervation" must accompany volition, James outlined the *ideo-motor theory* of voluntary action:

> "If we call the immediate psychic antecedent of a movement the latter's *mental cue*, all that is needed for invariability of sequence on the movement's part is a *fixed connection* between each several mental cue, and one particular movement. For a movement to be produced with perfect precision, it suffices that it obey instantly its own mental cue and nothing else, and that this mental cue be incapable of awakening any other movement. Now the *simplest* possible arrangement for producing voluntary movements would be that the memory-images of the movement's distinctive peripheral effects, whether resident or remote, themselves should severally constitute the mental cues, and that no other psychic facts should intervene or be mixed up with them" (James, 1890, Vol. 2, p. 497).

In deciding how strong a movement shall be made, we are guided by memory images of feelings of effort consisting of sensations from the muscular contractions, fixations of the larynx, chest, face, and body which attended earlier reactions to the stimulus before us. To James, nothing seemed so obvious to introspection as this:

> "When a certain degree of energy of contraction rather than another is thought of by us, this complex aggregate of afferent feelings, forming the material of our thought, renders absolutely precise and distinctive our mental image of the exact strength of movement to be made, and the exact amount of resistance to be overcome" (James, 1890, Vol. 2, p. 500).

Thus, James argued, we are able to explain the feeling of surprise if a heavy-seeming suitcase turns out, as we lift it, to be empty and very light. "*Surprise can only come from getting a sensation which differs from the one we expect*" (James, 1890, Vol. 2, p. 502).

## IMPORTANCE OF THE IDEA OF
## THE END OF ACTION

Are the "resident" and "remote" sensorial consequences of a movement equally important as "mental cues" in volition? James argued that in the early stages of learning a movement, the immediate (resident) kinaesthetic impressions are what come most strongly before consciousness. As the movement becomes more practiced, however, they should slip from consciousness and be replaced by anticipatory images of more remote consequences of the action. "What we are *interested* in is what sticks in our consciousness," argued James (1890, Vol. 2, p. 519), and what interests us are the ends which the movement is to attain:

> "Such an end is generally an outer impression on the eye or ear, or sometimes on the skin, nose, or palate. Now let the idea of the end associate itself definitely with the right motor innervation, and the thought of the innervation's *resident* effects will become as great an encumbrance as we formerly concluded that the feeling of innervation itself would be. The mind does not need it; the end alone is enough.
> "An end consented to as soon as conceived innervates directly the centre of the first movement of the chain which leads to its accomplishment, and then the whole chain rattles off *quasi*-reflexly" (James, 1890, Vol. 2, p. 519). [See Figure 2.1.]

James continually depended upon the reader's own introspections to bear him out. For example, in the context of the present argument, he said:

> "The reader will certainly recognize this to be true in all fluent and unhesitating voluntary acts. The only special fiat there is at the outset of the performance. A man says to himself, 'I must change my shirt,' and involuntarily he has taken off his coat, and his fingers are at work in their accustomed manner on his waistcoat-buttons, etc.; or we say, 'I must go downstairs,' and ere we know it we have risen, walked, and turned the handle of the door;—all through the idea of an end coupled with a series of guiding sensations which successively arise. It would seem indeed that we fail of accuracy and certainty in our attainment of the end whenever we are preoccupied with much ideal consciousness of the means" (James, 1890, Vol. 2, pp. 519–520).

The "idea of movement," then, which precedes a "voluntary" movement is "the anticipation of the movement's sensible effects, resident or remote, and sometimes very remote indeed" (James, 1890, Vol. 2, p. 521). The analysis of volition brings to the forefront the concept of end, aim, purpose, or goal of the action sequence.

## THE ACT OF WILLING

Turning to analysis of more complex instances of voluntary behavior, those which involve conflict, indecision, and deliberation prior to action, James again asks:

> "*Is the bare idea of a movement's sensible effects its sufficient mental cue . . . or must there be an additional mental antecedent, in the shape of a fiat, decision, consent, volitional mandate, or other synonymous phenomenon of consciousness, before the movement can follow?*" (James, 1890, Vol. 2, p. 522).

His answer is now qualified:

> "Sometimes the bare idea is sufficient, but sometimes an additional conscious element, in the shape of a fiat, mandate, or express consent, has to intervene and precede the movement. The cases without a fiat constitute the more fundamental, because the more simple, variety" (James, 1890, Vol. 2, p. 522).

We shall consider first the more simple cases and then turn to the complications which involve James' notion of "fiat" or "consent." The distinguishing feature of simple instances of volition is that action follows "*unhesitatingly and immediately* the notion of it in the mind" (James, 1890, Vol. 2, p. 522):

> ". . . The determining condition of the unhesitating and resistless sequence of the act seems to be *the absence of any conflicting notion in the mind.* Either there is nothing else at all in the mind, or what is there does not conflict. The hypnotic subject realizes the former condition. Ask him what he is thinking about, and ten to one he will reply 'nothing.' The consequence is that he both believes everything he is told, and performs every act that is suggested" (James, 1890, Vol. 2, p. 523).

Let us consider an example, one drawn from his own experience, that to James seemed "to contain in miniature form the data for an entire psychology of volition":

> "We know what it is to get out of bed on a freezing morning in a room without a fire, and how the very vital principle within us protests against the ordeal. Probably most persons have lain on certain mornings for an hour at a time unable to brace themselves to the resolve. We think how late we shall be, how the duties of the day will suffer; we say, 'I *must* get up, this is

ignominious,' etc.; but still the warm couch feels too delicious, the cold outside too cruel, and resolution faints away and postpones itself again and again just as it seemed on the verge of bursting the resistance and passing over into the decisive act. Now how do we *ever* get up under such circumstances? If I may generalize from my own experience, we more often than not get up without any struggle or decision at all. We suddenly find that we *have* got up. A fortunate lapse of consciousness occurs; we forget both the warmth and the cold; we fall into some revery connected with the day's life, in the course of which the idea flashes across us, 'Hollo! I must lie here no longer' —an idea which at that lucky instant awakens no contradictory or paralyzing suggestions, and consequently produces immediately its appropriate motor effects. It was our acute consciousness of both the warmth and the cold during the period of struggle, which paralyzed our activity then and kept our idea of rising in the condition of *wish* and not of *will*. The moment these inhibitory ideas ceased, the original idea exerted its effects" (James, 1890, Vol. 2, pp. 524–525).

THE IMPULSIVE NATURE OF CONSCIOUSNESS

The reason this simple conception of volition is not self evident, James felt, is because we so often have ideas which do not result in action. In every such case, he argued, we do not act because "other ideas simultaneously present rob them of their impulsive power" (James, 1890, Vol. 2, p. 525). Consciousness is "*in its very nature impulsive*," but the experience of "an express fiat" or "act of mental consent" comes in "when the neutralization of the antagonistic and inhibitory idea is required" (James, 1890, Vol. 2, p. 526).

"We do not have a sensation or a thought and then have to *add* something dynamic to it to get a movement. Every pulse of feeling which we have is the correlate of some neural activity that is already on its way to instigate a movement. Our sensations and thoughts are but cross-sections, as it were, of currents whose essential consequence is motion, and which no sooner run in at one nerve than they run out again at another. The popular notion that mere consciousness as such is not essentially a forerunner of activity, that the latter must result from some superadded 'will-force,' is a very natural inference from those special cases in which we think of an act for an indefinite length of time without the action taking place. These cases, however, are not the norm; they are cases of inhibition by antagonistic thoughts. When the blocking is released we feel as if an inward spring were let loose, and this is the additional impulse or *fiat* upon which the act effectively succeeds. . . .

". . . In all simple and ordinary cases, just as the bare presence of one idea prompts a movement, so the bare presence of another idea will prevent its taking place. Try to feel as if you were crooking your finger, whilst keeping it straight. In a minute it will fairly tingle with the imaginary change of position; yet it will not sensibly move, because *its not really moving* is also a part of what you have in mind. Drop *this* idea, think of the movement purely and simply, with all brakes off; and, presto! it takes place with no effort at all" (James, 1890, Vol. 2, pp. 526–527).

From the above paragraphs we gain a clearer picture of the difference between simple and more complicated instances of volition. *Consciousness is by its very nature impulsive. Ideas of acting are already impulses on the way to release of motor action.* When everything is running smoothly (as in habitual action) there is little or no consciousness of what is happening beyond the "mental cue" of the end. Action is delayed because there are conflicting impulses. Then there is consciousness of the conflicting ideas. The presence of conflicting ideas weakens the impulsive power of each of the separate tendencies. When the blocking is released, "*we feel as if an inward spring were let loose*" (James, 1890, Vol. 2, p. 527, italics added), and this is the additional experience of "fiat" or "consent" which so often accompanies volition. The principle of ideo-motor action applies throughout, but the process is complicated when antagonistic impulses are present. The resolution of conflict, however accomplished, is the event which corresponds to the feeling of "consent" or "fiat" in volition.

CONFLICT, DELIBERATION, AND DECISION

James turned next to a detailed analysis of that "peculiar feeling of inward unrest known as *indecision*" which occurs when "the mind is the seat of many ideas related to each other in antagonistic ways":

"As long as it lasts, with the various objects before the attention, we are said to *deliberate;* and when finally the original suggestion either prevails and makes the movement take place, or gets definitively quenched by its antagonists, we are said to *decide*, or to *utter our voluntary fiat* in favor of one or the other course. The reinforcing and inhibiting ideas meanwhile are termed the *reasons* or *motives* by which the decision is brought about" (James, 1890, Vol. 2, p. 528).

At every moment, the object of consciousness is extremely complex; it is "the existence of the whole set of motives and their conflict . . ." (James, 1890,

Vol. 2, p. 528). But there are moment to moment fluctuations in this totality.

". . . Certain parts stand out more or less sharply at one moment in the foreground, and at another moment other parts, in consequence of the *oscillations of our attention, and of the 'associative' flow of our ideas* [italics added]. But no matter how sharp the foreground-reasons may be, or how imminently close to bursting through the dam and carrying the motor consequences their own way, the background, however dimly felt, is always there; and its presence (so long as the indecision actually lasts) serves as an effective check upon the irrevocable discharge. The deliberation may last for weeks or months, occupying at intervals the mind. The motives which yesterday seemed full of urgency and blood and life to-day feel strangely weak and pale and dead. But as little to-day as to-morrow is the question finally resolved. Something tells us that all this is provisional; that the weakened reasons will wax strong again, and the stronger weaken; that equilibrium is unreached; that testing our reasons, not obeying them, is still the order of the day, and that we must wait awhile, patient or impatiently, until our mind is made up "for good and all." This inclining first to one then to another future, both of which we represent as possible, resembles the oscillations to and fro of a material body within the limits of its elasticity. There is inward strain, but no outward rapture. And this condition, plainly enough, is susceptible of indefinite continuance, as well in the physical mass as in the mind. If the elasticity give way, however, if the dam ever do break, and the currents burst the crust, vacillation is over and decision is irrevocably there" (James, 1890, Vol. 2, pp. 528–529).

OTHER FACTORS IN DECISION MAKING

James called attention to several tendencies that seemed to be "constant components of the web of motivation" in any decision requiring deliberation:

1. "Impatience of the deliberative state," that is, the impulse to decide and act "merely because action and decision are, as such, agreeable, and relieve the tension of doubt and hesitancy" (James, 1890, Vol. 2, pp. 529–530).

2. The "*dread of the irrevocable*" (p. 530), which opposes quick decision and, like the impulse to decide, influences not the content of a decision, but "when" it shall occur.

3. "The impulse to persist in a decision once made" (p. 530). Nowhere, argued James, do people differ more than in their tendency either to consider all decisions provisional or resolutely to consider any decision once made as final and irrevocable no matter what the consequence.

FIVE TYPES OF DECISION

James also distinguished five types of decision:

1. *The reasonable type*, in which the arguments pro and con seem to settle themselves in the mind and lead to one alternative course of action which can be adopted with little effort or constraint.

2. *Acquiescence determined from without*, in which some accidental external occurrence is allowed to shift the balance in one direction because we are weary of long hesitation.

3. *Acquiescence determined from within*, in which we find ourselves acting as if automatically in the direction of one of the horns of the dilemma and are caught up in the excitement of the sense of motion after a long and intolerable hesitation: "'Forward now!' we inwardly cry, 'though the heavens fall'"; as we follow "like passive spectators" (James, 1890, Vol. 2, pp. 532–533).

4. *Sudden change of heart*, in which, as a consequence of some sobering experience like grief or fear, the whole scale of values of our motives undergoes a sudden change which makes all trivial alternatives fade into nothingness.

5. *Effortful decisions*, in which

". . . we feel, in deciding, as if we ourselves by our own wilful act inclined the beam; . . . by adding our living effort to the weight of the logical reason which, taken alone, seems powerless to make the act discharge; . . . [or] by a kind of creative contribution of something instead of a reason which does a reason's work. The slow dead heave of the will that is felt in these instances makes of them a class altogether different subjectively from all the three preceding classes. . . . If examined closely, its chief difference from the three former cases appears to be that in those cases the mind at the moment of deciding on the triumphant alternative dropped the other one wholly or nearly out of sight, whereas here both alternatives are steadily held in view, and in the very act of murdering the vanquished possibility the chooser realizes how much in that instant he is making himself lose" (James, 1890, Vol. 2, p. 534).

DETERMINANTS OF THE STRENGTH
OF AN IMPULSE TO ACT

James has argued that "*consciousness* (or the neural process which goes with it) *is in its very nature impulsive*." Now we must consider his proviso: "*it must be sufficiently intense*" (James, 1890, Vol. 2, p. 535) to produce movement. Under ordinary circumstances, he stated, there may be habitual inhibitions that must be overcome. There is, for example:

". . . the native inertia, or internal resistance, of the motor centres themselves making explosion impossible until a certain inward tension has been reached and overpast. These conditions may vary from one person to another and in the same person from time to time. The neural inertia may wax or wane, and the habitual inhibitions dwindle or augment. The intensity of particular thought-processes and stimulations may also change independently, and particular paths of association grow more pervious or less so. There thus result great possibilities of alteration in the actual impulsive efficacy of particular motives compared with others" (James, 1890, Vol. 2, pp. 535–536).

What, we may now ask, are the states of mind which normally possess the most impulsive quality? James answers:

". . . either those which represent objects of passion, appetite, or emotion—objects of instinctive reaction, in short; or they are feelings or ideas of pleasure or of pain; or ideas which for any reason we have grown accustomed to obey so that the habit of reacting on them is ingrained; or finally, in comparison with ideas of remoter objects, they are ideas of objects present or near in space and time. Compared with these various objects, all far-off considerations, all highly abstract conceptions, unaccustomed reasons, and motives foreign to the instinctive history of the race, have little or no impulsive power. They prevail, when they ever do prevail, *with effort; and the normal*, as distinguished from the pathological *sphere of effort is thus found wherever non-instinctive motives to behavior are to rule the day*" (James, 1890, Vol. 2, p. 536).

In this answer, James speaks to an issue that is central in the contemporary psychology of motivation. It is the task of writing a law to account for the strength of a particular impulse to act. What are the several determinants of the strength of a tendency to act in a certain way? The details of his answer may later be compared with those advanced by other theorists whose work we consider in other chapters.

How, we ask, is a decision between alternatives arrived at? James answers:

"Each stimulus or idea, at the same time that it wakens its own impulse, must arouse other ideas (associated and consequential) with their impulses, and action must follow, neither too slowly nor too rapidly, as the resultant of all the forces thus engaged. Even when the decision is very prompt, there is thus a sort of preliminary survey of the field and a vision of which course is best before the fiat comes" (James, 1890, Vol. 2, p. 536).

According to James, "healthiness of will" (p. 536) requires the kind of survey or what we now call "scanning" of possibilities that is outlined in the above paragraph. "Unhealthiness of will" (p. 537) or "perversity of will" can come about in a number of ways. Action may come about too rapidly, before there has been an adequate scanning of possibilities and potential restraints. James referred to this as "precipitate" or "explosive will" (p. 537). And even when the survey of possibilities is complete, "perversity of will" may come about as a result of many causes—"too much intensity, or too little, here; too much or too little inertia there; or elsewhere too much or too little inhibitory power" (James, 1890, Vol. 2, p. 537).

ACTION AS THE RESULTANT OF CONFLICT

In elaborating his views about "perversity of the will," James considered actions observed from the outside as the *resultant* of inner conflict. This conception of action as a resultant is fundamental to an understanding of the relationship between "motivation" and "action" in all subsequent theories:

"It must be kept in mind, however, that since the resultant action is always due to the *ratio* between the obstructive and the explosive forces which are present, we never can tell by the mere outward symptoms to what *elementary* cause the perversion of a man's will may be due, whether to an increase of one component or a diminution of the other. One may grow explosive as readily by losing the usual brakes as by getting up more of the impulsive steam; and one may find things impossible as well through the enfeeblement of the original desire as through the advent of new lions in the path" (James, 1890, Vol. 2, p. 537).

James advanced this concept as a foundation for his treatment of the "explosive will" and the "obstructed will," cases of unusual impulsiveness or unusual inhibition of action. We miss the importance of the idea of action as a "resultant" if we fail to see that it applies to the resolution of any conflict. Observed action is always a resultant of impulsive and inhibitory tendencies. James employed this idea to help clarify what he meant by "the feeling of effort" in volition.

THE FEELING OF EFFORT IN VOLITION

There is a feeling of effort, he argued:

". . . whenever a rarer and more ideal impulse is called upon to neutralize others of a more instinctive and habitual kind; . . . whenever strongly explosive tendencies are checked, or strongly obstructive conditions overcome.

". . . We *feel*, in all hard cases of volition, as if the line taken, when the rarer and more ideal motives prevail, were the line of greater resistance, and as if the line of coarser motivation were the more pervious and easy one, even at the very moment when we refuse to follow it. . . .

"If in general we class all springs of action as propensities on the one hand and ideals on the other, the sensualist never says of his behavior that it results from a victory over his ideals, but the moralist always speaks of his as a victory over his propensities" (James, 1890, Vol. 2, p. 548).

What, we want to ask, determines the amount of effort? James answers:

"The very greatness of the resistance itself. If the sensual propensity is small, the effort is small. The latter is *made great* by the presence of a great antagonist to overcome. And if a brief definition of ideal and moral action were required, none could be given which would better fit the appearances than this: *It is action in the line of the greatest resistance*" (James, 1890, Vol. 2, p. 549).

Is the feeling of "volitional effort" something novel, something indeterminate which we, in some way, add to one side of the conflict (the "ideals") to overcome the more powerful "propensities"? James answers:

"The facts may be most briefly symbolized thus, *P* standing for the propensity, *I* for the ideal impulse, and *E* for the effort:

$$I \, per \, se < P.$$
$$I + E > P.$$

"In other words, if *E* adds itself to *I*, *P* immediately offers the least resistance, and motion occurs in spite of it.

"But the *E* does not seem to form an integral part of the *I*. It appears adventitious and indeterminate in advance. We can make more or less as we please, and *if* we make enough we can convert the greatest mental resistance into the least. Such, at least, is the impression which the facts spontaneously produce upon us" (James, 1890, Vol. 2, p. 549).

James recognized that the traditional issue of determinism versus free will is involved in his answer to questions about the "feeling of effort" which introspection finds in every difficult problem of choice. There was no question in James' mind that all "effortless" volitions are strictly determined:

". . . *effortless* volitions are resultants of interests and associations whose strength and sequence are mechanically determined by the structure of

that physical mass, [the] brain; and the general continuity of things and the monistic conception of the world may lead one irresistibly to postulate that a little fact like effort can form no real exception to the overwhelming reign of deterministic law. Even in effortless volition we have the consciousness of the alternative being also possible. This is surely a delusion here; why is it not a delusion everywhere?" (James, 1890, Vol. 2, p. 572).

And also:

"Decisions with effort merge so gradually into those without it that it is not easy to say where the limit lies. Decisions without effort merge again into ideo-motor, and these into reflex acts; so that the temptation is almost irresistible to throw the formula which covers so many cases over absolutely all. Where there is effort just as where there is none, the ideas themselves which furnish the matter of deliberation are brought before the mind by the machinery of association. And this machinery is essentially a system of arcs and paths, a reflex system, whether effort be amongst its incidents or not. The reflex way is, after all, the universal way of conceiving the business. The feeling of *ease* is a passive result of the way in which the thoughts unwind themselves. Why is not the feeling of effort the same?" (James, 1890, Vol. 2, p. 575).

Despite considerations such as these, which persuaded many of his contemporaries of the continuity of "voluntary behavior" with reflexive, instinctive, and habitual behavior "whose predetermination," James stated, "no one doubts" (James, 1890, Vol. 2, p. 575), he firmly held that "the question of freewill is insoluble on strictly psychologic grounds" (James, 1890, Vol. 2, p. 572):

"After a certain amount of effort of attention has been given to an idea, it is manifestly impossible to tell whether either more or less of it *might* have been given or not. To tell that, we should have to ascend to the antecedents of the effort, and defining them with mathematical exactitude, prove, by laws of which we have not at present even an inkling, that the only amount of sequent effort which could *possibly* comport with them was the precise amount which actually came. Measurements, whether of psychic or of neural quantities, and deductive reasonings such as this method of proof implies, will surely be forever beyond human reach. No serious psychologist or physiologist will venture even to suggest a notion of how they might be practically made. We are thrown back therefore upon the crude evidences of introspection on the one hand, with all its liabilities to deception, and, on the other hand, upon *a priori* postulates and probabilities" (James, 1890, Vol. 2, p. 572).

True to his own theory of volition, James asserted:

". . . taking the risk of error on our head, we must project upon one of the alternative views the attribute of reality for us; we must so fill our mind with the idea of it that it becomes our settled creed. The present writer does this for the alternative of freedom . . ." (James, 1890, Vol. 2, p. 573).

Since the grounds of this opinion were ethical rather than psychological, James did not pursue them further in his treatise on psychology. Nor shall we undertake more than a recording of this late-19th-century view. It narrowed the domain of "free will" much more than had Descartes (1637), who supposed it to be located in the pineal gland. Nevertheless it still allowed for the operation of "free effort" in deciding between the limited alternatives which the associative machinery of the brain brings to consciousness:

". . . the operation of free effort, if it existed, could only be to hold some one ideal object, or part of an object, a little longer or a little more intensely before the mind. Amongst the alternatives which present themselves as *genuine possibles*, it would thus make one effective. And although such quickening of one idea might be *morally and historically momentous*, yet, if considered *dynamically*, it would be an operation amongst those physiological infinitesimals which calculation must forever neglect" (James, 1890, Vol. 2, pp. 576–577).

## THE "SPRINGS OF ACTION"

### PLEASURE AND PAIN

It is always something of a surprise to contemporary psychologists to rediscover how thoroughly James anticipated the issues which have dominated the experimental psychology of learning and motivation from the turn of the century to the present. His analysis of what accounts for the impulsive or inhibitive power of an idea is one remarkable illustration of this:

"Objects and thoughts of objects start our action, but the pleasures and pains which action brings modify its course and regulate it; and later the thoughts of the pleasures and the pains acquire themselves impulsive and inhibitive power. . . . But as present pleasures are tremendous reinforcers, and present pains tremendous inhibitors of whatever action leads to them, so the thoughts of pleasures and pains take rank amongst the thoughts which have most impulsive and inhibitive power. The precise relation which these thoughts hold to other thoughts is thus a matter demanding some attention.

"If a movement feels agreeable, we repeat and repeat it as long as the pleasure lasts. If it hurts us, our muscular contractions at the instant stop. So complete is the inhibition in this latter case that it is almost impossible for a man to cut or mutilate himself slowly and deliberately—his hand invincibly refusing to bring on the pain. And there are many pleasures which, when once we have begun to taste them, make it all but obligatory to keep up the activity to which they are due" (James, 1890, Vol. 2, pp. 549–550).

These general ideas are certainly not original with James. They represent, however, a sophisticated statement of the traditional doctrine of hedonism in the context of deliberation about the neural basis of action. As widespread as the apparent influence of feelings of pleasure and pain on action is, James considered it a "premature philosophy" to treat pleasure and pain as the *only* spurs to action. They have, he reminds us, absolutely nothing to do with manifestations of instinct or emotional expression:

"Who smiles for the pleasure of the smiling, or frowns for the pleasure of the frown? Who blushes to escape the discomfort of not blushing? Or who in anger, grief, or fear is actuated to the movements which he makes by the pleasures which they yield? In all these cases the movements are discharged fatally by the *vis a tergo* which the stimulus exerts upon a nervous system framed to respond in just that way" (James, 1890, Vol. 2, p. 550).

The hedonist must not ignore the reflexive responses then called instinct; the habitual actions, which are performed with little or no consciousness of attendant or consequential pleasures or pains; and the *objects* of emotion like rage, love, or terror, which have a peculiar sort of impulsive power whether they be actually present to the senses or merely represented as ideas in consciousness. "The *impulsive quality* of mental states," James argued, "is an attribute behind which we cannot go. Some states of mind have more of it than others, some have it in this direction, and some in that" (James, 1890, Vol. 2, p. 551).

Over and over again, James reiterated that it is an essential characteristic of consciousness (or of the neural process underlying it) to instigate movement of some sort. Feelings of pleasure and pain have this characteristic; but so also do perceptions of objects and imaginations of objects. Thoughts of pleasure or of pain play no part in the activation of the initial instinctive actions which are performed without any prevision of ends. Nor do they play any role in so many of the daily routines which have become habitual which follow the principle of ideo-motor action:

> "How much more conducive to clearness and insight it is to take the *genus* 'springs of action' and treat it as a whole; and then to distinguish within it the species 'pleasure and pain' from whatever other species may be found!" (James, 1890, Vol. 2, p. 555).

James called attention to a complication in the relation of pleasure to action which he felt partly accounts for the general credence given the hedonistic doctrine. He put it this way:

> "An impulse which discharges itself immediately is generally quite *neutral* as regards pleasure or pain—the breathing impulse, for example. If such an impulse is arrested, however, by an extrinsic force, a great feeling of *uneasiness* is produced—for instance, the dyspnoea of asthma. And in proportion as the arresting force is then overcome, *relief* accrues—as when we draw breath again after the asthma subsides. The relief is a pleasure and the uneasiness a pain; and thus it happens that round all our impulses, merely as such, there twine, as it were, secondary possibilities of pleasant and painful feeling, involved in the manner in which the act is allowed to occur. These *pleasures and pains of achievement, discharge, or fruition* exist, no matter what the original spring of action be. We are glad when we have successfully got ourselves out of a danger, though the thought of the gladness was surely not what suggested to us to escape. To have compassed the steps towards a proposed sensual indulgence also makes us glad, and this gladness is a pleasure additional to the pleasure originally proposed. On the other hand, we are chagrined and displeased when any activity, however instigated, is hindered whilst in process of actual discharge. We are 'uneasy' till the discharge starts up again" (James, 1890, Vol. 2, pp. 555–556).

## PURSUED PLEASURE AND THE PLEASURE OF ACHIEVEMENT

It is, in James' words, the "*confusion of pursued pleasure with mere pleasure of achievement*" (James, 1890, Vol. 2, pp. 556–557) which makes the hedonistic theory of common sense so plausible. By "pursued pleasure" he meant a "pleasure *for the sake* of which" (James, 1890, Vol. 2, p. 556) an act is performed. This is the pleasure anticipated as a consequence of acting in a certain way. By "pleasure of achievement" he meant the incidental pleasure which attends performance of an act in the line of the present impulse and, contrariwise, the pain which would come if it is interrupted. The ordinary hedon-

ist, argued James, expresses the fact that action in the line of the present impulse seems the pleasantest course (witness the irritation when it is blocked in some way) by saying that we act for the sake of the pleasantness involved. But, he continued, for this sort of pleasure to be possible, or for the irritation of disruption to be possible, "*the impulse must be there already as an independent fact*" (James, 1890, Vol. 2, p. 557) to get the action started: "You cannot have your pleasure of achievement unless you have managed to get your impulse under headway beforehand by some previous means" (James, 1890, Vol. 2, p. 557).

The problem, as he saw it, becomes even more complicated when it is acknowledged that "*the pleasure of achievement may itself become a pursued pleasure*":

> "Take a foot-ball game or a fox-hunt. Who in cold blood wants the fox for its own sake, or cares whether the ball be at this goal or that? We know, however, by experience, that if we can once rouse a certain impulsive excitement in ourselves, whether to overtake the fox, or to get the ball to one particular goal, the successful venting of it over the counteracting checks will fill us with exceeding joy. We therefore get ourselves deliberately and artificially into the hot impulsive state. It takes the presence of various instinct-arousing conditions to excite it; but little by little, once we are in the field, it reaches paroxysm; and we reap the reward of our exertions in that pleasure of successful achievement which, far more than the dead fox or the goal-got ball, was the object we originally pursued" (James, 1890, Vol. 2, p. 557).

Granted, it is the pleasure of achievement that we sometimes pursue. This does not mean what the pleasure-philosophers seem to suppose, argued James, that always and everywhere it is pursuit of either a sensuous pleasure or the pleasure of achievement that is the mainspring of action. And as we do not always act for the sake of gaining some pleasure, neither do we act in order to escape the uneasiness of arrested action. The uneasiness which attends interrupted actions is "altogether due to the fact that the act is *already tending to occur* on other grounds" (James, 1890, Vol. 2, p. 558). The original bases for acting, whatever they were, provide the impetus for continuance, "even though the uneasiness of the arrest may upon occasion add to their impulsive power" (James, 1890, Vol. 2, p. 558).

## INTEREST AS DETERMINANT OF ATTENTION

James, we see, did not deny the importance of immediately felt or anticipated pleasures and pains in the motivation of action. Rather, he tried to bring in pleasure and pain under a broader conception which would embrace *all* of the springs of action. His view was that *any* idea which is able to compel attention and to dominate consciousness would influence action. If one must have a single name for the condition upon which the impulsive or inhibitive property depends, James proposed that the word be "*interest*":

> " 'The interesting' is a title which covers not only the pleasant and the painful, but also the morbidly fascinating, the tediously haunting, and even the simply habitual, inasmuch as the attention usually travels on habitual lines, and what-we-attend-to and what-interests-us are synonymous terms" (James, 1890, Vol. 2, pp. 558–559).

All ideas, as James conceived them, have relations with some path of action. Let any idea dominate for a moment, and let no other ideas displace it, then whatever motor effects belong to it will occur. This is what he argued in the case of instinct, emotion, in habitual ideo-motor action, and finally in the case of voluntary behavior which involves conflict, indecision, and choice:

> "In short, one does not see any case in which the steadfast occupancy of consciousness does not appear to be the prime condition of impulsive power. It is still more obviously the prime condition of inhibitive power. What checks our impulses is the mere thinking of reasons to the contrary—it is their bare presence to the mind which gives the veto, and makes acts, otherwise seductive, impossible to perform" (James, 1890, Vol. 2, p. 559).

## BASIC PROBLEM FOR A PSYCHOLOGY OF VOLITION

In closing his introspective analysis of volition, James stated:

> ". . . we find ourselves driven more and more exclusively to consider the conditions which make ideas prevail in the mind. With the prevalence, once there as a fact, of the motive idea the *psychology* of volition properly stops. The movements which ensue are exclusively physiological phenomena, following according to physiological laws upon the neural events to which the idea corresponds. The *willing* terminates with the prevalence of the idea; and whether the act then follows or not is a matter quite immaterial, so far as the willing itself goes. I will to write, and the act follows. I will to sneeze, and it does not. I will that the distant table slide over the floor towards me; it also does not. My willing representation can no more instigate my sneezing-centre than it can instigate the table to activity. But in both cases it is

as true and good willing as it is when I willed to write.\* In a word, volition is a psychic or moral fact pure and simple, and is absolutely completed when the stable state of the idea is there. The supervention of motion is a supernumerary phenomenon depending on executive ganglia whose function lies outside the mind" (James, 1890, Vol. 2, pp. 559–560).

The footnote to this paragraph, inserted at the asterisk (\*), is revealing of the kinds of controversies which arose as a consequence of reliance on the introspective method. In it, James notes that many persons say that where they disbelieve in the possibility of bringing about a certain effect, they cannot will it. Or perhaps different people attach different connotations to the word "will." James acknowledges: "When one knows that he has no power, one's desire of a thing is called a *wish* and not a will. The sense of impotence inhibits the volition" (James, 1890, Vol. 2, p. 560, fn.). This statement both illustrates the subtleties of introspective analysis and makes a point of some importance in connection with later theoretical conceptions of motivation which emphasize the important role of *expectations* about the consequences of actions. The final sentences of James' footnote nicely illustrate the irresolvable issues which characterized the introspective period of psychology and begin to suggest its inconclusiveness and ultimate sterility as a scientific method:

> "Only by abstracting from the thought of the impossibility am I able energetically to imagine strongly the table sliding over the floor, make the bodily 'effort' which I do, and to will it to come towards me. It may be that some people are unable to perform this abstraction, and that the image of the table stationary on the floor inhibits the contradictory image of its moving, which is the object to be willed" (James, 1890, Vol. 2, p. 560, fn.).

We thus reach the heart of James' conception of volition when we ask, as he did in identifying this as the central issue: *How does the thought of an act come to prevail stably in the mind?* The "volitional effort" of which he spoke (if there be such a thing) is clearly the effort involved in attending to an idea, of making it dominate consciousness. This is what James meant by the "fiat" or "consent"—the subjective experience which is equivalent to saying "let it be," which is the act of consciously "willing."

## A NEURAL MECHANISM FOR VOLITION

James concluded his psychology of "will" with a number of speculations about the kinds of neural arrangements that would be required to explain what introspection had revealed about volition. True to his conviction that what can be described in the language of conscious experience through introspection must, in principle at least, also be describable in the neurophysiological language, James titled his section on possible neural mechanisms, "The Education of the Will." Today we might call it, "The Neurophysiology of Learning." In it, he foreshadows the kind of analysis of connections between stimulus (S) and response (R) and the debate about possible neural mechanisms which was to dominate the theoretical orientation of many psychologists who turned from introspective analysis to experimental study of animal behavior, following Thorndike's classic investigation (1898) of how cats learn to get out of a puzzle box (see Chapter 5). Starting with the notion of instinctive reaction as blind, reflexive response to a given stimulus, he asked "*how can the sensory process which a movement has previously produced, discharge, when excited again, into the centre for the movement itself?*" (James, 1890, Vol. 2, p. 580). "To tell how this comes to pass," he stated, "would be to answer the problem of the education of the will in physiological terms" (James, 1890, Vol. 2, p. 580).

The task, as he saw it, was to begin to invent hypotheses about neural action to account for the formation of the new neural paths that were needed to explain volition as it is given to introspection. We shall state, with little comment, a number of his hypotheses simply to show the foreshadowing of subsequent treatments of these matters:

a. The connate (innate) neural paths all run one way, "*that is from 'sensory' cells into 'motor' cells and from motor cells into muscles, without ever taking the reverse direction.*" A corollary of this "law" is that no sensation has any tendency in advance of experience to awaken another sensation. "*There is no a priori calling up of one 'idea' by another; the only a priori couplings are of ideas with movements*" (James, 1890, Vol. 2, p. 581).

b. Once a motor cell (R) is fired by the sensation ($S_1$) to which it is innately connected, the kinaesthetic sensation ($S_2$) produced by the movement itself should continue to fire the motor cell (R). Motor contraction once initiated would continue indefinitely if it were not for other processes going on which inhibit the contraction. Thus "*inhibition is . . . an essential and unremitting element of our cerebral life*" (James, 1890, Vol. 2, p. 583).

In this connection, James stated that one great

inhibitor of the discharge of the sensation produced by a movement back into the motor cell causing the movement "seems to be the painful or otehwise displeasing quality of the sensation itself." Conversely, when the sensation is distinctly pleasant, that fact tends to further the tendency of the sensation produced by a movement to discharge back into the motor cell "to keep the primordial motor circle agoing" (James, 1890, Vol. 2, p. 583). In other words, if the consequence of a movement is a painful sensation, further movement is inhibited; if the consequence is a pleasant sensation, the movement continues.

The difficulty faced in trying to account for "pleasure" and "pain" in neural terms was immediately evident to James:

"Tremendous as the part is which pleasure and pain play in our psychic life, we must confess that absolutely nothing is known of their cerebral conditions. It is hard to imagine them as having special centres; it is harder still to invent peculiar forms of process in each and every centre, to which these feelings may be due. And let one try as one will to represent the cerebral activity in exclusively mechanical terms, I, for one, find it quite impossible to enumerate what seem to be the facts and yet to make no mention of the psychic side which they possess" (James, 1890, Vol. 2, p. 583).

The speculations about the role of "pleasure" and "pain" are interesting and instructive as to how this persistent dilemma seemed late in the 19th century:

"If the mechanical activities in a cell, as they increase, give pleasure, they seem to increase all the more rapidly for that fact; if they give displeasure, the displeasure seems to dampen the activities. The psychic side of the phenomenon thus seems, somewhat like the applause or hissing at a spectacle, to be an encouraging or adverse *comment* on what the machinery brings forth. The soul *presents* nothing herself; *creates* nothing; is at the mercy of the material forces for all *possibilities;* but amongst these possibilities she *selects;* and by reinforcing one and checking others, she figures not as an 'epiphenomenon' but as something from which the play gets moral support" (James, 1890, Vol. 2, p. 584).

c. "Potentialities of new paths are furnished by the fibres which connect sensory cells amongst themselves . . ." (James, 1890, Vol. 2, p. 584). The process by which new paths are formed is one in which the discharge of any sensory cell towards a motor cell tends to drain sensory cells behind it of whatever "tension" they may possess. The result is a new-formed path running from the "rearward" sensory cell to the "forward" sensory cell. When the rearward cell is later stimulated, the forward sensory cell will be immediately stimulated because of the new-formed path. As a result, *"when a sensation has once produced a movement in us, the next time we have the sensation, it tends to suggest the idea of the movement, even before the movement occurs"* (James, 1890, Vol. 2, p. 585). Now the sensation which was originally produced by the movement itself (the "idea" of the movement) is *antecedent* to the movement, so that when the motor cell which causes the movement discharges, it now drains the "tension" from the sensory cell corresponding to this sensation setting up a new path. Repetition will deepen the path. In time, the "idea" of the movement's sensory effects will have become an immediate and habitual antecedent of the movement itself. This, basically, is the condition James needed to explain what introspection seems to show, that the idea of the movement is what precedes its actual occurrence in instances of voluntary behavior.

### HYPOTHETICAL NEURAL MECHANISM OF AVOIDANCE (OR INHIBITION)

This type of analysis was extended to some of the more complicated problems James had discussed from the introspective side. We shall consider just one of them to capture the flavor of the beginnings of speculation about the neurophysiological underpinnings of motivational phenomena later treated experimentally. James considered the behavior of a child who sees a flame for the first time, reaches for it, is burned, and thereafter never reaches for it again: the problem of punishment and subsequent avoidance (or inhibition).

"The sight of the flame stimulates the cortical centre $S^1$ which discharges by an instinctive reflex path into the centre $M^1$ for the grasping-movement. This movement produces the feeling of burn, as its effects come back to the centre $S^2$; and this centre by a second connate path discharges into $M^2$, the centre for withdrawing the hand. The movement of withdrawal stimulates the centre $S^3$, and this, as far as we are concerned, is the last thing that happens. Now the next time the child sees the candle, the cortex is in possession of the secondary paths which the first experience left behind. $S^2$, having been stimulated immediately after $S^1$, drained the latter, and now $S^1$ discharges into $S^2$ before the discharge of $M^1$ has had time to occur; in other words, the sight of the flame suggests the idea of the burn before it produces its own natural reflex effects. The result is an inhibition of $M^1$, or an

overtaking of it before it is completed, by $M^2$" (James, 1890, Vol. 2, pp. 590–591). [See Figure 2.2.]

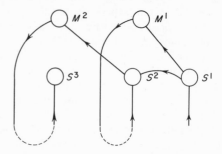

FIGURE 2.2    James' hypothetical neural mechanism to explain avoidance or inhibition. (*From James, 1890, Vol. 2, p. 591*)

We might say that the child's innate response to the imagined consequence of reaching, the burn ($S^2$), is withdrawal ($M^2$). This response is incompatible with his innate response, grasping ($M^1$), to a bright, flaming, object ($S^1$). The simultaneous presence of both ideas is enough to prevent the "willing" of the grasping movement in the period of indecision occasioned by the conflict between what *initially* were two blind, reflexive reactions to particular stimuli. The example captures the continuity from blind, reflexive response to the problem of volition. It also shows the interrelatedness of instinct, habit, volition, and even emotion if we consider the feeling of "fright" produced by the sudden withdrawal. These are the interrelated concepts James included under his broad heading, "the springs of action." They define many of the interrelated problems in contemporary psychology of motivation.

### SUMMARY: MOTIVATION CONCEIVED AS CONSCIOUS VOLITION

The introspective psychology of volition presented by James during the period when psychology was considered the "science of the mind" is easily understood. It is an elaborate description of what common sense conceives, in cruder terms, to be the process of motivation. The vivid descriptions of mental states, elaborated in the language of conscious experience (wishes, wants, desires, feelings, ideas, etc.), is congenial to the intuitive view of how behavior is caused. The conception of ideo-motor action, which highlights the importance of the idea of the end of action (commonly called "the goal") as the important "mental cue" in volition and acknowledges that long sequences of habitual actions "rattle off" automatically, is also intuitively compelling. Particularly congenial to common sense is the conception of consciousness as "fighter for ends," as the locus of deliberation and selection between alternative ends and of the most appropriate means to attain a given end. Perhaps the transition from common sense to the attitude of contemporary psychology begins as James argues that there is some neural process in the brain corresponding to every mental state and that the psychology of volition could be written in the language of neurophysiology, if we knew enough about the brain.

We begin our study of motivation with this review of James' treatment of volition because it is such a small step from the conception of common sense and because it conveys what the pre-experimental, introspective psychology of the late 19th century was like. We see the pervasive influence of Darwin's theory of evolution as James struggles to discover the adaptive significance of consciousness and advances the notion that consciousness functions like an organ evolved to steer a nervous system that has become too complex to regulate itself automatically. We see the influence of Darwin again and again as James feels compelled to link the phenomena of "mind," like emotion and will, to bodily processes and thus to suggest the continuity between the original, blind, reflexive impulses to action called instincts, the automaticity of habit, and the more "reasonable," deliberative, and selective process which characterizes conscious volition. We are introduced to a number of important concepts; instinct, habit, emotion, ideo-motor action, response-produced stimulus, pleasure as reinforcer, pain as inhibitor of behavior, and others. All of these concepts have since been refined, restated, and interwoven in the psychology of motivation. We catch the flavor of a period in which anecdotal evidence and the insufferable ambiguities of introspective analysis were tolerated as the "empirical" foundation of the science. In the Chapters which follow, we shall see how the conception of the problem of motivation and the method of study evolved as a consequence of subsequent developments.

# CHAPTER 3

# Indirect Analysis
# of Unconscious
# Motives

*"Humanity has in the course of time had to endure
from the hands of science two great outrages upon its
naïve self-love. The first was when it realized that our
earth was not the centre of the universe, but only a
tiny speck in a world-system of a magnitude hardly
conceivable. . . . The second was when biological research robbed man of his peculiar privilege of having
been specially created, and relegated him to a descent
from the animal world, implying an ineradicable animal nature in him. . . . But man's craving for gran-
diosity is now suffering the third and most bitter blow
from present-day psychological research which is endeavouring to prove to the "ego" of each one of us
that he is not even master in his own house, but that
he must remain content with the veriest scraps of information about what is going on unconsciously in
his own mind"* (Freud [1920],* 1943, p. 252).†

## INTRODUCTION TO SIGMUND FREUD
(1856–1939)

### THE POSSIBILITY OF UNCONSCIOUS
### MENTAL PROCESSES

Just one year before William James published his
*Principles*, a young Viennese physician who had
specialized in nervous diseases sat as a spectator
watching some astonishing hypnotic experiments and
demonstrations by Bernheim. Sigmund Freud had
decided to spend the summer of 1889 with him
perfecting his technique in hypnosis, a therapeutic
method which he had learned a few years earlier
from Charcot and which he had begun to find more
promising than any other in his attempt to treat
the neurosis called hysteria. Some years later, in his
*Autobiography*, he reports the impact of his experience that summer as a spectator of hypnotic phenomena: ". . . I received the profoundest impression of the possibility that there could be powerful

* In order to preserve a sense of the historical sequence
of ideas, the original date of publication is given in
brackets when a more recent and readily available source
is cited.
† Excerpts from Sigmund Freud, *A General Introduction to Psychoanalysis*, copyright 1920, are reprinted with
permission of George Allen & Unwin Ltd. and the
Liveright Publishing Corp.

mental processes which nevertheless remained hidden from the consciousness of men" (Freud, 1935, pp. 28–29).*

Freud was not the first to be struck by the idea of unconscious mental processes. But he was to make more of the idea than anyone before his time. As Freud conceived them, unconscious processes amounted to more than merely the automatic rattling-off without awareness of habitual action patterns. What impressed him most were phenomena which seemed to have all the essential characteristics of what James had called "volition" except one—consciousness. Freud was quick to observe that many of the symptoms his neurotic patients displayed, like repeated compulsive actions, seemed to correspond in all essentials with hypnotic phenomena. The neurotic often behaved, he said, "exactly like a subject under hypnotism whom Bernheim had ordered to open an umbrella in the ward five minutes after he awoke, but who had no idea why he was doing it" (Freud, [1920], 1943, p. 245).

## FIRST SCIENTIFIC RECOGNITION
### OF PSYCHOANALYSIS

Twenty years later, in 1909, Freud met William James briefly just a year before the latter's death. This helps us to pinpoint in time the first important impact of psychoanalytic ideas on the academic field of experimental psychology. It was on the occasion when Freud gave his first account of the development of the subject matter of psychoanalysis in five lectures before Clark University at Worcester, Massachusetts. This was the first official recognition of the possible importance to scientific psychology of psychoanalysis, a movement initiated by Freud within the field of medicine in the treatment of neurosis. For Freud, these lectures before a scientific audience in 1909 marked the end of a long period of work which had begun in almost complete isolation from medical colleagues who scorned his "fantastic" new ideas about the causes and treatment of neurosis. The official rebuke he faced was softened somewhat around 1902 when he began to gain some support from a small group which had gathered around him with the expressed intention of learning, practicing, and spreading psychoanalysis. The full significance to Freud of this first invitation to present his views to scientific colleagues can be appreciated from his own later reflections:

* Excerpts from Sigmund Freud's *Autobiography*, Copyright 1935, are reprinted by permission of W. W. Norton & Company, Inc.

"At that time I was only fifty-three, I felt young and healthy, and my short visit to the new world encouraged my self-respect in every way. In Europe I felt as though I were despised, but in America I found myself received by the foremost men as an equal. As I stepped on to the platform at Worcester to deliver my *Five Lectures upon Psycho-Analysis* it seemed like the realization of some incredible day-dream: psycho-analysis was no longer a product of delusion; it had become a valuable part of reality" (Freud, 1935, p. 104).

## BASIC CONTRIBUTIONS

During these twenty years, Freud had developed the foundation of his theories of resistance and repression, of the unconscious, of the aetiological significance of sexual life, and of the importance of infantile experience. "These," he stated, "form the principal constituents of the theoretical structure of psycho-analysis" (Freud, 1935, p. 76).

In addition, he had substituted the method of free association for hypnosis as the technique employed to recover memories of significant emotional experiences in the treatment of neurosis, and he had developed what he called the "art of interpretation" of mental content which he set forth in his classic work, *The Interpretation of Dreams* (1900). Furthermore, he had discovered that his method of analysis and his theoretical conception extended to the study of numerous little slips and mistakes which people often make and which common sense had always considered trivial and accidental. In 1904 he had published *The Psychopathology of Everyday Life* to show that the slips and errors of everyday life are not to be considered mere accidents having perhaps some physiological explanation but no other significance. He argued that slips, errors, accidents, and temporary lapses of memory, like dreams and neurotic symptoms, have a psychological significance that can be discovered and interpreted; all are motivated by unconscious wishes, intentions of the sort that are normally held to accompany the conscious process of volition. *Freud conceived it to be the work of psychoanalysis to discover why consciousness is denied to certain motives and to ascertain how and why their expression in conscious thought and action is possible only in incredibly disguised form.*

## SCOPE OF FREUD'S WORK

Freud's medical colleagues were to recoil from Freud's first arguments that neurotic symptoms represent the resolution of a mental conflict in which a wish, a motive, which has been banished from consciousness is expressed, that this wish seems invariably to be sexual in nature, and that the wish seems in all cases to date back to the earliest years of sexuality in childhood. How much more was the world to recoil from the implication of Freud's argument that dreams and occasional slips and errors, which are phenomena of *normal* mental life that occur in any healthy person, require the same inferences and assumptions. The implication of his discovery was crystal clear to Freud:

"If dreams turned out to be constructed like symptoms, if their explanation required the same assumptions—the repression of impulses, substitute-formation, compromise-formation, the dividing of the conscious and the unconscious into various psychical systems—then psycho-analysis was no longer a subsidiary science in the field of psychopathology; it was rather the foundation for a new and deeper science of the mind which would be equally indispensable for the understanding of the normal. Its postulates and findings could be carried over to other regions of mental happening; a path lay open to it that led far afield, into spheres of universal interest" (Freud, 1935, pp. 93–94).

Since 1909, when Freud first formally addressed a scientific audience, the term "psychoanalysis," which had originally been the name given by Freud to his new therapeutic method, has come to be employed by many as the name for a new field of inquiry—"the science of unconscious mental processes" (Freud, 1935, p. 144). Breuer had introduced Freud to the problems of hysteria and the temporary alleviation of physical symptoms following a catharsis in which forgotten experiences are reproduced under hypnosis. The therapeutic method called psychoanalysis substitutes free association and dream interpretation for hypnosis as the means of recovering significant emotional experiences. The implications of the concepts evolved in the treatment of neurosis are given extensive elaboration in books such as *Wit and its Relation to the Unconscious* (1905), *Totem and Taboo* (1913), *The Future of an Illusion* (1928), *Civilization and its Discontents* (1930), and other writings which turn to the analysis of aesthetics, religion, history, culture, and virtually every facet of human activity.

The complete story of Freud's work, from his early collaboration with Breuer in the 1880's to his extensive analyses of societal problems in later writings, is too long and too complex to tell in this introductory treatment. Nor shall we attempt to give an account of the elaborations and extensions of psychoanalytic ideas by those who have agreed and disagreed with Freud's original emphases, continuing, in their own clinical practice and treatment of neurosis, the work he began. Our limited objective is to consider Freud's discovery of the importance of unconscious determinants of thought and action as the first and most dramatic challenge to the commonsense conception of motivation. It demands a reorientation of thought about what constitutes the problem of motivation and how it should be studied. An overview of Freud's effort to construct an intelligible picture of the dynamics of mental conflict and his plausible arguments about how the motives of an adult have a history which dates back to earliest childhood will have an additional value. It will give us in bold outline a framework of thought within which the relationship among a number of subsequent fields of study within psychology may be seen. The Freudian scheme suggests how the study of learning and development of personality is related to the study of contemporaneous motivation and resolution of conflict, and how each of these fields of interest is related to the attempt to describe and measure how individuals differ in personality.

FREUD'S REACTION TO CRITICS

Contemporary attitudes about the significance of Freud's work for scientific psychology still range from uncritical conviction that the study of human motivation both began and ended with Freud, at one extreme, to an utter disregard of his major contributions, at the other, because his observations lacked quantified rigor and his concepts were often animistic, mentalistic, and ambiguous. There is no doubt that Freud considered himself a scientist and his work a contribution to science. He appreciated, as some of his ardent followers did not, that his original conceptions would be revised, extended, elaborated and probably supplanted by new and better ones as the science of psychology developed. A fair reading of his works will uncover, in addition to creative genius, a realistic skepticism about the life expectancy of some of his theoretical inventions. His reliance on introspection and anecdotal observation, we must remember, was common among psychologists of the late 19th and early 20th centuries, who had not yet learned how problems of human motivation might be subjected to experimental analysis. What Freud added to the same general method that James and other writers of the period employed were thousands of hours of intensive clinical observations of neurotic patients and a searching introspective self-analysis which provided the seed for new ideas and was, in turn, constantly guided by new conceptions as he began to develop them. No criticism pained Freud more than the frequent accusation that his concepts lacked *any* empirical foundation:

"Apart from emotional resistances, which were so easily explicable by the psycho-analytical theory that it was impossible to be misled by them, it seemed to me that the main obstacle to agreement lay in the fact that my opponents regarded psycho-analysis as a product of my speculative imagination and were unwilling to believe in the long, patient and unbiased work which had gone into its making. Since in their opinion analysis had nothing to do with observation or experience, they believed that they themselves were justified in rejecting it without experience. Others again, who did not feel so strongly convinced of this, repeated in their resistance the classical manoeuvre of not looking through the microscope so as to avoid seeing what they had denied" (Freud, 1935, p. 99).

Freud's reply to those who criticized the lack of precision in his concepts and explanatory schemes manifests the irritation of an explorer who could tolerate, where others could not, the ambiguity of his initial map of an unknown region. His writings reveal a conviction he shares with other scientists that improvement of basic concepts is essentially a bootstrap operation in which further and improved observation always plays the decisive role:

"Zoölogy and botany did not start from correct and adequate definitions of an animal and a plant; to this very day biology has been unable to give any certain meaning to the concept of life. Physics itself, indeed, would never have made any advance if it had had to wait until its concepts of matter, force, gravitation, and so on, had reached the desirable degree of clarity and precision. The fundamental concepts or most general ideas in any of the disciplines of science are always left indeterminate at first and are only explained to begin with by reference to the realm of phenomena from which they were derived; it is only by means of a progressive analysis of the material of observation that they can be made clear and can find a significant and consistent meaning. I have always felt it as a gross injustice that people always refuse to treat psycho-analysis like any other science. This refusal found an expression in the raising of the most obstinate objections. Psycho-analysis was constantly reproached for its incompleteness and insufficiencies, though it is plain that a science based upon observation has no alternative but to work out its findings piecemeal and to solve its problems step by step" (Freud, 1935, pp. 117–118).

CONTINUITY OF NORMAL AND
PATHOLOGICAL BEHAVIOR

The observations which provide the foundation of most of Freud's concepts are those which he (and later others) made in the study of neurosis and other pathological phenomena. His discovery that dreams, errors, and slips—the psychopathology of everyday life—provide a fund of observations from the domain of everyday activity to which these concepts apply equally well, allows us to consider these more familiar instances in our study of his method and basic concepts. Freud clearly believed that "normal" and "pathological" behavior were continuous:

"It must be true, as Jung expressed it so well in the early days when he was still an analyst, that neuroses have no peculiar content which belongs exclusively to them, but that neurotics break down at the same difficulties that are successfully overcome by normal people. This discovery was very far from being a disappointment. It was in complete harmony with another one: that the depth-psychology revealed by psycho-analysis was in fact the psychology of the normal mind. Our path had been like that of chemistry: the great qualitative differences between substances were traced back to quantitative variations in the proportions in which the same elements were combined" (Freud, 1935, pp. 112–113).

We shall turn first to Freud's analysis of slips, errors, and dreams for an essential knowledge of his method. Then we shall move on to some of his basic concepts—repression, the unconscious, and instinct—to catch the full impact of this first and most important transition from the viewpoint of common sense in the study of motivation.

## THE ANALYSIS OF EVERYDAY SLIPS AND ERRORS

PSYCHOANALYTIC CONCEPTION
OF MENTAL PHENOMENA

Freud was convinced that the sense he could make out of people's commonplace mistakes and errors was probably the most convincing evidence he could advance to win acceptance of his view that unconscious motives play a role in everyday activities as well as in neurotic disturbances. A look at his method of analysis of familiar slips and errors will afford us some basis for appreciating how the psychoanalytic conception of "mental phenomena" differed from that of common sense and the academic psychology (e.g., James) of the late 19th century:

"The psychoanalytical definition of the mind is that it comprises processes of the nature of feeling, thinking, and wishing, and it maintains that there are such things as unconscious thinking and unconscious wishing" (Freud, [1920], 1943, p. 23).

The kinds of everyday observations Freud called attention to include slips of the tongue, and slips of the pen in writing, instances in which the word spoken or written is clearly not the one consciously intended at the time; occasions when one misreads or mishears what is spoken; the temporary forgetting of names or intentions which under other conditions are remembered; the mislaying of objects; and finally even instances in which objects are "accidentally" destroyed. These familiar occurrences are, he argued, what common sense and other sciences consider "the refuse, so to speak, of the phenomenal world" (Freud, [1920], 1943, p. 26).

IMPORTANCE OF SMALL SIGNS

Freud anticipated that his critics would immediately feel that he attempted to make too much of too little—a mountain out of a molehill. To win assent for a fair hearing of his analysis of these apparently trivial incidents, he reminds us of the importance that we are already prepared to grant to very slight indications, as when a young man is assured of his lady's favor by a slight glance that is imperceptible to others or when the criminal investigator is elated to find a fingerprint at the scene of a crime. The young lover, he argued, does not expect a passionate public embrace; nor does the detective expect to find an autographed photograph of the murderer on the chest of the victim. Both are willing to make inferences of great import from very small signs, and so was Freud.

THE BASIC ASSUMPTION

In his approach to the analysis of slips and errors, as in his approach to all human behavior, Freud is a strict determinist. To break away from the conviction of the determination of natural phenomena at any single point, even in the case of so-called slips and accidents, he argued, is to overthrow the whole scientific outlook on the world. And for Freud, as we shall see, determinism in the realm of "mental phenomena" meant *all behavior is motivated*.

He considered first the usual excuses offered to explain slips and errors. They are normally attributed to fatigue, illness, a state of excitement, or concentration on something else. He admitted that these conditions sometimes increase the frequency of slips and errors. But, he argued (reminding us of James), we must consider the great many actions which can be carried out effectively with little or no attention. Absence of concentrated attention to what is being done or said seems not to be a very crucial determinant of whether the action will be carried out smoothly and effectively or marred by the intrusion of some mistake. And consider, he urged, "that mistakes may occur just on occasions when one is most eager to be accurate, that is, when a distraction of the necessary attention is most certainly not present" (Freud, [1920], 1943, p. 29). We cite one of his well-known examples of this: "For instance, the President of our Parliament once opened the session with the words 'Gentlemen, I declare a quorum present and herewith declare the session *closed*' " (Freud, [1920], 1943, p. 33).

In this context, many readers may recall some of the classic "bloopers" on radio which illustrate the same point. One of the most famous slips occurred in the early days of radio when the stentorial tones of a distinguished radio announcer introduced "The President of the United States, *Hoobert Heever*."

If we turn our attention to the result or *effect* of a slip, Freud argued, we find that in many cases the slip, itself, makes perfectly good sense. The President of the Parliament who expects no good to come from the session and wishes it were over, says so. In another of Freud's examples, "a lady, appearing to compliment another, says 'I am sure *you* must have *thrown* this delightful hat together' instead of 'sewn it together'" (Freud, [1920], 1943, p. 34). In still another, the printer setting type for a war correspondent's account of a meeting with a famous general whose drinking habits were well known, produces "this battle-scared veteran," and the next day's paper carries his correction with an apology saying "the words of course should have been 'the bottle-scarred veteran!'" (Freud, [1920], 1943, p. 30).

In these and many other examples that must come to mind, the meaning of the slip is apparent. If, Freud asserted, the great majority of errors should have meaning, then that would become the matter of central interest:

"All physiological and psycho-physiological conditions could then be ignored and attention could be devoted to the purely psychological investigations of the *sense*, that is, the meaning, the intention, in the errors" (Freud, [1920], 1943, p. 34).

It is not too early to clarify what Freud meant by the "meaning" of some action. As already suggested in this preliminary analysis of slips and errors, as is true also in the effort to understand neurotic symptoms and dreams, the goal of psychoanalytic interpretation of thoughts and actions is to discover their "meaning." Freud used this term as the equivalent of the *effect* produced by an action, its aim, its purpose, the motive it serves, its goal:

> "This is nothing else but the intention which it serves and its place in a mental sequence. In most of the cases we examined we could substitute for the word 'meaning' the words 'intention' and 'tendency' " (Freud, [1920], 1943, p. 38).

### INTERFERENCE OF COMPETING INTENTIONS

Sometimes slips of the tongue are not words which are meaningful in their own right. But what appears to be simply a meaningless and unintelligible utterance, Freud discovered, really represents the interference of two different intentions. A rather transparent example of this would be if the President of Parliament, instead of saying, "I declare the meeting *closed*," which is the exact opposite of his conscious intention, had said, "I declare the meeting *clopen*." In this hypothetical case, the slip would represent a compromise between the intention to say "open" and the intention to say "closed." Freud called attention to this type of distortion of names: ". . . They are attempts to liken the name to something derogatory or degrading, a common form of abuse, which educated persons soon learn to avoid but nevertheless do not willingly give up" (Freud, [1920], 1943, p. 40). The "meaning" of the distortion of a name is completely clear in cases where it is obviously deliberate as, for example, when during the heyday of "McCarthyism" the late Senator from Wisconsin referred to the distinguished Senator from Arkansas who had cast the only vote against an appropriation for his investigating committee as "Senator *Half*bright." Freud felt it did not go much beyond what is generally accepted "to assume that some such abusive intention may also be behind distortions of names produced by a slip of the tongue" (Freud, [1920], 1943, p. 40).

We have solved the riddle of errors, Freud argued, when we recognize that they are not accidents, but mental acts which have meaning: ". . . They arise through the concurrence—perhaps better, the mutual interference—of two different intentions" (Freud, [1920], 1943, p. 41).

### NATURE OF THE INTERFERING TENDENCY

What, we must now ask, is the nature of the purposes or tendencies which interfere with other intentions? What is the relation between the interfering tendency and the other one? Furthermore, how does one prove that an inference of a hidden motive is correct?

Freud was convinced that all instances of slips and errors could be attributed to some interfering motive. Fatigue, distraction, excitement, and disturbances of attention were acknowledged as factors to be considered, but only as frequent contributory influences. The resemblances between words and common associations between words were also considered important influences which facilitated a slip "by pointing out a path for it to take" (Freud, [1920], 1943, p. 43).

> "But if there is a path before me does it necessarily follow that I must go along it? I also require a motive to determining my choice and, further, some force to propel me forward. These sound-values and word associations are, therefore, just like the bodily conditions, the facilitating causes of slips of the tongue, and cannot provide the real explanation of them. Consider for a moment the enormous majority of cases in which the words I am using in my speech are not deranged on account of sound-resemblance to other words, intimate associations with opposite meanings, or with expressions in common use" (Freud, [1920], 1943, p. 43).

In all cases, he argued, we can unmistakenly ascertain the tendency which is interfered with by simply asking the person who committed the slip what he meant (intended) to say. But how is the *interfering tendency*, the conflicting motive, to be discovered?

In some cases we ascertain the interfering tendency by simply asking the person and find that he acknowledges having had the conflicting intention in mind immediately before speaking. For example, when the Parliamentarian had said, "I declare the session *closed*" (or "*clopen*"), he might have reported, if questioned, that it had just occurred to him how nice it would be if the session were about to close. In many cases of this sort which Freud examined, he felt that the interfering tendency is as definitely established as the one we are ready to admit as the speaker's conscious intention (the tendency suffering interference) at the time he speaks. Even in these, the most simple cases, Freud pointed out, one has to ask the speaker for some explanation, or the speaker himself might let the incident pass without seeking to explain it even to himself:

> "Being asked, however, he gave as his answer the first idea that occurred to him. And see now, this little intervention and the result of it consti-

tute already a psycho-analysis, a prototype of every psycho-analytic investigation that we may undertake further" (Freud, [1920], 1943, p. 44).

Should we now argue that an explanation that immediately pops into the person's head when he is asked is not necessarily the true reason, Freud would reply:

"It is remarkable how little respect you have, in your hearts, for a mental fact! Imagine that someone had undertaken a chemical analysis of a certain substance and had ascertained that one ingredient of it is of a certain weight, so and so many milligrams. From this weight, thus arrived at, certain conclusions may be drawn. Do you think now it would ever occur to a chemist to discredit these conclusions on the ground that the isolated substance might as well have had some other weight? Everyone recognizes the fact that it actually had this weight and no other, and builds further conclusions confidently on that fact. But when it is a question of a mental fact, that it *was* such an idea and no other that occurred to the person when questioned, you will not accept that as valid, but say that something else might as well have occurred to him! The truth is that you have an illusion of a psychic freedom within you which you do not want to give up. I regret to say that on this point I find myself in sharpest opposition to your views" (Freud, [1920], 1943, p. 45).

Common sense replies with still more pressing questions: What if the person vehemently denies having had any intention of the sort we might infer from his slip, even when he is trying to be most cooperative? Do we then accept his statement as evidence which refutes the interpretation? These questions, rooted in our intuitive conviction that the impulses we call purposes, intentions, or—more generally—motives should be conscious and reportable bring us to the point at which Freud's conception of motivation and his method of study begin to depart significantly from the traditional view which relies on introspection alone as the basic method for description of the contents of the mind.

INDIRECT EVIDENCE

Appreciating that to understand his answer to these questions we should have to transcend the intuitive conceptions which work so well for us in everyday life, and hoping that we shall suspend judgment until his view is fully developed, Freud would remind us that in court when the guilty man confesses, the judge usually believes him, but when he denies the crime, the judge does not believe him. In law, we are reminded, guilt is often determined on the basis of *indirect*, circumstantial evidence. In

terms of this analogy, Freud accepted as *"direct"* evidence of the suspected meaning of an error an immediate acknowledgement of the interfering intention by the person who had committed the error. And he admitted that the method of proof, if there is to be any proof, must be *"indirect"* when the subject refuses to admit an intention or is not present to provide any information.

As we now begin to examine the indirect method which Freud advanced to justify his inferences about motives hidden from consciousness and the new concepts which this new method of study produced, it is worth noting that the general logic which Freud advanced for making "theoretical" inferences is the same logic that finally evolved within experimental psychology after decades of debate about how the task of theory construction must proceed within psychology. Freud inferred the presence of a motive from an analysis of antecedent events which had influenced the person and then tested his inference against observations of the consequent behavior of the person. To acknowledge this foreshadowing of the logic of theory construction in experimental psychology is not to disregard the very important differences and contrasts between the qualitative clinical observations which were Freud's subject matter and the quantified descriptions of antecedent conditions and behavioral facts which are the subject matter of modern psychology. Not to acknowledge the correspondence in general logic for justifying theoretical inferences, on the other hand, would be to overlook the essential soundness of one of Freud's methodological innovations in the study of human motivation.

In justification of making inferences and producing indirect evidence to support assumptions about the presence of motives, which common sense always expects to find directly manifested in conscious awareness, Freud stated:

"It is a mistake to believe that a science consists in nothing but conclusively proved propositions, and it is unjust to demand that it should. It is a demand only made by those who feel a craving for authority in some form and a need to replace the religious catechism by something else, even if it be a scientific one. Science in its catechism has but few apodictic precepts; it consists mainly of statements which it has developed to varying degrees of probability. The capacity to be content with these approximations to certainty and the ability to carry on constructive work despite the lack of final confirmation are actually a mark of the scientific habit of mind" (Freud, [1920], 1943, p. 47).

## THREE INDIRECT INDICATIONS
## OF THE PRESENCE OF A MOTIVE

Freud prescribed three indirect ways of supporting inferences about the "hidden" motive, the interfering tendency, which is expressed in some kind of slip or error. Where, he asked, do we find the indications we seek?

"First, by analogy with similar phenomena not produced by error, as when we maintain that the distortion of a name by mistake has the same intention to ridicule behind it as intentional distortion of names. And then, from the mental situation in which the error arose, from our knowledge of the character of the person who commits it, and of the feelings active in him before the error, to which it may be a response. As a rule what happens is that we find the meaning of the error according to general principles; and this, to begin with, is only a conjecture, a tentative solution, proof being discovered later by an examination of the mental situation. Sometimes it is necessary to await further developments, which have been, so to speak, foreshadowed by the error, before we can find confirmation of our conjecture" (Freud, [1920], 1943, p. 47).

Let us examine this. First is the argument by analogy with similar phenomena when conscious intention is present. Freud means to extend "common sense," which attributes actions to conscious intentions, to include instances which in every respect appear comparable *except* in the absence of consciousness of intention. Second is the argument based on our knowledge of the mental situation and the character of the person who commits the error. Freud calls attention to the common practice of inferring how a particular person whom we know might feel in a given set of circumstances. If we know that the person has been exposed to ridicule and insult, we normally expect that he will feel angry and that what he then says or does is likely to reflect his hostile intentions. If we already knew that the President of the Parliament had good reason to lament the opening of the meeting because some cause with which he was identified was certain to suffer a defeat in the meeting, we ordinarily would infer that he would wish that the meeting could be postponed. Common sense, in other words, leads us to make inferences about how persons might feel and what they might want to do given certain *antecedent* conditions. A wife expects that her husband just home from an afternoon at the golf course will be hungry. A lawyer advances as sound infer-

ence the notion that the suspect being blackmailed might have had the motive to murder the blackmailer. This seems to be what Freud means when he says, "As a rule what happens is that we find the meaning of the error according to general principles; and this, to begin with, is only a conjecture, a tentative solution . . ." (Freud, [1920], 1943, p. 47). The wife is not surprised when her husband, home from the golf course, exclaims, "I'm famished." She had anticipated as much from her knowledge of the "antecedent conditions" and her quite ordinary inference that he should probably be hungry after an afternoon outdoors.

Finally, in stating that it is sometimes necessary to await further developments, to make further observations of the person's behavior to test the validity of the inference that such and such a motive is present, Freud makes it clear that in doubtful cases the supposition of a motive is treated as *an hypothesis subject to test against further observations* on the assumption that motives are normally expressed in subsequent actions. In this connection he presented illustrations of the following sort:

"I was once the guest of a young married couple and heard the young wife laughingly describe her latest experience, how the day after the return from the honeymoon she had called for her sister and gone shopping with her as in former times, while her husband went to his business. Suddenly she noticed a man on the other side of the street and, nudging her sister, said, 'Look, there goes Mr. K.' She had forgotten that this man had been her husband for some weeks. A shudder went over me as I heard the story, but I dared not draw the inference. Several years later the little incident came back to my mind after this marriage had come to a most unhappy end. . . .

"I know a woman now divorced from her husband who, in managing her money-affairs, frequently signed documents with her maiden name, many years before she really resumed it. I know of other women who lost their wedding-rings on the honeymoon and know, too, that the course of the marriage lent meaning to this accident. And now one striking example more, with a better ending. It is told of a famous German chemist that his marriage never took place because he forgot the hour of the ceremony and went to the laboratory instead of to the church. He was w se enough to let the matter rest with one attempt, and died unmarried at a ripe age" (Freud, [1920], 1943, pp. 52–53).

In all these instances, subsequent events provide further *indirect* evidence to support the inference of a hidden motive.

OUTLINE OF PSYCHOANALYSIS

Holding particulars aside for development in subsequent pages, we can see in outline form the general method of psychoanalysis in Freud's treatment of slips, lapses of memory, and other common mistakes. He begins with the assumption that all mental activity (and behavior) is determined and that the meaning or significance of any act is fully explained when the motive, the intention expressed, is discovered. In dealing with instances which do not seem to fit the general pattern of action preceded by *conscious* intention (i.e., the phenomenon of volition as described by James), he applies the same logic that common sense applies to the explanation of everyday actions. He makes plausible inferences from an analysis of what common sense would acknowledge to be relevant antecedent conditions. The supposition that such and such a motive must have been present, even though for some reason shut out of conscious awareness, is treated as a tentative hypothesis from which other consequences might be anticipated. If further behavioral consequences of the sort generally expected occur—again given the logic of common sense that intentions should influence subsequent actions—he considers their occurrence as *indirect* evidence supporting the original inference of motive. If such confirming consequences do not occur, and the individual still cannot confirm the inference of motive by direct acknowledgement of the intention, the supposition of motive must presumably continue to be treated as a conjecture still subject to confirmation, or must be considered incorrect. In all essential respects, this outlines the general method of psychoanalysis.

ACCUMULATED AND COMBINED ERRORS

Among slips and errors, which he considered the best commonplace examples of essentially the same processes he had observed in neurotic disturbances, Freud considered "accumulated and combined errors" as "the finest flowers of the species":

> "If we were only concerned to prove that errors had a meaning, we should have limited ourselves to them at the outset, for the meaning in them is unmistakable, even to the dullest intelligence, and strong enough to impress the most critical judgment. The repetition of the occurrences betrays a persistence which is hardly ever an attribute of chance, but which fits well with the idea of design. Further, the exchanging of one kind of mistake for another shows us what is the most important and essential element in the error; and that is, not its

form, or the means of which it makes use, but the *tendency* which makes use of it and can achieve its end in the most various ways" (Freud, [1920], 1943, p. 51).

The following paragraph provides a good example of an accumulated and combined error. It shows the *persistence* of the interfering tendency through a sequence of superficially dissimilar actions and clearly illustrates how the inference of motive by an external observer would account for the *interrelatedness* of many different actions:

Mr. X received a letter from a friend asking him to make a substantial monetary contribution to a cause they both considered worthy. The letter arrived at a time when Mr. X was temporarily rather financially embarrassed. To make a contribution at the time, though still possible, would have required the irritation of further severe restrictions on an already tight budget. But to admit his financial plight to the friend on the occasion of so worthy a cause seemed an even more insufferable alternative to Mr. X. Mr. X was plainly in conflict, particularly aggravated at having been asked at this particular time. After fumbling around a bit, considering the possibilities, he ruefully wrote a short note to his friend and mailed off a check. Or so he thought! A few days later he received a reply from his friend thanking him for the greeting and expression of willingness to contribute, with a pleasant reminder that he had forgotten to include the check. Again irritated, Mr. X insisted to himself that he had sent the check and was certain that he had a stub to prove it. Examination of his checkbook, however, revealed no entry. The check had not been written. Now somewhat flustered, Mr. X hurriedly wrote another note attempting to jolly-away the incident as one of those things attributable to his earlier haste in replying. In this state, he made out a check, inserted it in the envelope, and then felt compelled to make a special trip to the corner mailbox in order to hurry it on its way. Imagine the depth of his embarrassment a few days later to receive another note from his friend with the check attached. It had been made out for the appropriate amount but was not signed! Finally, with something like that great effort of attention to which James (see Chapter 2) had referred as the most striking characteristic of difficult acts of will, he signed the check, inserted it in an envelope, opened the envelope for a final inspection before mailing, and again felt compelled to make a special trip, this time to the post office, to hasten its delivery.

In this case, the interfering tendency was acknowledged by Mr. X, who had committed the series of blunders which began in his immediate irritable reaction to the request for a contribution. He had, in other words, consciously experienced the desire to find some way of avoiding having to make a contribution at that particular time. But he reported even more insistently that after due consideration he decided that he must make a contribution and that this was his conscious intention in each of the succeeding chapters of the episode of the check.

COMMON ELEMENT IN ALL SLIPS AND ERRORS

Errors of this type, about which the person readily admits consciousness of the competing wish before the incident, provided Freud with the clue he needed to find some common element which would also identify the interfering tendency when "the interfering tendency is likewise recognized by the speaker as his own, but he is not aware that it was active in him before the slip" (Freud, [1920], 1943, p. 57); and in a third group of errors, in which "the interpretation of the interfering tendency is energetically repudiated by the speaker; not only does he dispute that it was active in him before the slip, but he will maintain that it is altogether entirely alien to him" (Freud, [1920], 1943, p. 58).

In light of the basic assumption, with which we are already familiar, "that tendencies of which a speaker knows nothing can express themselves through him," the common element in the three groups of errors seemed unmistakable to Freud:

"In the first two groups the interfering tendency is admitted by the speaker; in the first, there is the additional fact that it showed itself immediately before the slip. But in both cases *it has been forced back. The speaker had determined not to convert the idea into speech and then it happens that he makes a slip of the tongue; that is to say, the tendency which is debarred from expression asserts itself against his will and gains utterance, either by altering the expression of the intention permitted by him, or by mingling with it, or actually by setting itself in place of it.* This then is the mechanism of a slip of the tongue" (Freud, [1920], 1943, pp. 58–59).

To bring the third group of errors into harmony with this mechanism which appropriately fits the first two groups, Freud needed only to assume that the three groups "are differentiated by the varying degrees to which the forcing back of an intention is effective" (Freud, [1920], 1943, p. 59). In other words, Freud assumed that:

". . . A tendency can still express itself by an error though it has been debarred from expression for a long time, perhaps for a very long time, has not made itself perceptible at all, and can therefore be directly repudiated by the speaker" (Freud, [1920], 1943, p. 59).

The common element is the suppression of a previous intention to say something (or to *do* something, in other kinds of errors). This, Freud stated, is the "*indispensable condition*" for the occurrence of a slip.

*In summary*, slips, errors, accidents, and other mistakes are conceived as actions which are meaningful, that is, purposive. They arise from mutual interference of two different intentions. One of these intentions, to be able to express itself by interfering with another, must "itself have been subject to some hindrance against its operation" (Freud, [1920], 1943, p. 59).

ERRORS CONCEIVED AS COMPROMISES

Errors are *compromises;* they represent partial satisfaction of each of the two intentions. In the incident of the check, Mr. X partially satisfied his conscious intention by going through the motions of sending the check; he also partially satisfied the suppressed intention to avoid a contribution at that particular time by a series of errors and omissions which delayed the actual contribution.

Freud considered this analysis of slips and errors as a model of the psychoanalytic method that is more fully developed in the analysis of dreams and in the attempt to understand neurotic symptoms. "You can perceive from these examples," he stated, "what the aim of our psychology is":

"Our purpose is not merely to describe and classify the phenomena, but to conceive them as brought about by the play of forces in the mind, *as expressions of tendencies striving towards a goal* [italics added], which work together or against one another. We are endeavouring to attain a *dynamic conception* of mental phenomena. In this conception, the trends we merely infer are more prominent than the phenomena we perceive" (Freud, [1920], 1943, p. 60).

Psychoanalysis is more concerned with discovering the genotype (the underlying dynamic or motive) than with mere description of the phenotype (the appearance of things, the observed action).

CAUTION CONCERNING OVERSIMPLIFIED INTERPRETATIONS

The lectures Freud gave to acquaint laymen with this new orientation always contained a warning against oversimplification in the interpretation one might make of the small "symptomatic actions" of one's friend. When discussing memory lapses—that is, the common error of forgetting to carry out some resolution—Freud insisted that the interfering tendency opposing the execution of the resolution was always an unwillingness. But, he also argued, "our own investigations show that this 'counter-will' may be of two kinds, either immediate or mediate" (Freud, [1920], 1943, p. 65). By this he meant that the counter tendency might be immediately related to the resolution in question, but needn't be. Some other, less obvious factor might be the cause of the aversion. There is, in other words, a danger of becoming too suspicious of one's absent-minded or error-prone friends and of doing them great injustice. To illustrate this, Freud stated:

". . . If someone forgets an appointment which he had promised and was resolved to attend, the commonest cause is certainly a direct disinclination to meet the other person. But analysis might produce evidence that the interfering tendency was concerned, not with the person, but with the place of meeting, which was avoided on account of some painful memory associated with it. Or if one forgets to post a letter the opposing tendency may be concerned with the contents of the letter; but this does not exclude the possibility that the letter in itself is harmless and becomes the subject of a counter-tendency only because something in it reminds the writer of another letter, written previously, which did in fact afford a direct basis for antipathy. It may then be said that the antipathy has been *transferred* from the earlier letter, where it was justified, to the present one where it actually has no object. So you see that restraint and caution must be exercised in applying our quite well-founded interpretations; that which is psychologically equivalent may in actuality have many meanings" (Freud, [1920], 1943, pp. 65–66).

THE MOTIVE OPPOSING RECOLLECTIONS

In the analysis of lapses of memory, whether they be of names that seem just on the tip of one's tongue, of resolutions to be carried out, or of incidents in the past, Freud felt that he had discovered a sufficiently large majority of cases of forgetting in which the "counter-will," or interfering intention, is acknowledged by the forgetful person to justify extending the assumption of a counter-force to those cases in which the forgetful person would not or could not confirm the presence of the inferred interfering tendency. This follows consistently the logic of his analysis of slips and other symptomatic actions. As to the motive for the tendency opposing recollections, he argued:

". . . We here for the first time encounter a principle which will later on reveal itself to be of quite prodigious importance in the causation of neurotic symptoms: namely, *the aversion on the part of memory against recalling anything connected with painful feelings that would revive the pain if it were recalled* [italics added]. In this endency towards *avoidance of pain* from recollection or other mental processes, this flight of the mind from that which is unpleasant, we may perceive the ultimate purpose at work behind not merely forgetting of names, but also many other errors, omissions, and mistakes" (Freud, [1920], 1943, p. 67).

In this connection, Freud recalled that Darwin was apparently so well aware of this principle that he made a golden rule of writing down every observation that seemed unfavorable to his theory.

The analysis of motivated forgetting of names and incidents leads immediately to the intricacies of the web of associations in which the forgotten item is anchored or embedded. It was in the effort to help patients recover memories of significant incidents in the past that Freud had first employed hypnosis in the treatment of neurosis. And it was for this same purpose that the method of free-association and the interpretation of dreams supplanted hypnosis in psychoanalytic treatment of neurosis.

THE INTERPRETATION OF DREAMS

THREE IMPORTANT CLUES

Three clues helped Freud to gain confidence in his conception of the confused dream of an adult as a compromise, analogous to a grossly distorted slip of the tongue, between the motive to sleep and some other persistent wish which, if directly expressed, would awaken the sleeper.

First, he called attention to those dreams in which the ringing of the alarm clock (or some other external stimulus) is blended into the content in such a way that its summons to arise goes unnoticed. What is the effect produced by the way in which an insistent external stimulus becomes a part of the dream? Sleep is preserved. The longing to continue in repose is satisfied. One of the functions of a dream, then, is to preserve sleep.

Second, he called attention to a phenomenon recognized by common sense and given the name "daydreams." To Freud, the most striking thing about these common day-time fantasies is that they should have been called "day*dreams.*" Unlike the dreams of nighttime, they are not hallucinatory experiences in which the dreamer is so caught up that all contact with outside reality is lost. Neither is the daydreamer asleep. So two of the central characteristics of dreams are missing. What, then, could be the possible correspondence which has led these acts of imagination, so common particularly in childhood and adolescence, to be called "daydreams"? Turning again to the *content* of the experience as the important clue, Freud stated:

"The content of these phantasies is dictated by a very transparent motivation. They are scenes and events which gratify either egoistic cravings of ambition or thirst for power, or the erotic desires of the subject. In young men, ambitious phantasies predominate; in women, whose ambition centres on success in love, erotic phantasies; but the erotic requirement can often enough in men too be detected in the background, all their heroic deeds and successes are really only intended to win the admiration and favour of women" (Freud, [1920], 1943, p. 88).

Daydreams are, in fact, transparent wish-fulfillments in which the subject, himself, is either the hero or obviously identified with the central character. Is this the characteristic they share with the hallucinatory experience which preserves sleep at nighttime? The difference between the fantasies we call "daydreams" and many dreams is striking; the content of one is so apparently meaningful and the content of the other is so typically bizarre.

Freud had already made great headway interpreting the confused content of dreams by his neurotic patients as grossly distorted expressions of some forbidden thought when he became fully aware of the existence of nocturnal dreams in which distortion is lacking: the dreams of children. This provided the third important clue.

The dreams of young children are so often short, clear, coherent, and easy to understand that very little in the way of interpretation is needed to see that the dream functions to preserve sleep by satisfying some persistent wish, an *internal* stimulus, which might otherwise awaken the sleeper. In support of his hypothesis, and to sustain the analogy with slips and errors, Freud presented evidence of how knowledge of some experience from the previous day in the life of a child (the antecedent conditions) justifies the inference of a persistent unfulfilled wish:

"(*a*) A boy of a year and ten months old had to present someone with a basket of cherries as a birthday gift. He plainly did it very unwillingly, although he had been promised some of them for himself. The next morning he told his dream: 'Hermann eaten all the cherries.'

"(*b*) A little girl of three and a quarter years went for the first time for a trip on the lake. When they came to land, she did not wish to leave the boat and cried bitterly; the time on the water had evidently gone too quickly for her. Next morning she said: 'Last night I was sailing on the lake' " (Freud, [1920], 1943, p. 114).

## DISTORTION NOT AN ESSENTIAL ELEMENT

In these and other simple and undisguised dreams of very young children Freud found the manifest content, like that of a daydream, to be a wish-fulfillment. Furthermore, it became apparent that "*distortion is not essential to the nature of the dream*" (Freud, [1920], 1943, p. 115). The dream "does not merely give expression to a thought, but represents this wish as fulfilled, in the form of an hallucinatory experience" (Freud, [1920], 1943, p. 116). As in the case of those dreams which dispose of the insistently ringing alarm clock, "the dream does not merely reproduce this stimulus, but, by a kind of living it through, removes it, sets it aside, relieves it" (Freud, [1920], 1943, p. 116).

He emphasized the similarities between dreams and errors:

"In the latter we distinguished between a disturbing tendency and one which is disturbed, the error being a compromise between the two. Dreams fall into the same category; the disturbed tendency can only, of course, be the tendency to sleep, while the disturbing tendency resolves itself into the mental stimulus which we may call the wish (clamouring for gratification), since at present we know of no other mental stimulus disturbing sleep. Here again the dream is the result of a compromise; we sleep, and yet we experience the satisfaction of a wish; we gratify a wish and at the same time continue to sleep. Each achieves part-success an part-failure" (Freud, [1920], 1943, pp. 116–117).

In addition to these dreams of childhood, there are also some dreams of adulthood in which no distortion is present and which are easily recognized as wish-fulfillments:

"These are dreams which are occasioned all through life by imperative physical needs—hunger, thirst, sexual desire—and are wish-fulfilments in the sense of being reactions to internal somatic stimuli" (Freud, [1920], 1943, pp. 118–119).

But what, we may now ask, of the many dreams which are so obviously confused and bizarre? Are they also to be considered wish-fulfillments? And, if so, how is their meaning ever to be discovered when it so frequently happens that one cannot even completely recall the dream? How is it to be subjected to analysis?

To begin with, Freud defined the dream as that which the person reports as his dream:

"Any disadvantage resulting from the uncertain recollection of dreams may be remedied by deciding that exactly what the dreamer tells is to count as the dream, and by ignoring all that he may have forgotten or altered in the process of recollection" (Freud, [1920], 1943, p. 76).

The "art of interpretation," which he developed following procedures already worked out to some extent in the treatment of neurotic symptoms, was considered by Freud to be a method of aiding the dreamer himself to report the meaning of the dream. The method is based on the premise that "the dreamer really does know the meaning of his dream; *only he does not know that he knows, and therefore thinks that he does not*" (Freud, [1920], 1943, p. 91).

To appreciate Freud's conviction, we must again refer to the profound influence on his later work of that summer in 1889 when he observed the phenomena of post-hypnotic suggestion. In his own words:

"In the year 1889 I was present at the remarkably impressive demonstrations by Liébault and Bernheim, in Nancy, and there I witnessed the following experiment. A man was placed in a condition of somnambulism, and then made to go through all sorts of hallucinatory experiences. On being wakened, he seemed at first to know nothing at all of what had taken place during his hypnotic sleep. Bernheim then asked him in so many words to tell him what had happened while he was under hypnosis. The man declared that he could not remember anything. Bernheim, however, insisted upon it, pressed him, and assured him that he did know and that he must remember, and lo and behold! the man wavered, began to reflect, and remembered in a shadowy fashion first one of the occurrences which had been suggested to him, then something else, his recollection growing increasingly clear and complete until finally it was brought to light without a single gap. Now, since in the end he had the knowledge without having learnt anything from any other quarter in the meantime, we are justified in concluding that these recollections were in his mind from the outset.

They were merely inaccessible to him; he did not know that he knew them but believed that he did not know. In fact, his case was exactly similar to what we assume the dreamer's to be" (Freud, [1920], 1943, pp. 92–93).

THE METHOD OF FREE ASSOCIATION

Freud's indirect method of asking the dreamer the meaning of his dream is called *free association.*

Unlike an ordinary slip of the tongue, a dream has a number of different elements. With some element of the dream as a starting point, Freud would ask the person to say exactly what came into his mind, "laying down the hard and fast rule that he must not withhold any association," even if it appears "that it is too unimportant, too absurd, too irrelevant or too unpleasant to speak of" (Freud, [1920], 1943, p. 104). And, as was also true when he accepted the first thought that popped into an individual's head when he was able to report the meaning of a slip, here too Freud stressed the importance of the very first association to some dream element. Freud considered the first association, and the chain of associations then called up by it, as the path to what he was searching for. He urged those who would consider this quite arbitrary "to have some respect for the *fact* that that one association, and nothing else, occurs to the dreamer when he is questioned" (Freud, [1920], 1943, p. 96). With the dream as his starting point, Freud found that the person would then begin to recall events which had happened recently, perhaps the preceding day, then less recently, until finally he had recalled some events which had happened in the distant past.

The process, as described by Freud, is very much like trying to recall a name which has been temporarily forgotten:

"When I forget a name temporarily, I am still certain that I know it, and by way of a détour through Bernheim's experiment, we are now in a position to achieve a similar certainty in the case of the dreamer. Now this name which I have forgotten, and yet really know, eludes me. Experience soon teaches me that no amount of thinking about it, even with effort, is any use. I can, however, always think of another or of several other names instead of the forgotten one. When such a substitute name occurs to me spontaneously, only then is the similarity between this situation and that of dream-analysis evident. The dream-element also is not what I am really looking for; it is only a substitute for something else, for the real thing which I do not know and am trying to discover by means of dream-analysis. Again the difference is that when I forget a name I know perfectly well that the substitute is not the right one, whereas we only arrived at this conception of the dream element by a laborious process of investigation. Now there also is a way in which, when we forget a name, we can by starting from the substitute, arrive at the real thing eluding our consciousness at the moment, i.e. the forgotten name. If I turn my attention to these substitute names and let further associations to them come into my mind, I arrive after a short or a long way round at the name I have forgotten, and in so doing I discover that the substitute I have spontaneously produced had a definite connection with, and were determined by, the forgotten name" (Freud, [1920], 1943, pp. 99–100).

## LATENT MEANING AND MANIFEST CONTENT DISTINGUISHED

Free association, beginning with a dream element, leads ultimately to *the latent meaning of the dream*, that is, to the underlying wish that is expressed in the distorted substitute, which comprises *the manifest content of the dream*. The dream as remembered and reported is not the "real thing" at all, but a distorted substitute, "which, by calling up other substitute-ideas, provides us with a means of approaching the thought proper, of bringing into consciousness the unconscious thoughts underlying the dream" (Freud, [1920], 1943, p. 103). Thus it matters little that the dream may be only partially recalled. If the dream is further distorted in the very process of being reported, "all that has happened is that a further distortion of the substitute has taken place, and this distortion itself cannot be without motivation" (Freud, [1920], 1943, p. 103).

## RESISTANCE

Freud invariably found that his patients would ignore the hard and fast rule not to withhold any association that came to mind. Often this opposition took the form of critical objections. Freud said this opposition, which he called *resistance*, attempted to suppress the very associations which "*without exception*" (Freud, [1920], 1943, p. 104) turned out to be the most important and most decisive for the discovery of the unconscious motive expressed in the dream. The amount of resistance varied in degree. It was related to the amount of distortion and to the length of the chain of associations needed to uncover the motive expressed in the dream.

Freud discovered that the unconscious wish expressed in the dream is one that has been denied entry into consciousness, that is, repressed, because its sexual or aggressive content and infantile char-

acter is abhorrent to the person. Thus he could view the active resistance to its discovery as another manifestation of the flight of the mind from the unpleasant, which he had also uncovered as the motive for the forgetting of names and resolutions.

## DREAM-CENSORSHIP

Dreams that seemed hopelessly confused and meaningless were finally interpreted and recognized to be grossly distorted expressions of repugnant wishes. A comparison of the *manifest content* of the dream, as originally reported by the dreamer, and the *latent thoughts*, which had to be discovered, revealed to Freud the extent to which dreams have undergone a process of "censorship." Freud considered the resistance encountered during the work of interpretation as one objective manifestation of this censorship and the distortion effected in the latent dream thoughts another. Just as the strength of resistance encountered during interpretation varies with each element of the dream, so too does the amount of distortion vary with each element of the whole dream:

> "A comparison of the manifest and the latent dream shows that certain latent elements are completely eliminated, others more or less modified, and others again appear in the manifest dream-content unaltered or perhaps even intensified" (Freud, [1920], 1943, p. 126).

What tendencies or motives are evident in this process of censorship? Freud based his answer to this question on the survey of the many dreams he had interpreted:

> "The tendencies which exercise the censorship are those which are acknowledged by the waking judgement of the dreamer and with which he feels himself to be at one. You may be sure that when you repudiate any correctly found interpretation of a dream of your own, you do so from the same motives as cause the censorship to be exercised and distortion effected, and make interpretation necessary" (Freud, [1920], 1943, p. 127).

## THE NATURE OF THE CENSORED MOTIVES

Consider now, in contrast, his general description (from the point of view of conscious, waking judgment) of the motives against which dream-censorship is exerted:

> "When we do this, we can only say that they are invariably of an objectionable nature, offensive from the ethical, aesthetic or social point of view, things about which we do not dare to think at all, or think of only with abhorrence. Above all are

these censored wishes, which in dreams are expressed in a distorted fashion, manifestations of a boundless and ruthless egoism; for the dreamer's own ego makes its appearance in every dream, and plays the principal part, even if it knows how to disguise itself completely as far as the manifest content is concerned. . . .

". . . The striving for pleasure—the libido, as we say,—chooses its objects unchecked by any inhibition preferring indeed those which are forbidden: not merely the wife of another man, but, above all, the incestuous objects of choice which by common consent humanity holds sacred—the mother and the sister of men, the father and the brother of women. . . . Desires which we believe alien to human nature show themselves powerful enough to give rise to dreams. Hate, too, rages unrestrainedly; wishes for revenge, and death-wishes, against those who in life are nearest and dearest—parents, brothers and sisters, husband or wife, the dreamer's own children—are by no means uncommon. These censored wishes seem to rise up from a veritable hell; when we know their meaning, it seems to us in our waking moments as if no censorship of them could be severe enough. . . . Depravity does not lie in the nature of dreams; in fact, you know that there are dreams which can be recognized as gratifying justifiable desires and urgent bodily needs. It is true that there is no distortion in these dreams, but then there is no need for it, they can perform their function without offending the ethical and aesthetic tendencies of the ego" (Freud, [1920], 1943, pp. 127–128).

It is clear from the above that without the censorship the attempt at fulfillment of these forbidden wishes in the hallucinatory experience of a dream would certainly awaken the sleeper in a state of shock and anxiety. This, in fact, argued Freud, is what often happens in those instances we refer to as "nightmares." The censorship is inadequate, and the function of the dream to preserve sleep is not served.

FACTORS INFLUENCING AMOUNT OF DISTORTION

Freud attributed the degree of distortion of dream elements to two factors. He found it greater the more shocking the wish and the more severe the demands of the censorship:

"Hence in a strictly brought up and prudish young girl, a rigid censorship will distort dream-excitations which we medical men would have recognized as permissible and harmless libidinous desires, and which the dreamer herself would judge in the same way ten years later" (Freud, [1920], 1943, p. 128).

This pithy statement contains within it the logic of an argument which later psychoanalysts and other students of behavior who followed Freud have advanced to temper his original emphasis of repressed *sexuality* as the seed of neurosis. Freud considered his explanation of dreams as parallel to his explanation of neurotic symptoms. In fact, his original suspicion that dreams had meaning arose after it had been discovered by Joseph Breuer in 1880–1882 that the symptoms of certain neurotic patients had meaning. In speaking of their symptoms, the patients often made references to their dreams. So Freud's acknowledgement that *censorship is a relative matter*, depending in part on the nature of the impulse and in part on the nature of the demands of censorship, which have their origin in the norms of the society in which the individual is reared, is of considerable importance. We must remember that Freud made his startling discoveries studying neurosis in late 19th-century Victorian society, which was particularly prudish about matters of sexuality. In other societies having more liberal standards about expression of sexuality, it is argued, one might find repressed hostility or the thwarting of other important motives to be the seed of neurotic conflict.

To those who are repelled by his assertions concerning the nature of the impulses ascribed to men as the causes of their dreams (and neurotic symptoms) Freud replied:

"I will say nothing of how you may appear in your own eyes, but have you met with so much goodwill in your superiors and rivals, so much chivalry in your enemies and so little envy amongst your acquaintances, that you feel it incumbent on you to protest against the idea of the part played by egoistic baseness in human nature? Do you not know how uncontrolled and unreliable the average human being is in all that concerns sexual life? Or are you ignorant of the fact that all the excesses and aberrations of which we dream at night are crimes actually committed every day by men who are wide awake? What does psycho-analysis do in this connection but confirm the old saying of Plato that the good are those who content themselves with dreaming of what others, the wicked, actually do?

"And now look away from individuals to the great war still devastating Europe: think of the colossal brutality, cruelty and mendacity which is now allowed to spread itself over the civilized world. Do you really believe that a handful of unprincipled placehunters and corrupters of men would have succeeded in letting loose all this latent evil, if the millions of their followers were not also guilty? Will you venture, even in these circumstances, to break a lance for the exclusion of evil from the mental constitution of humanity?

". . . It is no part of our intention to deny the

nobility in human nature, nor have we ever done anything to disparage its value. On the contrary, I show you not only the evil wishes which are censored but also the censorship which suppresses them and makes them unrecognizable. We dwell upon the evil in human beings with the greater emphasis only because others deny it, thereby making the mental life of mankind not indeed better, but incomprehensible. If we give up the one-sided ethical valuation then, we are sure to find a truer formula for the relation of evil to good in human nature" (Freud, [1920], 1943, pp. 130–131).

## THE DREAM WORK AND THE TASK OF INTERPRETATION

Freud referred to the process by which the latent dream is transformed into the manifest dream as the *dreamwork*. The reverse process, that of working back to the latent thoughts underlying the dream from the manifest content, is *the task of interpretation*. We have already seen how the method of free association is employed to recover the associative context which provides the material for analysis. Now, as we turn to Freud's ideas about the relations between the manifest content of a dream and the latent (unconscious) thoughts which are expressed in it, we begin to confront his broader conception of the nature of unconscious processes. He often asserted that the process of dream formation is equivalent to the process that is involved in the formation of neurotic symptoms. Hence, as we consider the concepts developed in the analysis of dreams we attend to the link between what is commonly considered "pathological" and "normal." It was Freud's contention that these same unconscious processes play a significant role in the determination of everyday "conscious" activities of the "normal" human adult.

In simple dreams of children, and in those of adults which, like daydreams, represent an undisguised fulfillment of some pressing but acceptable wish, the process of the dreamwork consists simply of transformation of a wish into an hallucinatory wish-fulfillment. In the case of confused and apparently meaningless dreams, which are more common among adults, the dreamwork, in addition, produces distortion and disguise of the latent wish. How is this accomplished?

Freud identified a number of relations between the manifest content of the dream and the underlying (unconscious) thought which describe how distortion is accomplished.

## CONDENSATION

First, the manifest dream is a kind of abbreviated translation of the latent thoughts. Some of the latent elements are omitted altogether. Others which have some common characteristic are blended together and expressed in the same manifest element of the dream. Still other latent thoughts suffer fragmentation; only a part, a suggestive allusion to the whole latent thought, is represented in the manifest dream. Freud referred to this first relationship between manifest and latent dream elements, and the process underlying it, as *condensation*.

## DISPLACEMENT

The second effect produced by the dreamwork is one of *displacement*. A latent element of the dream may be replaced, not only by a part of itself, but by something else which is remotely associated with it so that the manifest element is but a remote allusion to the underlying thought. In addition, the accent in the dream may be displaced from the most important element to another which is less important. This shifting of emphasis is further evidence of the operation of a censorship which would be best served if it were impossible to discover the thought alluded to in the manifest dream.

## TRANSLATION OF THOUGHTS INTO VISUAL IMAGERY

Third, the latent thoughts are translated into visual images. Objects and activities are given a concrete representation. Even abstract words and relations are usually represented in terms of visual images. Freud viewed this as evidence of a regressive process. The earliest material of thought, he argued, consists of sense-impressions and memory pictures. Only later do words become associated with these images and connected so as to form thoughts. In this *regressive translation of thoughts into images*, which retraces the development of thoughts from primitive sense impressions and memory images, all the more recent acquisitions of the thought process are stripped away.

## SECONDARY ELABORATION

A fourth mechanism of the dreamwork Freud called *secondary elaboration*. The results of condensation, displacement, and translation of thoughts into visual images are recombined into some kind of coherent whole which, in turn, further distorts the relationship between the manifest content and latent thoughts.

## SYMBOLISM

Finally, in addition to these several processes which serve to distort the meaning of the manifest dream, there is a constant relationship between certain manifest and latent elements called *symbolism*. The symbols employed in dreams (usually of sexual organs, objects, and activities) represent what Freud believed to be the universal language of the unconscious, a constant translation of latent thoughts into manifest elements which often makes it possible to interpret a dream even without recourse to free association to discover the link between manifest and latent elements. The method of interpretation based on a knowledge of symbolism, which Freud derived from folktales, myths, jokes, and the poetical use of language as well as from his study of dreams, and the method of free association were thus considered complementary techniques. Even after the work of free association is finished, certain dream elements remained meaningless unless they were interpreted as symbols:

> "It cannot fail to strike us that we arrive at a satisfactory meaning in every instance in which we venture on this substitution, whereas the dream remains meaningless and disconnected as long as we do not resolve to use this method. The accumulation of many exactly similar instances then affords us the required certainty . . ." (Freud, [1920], 1943, pp. 133–134).

Finding dreamers in possession of a symbolic and apparently universal mode of expression about which they consciously knew nothing served to enlarge Freud's conception of the scope of unconscious mental life:

> "Up till now we have only had to assume the existence of unconscious tendencies which are temporarily or permanently unknown to us; but now the question is a bigger one and we have actually to believe in unconscious knowledge, thought-relations, and comparisons between different objects, in virtue of which one idea can constantly be substituted for another. These comparisons are not instituted afresh every time, but are ready to hand, perfect for all time; this we infer from their identity in different persons, even probably in spite of linguistic differences" (Freud, [1920], 1943, p. 148).

## BROADENED CONCEPTION OF UNCONSCIOUS PROCESSES

Thus, in the analysis of dreams as in his analysis of neurotic symptoms, Freud found that he could not avoid the assumption "that there are processes and tendencies in mental life, of which we know nothing; have known nothing; have, for a very long time, perhaps even never, known anything about at all" (Freud, [1920], 1943, p. 132). The term *unconscious* took on fresh meaning. The qualifications "at the moment" or "temporary" seemed not to be essential attributes. The term referred to what is permanently beyond awareness in addition to what is merely "latent at the moment."

## REGRESSIVE NATURE OF DREAMS

We might suppose the unconscious processes inferred in the analysis of dreams to have belonged to an earlier phase of intellectual development. Because of this, Freud referred to the form of expression in dreams as *archaic* or *regressive*. He supposed that the symbolic mode of expression might even be regarded as a racial heritage. And, he argued, the regressive tendency in dreaming is one of substance as well as form. The wish expressed in distorted and disguised form may be one that has long been denied access to consciousness, that is, repressed.

## COMPONENTS OF LATENT DREAM THOUGHTS

The latent dream thoughts are made up of two components: some "residue" from the activities of the previous day—perhaps, but not always, some latent wish that has remained unsatisfied from the waking hours; *and* a repressed wish-impulse, often one having its origin in the distant past experience of the dreamer, with which the "residue" of thoughts from the previous day has made contact.

# THE MEANING OF "UNCONSCIOUS"

## CONSCIOUS, PRECONSCIOUS, AND UNCONSCIOUS

Freud's conception of "the unconscious" is the great challenge to the common-sense view that behavior is to be explained in terms of an act of conscious volition which precedes it. As his ideas evolved about dynamic processes that are beyond immediate awareness, Freud sought to extend and clarify his meanings. The term *conscious* was applied to that which is immediately present to consciousness and of which we are aware. He needed some term to designate that which is now absent from consciousness, but which may be brought into consciousness with little difficulty. He employed the term *preconscious* to stand for latent thoughts of this kind which he had often referred to as "temporarily unconscious" or "unconscious at the moment." The term *unconscious* could then be reserved for those mental activities which are particularly resistant to being brought into immediate awareness:

"It is by no means impossible for the product of unconscious activity to pierce into consciousness, but a certain amount of exertion is needed for this task. When we try to do it in ourselves, we become aware of a distinct feeling of *repulsion* which must be overcome, and when we produce it in a patient we get the most unquestionable signs of what we call his *resistance* to it. So we learn that the unconscious idea is excluded from consciousness by living forces which oppose themselves to its reception, while they do not object to other ideas, the preconscious ones. Psycho-analysis leaves no room for doubt that the repulsion from unconscious ideas is only provoked by the tendencies embodied in their contents. The next and most probable theory which can be formulated at this stage of our knowledge is the following. *Unconsciousness is a regular and inevitable phase in the processes constituting our mental activity; every mental act begins as an unconscious one, and it may either remain so or go on developing into consciousness, according as it meets with resistance or not* [italics added]. The distinction between preconscious and unconscious activity is not a primary one, but comes to be established after repulsion has sprung up" (Freud, [1912], 1949, Vol. IV, pp. 26–27).*

LIMITED CONSCIOUSNESS IN EXECUTION
OF POST-HYPNOTIC SUGGESTION

With our preliminary understanding of resistance, as Freud conceived it, we can profitably re-examine the illustration of post-hypnotic suggestion to which he constantly referred. The full implication of acknowledging the existence of such unconscious processes is unavoidable.

". . . A person is put into a hypnotic state and is subsequently aroused. While he was in the hypnotic state, under the influence of the physician, he was ordered to execute a certain action at a certain fixed moment after his awakening, say half an hour later. He awakes, and seems fully conscious and in his ordinary condition; he has no recollection of his hypnotic state, and yet at the pre-arranged moment *there rushes into his mind the impulse to do such and such a thing, and he does it consciously, though not knowing why*. It seems impossible to give any other description of the phenomenon than to say that the order had been present in the mind of the person in a condition of latency, or had been present unconsciously, until

* Excerpts from Sigmund Freud, *Collected Papers*, Vol. IV, 1949, are reprinted with permission of the Hogarth Press Ltd. and Basic Books, Inc.

the given moment came, and then had become conscious. *But not the whole of it emerged into consciousness: only the conception of the act to be executed. All the other ideas associated with this conception—the order, the influence of the physician, the recollection of the hypnotic state—remained unconscious even then*" (Freud, [1912], 1949, Vol. IV, p. 23, italics added).

The subject who is given a post-hypnotic suggestion is normally also instructed while under hypnosis that he will not remember what has transpired when he awakens. Nevertheless, he later carries out the action suggested to him. The impulse to act in a certain way bursts into consciousness at the appropriate time, and the action is executed. This much fits James' introspective analysis of volition. The idea of the act dominates consciousness. However, something is missing. The "reasons" for wanting to perform the act—what common sense would ordinarily call the "motives" for the action—do not burst into consciousness. The instruction to the subject that he will not remember what has transpired functions like what Freud called resistance. Consciousness is denied to the thoughts of the surrounding circumstances that would normally give the person a "rationale" for his action.

INADEQUACY OF INTROSPECTIVE ANALYSIS
OF CONSCIOUS EXPERIENCE

In light of Freud's discovery that various thoughts differ in degree of resistance to entry into consciousness—depending upon the severity of standards applied by the censor and the shockingness of the content of the thought—is it not likely that only the most acceptable "reasons" for acting in certain ways will easily gain consciousness during the waking life of any normal individual? Are not many of the explanations we make to ourselves and to others of our own everyday actions to be considered "rationalizations" which have suffered some of the same distortions so strikingly evident in dreams?

THE RELATION OF CONSCIOUS
AND UNCONSCIOUS THOUGHT

Freud used the analogy of the production of a finished picture in photography to describe the relation of conscious and unconscious activity:

"The first stage of the photograph is the 'negative'; every photographic picture has to pass through the 'negative process,' and some of these negatives which have held good in examination are admitted to the 'positive process' ending in the picture" (Freud, [1912], 1949, Vol. IV, p. 27).

The photographer who examines many negatives, deciding that some shall be turned into positive prints and others not, functions like the "censorship." There are many techniques available to the photographer for removing minor blemishes in an otherwise adequate negative before a positive print is made. Furthermore, in making the positive print, the photographer may control the lighting with filters and employ other devices to give a special accent, a highlight here, and a shading into the imperceptible background there, of other less desirable features. In other words, in addition to complete rejection of a negative, the photographer, like the "censorship" in Freud's conception, can produce a partially accurate reproduction of what is in the negative by completely removing certain blemishes and by offering more or less "resistance" to other elements. The photographer also has it in his power to crop several different negatives and by combining them in novel ways to make a positive print that is a completely distorted version of what the several negatives contain. It is an instructive analogy.

## DEFENSE OF ASSUMPTION
## OF UNCONSCIOUS PROCESSES

Freud's dethronement of consciousness as the center of interest for scientific psychology, coming as it did during a period when introspective description of the contents of the conscious mind was the main preoccupation of many academic psychologists, met with substantial "resistance." In 1915, in a paper titled "The Unconscious," he sought to meet the objections of critics who disputed his assumption of an unconscious system "for purposes of scientific work." He acknowledged that we arrive at a knowledge of the unconscious only indirectly through analysis of conscious products which have undergone the kinds of transformations and translation into acceptable form which he had presumed. But he saw the assumption of such unconscious processes as an unavoidable necessity for scientific psychology:

"It is necessary because the data of consciousness are exceedingly defective; both in healthy and in sick persons mental acts are often in process which can be explained only by presupposing other acts, of which consciousness yields no evidence. These include not only the parapraxes [i.e., slips and errors] and dreams of healthy persons, and everything designated a mental symptom or an obsession in the sick; our most intimate daily experience introduces us to sudden ideas of the source of which we are ignorant, and to results of mentation arrived at we know not how. All these

conscious acts remain disconnected and unintelligible if we are determined to hold fast to the claim that every single mental act performed within us must be consciously experienced; on the other hand, they fall into a demonstrable connection if we interpolate the unconscious acts that we infer. A gain in meaning and connection, however, is a perfectly justifiable motive, one which may well carry us beyond the limitations of direct experience. When, after this, it appears that the assumption of the unconscious helps us to construct a highly successful practical method, by which we are enabled to exert a useful influence upon the course of conscious processes, this success will have won us an incontrovertible proof of the existence of that which we assumed. We become obliged then to take up the position that it is both untenable and presumptuous to claim that whatever goes on in the mind must be known to consciousness" (Freud, [1912], 1949, Vol. IV, p. 99).

Freud forced his critics to consider what a small content is embraced by consciousness at any given moment. Are all the latent memories which can be brought into consciousness no longer to be described as *mental* processes? Are they to be treated only as "residues of somatic processes from which something mental can once more proceed" (Freud, [1912], 1949, Vol. IV, p. 100)? To him the conventional identification of *mental* activity with *conscious* activity seemed "thoroughly unpractical" (Freud, [1912], 1949, Vol. IV, p. 100). It both "overestimates the part played by consciousness" (Freud, [1912], 1949, Vol. IV, p. 100) and arbitrarily forces the psychologist to give up the task of developing a picture of the continuity of psychological processes in *psychological* terms. He felt there was little to be gained by merely acknowledging, in principle, that some *physical* process might be posited to account for memory and the other phenomena he wished to refer to as unconscious *mental* processes:

"Now, as far as their physical characteristics are concerned, they are totally inaccessible to us: no physiological conception nor chemical process can give us any notion of their nature. On the other hand, we know for certain that they have abundant points of contact with conscious mental processes; on being submitted to a certain method of operation they may be transformed into or replaced by conscious processes, and *all the categories which we employ to describe conscious mental acts, such as ideas, purposes, resolutions and so forth, can be applied to them*. Indeed, of many of these latent states we have to assert that the only point in which they differ from states which are conscious is just in the lack of consciousness of them. So we shall not hesitate to treat them as objects of psychological research, and that in the most intimate connection with conscious mental acts" (Freud, [1912], 1949, Vol. IV, pp. 100–101, italics added).

Freud's goal was to develop a consistent "psychology" without reference to possible neurophysiological concomitants of "mental" activities which, though he would readily admit in principle, seemed not, in his time at least, to promise much immediate gain in study of psychological problems. He felt that the stubborn denial of the "mental quality" of latent processes could probably be attributed to the fact that outside of psychoanalysis, very few of the relevant phenomena have been objects of study:

"Anyone who is ignorant of the facts of pathology, who regards the blunders of normal persons as accidental, and who is content with the old saw that dreams are froth need only ignore a few more problems of the psychology of consciousness in order to dispense with the assumption of an unconscious mental activity. As it happens, hypnotic experiments, and especially post-hypnotic suggestion, had demonstrated tangibly even before the time of psycho-analysis the existence and mode of operation of the unconscious in the mind" (Freud, [1912], 1949, Vol. IV, p. 101).

THE IMPUTATION OF CONSCIOUSNESS
TO ANOTHER PERSON

Having argued that it is a scientific necessity to assume unconscious processes if psychology is to get along with its explanatory task, Freud then attempted to establish the legitimacy of his inference. His argument appealed to his critics to recognize that the common belief that some other person has *conscious* experiences like one's own is no less of an inference than the one which he now proposed:

"The assumption of an unconscious is, moreover, in a further respect a perfectly *legitimate* one, inasmuch as in postulating it we do not depart a single step from our customary and accepted mode of thinking. By the medium of consciousness each one of us becomes aware only of his own states of mind; that another man possesses consciousness is a conclusion drawn by analogy from the utterances and actions we perceive him to make, and it is drawn in order that this behaviour of his may become intelligible to us. (It would probably be psychologically more correct to put it thus: that without any special reflection we impute to everyone else our own constitution and therefore also our consciousness, and that this identification is a necessary condition of understanding in us.) This conclusion—or identification—was formerly extended by the ego to other human beings, to animals, plants, inanimate matter and to the world at large, and proved useful as long as the correspondence with the individual ego was overwhelmingly great; but it became more untrustworthy in proportion as the gulf between the ego and non-ego widened. To-day, our judgement is already in doubt on the question of consciousness in animals; we refuse to admit it in plants and we relegate to mysticism the assumption of its existence in inanimate matter. But even where the original tendency to identification has withstood criticism—that is, when the non-ego is our fellow-man—the assumption of a consciousness in him rests upon an inference and cannot share the direct certainty we have of our own consciousness.

"Now psycho-analysis demands nothing more than that we should apply this method of inference to ourselves also—a proceeding to which, it is true, we are not constitutionally disposed. If we do this, we must say that all the acts and manifestations which I notice in myself and do not know how to link up with the rest of my mental life must be judged as if they belonged to someone else and are to be explained by the mental life ascribed to that person. Further, experience shows that we understand very well how to interpret in others (*i.e.* how to fit into their mental context) those same acts which we refuse to acknowledge as mentally conditioned in ourselves. Some special hindrance evidently deflects our investigations from ourselves and interferes with our obtaining true knowledge of ourselves" (Freud, [1912], 1949, Vol. IV, p. 102).

MENTAL OPERATIONS LACKING
IN QUALITY OF CONSCIOUSNESS

Freud acknowledged that this method of inference does not lead to the discovery of an unconscious system, as he conceived it, but to another consciousness of which a person is himself unconscious. He meant to describe unconscious processes in the same language one ordinarily applies to conscious states. In this limited sense, the inference of an unconscious system of ideas and wishes is no more than an extension of the conventional, intuitive categories of common sense to influences of which a person is unaware. But, Freud argued:

". . . We have to take into account that analytic investigation reveals some of these latent processes as having characteristics and peculiarities which seem alien to us, or even incredible, and running directly counter to the well-known attributes of consciousness. This justifies us in modifying our inference about ourselves and saying that what is proved is not a second consciousness in us, but the existence of certain mental operations lacking in the quality of consciousness" (Freud, [1912], 1949, Vol. IV, p. 103).

In other words, these unconscious mental processes, though generally describable in terms which are normally used in reference to conscious mental states and therefore appropriately considered "mental," may nevertheless differ in certain important respects from conscious activities in the way they operate. Concluding his argument, Freud stated:

"In psycho-analysis there is no choice for us but to declare mental processes to be in themselves unconscious, and to compare the perception of them by consciousness with the perception of the outside world through the sense-organs; we even hope to extract some fresh knowledge from the comparison. The psycho-analytic assumption of unconscious mental activity appears to us, on the one hand, a further development of that primitive animism which caused our own consciousness to be reflected in all around us, and, on the other hand, it seems to be an extension of the corrections begun by Kant in regard to our views on external perception. Just as Kant warned us not to overlook the fact that our perception is subjectively conditioned and must not be regarded as identical with the phenomena perceived but never really discerned, so psycho-analysis bids us not to set conscious perception in the place of the unconscious mental process which is its object. The mental, like the physical, is not necessarily in reality just what it appears to us to be. It is, however, satisfactory to find that the correction of inner perception does not present difficulties so great as that of outer perception—that the inner object is less hard to discern truly than the outside world" (Freud, [1912], 1949, Vol. IV, p. 104).

The analogy drawn in this last paragraph provides a clear statement of the important implication of Freud's conception of unconscious processes. Just as our conscious perception of a falling apple must not be confused with the physical phenomenon which Newton had to infer to account for that subjective experience, the ideas, feelings, and intentions of which we are conscious must not be confused with the underlying psychological phenomena which produces them, of which we are entirely unconscious. In both cases, conscious experience gives the appearance of things. It is the task of science to go beyond appearances—to construct, by means of inference, a picture of the underlying phenomena.

SPECIAL CHARACTERISTICS
OF UNCONSCIOUS PROCESS

The unconscious was treated by Freud as a separate system of mental activities. It was conceived as the domain of instinctual impulses, pressing for discharge and immediate gratification. That is to say, the unconscious is the domain of wish-impulse. By the process of displacement, the impulsivity

(which Freud called *cathexis*) of one wish could be surrendered to another. By the process of condensation, one wish-impulse might appropriate the impulsivity of several others. Freud proposed to regard these two processes as the distinguishing marks of the *primary process* in the mind in contrast to the reality-oriented and logic-bound *secondary process* which characterizes the preconscious and conscious systems.

In the unconscious, as Freud conceived it, opposite impulses could exist side by side, exempt from mutual contradiction:

"When two wishes whose aims must appear to us incompatible become simultaneously active, the two impulses do not detract one from the other or cancel each other, but combine to form an intermediate aim, a compromise" (Freud, [1912], 1949, Vol. IV, p. 119).

In this system there is no negation, no doubt, no uncertainty, no sense of time or temporal ordering of activities, no contact with reality. All these are characteristics of the preconscious and conscious systems which control action and through which the wish-impulse must be transmitted if it is to be satisfied. Left to itself, said Freud, the unconscious system would not be able to bring about any purposive muscular action with the exception of those already organized as reflexes.

There is, we see, more to the unconscious as Freud conceived it than the mere absence of conscious awareness of the idea representing a tendency, but we must now move on to some of Freud's other conceptions which also have had a profound effect on the subsequent study of motivation.

THE INSTINCTUAL ORIGINS
OF MOTIVES

In 1915, Freud also set forth his conception of what James had earlier referred to as "the springs of action," in a paper entitled "Instincts and their Vicissitudes." It is an important paper in the history of psychology, for it contains the essential ideas of the theory later known as *drive-reduction*, which was formally developed by Clark Hull (1943) to explain experimental facts of learning and behavior in lower animals. We shall begin with Freud's conception of "instinct," its relationship to a fundamental assumption he made about the neurophysiological process underlying all behavior, and its relationship to what common sense calls "pleasure" and "pain." Then we shall survey Freud's various schemes for classification of instincts and his skeptical attitude about the sufficiency of any of these schemes.

## INSTINCT (OR NEED) CONCEIVED AS PERSISTENT INTERNAL STIMULUS

Writing some fifty years after Darwin, in the heyday of "armchair" explanations of human behavior in terms of instinct, Freud seemed almost apologetic as he first approached the analysis of this "conventional but still rather obscure basal concept . . . which is nevertheless indispensable to us in psychology" (Freud, [1915], 1949, Vol. IV, p. 61). He begins, as did James, with the concepts of *stimulus* and *reflex-arc* taken over from physiology; the notion that a stimulus applied from the outer world is discharged by action which removes the organism out of range of the stimulus. But hunger, thirst, and the sexual impulses to which Freud referred as "instinctual" impulses do not originate in the outer world. They were to be considered stimuli having an internal origin:

". . . A strong light striking upon the eye is not a stimulus of instinctual origin; it is one, however, when the mucous membrane of the oesophagus becomes parched or when a gnawing makes itself felt in the stomach. [Footnote:] Assuming, of course, that these internal processes constitute the organic basis of the needs described as thirst and hunger" (Freud, [1915], 1949, Vol. IV, p. 61).

What are some of the differences between external and internal "stimuli to the mind"? External stimuli have a momentary impact and may be discharged by a single appropriate action. The impacts may be repeated "and their force may be cumulative," but that does not alter the fact that external stimuli may be easily removed by some immediate action. "An instinct, on the other hand, never acts as a momentary impact but always as a constant force"; and since it originates within the organism, "no flight can avail against it" (Freud, [1915], 1949, Vol. IV, p. 62). Freud suggested that these internal stimuli which cannot be dispelled by simple flight might more appropriately be called "*needs*":

"A better term for a stimulus of instinctual origin is a 'need'; that which does away with this need is 'satisfaction.' This can be attained only by a suitable (adequate) alteration of the inner source of stimulation" (Freud, [1915], 1949, Vol. IV, p. 62).

Freud supposed that very early in the life of any organism it will detect that some stimuli are removed by some simple action of the muscles, as in flight,

while others persist undiminished. This would provide one basis for discriminating between the inner and outer worlds.

## ASSUMED EXCITATION-REDUCING FUNCTION OF NERVOUS SYSTEM

Freud made explicit the basic postulate which was to guide his inquiry into the psychological phenomena arising when an instinct, or inner need, is aroused. The postulate, he said, "is of a biological nature, and makes use of the concept of 'purpose' (one might say, of adaptation of the means to the end). . . ."

". . . The nervous system is an apparatus having the function of abolishing stimuli which reach it, or of reducing excitation to the lowest possible level: an apparatus which would even, if this were feasible, maintain itself in an altogether unstimulated condition" (Freud, [1915], 1949, Vol. IV, p. 63).

Broadly speaking, the task of the nervous system as Freud conceived it was "*to master stimuli.*"

The simple physiological reflex scheme is greatly complicated by the introduction of this concept of instinct or "need." James had held, we recall, that the mechanism of instinct was essentially that of the reflex-arc: external stimulus evokes some unlearned reaction. Freud's view was different:

"External stimuli impose upon the organism the single task of withdrawing itself from their action: this is accomplished by muscular movements, one of which reaches the goal aimed at and, being the most appropriate to the end in view, is thenceforward transmitted as an hereditary disposition. Those instinctual stimuli which emanate from within the organism cannot be dealt with by this mechanism. Consequently, they make far higher demands upon the nervous system and compel it to complicated and interdependent activities, which effect such changes in the outer world as enable it to offer satisfaction to the internal source of stimulation . . ." (Freud, [1915], 1949, Vol. IV, p. 63).

## THE PLEASURE PRINCIPLE

Freud then offered a tentative hypothesis relating his physiological assumption that reduction of excitation is the goal of all action to his psychological *pleasure principle:*

". . . When we find further that the activity of even the most highly developed mental apparatus is subject to the pleasure-principle, *i.e.* is automatically regulated by feelings belonging to the pleasure-'pain' series, we can hardly reject the further postulate that these feelings reflect the manner in which the process of mastering stimuli takes place. This is certainly so in the sense that 'painful' feelings are connected with an increase and pleasurable feelings with a decrease in stimulation" (Freud, [1915], 1949, Vol. IV, p. 64).

While this conception pervades most of Freud's writings, and much of the subsequent psychology of motivation, we would miss the tentative attitude Freud had about this conjecture as he did about so many of his guiding concepts if we failed to consider his immediate qualification:

> "Let us, however, be careful to preserve this assumption in its present highly indefinite form, until we succeed, if that is possible, in discovering what sort of relation exists between pleasure and 'pain,' on the one hand, and fluctuations in the quantities of stimuli affecting mental life, on the other. It is certain that many kinds of these relations are possible, some of them by no means simple" Freud, [1915], 1949, Vol. IV, p. 64).

The instinct (or biological need) conceived as a persistent internal stimulus appeared to Freud to be a concept which linked the "mental" and the "physical":

> "If we now apply ourselves to considering mental life from a biological point of view, an 'instinct' appears to us as a borderland concept between the mental and the physical, being both the mental representative of the stimuli emanating from within the organism and penetrating to the mind, and at the same time a measure of the demand made upon the energy of the latter in consequence of its connection with the body" (Freud, [1915], 1949, Vol. IV, p. 64).

CHARACTERISTICS OF AN INSTINCT (OR NEED)

What terms are to be used in reference to an instinct or need? Freud suggested four: *source*, *impetus*, *aim*, and *object*.

The term *source* refers to "that somatic process in an organ or part of the body from which there results a stimulus represented in mental life by an instinct" (Freud, [1915], 1949, Vol. IV, p. 66).

The term *impetus* refers to its impulsive quality, its strength—"its motor element, the amount of force or the measure of the demand upon energy which it represents" (Freud, [1915], 1949, Vol. IV, p. 65).

The *aim* of an instinct is always satisfaction, "which can only be obtained by abolishing the condition of stimulation in the source of the instinct" (Freud, [1915], 1949, Vol. IV, p. 65).

By the *object* of an instinct, Freud meant "that in or through which it can achieve its aim" (Freud, [1915], 1949, Vol. IV, p. 65). This was the most variable thing about an instinct. The *means* of satisfying some need is not originally connected with the need. It becomes an object (a preferred means) "only in consequence of being peculiarly fitted to provide satisfaction" (Freud, [1915], 1949, Vol. IV, p. 65). The object (or means of attaining satisfaction) may be changed any number of times during the course of life. This, in fact, is what Freud refers to when he speaks of the "vicissitudes" of instincts. The substitutability of objects, or means, reflects the capacity for *displacement*. And the possibility that the same object may serve in attaining satisfaction of more than one instinct is the process of *condensation*. Freud referred to a particularly close attachment of an instinct to its object as a *fixation*. In other words, the term fixation refers to a resistance to change from some preferred means of satisfying an inner need to another.

Although the source of an instinct, the condition in the body which gives rise to the persistent inner stimulus, is what gives the instinct its distinct and essential character (e.g., hunger versus thirst), Freud believed, "The study of the sources of instinct is outside the scope of psychology . . ." (Freud, [1915], 1949, Vol. IV, p. 66). He firmly held that a more exact knowledge of the sources of instinct is not needed for psychological investigation. The source may often be inferred from some "intermediate aim" (like eating) which is closely related to the ultimate aim of the instinct called hunger. Freud referred to what common sense might call the goals of hunger and thirst, viz., eating and drinking, as the "nearer or intermediate aims," the ultimate aim being always satisfaction through abolishment of the particular internal stimulation which is the source.

CLASSIFICATION OF INSTINCTS

"Now what instincts and how many should be postulated?" Freud asked (Freud, [1915], 1949, Vol. IV, p. 66). It is probably more important that we grasp his attitude concerning such a question than the details of any one of the several answers he gave to it during the long course of his work:

> "There is obviously a great opportunity here for arbitrary choice. No objection can be made to anyone's employing the concept of an instinct of play or of destruction, or that of a social instinct, when the subject demands it and the limitations of psychological analysis allow of it. Nevertheless, we should not neglect to ask whether such instinc-

tual motives, which are in one direction so highly specialized, do not admit of further analysis in respect of their sources, so that *only those primal instincts which are not to be resolved further could really lay claim to the name*" (Freud, [1915], 1949, Vol. IV, pp. 66–67, italics added).

His earliest proposal was that the prime movers should be thought of as falling into two groups: "the *self-preservative* or *ego*-instincts and the *sexual* instincts" (Freud, [1915], 1949, Vol. IV, p. 67). The latter category included all the sensual pleasure-seeking activities apparent in man, from infancy on into adulthood, which finally become organized about heterosexual activity leading to reproduction and survival of the species. The Darwinian influence could not be more obvious. But, Freud made it very clear that this proposition did not have the weight of a necessary postulate:

". . . It is merely an auxiliary construction, to be retained only so long as it proves useful, and it will make little difference to the results of our work of description and classification if we replace it by another" (Freud, [1915], 1949, Vol. IV, p. 67).

And replaced it was. The classification of prime movers into ego instincts and sexual instincts had arisen as Freud evolved his initial theory about the causes of psychoneuroses. Freud had discovered that the root of hysteria and obsessional neurosis, the so-called transference neuroses, was always "a conflict between the claims of sexuality and those of the ego" (Freud, [1915], 1949, Vol. IV, p. 67). It was the kind of conflict we have become familiar with in Freud's treatment of distorted dreams, a conflict between a repressed wish-impulse and those opposing (the force of the censorship) with which the person himself feels identified. In Freud's earliest theory of the neurotic conflict, the impulsivity of the represssed infantile wish at the core of neurosis was attributed to sexual instinct, and the impulsivity of the repressing tendency was derived from ego instincts, the self-preservative tendencies.

A little later, when Freud began to study narcissistic psychoneuroses, he changed his system of classification of instincts from a dualism to a monism. *Libido* became the single energy of an all-pervasive sexual instinct which could be directed either towards the self (self-love) or towards some other object. The two sides of the neurotic conflict were then accounted for in terms of narcissistic libido and object-libido. Still later considerations made Freud discontent with assuming the existence of only a single class of instincts. In later years, he combined the self-preservative or ego instincts and those which lead to preservation of the species (the sexual instincts) under the concept of *Eros* and posited a separate instinct of destruction, *Thanatos*. Thus he embraced the phenomena of aggression and the destructiveness which surrounded him at the time of the First World War.

GENESIS OF HUMAN MOTIVES

A detailed analysis of Freud's reasons for changing his classification of the instincts would lead us far astray of our present purpose. It is sufficient to note that he considered the springs of action, the sources of the impulses we call motives, to be imperative internal stimuli; that he emphasized the substitutability of means, or objects, which could satisfy the need; and that his theory of the psychosexual genesis through the now well-known oral, anal, and genital stages is a description of the variety of forms of sensual (sexual) satisfaction, organ pleasures, available during infancy and childhood. In his theory of psychosexual development, a point of major interest is his conception of how the expression of infantile sexual and hostile impulses come to be inhibited and repressed, and how displacement to other than the original objects comes about. Those displacements which are socially acceptable and which contribute to the attainment of some socially useful end were called *sublimations*. Thus, in brief, Freud attempted to account for the instinctual origins of all the motives which characterize the normal adult as well as the repressed infantile impulses which are both the seed of neurotic disturbance and the censored wishes expressed in the dreams of the healthy.

THE MOTIVATION OF DIRECTED ACTIONS

We have seen how Freud coordinated his conception of the nervous system as a machine geared to reduce excitations with the feelings of pleasure and pain, and how he emphasized that the psychological principle corresponding to the physiological principle of stimulus-reduction was the pleasure principle. It is also important to see how he related these ideas to the overt behavior of a person in relation to some object:

"When the object becomes a source of pleasurable feelings, a motor tendency is set up which strives to bring the object near to and incorporate it into the ego; we then speak of the 'attraction' exercised by the pleasure-giving object, and say that we 'love' that object. Conversely, when the object is the source of painful feelings, there is a tendency which endeavours to increase the distance between object and ego and to repeat in relation to the former the primordial attempt at flight from the external world with its flow of stimuli. We feel a 'repulsion' from the object, and hate it; this hate can then be intensified to the point of an aggressive tendency towards the object, with the intention of destroying it" (Freud, [1915], 1949, Vol. IV, pp. 79–80).

## REPRESSION AND ANXIETY

"One of the vicissitudes an instinctual impulse may undergo," wrote Freud, "is to meet with resistances the aim of which is to make the impulse inoperative" (Freud, [1915], 1949, Vol. IV, p. 84). We have already discussed the concept of resistance in Freud's treatment of slips and dreams. It is the tendency opposed to admission of certain ideas which arise during free association. It is the source of critical objections by the patient as the work of interpretation of dreams proceeds. Now we turn to a related process, perhaps the key concept in psychoanalytic theory, *repression:* ". . . *The essence of repression lies simply in the function of rejecting and keeping something out of consciousness*" (Freud, [1915], 1949, Vol. IV, p. 86).

How can an instinctual impulse suffer such a fate, asked Freud? In keeping with the pleasure principle, this could only come about if the attainment of the aim of the instinct should produce pain instead of pleasure. What, then, are the peculiar circumstances which change the pleasure of satisfaction into pain? This is how Freud phrased the paradox.

He dismissed the possibility that repression might occur merely because the instinctual impulse became too intense as a consequence of lack of opportunities for satisfaction. Certainly hunger keeps up its constant gnawing tension even when its intensity is extreme. And the physical pain caused by disease of organs or injury does not cease as a function of its great intensity. It is reduced only by appropriate drugs or sufficient distractions, but even then it persists in the background.

The clue to understanding the process of repression, Freud felt, comes from many clinical examples of the sort we have considered. These are instances in which satisfaction of some wish-impulse would be possible were it not for some other competing tendency with which the impulse is irreconcilable. *Repression occurs when the tendency of avoiding some pain which would attend the gratification of the impulse*

*has acquired more strength than the pleasure of gratification.*

### PRIMAL REPRESSION AND REPRESSION PROPER

A *primal repression*, the first phase of repression, "consists in a denial of entry into consciousness to the mental (ideational) presentation of the instinct" (Freud, [1915], 1949, Vol. IV, p. 86). A second phase of repression, called *repression proper*, refers to the same fate suffered by mental derivatives of the repressed idea. The derivatives are other ideas that are in some way linked to it by associative connections. (Recall the earlier injunction not to oversimplify the problem of interpretation.)

We have already seen how repressed impulses continue to function in the formation of dreams. Though *the idea representing the impulse* is barred from consciousness, the repressed wish may, through displacement, produce remote substitute ideas. These remote derivatives are not denied access to consciousness.

### EARLY CONCEPTION OF ANXIETY
### AS THE CONSEQUENCE OF REPRESSION

In this, his original conception of repression, Freud emphasized the barring from consciousness of *the idea* representing some unacceptable impulse. He considered the spread of repression to other closely associated ideas and called attention to the process of displacement which accounts for the remote substitutes that are represented in consciousness. Furthermore, *he explained the affect of anxiety*, which he had observed in neurotic patients whose troubles were rooted in the repression of sexual impulses, *as a consequence of repression*. That is, in his earliest theorizing, he held that the excitation of the repressed instinctual impulse was transformed, as a result of repression, into the affect of anxiety, like so much steam escaping from the lid of the boiling kettle.

### LATER CONCEPTION OF ANXIETY
### AS THE CAUSE OF REPRESSION

Not until 1936 in a book called *The Problem of Anxiety* did he finally work out the relationship between anxiety, inhibition, repression, and resistance to his own satisfaction. This later conception of anxiety clarified the dynamics of censorship and substantially influenced the experimental psychology of motivation. Freud finally saw that *the flight of the mind from the painful is a flight from anxiety* that is directly analogous to the physical flight of a person made anxious by some external threat. "Anxiety," he asserted, "is undeniably related to expectation; one feels anxiety *lest* something occur" (Freud, 1936, p. 112). In the case of realistic anxiety, or fear, the object which gives rise to the feeling of anxiety is known; it is some external threat. The anxiety is allayed by physical flight, avoidance. But neurotic anxiety has the character of indefiniteness and objectlessness. The person does not know why he is anxious because its object is unconscious. *Instinctual demands become an internal danger* "only because of the fact that their gratification would bring about an external danger—because, therefore, this internal danger represents an external one" (Freud, 1936, p. 116).

Freud, searching for the function of anxiety, noted that it arises in situations of impending danger. He conceived it to be a primitive response to a situation in which the individual is helpless in the face of ever-increasing, painful stimulation. He was inclined to view the trauma of birth as the prototype experience. At birth the neonate is for the first time exposed to intense stimulation with which it has no capacity to cope. So, too, is the infant helpless in the face of the recurrent internal stimulations which constitute the instinctual demands of hunger and thirst which are allayed by the ministrations of a mother:

> "If the infant longs for the sight of the mother, it does so, surely, only because it already knows from experience that she gratifies all its needs without delay. The situation which the infant appraises as "danger," and against which it desires reassurance, is therefore one of not being gratified, of an *increase of tension arising from non-gratification of its needs*—a situation against which it is powerless" (Freud, 1936, p. 76).

From this situation of helplessness in early childhood is derived the anxiety elicited by the threat of loss of love, which is produced by parental disapproval for expressing certain sexual and hostile impulses in infancy and early childhood. Thus instinctual demands themselves become a threat to be averted. The denial of the ideational representations of these impulses to consciousness, that is, repression, is a flight from the anxiety which signals the impending danger. Anxiety, in other words, is the *cause* (the motive) of repression and not its consequence, as he had originally supposed. Anxiety is reduced when the danger is averted. Anxiety is aroused as a signal, whenever the forbidden impulses again threaten to break into consciousness. Thus, anxiety is the motive power of the censorship

and of the resistance confronted in the task of interpretation of dreams and symptoms, the unpleasant state to be averted, which motivates so many of the defensive self-deceptions that Freud's pioneering investigations had uncovered:

> "It then seems evident that the defensive process is analogous to flight, by means of which the ego avoids a danger threatening from without, and that it represents, indeed, an attempt at flight from an instinctual danger" (Freud, 1936, p. 87).

## CONCLUDING SURVEY

### THE IMPACT OF PSYCHOANALYTIC CONCEPTS

There is obviously much more to the superstructure of psychoanalytic theory than we can cover with profit in an introductory treatment. Freud's basic ideas have been elaborated and extended by many others who have followed his lead in the clinical treatment of neurosis. Psychoanalytic theory is a lively contemporary system of thought, a conceptual scheme which many psychiatrists and clinical psychologists have found more suited to their practical task of helping the emotionally distressed than any other scheme that has been devised. It is, as we shall see in later chapters, a rich source of guiding hypotheses for contemporary research on motivation and the development of personality. But to pursue our discussion of psychoanalytic concepts any further here would lead us from the purpose of these introductory chapters: viz., to make the transition from the viewpoint of common sense to the viewpoint of contemporary scientific psychology concerning the problem of motivation. Freud's pioneering effort does not complete the transition. It begins it. The methods and concepts he introduced do not represent the final word on the subject, but the beginning of an objective orientation towards the whole problem of human motivation and a set of general hypotheses that are too important and too much of a challenge to long-accepted views to ignore.

### TENTATIVE NATURE OF FREUD'S CONCEPTIONS

Nothing is more instructive in the writings of Freud than those passages which show his own perspective concerning his contributions to a science of motivation. The constant reminders that certain theoretical constructions are to be held as tentative working hypotheses reveal the working attitude of a scientist who appreciated his place in the history of a scientific psychology. We may take as a good example of this, the statements which conclude his work on the final revision of the classification of instincts and which contain a very speculative treatment of the implications of his concept of death instinct:

> "We must be patient and wait for other means and opportunities for investigation. We must hold ourselves too in readiness to abandon the path we have followed for a time, if it should seem to lead to no good result. Only such 'true believers' as expect from science a substitute for the creed they have relinquished will take it amiss if the investigator develops his views further or even transforms them.
> "For the rest we may find consolation in the words of a poet for the slow rate of progress in scientific knowledge:
>
> 'Whither we cannot fly, we must go limping.
> The Scriptures saith that limping is no sin.'*
>
> * (Rückert in the 'Mahamen des Hariri')" (Freud, 1922, p. 83).

### THE EMPIRICAL FOUNDATION
### OF PSYCHOANALYTIC CONCEPTS

Freud, the empiricist, scrutinized the novel facts which had come to light as he employed the method of free association with his patients. It is a good idea for us to have firmly in mind the special kinds of observations which provide the foundation for his theorizing:

> "In psycho-analytic treatment nothing happens but an exchange of words between the patient and the physician. The patient talks, tells of his past experiences and present impressions, complains, and expresses his wishes and his emotions. The physician listens, attempts to direct the patient's thought-processes, reminds him, forces his attention in certain directions, gives him explanations and observes the reactions of understanding or denial thus evoked" (Freud, [1920], 1943, p. 19).

This was Freud's "laboratory." These are the facts he sought to explain. Freud, the theorist, let his creative imagination work over the details of these novel clinical observations and let the hunches suggested by them carry over to the interpretation of many other more general observations he made of how children and adults behave in everyday life. He followed the implications of an idea as far as it would take him: "One may surely give oneself up to a line of thought, and follow it up as far as it leads, simply out of scientific curiosity . . ." (Freud, 1922, p. 76).

However, he realized the pitfalls of straying too far from the observations which gave birth to the idea:

"We know that the final result becomes the more untrustworthy the oftener one does this in the course of building up a theory, but the precise degree of uncertainty is not ascertainable. One may thereby have made a brilliant discovery or one may have gone ignominiously astray" (Freud, 1922, p. 77).

There is much more healthy scientific skepticism in Freud's writings, and clearer perspective concerning his place in the development of a scientific psychology, than one might gather from the doctrinaire attitudes that are often attributed to him by critical commentators and evident in many who consider themselves his devoted followers.

### SUMMARY: THE CHALLENGE
### TO TRADITIONAL IDEAS

What is the fundamental challenge to the traditional mode of thought in Freud's discoveries and arguments? It is, without question, a shattering of the belief that the set of dictionary terms which refer to conscious feelings, thoughts, and intentions provides an adequate scheme for explaining what "causes" people to behave the way they do. In simple terms, it is the assertion that the contents of consciousness do not contain the full explanation of a person's actions. The introspective psychology of the late 19th century had not departed from the traditional framework of thought about why people act as they do in referring purposeful actions to what is in consciousness at the time. Freud, in contrast, demotes consciousness to the status of a probably distorted resultant of the clash of more primitive impulses and a "decision process" that is beyond awareness, not available to introspective survey—in brief, unconscious.

Where the untutored curiosity of common sense is satisfied by asking the person his intentions, acknowledging that at times (as in a murder trial) there may be a good deal of natural resistance to overcome in getting the person to break down and confess his true motive, Freud had discovered a new kind of resistance which often prevents even the individual himself from knowing his own motives. The whole point of the indirect methods of psychoanalysis—the "questioning" of a person by means of the method of free association, the interpretation of what appears to be the symbolic language of dreams, and the emphasis given what appear to be reasonable inferences based on knowledge of antecedent conditions which may have influenced the person and on observations of consequent actions—

is to overcome this resistance, which maintains the repression of what is unconscious.

Underlying Freud's viewpoint is the general assumption that all thought and action is strictly determined. To him this meant it is motivated, or purposive, in the same sense that traditional thought would employ these terms in reference to acts of conscious will. But Freud's assumption embraces phenomena that common sense had held to be unmotivated, accidental, irrational, meaningless—the symptoms and absurd actions of people classified neurotic, the ridiculously confused dreams of the normal adult, and those many slips, errors, and lapses of memory that were waved aside as humorous little everyday incidents but lacking in significance.

Freud relied on his discovery of meaning in the psychopathology of everyday life to win general assent to the idea that the so-called "normal" and "pathological" are not qualitatively different realms of behavior, but that the same principles apply to both. This would mean, in light of what had been learned about the distortions and incompleteness of consciousness from analysis of the striking examples, that we should distrust the simple explanations we ordinarily give to ourselves and others of everyday actions in terms of conscious motives. It is this important implication which provoked a change in the orientation of psychologists towards the whole problem of human motivation and how it should be studied. Consider, as illustrative, some statements from a book by the American psychologist E. B. Holt, published in 1915, which argued the thesis that "The Freudian Wish" (the title of his book) was the basic causal category that the "science of the mind" had previously lacked:

"Illustrations of the influence of more or less suppressed 'wishes' on all phases of life could be multiplied without number; for in fact life itself *is* nothing but these wishes working themselves out in action. Some of them are 'conscious,' others 'preconscious,' while others are hidden more deeply in the once mysterious levels of the subconscious (Holt, 1915, pp. 39–40).
". . . Thought, that is, conscious thought, is so little complete as to be scarcely any index to a man's character or deeds. This is Freud's doctrine of the unconscious; although Freud is by no means the first to discover or to emphasize the unconscious. A man's conscious thoughts, feelings, and desires are determined by unconscious thoughts or 'wishes' which lie far deeper down, and which the upper, conscious man knows nothing of. . . . In fact, conscious thought is merely the surface foam of a sea where the real currents are well beneath

the surface. It is an error, then, to suppose that the 'secret behind' a man's actions lies in those thoughts which he (and he alone) can 'introspectively survey.' We shall presently see that it is an error to contrast thought with action at all" (Holt, 1915, pp. 88–89).

And what are these "real currents" that are well below the surface in the view of the first depth psychologist? They are the most primitive of sensual pleasure-seeking tendencies, destructive impulses, and all the other biological imperatives that common sense had traditionally attributed to animals and contrasted with the higher purposes of rational men. Add to this *potpourri* one more ingredient, anxiety, and we have the other side of the pervasive conflict which Freud detected. This list gives a complete picture of the Freudian scheme of the basic springs of human thought and action. The so-called loftier conscious motives of men are to be treated as the results of this conflict, as compromise interests in substitute goals and substitute activities which represent displacements of the more primitive impulses to more acceptable objects.

How, we must now finally come to ask, are we to decide whether this, the Freudian psychology, is a truer picture than that provided by conventional wisdom? In asking this question, we provide the impetus we need to get on to the other transitions in orientation from common sense to scientific viewpoint which will take the question out of the realm of heated argumentation. The matter of settling disputes about the adequacy of inferences, assumptions, and proposed explanatory schemes lies at the core of what we call science. And the further steps in transition of our viewpoint from that of common sense to that of experimental-theoretical science still remain before us.

## A PRELUDE TO SUBSEQUENT CHAPTERS

To set the stage for subsequent chapters we might stop to ask, "What is to be our criterion for acceptance or rejection of Freud's theory, or, for that matter, of any other theories of motivation that are advanced?" We are helped to see the need for further clarification in the method of study and to an understanding of the role of science by some ideas presented in an essay concerning the various ways of justifying belief by the philosopher Charles Peirce (1877).

## FOUR METHODS OF JUSTIFYING BELIEF

Peirce identified four methods which have been employed in the history of mankind. The first, and most primitive, he called *the method of tenacity*. If this is the way we go about deciding what to believe and what not to believe, we merely cling tenaciously to our customary beliefs. We may not know how we came to have them, nor do we care. Our primary consideration is to avoid the anxiety of doubt which would threaten us if we were to admit for a minute that there is any degree of uncertainty about our present state of knowledge.

A second method of justifying opinion is called *the method of authority*. We may already be prone to think of Freud as the greatest authority of all time on the matters at hand, in which case we may have already taken up these new conceptions as our own and set our sights to learn all there is to know about psychoanalysis. It is perhaps more likely, if this is our favorite method of justifying opinion, that we have already rejected Freud's views because they do violence to other beliefs behind which even greater authority stands. If this is our method, the whole matter hinges on our choice of authorities— if we are fortunate enough to have a choice. We are not likely to care at all how the authority came to have his opinion. And we are certain to find some worthy authority behind any side of any controversial issue. At least this would seem to be the lesson of history, from the time the earth was generally considered flat, through ages in which witches believed to be possessed of demons were also believed in need of a little burning, through the famous Scopes trial which had to do with the legitimacy of teaching Darwin's theory of evolution in the schools, into the present and its areas of ignorance and controversy.

If, on the other hand, we have already learned to despise authority as an adequate criterion of belief, we may wish to employ the more rational method developed by the learned men of ancient times who put the greatest stress on straight thinking. This is *the method of* a priori *reason*. The question we ask of Freud's basic ideas is this: Are they intuitively compelling? Are these basic ideas of his to be considered self-evident truths which break upon us with such clarity and distinctness that we must hold them as our basic premises from which all particulars about human motivation can be logically derived? The only rub with this method, as with the other two we have briefly considered, is that none of them

is designed to overcome disagreements. None of them provides for the correction of a false opinion. Two tenacious men who disagree will argue interminably and probably, in the end, come to blows. The same is likely if we appeal to authorities, since authorities have a habit of being in disagreement. And while it is unlikely that raw power would ever become the final criterion of truth when the two men in disagreement are ones who value reason so dearly they choose to argue logically (that is, deductively) from self-evident assumptions as their method of proof, it is equally unlikely that they would ever break their deadlock about particulars if their taste in what is intuitively self-evident should be at variance to begin with. How, then, do we decide if Freud has given us a truer picture than what common sense provides?

Peirce concluded his essay with a fourth method, the empirical method, or the *method of science*. (We shall overlook the fact that it is currently unfashionable to speak of "the" method of science, as if it were a set of rules for playing a game that is neatly laid out in some handbook, in order to appreciate Peirce's central point.) When this method is employed, he meant to point out, empirical observations or matters of fact, about which men can much more readily agree, become the final criterion:

"It is not to be supposed that the first three methods of settling opinion present no advantage whatever over the scientific method. On the contrary, each has some peculiar convenience of its own. The a priori method is distinguished for its comfortable conclusions. It is the nature of the process to adopt whatever belief we are inclined to, and there are certain flatteries to the vanity of man which we all believe by nature, until we are awakened from our pleasing dream by rough facts. The method of authority will always govern the mass of mankind; and those who wield the various forms of organized force in the state will never be convinced that dangerous reasoning ought not to be suppressed in some way. . . . Singularly enough, the persecution does not all come from without; but a man torments himself and is oftentimes most distressed at finding himself believing propositions which he has been brought up to regard with aversion. The peaceful and sympathetic man will, therefore, find it hard to resist the temptation to submit his opinions to authority. But most of all I admire the method of tenacity for its strength, simplicity, and directness. Men who pursue it are distinguished for their decision of character, which becomes very easy with such a mental rule. They do not waste time in trying to make up their minds what they want, but, fastening like lightning upon whatever alternative comes first, they hold it to the end, whatever happens, without an instant's irresolution. This is one of the splendid qualities which generally accompany brilliant, unlasting success. It is impossible not to envy the man who can dismiss reason, although we know how it must turn out at last.

"Such are the advantages which the other methods of settling opinion have over scientific investigation. A man should consider well of them; and then he should consider that, after all, he wishes his opinions to coincide with the fact, and that there is no reason why the results of those three first methods should do so. To bring about this effect is the prerogative of the method of science" (Peirce, 1877, pp. 13–14).

THE SELF-CORRECTIVE NATURE OF SCIENCE

When it is the method of science that we wish to follow, empirical facts come in to settle the matter of whether or not a particular theory is to be accepted or not. But for this to happen, the concepts which comprise the theory must be stated with great clarity, and their interrelations and implications must be spelled out with equal precision. The conceptual scheme must be capable of generating unambiguous hypotheses which can actually be tested against pertinent empirical observations. This critical relationship between theory, which is an invention of the human mind, and factual evidence is what distinguishes the method of science from the methods of tenacity, authority, and *a priori* reason. The unique feature of the scientific method is that *it is self-corrective*. If a scientific theory is incorrect, hypotheses derived from it will not be supported by factual evidence.

The further transitions in thought about motivation, to which we turn in the next two chapters, have to do with improving the clarity of basic concepts and theoretical assertions about motivation, and seeing the vital role of experimentation in the study of motivation, and clarifying of the question of what constitutes factual evidence about motivation. These were transitions in orientation which it took psychology many years to work out. We shall try to accomplish them within the next two chapters.

The excerpts from Freud's works which are included in this chapter are taken from his *Collected Papers*, a translation published some forty years ago. A more accurate rendering of the original will be found in the current *Standard Edition of the Complete Psychological Works of Sigmund Freud*, newly revised and largely retranslated under the editorship of James Strachey.

# CHAPTER 4

# Conceptual

# Analysis

# of Motivation

# and Conflict

*"For thousands of years man's everyday experience with falling objects did not suffice to bring him to a correct theory of gravity. A sequence of very unusual, man-made experiences, so-called experiments, which grew out of the systematic search for the truth were necessary to bring about a change from less adequate to more adequate concepts. To assume that first-hand experience in the social world would automatically lead to the formation of correct concepts or to the creation of adequate stereotypes seems therefore unjustifiable"* (Kurt Lewin, 1948, pp. 60–61).*

The work of Kurt Lewin (1890–1947), which we consider in this chapter, represents an explicit attempt to draw on knowledge of the historical development of physical science for clues as to how obstacles to progress in psychology might be overcome. Conceived early in the 1920's, the viewpoint advanced by Lewin and his co-workers is now familiarly known as the field-theoretical approach, or Field Theory. It arose out of Lewin's conviction that psychology needed to adopt the "Galilean mode of thought" to overcome the limitations of intuitive conceptions and traditional ways of thinking which now obstruct the development of behavioral science as they once delayed the development of physical science.

Lewin always held that his approach, Field Theory, should be characterized as a method: "namely, a method *of analyzing causal relations and of building scientific constructs*" (Lewin, 1951, p. 45). Field Theory constitutes a reorientation in approach to the problem of motivation and other psychological problems which have been encompassed by it since Lewin's early work. It is deliberately modeled after the method of analysis employed by Galileo centuries ago in overcoming the traditional Aristotelian ideas about the cause of physical motion. To appreciate fully Lewin's conception of motivation, we ought first attempt to see, as he did, how the traditional (Aristotelian) mode of thought still pervades common sense about motivation as it once pervaded ideas about the cause of movement in physical objects, and how the Galilean orientation is different.

* Excerpts from Kurt Lewin, *Resolving Social Conflicts*, copyright 1948, Harper & Row, Publishers, Incorporated, are reprinted by permission.

## THE GALILEAN MODE OF THOUGHT

Galileo (1564–1642) is generally recognized as the father of modern science. In tracing the growth of ideas in the evolution of physics, Einstein and Infeld say this of Galileo's contribution:

> "The discovery and use of scientific reasoning by Galileo was one of the most important achievements in the history of human thought, and marks the real beginning of physics. This discovery taught us that intuitive conclusions based on immediate observations are not always to be trusted. . . .
> "Human thought creates an ever-changing picture of the universe. Galileo's contribution was to destroy the intuitive view and replace it by a new one" (Einstein and Infeld, 1951, pp. 7 and 9).

### INTUITIVELY COMPELLING VIEWS OF ARISTOTLE

The "intuitive view" of the world to which they refer is the Aristotelian conception of physical reality. It had been accepted as the final word for centuries prior to Galileo. According to Aristotle, man's earthly environment is composed of four elements: Earth, Water, Fire, and Air. Each earthly element has a natural place which it tends to seek: Water and Earthly bodies fall; Air and Fire rise. The motions of any object were believed to be produced by a tendency that is an inherent property of the object itself. The "Natural" motion of an Earthly object was observed to be vertical, downward towards the center of the earth, which was then thought to be the center of the universe. Any motion other than this "Natural" motion required the continued application of effort or some external force. The speed of "Natural" motion was believed to depend upon the amount of Earth in the falling object. In other words, heavy objects were believed to fall faster than light objects because they contain more Earth. The "irregular" motion of a rock shot from a catapult, for example, was explained by assuming that the external force from the catapult persists for a short time after the impact and then "wears out," at which point the "Natural" tendency of the object to fall vertically takes over, and the object falls to earth. These are examples of intuitive conclusions that may be arrived at through much qualitative observation if one attempts, as Aristotle did, to abstract from many different instances the general (lawful) tendency which *most frequently* characterizes the behavior of an object.

One might even arrive at still another Aristotelian conclusion. Since none of the terrestrial motions manifest the "perfect" circular paths observed by the ancients in heavenly bodies, terrestrial motions must be considered a lower order of motion, *different in kind* from the "higher" motions of heavenly bodies. The causal tendencies which are intrinsic to different objects were believed to depend solely upon *the class* to which each belongs.

It is probably not surprising that all of these Aristotelian generalizations seem to check with our own untutored observations and intuitive conclusions. Smoke (from Fire) and balloons (full of Air) do generally tend to rise. Heavier bodies (full of Earthy substance) do generally tend to fall vertically. The apparent motions of the moon and sun around the earth each day do seem a good deal more regular and "perfect" than the irregular paths of projectiles and other moving things at the earth's surface. And everyone knows it requires external force to move an object. Witness the effort required to rearrange furniture. The piano, for example, soon ceases to move when the push is withdrawn. Furthermore, heavier objects do seem to fall a lot faster than light objects. In a summer storm, a broken branch hits the ground a good deal sooner than some of the leaves that have shaken loose. All of this seems satisfactory. Where is the rub? What is the nature of so-called "scientific reasoning," which Galileo is given so much credit for having discovered and which is supposed to have instigated a revolution in thought?

### GALILEAN THOUGHT TRANSCENDS OBSERVATIONS

The disciplined use of creative imagination, which transcends intuitive conclusions drawn from observation of actual happenings, may strike us as the first and most important characteristic of the Galilean mode of thought. Galileo considered the problem of the force required to move an object at the earth's surface and the problem of free-falling bodies. Let us follow his line of thought to grasp the essentials of his method of analysis.

Consider, first, a wagon on a flat road. Granted, it takes a push to move it. Yet sometimes the wagon will roll farther before stopping after a sudden push than at other times. If the road, though flat, is muddy, the wagon will hardly roll at all. On the other hand, if the road is a firm pavement, the wagon will roll farther even though the force from the push is the same. Why? The stickiness of the road (the friction), which is greater when the road is muddy, must act like another push, another force, but in the opposite direction. This is what must slow down the wagon faster on a muddy road than on a pavement.

How can we make the wagon roll even farther before coming to a stop without increasing the force of our initial push? Quite clearly, we can make sure the wheel-bearings are well oiled, and we can also attempt to slicken the road, perhaps by waiting until just after a freezing rain. So far, Galileo and we with him have drawn from our memory of past happenings. We have not really gone beyond our own observations of things that have actually happened in the past.

AN EXPERIMENT IN THOUGHT

At this point, however, Galileo departed from his memory images of frequently observed past happenings to create, in thought, a completely novel happening. "What if," he asked himself, the road should be perfectly smooth, without any friction to slow the wagon? The resting wagon should begin to move when we apply the external force to it, but then since the opposing force is now zero, it should continue to move indefinitely at a uniform speed. We must conclude that Aristotle was wrong in assuming that some continued application of external force is needed to maintain a horizontal motion and that the force would "wear out" when withdrawn. It now strikes us that the "natural" condition of an object is to maintain its present state of uniform motion (or rest) unless some external force is introduced to *change* it. The initial push increases the speed from zero (at rest), and then the opposing force of friction changes the speed back to zero. In other words, the observed motion of the wagon following a push, and probably all other motions as well, depend a good deal on the *immediate external conditions* affecting them.

This imaginative conclusion of Galileo was stated formally a generation later by Isaac Newton as the *law of inertia*, the first law of motion. It was arrived at only by transcending, in a creative and imaginative way, the appearance of things actually observed in past experience. The unique event imagined by Galileo, which cannot actually be made to happen because it is impossible to remove all external influences on a rolling cart, is often referred to as an "idealized experiment," or an "experiment in thought." It provides a conclusion that is certainly consistent with observations of what happens when a surface is made slicker and slicker, but speculative thought was needed to reach it.

ROLE OF ACTIVE, EMPIRICAL EXPERIMENTATION

A second important feature of the Galilean mode of thought, which is suggested in the preceding paragraphs, becomes more obvious when we consider Galileo's quarrel with the Aristotelian doctrine that the lawfulness of freely falling bodies is to be attributed *solely* to their inherent property (if they are classified as Earthly bodies) to fall vertically. If Aristotle is correct, the falling motion should not be systematically affected by any condition that is external to the body itself.

Galileo, and some of his precursors, were led to suspect that falling objects tend to fall faster the longer they fall. If the motion is fully explained as an inherent tendency of the object, the speed of fall should depend only upon how much Earthly substance the object contains. The distance traveled in a fall should be directly proportionate to how long the object is in motion. That is, if a given body were to fall 10 feet each second for 10 seconds, it should fall a total distance of 100 feet. If it were to fall only five seconds, that is, half as long, then it should fall only 50 feet, half the distance. On the other hand, if an object speeds up as it falls, which would mean that its motion is influenced by some factor other than its own inherent tendency, then the object which falls for ten seconds should fall more than twice the distance of one which falls for only five seconds. This was Galileo's argument, and this time the experiment imagined in thought could be performed. Through active intervention in the normal flux of things, the event needed to test the two arguments can be made to happen by arranging the appropriate conditions. Lawfulness, we must note, is now sought not only in natural events which occur with relatively great frequency, but also in very unique events that literally have to be created first in thought and then brought about through actual experiment.

HOMOGENIZATION OF THE SUBJECT MATTER

Guided by the belief that the same laws of motion would apply to events that are superficially different in appearance, Galileo felt no qualms about slowing down the motion of a freely falling body, which is too fast to observe with much precision. He decided to roll balls down an inclined plane, making appropriate measurements of the distance traversed and crudely timing the duration of motion by counting the beat of his own pulse from the beginning to the end of the roll. No better clocks were then available. The results of this famous experiment supported Galileo's hypothesis that time had a systematic (lawful) influence on the speed of a falling object. The measured distances traversed by balls rolling down an inclined plane were greater than expected if the speed was constant, as Aristotle had supposed. The distances were, in fact, always proportional to the square of the time ($t^2$) multiplied by a different constant value which depended upon the particular degree of slope employed: $d = Kt^2$. In other words, both time (duration of motion) and the slope of the plane had a lawful relationship to the motion of the falling object. Both factors are *external* to the inherent property which Aristotle had designated as the sole cause of motion. Galileo was able to deduce that the change in speed of the ball must mean that some *external* force is constantly active during the time of the fall, producing a constant change in motion just as the pushing of a wagon produces a *change* in its horizontal motion. A generation later, following the "Galilean mode of thought," Newton formulated the basic laws of motion and the universal law of gravitational force which explains not only the steadily increasing speed of a freely falling Earthly object, but also the "more perfect" orbits of all heavenly bodies, supposed by Aristotle to follow a separate and "higher" principle of motion.

## COMPARISON OF ARISTOTELIAN AND GALILEAN MODES OF THOUGHT

How can we characterize some of the differences between the Aristotelian and Galilean modes of thought? In one respect, they differ as the occupations of newspaper reporter and author differ. The one is limited to what has actually happened in the natural flux of daily events. The reporter would be fired if he began to try to make the news himself (by robbing a bank) or of including the possible relevance of some imagined events in his daily copy. The other is not so constrained. He may imagine novel events that have never really happened. In fact, an author is expected to consider *creative imagination a central feature of the job.*

We might also say that the Aristotelian orientation is a backward-looking and, therefore, a limited empirical method. Only the observation of natural historical events plays any significant role in the search for lawfulness. In contrast, the Galilean orientation, though beginning with a backward glance, is essentially a *forward-looking, unlimited*

*empirical method* in that it is actually more concerned with unique events that have not already occurred but might be made to occur in the future by the *active, creative intervention of the scientist in the normal flux of events.* An experiment in science is a completely novel occurrence that is made to happen for the first time because it is related in some important way to the ideas the scientist has begun to develop. Galileo's student, Torricelli, for example, discovered that Aristotle was wrong in asserting that "nature abhors a vacuum" merely by filling a long glass tube with mercury and inserting the open end of the tube in a plate of mercury for the first time in history. So far as anyone knows, he was the first man *to see* a vacuum. Even the imagined results of "idealized experiments" that cannot actually be performed play a significant role in the Galilean search for lawfulness.

Aristotelian thought is essentially a process of abstraction and classification in which lawfulness is identified with the most common and frequently appearing tendency of an object, which, like the sheep, must be separated from the many slight variations which characterize the many particular instances, the goats. The latter are dismissed as unlawful, accidental—that is, as irrelevant and immaterial in the search for lawfulness. (We have already considered how the conventional wisdom treated slips and errors as accidents before Freud.) In contrast, the Galilean mode of thought *demands much more concreteness in the description of particular instances to begin with.* The *minor variations* between two instances which otherwise show essentially the same trend *are matters of great interest*, for lawfulness is sought in the total event, the object in relation to its immediate external surroundings. And then, the Galilean mode of thought is distinctly different: it is essentially a process of creative invention which *constructs a picture of the underlying reality that must be assumed to account for the observed behavior of the object.* It asks what kind of lawful relations of the object (with its properties) to its immediate external environment must be assumed to account for the differences as well as the similarities which appear on different occasions.

The Aristotelian orientation is passive. The observer listens as nature speaks. *The Galilean orientation is active.* Through experiment, it questions nature in ways that she has never before been questioned, and, in the words of Claude Bernard (1813–1878) who was the founder of experimental medicine, "forces her to unveil herself."

## MATHEMATICS: THE VEHICLE OF SCIENTIFIC THOUGHT

To phrase meaningful questions, the scientist must first manipulate in thought the many possibilities that have not already been observed in the normal flux of past events. He may think in terms of vague impressions, the images left in memory from observations of the past. He may think in terms of words, which describe, more or less ambiguously, the events he has in mind. Or he may think in terms of precisely defined mathematical concepts which correspond to the events he has in mind and thus provide *a conceptual model of the empirical events* he studies. The thoughtful analysis of physical reality which Einstein referred to as "scientific reasoning" was as disciplined and precise in the time of Galileo and Newton as the Euclidean geometry which provided the conceptual framework for thinking about the positions of objects in space, the path of motion, distances, and the mathematical concept of vectors which was employed to represent the direction and speed of motion, and the direction and magnitude of the forces causing motion. Later, when new problems arose for which the original model proved inadequate, post-Galilean scientists, convinced of the value of symbolic, mathematical representation of natural phenomena, invented new abstract schemes for thought, new systems of mathematics (e.g., the calculus) to provide the tools they needed for further creative work in the construction of a useful conceptual picture of physical reality.

## CONCEPTUAL REPRESENTATION OF EMPIRICAL PHENOMENA

A conceptual (mathematical) representation of empirical phenomena is like a road map. One may sit down before a trip with a good road map and plot out the various possibilities that may later be experienced by actually taking the trip. The adequacy of the road map can be tested by actually taking the trip, as planned the night before in thought. If it is a good map, one arrives at the mountains or the sea on schedule, when the directions have been accurately followed. If, however, one follows a plan devised on the assumption that the map provides a valid picture of the geography of the region only to become hopelessly lost in the desert when expecting to reach the mountains or the sea, one throws down the map in disgust and looks for a better one before the next trip. If the land is uncharted, explorers will attempt to construct a crude map for others who follow. It will be improved as its inaccuracies are noted and corrected. Certainly a road map is a better guide in planning a long trip to some unfamiliar place than a plan based on vague past impressions from other trips, or a plan which relies on the long, involved, and so often misleading verbal directions one might receive from a friend over the telephone.

A good road map is a scaled-down version of the relations between cities, mountains, rivers, and oceans that actually exist in a particular geographic region. The lines representing highways represent the actual direction and distance that must be traveled. The "mapping" of the path of motion and the action of physical forces in terms of appropriate mathematical concepts is another of the most important and useful features of the post-Galilean mode of thought in science.

# THE NEED FOR A GALILEAN OUTLOOK IN PSYCHOLOGY

## IS RIGOROUS MEASUREMENT THE FIRST STEP?

When Kurt Lewin (beginning in the early 1920's) considered the differences between Aristotelian and post-Galilean physics, he saw that the obvious difference between the inexactness of Aristotelian doctrine and the highly quantified exactness of contemporary physics is really secondary to the more fundamental difference in orientation. We are misled, he argued, to consider rigorous measurement and quantification the hallmark of science. We must remember that clocks, as we know them, and many other refined measuring devices which now produce the exactness of contemporary physical science were a consequence, not the cause of the Galilean revolution in thought. Lewin was not impressed with the dedication to quantified measurement, apparently for its own sake, that characterized much of the experimental psychology of his day. He was more troubled in discovering the extent to which Aristotelian dichotomies, the Aristotelian concept of cause, and the Aristotelian concern with statistical frequency still characterized the orientation of many psychologists who had otherwise assimilated the post-Galilean emphasis on refinement of measurement. This, he felt, was like expecting the cart to pull the horse.

## HOMOGENIZATION OF SUBJECT MATTER OF BEHAVIORAL SCIENCE

Lewin called attention to the breakdown of qualitative, valuative distinctions between phenomena and the homogenization of the subject matter of physical science following Galileo. The motions of heavenly bodies and terrestrial bodies were no longer treated as separate and distinct classes of phenomena to be explained in terms of separate principles, the one a higher form, the other a lower form in terms of some irrelevant evaluative preconception. We have already touched upon several encouraging examples of a comparable homogenization of the subject matter of behavioral science: first, when Darwin's theory of evolution destroyed the traditional evaluative distinction between "rational man" and "irrational animal" and instigated the search for principles of behavior which apply to both; second, when Freud destroyed the traditional dichotomy of "normal" (or sane) and "pathological" (or insane) by treating the psychopathology of everyday life and more extreme forms of disturbance as behavior that is meaningful in the same sense that going to bed when tired or eating when hungry is meaningful. These are advances, but many other traditional, qualitative dichotomies still exist.

## CONFUSION REGARDING CAUSALITY, TELEOLOGY, AND DIRECTIONAL CONCEPTS

The real crux of the matter for Lewin was the dramatic change in the Galilean orientation concerning the idea of causality. For Aristotle, the cause of motion was some unchanging, inherent property of the object itself. The Aristotelian concept of the cause of motion finds a direct parallel in the late 19th-century concept of instinct as the cause of behavior and even in some unrefined contemporary views that behavior is to be understood as a direct expression of basic personality traits or needs. Lewin called attention to the parallel in discourse on instinct and how Aristotle had spoken of falling objects:

"... The object strives toward a certain goal; so far as movement is concerned, it tends toward the place appropriate to its nature. Thus heavy objects strive downward, the heavier the more strongly, while light objects strive upward" (Lewin, 1935, pp. 27–28).*

* Extracts from *A Dynamic Theory of Personality*, by Kurt Lewin, are used by permission. Copyright 1935. McGraw-Hill Book Company.

Is the essential difference between Aristotelian and Galilean conceptions of motion that Aristotle's teleological explanations assumed a direction of events toward a goal which Galilean causal explanation does not recognize? Many psychologists, forgetting the Newtonian principle of gravitational attraction, have argued that this is the essential issue. Lewin argued that this is not an essential difference, for the causal explanations of modern physics clearly use *directional* concepts which are mathematically described as vectors:*

"Physical force, which is defined as 'the cause of a physical change,' is considered a directed, vectorial factor. In the employment of vectorial factors as the foundation of dynamics there is thus no difference between the modern and the Aristotelian view" (Lewin, 1935, p. 28).

The real difference, and the one of paramount importance for Lewin as he considered the psychological problem of motivation,

"... lies rather in the fact that *the kind and direction of the physical vectors in Aristotelian dynamics are completely determined in advance by the nature of the object concerned.* In modern physics, on the contrary, *the existence of a physical vector always depends upon the mutual relations of several physical facts, especially upon the relation of the object to its environment*" (Lewin, 1935, p. 28, italics added).

## IMPORTANCE OF IMMEDIATE ENVIRONMENTAL INFLUENCES

As we have seen, the Aristotelian view is that the cause of behavior is an inherent property of the object which belongs to that object once and for all, irrespective of the surroundings at any given time. Lewin pointed out that in modern physics, not only is the upward tendency of a lighter body or the downward tendency of a heavy body derived from the relation of the body to its immediate environment, but even the important properties of the object itself (like the mass which is measured by weight) depends upon such a relation. It is the force of gravity on the object when put on a scale that provides the measure of its mass.

As Lewin saw it, the decisive revolution in thought came to clearest expression in Galileo's classic investigations of the law of falling bodies, which we have touched upon briefly. Galileo focused attention, not on the heavy body itself, but on the process

* A mathematical vector is represented as →. The arrow indicates direction, the length of line the speed of motion or magnitude of force.

of falling and movement on an inclined plane as it was effected by the inclination of the plane, the time of the fall, and other factors in the immediate surroundings. Lewin argued, even the idea of

". . . resorting to the [study of] slower movement upon an inclined plane presupposes that the dynamics of the event is no longer [seen as] related to the isolated object as such, but is seen to be dependent upon the whole situation in which the event occurs" (Lewin, 1935, p. 29).

The dependence of motion upon the essential characteristics of the situation—time and the slope of the plane—became the center of importance in Galileo's experimental observations and in his invention of new explanatory concepts.

ARE THE PROPERTIES OF THE
OBJECT INSIGNIFICANT?

Lewin *did not* conclude from this examination of the Galilean mode of thought that the nature of the object becomes insignificant. In psychology, that would be tantamount to saying there are no stable attributes of personality which need to be taken into consideration. We must remind ourselves, as Lewin no doubt did, that concepts like mass, which refer to properties of particular physical objects, have continued to be essential in the physical sciences. His conclusion was:

"The properties and structure of the object involved remain important also for the Galilean theory of dynamics. But the situation assumes as much importance as the object. *Only by the concrete whole which comprises the object and the situation are the vectors which determine the dynamics of the event defined*" (Lewin, 1935, pp. 29–30).

BEHAVIOR AS A FUNCTION OF
THE TOTAL SITUATION

This conclusion was phrased for psychology in a programmatic equation for which Lewin is famous, $B = f(P,E)$. The equation says that behavior ($B$) must always be considered the result of interaction between the person ($P$) and his immediate psychological environment ($E$). This, it is clear, is an exact reversal of the Aristotelian mode of thought in psychology, which is to abstract from the total situation the "accidental" disturbing influences in order to understand the essential nature of the object and the direction of its goal. An appreciation of the importance of constantly recognizing that a person's behavior is determined by the *immediate* relationship between the person and his environment was the foundation of Lewin's criticism of the "historical approach" in psychology. It so often seeks the cause of present action in the past history of the individual, as Aristotle sought his explanations in observations of the most frequently appearing characteristics of an object's past behavior.

THE PRINCIPLE OF CONTEMPORANEITY

Lewin began to stress *the principle of contemporaneity: the only determinants of behavior at a given time are the properties of the person and his psychological environment at that time.* This argument does not deny that past experience affects present behavior. Rather it stresses that whatever the influence of the past history of an individual, it must be represented as an effect that is now actively present in the contemporaneous interaction of the person ($P$) and his immediate environment ($E$).

SKEPTICISM CONCERNING PHYSICAL AND
PHYSIOLOGICAL CONCEPTS IN PSYCHOLOGY

A Galilean view of psychological dynamics, or motivation, does not mean that psychology should become a branch of physics and begin to view the behaving person as a physical machine exposed to physical forces. Like Freud, Lewin was skeptical of attempts to develop a theory of motivation in terms of physical or physiological concepts. The task, as he saw it, was to develop a workable representation of a concrete *psychological* situation including the condition of the individual and the structure of the psychological situation for him at that time. In this connection, Lewin recognized—far earlier than most psychologists—the essential role of abstract, mathematical conceptualization in post-Galilean physical science and the need for a comparably adequate system of concepts for representation of the problem of motivation. Can something as useful as Euclidean geometry and mathematical vectors in the study of motion be developed for analysis and creative thought about the psychological problem of motivation? Are there any available systems of mathematics that already contain concepts and relations that correspond to the problems of psychology to provide a conceptual model as Euclidean geometry once provided the model for the physical problem of motion? These were the questions he asked.

THE HOPE OF MATHEMATICAL PSYCHOLOGY

If it could be accomplished, a mathematical representation of the psychological situation containing the person ($P$) and his immediate environment

(*E*) would make it possible to represent the subtle differences between one event and another with great clarity and precision. This would greatly refine the kind of description of events that is possible with words and traditional Aristotelian dichotomies. As in physics, the functional concepts of some form of mathematics would enable psychology to make its way from exact description of individual cases and particular instances back to general laws, and from general laws to a description of the essential details of any specific case. This, Lewin felt, is the kind of demand that post-Galilean physical science made upon itself, and one that psychology should attempt to emulate. He undertook the task himself, anticipating by about twenty years the general recognition of the importance of mathematical models in psychology.

SEARCH FOR "BASIC ELEMENTS
OF CONSTRUCTION"

To Kurt Lewin it seemed that the essential work of a scientist was to translate phenomena, as observed, into a workable set of concepts (Cartwright, 1951, p. ix). Concepts are needed merely to describe what is observed, and to construct an adequate explanation of what is observed. Lewin devoted primary attention to the task of finding what he called "*the basic elements of construction*" for psychology. Just as a builder needs bricks, cement, wood, nails, and other basic materials, the psychologist must be equipped with a set of basic concepts in terms of which he can construct a picture of the events he studies. The chemist, when asked, "What is the chemical nature of this thing?" answers in terms of basic chemical elements and their properties. The physicist answers a similar question in terms of the basic physical constructs he has found useful. Like them, Lewin argued, psychologists must transcend appearances and intuitive conclusions and describe psychological events in terms of basic *psychological* constructs and properties. He did not believe it would be fruitful to turn to neurophysiology and the concepts of stimulus and response, as James (see Chapter 2) and many subsequent psychologists did, for the basic elements of construction.

THE CONCEPT OF LIFE SPACE

Guided by the belief that behavior must always be considered the result of interaction between a person and his environment ($B = f(P,E)$) and the principle of contemporaneity, Lewin advanced the concept of *life space* to refer to the totality of coexisting facts which influence the behavior of a person at a particular time. In other words, $B = f(P,E) = f(Lsp)$: behavior is a function of the life space at a given time.

What are the essential characteristics of behavior that need to be represented in the life space? First, behavior always occurs in the context of a particular environment and is influenced by that environment. Second, behavior is directed.

THE PSYCHOLOGICAL ENVIRONMENT

To say, "The child is playing," is an inadequate description of his behavior. It lacks concreteness. A child does not just play; he plays with particular toys that are immediately accessible. A man does not work in a vacuum; he works at something, in a particular setting, at a particular time. The environment in which behavior occurs and to which reference must be made merely to describe the behavior must be adequately represented in the life space.

How is the environment to be conceived? Is it the physical environment surrounding the person that needs to be represented to describe and to make sense out of what the person is doing? Definitely not, argued Lewin. The environment which influences the person's behavior is the world *as it exists for him at the time*. The psychological environment, as conceived by Lewin, was meant to represent both what the person consciously perceives and other environmental influences that might be outside of conscious awareness.

The psychological environment of one person does not always correspond to the geographic environment as it might be described by a disinterested observer who has made careful measurements of all its physical characteristics. Consider an example made famous in the writings of the Gestalt psychologist, Koffka, whose treatment of the problem of perception greatly influenced Lewin. Late at night, high in the Swiss Alps, a lone horseback rider hurries through a blizzard which is becoming more severe at every moment. The horse is tired. The rider knows that the storm may well continue to rage through the night, making the roads impassable. Though a stranger in these parts, the rider has often heard stories of persons who were stranded and frozen to death in such a blizzard. He is dreadfully concerned. Suddenly, far ahead in the distance he sees a faint speck of light—an inn! As he approaches the speck of light, he sees stretching before him a vast snow-covered plain and the safety of the inn across the plain. He urges his horse forward, through the blizzard to safety. Finally he arrives at the inn, tired but greatly relieved. As he approaches the door of the inn, he is met by the innkeeper, whose face is white with anxiety. The innkeeper sits down and utters a gasp. He knows the rider has just ridden across the great lake that usually is not solidly frozen over. He knows the horseback rider is lucky not to have broken through the thinly frozen ice and drowned. Had the innkeeper been the man on horseback, he certainly would have taken a very circuitous route around the treacherous lake and not directly over what to the visitor had *appeared* an open plain to safety.

Were we to attempt to make sense out of the horseback rider's behavior in terms of the innkeeper's knowledge of the geography, we should conclude that he is mad, or at best, extremely foolhardy. We should be very surprised to find him a cautious and prudent man. Only when he told us of his "misconception" should we feel that his behavior was, indeed, understandable.

GEOGRAPHIC AND PSYCHOLOGICAL
ENVIRONMENT DISTINGUISHED

The distinction between the *geographic*, or *physical* environment and the *psychological* environment is one that we have already discovered in our own experience. Everyone can recall the time he reached down with muscles taut to pick up a very heavy suitcase only to have the suitcase spring into the air because it was, in fact, empty. We also recall the feeling of surprise which occurs when, after we have entered an elevator and pressed the button marked "up," the floor gives way under our feet. The surprise can be attributed to the fact that we mistakenly expected the elevator to move upward, when in fact it moved downward because someone had previously pushed the "down" button.

The environment, *as it exists for the person at the time*, defines alternative courses of action which he may undertake. Consider still another illustration. A recent news story makes the point dramatically. It is reported that a warehouse was robbed by a gang of burglars who locked the two night watchmen in the trunks of two automobiles standing in the parking lot. The next morning, one of the night watchmen attracted attention by banging on the inside of the trunk in which he was locked. He had survived the night by breathing air from the spare

tire. The other man was less fortunate; he had suffocated. One man had found himself hopelessly trapped and suffocating in the crowded trunk of an automobile with a tire and some tools that were inadequate for making a hole to let in some fresh air. The other, in much the same physical environment, lived through the night by breathing the air contained in the spare tire. Can the behavior of the two men be explained without taking into account the difference in the psychological environments of these two men? The psychological environment of one man contained a storage tank of air; the less fortunate man's psychological environment, though it contained a full spare tire, did not.

## THE DIRECTION OF BEHAVIOR

The second essential characteristic of behavior which needs to be represented in the life space is direction. Any description of behavior, so argued Lewin, requires the concept of direction. Changes of behavior must be represented as movement *from* one activity *to* another just as physical motion is represented as movement *from* an initial position *to* some other position in physical space. The *from-to* character of physical motion is represented as direction. Certainly the most common examples of behavior in progress towards some goal or away from some threat have this same directional character.

Lewin sought to represent the position of a person in relation to potential goals or potential threats in his immediate psychological environment in terms of a form of mathematics called topology. Thus, the area in which the horseback rider in our first example was traveling might be represented as one topological region, the open plain before him as another, and the distant inn as another. (See Figure 4.1.) The rider's behavior may then be represented as a path (a line) which traverses the intermediate region between his initial location and his destination. The situation as it might have existed for the innkeeper, had he been caught out in the same storm, would be represented differently. The life space of the innkeeper would contain an insurmountable barrier in the region corresponding to what the other man had perceived as an open plain. The innkeeper's path toward the inn would have been a roundabout route, as shown in Figure 4.2. The two men would have pursued different means to the same end. Yet *direction towards the inn* would be an appropriate description of the behavior in each case.

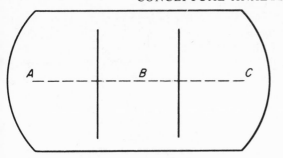

FIGURE 4.1 Topological representation of the initial location of the horseback rider (region A), the open plain before him (region B), and his goal, the distant inn (region C). His behavior is represented as a path (a line) *from A, through B, to C.*

Because the psychological direction of behavior does not always correspond to physical direction (as, for example, in the case of the innkeeper taking a roundabout route), Lewin realized that direction in the life space must be represented differently than direction as employed in physics in reference to a rolling ball in physical space. The shortest psychological distance between two regions is not often a straight line as it is in the Euclidean geometry which represented positions and directions in physical space very adequately for Galileo and Newton.

Inspired by the way physicists had come to realize their need for a new type of geometry to supplant Euclidean geometry when the theory of relativity was developed by Einstein in this century, Lewin faced with optimism the comparable task of trying to develop a suitable type of geometry for the problems of psychology. He attempted to work out the axioms for such a geometry which would serve

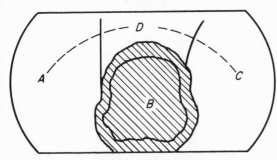

FIGURE 4.2 Topological representation of the initial location of the innkeeper, had he been caught in the storm (region A), showing the insurmountable obstacle before him (region B), an area of safe travel around the obstacle (region D), and his goal, the distant inn (region C). His behavior is represented as a roundabout path (a line) *from A, through D, to C.*

as a model for the life space. We will consider only a few of the fundamental ideas in Lewin's treatment of the possible directions of behavior.

DIRECTION TOWARD SOME OTHER REGION

If a boy were walking to the store to buy a piece of candy, we might describe the direction of his behavior as "going to the store." In a topological representation of the situation (see Figure 4.3) the

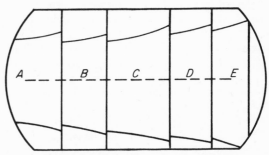

FIGURE 4.3 Topological representation of the behavior described as "going to the store." The concept of direction refers both to the whole sequence of activities which comprise the path from the beginning, A, to the end, E, and to the immediate next step in the path. Thus, behavior of the boy in region A may be described as directed toward the end, $d_{A,E}$, and as directed toward the immediate next step, $d_{A,B}$, which is a means to the end.

boy is located in region $A$. He must traverse the intermediate regions $B$, $C$, $D$, before arriving at the store, which is represented as region $E$. The *direction* of his behavior is a characteristic of the whole path $A,E$. We can describe the boy's behavior as having the direction from $A$ to $E$, that is, as $d_{A,E}$. But *the concept of direction refers also to a characteristic of the path in region $A$: the immediate direction from $A$ to $B$, that is, $d_{A,B}$.* The immediate direction of his behavior refers to the initial step of the path, the very next action which will occur. The next step, $A,B$ (which is read "from $A$ to $B$"), is a segment of the whole path $A,E$ (which is read "from $A$ to $E$"). We might say, the boy is walking from the porch ($A$) of his house to the front gate ($B$) in order to go to the store ($E$). If the situation did not change as the boy proceeded to the store, the immediate direction would change as he went along. First it would be $d_{A,B}$, then $d_{B,C}$, then $d_{C,D}$, and finally $d_{D,E}$. At every point, the concept of direction applies both to the goal-directedness of the whole sequence of actions ($d_{A,E}$) and to the immediate next step ($d_{A,B}$) which serves as a means to that end.

We must remember that the concept of direction in the life space is intended to describe behavior at a particular time. The situation might change as the boy proceeds to the store. After finishing the first two steps of the original path toward the store, he might be influenced by an *unexpected* happening, some factor that was "alien to" (that is, outside) the initial life space (Lewin, 1938, p. 33). For example, a friend might drive by in an auto and offer him a lift. The structure of the situation would then change. The life space at that moment might contain a third step toward the goal that had not been part of the original path. In other words, we must remember: (a) that the statement "he is going to the store" ($d_{A,E}$) describes the behavior of the boy as directed toward some distant goal *at a particular time;* (b) that this statement refers also to the direction of the immediate next step along the path, which is $d_{A,B}$; and (c) that the situation might change before the whole sequence of action has been completed.

Let us suppose that the life space of the boy contained three paths from A to E at the outset, that is, three means of getting from the front porch to the store. (See Figure 4.4.) The *immediate* direc-

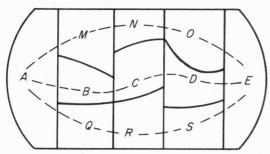

FIGURE 4.4   Topological representation of three paths from A to E. The immediate direction of the three paths is different in region A, i.e., $d_{A,M}$, $d_{A,B}$, $d_{A,Q}$, but each presents a step in a path toward E having the direction $d_{A,E}$.

tions of the three paths are different ($d_{A,B}$, $d_{A,M}$, $d_{A,Q}$), even though each path represents going to the store ($d_{A,E}$). A little later we shall turn to the question of what determines the immediate direction of locomotion, or behavior, in such a case.

### PSYCHOLOGICAL DISTANCE: A CHARACTERISTIC OF A PATH OF ACTION

Another important characteristic of the path from A to E in our example of the boy going to the store is the *psychological distance* from A to E, or from A

to any intermediate region like C. Lewin employed the symbol e to refer to the psychological distance between two regions in the life space. The concept of distance refers to the whole path between two regions. Thus the distance from A to E ($e_{A,E}$) refers to the number of intermediate regions (or more precisely, the number of boundaries between regions) which must be traversed in going from A to E. This distance, $e_{A,E}$, is greater than $e_{A,B}$, or $e_{A,C}$, or the distance of any segment of the whole path.

### DIRECTION AWAY FROM SOME OTHER REGION

Suppose a boy is running away from a fire some distance from him. At the moment we choose to describe his behavior, he is located in activity region A (running up the basement stairway), and the fire is spreading from the furnace, as represented in region B of Figure 4.5. The direction of his behavior

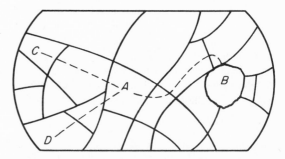

FIGURE 4.5   Representation of behavior directed away from a threat. The direction of behavior in region A, away from region B, is designated $d_{A,-B}$. This is equivalent to the direction toward any other region X, $d_{A,X}$, which is more distant from B than A is. In this example, $d_{A,-B} = d_{A,C}$ and $d_{A,-B} = d_{A,D}$. Both regions C and D are more distant from region B than region A is.

in A, away from B, is designated $d_{A,-B}$. The direction in A away from B ($d_{A,-B}$) is defined by Lewin as equivalent to the direction *from A to* any other region X which is more distant from B than A is, that is, as direction $d_{A,X}$. Lewin cautioned that the direction "away from" should not be confused with "opposite direction." He supposed:

> "There are even cases in which the direction in A away from B is equal to the direction in A toward B ($d_{A,-B} = d_{A,B}$). This rather paradoxical equation arises in situations where one can reach a greater distance from B only by first passing through B" (Lewin, 1938, p. 52).

In this connection, we call to mind the behavior of a cornered animal when terror gives way to direct attack. Lewin referred to this as the so-called "flight forward," an attempt in desperate situations to break through in the direction towards the enemy.

We must note that the direction "away from" is a *many-valued* direction. That is, "$d_{A,-B}$ implies $d_{A,X}$ (where $X$ is more distant)" means that there may exist more than one other activity (region $X$) which is farther from $B$ than $A$ is. For example, a prize fighter can duck his head to the left (region $X_1$) or to the right (region $X_2$) to avoid a punch.

DIRECTION AWAY FROM THE PRESENT REGION

Here Lewin considered the case of a person who finds himself engaging in some "unpleasant" activity and is attempting to escape from it. The direction in region $A$ away from region $A$ ($d_{A,-A}$) is defined as equivalent to the direction $d_{A,X}$ as long as $A$ and $X$ are not identical. The direction away from $A$ ($d_{A,-A}$) is the same as the direction *from A to* some other region $X$ ($d_{A,X}$) when the distance between $X$ and $A$ is greater than the distance from $A$ to $A$, which is zero. Here again, the immediate direction of behavior is not specified in terms of some *particular* next step as it is when direction towards a distant goal implies a *particular* next step $d_{A,B}$. (See Figure 4.3.) The direction of behavior away from some other region or away from the present region is described in terms of what, specifically, *does not* happen rather than what, specifically, *does* happen next.

DIRECTION TOWARD THE PRESENT REGION

We now consider the case of a person who is "enjoying" his present activity. An adequate description of the direction of his behavior requires that we represent it as sustained or continued. According to Lewin, the direction "to stay in a region" ($d_{A,A}$) may be considered equivalent to the direction "*opposed* to leaving this region," which Lewin represented as $\bar{d}_{A,-A}$. The concept of direction as referring to a change *from* one activity *to* another is thus maintained. The direction of the behavior of a child engrossed in play, an adult reading a good book, a scientist immersed in his work, any hungry person beginning a good meal, all may be described as $d_{A,A}$, or as a direction *opposed* to doing anything else, which is written $\bar{d}_{A,-A}$ (or $\bar{d}_{A,X}$).

## SUMMARY: THE DESCRIPTION OF BEHAVIOR

Before introducing concepts which might help to *explain* a person's behavior, we must face the task of how the behavior we observe and seek to explain is to be *described*. To Lewin, the essential characteristics of behavior were: (a) behavior always occurs in a particular environment; (b) behavior is directed.

The environment in which the behavior of a person occurs is not the physical environment as it might be described after very precise observations and measurements of all the physical and geographic properties of the immediate surroundings. Instead, the environment must be considered from the viewpoint of the person whose behavior we study, *as it exists for him at the time*. The psychological environment contains properties which the person attributes or imputes to his surroundings, consciously or unconsciously.

The concept of direction refers to change *from* one activity *to* another. Activities are represented as regions in the life space of the person at the time. A direction is thus always defined in terms of two regions. One region represents the activity in progress which contains the person at the time. The other is the region toward which or away from which the person moves. In considering the possible directions of behavior, Lewin has tried to represent: (a) the case of an activity which is a means to some distant end, which may be described as the *direction towards some goal;* (b) the case of activity that is a means of avoiding something, which may be described as the *direction away from some distant region;* (c) the case of activity which is an escape from the immediate activity, which is described as the *direction away from the present region;* (d) the case of activity which is sustained or prolonged, which is described as the *direction towards the present region* (or as the direction *opposed to* away from the present region).

## THE MOTIVATION OF BEHAVIOR

PSYCHOLOGICAL FORCE

Now, having clearly in mind how Lewin conceived behavior as directed and to be represented as *locomotion* of the individual from one region of activity to another in the life space, we may turn to his treatment of the determinants of locomotion.

The motions of physical objects are governed by physical forces. Why can't the "wants" and "intentions" of an individual, whether they be conscious or unconscious, be represented as *psychological forces* acting on the individual to produce the changes we observe in behavior that are represented as loco-motions in the life space?

### FORCE REPRESENTED AS A VECTOR

Lewin employed the mathematical concept of vector ($\rightarrow$) to represent a psychological force in the life space. The conceptual properties of a psychological force are: direction, strength, and point of application. The *direction of force* is indicated by the arrow; the *strength of force* by the length of the vector; and the *point of application* is a region in the life space, usually the one which represents the present position of the person.

If a child sees a toy on the floor some distance from him and *wants* to play with it, the situation might be represented as in Figure 4.6A. The direction of the force implies that he is motivated to locomote in that direction. The strength of the force, as indicated by the length of the vector, implies the vigor of locomotion. The basic idea is to link the actual locomotions which represent behavior to the psychological forces which produce them. But it is very difficult to conceive of a situation in which only one psychological force would be influencing a person. As Freud so often emphasized, behavior is "overdetermined." If the situation illustrated in Figure 4.6 were an actual situation, the child might already be playing with some other toy which interests him. This would have to be represented as a force towards the present activity region having the direction $d_{A,A}$ or, as we have seen, as a force $f_{\overline{A,-A}}$ opposed to leaving the activity. This force, $f_{\overline{A,-A}}$, would oppose the force $f_{A,C}$ towards the new toy ($C$). Let us assume that such a counterforce

exists for the child, but that it is weaker than his interest in the new toy as represented by $f_{A,C}$, as shown in Figure 4.6B. Our representation of the situation implies that the "resultant" of the two forces should favor the child's moving towards the new toy. In other words, *the actual locomotion of the child reflects the strength of the resultant force ($f^*$) rather than the strength of any single force active at the time.* A resultant force having the direction $d_{A,C}$ is indicated by the asterisk: $f^*_{A,C}$.

### LOCOMOTION RELATED TO THE RESULTANT OF FORCES

Lewin stated the coordination of psychological forces with locomotion as follows:

> "If the resultant of psychological forces acting on a region is greater than zero, there will be a locomotion in the direction of the resultant force, or the structure of the situation will change so that the change is equivalent to such a loco-motion" (Lewin, 1938, p. 85).*

This definition, which links locomotion to result-ants of forces, may be stated symbolically: If $\Sigma f_{A,X} = f^*_{A,B}$ and $|f^*_{A,B}| > 0$, then $v_{A,B} > 0$. This is read, if the directions and strengths of all forces are taken into account by adding the vectors which represent them ($\Sigma f_{A,X}$) and this produces a resultant force from region $A$ to region $B$ ($f^*_{A,B}$), and the strength of this resultant force ($|f^*_{A,B}|$) is greater than zero, then the tendency to locomote (the

---

* Excerpts from Kurt Lewin, *The Conceptual Representation and the Measurement of Psychological Forces,* 1938, are reprinted by permission of Duke University Press.

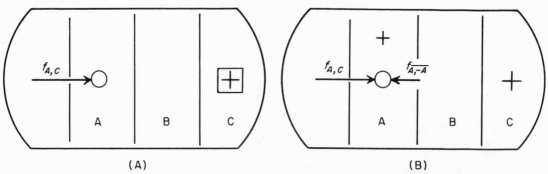

(A)          (B)

FIGURE 4.6    Representation of situation which exists when a child sees a toy and wants to play with it. In Part A, this state of affairs is described as one in which the psychological force, $f_{A,C}$, produces a tendency to locomote from A to C. Part B takes into account the child's present interest in activity A when he is attracted to a new toy, C. His present interest is represented as a force opposed to leaving the initial activity, $f_{\overline{A,-A}}$, and hence opposed to the force, $f_{A,C}$, which is di-rected toward the new toy.

velocity) from $A$ to $B$ is greater than zero ($v_{A,B} > 0$).

The reversal of this definition, which coordinates resultant of forces and locomotion, is also assumed to hold. Every psychological locomotion (or change of structure of the situation equivalent to such a locomotion) is due to the resultant of forces in its direction. That is, if $v_{A,B} > 0$, then a resultant $f^*_{A,B} = \Sigma f_{A,X}$ exists such that $|f^*_{A,B}| > 0$.

Already, we begin to anticipate some of the difficult problems which lie ahead. For example, is the resolution of conflict between different psychological forces to be merely a matter of *adding* the various forces together as in physics? We imagine not, since people often face choices between incompatible alternatives and must *decide* on either one course of action *or* another instead of some compromise. If a student resolves the conflict between going to a movie and continued study in favor of the movie, he does not simply walk very slowly to the movie because the resultant force towards the movie is now relatively weak. He may have trouble deciding, but once the decision is made, he gets going so as not to be last in line. (Recall James: "Forward—though the heavens may fall!") Lewin and his co-workers recognized this problem, and they have worked out a solution to it, a theory of decision. But let us put these complex questions out of mind until we have a firm grasp of the basic elements of construction as they apply to the most simple cases. This, after all, is the way one should proceed in following the "Galilean mode of thought."

## THE DETERMINANTS OF FORCE

We now have in mind how psychological forces influence locomotion (behavior). Let us turn to the question of what factors account for these forces. In our example above, it was the attractive toy that sparked the child's interest. We may imagine that the toy might have appeared either more attractive or less attractive to the child and that the force towards the toy should be affected by this. We may also imagine what might have occurred if instead of a toy the child had noticed a growling dog.

### VALENCE

Lewin represented the attractive or repulsive quality of an object or activity for a person by means of the concept of *valence:* "A region $G$ which has a valence ($Va(G)$) is defined as a region within the life space of an individual $P$ which attracts or repulses this individual" (Lewin, 1938, p. 88). A region of positive valence (an attraction) is indicated by a plus sign ($+$). A region of negative valence (a repulsion) is indicated by a minus sign ($-$). Positive and negative valences are defined in terms of the *direction* of the force which they engender.

*Definition of positive valence:*
$$\text{If } Va(G) > 0, \text{ then } |f_{P,G}| > 0.$$

This is read, if the valence of a region is greater than zero—that is, if it has a positive value ($+$)—then the strength of force on the person *towards* that region is greater than zero.

*Definition of negative valence:*
$$\text{If } Va(G) < 0, \text{ then } |f_{P,-G}| > 0.$$

This is read, if the valence of a region is less than zero—that is, if it has a negative value ($-$)—then the strength of force on the person *away from* that region is greater than zero.

In connection with the concept of valence, Lewin stated:

> "The concept of valence as defined [above] . . . does not imply any specific statement concerning the origin of the attractiveness or the repulsiveness of the valence. The valence might be due to a state of hunger, to emotional attachment, or to a social constellation. The final goal related to a valence might be a consumption like eating a cake; it might be the joy of watching a performance at a theater; a negative valence might be based on the fear of being defeated in a competition. The statement that a certain region of the life space has a positive or negative valence merely indicates that, for whatever reason, at the present time and for this specific individual a tendency exists to act in the direction toward this region or away from it" (Lewin, 1938, p. 88).

These definitions relate the concept of valence to force, but a valence is not identical with a force. It is only one of the factors which determine the force.

### PSYCHOLOGICAL DISTANCE

Another factor which influences force is the psychological distance ($e$) between the person ($P$) and the valent region ($G$)—that is, $e_{P,G}$. For example, the growing excitement of a child as he approaches the zoo with his father may cause him to break away and run the last few steps to the gate. And the fear of a growling dog diminishes as one moves a safe distance from it. In other words, the strength of force is related to both the valence of a region and the psychological distance between the person and that region.

$$|f_{P,G}| = f(Va(G)) \times \frac{1}{e_{P,G}} = f\left(\frac{Va(G)}{e_{P,G}}\right)$$

The strength of force is proportionate to the valence; it is stronger the greater the magnitude of valence. The force is inversely proportionate to the psychological distance; it becomes stronger as the psychological distance *decreases*.

### FORCE FIELD

Since a valence ($Va(G)$) produces a force upon the person in the activity region where he is located either towards or away from the valent region, and this force depends upon the psychological distance from the valent region, we can proceed to determine systematically for every other activity region of the life space what the direction and strength of force upon the person would be *if* the person were in that region. Obviously there would be no psychological force acting upon the person unless he were located in a certain region. Nevertheless we can imagine what that force would be. This is what Lewin meant by a "force field": "A force field correlates to every region of a field the strength and direction of the force which would act on the individual if the individual were in that region" (Lewin, 1938, p. 90).

We begin now to understand why the life space is often referred to as the *psychological field* of a person and why the Lewinian approach came to be known as the field-theoretical approach, or *Field Theory*. Figure 4.7 shows that we may now amplify our definition of a positive valence: *a positive valence*

*corresponds to a force field where all forces are directed toward the same region*. This figure also allows us to redefine a negative valence: *a negative valence corresponds to a force field where all forces are directed away from the same region*.

We see the close relation between valence and force. Yet a valence is not a force. A valence has no direction, merely strength. A valence corresponds to a force field. A force, however, has both strength and direction, depending upon the magnitude of the valence *and* psychological distance. A force is represented as a vector implying a tendency to locomote in a given direction.

We have considered how a positive valence together with psychological distance accounts for forces on the person having the direction *towards* some region ($f_{P,G}$) and how negative valence together with psychological distance accounts for forces on the person having the direction *away from* ($f_{P,-G}$). We still have to consider how valence produces forces having the direction *away from* the present region ($d_{A,-A}$) and the direction *towards the present region* ($d_{A,A}$).

The force fields in Figure 4.8 help us to understand these two cases. A child might be involved in some activity which he greatly dislikes, in region $A$ on the left side of Figure 4.8. The force corresponding to the negative valence ($Va(A)$) will in this case be $f_{A,-A}$, or $f_{A,X}$. (See p. 77.) It accounts for the tendency to escape. If, however, the child is immersed in play activity which he greatly enjoys, we represent this by imagining him in region $G$ on the right side of Figure 4.8. It would at first appear that the child in a region of positive valence is exposed

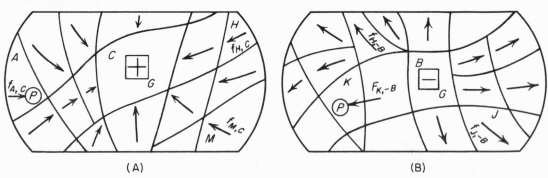

(A)    (B)

FIGURE 4.7   Positive and Negative central force fields. In Part A, the person, P, is located in A and the goal, G, in C. The forces $f_{A,C}$, $f_{H,C}$, and $f_{M,C}$, correspond to $Va(G)$ when P is located in regions A, H, or M, respectively. All forces are directed toward G. In Part B, the person, P, is located in K, and B is a region of negative valence. The forces $f_{K,-B}$, $f_{J,-B}$, and $f_{H,-B}$, correspond to $Va(G)$ when P is located at K, J, or H, respectively. All forces are directed away from G. (After Lewin, 1938)

to the pressure of a great number of competing forces. Yet intuitively we feel that this should not be a region of great conflict. It is supposed to represent the region of enjoyable activity. Lewin took account of this difficulty. All of the approach forces shown are defined as having the direction from some region outside $G$ towards $G$. *The point of application of each of these forces lies outside G. Hence, these forces do not influence the child who is already in region G. They would, however, have an immediate influence should he begin to locomote out of region G.* The force acting on an individual who is located in a region $G$ of positive valence is formally given as $f_{G,G}$, but we should remember that this force ($f_{G,G}$) is *"in itself not a tendency to a directed action but merely a tendency which is opposed to leaving the present region G, that is, opposed to $f_{G,-G}$"* (Lewin, 1938, p. 175).

This conception helps to explain the well-known tendency of persons to sustain what common sense refers to as enjoyable activity and to resist forces to stop and to do something else, as a child does a call from play, yet it raises another important question that we must, in time, consider: Would activity in a positively valent goal region continue indefinitely if it were not for the influence of other stronger forces to do something else?

## TENSION AS AN INDIRECT DETERMINANT OF FORCE

So far we have concentrated on the environmental determinants of psychological force—the attractive or repulsive object or activity, and the distance of the person from it. Is this not as one-sided as the Aristotelian preoccupation with the properties of the behaving object, that is, the attempt to explain behavior only in terms of properties of the person? Lewin's programmatic equation, $B = f(P,E)$, suggests that the condition of the person should have something to do with the psychological forces which influence his behavior. Lewin in fact argued that the person ($P$) and environment ($E$) are interdependent; the condition of the person ($P$) is often influenced by the environment ($E$)—that is, $P = f(E)$—and the psychological environment of the person is often influenced by the prior condition of the person—that is, $E = f(P)$. For example, after a long day of vigorous exercise, a person is hungry and this greatly strengthens his interest in food. On the other hand, after a good hearty meal there comes a point where even another bite of a delicious lemon pie is impossible. Lewin did not ignore the present condition of the person as one of the important determinants of psychological forces. He considered two factors which are basic for that part of the life space which represents the person: (a) the structure of the person, and (b) tension.

Lewin considered the person as a system of interdependent subsystems which may be represented as subregions within that region of the life space standing for the person. Thus one could speak of the *degree of differentiation* within the person as one of the important structural properties of the person. Individual differences in degree of differentiation and in type of structure are important matters in the study of personality. More important to the study of motivation is one of the outstanding characteristics of a subsystem within the person, as conceived by Lewin: namely, its state of *tension* ($t$).

*Lewin represented a "need" in the state of hunger in the life space as a system in a state of tension, and*

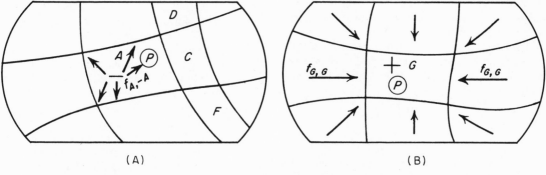

( A )                                            ( B )

FIGURE 4.8 Forces when in a region of negative or positive valence. In part A, the person, P, is located in a region of negative valence, A. The force $f_{A,-A}$ is equal to a force $f_{A,X}$ toward the region of different activity, D, C, or E. In Part B, the person, P, is located in a region of positive valence, G. The force $f_{G,G}$ is equivalent to a force $f_{G,-G}$, i.e., one opposed to leaving the present region G. (*After Lewin, 1938*)

*the satisfaction of that "need" as a release of the tension within the system.* He suggested that the force towards food is stronger when the person is hungry than when his hunger has been satisfied, and the force towards water stronger when thirsty, *because the inner-personal regions of a person are related to certain valences in the environment.* The valence of food objects and the activity of eating is affected by hunger; the valence of water and other liquids and the activity of drinking is affected by thirst. However, the existence and the strength of a valent region of the psychological environment does not depend solely upon the tension (i.e., need) of the person. Only in cases of hallucination, as when there is extreme thirst on a desert, does thirst alone seem responsible for the existence of a region of high valence containing water in the person's psychological environment. Commonly, the existence and valence of regions in the life space are greatly influenced by what Lewin referred to as "alien" factors which lie outside the life space in the immediate physical or geographic environment. In other words, both the physiological condition of the person called "hunger" and properties of the perceived physical reality called "an apple" influenced the valence of the apple in an individual's life space:

> "More specifically, the valence $Va(G)$ which an object of activity $G$ possesses for a person at a given time depends upon the character and state of the person $P$, and upon the perceived nature of the object or activity $G$; $Va(G) = F(t,G)$" (Lewin, 1938, p. 107).

Accordingly, forces towards food and eating are affected by the condition of the person *indirectly* via the influence of tension systems $(t_g)$ on the valence of potential goal objects and activities. The valence of a goal determines the force field.

The interaction of person $(P)$ and environment $(E)$ in the determination of psychological force is clearly shown when we consider, now, Lewin's basic conception of psychological force:

$$f_{P,G} = \left( \frac{Va(G)}{e_{P,G}} \right) = \left( \frac{t,G}{e_{P,G}} \right).$$

In Lewin's words, ". . . the force for a locomotion depends on the need or the tension of the person; on those non-psychological factors which affect the existence of the valence; and on the relative position of the person and the valence" (Lewin, 1938, p. 107). Instead of attempting to explain behavior as the direct result of some internal

need, instinct, or some other inherent property of the person (in Lewin's opinion, the worst form of Aristotelian mode of thought in psychology), he stressed the determinative role of the immediate environment by emphasizing the *indirect* link between the condition of the person (a system in a state of tension $(t_g)$) and the force which accounts for a tendency to act in a certain way. The need of the person is linked with certain properties of the environment, viz., $Va(G)$. It is the immediate environment which then determines behavior.

THE SIMILARITY OF LEWIN'S PSYCHOLOGICAL
FORCE AND NEWTON'S GRAVITATIONAL FORCE

The extent to which Lewin was influenced by the post-Galilean physics of motion may be surmised by comparing Newton's principle of gravitational force with Lewin's principle of psychological force. According to Newton, the force of gravity on an object having a certain mass $m$ is proportionate to the product of this mass and a corresponding property $M$, the mass of the attracting object, and inversely proportionate to the square of the distance between them $(R^2)$, times a constant value $G$:

*Newton:* Gravitational Force $= G \dfrac{mM}{R^2}$

*Lewin:* Psychological Force $= F \left( \dfrac{t,G}{e_{P,G}} \right).$

Both principles say that force is positively related to some property (or condition) of the behaving object and a related property in some object in the environment which attracts. Both principles say that force is weaker the greater the distance. The force of gravity propels a meteor towards the earth; a psychological force propels the hungry man towards his supper. The similarity is striking.* Yet one very important difference has troubled psychologists who believe that *enduring* attributes of personality should have some influence on an individual's motivation. In physics, the mass of an object, as inferred from the measure called weight, is considered a constant inherent property of the object. The tension system $(t_g)$ which represents the person in the Lewinian scheme is a very transient condition. Hunger and thirst arise as a consequence of the metabolic process and are removed by eating and drinking. Are we to

---

* Even more striking is the similarity of Lewin's conception of psychological force and the later physical principles of electrical and magnetic attraction, which account for both attraction and repulsion as does the Lewinian principle.

assume there are no stable properties of the person, like the mass of a physical object, which have any motivational significance?

This is an important question to keep in mind. It will arise again when we review the development of motivational concepts in studies of animal behavior. We shall return to the problem again in the final chapter, after considering what has been learned about individual differences in motivation. But now, having introduced some of the basic elements of construction which Lewin advanced, it is time to turn to some of the experiments which suggested and shaped the concepts we have been considering.

It would be a mistake to assume that this conception of motivation sprang fullblown from Lewin's head. We have examined his concepts and principles as they were stated in 1938, after about 20 years of experimental analysis of motivation by Lewin and many co-workers. To illustrate the role of experimentation and to concretize many of the ideas we have discussed, let us turn to experimentation related to an issue that was of central importance in Freud's analysis of the psychopathology of everyday life and in his theory of dreams: the persistence of an unfulfilled wish.

## RESUMPTION AND RECALL OF INTERRUPTED ACTIVITIES

One of the most important ideas advanced by Freud is that wishes persist until they are satisfied. His explanation of dreams, slips, errors, and accidents rests on the assumption that an unfulfilled wish, whether conscious or not, continues to influence thought and action until it is satisfied. Some of the earliest experiments undertaken by Lewin and his co-workers had to do with this basic assumption about motivation. The experiments were designed to determine whether an "intention to do something" could be conceived as a system in tension (i.e., as a *quasi*-need) and "satisfaction of the intention"— that is, the completion of the activity—as the discharge of tension. We already know that in the Lewinian scheme a tension system ($t_g$) is one of the determinants of psychological force ($f_{P,G}$). A tension system within the person ($t_g$), corresponding to "an intention," is one of the factors which influences the valence ($Va(g)$) of the activity or object which represents the "goal" of the person; and $Va(g)$ is the major determinant of force ($f_{P,G}$), the tendency of $P$ to locomote towards the goal region.

Let us now turn to some of these early experiments

that were guided by the idea that what common sense calls "wish," "want," or "intention" should be thought of as a system in tension, and "satisfaction of the wish" as reduction of tension. After describing the initial experiments and their results, we will consider Lewin's theoretical explanation of the results in terms of the conception of motivation we have just reviewed.

### THE ZEIGARNIK EFFECT

It is said that the first of these experiments, performed by Bluma Zeigarnik between 1924 and 1926, was suggested by an observation Lewin and his students had made at lunch one day. Their waiter had an incredible memory for the details of everyone's luncheon order until after they had paid the checks. If questioned a few minutes later, however, he could not recall what each person had been served. This suggested that the intention to carry out the activity of serving each person the meal he had ordered and collecting payment could be considered a system in tension that sustained goal-directed thought and action only until the activity was accomplished and the "tension" was discharged.

Zeigarnik designed an experiment to test the adequacy of this conception. She devised a number of different tasks (puzzles, problems, etc.) for student subjects to perform. During the experimental session, each student was invited to work at the tasks. The subject was allowed to continue some of the activities until they were clearly completed. For example, work at a puzzle might continue until the solution was clearly attained. But some of the activities were informally interrupted before they were finished. The experimenter interrupted by simply asking the subject to work at some other task instead. After the subject had worked on all of the tasks for a while, finishing some of them but not finishing others, the various tasks were collected and put out of sight. Then Zeigarnik asked the subject in an informal way if he could recall some of the activities he had worked on. Typically the subject described a number of the tasks immediately. Then, however, he would have to pause and think carefully before being able to recall any more. Zeigarnik found, as she had expected, that the number of *unfinished* tasks which were recalled (particularly during the "spontaneous" period before the pause) greatly exceeded the number of completed tasks that were recalled. In fact, the ratio of recalled unfinished tasks to recalled completed tasks, ($RU/RC$), for a sizable number of subjects averaged about 1.9. In other words, the number of *unfinished* tasks recalled was almost twice as large as the number of completed tasks recalled. This phenomena, which has been repeatedly observed when Zeigarnik's procedure is carefully followed, is now commonly referred to as "*the Zeigarnik effect*" (Zeigarnik, 1927).

SPONTANEOUS RESUMPTION OF
INTERRUPTED ACTIVITY

A short time later, Ovsiankina repeated the experimental procedure in all its essential details but one. Instead of putting the tasks away after the subject had worked on all of them, having finished some but not others, Ovsiankina provided an interval of time for free activity. While the experimenter attended to other matters, as if getting ready for some further activity, the subject had an opportunity to resume work at any one of the tasks "spontaneously." Ovsiankina discovered that subjects spontaneously resumed the activities which had been interrupted prior to completion. In other words, the intention to complete the task persisted beyond the point of interruption and clearly influenced subsequent "spontaneous" action (resumption) as it had influenced subsequent thought (recall) in the experiment by Zeigarnik. These experimental results are strikingly similar to the manifestations of unfulfilled wishes and intentions in dreams (thought) and actions (slips, errors, accidents) which Freud had considered of great significance (Ovsiankina, 1928).

How are these experimental facts concerning the tendency to recall and resume interrupted activities explained by the Lewinian conception of motivation?

"*Assumption 1:* The intention to reach a certain goal $G$ (to carry out an action leading to $G$) corresponds to a tension ($t$) in a certain system ($S^G$) within the person so that $t(S^G) > 0$" (Lewin, 1951, p. 9).*

(This assumption says that the observable syndrome popularly called "intention" should be represented in the life space as a system in tension.)

"*Assumption 2:* The tension $t(S^G)$ is released if the goal $G$ is reached" (Lewin, 1951, p. 9).

That is, $t(S^G)$ equals zero if $P$ reaches $G$. (This assumption says that what is popularly called "satisfaction" should be represented in the life space

* Excerpts from *Field Theory in Social Science* by Kurt Lewin, copyright 1951 by Harper & Row, are reprinted by permission.

as a discharge or reduction of tension when $P$ reaches the goal region.)

Recalling that $t(S^G)$ is one of the factors which determines the valence of some region ($Va(G)$) and that $Va(G)$ in part determines the force acting on the person towards the goal ($f_{P,G}$), we continue:

"*Assumption 3:* To a need for $G$ [or intention to reach $G$] corresponds a force $f_{P,G}$ acting upon the person and causing a tendency of locomotion towards $G$:

$$\text{if } t(S^G) > 0 \text{ [then] } f_{P,G} > 0\text{''}$$

(Lewin, 1951, p. 10).

"*Assumption 3a:* A need [or intention] leads not only to a tendency of actual locomotion towards the goal region but also to thinking about this type of activity; in other words the force $f_{P,G}$ exists not only on the level of doing (reality) but also on the level of thinking (irreality);

$$\text{if } t(S^G) > 0 \text{ [then] } f_{P,R} > 0$$

where $R$ means recall" (Lewin, 1951, p. 10).

"*Derivation I:* The tendency to recall interrupted activities should be greater than the tendency to recall finished ones" (Lewin, 1951, p. 10).

This derivation follows from the following considerations:

"We indicate any completed task by $C$, any unfinished one by $U$, and the corresponding systems by $S^C$ and $S^U$ respectively. We can then state
    (a) $t(S^U) > 0$ according to [Assumption 1]
    (b) $t(S^C) = 0$ according to [Assumption 2]
Hence (c) $f_{P,U} > f_{P,C}$ according to [Assumption 3a], . . . there is a greater tendency to [think about and] recall spontaneously unfinished tasks than finished tasks" (Lewin, 1951, p. 10).

The derivation for resumption of interrupted tasks is essentially the same. In this case, when opportunity is provided for further activity, $f_{P,U} > f_{P,C}$ is manifested in spontaneous overt action.

EFFECT OF DIFFERENCES IN INTENSITY OF NEED

The assumption that an individual's "need" or "intention" is to be represented in the life space as a tension system $t(S^G)$ can be elaborated to include the notion that the *amount* of tension is greater the stronger the "need" or "intention"— that is, $t(S^G) = F$ (strength of "need" for some goal). Accordingly, the amount of tension ($t(S^G)$) influences the strength of force towards the goal ($|f_{P,G}|$). Thus if a person is strongly motivated to complete a task and is interrupted, the residual tension and persistent force $f_{P,G}$ towards resumption or recall should be greater than if the initial tendency to complete the task is weaker. In other words, $RU/RC$, the Zeigarnik effect, is greater the stronger the initial need or intention.

Zeigarnik found that subjects who could be characterized as "ambitious" in terms of their general behavior (without regard to their Zeigarnik quotient) showed a much greater recall of interrupted activities than other subjects whose general behavior suggested they were not personally involved in the task. The Zeigarnik quotient ($RU/RC$) averaged 2.75 for "ambitious" subjects and only 1.03 for those who were judged "not involved" in the task. The latter group, in other words, recalled interrupted and completed activities about equally well.

Marrow (1938) conducted an experiment which repeated the essential details of the Zeigarnik experiment with college students who had volunteered to participate in an experiment. Some of these subjects were given instructions similar to those employed by Zeigarnik. Others, however, were given special instructions that were deliberately designed to heighten competitive interest. They were urged, at the outset, to do their best, and during the performance of the tasks, the experimenter made either encouraging or discouraging comments that were calculated to strengthen the subject's "intention" to do well at the tasks. The latter groups, in which interest in completing the tasks had been heightened by deliberate experimental procedures, showed a substantially greater average Zeigarnik effect than the "control group" which had been given more neutral instructions.

These two experiments show that differences in strength of the tendency to reach some goal, whether it be the result of characteristic differences between individuals in strength of "ambition" or a temporary heightening of motivation that is attributable to factors in the immediate environment, do affect recall of interrupted tasks as expected if (a) what common sense calls strength of need or intention is represented in the life space as amount of tension ($t(S^G)$), and (b) amount of tension ($t(S^G)$) affects the strength of force ($f_{P,G}$).

THE NEED FOR PRECISION IN EXPERIMENTATION AND DESCRIPTION OF AN EVENT

Consideration of one of the difficulties often encountered in performing the Zeigarnik experiment will help us to appreciate the concern over details that is a characteristic of "the Galilean mode of thought." We may recall that the concept of inertia in physics is based on the result of an imaginary or idealized experiment that can only be crudely approximated in an actual experiment by removing as many sources of friction as possible. And Galileo's law of free-falling bodies, which leads to the prediction that a feather and a baseball will fall to earth at the same speed, can be verified only by reducing the resistance of the air to zero. Similar difficulties arise in attempting to conduct an experiment to shown that an "intention" may be represented as $t(S^G)$, and "satisfaction of an intention" as discharge of tension.

One difficulty arises in the attempt to minimize the influence of other factors which might affect the person at the time he is asked to recall the activities he has performed. Some investigators have tried without success to reproduce Zeigarnik's findings. One of the troubles is that they have forgotten that behavior (locomotion in the life space) is not the result of any single force, but of the resultant of all forces active at the time.

The critical detail in performance of an experiment on recall or resumption of interrupted activities is the need to minimize the influence of other forces at the time of resumption or recall so that the behavior of the person reflects as clearly as possible only the relative strength of $f_{P,U}$ (force towards the unfinished tasks) and $f_{P,C}$ (force towards the completed tasks). In the experiment on resumption of tasks, the experimenter should do nothing that would indicate that he expects the subject to resume activity or that resumption is forbidden. The idea is to observe the "spontaneous" tendency to resume the activity that would normally occur in everyday life if the subject were "free" to do so. But in the experiment on recall, the experimenter must ask the subject to report what he might otherwise be "spontaneously" thinking about privately. This request for recall should, according to the theory, produce a new intention to remember the tasks. This new intention must be represented in the life space as another $t(S^G)$, which gives rise to a second force to recall the tasks. We shall refer to it as an induced force, $if_{P,R}$. The induced force to recall, $if_{P,R}$, is non-selective. That is, it is directed towards recall of all tasks whether or not they have been completed or interrupted ($if_{P,U} = if_{P,C}$). So the resultant force which accounts for recall of unfinished tasks must equal $if_{P,U} + f_{P,U}$, and the resultant force which accounts for recall of completed tasks must equal $if_{P,C} + f_{P,C}$. Consequently the observed ratio

$$\frac{RU}{RC} = F\left(\frac{if_{P,U} + f_{P,U}}{if_{P,C} + f_{P,C}}\right).$$

If the induced force is very weak, as it would be if the subject felt that the experimenter attached no importance to his behavior at the time of recall but considered the request for recall as just an after-thought, then the "spontaneous" recall of finished and unfinished activities should reflect fairly accurately the relative strengths of $f_{P,U}$ and $f_{P,C}$. If, however, the induced force to recall should be very strong, as it might be if the experimenter conveyed to the subject that this was a test of memory or the most important part of the experiment, then the very strong induced force to recall all activities could virtually wipe out what otherwise might be a very slight differential in the strength of the two forces, $f_{P,U}$ and $f_{P,C}$. For example, if $f_{P,U} = 2$ and $f_{P,C} = 0$, the ratio $RU/RC = 3/1$ when the induced force to recall, $if_{P,R}$, is 1; but $RU/RC = 12/10$ when $if_{P,R}$ is 10.

It may be deduced from the Lewinian theory which links behavior (locomotion) to the resultant of forces, that: "The more the recall loses its spontaneity and becomes the result of the experimenter's instruction, the more the Zeigarnik quotient approaches 1" (Lewin, 1951, p. 19). Zeigarnik had observed that for subjects who had experienced the experiment as a memory test, $RU/RC = 1.5$; whereas for others who later reported that they had recalled in the mode of "telling about" what they had done, the ratio was 2.8. A person on the witness stand in court can, with some coaxing, recall many of the details of the preceding day. In sleep, with no induced force to recall, his thought (the dream) is only of unfulfilled wishes.

THE SUBJECTIVE NATURE OF THE GOAL

So far, we have treated the person's goal in these experiments as equivalent to actual completion of some specific task set for him by the experimenter. The concept of tension system ($t(S^G)$) refers to the specific "intention to complete a task" that is assumed to occur in a cooperative subject after the experimenter has given him certain preliminary instructions and presented him with a task to perform. We have begun our conceptual description of the event with a common-sense assumption that, given these instructions, the subject will now intend to work on the task in order to complete it.

A number of the early experiments on the effects of interruption of activity called attention to the importance of distinguishing the goal as it might be defined from the point of view of the experimenter or an outside observer from the goal as it exists in the life space of the person whose behavior we study. Lewin had emphasized that the behavior of a person must be explained in terms of the psychological environment as it exists for the person at the time. The momentary goal of the person must be represented as it exists for him, as a region in the life space having valence at the time.

Marrow (1938) performed an experiment which dramatizes the difference between the objective events of completion and interruption of a task, on the one hand, and attainment or non-attainment of a goal from the viewpoint of the person we study. The essential procedures of the interruption-of-tasks experiment were followed except for the following changes: subjects were told that the experimenter was merely interested in seeing whether or not they were able to carry out the tasks effectively and that *he would interrupt them when they had satisfactorily demonstrated their ability.*

This critical change in the preliminary instruction meant that the goal, as represented in the life space of the subject, should now be located in the region "being interrupted by the experimenter." The interruption would mean he had shown a mastery of the material. Having to continue working at the task until it was objectively finished would mean that this goal region had not been attained. Tension should be discharged when the person reaches *his* goal, and *his* goal, "success," corresponds to the event of being interrupted. Paradoxically, this means that at the end of the work period, the residual force $f_{P,G}$ should be *weaker* for tasks that have actually been interrupted by the experimenter than for tasks which have been carried through to an objective completion. Objective completion of a task now corresponds to non-attainment of the goal-region and non-discharge of tension as it is defined in the life space of the subject. Marrow found, as predicted, that subjects recalled more of the tasks they had finished in an objective sense than the tasks that had been interrupted before they had finished.

If an outside observer had identified the tasks as Unfinished or Completed in terms of their *objective appearance* at the end of the experiment, he would have found $RU/RC = .74$. However, determining the Zeigarnik quotient in terms of attainment and non-attainment of the goal *as defined in the life space* (Recall of tasks when goal is not attained/Recall of tasks when goal is attained) would produce a value above 1.00 (in this case 1.35), a value more comparable to the results of the other experiments in which the "psychological goal" did correspond with the fact of completion.

We must conclude from this experiment that attainment of a goal as defined in the life space of the person is accompanied by the discharge of tension and that non-attainment of a goal as defined in the life space is the essential condition for continued tension and the persistent force $f_{P,G}$ that is "normally" manifested in recall and resumption of interrupted activities.

### RELATION OF SPECIFIC EXPERIMENTAL FACTS TO GENERAL THEORETICAL PRINCIPLES

The experiments on recall and resumption of interrupted activities in these especially contrived experimental situations can be considered very simple instances of the persistence of unfulfilled wishes. Nevertheless, they provide evidence concerning a general principle that should apply no matter what the nature of an individual's goal. Zeigarnik had suggested that subjects in her experiments were probably motivated to complete the tasks by ambition, a desire to please the experimenter by following instructions, and, perhaps, intrinsic interest in some of the activities. The qualitative nature of the goal was probably somewhat different for different subjects. Thus for some, completion of the task might have meant "success"; for others, completion might have meant "approval of the experimenter." Whatever the qualitative nature of the goal, the consequence of interruption of the activity before that goal had been attained was, as these experiments have shown, continued goal-directed thought and action. Whatever the qualitative nature of the experienced satisfaction which accompanied completion of tasks, these experiments were designed to show that it is useful to think of "satisfaction" as reduction of tension and, given the relation of $t(S^G)$ to $f_{P,G}$, as equivalent to a reduction of the goal-directed force on the person.

Most of the Freudian illustrations of persistence of unfulfilled wishes have to do with thwarted sexual and aggressive needs, for these were the kinds of activity most frequently prohibited in the late Victorian society which produced the neurotic persons Freud studied so intensively. We would miss the point of experimentation in psychology if we failed to see that these simple experiments, like the very simple experiments on motion in physics, are intended to throw some light on a general principle which should apply to all instances of motivated behavior. *The importance of an event in science does not depend upon the frequency of its occurrence under natural conditions nor upon its contemporary social significance, but upon its relation to a conceptual scheme that does have general significance.* This is as true for psychology as for physics, chemistry, and the other advanced experimental sciences.

## SUBSTITUTE ACTIVITY AND SUBSTITUTE SATISFACTION

Psychoanalytic investigations of motivation call attention to many instances of substitution when expression of the original need or wish is blocked. A new activity is instigated and the original wish is satisfied in some activity other than the activity which defined the original goal. The worker may inhibit his anger and not hit the boss, but take it out instead on a fellow worker, or even kick the proverbial cat. The concept of tension system ($t(S^G)$) is useful in dealing with the problem of substitution.

### STRUCTURE OF SUBSYSTEMS WITHIN A PERSON

Lewin attributed certain additional properties to the subsystems within the person which he employed to represent "needs" and "intentions" in the life space. We recall that he thought the person should be represented as a *set* of subsystems, the structure and content of which might differ from one person to the next. These "inner-personal regions," like any other regions in the life space, have certain positions relative to each other. Some are immediately adjacent (i.e., closely associated). Others are separated by intervening regions (i.e., less closely associated). The boundaries between inner-personal regions might be conceived as relatively permeable. This would mean that tension in one system could flow through the boundary into an immediately adjacent region. Lewin assumed, as part of his theory, that if the boundary between two adjacent systems $S^1$ and $S^2$ was relatively permeable, but one of them contained more tension than the other ($t(S^1) > t(S^2)$), there would exist a tendency to change so that $t(S^1) = t(S^2)$. In other words, he assumed a tendency towards equalization of tension in neighboring (associated) systems. This equalization process depends upon the fluidity of the boundary and time.

## SUBSTITUTE VALENCE

These ideas provide a way of representing the possibility that sometimes a "need" or "intention" for one goal is satisfied by a substitute activity. If the tension corresponding to an unfulfilled wish $t(S^1)$ were to flow into some other system $S^2$, then this second system in tension, $t(S^2)$, would increase the valence of its corresponding goal or activity $Va(G^2)$, producing a force $f_{P,G^2}$ towards a "substitute goal." We refer to this as an instance of *substitute valence, SVa(G)*. If the "*substitute goal*" $G^2$ is actually attained, the tension $t(S^2)$ is discharged. In common-sense terms, this would represent partial satisfaction of the original need or intention that had been represented by $t(S^1)$.

## SUBSTITUTE VALUE

The experiment designed by Ovsiankina provides a technique for investigating the *substitute value* of different types of activities. If, as Ovsiankina had shown, persons tend to resume interrupted activities when given the opportunity, the substitute value of some other activity can be discovered by having the subject perform a second activity after being interrupted on the initial activity but before he is given an opportunity to resume it. If the tendency to resume the initial activity is reduced, this indicates the extent of the substitute value of the intervening activity. In other words, if a child initially has his heart set on having a dog but this desire is satisfied by being given a cat, we should expect him to stop asking for a dog and pestering the neighbor's dog after he is given the cat. On the other hand, if the cat has no substitute value, the child should continue to seek a dog even after being presented with a cat.

## INITIATION OF SUBSTITUTE ACTIVITY

In some early studies of frustration and anger, Dembo (1931) had observed what clearly appeared to be the initiation of a substitute activity. An individual trying to throw rings over a bottle but without success would, at last, go to the door and throw rings over the coat hooks. A child unable to reach a flower which was her immediate goal "spontaneously" grabbed another flower from a nearby vase. The substitute actions spring from the tension system which corresponds to the initial "desire." The assumed flow of tension from $S^1$ to $S^2$ would account for the substitute valence $SVa(G^2)$, since $Va(G) = f(t_0,G)$. And $SVa(G)$ would then pro-

duce the force that is manifested in the initiation of a substitute action.

## SUBSTITUTE VALENCE AND SUBSTITUTE VALUE DISTINGUISHED

We would expect that the original tension system should be discharged through the substitute action, either completely or in part. But this is not always the case. The new activity, though attractive at a distance, may not, in fact, have *substitute value* when the person gets to it. The new activity may not satisfy the original need or intention even though it occurred because the new activity appeared attractive to the person (i.e., it had *substitute valence*). The distinction between *substitute valence* and *substitute value* is a very important one.

Suppose that in Freud's famous illustration of Herman and the cherries (page 47), Herman, after giving the bowl of cherries (which he wanted) to his little girl friend, had grabbed an apple from a table decoration and taken a quick bite only to find it made of wax! This would illustrate the difference between substitute valence and substitute value. Because the desire to eat the cherries is thwarted, an object similar in appearance to an apple looks very attractive and edible, $SVa(G)$. But when the force toward that object brings Herman to the substitute goal region, the situation changes. It is a wax object with $SV = 0$. The original tension is not reduced.

## EFFECT OF INTERRUPTION ON VALENCE OF SIMILAR ACTIVITIES

Cartwright (1942) has presented experimental evidence which supports the view that initiation of a substitute activity can be attributed to a change in valence of some new goal or activity by spread of tension from one system to another. He studied changes in ratings of the attractiveness of an initial activity and other activities following interruption of the initial activity. Subjects were asked to rate the attractiveness of various tasks on a scale from $-100$ to $+100$ before and after performance. They were told that the experimenter's purpose was only to know which of the tasks among the set lying on a table the subject wanted to do next. At the end of the experiment, the subjects were also asked to rate the *similarity* of tasks to each of three they had actually been given an opportunity to perform. Thus the experimenter was able to study changes in attractiveness ratings of the tasks actually performed and ones perceived as similar or different.

Following interruption, the attractiveness of the

interrupted task rose much more frequently than it fell. This is consistent with the tendency to resume interrupted activities discovered by Ovsiankina. And when the attractiveness of the initial activity rose, those activities perceived as *similar* became more attractive 57 per cent of the time and less attractive only 15 per cent of the time. Tasks perceived as *different* rose and fell in attractiveness about equally often (29 per cent and 26 per cent respectively). From this we may surmise that the tasks perceived as similar to the initial task which had been interrupted might have been undertaken as substitute activities if the subjects had been given this opportunity.

FACTORS WHICH INFLUENCE SUBSTITUTE VALUE

Turning now from the problem of *substitute valence* to the problem of *substitute value*, we may consider the results of experiments which utilized the design of the resumption-of-interrupted-tasks experiment to discover some of the factors which influence the substitute value of an activity. The subject is allowed to complete a second activity *after* being interrupted prior to completion of an initial activity. The subsequent resumption of the initial activity implies that the second activity has no substitute value. Non-resumption of the initial activity implies that it does have substitute value.

The tendency to resume the initial activity is reduced when the intervening activity is similar to the initial activity. Thus *similarity* influences both substitute valence and substitute value.

The *difficulty* of the second activity also influences its substitute value. Lissner (1933), for example, found that if a person was interrupted while putting mosaic blocks together and the second task of making a mosaic pattern was easy, the resumption of the initial activity was 100 per cent. When the second task of making a mosaic pattern was relatively more difficult, the resumption of the initial activity dropped to 42 per cent.

In comparing the substitute value of real (overt) action versus irreal (thought) activities like talking about the task or making up a story in which the initial task was completed in fantasy, Mahler (1933) found that substitute value was generally greater the greater the *reality* of the intervening activity.

LEWINIAN CONTRIBUTION TO UNDERSTANDING
OF SUBSTITUTION

From psychoanalysis we learn something of the complicated fabric of dynamic relationships between activities which substitute for one another. The Freudian concept of sublimation, for example, refers to the substitute value of socially acceptable activities for underlying needs that are not permitted direct expression. The Lewinian contribution is not a simple formula for deciding in advance what activities are likely to be attempted as substitute activities or what activities are likely to produce substitute satisfaction for a particular person in a given instance. Rather, it is: (a) the development of a conceptual scheme which attempts to explain how substitute actions come to be initiated and what substitute satisfaction means; and (b) an experimental method for determining whether or not one activity or goal has substitute value for another.

*Substitute value* is formally defined as follows: the substitute value ($SV$) which an activity or goal $G^2$ has for the activity or goal $G^1$ is defined by the extent to which "consumption" of $G^2$ ($cons\ G^2$) satisfies the need for $G^1$, that is, decreases the tension $t(G^1)$:

$$\text{``}SV(G^2 \text{ for } G^1) > 0, \text{ if } t(G^1) = F\left(\frac{1}{cons\ (G^2)}\right)\text{''}$$

(Lewin, 1938, p. 163).

The tentative conclusion reached in early experiments on substitution was that substitute value is greater the more the substitute action corresponds not to a new goal, but to another way of reaching *the original inner goal* of the person. Again, we must consider the nature of the inner goal of the person, what Freud often referred to as the "meaning" of the activity for the person.

RESOLUTION OF CONFLICT

Having in mind the simple elements of construction advanced by Lewin, we may proceed to the analysis of more complicated instances of motivation. We remember Freud's continual emphasis of the point that behavior is "overdetermined." Often, several different "intentions" may combine to produce a greater force in a given direction than the force corresponding to any single intention. Freud called this "condensation." For example, a child may be hurrying home from school both because he wants to play and because he is hungry for some of mother's chocolate cake. He is more strongly motivated to get home than if he were only concerned with getting out to play. Just as often, however, intentions clash. If the region of play activity is the local playground which is east of school and home is to the west, the child must decide what to do, or at least what to do first. This is a very simple instance of conflict. Most life situations are more complex.

OVERLAPPING SITUATIONS

In linking psychological forces to behavior, which is represented as locomotion in the life space (see p. 78), Lewin assumed that behavior depends upon the resultant of forces. Instances of conflict between *mutually incompatible forces* are to be represented as *overlapping fields of force* or *overlapping situations*. "Thus," as he saw it, "the dominant problem is that of determining the resultant of the forces of the overlapping fields at a given point" (Lewin, 1938, p. 175). We turn, then, to the resolution of conflict as conceived by Lewin and his co-workers. The question we seek to answer is: How does the resolution of conflicting forces come about?

DETERMINATION OF THE RESULTANT OF FORCES

In physics, the resolution of forces which explains the motion of physical objects is a simple matter of adding the vectors which represent the direction and strength of the several forces. The sum of the vectors gives the resultant motion of the physical object. But the life space, we must recall, is a representation of the person in his immediate *psychological* environment and of the *psychological* forces which momentarily influence him. The geometry and analysis of resultant of vectors which suit physical space do not apply to the life space. If they did, this would be equivalent to saying that the result of psychological conflict is always an action which simultaneously satisfies all of the competing motives which influenced the person— that is, an action that is a compromise reflecting all of the individual's current goals. Freud called attention to such compromises in the formation of dreams and in the case of slips, errors, and accidents. But we know from our own experience that this does not always occur in everyday actions. Sometimes, however, an "ideal" solution to a motivational conflict does occur. A person may face what initially appears a situation in which he has to choose between two goals, but a way of "having his cake and eating it too" may occur to him. Lewin illustrated this possibility in terms of a student who wishes to prepare for an examination but would also like to spend the evening with a friend. If it occurs to the student that he might combine both goals by interesting the student in the topic of his

studies, the situation is no longer one of conflict. The two forces which correspond to the original intentions are now directed towards the same goal region, "studying for the examination in the presence of his friend" (Lewin, 1938, p. 176). This merely reminds us that in a given circumstance the life space of two individuals may be very different, a problem we have considered in the example of the two night watchmen locked in the automobile trunks. It occurred to one of them that there was air in the spare tire. The problem of immediate interest is to understand how a conflict and its resolution is represented in the life space when an ideal solution or compromise is impossible or does not occur to the person.

The general principle of resolution of conflict between mutually incompatible forces of unequal strength is *the stronger force is dominant*. The direction of the resultant of forces corresponds to the direction of the stronger force. We may consider an example of overlapping situations as it would be represented by Lewin. (See Figure 4.9.) A child simultaneously wants to go downtown to a movie, $f_{P,M}$; wants to play with his trains in the basement, $f_{P,T}$; and wants to read his new book in the living room, $f_{P,B}$. He stands in the living room wondering

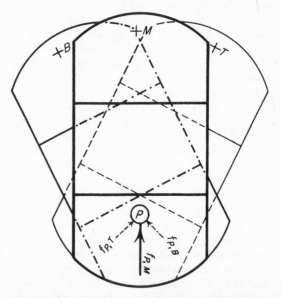

FIGURE 4.9  Overlapping situations. A child, P, wants to go to a movie, $f_{P,M}$; to play with his trains, $f_{P,T}$; and to read a book, $f_{P,B}$. The immediate directions of the forces are different. The direction of the resultant force is equivalent to the direction of the dominant (i.e. strongest) force, $f_{P,M}$.

what to do. The immediate directions of the three forces are clearly different and incompatible: go out the front door; go through the dining room to the basement stairs; sit down in a chair. Let us suppose the movie is most attractive and, though a greater distance from him, produces the strongest force. The resolution of the conflict depends upon the relative strengths of the three forces. *The direction of the resultant force is equivalent to the direction of the strongest or dominant force.* If the child begins to go to the movie without coming to a clearcut decision, he may move rather slowly and hesitantly because the other two forces are still in active opposition. When, however, a clearcut decision is made, Lewin assumed that this corresponded to a reduction of the *potency* of the overlapping situations which represent the unchosen alternatives. They would cease to exist as influences on the child's behavior. Thus a resolution of forces may occur: (a) without a clearcut decision, in which case the other forces continue to impede locomotion in the direction of the resultant of forces; (b) or in a clearcut decision, in which case the potency of the opposing forces is substantially or completely reduced.

It is now clear that the resultant of forces is arrived at, not as in physics, by first determining the resultant of any two of the forces (by adding their vectors) and then determining the final resultant when this combined force is added to the third force. Instead, the process by which the resultant of psychological forces is arrived at is essentially one of comparison. The relative strengths of $f^1$ and $f^2$ are compared, the stronger winning out. Then, whichever was dominant is compared with $f^3$. The resultant of forces is the strongest or most dominant force. On this basis, the direction of action is determined when there exist alternative means to the same goal or when there exist a number of incompatible goals.

## TYPES OF CONFLICT

*Lewin defined a conflict situation as one in which the forces acting on the person are opposite in direction and about equal in strength.* Three simple cases will be considered. The person may be located between two positive valences, between two negative valences, or a positive and negative valence may lie in the same direction. These are instances of conflict between the *driving forces* produced by the positive and negative valences. We consider each in turn.

## APPROACH-APPROACH CONFLICT

The person is attracted to mutually incompatible goals. A child, for example, has to choose between going to a picnic ($G^1$) and playing with his friends at home ($G^2$). (See Figure 4.10.) At the point in the life space where the conflict exists, the strength of the force to approach $G^1$ is exactly equal to the strength of the force to approach $G^2$. Consider now that strength of force is greater the greater the valence of a goal and the smaller the psychological distance from it: Force = $F(Va(G)/e_{P,G})$. This means that approach-approach conflicts should be relatively easily resolved. Any fortuitous influence which might momentarily bring the person a little closer to one of the goals than the other should produce a resolution of the approach-approach conflict. Why? Because as soon as the person is a little closer to one of the goals than to the other, the force towards the closer goal will become stronger and the force towards the farther goal will become weaker. The

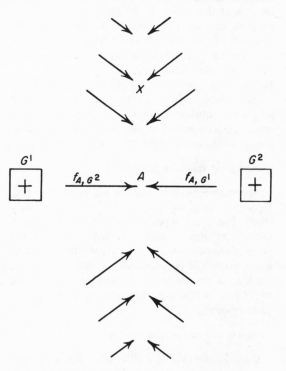

FIGURE 4.10 Approach-approach conflict. In region A, the strength of force toward $G^1$ ($f_{A,G^1}$) is equal to the strength of force toward $G^2$ ($f_{A,G^2}$). If the person were in region X, the resultant of forces would direct him to A, the region of unavoidable conflict, which is nearer to both $G^1$ and $G^2$ than X is. (*After Lewin, 1938*)

resultant of forces will then be equivalent to the direction of the force towards the closer goal. As he begins to locomote towards the closer goal, the force in this direction increases even more and the opposing force continues to weaken. The *equilibrium* which existed at the point of conflict is called *unstable* because it is so easily broken by any additional influence which brings the person closer to one or the other goal. In the moment of conflict between two pieces of lemon meringue pie in the cafeteria line, a little jolt from the person behind is enough to resolve the approach-approach conflict by bringing one of the two equivalent pieces a little nearer.

THE REGION OF UNAVOIDABLE CONFLICT

Figure 4.10 shows the field of forces produced by the two positive valences. Recall that because force is a function of valence and psychological distance, it is possible to represent the force which would influence the person at any point in the life space *if* he were at that point. If the child in our example were at the point designated $X$, the immediate direction of the resultant of forces might be $d_{X,A}$, since the forces combine to direct him to a region that is simultaneously closer to both of the goals. He has not reached "*the region of unavoidable conflict*" until he reaches region $A$, where the two forces are equal and opposite in direction. From region $A$, locomotion in any direction brings him farther away from at least one of the two goals.

MEANING OF STABLE EQUILIBRIUM

Approach-approach conflicts are easily resolved. Hence the time to reach a decision is relatively short. The other types of conflict are not easily resolved because a *stable equilibrium* exists at the point of conflict. That is, any factor which momentarily moves the person from the point of conflict produces a change in the relative strengths of the two forces which immediately returns him to the point of conflict.

AVOIDANCE-AVOIDANCE CONFLICT

Consider the case of a child who stands between two negative valences. He is threatened with punishment $-G^1$ if he does not perform a certain disagreeable task $-G^2$. If at any moment he should begin to move away from the threatening punishment $(-G^1)$ towards the disagreeable task $(-G^2)$, the force $f_{P,-G^2}$ would increase in strength because it is now closer

and the force $f_{P,-G^1}$ would weaken because $-G^1$ is now farther away. Hence the resultant of forces would be directed away from the disagreeable task $(G^2)$ back to the region of unavoidable conflict.

We should expect vacillation, back and forth, "between the devil and the deep blue sea" to characterize behavior when avoidance-avoidance conflict exists. However, considering the fields of forces generated by the two negative valences, as in Figure 4.11, we see that should some fortuitous occurrence move the child in a psychological direction that is simultaneously away from both of the two threatening regions, point $Y$ in Figure 4.11, then the conflict

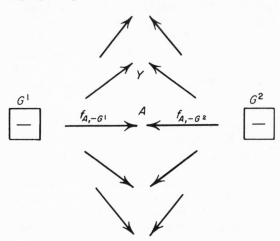

FIGURE 4.11    Avoidance-avoidance conflict. In region A, the strength of force away from $G^1$ $(f_{A,-G^1})$ is equal to the strength of force away from $G^2$ $(f_{A,-G^2})$. If the person were in region Y, the forces would combine to produce the resolution of conflict called "leaving the field."

would be readily resolved by his "*leaving the field*." The two forces would combine to propel him away from both of them. In this connection, we might imagine Huckleberry Finn sneaking out the window of the classroom when the teacher turns his back. The concept of "*leaving the field*" was proposed by Lewin as a possible conceptual representation of the flight from reality which so often seems to characterize the behavior of persons who are caught in the web of unresolvable conflict between negative valences.

APPROACH-AVOIDANCE CONFLICT

Lewin illustrated the case of a person at a distance from some region which was both positively and negatively valent with the example of a child seeking his little boat in the ocean waters a few feet from shore. The child is directed towards the toy ($G^1$), which has positive valence, but away from the threatening splashing waves ($-G^2$), which have negative valence but are represented in the same region of the life space as the toy. The child runs up to the water; then, frightened, he dashes back again. Then, being quite a distance from the water, he darts back again only to return a moment later without the toy. This, again, is an instance of stable equilibrium.

One further assumption is introduced to explain this type of conflict: *the magnitude of an avoidance force decreases more as a result of psychologica. distance than the magnitude of an approach forcel* This relationship is shown graphically in Figure 4.12. The point of conflict (where the two forces are equal in strength but opposite in direction) is designated $E$. The assumption of a steeper gradient of avoidance force means that the magnitude of the

negative valence must be greater than the magnitude of the positive valence. The child must be more afraid of the waves than he is attracted to the toy. Otherwise no conflict would exist. The vacillation about the point of conflict is again explained in terms of the changes in the strengths of the two forces as the person gets nearer to or farther from the region about which he is *ambivalent*.

We might consider another example of approach-avoidance conflict to explore another implication of Lewin's conception of it. Suppose a child was attracted to a dog whose leash was attached to a spike in the ground in the middle of a large front yard. Suppose also, that the child was also frightened because he had already been nipped by another dog. We should expect the region of unavoidable conflict to extend all about the dog in a sweeping circle as in Figure 4.13. The dotted line around the dog is

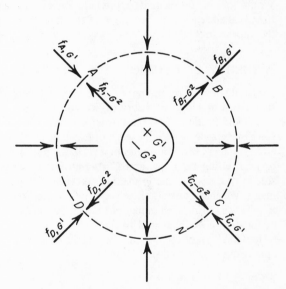

FIGURE 4.13 Zone of equilibrium in approach-avoidance conflict. In regions A, B, C, D and others falling on the line of equilibrium, N, the force toward $G^1$ is equal to the force away from $G^2$ (*After Lewin, 1938*)

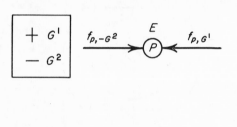

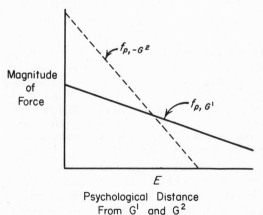

Magnitude of Force

$E$

Psychological Distance From $G^1$ and $G^2$

FIGURE 4-12 Approach-avoidance conflict. In region E, the strength of force toward $G^1$ ($f_{P,G^1}$) is equal to the strength of force away from $G^2$ ($f_{P,-G^2}$). The assumption that the magnitude of an avoidance force decreases more as a result of psyhcological distance than the magnitude of an approach force is shown graphically below.

the zone or region of equilibrium. The resultant force is zero throughout this region. In his vacillation, back and forth about the point of conflict, the child might locomote in a circular path around the dog. In a sense, he is trapped at a certain distance from the region which has both positive and negative valence. He can't do with it, and he can't do without it!

In the case of avoidance-avoidance and approach-avoidance conflict, the stable equilibrium can be broken only by some change in the situation. Some change in forces must occur, as would be the case, for example, if the child's father appeared and took him by the hand, thus reducing his fear of the dog, while he patted its head.

Given this conception of the various types of conflict and the principle that force is a function of both valence and psychological distance, one may begin to consider what would happen if the magnitude of the negative valence were very much greater than the magnitude of the positive valence in an instance of approach-avoidance conflict. Would extreme fear of punishment in relation to the attractiveness of an activity so increase the strength of the avoidance force that the individual would not even think of locomoting towards the goal region? Would this be an adequate representation of what Freud called repression, "the flight of the mind from the unpleasant"?

## A THEORY OF DECISION

The theory of resolution of forces was finally stated as a quantitative theory of decision by Cartwright and Festinger (1943) following clarification of some of its basic ideas in the work of Escalona (1940) and Festinger (1942) in studies of level of aspiration, or goal-setting behavior, and Cartwright (1941) in studies of decision-time in making perceptual judgments. We shall consider these two types of decision to advance our understanding of how the resolution of forces comes about and to illustrate the experimental analysis of conflict in what might otherwise appear quite unrelated problems.

DECISION IN A PERCEPTUAL
DISCRIMINATION TASK

The measurement of reaction time and time taken to make a judgment in studies of perceptual discrimination is as old as experimental psychology itself. Cartwright argued that the increase in time it takes to make difficult perceptual judgments can be considered an instance of conflict and resolution of psychological forces. When a person is asked to judge whether one line is longer or shorter than another line, he has to choose between "saying longer" (L) and "saying shorter" (S). It is generally assumed that a cooperative subject wants to be right, so his goal in an experiment on perceptual judgment is "to be right." The goal region "being

right" possesses positive valence for him, and the region "being wrong" possesses negative valence. Thus, if the line he is asked to judge is perceived as longer, there is a force towards "saying longer" ($f_{P,L}$) because "saying longer" is the path to the positively valent goal region. There is also a force away from "saying shorter" ($f_{P,-S}$) because "saying shorter" leads to the negatively valent region, as shown in Figure 4.14. Since the directions of the

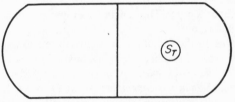

Perceived as Shorter        Perceived as Longer
PHENOMENAL FIELD

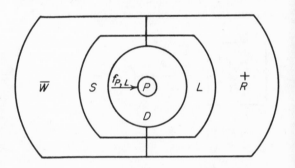

FIELD OF ACTION

FIGURE 4.14  The phenomenal field and the field of action when the variable stimulus is clearly longer than the standard. P stands for person, D for the activity of deciding, S for "saying 'shorter,'" L for "saying 'longer,'" W for "being wrong," and R for "being right." The force acting upon P has the direction toward L because L is a part of R and R possesses a positive valence. (From Cartwright, 1941)

two forces are equivalent, the person says "longer" without hesitation. If the stimulus is perceived as shorter, the situation is represented in a similar way, but now the resultant force is directed towards "saying shorter," which leads to the goal region "being right."

Conflict arises when a subject is asked to judge a line that appears virtually the same size as the line to which it is compared. The subject is *uncertain* as to whether it is longer or shorter. The activity region "saying longer" is now contained in two overlapping situations. In one of them, "saying longer" leads to "being right"; in the other, however, "saying longer" leads to "being wrong." The same is true of "saying shorter." The overlapping situations are represented as in Figure 4.15. Since the forces on the

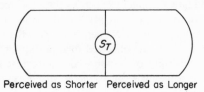

Perceived as Shorter   Perceived as Longer

PHENOMENAL FIELD

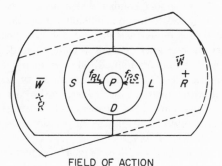

FIELD OF ACTION

FIGURE 4.15 A topological representation of a judgment when the stimulus is perceived as falling on the border between categories. Here two overlapping situations are operating simultaneously. The person is placed in a conflict of two opposing forces. No locomotion can occur so long as the situation remains unchanged. (*From Cartwright, 1941*)

person are now in opposition, the time required to make a judgment should be increased. The person is not sure which path to take to arrive at his goal, "being right." He cannot choose either alternative as long as the two forces are exactly equal. *It is assumed that fluctuation in the strength of forces must occur and that time is required to upset the initial balance of forces.* If the fluctuation of forces occurs as often in one direction as in the other, the subject should say "longer" and "shorter" equally often when asked to judge this particular stimulus a number of different times. Thus Cartwright predicted that judgment time should be longer for that stimulus which is called "longer" and "shorter" an equal number of times on repeated presentations than for any other stimulus.

When a person experiences a conflict, which is represented as overlapping situations, it is assumed that the strength of each force depends upon the weight or *potency* of each situation ($Po(S)$) for the subject. The strength of the *effective force* ($^of_{P,G}$) is equal to the strength of that force if only one situation existed multiplied by its potency:

$$^of_{P,G} = f_{P,G} \times Po(S)$$

*Potency is determined by the subject's feeling of probability (his expectancy) that his judgment is correct.* The sum of potencies is arbitrarily set at 1.00. Thus, if there is only one situation (and no conflict), $Po(S)$ equals 1.00. If there are two overlapping situations and the person feels some degree of uncertainty as to which path will lead to his goal, "being right," the strength of his expectancy that each of the alternatives will lead to the goal determines the potency of each situation, and the sum of the two potencies equals 1.00. If the person feels that the two alternatives are equally probable, then the potency of each situation is .50, and the effective forces are half as strong as each taken singly.

It is assumed that the potency of a situation fluctuates in time, as often in one direction as the other, about an average value. In other words, at one instant the subject is a little more certain, at the next instant a little less certain, that a particular path of action will lead to his goal. These fluctuations are assumed to be distributed normally about the average value. This means that at any moment a small fluctuation in either direction is much more likely than a large fluctuation. As a consequence of fluctuations in degree of certainty, or potency, the effective forces fluctuate in strength from moment to moment. When the potency of one alternative fluctuates upward, the potency of the other fluctuates downward, creating a difference between the *effective* forces.

In Cartwright and Festinger's (1943) quantitative theory of decision, it is further assumed that the *difference* between effective forces must reach a certain critical magnitude before a decision is reached. The subject, in other words, wishes to be reasonably more certain of one of the alternatives than another before acting. Due to the fluctuation of potencies, this critical difference between the strength of effective forces will come about in time, and a decision will be made. Thus when the potencies of two alternatives are equal (each has an average value of .50), the normal fluctuation of potency, and hence of effective forces, will *in time* produce a difference between the two effective forces which exceeds the critical magnitude of difference required for decision.

But the time required will be greater than if the degree of certainty is initially greater, say .70 for one alternative as against .30 for the other. When the potency of each alternative is .50, the critical difference in effective forces will come about only when one of the infrequent large upward fluctuations in potency of one of the alternatives occurs. When the potencies are quite a bit different to begin with, the more frequent small upward fluctuations or even the slight downward fluctuations in the potency of the dominant alternative still produces a difference between the effective forces that is greater than the critical difference needed to reach a decision. Thus, judgment time decreases the more unequal the two stimuli are initially perceived to be.

The essential ideas in this theory of decision may be summarized:

a. Conflict between incompatible forces is represented in the life space as overlapping situations, that is, as if the person were simultaneously in two different situations.

b. The strength of *effective forces* depends upon how much weight or *potency* each of the overlapping situations has for the person.

c. The concept of *potency* refers to how certain the person feels that each path of action will lead to his goal. The sum of potencies is therefore always equal to 1.00 (complete certainty).

d. The feeling of certainty (i.e., potency) is assumed to fluctuate in a normal manner.

e. As a result, the strength of effective forces fluctuates from moment to moment.

f. A certain minimal difference between effective forces must occur before a decision is reached.

g. It takes more time for this minimal difference between effective forces to come about when the occurrence of such a difference requires a relatively large (and therefore infrequent) fluctuation in the potencies of alternatives, that is, when the potencies are equal or nearly equal to begin with.

This theory of decision explains a number of the details of results in studies of perceptual judgment when subjects are given a number of opportunities to judge the same stimulus. Most obvious is the fact that a subject will say "longer" 100 per cent of the time when the stimulus is very obviously longer than the one to which it is compared, but the frequency of saying "longer" will gradually drop as the stimulus is perceived as more nearly equal that of the comparison stimulus until he says "longer" only 50 per cent of the time. Then, the frequency of saying "longer" will continue to drop gradually to zero as the line becomes obviously shorter. In other words, *conflict exists even when the potencies of two alternatives are not exactly equal.* The assumption of fluctuation in potency explains why a stimulus that is physically shorter than the standard stimulus is sometimes said to be longer by the subject. Secondly, judgment time increases as the observed frequency of response ("longer" or "shorter") falls from 100 per cent to 50 per cent. The theory of decision explains the observed relationship between actual probability of response and judgment time, or, as it is sometimes called, *the latency of response.*

PROCEDURE IN STUDY OF LEVEL OF ASPIRATION

We have considered the theoretical analysis of a simple motivational conflict which arises when a person is asked to make a difficult perceptual discrimination. Let us turn now to another type of conflict, the one a person faces when trying to decide what goals to set for himself, whether to try tasks that appear very difficult to accomplish or to be content with success at much easier tasks. We will see that the same basic elements of construction and theory of decision apply to the decision involved in setting a *level of aspiration.*

The concept of "*level of aspiration*" was first introduced by Dembo (1931) in reference to *the degree of difficulty of the goal towards which a person is striving.* Experimental results stemming from her observations and those of Hoppe (1930), who performed the first experimental analysis of aspirational phenomena, spurred many others to investigate the factors which influence goal-setting behavior. It will help to concretize our discussion of level of aspiration to consider first the kind of experimental procedure that was evolved in the study of this problem.

A subject is given a task in which different levels of accomplishment are clearly possible. It might be a set of arithmetic problems with a five-minute work period to complete as many as possible. It might be a ringtoss game with distances from the peg clearly marked on the floor. It might be a dart-throwing game in which the distance from the target is fixed and the target consists of a set of concentric rings with the highest score of 10 for hitting the smallest ring at the very center and the lowest score of 1 for hitting just inside the largest, outermost ring. We shall consider the dart-throwing example as our reference experiment.

What is a typical sequence of events? The subject takes careful aim and throws the first dart. Let us suppose he hits ring 6. This defines his *initial level of performance*. Now he may be asked, "What score are you going to *try* for on the next shot?" He may answer, "I am going to try for 8." This statement defines his *level of aspiration*. Now he shoots again. If he attains 9, he may experience *the feeling of success*. If he attains only 5, he may experience *the feeling of failure*, or "disappointment." Whatever the level of his new performance and his reaction to that performance, we again ask, "What score are you going to *try* for on the next shot?" At this point, he may decide to leave the activity altogether, or he may set a new level of aspiration that is above, below, or at the same level as his immediate past performance. The experimenter records the level of each performance and the stated levels of aspiration. He may also note other matters of interest like the time taken to come to a decision, or spontaneous remarks and activities which constitute expressions of feelings of success, failure, or a desire to leave the activity altogether. The experimenter may also vary the question he asks the subject, sometimes asking "What score do you *expect* to make?" or "What score would you *like* to make?"

ISSUES INVOLVED IN STUDIES OF ASPIRATION

Many of the issues we have already touched upon are involved in the study of level of aspiration: the subjective nature of an individual's goal; the dis-charge of tension (feelings of success) when that goal is attained; the problem of conflict, decision, choice; the influence of immediate past experience on the subsequent life space. Figure 4.16 summarizes the typical time sequence and calls attention to the two critical problems:

(a) What determines a level of aspiration?

(b) What are the reactions to achieving or not achieving the level of aspiration?

DEFINITION OF LEVEL OF ASPIRATION

One of the earliest investigators, Frank (1935, p. 119), provided a definition of level of aspiration which is now generally accepted: "*the level of future performance in a familiar task which an individual, knowing his level of past performance in that task, explicitly undertakes to reach.*" In the task we are using as a reference experiment, it is normally as-sumed that the subject's verbal statement of aspira-tion corresponds to the goal he really intends to reach at the time he shoots. He might, however, really like to hit the very center of the target and be aiming at it when he shoots. We refer to this as his "*ideal goal*" to distinguish it from his "*action goal*," which is stated in answer to the question, "What score are you going *to try for* on the next shot?"

Many investigators have considered the verbal statement of aspiration an adequate approximation

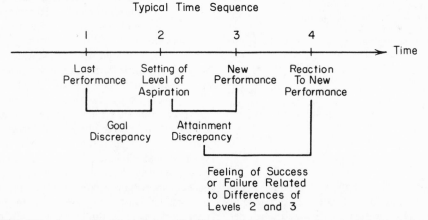

FIGURE 4.16  Four main points distinguished in a typical sequence of events in a level-of-aspira-tion situation: last performance, setting of level of aspiration for the next performance, new per-formance, and the psychological reaction to the new performance. The difference between the level of the last performance and the level of the new goal is called goal discrepancy; the dif-ference between the goal level and that of the new performance is called attainment discrepancy. This difference is one of the bases of the reaction at point 4. (*From Kurt Lewin, Tamara Dembo, Leon Festinger, and Pauline Snedden Sears, "Level of Aspiration," in* Personality and the Behavior Disorders—A Handbook Based on Experimental and Clinical Research, Volume One, *edited by J. McV. Hunt. Copyright 1944 The Ronald Press Company*)

of the "action goal" in light of some of the other virtues of this experimental procedure. Often, however, *the level of aspiration or action goal is inferred from the actual behavior of the individual in a choice among tasks which differ in difficulty.* For example, the dart-throwing game might be arranged so that there is only one small circular ring for a target but the subject wins a higher number of points for hitting it from a greater distance. He must, in other words, clearly reveal his action goal by choosing to shoot from 10 feet away or from 5 feet away. The results using both procedures are generally equivalent.

THE GOAL DISCREPANCY

Figure 4.16 calls attention to the measure that is most frequently employed to describe a subject's level of aspiration, the "*goal discrepancy.*" The "*goal discrepancy*" *is determined by subtracting the immediate past performance from the new level of aspiration.* The goal discrepancy is positive if the new level of aspiration is above the level of immediate past performance. If the new level of aspiration lies below the level of past performance, the goal discrepancy is negative.

TYPICAL RESULTS IN STUDY OF ASPIRATION

The most typical result of early studies of level of aspiration is summarized by Lewin *et al.* as follows:

"Experimental work on the level of aspiration has brought out the variety of influences which are present for a single decision as to action goal. Some of these influences are probably rather stable and permanent in their effects; i.e., their value will be much the same for all individuals of a given culture in a variety of competitive situations. It has been found, for example, that nearly all individuals of western culture, when first exposed to a level of aspiration situation, give initially a level of aspiration which is above the previous performance score, and under most conditions tend to keep the goal discrepancy positive" (Lewin *et al.*, 1944, p. 337).

Another very typical result is that the level of aspiration is generally raised when performance attains the level of aspiration and lowered when performance falls below the level of aspiration. Jucknat (1937), for example, employed two series of 10 mazes which differed in difficulty. One series of mazes was solvable; the other series was not. Thirty children were the subjects. In the solvable series, 76 per cent of the shifts in aspiration were upward and 24 per cent downward. In the nonsolvable series, 84 per cent of the shifts were downward and only 16 per cent

were upward. In other words, in one condition 76 per cent and in the other 84 per cent of the changes in aspiration were "typical" changes. Festinger (1942) observed that after attainment of the level of aspiration there were 51 per cent raisings, 41 per cent staying on the same level, and 8 per cent lowerings of the level of aspiration. After nonattainment of the level of aspiration, it was raised 7 per cent, stayed the same 29 per cent, and lowered 64 per cent of the time. Jucknat carried this type of analysis a step further by judging the reaction of the subject to attainment or nonattainment of his level of aspiration. He attempted to infer the extent of the subject's feelings of success and failure. Results showed that the tendency to raise the level of aspiration is greater the stronger the feeling of success, and the tendency to lower aspiration is greater the stronger the feeling of failure.

The predominant tendency of subjects to maintain a moderate positive goal discrepancy, that is, a level of aspiration that is a little above past performance, and to raise aspiration following success and to lower it following failure has been observed by many investigators dealing with representative samples of school children and college students as subjects.

ATYPICAL RESULTS IN STUDY OF ASPIRATION

Following the Galilean mode of thought, we consider the "atypical" cases of equal importance. P. S. Sears (1940) studied selected groups of children who had very different histories of success and failure in schoolwork. Children with a past history of success showed very little variability in aspiration. Most of them maintained the "typical" small positive goal discrepancy. Children with past histories of failure, however, showed a much higher average goal discrepancy, and variability within this group of subjects was very substantial. Some had very high positive goal discrepancies; they set their levels of aspiration way above their immediate past performances. Others had negative goal discrepancies; they set their levels of aspiration below their immediate past performances. Similar "atypical" patterns of aspiration have been observed in later clinical studies of level of aspiration. Eysenck and Himmelweit (1946), Himmelweit (1947), and Miller (1951), for example, have found that persons clinically diagnosed as "hysteric" tend to maintain a negative goal discrepancy (a very low level of aspiration) while persons diagnosed as "neurasthenic" tend to maintain an extremely high positive goal discrepancy (aspirations that are far above the level of their past performance). In these studies, "normal" control groups show the typical moderate positive goal discrepancy. Rotter (1943, 1954) has found that atypical patterns of changes following success and failure tend to be associated with atypical goal discrepancies. The level of aspiration is, in other words, a sensitive measure of how individuals differ in motivation and in the resolution of conflict.

LEVEL OF ASPIRATION AS A CHOICE SITUATION

A theoretical conception of level of aspiration was first presented by Escalona (1940) and elaborated by Festinger (1942). It is often referred to as the "*resultant valence theory*" of level of aspiration. We shall follow the statement of theory presented in Festinger (1942) and further amplified by Lewin, Dembo, Festinger, and P. S. Sears (1944).

The psychological situation of a person at the moment he is asked to state his level of aspiration can be characterized as a choice situation. He must decide whether he will choose a more difficult level, an equally difficult level, or an easier level. If the choice involves different types of activity—for example, target shooting versus arithmetic problems versus solving puzzles—a great number of factors will influence the valences or attractiveness of the several goals. In the experimental study of level of aspiration, the situation is simplified somewhat by the fact that the general character of the activity is held constant. The choice is determined by the valences which *different levels of difficulty within the same activity* have for the person. Each level of difficulty may be represented as a separate activity or goal region in the life space of the person. The choice of a particular goal region L, that is to say, the level of aspiration, will be determined by the resultant force towards L ($f^*_{P,L}$).

The individual faces the possibility of succeeding or failing whatever level he chooses, so the *positive valence of future success* and the *negative valence of future failure* become basic determinants of his decision. Some tasks may appear so easy that performance of them would not produce any appreciable feeling of success. If, for example, an adult were asked to solve three simple arithmetic problems and given an hour to do it, the prospect of success would have zero valence. Within the range of difficulty that taxes the subject's ability, however, *the attractiveness of success seems to increase with the level of difficulty*. Similarly, the valence of failure at a task that is "humanly impossible" is zero, but

within the range of activities that provide some challenge to one's ability, *the negative valence of failure is greater the less difficult the task*. If the valences of success ($Va_{succ}$) and failure ($Va_{fai}$) were alone responsible for the decision as to what level of difficulty to choose, everyone should choose the most difficult task. This follows because the force towards success ($f_{P,succ}$) would be stronger and the force away from failure ($f_{P,-fai}$) would be weaker the more difficult the task, within the limited range of difficulty which can effectively challenge the person's ability. But everyone does not choose the most difficult task. Why not?

This problem is resolved by making use of the concept of *potency*, which is essential in the theory of decision. Escalona (1940) first suggested that it is doubtful whether the desirability of success and the undesirability of failure at a given level of performance are both present in the life space of the person with equal effectiveness at all times. The desirability of success is the uppermost consideration if success seems most probable, but the undesirability of failure is the uppermost consideration if failure seems most probable.

> "*The subject's expectancy of success and failure at a given level of performance . . . will define the relative potency of the valences of success and failure at that level.* At easy levels the probability of success is very high and so the potency of the positive valence of success will be great and the potency of the negative valence of failure correspondingly small" (Festinger, 1942, pp. 238–239, italics added).

At each level of difficulty, then, there must be an effective force towards success, $^of_{P,succ_L}$, which is determined by $Po_{succ_L} \times Va_{succ_L}$, and an effective force away from failure, $^of_{P,-fai_L}$, which is determined by $Po_{fai_L} \times Va_{fai_L}$. The resultant force ($f^*_{P,L}$) for a given level of difficulty is determined by the equation:

$$f^*_{P,L} = {^of_{P,succ_L}} + {^of_{P,-fai_L}}$$
$$= (Po_{succ,L} \times Va_{succ,L}) - (Po_{fai,L} \times Va_{fai,L}).$$

The particular region L toward which the resultant force $f^*_{P,L}$ is greatest will be chosen as the goal region. In other words:

Level of aspiration = L at which $f^*_{P,L}$ = maximum.

In brief, the level of aspiration is considered the resolution of a conflict in which three factors are of major importance: (a) the attractiveness of success; (b) the repulsiveness of failure; and (c) the cognitive factor of a probability judgment ($Po_{succ}$ and $Po_{fai}$). The person is conflicted about undertaking any task when feelings of success or feelings of failure are possible outcomes. In setting his level of aspiration, he is simultaneously confronted with a number of different levels of difficulty, which may be represented as separate activity regions in the life space. This is shown in Figure 4.17.

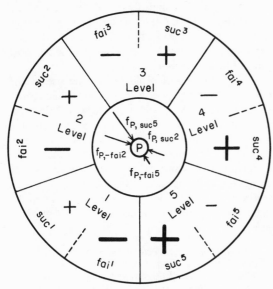

FIGURE 4.17　The difference in the attractiveness of the various difficulty levels 1 to 5 of the activity determined by the valence of future success (*suc*) and failure (*fai*) at that level. The valence of success increases while that of failure decreases with increasing difficulty level. Correspondingly the force toward success—for instance, $f_{P,suc^5}$—is greater than the force $f_{P,suc^2}$ on level 2. The force away from failure, $f_{P,-fai^5}$, is smaller than $f_{P,-fai^2}$. Therefore, the total valence of the more difficult level is higher than that of the easier level. (*From Kurt Lewin, Tamara Dembo, Leon Festinger, and Pauline Snedden Sears, "Level of Aspiration," in* Personality and the Behavior Disorders—A Handbook Based on Experimental and Clinical Research, Volume One, *edited by J. McV. Hunt. Copyright 1944 The Ronald Press Company*)

Following Festinger (1942), we may review in turn each of the factors which influences the decision with reference to Figure 4.18:

"(1) *Valence of success* ($Va_s$) is defined as the positive valence of future success as it appears to the person when setting his goal. This valence would be very low, or perhaps zero at the very easy levels and would rise to a maximum at the

difficult levels of performance. It is probably an S shaped curve because the areas of too difficult and too easy performance seem only slightly differentiated with regard to valence.

"(2) *Valence of failure* ($Va_f$) is similarly defined as the negative valence of future failure as it appears to the subject when setting his goal. This curve would be high at the easy levels and low at the difficult levels.

"(3) *Expectancy of success* ($Po_s$) is defined as the judgment of the individual at the time when he sets his goal as to the probability of reaching a given level of performance. This curve would be high at the easy levels (the individual would feel sure he could score at least that much) and would be very low at the difficult levels (the individual would be sure he could not score that much). The maximum value of this curve (practical certainty) is unity.

"(4) *Expectancy of failure* ($Po_f$) is correspondingly defined as the subjective probability of failure at the time of setting the goal. Mathematically, the $Po_f = 1 - Po_s$. Psychologically this is not necessarily so although on the whole it is approximately correct: the expectation of failure decreases as the expectation of success increases" (Festinger, 1942, pp. 239–240, italics added).

The curve of the resultant force in Figure 4.18, which is based on the values assumed for each of the separate factors also plotted in Figure 4.18, shows the level of aspiration at the point where $f^*_{P,L} = $ maximum.

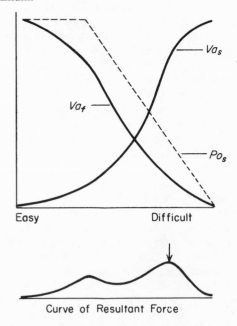

Curve of Resultant Force

FIGURE 4.18　Derivation of the resultant force ($f^*_{P,L}$) from a set of valence and potency curves of given value (*From Festinger, 1942*)

A NUMERICAL ILLUSTRATION

Table 4.1 is a numerical illustration of the determination of level of aspiration. Arbitrary values are assigned to $Va_s$ and $Va_f$ in keeping with the assumptions that $Va_s$ increases and $Va_f$ decreases as the level of difficulty increases. The level of immediate past performance is assumed to be 7 in this illustration. The resultant force is greatest at 8, hence 8 is the level of aspiration. The goal discrepancy is +1.

Early studies of level of aspiration showed the influence of group norms and other factors on the level of aspiration. They are treated as factors which influence the height or shape of the curve of $Va_s$ and $Va_f$ or influence the person's expectations, $Po_s$ and $Po_f$, to bring about changes in the shape of the curve of resultant forces. Similarly, the effects of individual differences in motivation were given some consideration:

"Great differences exist among people in regard to the degree to which they are ruled by the tendency to avoid failure or by the tendency to seek success. Some people appear very much afraid of failure and to them the possibility of failure is uppermost in their minds" (Lewin *et al.*, 1944, p. 366).

We recall that the momentary strength of an individual's desire to succeed or to avoid failure would be represented in the life space as a system in a state of tension ($t_g$) which influences $Va_g$. Table 4.2 shows what might be expected to happen if the values of $Va_f$ which appear in Table 4.1 were to be doubled. Such would be the case if failure were very threatening to a person. The resultant force for the person whose conflict is represented in this table is greatest at level 10. This means the goal discrepancy would be +3, like the "atypical" cases of very high positive goal discrepancy observed in some of the studies of persons who might be more sensitive about failure because they have failed frequently in the past (e.g., P. S. Sears, 1940). The other "atypical" response, a negative goal discrepancy, could come about as a consequence of some other combination of valences and potencies. We shall consider a contemporary refinement of this scheme in Chapter 9.

## RELATIONSHIP BETWEEN STUDIES OF ASPIRATION AND EFFECTS OF INTERRUPTION OF TASKS

AN EXAMPLE OF HOMOGENIZATION OF SUBJECT MATTER

One of the most interesting features of the Lewinian conception is its applicability to both the problem of decision, which traditional thought explains as a deliberate and conscious mental calculus

TABLE 4.1

Numerical illustration of the determinants of level of aspiration (Based on Lewin *et al.*, 1944, p. 358)

| Levels of possible objective | Tendency to approach success | | | Tendency to avoid failure | | | Resultant tendency $f^*_{P,lev}$ | |
|---|---|---|---|---|---|---|---|---|
| | $Va_{succ} \times Po_{succ} = {}^o f_{P,succ}$ | | | $Va_{fai} \times Po_{fai} = {}^o f_{P,-fai}$ | | | | |
| Too difficult ↑ 15 | 10 | 0 | 0 | 0 | 100 | 0 | 0 | |
| 14 | 10 | 0 | 0 | 0 | 100 | 0 | 0 | |
| 13 | 10 | 0 | 0 | 0 | 100 | 0 | 0 | |
| 12 | 10 | 0 | 0 | 0 | 100 | 0 | 0 | |
| 11 | 10 | 5 | 50 | 0 | 95 | 0 | 50 | |
| 10 | 9 | 10 | 90 | 0 | 90 | 0 | 90 | Level |
| 9 | 7 | 25 | 175 | −1 | 75 | −75 | 100 | of |
| 8 | 6 | 40 | 240 | −2 | 60 | −120 | 120 | aspiration ↓ |
| 7 | 5 | 50 | 250 | −3 | 50 | −150 | 100 | ↖Goal ↙discrepancy |
| 6 | 3 | 60 | 180 | −5 | 40 | −200 | −20 | ↑ Level of |
| 5 | 2 | 75 | 150 | −7 | 25 | −175 | −25 | past |
| 4 | 1 | 90 | 90 | −9 | 10 | −90 | 0 | performance |
| Too easy 3 | 0 | 95 | 0 | −10 | 5 | −50 | −50 | |
| 2 | 0 | 100 | 0 | −10 | 0 | 0 | 0 | |
| ↓ 1 | 0 | 100 | 0 | −10 | 0 | 0 | 0 | |

TABLE 4.2

Determinants of level of aspiration when the negative valence of failure is relatively high. *The values of subjective probability of success and failure are the same as in Table 4.1, but the negative valence of failure is doubled.* (Based on Lewin *et al.*, 1944, p. 365)

| Levels of possible objective | Tendency to approach success $Va_{succ} \times Po_{succ} = {}^of_{P,succ}$ | | | Tendency to avoid failure $Va_{fai} \times Po_{fai} = {}^of_{P,-fai}$ | | | Resultant tendency $f^*_{P,lev}$ | |
|---|---|---|---|---|---|---|---|---|
| Too difficult ↑ 15 | 10 | 0 | 0 | 0 | 100 | 0 | 0 | |
| 14 | 10 | 0 | 0 | 0 | 100 | 0 | 0 | |
| 13 | 10 | 0 | 0 | 0 | 100 | 0 | 0 | |
| 12 | 10 | 0 | 0 | 0 | 100 | 0 | 0 | Level |
| 11 | 10 | 5 | 50 | 0 | 95 | 0 | 50 | of |
| 10 | 9 | 10 | 90 | 0 | 90 | 0 | 90 | aspiration |
| 9 | 7 | 25 | 175 | −2 | 75 | −150 | 25 | Goal |
| 8 | 6 | 40 | 240 | −4 | 60 | −240 | 0 | discrepancy |
| 7 | 5 | 50 | 250 | −6 | 50 | −300 | −50 | |
| 6 | 3 | 60 | 180 | −10 | 40 | −400 | −220 | Level of |
| 5 | 2 | 75 | 150 | −14 | 25 | −350 | −200 | past |
| 4 | 1 | 90 | 90 | −18 | 10 | −180 | −90 | performance |
| Too easy 3 | 0 | 95 | 0 | −20 | 5 | −100 | −100 | |
| 2 | 0 | 100 | 0 | −20 | 0 | 0 | 0 | |
| ↓ 1 | 0 | 100 | 0 | −20 | 0 | 0 | 0 | |

which balances potential satisfactions against potential losses in arriving at "rational" choice, and the problem of the persistence of unfulfilled wishes, which Freud often referred to as the tendency of an impulse to seek expression until satisfied. The life space represents the totality of factors which have an immediate influence on behavior, whether the person is conscious of them or not. Application of the same constructs and same explanatory principles to these apparently different phenomena provides an excellent illustration of the homogenization of subject matter which is characteristic of the Galilean mode of thought. This does not exclude the possibility of important differences between conscious and unconscious processes. Rather, it represents the same kind of conviction that dominated Galileo and other early physicists that the basic concepts needed to explain terrestrial motion would apply equally well to "heavenly" motions and that the apparent differences could be represented as different conditions using the same basic elements of construction. Thus the conceptual picture of what influences the person as he recalls an interrupted task, initiates a substitute activity, faces a difficult perceptual discrimination, or sets his level of aspiration is different in each case, but the elements of construction and basic principles are the same. We shall find this same conviction among psychologists who have undertaken systematic experimental analysis of motivation in lower animals because it affords much greater opportunity for experimental control and manipulation of relevant conditions than is possible with human subjects (see Chapters 6 and 7).

Guided by the conviction that the basic concepts and principles are general, Lewin and his co-workers have extended their application to problems of interpersonal relations, social forces, group dynamics, and many other broader social psychological problems which fall beyond the scope of our present interest in the study of motivation. (See Cartwright, 1959.)

PREVALENCE OF TENDENCIES TO SEEK
SUCCESS AND TO AVOID FAILURE

A second and more immediately relevant relationship between studies of level of aspiration and studies of the effects of interruption of tasks is the extent to which the tendency to seek success and the tendency to avoid failure are involved in both. The theory of level of aspiration highlights the importance of individual differences in motivation having to do with achievement and failure. It suggests how both "typical" and "atypical" aspirations might be explained in terms of differences in the magnitude of valences of success and failure or differences in the relative potencies of these two goals. Until now we have not considered the fact that similar "atypical" effects were observed in several of the early studies involving interruption of tasks. These were effects which focus attention on *the problem of accounting for individual differences in the psychological goals of subjects who are exposed to the same experimental instructions*, that is, to the same immediate geographic-environmental influences. Let us consider a few examples.

One important early study of the effects of interruption on recall was performed by Rosenzweig (1943). He sought to use the Zeigarnik technique to study Freud's theory of repression, the flight of the mind from recollection of painful events. Rosenzweig assumed that if subjects were given various activities to perform and the importance of these activities was emphasized in preliminary instructions by making them to appear to be tests of very important personal attributes like intelligence, then the intentions to succeed and to avoid failure should be very strong. Furthermore, if the procedure of interruption were made to appear to the subject that he had failed an important test, then, at the time of recall the subject should experience a conflict between the persistent wish to complete the task and the tendency to avoid thinking about it because that would reawaken the embarrassment and shame of a failure experience. In all essential details, Rosenzweig's experimental procedure seems very similar to that employed by Marrow (see page 85) when he induced a stronger intention to complete tasks by making the situation competitive and offering encouraging and discouraging remarks to sustain the competitive atmosphere. Marrow, you recall, had found that this procedure produced a much greater Zeigarnik effect than more neutral preliminary instructions. Rosenzweig, however, found that the average Zeigarnik quotient was less than 1.00, which meant that his subjects recalled more of the tasks they had actually completed than those which had been interrupted. He interpreted this result to mean that the subjects had repressed thoughts about their "failures" and had, instead, favored the recall of their "successes."

In the Lewinian scheme, this result can be interpreted *after the fact* by positing a force away from failure, $f_{P,-F}$, if one assumes that the event of interruption constituted a negatively valent experience of failure in the life space of the subject. At the time of recall, the force away from failure ($f_{P,-F}$) would oppose the "normal" force towards recall of unfin-

ished activities ($f_{P,U}$) corresponding to the strong unsatisfied desire of the subject to succeed. Thus when the experimenter asked the subject to recall the tasks, the induced force to recall tasks would produce a resultant force which favored recall of completed tasks.

Rosenzweig observed that some of his subjects tended to show the familiar Zeigarnik effect even in this rather stressful situation. They manifested what he called a *"need-persistive"* reaction to failure in contrast to the more prevalent *"ego-defensive"* reactions of the other subjects.

## RELATIVE NEGLECT OF INDIVIDUAL DIFFERENCES IN PERSONALITY

It is not our intention to pursue the implications of the Rosenzweig experiment, and many others which soon followed, showing contradictory patterns of results that were apparently attributable to individual differences in personality, until a later chapter which will deal explicitly with individual differences in motivation. Here, however, we must begin to note the troublesome problem which arose very early in the context of experiments by Lewin and his co-workers and which is inadequately treated in Lewin's conceptual scheme of motivation: namely, the extent to which the subjective goal of the person in a particular geographic situation apparently depends upon characteristics of his personality. The programmatic equation, $B = f(P,E) = f(Lsp)$, clearly implies that certain "properties of the person," his personality, together with immediate environmental influences, should combine to produce the forces that are represented in the life space. But in the theoretical conception and experimental analysis of motivation, Lewinians consider only the momentary and temporary condition of the person, which is represented as $t(S^G)$. And in most cases, $t(S^G)$ is assumed to be roughly equivalent for all subjects exposed to the same experimental instructions and arrangements in the course of conducting the experiment.

Again in Cartwright's (1942) study of changes in attractiveness of activities following interruption (see page 88), the observed changes in attractiveness of the initial and similar tasks highlight the importance of individual differences in personality. Some subjects in this experiment were given special instructions designed to induce feelings of failure when they were interrupted or feelings of success when they completed a task. Cartwright considered the fact that for some subjects the attractiveness of a task *decreased* after interruption:

"Spontaneous remarks by the subjects lead the experimenter to believe that some subjects viewed interruption as an escape from certain failure. These subjects seemed to want to avoid the interrupted task. To investigate this possibility an interview was introduced at the end of the experimental session and eighteen of the subjects were asked whether at the point of interruption they had anticipated success or failure. The changes in attractiveness in these two groups were distributed among the subjects as follows:

|  | N | Increase | Decrease | No Change |
|---|---|---|---|---|
| Anticipation of success | 11 | 7 | 1 | 3 |
| Anticipation of failure | 7 | 0 | 4 | 3 |

". . . It cannot be stated too strongly that future studies dealing with the effects of interruption, whether concerned with resumption or with memory, cannot fail to pay strict attention to the method of interruption and to the subject's expectations of success or failure" (Cartwright, 1942, p. 6).

Considering the results when subjects had been exposed to procedures that were especially designed to induce feelings of failure, Cartwright states:

". . . For the largest group of subjects, failure acted to reduce the attractiveness of the tasks on which the failure was experienced. Further, just as when failure was anticipated the reduction of attractiveness affected a whole category of activities. "A fairly sizable group of subjects raised the preference-rating after failure, thus demonstrating the necessity for a theory of failure which can account for both increases and decreases in attractiveness. Interviews with the subjects seemed to indicate clearly that many subjects who raised the preference-rating viewed the experimenter's evaluation of their performance not as failure but rather as an obstacle on the way to their goal. For these subjects failure acted much like interruption. Other subjects seemed to want to 'erase' the failure by subsequent success on the same activity. (Footnote: For this second group of subjects it is possible that one could speak of a 'need for success.') For both groups of subjects a tension system could be assumed with its spread to neighboring regions increasing the attractiveness of the similar tasks . . ." (Cartwright, 1942, pp. 11–12).

## CRITIQUE OF THE LEWINIAN CONTRIBUTION

In these and other early experiments which begin to spell out the behavioral implications of Lewin's basic concepts, the issue of individual differences in motivation arises as a stubborn problem. Lewin had intended to develop a set of concepts which would allow accurate description of individual cases within the framework of general laws. No one has stated more clearly how the individual case and the systematic principles of motivation should, in principle, be related:

"A law is expressed in an equation which relates certain variables. Individual differences have to be conceived of as various specific values which these variables have in a particular case. In other words, general laws and individual differences are merely two aspects of one problem; they are mutually dependent on each other and the study of the one cannot proceed without the study of the other" (Lewin, 1946, p. 794).*

Yet in the experimental work of the Lewinian program, the systematic search for general concepts and laws did attempt to proceed without much attention to the influence of relatively stable differences in personality on motivation in particular situations. As a consequence, this question constantly arises: How is the investigator to know what the momentary goals, valences, and potencies will be for a given subject in a given situation? Putting together all we have learned, we find that a complete statement of the determinants of effective force in a given situation is:

$$\text{Effective Force} = {}^\circ f = \frac{Va(G) \times Po(G)}{e_{P,G}},$$

where 
$$Va(G) = F(t_g, G)$$

This equation tells us that the momentary strength of the person's "need" or "intention" ($t_g$), the strength of his "expectancy" ($Po$), the psychological distance from the goal ($e_{P,G}$), and the perceived character of the goal itself ($G$) all must be represented as determinants of the effective force on the person towards the goal. But how is the investigator to know in advance what the intention of a subject is likely to be when given certain instructions for a task, or how the subjective goals of one subject may differ from those of another in the same objectively defined environment?

In his reaction against the Aristotelian mode of thought in psychology, which often attempts to explain behavior solely or primarily in terms of inherent properties of the person called instinct, habit, trait, or need, Lewin excluded any systematic reference in his principle of force to relatively enduring attributes of a person which might be assessed be-

* Excerpts from Kurt Lewin, Behavior and development as a function of the total situation, in L. Carmichael (Ed.), Manual of Child Psychology, copyright 1946, John Wiley & Sons, Inc., are reprinted with permission.

forehand to afford prior knowledge of which subject, for example, would attach a greater valence to success than to failure, or for which subject the potency of failure in the level of aspiration experiment might be particularly strong. Lewin seemed to forget what he had already acknowledged, that even in post-Galilean physics, whose orientation he sought to capture for psychology, certain enduring, inherent properties of objects like *mass* were systematically represented in the basic laws and given as much attention in experimentation as immediate environmental influences.

INADEQUATE EMPIRICAL DEFINITION OF CONCEPTS

An extension of this type of criticism calls attention to the fact that although the conceptual properties of the various constructs and their interrelationships have been clearly formulated, the definition of the observable events which these constructs are supposed to represent in the life space is not treated with anywhere near the same precision. To take a concrete example, the formal concept of tension $(t_g)$ is coordinated to the psychological concept of "need" or "intention," but the observable events which define these terms is indeed very ambiguous. The empirical events to which Lewin referred the term "need" are "those acts or behavior which generally are recognized as a syndrome indicating a need" (Lewin, 1938, p. 99). But is the "syndrome indicating a need" well defined by common sense?

In a recent critical essay, Estes (1954) has emphasized the importance of a sound empirical foundation as a base for any undertaking like that of Lewin which seeks to find a mathematical model to fit it. In reference to the weakness of the link between Lewinian concepts and observable events he states:

"... Lewin has had to take as his empirical base a hodge podge of terms taken over from classical psychological literature and from vernacular, and then proceed to coordinate these terms to terms in the mathematical system" (Estes, 1954, pp. 324–325).

When everyday experiential terms like "intention," "satisfaction," and "expectation" are employed to designate what is to be represented in the life space, the testability of the theory is open to question. How can any specific hypothesis derived from a theory be tested if the experimenter is uncertain as to what specific observable event he can point to as evidence that such and such an "intention," "satisfaction," or "expectation" did, in fact, occur for a particular subject at a particular time? How, in other words, can the life space of a person be adequately defined so that predictions derived from the theory can be tested?

This is the kind of tough-minded criticism advanced by many contemporary investigators, particularly those who have undertaken the experimental analysis of motivation in nonintrospective and nontalking animals. To them the matter of central interest is precise definition of concepts in terms of *observable* features of the geographic environment and organic conditions which affect the subject, and precise definition of the *observable* behavioral consequences.

DEFINING THE LIFE SPACE AT A GIVEN TIME

Lewin did not minimize the problem of defining the life space, or field, at a given time. He realized that, in order to provide an adequate conceptual description of the psychological situation facing a person, the basic elements of construction needed to be linked or coordinated in an unambiguous way to observable events, so that the scientist could make accurate inferences. Yet *he was convinced that the matter of developing a coherent scheme of interrelated concepts deserved primary attention.* He believed that crude and approximate empirical definitions of his concepts would provide an adequate impetus for the type of experimental analysis needed to improve the precision of the empirical definitions. We recall his argument that the precision in observation and measurement of empirical events which now characterizes contemporary physical science was not the cause but the effect of the fundamental reorientation of thought accomplished by Galileo. To him, in other words, it was a matter of putting first things first. His general answer to the question "How does one go about defining the life space of a person at a given time?" will help us to understand how the study of learning and development and the measurement of individual differences relate to the study of motivation. These topics are taken up in subsequent chapters. Lewin stated:

"If one has to derive behavior from the situation at that time, a way has to be found to *determine* the character of the 'situation at a given time.' ...

"To determine the properties of a present situation or—to use medical terminology—to make a diagnosis, one can follow two different procedures: One may base one's statement on conclusions from history (*anamnesis*), or one may use diagnostic *tests of the present.*

"To use a simple example: I wish to know whether the floor of the attic is sufficiently strong to carry a certain weight. I might try to gain this knowledge by finding out what material was used when the house was built ten years ago. As I get reliable reports that good material has been used, and that the architect was a dependable man, I might conclude that the load probably would be safe. If I can find the original blueprints, I might be able to do some exact figuring and feel still more safe.

"Of course, there is always a chance that the workmen have actually not followed the blueprints, or that insects have weakened the woodwork, or that some rebuilding has been done during the last ten years. Therefore, I might decide to avoid these uncertain conclusions from past data and to determine the present strength of the floor by testing its strength now. Such a diagnostic test will not yield data which are absolutely certain; how reliable they are depends upon the quality of the available test and the carefulness of testing. However, the value of a present test is, from the point of view of methodology, superior to that of *anamnesis*. An *anamnesis* includes logically two steps: namely, the testing of certain properties in the past (of the quality, size, and structure of the woodwork) and the proof that nothing unknown has interfered in the meantime; in other words that we have to deal with a 'closed system.' Even if a system is left untouched by the outside, inner changes occur. Therefore, in addition, the laws governing these inner changes have to be known if the properties of a situation are to be determined through an *anamnesis*.

"Medicine, engineering, physics, biology are accustomed to using both methods, an inquiry into the past and a test of the present. But they prefer the latter whenever possible" (Lewin, 1951, pp. 48–49).

THE HISTORICAL APPROACH

The *historical approach* is the method employed in psychoanalytic investigations of the person's life history when the individual, through free association, helps to provide relevant information concerning critical life experiences from which inferences concerning his present personality are made. The historical approach is also the method evolved in study of animal behavior, in which the investigator attempts to control the sequence of life experiences in order to discover the principles of change, thus providing a basis for valid inference of the animal's present state.

DIAGNOSTIC TESTS

The *method of diagnostic testing* is the approach which has characterized the mental-test movement in psychology from the time of the earliest interest in measurement of reaction time and intelligence. It has, over the years, produced countless tests and techniques for assessment of various attributes of personality. One of the great paradoxes in the history of psychology is that the study and assessment of individual differences has been, until very recently, completely isolated from the experimental analysis of motivation and the quest for a systematic conception of the process of motivation.

THE LEWINIAN EMPHASIS

Lewin's *ahistorical* emphasis and his method of going about the task of developing concepts has helped us to define the problem of motivation and has shown the role of experimentation. His appreciation of the need for conceptual clarity and the need for mathematical concepts in psychology, which ran well ahead of that of his colleagues in the field, is now an important component of the scientific attitude of contemporary psychology. Beginning with the familiar experiential language of motivation, Lewin emphasized that we must give up these vaguely defined concepts in favor of other more precisely defined concepts which are interrelated in a coherent scheme of thought. He was mainly concerned with the *conceptual definitions* of psychological terms.

Another transition in thought, however, is required to complete the bridge from common sense to the contemporary scientific attitude. We must turn to the equally important task of clarifying the problem of motivation and definition of concepts in terms of observable environmental events and observable features of behavior. Scientific concepts must refer unambiguously to the procedures and operations performed by the scientist when he employs the concepts in an experiment. He must know how to use his concepts in reference to concrete, observable environmental conditions and in reference to concrete and measurable features of observable behavior. Psychological concepts must, in other words, be given unambiguous empirical, or *operational definitions*.

The transition from viewing the problem of motivation as it is generally described in terms which refer to inner experiences to definition of the problem in more objective terms was a natural consequence of turning attention to the systematic study of animal behavior. What possible meaning can be attached to terms like "purpose," "emotion," "knowledge," "expectation," and other experiential terms when the subject of study is an animal for which the method of introspective analysis and verbal report is impossible? In the next chapter, we turn to the work of another great teacher, which in point of time overlaps that of Lewin, for the answer to this question.

# CHAPTER 5

# Experimental

# Analysis

# of Purposive

# Behavior

*"All that can ever actually be observed in fellow human beings and in the lower animals is behavior. Another organism's private mind, if he have any, can never be got at. . . .*

*"The behaviorism here to be presented will contend that mental processes are most usefully to be conceived as but dynamic aspects, or determinants, of behavior. They are functional variables which intermediate in the causal equation between environmental stimuli and initiating physiological states or excitements, on the one side, and final overt behavior, on the other"* (Tolman, 1932, p. 2).*

## INTRODUCTION TO STUDY OF ANIMAL BEHAVIOR

We turn now to the experimental study of behavior in lower animals which began around 1900. Our objective in this chapter is two-fold: first, to understand the transition in thought about the problem of motivation that came about as a result of studying organisms that could neither talk nor introspect; second, to begin to gain some historical perspective concerning the still unsettled theoretical issues in the psychology of motivation which grow out of systematic experimentation with animals, mainly the rat.

Neither Freud nor Lewin questioned the idea that behavior is purposive or goal-seeking in character. The Lewinian scheme provides a way of describing the immediate behavior of a person as either directed towards some anticipated goal or away from some anticipated threat on the one hand, or as an activity that is immediately enjoyable (i.e., activity in the goal region) or immediately disenjoyable and to be escaped from (i.e., activity in a negatively valent region). In other words, behavior is always considered as representing some phase in a goal-directed sequence. This conception is so congruent with intuitive ideas about behavior that it is surprising to find that it took about 20 years of psychological research with animals before the purposive characteristics of gross adjustive behavior in animals even began to attract serious experimental interest. We may come to undetstand the reason for this by re- viewing the main guiding ideas from the past and the innovations in method of study which molded the interest and conceptions of psychologists during the early days of experimental research with animals.

### THE NEED FOR CLARITY IN EMPIRICAL DEFINITION OF CONCEPTS

The work of Lewin and his students helps us to appreciate the need for a coherent conceptual scheme in scientific study of motivation. At least, it gives us a picture of what a clearly articulated theory of motivation might be like. Now, as we begin to consider the methods and ideas evolved in the study of animals, we will discover an equally important and complementary emphasis: a recognition of the need for clarity in the *empirical* definition of motivational problems and concepts. Scientific study requires both. We shall see how questions about motivation that are originally phrased in the subjective terms of everyday language have to be stated more objectively from the very outset when the subject of study is an animal. They must be restated as questions about characteristics of an animal's behavior in relation to features of its immediate environment and organic conditions that can be observed from outside and controlled or manipulated in experiments. Later in the chapter we shall see how explanatory concepts much like those advanced by Lewin in reference to human motivation evolved out of an intensive analysis of the observable characteristics of animal behavior.

A brief survey of the major issues which arose in the early studies of animal behavior will introduce the historical antecedents of some of the controversial issues that are still not completely resolved in contemporary research on motivation. With the Lewinian conception as our preliminary guide, we can see how some of the initial guiding ideas in research with animals actually obstructed experimental interest in the problem of motivation as distinct from the problem of learning for quite some time.

As psychologists began to turn to experimentation with lower animals around 1900 and thereafter, they were literally forced to become much more objective in their approach. When the subject of study can neither introspect nor talk about its private thoughts and feelings, if indeed it has any, many intuitive presumptions which are likely to go unnoticed when the subject is human become the most important issues. It seemed acceptable to both Freud and Lewin to speak of a person's "wishes" and "intentions" to reach some goal. They took for granted, as common sense does, that human thought and action is generally purposive—that is, directed towards ends. Their analyses of motivational problems begin with this assumption. But what, if anything, do familiar terms like "wish," "intention," "purpose," or "satisfaction" mean in reference to the behavior of lower animals? How can the scientific investigator possibly know if an animal has an "intention" or "desire" to reach some goal?

### ESCHEWING OF ANTHROPOMORPHISM

In their early efforts to overcome a natural inclination towards anthropomorphism, the attribution of human qualities to lower animals, psychologists deliberately eschewed the use of terms suggesting a human-like consciousness in lower animals. They wanted to begin their analysis with systematic observations of animal *behavior*, rather than with a fund of preconceptions based on their own introspections. They were intent on discovering how the behavior of an animal changed as a result of past experience and how the animal's behavior was influenced by factors that they could control in experiments. As outside observers who could never look within to see what, if any, private thoughts and feelings the animal experienced as it behaved, they were forced to invent plausible hypothetical pictures of the processes which intervened between the environmental influences to which an animal was exposed, which they could see and control, and the animal's behavior, which they could see and measure. To the extent that they were able to free themselves from the tendency to anthropomorphism, they were also free from the bondage of traditional intuitive ideas which so often go unquestioned when the subject of study is another human being like the investigator himself. One of the most important things they soon learned was that if hypothetical explanatory concepts were to be of any real value, they had, above all else, to be precisely defined in terms of observable antecedent events and behavior that could be measured from the outside. This emphasis on objectivity, on the need for clarity in the *empirical* meanings of motivational concepts, has since been absorbed by psychologists as another important component of the scientific orientation whether the subject of study is animal or human. It represents one more advance, perhaps the most fundamental of all, from the intuitive ideas of common sense to the working orientation of contemporary behavioral scientists.

## BEGINNING OF EXPERIMENTATION WITH ANIMALS

The experimental study of animal behavior began with the pioneering investigations of associative processes in animals by Edward L. Thorndike in 1897–1898. Thorndike was interested in "animal intelligence," not motivation. We shall see that he took motivation for granted in studies that were designed to enable him to observe how an animal learned to perform the response that got it out of a problem box to a food reward outside. Thorndike's innovation in method of study can be appreciated from the fact that the only place he could find to house the chickens with which he began his explorations as a graduate student at Harvard was in the basement of the home of William James. The continuity in ideas from James (see Chapter 2) to Thorndike will be readily apparent.

Within a year or so after Thorndike had begun his work, the Russian physiologist, I. P. Pavlov, independently developed another important method of study which also focused attention upon associative processes. Pavlov and his co-workers observed that dogs, who normally salivate when food or acid is placed in the mouth, quickly learned to salivate in response to some previously neutral stimulus like a bell which has frequently preceded placement of food or acid in the mouth. Pavlov, too, was mainly concerned with an aspect of "intelligence," the associative process, and not with motivation. A good many years were to pass before psychologists were to appreciate fully how the initial observations of both Thorndike and Pavlov were as much related to the problem of motivation as to the problem of learning. Having reviewed the later work of Lewin first, we are perhaps in a position to anticipate the turn of events.

### ORIGINAL EMPHASIS: THE PROBLEM OF LEARNING

As we turn now from a survey of what Freud had learned about human motivation from clinical observations, and the conceptual clarifications in reference to human motivation that were advanced by Lewin in the 1920's and 1930's, back to Thorndike and subsequent work with animals, we are reminded that we return in time again to the late 1890's to pick up what was later to become the main thread of experimental research on motivation in America. The experimental study of animal behavior, which focused initially almost completely on the problem of how animals learn, ultimately provides an independent source of ideas about motivation. It should be considered another starting point.

Our first task is to see how a recognition of the problem of motivation as distinct from the problem of learning gradually began to emerge as research with animals developed and new methods of study were conceived. It is a complicated chapter in the history of psychology, one that has always been written from the viewpoint of a primary interest in learning theory. We shall have to restrict our attention to some of the major ideas and developments which, in light of our knowledge of the later course of events, seem to provide a foundation for understanding the subsequent evolution of concepts having to do with motivation. Then in the next chapter, having undergone the several transitions in thought needed to appreciate contemporary work on motivation, we shall begin to outline the systematic developments within the field of animal research from 1940 to the present before turning to contemporary developments in the study of human motivation in later parts of the book. We shall see that the problem of motivation which for so many years was subordinate to an interest in learning has now taken the center of the stage in systematic research with animals.

## SOME MAJOR ISSUES DURING THE FORMATIVE YEARS

Looking back, we can identify three controversial issues in this formative period of American psychology that have in one way or another influenced the subsequent study of motivation. It will be helpful to put a spotlight on them in advance.

### INTROSPECTION VERSUS OBSERVATION OF BEHAVIOR

The rapid growth of interest in the behavior of lower animals, inspired by the implications of Darwin's theory of evolution, brought to a head a basic methodological issue that psychology had to resolve as it attempted to break away from its prescientific moorings in philosophy and find a rightful place among the empirical sciences. One of the distinguishing features of empirical science is that the subject matter, that is, the facts to be explained, is public. The subject matter of science consists of observable empirical events. What this means is very simple to understand. Two or more observers can watch what is happening as a ball rolls down an inclined plane or as solutions are mixed in a test tube in a chemistry laboratory. The empirical facts are relationships be-tween concrete happenings "out there" in open view where the crudities of initial observations and de-scriptions can, in time, give way to more precise and agreed-upon procedures for measurement as the science develops.

In contrast to these examples of empirical happen-ings in the physical sciences, let us recall James' introspective observations concerning the contents of his own consciousness when "voluntarily" getting out of bed on a cold morning. What other observer could look over his shoulder to verify the observa-tion that it is the absence of any competing idea in his consciousness that finally produces his getting up? What is the scientific status of introspective observations concerning the nature of one's own private thoughts and feelings? How can study of them find a place among the objective experimental sciences? These were the questions which began to arise as psychology pressed towards an acceptable methodology.

It soon became apparent that the kinds of observa-tions that Thorndike and others were beginning to make of cats struggling to get out of problem boxes and of rats running through mazes constituted a more objective subject matter for psychology than introspective descriptions of consciousness. Like the subject matter of the well-founded natural sciences, the behavior of some other organism was "out there," open to public inspection. Observations of behavior could be verified by independent observers; introspective observations could not. This was the essential point of an argument about methodology that was finally made explicit by John Watson in 1912 as he initiated the movement he called "Behav-iorism." It sounded the death knell of the older "introspective" psychology which had considered the systematic description of the private contents of consciousness to be the main business of psychology. The "Behaviorists" vigorously opposed any last rem-nants of concepts which suggested private "mental" entities or events which could be studied only through introspection and which raised the ancient issue of a mind-body interaction. In time, the need for objectivity, which was the central point of their argument, though not all of the excesses of their early viewpoint, was generally accepted. Psycholo-gists no longer quarrel with the notion that the em-pirical foundation of a scientific psychology is what people and animals do, their behavior (including, of course, their verbal behavior) in relation to observa-ble features of their environment and their organic

condition rather than descriptions of the private contents of one's own consciousness. On this matter of objectivity, the psychologists who studied animal behavior experimentally were in complete accord. But on two other matters there was, as we shall see, considerable disagreement.

## "ASSOCIATION" VERSUS "PURPOSE" AS GUIDING IDEAS

Some investigators plunged into the task of ex-perimentation with animals guided by the presump-tion that the explanation of behavior was to be found in what the 18th-century philosophers had called "the association of ideas." During the 19th century, physiology had provided what seemed a scientifically respectable objectification of this pre-scientific doctrine in the concept of the reflex-arc, the neural connection between a stimulus and a response, and a picture of the brain as the physical locus of neural associations and interactions be-tween them. We have already seen how James had pounced on the possibility of translating "association of ideas" into neural linkages in his speculations about both habit and volition (see Chapter 2). The new experimental methods of Thorndike and Pavlov turned the guiding idea of neural association between stimulus and response into an empirically fruitful working hypothesis. Experiments could be performed to study the growth of neural associations. No wonder that the problem of associative learning quickly came to dominate the interests and atten-tion of psychologists and that many of them, like Watson, the father of behaviorism, should see in S-R the basic unit for analysis of *all* psychological problems. James' treatment of habit foreshadowed the trend.

On the other hand, the observations of some other psychologists during this formative period seemed colored from the outset by another presumption carried over from the past: the idea of "purpose." This traditional notion that thought and action is directed towards and guided in some way by an end, or goal, is evident, for example, in James' treatment of both instinct and volition. The 19th-century concept of instinct as an innate tendency towards some end or goal lent a technical ring to the early arguments of "purposivists," but those who held this viewpoint were handicapped in not having any new and exciting experimental method to rival those of Thorndike and Pavlov during the early decades of this century. A speculative doctrine of instinct was advanced by William McDougall

(1908) to provide social psychology with an underlying dynamic to account for the springs of human action. It was the forerunner of the concept of *drive* which gained currency in the 1920's when suitable methods for empirical study were finally developed.

The "associationists," among whom we find Thorndike and Pavlov, the major innovators in method of study, and Watson, who became the leading spokesman of "Behaviorism," focused attention on the observable change in an animal's response to some stimulus as a function of experimentally controlled past experience. This concretized the problem of *learning* as they conceived it. The "purposivists," on the other hand, for a long time did little more than argue from the sidelines that the immediate response to some stimulus must always be viewed in the larger context of the animal's active striving for some goal. This, in their view, was the central characteristic of ongoing behavior. While the associationists had gotten off to a fast start in the experimental analysis of behavior, William McDougall kept the purposivist viewpoint alive, citing as illustrative evidence problems like that of the hunting dog tracking its prey, sniffing here, looking there, actively searching for the prey and attending only to those stimuli that lead on to the final goal. For the "purposivists," what was later to be recognized as the problem of motivation always seemed of primary importance. To them, animal intelligence and particular associations between stimuli and responses had to do with *means;* instinct, on the other hand, had to do with the more fundamental problem of the basic springs of action and the problem of *ends.*

THE NEED FOR PHYSIOLOGICAL
EXPLANATORY CONCEPTS

Psychologists of this period and subsequently have also disagreed concerning the necessity of using neurophysiological concepts to explain their observations concerning behavior in relation to stimulating conditions. Those who began with the concept of the neural reflex as their model, and with the idea that descriptions of neural functions must replace descriptions of consciousness, quite naturally were disposed to encourage the affinity of psychology and physiology. They had, in fact, a neurophysiological concept as their guiding hypothesis. In comparison, the "purposivists" were in the unenviable position of arguing a doctrine that smacked of the traditional "mentalism" and that had no comparable neurological basis. However, Edward C.

Tolman, who became the effective spokesman for the purposivist viewpoint in the 1920's, developed a scientifically respectable logic for the construction of psychological theory in terms of inferred "psychological" variables which intervene between observable stimulus and response without appealing to presumed underlying neurophysiological mechanisms and processes. His view was similar in this respect to that of both Freud and Lewin, who felt the need to develop psychological theory in its own right without explicit appeal to underlying neurophysiological process.

PLAN OF THE REMAINDER
OF THE CHAPTER

We shall begin with some descriptions of the methods, observations, and concepts of Thorndike and Pavlov. The early work of these two men did much to mold the viewpoint of subsequent workers interested in problems of animal learning and behavior. We must recognize that it is in the context of research on associative learning that the problem of motivation finally emerges as a separate problem for experimental research on animals. The work of Thorndike and Pavlov will provide a background for a short review of McDougall's ideas about instinct and purpose and a discussion of the concept of "drive" as it was originally introduced by Woodworth in 1918 as the name for what was then recognized as a separate problem that the "associationists" had previously neglected.

A major portion of the chapter will then be devoted to the "purposive behaviorism" developed by Edward Tolman during the period 1920–1935. This was the period during which Lewin also began his systematic work in Germany. Tolman's writings span the period in which psychologists interested in systematic study of animal behavior were beginning to see how "emotion," "knowledge," "memory," and "purpose"—the traditional problems of "introspective" psychology—could still be identified *in* the behavior of animals as they ran through mazes and struggled to get out of problem boxes. Tolman showed how it was first a matter of appreciating that these mentalistic-sounding terms, even when used in reference to human behavior, refer to identifiable characteristics of overt behavior, and then a matter of studying how these observable characteristics of behavior are influenced by prior training and other antecedent conditions that the investigator can observe and control. His work illustrates how one may work up from careful observations of overt behavior in relation to observable antecedent conditions to an explanatory scheme very much like that advanced by Lewin, who was studying human subjects. In the definition of problems and in the working out of a logic for systematic theory construction, Tolman's work provided the challenge and also set the stage for the subsequent systematic development of *S-R* behavior theory. Tolman's work complements that of Lewin. The theoretical views of the two men were very similar. And since one of them emphasized *the need for conceptual clarity* and the other *the need for objectivity*, together their methodological views more adequately represent the orientation of contemporary psychologists than either by itself.

## THORNDIKE'S INVESTIGATIONS OF ANIMALS IN PUZZLE BOXES

Following Darwin, speculation was rife as to whether or not animals lower on the phylogenetic scale could reason. Some writers of the late 19th century argued affirmatively in terms of anecdotal evidence. They cited cases in which animals had been known to perform marvelous acts of "intelligence." But the biases in sampling of cases (after all, only the unusual incidents were even noticed), the inaccuracies of "general" observation, and the distortions of human memory seemed all too obvious to E. L. Thorndike when he became interested in this question. He saw the need of turning to experimental observations under controlled conditions and with substantial numbers of randomly selected animals to get a justifiable answer to the question. His systematic use of special devices for setting standard problems for animals to solve and his quantified observations of the time it took an animal to perform the "correct" response on repeated trials represent the turning point in method of settling arguments about the causes of animal behavior. The invention of the maze and many other devices suited to study of learning and motivation in animals were soon to follow.

Our interest in surveying Thorndike's method, his observations, and the concepts which arose from some of these earliest experimental facts concerning animal behavior is twofold. First, it will give us a clear picture of the kinds of methods and facts which constitute another independent beginning point in the study of motivation. Second, it will show how the notions of common sense which guided the in-

itial investigations and pervaded the initial attempts to explain animal behavior began to give way to more precise and objectively defined concepts almost as soon as disciplined empirical inquiry got underway.

### THE METHOD OF STUDY

A passage from Thorndike's book *Animal Intelligence* (1911), which reproduced the reports of the investigations he had undertaken beginning in 1897–1898, provides a good overview of his method of study:

"After considerable preliminary observation of animals' behavior under various conditions, I chose for my general method one which, simple as it is, possesses several other marked advantages besides those which accompany experiment of any sort. It was merely to put animals when hungry in inclosures from which they could escape by some simple act, such as pulling at a loop of cord, pressing a lever, or stepping on a platform. . . . The animal was put in the inclosure, food was left outside in sight, and his actions observed. Besides recording his general behavior, special notice was taken of how he succeeded in doing the necessary act (in case he did succeed), and a record was kept of the time that he was in the box before performing the successful pull, or clawing, or bite. This was repeated until the animal had formed a perfect association between the sense-impression of the interior of that box and the impulse leading to the successful movement. When the association was thus perfect, the time taken to escape was, of course, practically constant and very short. . . .

"Enough different sorts of methods of escape were tried to make it fairly sure that association in general, not association of a particular sort of impulse, was being studied. Enough animals were taken with each box or pen to make it sure that the results were not due to individual peculiarities. None of the animals used had any previous acquaintance with any of the mechanical contrivances by which the doors were opened. So far as possible the animals were kept in a uniform state of hunger, which was practically utter hunger" (Thorndike, 1911, pp. 26–27).

In a footnote to this passage, Thorndike explained that his phrase "practically utter hunger" referred not to a state of near starvation, but to the condition of the animal after fourteen hours without food. Hunger was maintained at this relatively constant level by giving the animal only a very small food reward after each trial and then by not testing him too many times in any one day.

Typical of the puzzle boxes used by Thorndike is the one shown in Figure 5.1. Each box was about 20 inches long, 15 inches wide, and 12 inches high.

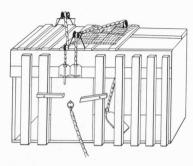

FIGURE 5.1   The puzzle box employed by Thorndike in the classic studies of trial-and-error learning (*From Thorndike, 1911*)

The door was pulled open by a weight attached to a string which ran over a pulley and was fastened to the door when the animal loosened the bolt or bar which held it. Experiments were conducted using these boxes with cats and dogs, and also with chickens, fish, and monkeys in somewhat different types of arrangements.

ORIGINAL RESULTS IN STUDY
OF SELECTIVE LEARNING

A general description of the behavior of 13 cats observed in the earliest experiments is given by Thorndike as follows:

"The behavior of all but [subjects number] 11 and 13 was practically the same. When put into the box the cat would show evident signs of discomfort and of an impulse to escape from confinement. It tries to squeeze through any opening; it claws and bites at the bars or wires; it thrusts its paw out through any opening and claws at everything it reaches; it continues its efforts when it strikes anything loose and shaky; it may claw at things within the box. It does not pay very much attention to the food outside, but seems simply to strive instinctively to escape from confinement. The vigor with which it struggles is extraordinary. For eight or ten minutes it will claw and bite and squeeze incessantly. With 13, an old cat, and 11, an uncommonly sluggish cat, the behavior is different. They did not struggle vigorously or continually. On some occasions they did not even struggle at all. It was therefore necessary to let them out of the box a few times, feeding them each time. After they thus associate climbing out of the box with getting food, they will try to get

out whenever put in. They do not, even then, struggle so vigorously or get so excited as the rest. In either case, whether the impulse to struggle be due to an instinctive reaction to confinement or to an association, it is likely to succeed in letting the cat out of the box. The cat that is clawing all over the box in her impulsive struggle will probably claw the string or loop or button so as to open the door. And gradually all the other nonsuccessful impulses will be stamped out and the particular impulse leading to the successful act will be stamped in by the resulting pleasure, until, after many trials, the cat will, when put in the box, immediately claw the button or loop in a definite way.

"The starting point for the formation of any association in these cases, then, is the set of instinctive activities which are aroused when a cat feels discomfort in the box either because of confinement or a desire for food. This discomfort, plus the sense-impression of a surrounding, confining wall, expresses itself, prior to any experience, in squeezings, clawings, bitings, etc. From among these movements one is selected by success" (Thorndike, 1911, p. 36).

Thorndike noted that a cat which had learned to escape from one box by clawing will show a much greater tendency to claw at things in a second box "than it instinctively had at the start" (p. 36). The impulses associated with the feeling of confinement and sense-impressions of one box was, in other words, transferred to other similar boxes.

Thorndike used the term *instinctive* only to refer to "any reaction which an animal makes to a situation *without experience*" (p. 37). He made it clear that within the confines of his observations, this meant the initial responses which were observed in the box whether they were innate or had been acquired in earlier experiences that were not subject to observation. He used the term *impulse* to refer to the "*direct feeling of the doing*," the tendency to respond itself, "as distinguished from the *idea of the act done*" which James had spoken of in connection with voluntary action. The stamping in, of which Thorndike spoke, was the presumed strengthening of the neural bond between $S$ (sense-impression) and $R$ (impulse to respond).

Thorndike kept careful track of the amount of time it took the cat to perform the "successful" response on subsequent trials. He then plotted "time-curves" as shown in Figure 5.2. These "time-curves," or learning curves as they were soon to be called, summarize what Thorndike felt he had observed:

"Starting, then, with its store of instinctive impulses, the cat hits upon the successful movement, and gradually associates it with the sense-impres-

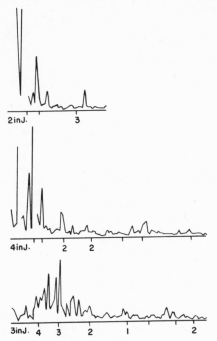

FIGURE 5.2 Examples of the time curves (learning curves) obtained by Thorndike in the earliest studies of selective learning. Each of the curves, for three different animals, shows a decrease in amount of time taken to perform the correct response after a number of re-warded trials. (*From Thorndike, 1911*)

sion of the interior of the box until the connection is perfect so that it performs the act as soon as confronted with the sense-impression" (Thorndike, 1911, p. 38).

The results of experiments with dogs were very similar. Some minor differences, however, were noted:

"A dog who, when hungry, is shut up in one of these boxes is not nearly so vigorous in his struggles to get out as is the young cat. And even after he has experienced the pleasure of eating on escape many times he does not try to get out so hard as a cat, young or old. He does try to a certain extent. He paws or bites the bars or screening, and tries to squeeze out in a tame sort of way. He gives up his attempts sooner than the cat, if they prove unsuccessful. Furthermore his attention is taken by the food, not the confinement. He wants to get *to* the food, not *out of* the box. So, unlike the cat, he confines his efforts to the front of the box. It was also a practical necessity that the dogs should be kept from howling in the evening, and for this reason I could not use as motive the utter hunger which the cats were made to suffer. In the morning, when the experiments were made, the

dogs were surely hungry, and no experiment is recorded in which the dog was not in a state to be willing to make a great effort for a bit of meat, but the motive may not have been even and equal throughout, as it was with the cats" (Thorndike, 1911, p. 59).

Chicks were placed in a confining pen made by laying books on end. They were given an opportunity to run up an inclined plane on one side from which they could jump down to be with their fellows and get to food spread outside the pen. Their behavior was very similar to that of the cats and dogs which had been confined in boxes:

"The behavior of the chicks shows the same general character as that of the cats, conditioned, of course, by the different nature of the instinctive impulses. . . . When taken from the food and other chicks and dropped into the pen he shows evident signs of discomfort; he runs back and forth, peeping loudly, trying to squeeze through any openings there may be, jumping up to get over the wall, and pecking at the bars or screen, if such separate him from the other chicks. Finally, in his general running around he goes up the inclined plane a way. He may come down again, o he may go on up far enough to see over the top of the wall. If he does, he will probably go running up the rest of the way and jump down. With further trials he gains more and more of an impulse to walk up an inclined plane when he sees it, while the vain running and pecking, etc., are stamped out by the absence of any sequent pleasure. Finally, the chick goes up the plane as soon as put in. In scientific terms this history means that the chick, when confronted by loneliness and confining walls, responds by those acts which in similar conditions in nature would be likely to free him. Some one of these acts leads him to the successful act, and the resulting pleasure stamps it in. Absence of pleasure stamps all others out. The case is just the same as with dogs and cats" (Thorndike, 1911, pp. 63–64).

For Thorndike, the point of these comparisons, which he pursued at greater length, was to reveal the nature of differences in "intelligence" among various species. Our interest, on the other hand, is to become familiar with the experimental method which Thorndike had introduced and the experimental observations upon which he based the famous *"law of effect"* to explain the "stamping in" of associations between stimuli and "successful" responses and the "stamping out" of associations between stimuli and "unsuccessful" responses. The law of effect has been a matter of central interest and controversy ever since these pioneer investigations of animal behavior.

## BASIC ASSUMPTIONS

In approaching the task of explaining what he had observed, Thorndike's fundamental premise was *"behavior is predictable"*:

"The first law of behavior, one fraction of the general law of the uniformity of nature, is that with life and mind, as with mass and motion, the same cause will produce the same effect,—that *the same situation will, in the same animal, produce the same response,*—and that *if the same situation produces on two occasions two different responses, the animal must have changed"* (Thorndike, 1911, p. 241).

The apparently random behavior of a neonate was believed to be as strictly determined as later behavior "stamped in" by learning experience. Thorndike referred to this idea as "the law of original behavior, or the law of instinct":

"*. . . to any situation an animal will, apart from learning, respond by virtue of the inherited nature of its reception-, connection- and action-systems*" (Thorndike, 1911, p. 243).

## THE LAW OF EFFECT AND THE LAW OF EXERCISE

The concrete fact which required explanation in these early puzzle-box studies was the gradual decrease in time taken to perform the correct response on subsequent trials. In his original statement of the "provisional laws of acquired behavior or learning," Thorndike added a new principle—*the law of effect*—to the long-recognized principle of frequency of repetition. It was this new principle, highlighting the role of reward and punishment in the learning process as Thorndike conceived it, which influenced educational practice in the schools. Heretofore, classroom methods had leaned completely upon drill and repetition alone as the key to learning and memory. And it was this new principle which accounts for the entanglement of ideas about motivation and ideas about the process of learning in so much subsequent research on how changes in behavior of animals are brought about:

**The Law of Effect.** "*Of several responses made to the same situation, those which are accompanied or closely followed by satisfaction to the animal will, other things being equal, be more firmly connected with the situation, so that, when it recurs, they will be more likely to recur; those which are accompanied or closely followed by discomfort to the animal will, other things being equal, have their connections with that situation weakened, so that, when it recurs, they will be less likely to occur. The greater the satisfaction or discomfort, the greater the strengthening or weakening of the bond.*

**The Law of Exercise.** "*Any response to a situation will, other things being equal, be more strongly connected with the situation in proportion to the number of times it has been connected with that situation and to the average vigor and duration of the connections*" (Thorndike, 1911, p. 244).

## IS THE LAW OF EFFECT HEDONISTIC?

The references to "satisfaction" and "discomfort" as major determinants of whether or not a tendency to respond ($R$) to a given situation ($S$) will be strengthened or weakened makes the Law of Effect sound like a restatement of the traditional hedonism of common sense. The influence of traditional thought is obvious; but the difference between Thorndike's Law of Effect and the conventional hedonism, while subtle, is, nonetheless, very important. As outlined in James (see p. 30), the traditional intuitive view was that behavior is undertaken *in order to* experience feelings of pleasure or *in order to* avoid feelings of discomfort. If Thorndike's view is at all hedonistic, its most striking characteristic is that *it is a hedonism of the past*. The animal getting out of the puzzle box promptly after a number of previously rewarded trials is not, in Thorndike's view, dominated by thoughts of impending pleasant feelings. This is not the explanation of why it performs the correct response quickly. Rather, it performs the correct response almost immediately because the connection between that particular response ($R$) and the sense impressions of the box ($S$) which calls it forth has been *selectively strengthened* by the satisfaction which has *previously* followed it. In other words, the response most likely to occur in a given situation today is the one which has been most frequently rewarded in the past. Given the stimulus situation and the strengthened $S$-$R$ bond, the animal is now, without any foresight of consequences, *compelled* to perform the response. That was Thorndike's view.

## IS THE LAW OF EFFECT CIRCULAR?

Some critics of Thorndike mistakenly believed that his reference to mentalistic-sounding events like "satisfaction" and "discomfort" as the conditions which strengthened and weakened connections between $S$ and $R$ made the Law of Effect immune from disproof. Whenever learning was observed, they argued, it could be referred to the satisfaction that must have followed the response. Whenever learning did not occur, it could be referred to some "discomfort" or "annoyance." Since animals cannot talk about their private feelings, who could contradict these assertions?

Thorndike's logic was a step or two ahead of that of some of his critics who may have turned too quickly from his writings because he had continued to use the common-sense language which seemed to them to smack too much of private mental events. He recognized the need for further definition of what was meant by the central phrases in his law of effect which describe the consequences of a response as "satisfaction" or "discomfort."

OBJECTIVE DEFINITIONS OF "SATISFYING"
AND "ANNOYING" STATES OF AFFAIRS

Very early in the book on *Animal Intelligence* he stated, "the studies reprinted in this volume produced in their author an increased respect for psychology as the science of behavior" and "a willingness to make psychology continuous with physiology . . ." (Thorndike, 1911, p. 5). He went on to say that he would attempt "to show further that psychology may be, at least in part, as independent of introspection as physics is" (p. 5). So he realized that "satisfaction" and "discomfort" or "annoyance," which sound like private feelings which can be got at only through introspection (impossible in animals), required more objective meanings. His own words on the subject merit careful attention because they show how *psychologists began to translate terms which heretofore had been used in reference to private thoughts and feelings into a more objective language, thus paving the way for a behavioristic psychology of motivation:*

"By a satisfying state of affairs is meant one which the animal does nothing to avoid, often doing such things as attain and preserve it. By a discomforting or annoying state of affairs is meant one which the animal commonly avoids and abandons.
"*The satisfiers for any animal in any given condition cannot be determined with precision and surety save by observation.* Food when hungry, society when lonesome, sleep when fatigued, relief from pain, are samples of the common occurrences that what favors the life of the species satisfies its individual members. But this does not furnish a completely valid rule.
"The satisfying and annoying are not synonymous with favorable and unfavorable to the life of either the individual or the species. Many animals are satisfied by deleterious conditions. Excitement, overeating, and alcoholic intoxication are, for instance, three very common and very potent satis-

fiers of man. Conditions useful to the life of the species in moderation are often satisfying far beyond their useful point: many conditions of great utility to the life of the species do not satisfy and may even annoy its members.
"The annoyers for any animal follow the rough rule that alterations of the animal's 'natural' or 'normal' structure—as by cuts, bruises, blows, and the like,—and deprivations of or interferences with its 'natural' or 'normal' activities,—as by capture, starvation, solitude, or indigestion,—are intolerable. But interference with the structure and functions by which the species is perpetuated is not a sufficient criterion for discomfort. Nature's adaptations are too crude" (Thorndike, 1911, pp. 245–246).

It is clear that Thorndike believed it possible to refer the subjective terms of everyday language to more objective, behavioral events, a conviction that is more explicit in the later work of Tolman. Thorndike outlined a method by which one could discover what is "satisfying" or "annoying" for an animal "in any given condition." One merely had to observe whether or not an animal, when given an opportunity, "does nothing to avoid, often doing such things as attain and preserve" the activity in question. For example, if a piece of fish is placed on the floor before a cat that hasn't eaten for some hours or before one that has just finished eating a large meal, the presence and vigor of a tendency to approach and preserve the activity of eating, should we try then to snatch the food away, is the objective definition of a "satisfier." Similar observations could be made of an animal placed on an electric grid through which an electric current is passing. The immediate escape and/or the effort that would be required to restrain the animal's vigorous attempt to escape give substantive meaning to the concept of an "annoying state of affairs" as one the animal "commonly avoids and abandons."

NEUROPHYSIOLOGICAL SPECULATION

We also see in this early search for a simple rule that would define all satisfiers and annoyers some skepticism about the possibility that only what enhances the possibility of survival should yield satisfaction and only what is injurious to the organism or the chance of species survival should produce discomfort. We shall find that this problem has continued to command attention of research workers and that, to date, no completely adequate solution to it has been presented.

Following the procedure that Thorndike suggested, we may discover that a given activity is "satisfying" (e.g., eating food when hungry) or "annoying" (e.g., standing on an electrified grid) through observation of an animal's behavior. This gives an empirical definition of what will function as a satisfier (a reward) or an annoyer (a punishment) in a learning experiment. But there remains the question *why? Why* is eating when hungry "satisfying" and getting shocked "annoying"? Like James before him and many others who were to become interested in *this* kind of question, Thorndike turned to neurophysiology for the answer. These were some of his earliest conjectures:

"Satisfaction and discomfort, welcoming and avoiding, thus seem to be related to the maintenance and hindrance of the life processes of the neurones rather than of the animal as a whole, and to temporary rather than permanent maintenance and hindrance. . . .

"The connections formed between situation and response are represented by connections between neurones and neurones, whereby the disturbance or neural current arising in the former is conducted to the latter across their synapses. The strength or weakness of a connection means the greater or less likelihood that the same current will be conducted from the former to the latter rather than to some other place . . .

"As a provisional hypothesis to account for what satisfies and what annoys an animal, I suggest the following:—

"A neurone modifies the intimacy of its synapses so as to keep intimate those by whose intimacy its other life processes are favored and to weaken the intimacy of those whereby its other life processes are hindered. The animal's action-system as a whole consequently does nothing to avoid that response whereby the life processes of the neurones other than connection-changing are maintained, but does cease those responses whereby such life processes of the neurones are hindered" (Thorndike, 1911, pp. 246–247).

These conjectures about connections between neurones and other neurones at their point of juncture, the synapse, illustrate the underlying conviction shared by many psychologists that psychology and neurophysiology should be continuous. It is an attitude already evident in James' discussion of possible neurophysiological concomitants of habit, volition, and emotion, and one shared by the great majority of subsequent workers in the field of animal behavior. This orientation derives from the close affinity of experimental psychology and the experimental science of physiology which was its forerunner early in the 19th century. In their quest for respectable explanatory concepts to take the place of "mentalis-tic entities" which raise the awkward and insoluble metaphysical problem of how "mind" and "body" can interact, the early behaviorists were little deterred by the fact that some of the neurophysiological conceptions which to them seemed firm ground were themselves incomplete, suppositional, and in need of substantially more empirical verification. Subsequent neurophysiological research has, in fact, shown the simple reflex-arc and telephone switchboard image of the brain's function to be incorrect (Pribram, 1960).

SUMMARY

Thorndike's work begins the experimental analysis of animal behavior. His record of the time taken to perform the correct response in succeeding trials defines the change in "strength" of the tendency to perform that response in that situation. His findings directed attention to the "trial-and-error" nature of problem solving in animals. The matter of central interest is the *assumed* change in the neural connection between stimulus and response. Running through his descriptions of what he had observed are references to the animal's hunger and obvious "discomfort" in the problem box, the dog's greater attention to the food and the assumption that the dog more than the cat "wants to get to the food and not out of the box," etc. *But these references to motivation are of secondary interest; they come in only as further descriptions of the initial condition of the animal.* That is, "discomfort plus sense impressions of the box" account for the initial responses which are called forth, one of which will be strengthened relative to the others by reward. Food is a "satisfier" or reward for a hungry animal. We can tell this by observing how hungry animals normally will behave in reference to food: they will approach it and will attempt to preserve the activity of eating. But again these observations, for Thorndike, only serve to define food as a potential *reward* for a hungry animal, i.e., something which will strengthen the connection between the stimulus, *which he conceived to be the impetus for action*, and some particular response. The animal is changed after a rewarded trial. Specifically, what has happened is that the connection between the test situation and a particular response is now stronger. It will be performed sooner on a later occasion in that situation. Finally, after repeated trials, it will become a habit and "rattle off" automatically, as James had put it.

## PAVLOV'S EXPERIMENTS ON SALIVARY CONDITIONING

### THE GUIDING ORIENTATION

The work on salivary conditioning in Pavlov's Petrograd laboratory gradually became known to American psychologists in the early decades of this century even though a full translation of his work, *Conditioned Reflexes*, was not available until 1927. Pavlov's orientation was soon shared by many psychologists who had begun to devote their energies to experimental analysis of animal behavior, for his conception of *conditioned responses* reinforced interest in the association between stimulus and response already deriving from Thorndike's work. We may capture the underlying assumption in the work, and the writings of behaviorists like Watson who were greatly influenced by it, from Pavlov's own words:

"Three hundred years ago Descartes evolved the idea of the reflex. Starting from the assumption that animals behaved simply as machines, he regarded every activity of the organism as a *necessary* reaction to some external stimulus, the connection between the stimulus and the response being made through a definite nervous path: and this connection, he stated, was the fundamental purpose of the nervous structures in the animal body. This was the basis on which the study of the nervous system was firmly established. . . .

"Our starting point has been Descartes' idea of the nervous reflex. This is a genuine scientific conception, since it implies necessity. It may be summed up as follows: An external or internal stimulus falls on some one or other nervous receptor and gives rise to a nervous impulse; this nervous impulse is transmitted along nerve fibers to the central nervous system, and here, on account of existing nervous connections, it gives rise to a fresh impulse which passes along outgoing nerve fibers to the active organ, where it excites a special activity of the cellular structures. Thus a stimulus appears to be connected of necessity with a definite response, as cause with effect. . . .

". . . The starting point for the present investigation was determined in particular by the study of two reflexes—the food or 'alimentary' reflex, and the 'defence' reflex in its mildest form, as observed when a rejectable substance finds its way into the mouth of the animal. As it turned out, these two reflexes proved a fortunate choice in many ways. Indeed, while any strong defence reflex, *e.g.*, against such a stimulus as a powerful electric current, makes the animal extremely restless and excited; and while the sexual reflexes require a special environment—to say nothing of their periodic character and their dependence upon age—the alimentary reflex and the mild defence reflex to rejectable substances are normal everyday occurrences.

"It is essential to realize that each of these two reflexes—the alimentary reflex and the mild defence reflex to rejectable substances—consists of two distinct components, a motor and a secretory. Firstly the animal exhibits a reflex activity directed towards getting hold of the food and eating it or, in the case of rejectable substances, towards getting rid of them out of the mouth; and secondly, in both cases an immediate secretion of saliva occurs, in the case of food, to start the physical and chemical processes of digestion and, in the case of rejectable substances, to wash them out of the mouth. We confined our experiments almost entirely to the secretory component of the reflex: the allied motor reactions were taken into account only where there were special reasons. The secretory reflex presents many important advantages for our purpose. It allows of an extremely accurate measurement of the intensity of reflex activity, since either the number of drops in a given time may be counted or else the saliva may be caused to displace a coloured fluid in a horizontally placed graduated glass tube. It would be much more difficult to obtain the same accuracy of measurement for any motor reflex, especially for such complex motor reactions as accompany reflexes to food or to rejectable substances. Even by using most delicate instruments we should never be able to reach such precision in measuring the intensity of the motor component of the reflexes as can easily be attained with the secretory component. Again, a very important point in favour of the secretory reflexes is the much smaller tendency to interpret them in an anthropomorphic fashion—*i.e.*, in terms of subjective analogy. Although this seems a trivial consideration from our present standpoint; it was of importance in the earlier stages of our investigation and did undoubtedly influence our choice" (Pavlov, 1927, pp. 4, 7, 17–18).*

### EXPERIMENTAL PROCEDURE

The animal was prepared for study by subjecting it to a minor operation which diverted the duct of the parotid gland so that saliva would flow through an opening in the cheek into a glass funnel cemented on the cheek to collect it. The dog was trained to stand quietly while loosely harnessed on a table in a room that had been insulated against distracting noises. The experimenter observed the dog from an adjoining room through a small window. Stimuli were presented to the dog by means of automatic devices.

* Extracts from I. P. Pavlov, *Conditioned Reflexes*, copyright 1927, are reprinted by permission of the Clarendon Press, Oxford.

## UNCONDITIONED REFLEX

Pavlov referred to innate or unlearned responses as *unconditioned reflexes*. For example:

"Food is suddenly introduced into the dog's mouth; secretion begins in 1 to 2 seconds. The secretion is brought about by the physical and chemical properties of the food itself acting upon receptors in the mucous membrane of the mouth and tongue. It is purely reflex" (Pavlov, 1927, p. 23).

## CONDITIONED REFLEX

He used the term *conditioned reflex* in reference to the salivary reaction elicited by some stimulus as a result of prior training, and he referred to an otherwise neutral stimulus which had taken on the power of eliciting a "conditioned" salivary response as a "signal." For example, if a dog was stimulated by the sound of a metronome for several seconds and then immediately presented with food on several occasions, the sound of the metronome alone would subsequently produce a salivary reaction:

". . . When the sounds from a beating metronome are allowed to fall upon the ear, a salivary secretion begins after 9 seconds, and in the course of 45 seconds eleven drops have been secreted. The activity of the salivary gland has thus been called into play by impulses of sound—a stimulus quite alien to food. The activity of the salivary gland cannot be regarded as anything else than a component of the alimentary reflex. Besides the secretory, the motor component of the food reflex is also very apparent in experiments of this kind. In this very experiment the dog turns in the direction from which it has been customary to present the food and begins to lick its lips vigorously" (Pavlov, 1927, p. 22).

In this example, "the sound of the metronome is the signal for food and the animal reacts to the signal in the same way as if it were food; no distinction can be observed between the effects produced on the animal by the sounds of the beating metronome and showing it real food" (p. 22). But, as Pavlov pointed out, even the response to sight of real food at a distance must be considered a conditioned reflex. In one experiment, several puppies were taken from their mother and fed only milk for a considerable time. When the puppies were a few months old, they were prepared for the conditioning experiment. Then the puppies were first shown some solid food—bread or meat—but no salivary secretion was evoked:

"It is evident, therefore, that the sight of food does not in itself act as a direct stimulus to salivary secretion. Only after the puppies have been allowed to eat bread and meat on several occasions does the sight or smell of these foodstuffs evoke the secretion" (Pavlov, 1927, p. 23).

## OTHER BASIC CONCEPTS

Pavlov identified the conditions under which new conditioned reflexes would be established. The external stimulus which was to become the "signal" in a conditioned reflex had to *precede* and *overlap* in point of time the action of an effective unconditioned stimulus. Thus the occurrence of food in the mouth following the onset of the ticking of a metronome is what *reinforced* the connection between the previously neutral ticking sound and the salivary response which is the unconditioned response to food itself. Pavlov also discovered that repeated application of a conditioned stimulus when not followed by the reinforcement of an unconditioned stimulus produced a progressive weakening of the reflex to the conditioned stimulus. This he referred to as *experimental extinction* of the conditioned reflex. Subsequent evidence of elicitation of the conditioned response after experimental extinction was called *spontaneous recovery*. Spontaneous recovery decreases after successive instances of experimental extinction.

## CONCEPTION OF BRAIN FUNCTION

Pavlov defended his use of the term "reflex" (which had previously been reserved for innate tendencies) in reference to these *acquired* connections between stimuli and responses in a way that further conveys to us the then current conception of how the brain functioned:

"We may take the telephone installation as an illustration. Communication can be effected in two ways. My residence may be connected directly with the laboratory by a private line, and I may call up the laboratory whenever it pleases me to do so; or on the other hand, a connection may have to be made through the central exchange. But the result in both cases is the same. The only point of distinction between the methods is that the private line provides a permanent and readily available cable, while the other line necessitates a preliminary central connection being established. In the one case the communicating wire is always complete, in the other case a small addition must be made to the wire at the central exchange. We have a similar state of affairs in reflex action. The path of the inborn reflex is already completed at birth; but the path of the signalizing reflex has still to be completed in the higher nervous centers. We are thus brought to consider the mode of formation of new reflex mechanisms. A new reflex is formed inevitably under a given set of physiological conditions, and with the greatest ease, so that there is no need to take the subjective states of the dog into consideration. With a complete understanding of all the factors involved, the new signalizing reflexes are under the absolute control of the experimenter; they proceed according to as rigid laws as do any other physiological processes, and must be regarded as being in every sense a part of the physiological activity of living beings" (Pavlov, 1927, pp. 24–25).

Here, it seemed to Pavlov and many early behaviorists, was a conception of how *new* connections were established within the cerebral hemispheres to explain how the simple innate reflex activities of the neonate might provide a foundation for the development of the complicated action patterns of later life. In Pavlov's words:

"Conditioned reflexes are phenomena of common and widespread occurrence: their establishment is an integral function in everyday life. We recognize them in ourselves and in other people or animals under such names as 'education,' 'habits,' and 'training': and all of these are really nothing more than the results of an establishment of new nervous connections during the post-natal existence of the organism. They are, in actual fact, links connecting definite extraneous stimuli with their definite responsive reactions. I believe that the recognition and the study of the conditioned reflex will throw open the door to a true physiological investigation probably of all the highest nervous activities of the cerebral hemispheres . . ." (Pavlov, 1927, p. 26).

We observe in Pavlov's work what we have already observed in Thorndike's early work: a restriction of interest to the change in response to some stimulus. For both men, the stimulus is explicitly accepted as the "cause" of the response. All other matters are considered in relation to what is assumed from the outset to be the basic issue—how the connection between a stimulus and a response is established and changed. All complex forms of behavior were to be conceived as long and integrated chains of *S-R* units which, after considerable prior experience, would rattle off as habitual action patterns.

SOME POTENTIALLY SIGNIFICANT
"ATYPICAL" RESULTS

In the background, however, are some observations made by Pavlov, the full importance of which could only be appreciated later when a broader conception of the basic characteristics of animal behavior had been accepted. We include a few of them here to foreshadow and give substance to some of the ideas of the "purposivists" which will soon be presented, and to forestall any oversimplified notions as to what is involved in establishing a conditioned salivary response, or for that matter, any kind of conditioned response:

"If the dog is mostly drowsy during the experiments, the establishment of a conditioned reflex becomes a long and tedious process, and in extreme cases is impossible to accomplish. The hemispheres [*of the cerebral cortex*] must, however, be free from any other nervous activity, and therefore in building up a new conditioned reflex it is important to avoid foreign stimuli which, falling upon the animal, would cause other reactions of their own. If this is not attended to, the establishment of a conditioned reflex is very difficult if not impossible. Thus, for example, if the dog has been so fastened up that anything causes severe irritation, it does not matter how many times the combination of stimuli is repeated, we shall not be able to obtain a conditioned reflex. . . . It is obvious that this must be so, when we consider that even in the most favorable circumstances the experimental conditions themselves will be sure to provoke numerous different reflexes—*i.e.*, will give rise to one or other disturbing activity of the hemispheres" (Pavlov, 1927, p. 28).

Perhaps even more to the point of our interest are some of Pavlov's comments about the effect of hunger on the setting up of a conditioned salivary response:

"Some unconditioned stimuli may be permanently weak, others may display a weakness which is only temporary—varying with the condition of the animal. As an example of the last we may take food. In the hungry animal food naturally brings about a powerful unconditioned reflex, and the conditioned reflex develops quickly. But in a dog which has not long [ago] been fed the unconditioned stimulus has only a small effect, and alimentary conditioned reflexes either are not formed at all or are established very slowly" (Pavlov, 1927, pp. 31–32).

Just as Thorndike had noted that food is a satisfier only for a hungry animal, Pavlov had found that food is an *effective* stimulus for the salivary reflex only when the animal is hungry.

Still further evidence to suggest the importance of the momentary goal-seeking tendency of the dog during the course of the conditioning experiment is contained in some further observations of Pavlov:

"In one case an experiment may be running quite smoothly, and suddenly all conditioned reflexes begin to fail, and finally disappear altogether. The dog is taken out, allowed to urinate, and then all the reflexes return to normal. Evidently stimulation of the center for micturition had inhibited the conditioned reflexes. Another example may be chosen in the season when the females are in heat. If the males have been housed near the females before the experiment, it is found that all their conditioned reflexes are inhibited in greater or less degree. It is obvious in this case that the inhibition derives from the sexual centres in the hemispheres. In face of such numerous potential sources of inhibition we see that our term of 'conditioned' reflexes is very appropriate. Yet these conditions can readily be controlled, and the disquieting factors can be eliminated" (Pavlov, 1927, p. 47).

To those who held the view that the association of stimulus and response was the prototype of all learning, and the elicitation of a response by a stimulus the model for explanation of all behavior, these "disquieting factors" were so many extraneous reflexes which needed to be controlled to show the lawfulness of behavior in the simplest case. Pavlov, in fact, referred to the inordinate strength of the "freedom reflex" in one dog which could not tolerate being harnessed on the platform.

To others struck with the purposive character of ordinary behavior, the ease of establishing a conditioned salivary response with a hungry dog but not with one recently fed, and the absence of a conditioned salivary response when the animal is apparently much more intent on doing something else like getting off the stand to urinate or reaching the females who are in heat seems to highlight the problem of motivation that was completely ignored by the early associationists.

## McDOUGALL'S CONCEPTION OF BEHAVIOR, PURPOSE, AND INSTINCT

William McDougall (1871–1938) was the most vigorous and popular critic of the mechanistic viewpoint which had been molded by the important experiments and arguments of Thorndike, Pavlov, and others who had adopted the stimulus-response mode of thought. In his *Introduction to Social Psychology* (1908) and again in his *Outline of Psychology* (1923) he developed fully the argument of those whose guiding idea from the past was "purpose." We shall briefly review his conception of behavior, ideas about purpose, and doctrine of instinct.

### THE MARKS OF BEHAVIOR

In contrast to "associationists," who focused attention upon the details of the relation between stimulus and response, the "purposivists" were concerned primarily with characteristics of the broad trend of behavior. McDougall, by 1923, had distinguished seven major characteristics or marks of the actions of living things:

1. *"A certain spontaneity of movement"* (McDougall, 1923, p. 44). Even if it is true that every action is a reaction to an external or internal stimulus, he argued, it is even more evident that a train of behavior once initiated often continues independently of the initiating stimulus:

"A momentary noise, such as the snapping of a twig, may send a rabbit scurrying to his burrow, put to flight a flock of birds, and throw the timid deer into the attitude and motions of alert watchfulness; or the taking of my hat from its peg, or a single word uttered, may provoke in my dog a violent and prolonged outburst of activity, a general excitement which may long persist and may break out afresh many times" (McDougall, 1923, p. 44).*

And here, he said, we have the second mark of behavior:

2. *"The persistence of activity independently of the continuance of the impression which may have initiated it"* (McDougall, 1923, p. 44). The particular movements, McDougall argued, are not predictable in detail, but the general character and final outcome of a long chain of movements are predictable under particular conditions. This, then, is a third feature of behavior:

3. *"Variation of direction of persistent movements"* (McDougall, 1923, p. 45). And, he went on, when a change in the situation is brought about by the sequence of movements, the train of activity typically ceases and gives way to a new and different train of activity. Thus:

4. *"Coming to an end of the animal's movements as soon as they have brought about a particular kind of change in its situation"* (McDougall, 1923, p. 45).

In connection with this end-situation, or goal, there is another distinguishing feature of behavior:

5. *"Preparation for the new situation toward the production of which the action contributes"* (McDougall, 1923, p. 45). The dog aroused by the master's

* Extracts from William McDougall, *Outline of Psychology*, copyright 1923, are reprinted by permission of Charles Scribner's Sons.

call from outside the door, McDougall argued, keeps looking at the door or scratching it—waiting for it to open.

McDougall called attention to the difficulty in trying to describe actions showing these five marks of behavior, particularly the latter three, in purely objective terms:

> "We naturally say that the animal is seeking and anticipating the new situation which is the natural end or goal of its behavior, and that it directs its actions toward this goal" (McDougall, 1923, p. 46).

For McDougall, this constant goal-directedness of behavior was to be taken as the manifestation of "mind" or "mental activity."

6. "*Some degree of improvement in the effectiveness of behavior, when it is repeated by the animal under similar circumstances*" (McDougall, 1923, p. 46) was listed as the sixth mark of behavior and further evidence of mental activity. This, of course, is what Thorndike had observed in his experiments. To complete the list and to distinguish the viewpoint of the purposivist from that of the associationist who focused attention upon reflex actions, as did Pavlov, McDougall listed:

7. "*A reflex action is always a partial reaction, but a purposive action is a total reaction of the organism*" (McDougall, 1923, p. 56, italics added). This called attention to evidence such as that considered earlier, when one of Pavlov's dogs, given the conditioned stimulus, failed to salivate until it was allowed to leave the table to urinate. For McDougall, this type of observation typified the point that purposive actions involve the whole organism and override the effects of particular momentary stimuli.

When movements of a human being exhibit these various characteristics, McDougall argued, "we do not hesitate to infer that they are purposive; by which we mean that they are made for the sake of attaining their natural end, and that this end is more or less clearly anticipated or foreseen" (McDougall, 1923, p. 47). He believed that the same inference could be made when the behavior of lower animals shows these characteristics, though he admitted that in lower forms of behavior there might be only a "vague anticipation of the goal" (McDougall, 1923, p. 48).

MC DOUGALL'S CONCEPT OF PURPOSE

His view is succinctly summarized in this paragraph:

> "Purposive action is, then, action that seems to be governed or directed in some degree by prevision of its effects, by prevision of that which still lies in the future, of events which have not yet happened, but which are likely to happen, and to the happening of which the action itself may contribute. *Purposiveness in this sense seems to be of the essence of mental activity;* and it is because all actions which have the marks of behavior seem to be purposive, in however lowly and vague a degree, that we regard them as expressions of Mind" (McDougall, 1923, pp. 48–49).

For McDougall, *purposive action* was clearly the most fundamental category for all psychology.

THE DOCTRINE OF INSTINCT

McDougall conceived "Instinct" as "native or inborn capacity for purposive action" and "Intelligence" as "the capacity to improve upon native tendency in the light of past experience" (McDougall, 1923, p. 71). The former and, to his way of thinking, the more fundamental problem had to do with the *ends* of behavior; the latter, the problem which interested the associationists, with the *means* of attaining the innately given ends. He referred to his theory that all animal and human behavior is purposive and that purposive action is fundamentally different from mechanical process as the *Hormic* theory. The Greek word "horme" means a vital impulse or urge to action.

An instinct was conceived as a mental structure, as "a mental disposition, whose nature is revealed to us in, and inferred by us from, the modes of behavior and of experience which it determines" (McDougall, 1923, p. 106). When an instinct is excited, he argued, the organism becomes completely absorbed in its endeavor towards the goal of the instinct. The absorption of the organism is complete. We call this "attention," and the characteristic form of excitement accompanying the arousal of a particular instinct, we call "emotion." In summary, McDougall stated:

> "We may therefore define "an instinct" as an innate disposition which determines the organism to perceive (to pay attention to) any object of a certain class, and to experience in its presence a certain emotional excitement and an impulse to action which find expression in a specific mode of behavior in relation to that object" (McDougall, 1923, p. 110).

Like James before him, McDougall considered the problem of conflict among simultaneously aroused instincts and concluded, as did James, that there would then be indecision, alternation of movements, etc., until one tendency finally came to dominate and govern the behavior of the whole organism. Instincts were not to be identified in terms of particular motor responses. Motor responses were considered mere instrumentalities in the service of any and all instincts. Rather, an instinct was to be defined "by the nature of the goal, the type of situation, that it seeks or tends to bring about, as well as by the type of situation or object that brings it into activity" (*ibid.*, p. 119). The quality of the emotion which accompanies the arousal of a particular instinctive impulse in man could be considered the clue as to what instinct is at work.

McDougall's list of the basic springs of action is not unlike that of James before him: Parental Instinct (which he considered the only altruistic factor in human nature), Instinct of combat (pugnacity), Curiosity, Food-seeking (including also thirst), Repulsion (avoidance, disgust), Escape (with the primary emotion of fear), Gregarious instinct, Primitive passive sympathy, Self-assertion, Submission, Mating, Aquisitive Instinct, Constructive Instinct, Instinct of Appeal.

The list is of less importance to us than the conception behind the list: actions are viewed as expressions of basic, innate, goal-directed tendencies. Here is the "Aristotelian" doctrine of instinct which Lewin (see Chapter 4) criticized so forcefully.

This, then, was the nature of the argument advanced by the "purposivists" as Thorndike, Pavlov, and others were introducing the methodological innovations needed to establish an experimental science of animal behavior. It is best summarized in a quotation from McDougall's 1908 book which he saw fit to reprint when he refined his conception in 1923:

". . . the instincts are the prime movers of all human activity; by the conative or impulsive force of some instinct . . . , every train of thought, however cold and passionless it may seem, is borne along toward its end, and every bodily activity is initiated and sustained. The instinctive impulses determine the ends of all activities and supply the driving power by which all mental activities are sustained; and all the complex intellectual apparatus of the most highly developed mind is but a means towards these ends, is but the instrument by which these impulses seek their satisfactions, while pleasure and pain do but serve to guide them in their choice of the means.

"Take away these instinctive dispositions, with their powerful impulses, and the organism would become incapable of activity of any kind; it would lie inert and motionless, like a wonderful clockwork whose mainspring had been removed or a steam-engine whose fires had been drawn. These impulses are the mental forces that maintain and shape all the life of individuals and societies, and in them we are confronted with the central mystery of life and mind and will" (McDougall, 1908, p. 44).*

## INSTINCT REPLACED BY THE CONCEPT OF DRIVE

In 1918, catching the merits of both sides of the argument between "associationists" and "purposivists," R. S. Woodworth published a little book entitled *Dynamic Psychology* which advanced certain general ideas that were to set the stage for more sophisticated theoretical analysis and experimentation with animals. It had long been Woodworth's view that what psychology needed was a "motivology." Influenced in part by Freud, he recognized the need for something more than the simple model of reflex-arc, yet something more defensible than the vague descriptive doctrine of instinct to account for "the springs of action." He urged the development of a "dynamic psychology" that would attempt "to gain a clear view of the action or process in the system studied both in its minute elements" (what the associationists were interested in) "and in its broad tendencies" (what the purposivists called attention to) (Woodworth, 1918, p. 35).

### THE PROBLEMS OF "MECHANISM" AND "DRIVE"

Woodworth distinguished two fundamental problems for such a psychology. They were, in fact, the two problems which those interested in *S-R* bonds, on the one hand, and those interested in instinct and purpose, on the other, had already given special emphasis. He referred to the first as the problem of "mechanism," and for the second, he coined the term "drive." The concept of drive was soon to replace the concept of instinct in the psychologist's glossary of important terms. Later still, the term "drive" was to take on a very precise theoretical meaning in the behavior theory of Clark L. Hull (1943). For these reasons, it is of some importance to appreciate Woodworth's original use of the term.

The problem of *mechanism* is the problem of how we do a thing; the problem of *drive* is "the problem of what induces us to do it":

* Reprinted from William McDougall, *An Introduction to Social Psychology*, 5th Edition, copyright 1908, by permission of Methuen & Co. Ltd.

"Take the case of the pitcher in a baseball game. The problem of mechanism is the problem how he aims, gauges distance and amount of curve, and coordinates his movements to produce the desired end. The problem of drive includes such questions as to why he is engaged in this exercise at all, why he pitches better on one day than on another, why he arouses himself more against one than against another batter, and many similar questions. . . .

"This distinction between drive and mechanism may become clearer if we consider it in the case of a machine. The drive here is the power applied to make the mechanism go; the mechanism is made to go, and is relatively passive. Its passivity is, to be sure, only relative, since the material and structure of the mechanism determine the direction that shall be taken by the power applied. We might speak of the mechanism as reacting to the power applied and so producing the results. But the mechanism without the power is inactive, dead, lacking in disposable energy" (Woodworth, 1918, pp. 36–37).*

DRIVE RELATED TO CONSUMMATORY REACTION

Taking a simple reflex as his example, Woodworth stated:

"The whole reflex mechanism, consisting of sense organ, sensory nerve, center, motor nerve, and muscle, can be thought of as a unit; and its drive is then the external stimulus" (Woodworth, 1918, p. 38).

But, he argued, if all behavior were a matter of simple reflex activity, we should not need to make the distinction between "drive" and "mechanism." The problem, as he saw it, was one of working up from the notion of "drive" as an external stimulus to "drive" as inner motive force. In this respect, Woodworth's conception resembles that advanced by Freud (1917), who argued that an instinct (or need) should be considered a persistent *inner* stimulus. But, as Woodworth continued the development of his conception of drive, it is clear that what he had in mind was (a) an activity in one neural mechanism, which (b) outlasted the external stimulus that had aroused it, and (c) in turn facilitated the action of some other neural mechanism. He illustrated his meaning in terms of the distinction between "preparatory" and "consummatory" reactions that had been advanced by the physiologist Sherrington. We may, in this connection, think back to the description of the behavior of Thorndike's cats as they struggle to get out of the box (preparatory reactions) and

* Excerpts from Robert Sessions Woodworth, *Dynamic Psychology*, copyright 1918, are reprinted by permission of Columbia University Press.

then finally get out to eat the food (consummatory reaction).

"A consummatory reaction is one of direct value to the animal—one directly bringing satisfaction—such as eating or escaping from danger. The objective mark of a consummatory reaction is that it terminates a series of acts, and is followed by rest or perhaps by a shift to some new series. Introspectively, we know such reactions by the satisfaction and sense of finality that they bring. The preparatory reactions are only mediately of benefit to the organism, their value lying in the fact that they lead to, and make possible, a consummatory reaction. Objectively, the mark of a preparatory reaction is that it occurs as a preliminary stage in a series of acts leading up to a consummatory reaction. Consciously, a preparatory reaction is marked by a state of tension.

"Preparatory reactions are of two kinds. We have, first, such reactions as looking and listening, which are readily evoked when the animal is in a passive or resting condition, and which consist in a coming to attention and instituting a condition of readiness for a yet undetermined stimulus that may arouse further response. The other kind consists of reactions which are not evoked except when the mechanism for a consummatory reaction has been aroused and is in activity. A typical series of events is the following: a sound or light strikes the sense organ and arouses the appropriate attentive reaction; this permits a stimulus of significance to the animal to take effect—for example, the sight of prey, which arouses a trend towards the consummatory reaction of devouring it. But this consummatory reaction cannot at once take place; what does take place is the preparatory reaction of stalking or pursuing the prey. The series of preparatory reactions may be very complicated, and it is evidently driven by the trend towards the consummatory reaction. That there is a persistent inner tendency towards the consummatory reaction is seen when, for instance, a hunting dog loses the trail; if he were simply carried along from one detail of the hunting process to another by a succession of stimuli calling out simple reflexes, he would cease hunting as soon as the trail ceased or follow it back again; whereas what he does is to explore about, seeking the trail, as we say. This seeking, not being evoked by any external stimulus (but rather by the absence of an external stimulus), must be driven by some internal force; and the circumstances make it clear that the inner drive is directed towards the capture of the prey.

"The dog's behavior is to be interpreted as follows: the mechanism for a consummatory reaction, having been set into activity by a suitable stimulus, acts as a drive operating other mechanisms which give the preparatory reactions. Each preparatory reaction may be a response in part to some external stimulus, but it is facilitated by the drive towards the consummatory reaction. Not only are some reactions thus facilitated, but others which in other circumstances would be evoked by external stimuli are inhibited. The dog on the trail does not stop to pass the time of day with another dog met on the way; he is too busy. When an animal or man is too busy or too much in a hurry to respond to stimuli that usually get responses from him, he is being driven by some internal tendency.

" 'Drive' as we have thus been led to conceive of it in the simpler sort of case, is not essentially distinct from "mechanism." *The drive is a mechanism already aroused and thus in a position to furnish stimulation to other mechanisms. Any mechanism might be a drive. But it is the mechanisms directed towards consummatory reactions—whether of the simpler sort seen in animals or of the more complex sort exemplified by human desires and motives—that are most likely to act as drives.* Some mechanisms act at once and relapse into quiet, while others can only bring their action to completion by first arousing other mechanisms. But there is no absolute distinction, and it will be well to bear in mind the possibility that any mechanism may be under certain circumstances the source of stimulation that arouses other mechanisms to activity.

"The inadequacy of either consciousness or the behavior psychology, in their narrower formulations at least, is that they fail to consider questions like these. Their advantage as against a dynamic psychology is that they are closer to observable phenomena. *Behavior we can observe, consciousness we can observe with some difficulty, but the inner dynamics of the mental process must be inferred rather than observed.* Even so, psychology is in no worse case than the other sciences. They all seek to understand what goes on below the surface of things, to form conceptions of the inner workings of things that shall square with the known facts and make possible the prediction of what will occur under given conditions. A dynamic psychology must utilize the observations of consciousness and behavior as indications of the "workings of the mind"; and that, in spite of formal definitions to the contrary, is what psychologists have been attempting to accomplish since the beginning" (Woodworth, 1918, pp. 40–43, italics added).

SELECTIVE AND CONTROL FUNCTIONS OF DRIVE

In another analogy offered to illustrate another important feature of the distinction he was trying to make between the problem of "mechanism" and the problem of "drive," Woodworth compared a living organism to a manufacturing plant. The big, complex plant is equipped to deal with many raw materials in a variety of ways to turn out a variety of finished products. It consists of a variety of specific mechanisms and special linkages between them that can be adapted to meet the "*demands*"

made upon it. New "*demands*" may arise which require the development of new mechanisms. An inventory of the total equipment of the plant would show that at any given time, only part of it is in action; the remainder is in a resting condition waiting some future demand. In terms more descriptive of what happens in a man or animal, the resting equipment is put into action by something acting on it like a stimulus:

"A man carries around with him a vast assortment of possibilities of action. The best conception of a 'possibility of action' is undoubtedly that of a neural mechanism so connected with other neural mechanisms and with the sense organs and muscles as to give the action when aroused. The question now before us is as to what determines which of the many possible actions shall become actual at a given time—as to how some are activated while others are left inactive—as to the arrangement by which drive is at any moment applied to certain mechanisms and not to others. It is a question of selection, management, and control" (Woodworth, 1918, p. 106).

In Woodworth's view, the fundamental thing in selection was the linkages, provided by nature or past experience, between actions and their exciting stimuli. "Actions are *reactions*" (p. 106), he asserted in general agreement with the position of the "associationists," but the mechanism for a reaction remains in a resting condition unless the stimulus awakening it occurs. "Thus," he argued, "the selective agency is very largely to be sought in the situation confronting the animal or man" (p. 107). Little more would need to be said regarding selection if each stimulus was simply joined to one reaction and if stimuli always came to the organism one at a time. But, he pointed out, neither of these things is true. The same stimulus may be linked to several different reactions, and the same act with several different stimuli. Furthermore, the situation presented to the organism at any time is nearly always very complex, presenting elements that are capable of acting as stimuli to many different reactions. Under these conditions, as for example in the case of Thorndike's cat in the puzzle-box, the problem of selection is much more complicated. The situation confronted by Thorndike's cat is complex to begin with:

". . . confinement, food outside, bars, spaces, and other points that can be attacked. The cat possesses a variety of reactions to this situation. It brings out its reactions in succession, attacking first one and then another part of the cage—or, as we might also say, responding first to one and then to another feature of the situation. Some one feature has an advantage over the others, and gets itself responded to first; but it loses its advantage when reaction to it does not bring the consummation at which the animal is aiming, and some other feature takes its turn as the stimulus evoking the next reaction. As related to the problem of selection, the cat's behavior shows: (1) several possible reactions to the same situation; (2) the occurrence of the reactions one at a time and not simultaneously; (3) an advantage of some of these over others; (4) that, on being thrown back defeated from one line of attack, the cat becomes responsive to other features which at first did not arouse reaction; and (5) that all of these reactions are of the nature of preparatory reactions, leading towards the consummation of escape and eating, and that without the drive towards this consummatory reaction, none of these particular preparatory reactions would be evoked, but still others, such as lying down and purring, might take their place. Simple animal behavior thus furnishes a fairly complete outline of the psychology of selection and control . . ." (Woodworth, 1918, pp. 107–108).

These, then, were some of the complications in behavior that seemed to require the notion of inner drive as a selecting agent:

1. Multiple possibilities of reaction to the same external stimulus.

2. The mutual exclusion of alternative (incompatible) responses.

3. The advantage possessed by one alternative reaction over others.

4. The shifting of advantage from one reaction to another.

In Woodworth's view, the last of these, a checking of the reaction which had the initial advantage in favor of another, was the most characteristic thing about the selectivity evident in Thorndike's cats and similar problem-solving behavior. It implied "a trend in a certain direction":

"When the cat, squeezing between the bars of a cage and meeting resistance, turns to some other point of attack, it is because, in common speech, it is trying to get out. It is this tendency towards escape and securing the food placed outside— whatever form the tendency may take in the cat's consciousness—that controls its reactions to the various features of the situation confronting it. Without this tendency, it would not attack the parts of the cage as it does, nor restlessly shift from one reaction to another till some one gave success. This tendency to escape is a mechanism aroused by the stimulus of confinement with food outside; once aroused and not immediately satisfied, it acts as a drive to the mechanisms that produce the various specific reactions of the cat to

different parts of the cage. It acts as a reinforcement to certain reactions, selecting them one after another; and it acts as an inhibition to other reactions, preventing the cat, for example, from reacting to a convenient spot by lying down there. The drive acts as a selective agency, as a controlling agency.

". . . A rat, on being first placed in a strange maze, reacts by exploration; after once finding food, it behaves in quite a different way, without random exploration but with urgency and haste. It has got a drive which eliminates otherwise preferred reactions and greatly increases the energy of behavior" (Woodworth, 1918, pp. 120–121).

In further development of his concept of "the selective force of drives," Woodworth extended it in illustrative examples to all phases of human behavior, particularly to observation and mental work. The stimuli observed and responded to in any given situation, he argued, are not determined only by such factors as the intensity of suddenness, and movement of a stimulus and preformed habits, but as much by the "interest" that is momentarily dominant. The question a person is trying to answer, for example, in part determines what stimuli he will observe and respond to. In this, Woodworth was referring to the very kind of issue with which we are concerned in this chapter, viz., the extent to which guiding ideas from the past account for the selectivity in the early observations of "associationists" and "purposivists" alike in their study of how animals behave.

MOTIVE: A TENDENCY TOWARDS
A CERTAIN END-REACTION

A few years later, in what became a very influential general introductory textbook for psychology, Woodworth (1921) developed further his idea that what the *S-R* type of psychology needed to be complete was some account of the inner tendency towards some end or goal which, together with momentary stimulation, determined the response. (See Figure 5.3.) This time, searching for the most appropriate term to use in reference to "*internal* states that *last* for a time and *direct* action" (p. 71), Woodworth favored the term "motive" instead of "drive":

" 'Purpose' is not the best general term to cover all the internal factors that direct activity, since this word rather implies foresight of the goal, which demands the intellectual ability to imagine a result not present to the senses. This highest level of inner control over one's behavior had best be left for consideration in later chapters on imagination and will. There are two levels below this. In

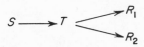

FIGURE 5.3   The stimulus-response scheme complicated to allow for the existence of *T*, an inner motive or tendency, which, aroused by an external stimulus, itself arouses a motor response. If the reaction-tendency were linked so firmly to a single response as to arouse that response with infallible certainty and promptness, then it would be superfluous for psychology to speak of a tendency at all. But often quite a series of responses, $R_1$, $R_2$, etc., follows upon a single stimulus, all tending toward the same end result, such as escape, and then the notion of "tendency" is by no means superfluous. *(From Woodworth, Psychology: A Study of the Mental Life, 1921, Holt, Rinehart and Winston, Inc., p. 71)*

the middle level, the individual has an inner steer towards a certain result, though without conscious foresight of that result. At the lowest level, we can scarcely speak of the individual being directed towards any precise goal, but still his internal state is such as to predispose him for certain reac-actions and against other reactions.

"The lowest level, that of organic states, is typi-fied by fatigue. The middle level, that of internal steer, is typified by the hunting dog, striving to-wards his prey, though not, as far as we know, having any clear idea of the result at which his actions are aimed. The highest level, that of con-scious purpose, is represented by any one who knows exactly what he wants and means to get.

"No single word in the language stands out clearly as the proper term to cover all three levels. 'Motives' would serve, if we agree at the outset that a motive is not always clearly conscious or definite, but may be any inner state or force that drives the individual in a given direction. 'Wants' or 'needs' might be substituted for 'motives,' and would apply better than 'motives' to the lowest of our three levels. 'Tendencies,' or 'tendencies to reaction,' carries about the right meaning, namely that the individual, because of his internal state, tends towards a certain action. 'Determining tend-encies' (perhaps better, 'directive tendencies') is a term that has been much used in psychology, with the meaning that the inner tendency determines or directs behavior. Much used also are 'adjustment' and 'mental set,' the idea here being to liken the individual to an adjustable machine which can be set for one or another sort of work. Often 'prepa-ration' or 'readiness for action' is the best expres-sion" (Woodworth, 1921, pp. 71–72).*

We do not review all these various possible terms to bewilder the reader but to give him an apprecia-

* Excerpts from Robert Sessions Woodworth, *Psy-chology, A Study of Mental Life*, copyright 1921, are reprinted by permission of Holt, Rinehart and Winston, Inc.

tion of the fact that around 1920, psychologists who generally favored the stimulus-response type of an-alysis were beginning to recognize the need of some-thing more in their explanations of behavior. The guiding concept, rather than the verbal label used to identify it, is important. We will see this concept reflected in many later developments:

"In general, a motive is a tendency towards a certain end-result or end-reaction, a tendency which is itself aroused by some stimulus, and which persists for a time because its end-reaction is not at once made. The end-reaction is not made at once because it can only be aroused by an ap-propriate stimulus, acting in conjunction with the motive. But the motive, persisting in its inner activity, facilitates reactions to certain stimuli and inhibits others. The reactions it facilitates are preparatory to the end-reaction, in that they pro-vide the necessary conditions for that reaction to occur, which means that they bring to bear on the individual the necessary stimulus which can arouse the end-reaction. The restlessness that characterizes an individual driven by an inner motive gives way to rest and satisfaction when the end-result is reached.

"Motives range from the primitive or primal, like hunger, to the very advanced, such as zeal for a cause. They range from the momentary, illus-trated by the need for more light in reading, to the great permanent forces of life, like *amour propre* and *esprit de corps*. But the permanent motives are not always active; they sleep and are awakened again by appropriate stimuli" (Woodworth, 1921, pp. 84–85, italics added).

A NEW FORMULATION: S-O-R

In acknowledging that "you cannot predict what response will be made to a given stimulus unless you know the organic state present when the stim-ulus arrives" (Woodworth, 1921, p. 74), Woodworth complicated the oversimplified *S-R* formula of the early associationists. His *S-O-R* conception, where *O* refers to the momentary characteristics of the behaving organism, paved the way for a more sophis-ticated experimental analysis of animal behavior which would begin to turn these general conjectures and speculations of the past into a more coherent conceptual scheme tied to the details of experimental observations.

THE PURPOSIVE BEHAVIORISM
OF EDWARD C. TOLMAN

AN ALTERNATIVE APPROACH

Like Thorndike, Pavlov, Watson, and most other experimental psychologists of the period, Woodworth found it useful *to think* in terms of stimulus, response, and plausible neurophysiological mechanisms within *O* when analyzing behavioral problems. Yet another equally objective orientation was suggested in Thorndike's initial attempt to state what it means to say that something is a "satisfier" or an "annoyer" in a learning experiment. (See p. 116.) He had stated in behavioral terms, even more clearly than in neurophysiological terms, what these mentalistic-sounding terms mean. This suggests an approach which might begin by translating the traditional language of private thoughts and feelings into a more objective behavioral language. Then the study of traditional psychological problems, now defined in terms of characteristics of observable behavior, might proceed, but without preconceptions or guesses as to the nature of underlying neurophysiological mechanisms.

As this kind of approach finally evolved in the type of behavioristic psychology advocated by Edward C. Tolman during the 1920's and 1930's, it constituted a viewpoint which agrees in principle with that of Freud and Lewin, but Tolman, working with animals, was forced to place much greater emphasis on the *empirical* definitions of his concepts. He acknowledged that neurophysiological processes underlie all behavior, but he did not think it the psychologist's job to discover what these processes and mechanisms are. He conceived the task of the psychologist to be that of analyzing the *observable* characteristics of behavior in relation to *observable* features of the environment and past experience. Once the important traditional issues of "purpose," "knowledge," "emotion," and so forth, had been identified with observable characteristics of behavior, experimental analysis could be undertaken to discover lawful relationships between observable antecedents and these characteristics of behavior. Then, instead of inventing hypothetical neurophysiological processes to account for what was hidden from the external observer, the psychologist could as easily invent hypothetical "psychological" variables and processes intervening between the observable stimulus and the response. But these *intervening variables*, invented to account for what was going on within the *O* of Woodworth's *S-O-R* formula, would be carefully defined in terms of observable antecedents and the behavioral effects which they produced and from which they were also to be inferred.

Much later, Tolman (1959) admitted that what he had always been trying to do was rewrite a commonsense mentalistic psychology in objective, behavior-

istic terms. We may, therefore, anticipate that his conception of what went on within the *O* to determine the response to some stimulus might come to resemble, in many ways, the Lewinian life space.

THE CONCEPT OF MOLAR BEHAVIOR

To begin with, Tolman, like McDougall, held that the interaction of an organism with its environment consists of more than molecular muscle movements and glandular secretions. This, after all, is what the term *response* must mean if one is to be completely consistent in the view that behavior is to be understood in terms of neural connections between *stimulus* and *response*. Tolman was interested in *molar* behavior—the broader adjustments and accomplishments of the whole organism in relation to its environment as distinct from the isolated bits that make it up, such as the salivary response to which Pavlov had directed attention. In Tolman's view, *molar* behavior was the proper subject matter of psychology and a subject matter which presented a new and unique set of properties all its own:

" 'A rat running a maze; a cat getting out of a puzzle box; a man riding home to dinner; a beast of prey stalking its quarry; a child hiding from a stranger; a woman doing her washing or gossiping over the phone; a pupil marking a mental test sheet; a psychologist reciting a list of nonsense syllables; myself and my friend telling one another our thoughts and feelings.' These are *behaviors*. And it is to be noted that in mentioning no one of them have I referred to, or, I blush to confess it, for the most part even known, what were the exact muscles and glands, sensory nerves and motor nerves involved. For these responses somehow had other sufficiently identifying properties of their own. And it is these other properties in which, as a behaviorist, I am interested" (Tolman, 1926, pp. 353–354).

TOWARDS A "PSYCHOLOGICAL" BEHAVIORISM

The two orientations in study of behavior differ most strikingly in the priority they give to translation of psychological problems into the language of neurophysiology. Physiological behaviorism (or physiological psychology) makes this the first order of business. It sometimes proceeds as if there were no other alternative. The other orientation, which has gained many adherents in recent years, particularly as the role of mathematics in behavioral science has become more fully appreciated, was then referred to by Tolman as *"psychological"* behaviorism. A "psychological" behaviorism proceeds from the vaguely defined concepts of common-sense towards better-defined concepts and the construction of a more coherent explanatory scheme than common sense provides, but without explicit reference to the neurophysiological mechanisms underlying the inferred "causal" variables. Tolman once stated the attitude of the "psychological" behaviorist as follows:

"Science demands, of course, in the end, the final development of both sorts of behaviorism. And the facts and laws of physiological behaviorism, when obtained, will presumably provide the explanation for the facts and laws of psychological behaviorism. But the psychological facts and laws are also to be gathered and established in their own right. *A psychology cannot be explained by a physiology until one has a psychology to explain.* Further, it appears to me that it is primarily the job of us psychologists, or at any rate of the "purer" among us, to gather the psychological facts and laws and to leave it to our less pure physiologically minded brethren to gather the neurological, glandular, and biochemical data which underlie such psychological facts and laws" (Tolman, [1936], 1951, p. 118, italics added).

Let us turn, then, to the systematic views which Tolman developed and also called a *"purposive behavorism,"* to highlight his conviction that goal-seeking was the most striking characteristic of *molar* behavior; and an *"operational behaviorism,"* to emphasize that even though subjective-sounding terms like "purpose" and "expectation" might be employed, his psychology would be "one which seeks to define its concepts in such a manner that they can be stated and tested in terms of concrete repeatable operations by independent observers" (Tolman, 1951, p. 115).

OPERATIONAL DEFINITION

An *operational definition* of a psychological concept is one which gives its meaning in terms of the concrete procedures (or operations) employed by the investigator to gain the empirical observations which justify its use. We met this issue in the last chapter in the criticism of some of the Lewinian concepts. The question raised was: How can you know, for example, when a person has an "intention" that is to be represented in the Lewinian life space as a tension system? Thorndike's method of defining "satisfying" and "annoying" states of affairs in objective, behavioral terms has already introduced us to some empirical, or operational definitions of psychological concepts. Thorndike specified what concrete observable events the terms "satisfier" and "annoyer" refer to and what we must do (the opera-

tions) to gain those observations. The task of stating clear and unambiguous operational definitions of terms became a matter of central interest to Tolman and to all subsequent scientific psychology. Tolman speaks for that period between World War I and World War II when psychologists interested in the broad problems of motivation and action began to realize that they could do more than speculate about the phenomena and offer discursive interpretations based on general observations. It was time to begin to study the phenomena empirically and to bring the guiding ideas of the past into contact with the details of observations of behavior made under controlled experimental conditions.

OBJECTIVE DEFINITIONS OF TRADITIONAL PSYCHOLOGICAL TERMS

We can gain an important insight into how Tolman went about the task of translating terms which had been traditionally used in reference to private feelings into objective behavioral terms from his analysis of emotion, which was published in 1923 during the formative years of his viewpoint. We have already seen how emotion is treated from the introspective side in the work of both James and Freud, and the James-Lange theory of emotion is an illustration of the attempt to get at the underlying neurophysiological mechanism. How does a *molar* behaviorist view the problem?

Tolman asked himself these kinds of questions: How can we study emotions in children or subhuman organisms who cannot introspect to report the nature of their feelings? Must the problem be written off as one that cannot be solved? Or is there a way of identifying what traditional language calls emotion in terms of something external, the behavior exhibited, the observable stimulus conditions, or the relation of the behavior to the stimulus conditions?

His attempt to answer these questions forced him to ask even more basic questions. Suppose we are dealing with an adult who tells us that he "feels" angry or afraid? If he is "feeling" angry and says so, how can we possibly know what he means? We seem to know something about him, for we act on the basis of this kind of information in everyday life. But how is it possible that we know what he means by "feeling angry"? His private feelings are not now, nor have they ever been exposed directly to our view. We cannot get inside him to see what it is he calls anger, as distinct from fear, love, or any other "emotion." How did the connection between some particular word, "anger," and some particular emotional state arise in the first place? The gist of Tolman's argument follows. It gives the basic logic of his orientation:

"Suppose we turn to the young child learning to talk. He hears the words 'anger' or 'angry' in certain situations. I behave angrily and he is told that I am 'angry.' The child cannot get inside me nor directly experience my anger. *The one thing therefore which can ultimately identify the word for him and give it its meaning, must be something about my behavior or the situation which produces it, or both* [italics added]. Or, again, he exhibits anger in his behavior and is told that he is 'angry.' Again *the word must get its identification and meaning from something about the behavior situation and from that only* [italics added]. But, perhaps you will say that since in this second case the child does directly experience his own conscious emotion, as such, this time the meaning of the word will get directly attached by him to the conscious state as such. Very good. But, be it noted, *this conscious state when you tell him that he is angry no more gets directly into you than did your conscious state, when you are angry, get directly into him* [italics added]. It was only because he was *behaving* in such and such a way that you knew that he was angry and told him so. You could not see his anger any more than he could see yours. In both cases it was only what may perhaps be called the *behavior analogue* of the emotion which was the common term mediating between you. *Hence, ultimately, it seems to be this behavior analogue which defines, if not your meanings for, at any rate your uses of, the word*" [italics added] (Tolman, 1923, p. 218).

Let us review the argument. Whatever the internal cues which lead a person (one of Freud's patients, for example) to say, "I feel angry," these cues are completely private. They have never been "observed" by any other person. How then can the expression "I feel angry" communicate anything to another person? We know it does. But *what* is communicated? When we consider the conditions under which the child must have first learned to use the word, we find that both child and parent observed the same external occurrence, the behavior of one or the other in some situation, to which the verbal response "anger" is made by the parent who already knows the conventional name for that kind of external occurrence. If, when the child is behaving in a way that the parent might call "angry," he, the child, also experiences some distinctive internal (and private) sensation, then both the common external cue (the observed behavior-situation) and the private internal cue (the sensations which James supposed comprise what is called the feeling) are

associated with the same verbal response, the word "angry":

"When an instrospecting organism reports that he is angry, what you thereby know and identify is not his conscious state as such (which never gets into you) but rather that he is in a condition which makes him likely to behave in a certain way. You know that he is probably going to behave in the way which determined your and his original acquisition of the word. Introspection, no more than any other type of behavior, can display directly to you the 'private contents' of the other person's mind" (Tolman, 1923, pp. 218–219).

The same argument can be applied to account for how one initially learns to use the words "fear" or "love" to label other emotional states. And for that matter, the same logic should apply to the original meanings of all other terms which in everyday language are commonly used to refer to private thoughts and feelings, viz., want, desire, idea, purpose, intention, expectation, satisfaction, and all the other terms which make up the familiar experiential language of motivation. In each case, if Tolman's logic is applied, *there must initially be some external behavioral referent for these terms*, common to child and parent, else how could individuals who have never had direct contact with each other's private thoughts and feelings have any notion of what the other means when he uses them?

A complication arises in that the adult who might report he "feels" angry does not necessarily behave like the "angry" child. We already know that much of psychoanalytic theory is an effort to account for the indirect and disguised expressions of the original infantile tendencies. Tolman acknowledged this kind of complication in stressing a second point about emotion:

"It is not the actually exhibited behavior, as such, which constitutes, behavioristically speaking, the emotion, but rather the *readiness* or *drive* for such a behavior—a readiness or drive which, as a result of acquired habits, may come to vent itself sometimes in quite other than the original, and initially defining behavior.* *But it is only through tracing these other behaviors back to the initial and defining behavior that we know what emotion they express* [italics added].
Footnote: * "The introspective speech reaction constitutes one of the most common of these acquired behaviors" (Tolman, 1923, p. 219).

In other words, the adult, responding to private internal cues (his inner sensations) which occurred originally in conjunction with certain external cues of a behavior-situation at which time the verbal label "anger" was first associated with both, may now say, "I feel angry" (meaning, "I am ready to strike out at someone") even though this particular response may now be inhibited in favor of some later-acquired response.

Tolman concluded from this type of analysis that the study of emotions in introspecting organisms has much the same status as its study in non-introspecting animals:

> "The introspective study of emotions no more than any other study of them gets directly at private mental contents. *For both types* [italics added] of study the emotion is in the last analysis defined, characterized, and identified in terms of a *behavior* situation" (Tolman, 1923, p. 219).

Tolman then analyzed the results of Watson's (1919) classic study of the unlearned emotions of infants which attempted to identify the stimuli and responses of fear, rage, and love. (See Table 5.1.) How is it, he asked, that Watson or anybody else could recognize these as "fear," "rage," and "love"?

"The distinguishing characteristics hardly seem to lie in the individual stimuli as such. It would be no outrage, to my conception of fear, at least, if none of the listed stimuli had actually happened to evoke fear, or indeed, if other quite different stimuli had evoked it. If the dropping of the child had caused not fear but anger, I should have felt no particular surprise. Indeed the same may be said for any of the other stimuli. It can hardly then be the stimuli as such that defined the emotions. But neither does it seem to have been the responses, *merely as such*, that defined them. Sudden catching of the breath, random clutching (i.e., the grasping reflex), blinking of eyelids, puckering of the lips, crying, flight and hiding, these, just as such and such muscle contractions, do not define fear. Catching of the breath, merely as catching of the breath, grasping, merely as grasping, blinking, merely as blinking, puckering, merely as puckering, crying, merely as crying, running away, merely as running away, and hiding, merely as hiding, might severally occur in any one of numerous *non*-fear situations. When, however, we take them all altogether and evaluate them not merely as involving such and such muscle contractions, but rather as obviously calculated to produce, to be

TABLE 5.1

Tolman's summary of the Watsonian definition of emotions in terms of particular eliciting stimuli and particular characteristics of response (From Tolman, 1923)

### FEAR

| *Stimuli* | *Responses* |
|---|---|
| Suddenly removing all means of support (dropped from the hands to be caught by an assistant). | Sudden catching of breath. |
| Loud sound. | Clutching (grasping reflex). |
| Sudden push or slight shake (when just falling asleep or just waking up). | Blinking of eyelids. |
| Sudden pulling of supporting blanket (when just going to sleep). | Puckering of lips. |
|  | Crying. |
|  | In older children, possibly flight or hiding (not yet observed by Watson as original reactions). |

Any or all of the responses can apparently appear for any one of the stimuli (the account is perhaps not altogether clear upon this point). The grasping reflex, however, invariably appears when the child is dropped.

### RAGE

| *Stimuli* | *Responses* |
|---|---|
| Hampering the infant's movements, i.e., holding of face or head; or holding arms tightly to sides. This "is the factor which apart from all training brings out the movements characterized as rage." | Crying. |
|  | Screaming. |
|  | Body stiffening. |
|  | Fairly well coördinated slashing or striking movements of the hands and arms. |
|  | Feet and legs drawn up and down. |
|  | Holding breath. |
|  | In older children, kicking, slapping, pushing. |

### LOVE

| *Stimuli* | *Responses* |
|---|---|
| Stroking or manipulation of an erogenous zone. | If the infant is crying, crying ceases. |
| Tickling. | A smile appears. |
| Shaking. | Attempts at gurgling and cooing. |
| Gentle rocking. | In slightly older children, the extension of the arms. |
| Patting. |  |
| Turning on stomach across attendant's knee. |  |

appropriate for, such and such a reaction back upon the stimuli which produced them, then they *do* indicate fear.

"It is not a response, *as such*, nor a stimulus situation, *as such*, that constitutes the behavior definition of an emotion, but rather the response as affecting or calculated to affect the stimulus situation" (Tolman, 1923, pp. 222–223).

The responses listed under fear in Table 5.1 seemed to Tolman "to be of a nature to *protect* the organisms from exciting stimuli of one sort or another" (p. 223). Those listed under anger all seemed to him "appropriate for another type of back action upon the exciting stimulus, viz: the destruction of the latter" (p. 223). In one respect, then, fear and anger are alike:

"Fear and anger are alike in that they both cause the removal of the stimulus, but they are different in that whereas the behavior situation which defines fear is one in which the organism is merely protected against, the behavior situation which defines anger is primarily one in which the stimulus is destroyed. The one operates by leading away from, the other by leading towards and destroying" (Tolman, 1923, p. 223).

And what of the responses listed under love in Table 5.1? They all seem appropriate for the further continuation of the stimulus:

"The stopping of crying, smiling, cooing, gurgling, the stretching out of the arms are one and all, given a social environment, responses calculated either to leave the stimulating condition undisturbed or actually to reach out and get more of it" (Tolman, 1923, p. 223).

Tolman asserted that all response tendencies fell into one of two classes, "of 'tending to remove' or of 'tending to continue and get more of' the stimulus" (p. 224). Fear and anger fall in the former class and love in the latter.

This is probably enough to illustrate how Tolman searched for the defining characteristics of the behavior-situations which provide the initial basis for the labeling of "feelings." In the case of each of the three emotions fear, anger, and love, he said:

". . . It appears that the thing which is characteristic and which defines it for us as an instance of such and such an emotion is not the nature of the individual stimuli, as such, nor the nature of the individual responses, as such, but rather the gross *behavior result*, i.e., the nature of the back-action of the responses upon the stimuli" (Tolman, 1923, p. 224).

We can clarify what Tolman was getting at in this analysis of emotion by recalling an occasion on which we ourselves have said something like this: "Look out, that cat is *angry!*" or, "The chipmunk is *frightened*," or, "Our dog *loves* children." What seems to justify our use of these terms? Is it not the behavior of the animal in relation to some object in its immediate environment that provokes these verbal reactions? The cat with its upraised paw *as if* about to strike the youngster who is pulling its tail; the chipmunk poised *as if* to scamper away and up the nearest tree as our footsteps rustle the leaves on the ground; the dog, with tail wagging and pulling at the leash *as if* to jump up to lick the faces of the children just back from school. We infer from our observation of the animal's behavior in relation to some object in its environment that its feelings (we naïvely assume that it has feelings) must correspond to our own when we strike out at some irritant, run away from some threat, or greet a returning friend. What is more, our attribution of conscious feelings to other human beings involves no less of an inference, as Freud pointed out. (See p. 55.) In every case of this sort, Tolman would say, *the mentalistic-sounding terms of our everyday language must refer initially, and implicitly in our use of them, to some observable characteristics of a defining behavior-situation.*

Thus, it would seem that we can literally turn the problem of motivation as common sense understands it *inside-out* by rediscovering the original behavioral referents of familiar emotional and motivational terms. Isn't this, after all, what Thorndike did in defining what he meant by "a satisfying state of affairs" and "an annoying state of affairs"? Something is called satisfying in everyday discourse if it is the kind of thing we like to do, that is, if it is something we *would* do if given the opportunity—like eating when hungry. Something is called annoying in everyday language if it is the kind of thing we dislike staying in the presence of, that is, if it is something we *would* get away from quickly if given the opportunity—like a buzzing bee.

This initial step will get the problems outside, where they can be studied objectively. After this step is accomplished, the characteristics of behavior in relation to features of the environment, past experience, and organic state can be subjected to systematic experimental analysis to discover what factors affect the behavior in question. We may anticipate that the initial, merely descriptive concepts of common sense will soon give way to more useful, explanatory concepts as more precise and systematic observations are made.

In a general way, we have outlined the strategy which Tolman also employed in his analysis of the mentalistic-sounding concept of "purpose," which is so deeply embedded in intuitive explanations of behavior. Tolman identified the characteristics of behavior which give empirical meaning to this term, and then he undertook a systematic study of "purposive behavior." In the course of his work, he came upon other terms like "memory," "knowledge," "expectation," which refer to "mental" states in common-sense use. His big problem was to identify, as Thorndike had, with "satisfaction" and "annoyance," the features of behavior to which these traditional terms refer. Once the problem involved in the common use of the term had been turned *inside-out* and conceived as a behavioral problem, the task of experimental analysis and the invention of more useful concepts and explanatory schemes could follow.

MENTALISM VERSUS BEHAVIORISM

In the very first chapter of his major systematic work, *Purposive Behavior in Animals and Men* (1932), Tolman gives a succinct statement of the objective orientation which had replaced the subjective orientation of traditional psychology and common sense:

"The mentalist is one who assumes that 'minds' are essentially streams of 'inner happenings.' Human beings, he says, 'look within' and observe such 'inner happenings.' And although sub-human organisms cannot thus 'look within,' or at any rate cannot report the results of any such lookings within, the mentalist supposes that they also have 'inner happenings.' The task of the animal psychologist is conceived by the mentalist as that of inferring such 'inner happenings' from outer behavior; animal psychology is reduced by him to a series of arguments by analogy.

"Contrast, now, the thesis of behaviorism. For the behaviorist, 'mental processes' are to be identified and defined in terms of the behaviors to which they lead. 'Mental processes' are, for the behaviorist, naught but inferred determinants of behavior, which ultimately are deducible from behavior. Behavior and these inferred determinants are both objectively defined types of entity. There is about them, the behaviorist would declare, nothing private or 'inside.' Organisms, human and sub-human, are biological entities immersed in environments. To these environments they must, by virtue of their physiological needs, adjust. Their 'mental processes' are functionally defined aspects determining their adjustments. For the behaviorist all things are open and above-board; for him, animal psychology plays into the hands of human psychology" (Tolman, 1932, p. 3).

THE DESCRIPTIVE PROPERTIES OF MOLAR BEHAVIOR

Shortly after Tolman advanced the analysis of emotion which we have considered in order to become familiar with his point of view, he began to work out behavioristic definitions of terms like "purpose" and "ideas" which were rooted in psychology's mentalistic tradition. Running counter to the *S-R* orientation which had already taken hold as the dominant viewpoint of American psychology, he was feeling his way towards an acceptable method of dealing with traditional psychological concepts and problems within the framework of an objective psychology. His discussion of "purpose" and "ideas" refers to the experimental observations of Thorndike and other psychologists who, like himself, had begun to accumulate evidence concerning the behavior of rats in mazes of all sizes and descriptions.

MOLAR BEHAVIOR IS PURPOSIVE

Like McDougall, Tolman was convinced that an adequate description of what an animal is doing must always make reference to some end (goal) towards which or away from which the animal is, at the time, moving. He put the idea this way:

"When an animal is learning a maze, or escaping from a puzzle box, or merely going about his daily business of eating, nest building, sleeping, and the like, it will be noted that in all such performances a certain *persistence until* character is to be found. Now it is just this *persistence until* character which we will define as purpose. . . .

". . . When one observes an animal performing, one knows nothing concerning possible 'contents' in the latter's 'mind' and to assume such contents seems to us to add nothing to one's description. One does, however, see certain aspects of the behavior itself which are important and for which the term 'purpose' seems a good name. And there is no additional explanatory value, we should contend, in making the further assumption that such responses are accompanied by a mentalistic something, also to be known as 'purpose.'

"It is, then, the argument of this paper that wherever the purely objective description of either a simple or complex behavior discovers a *persistence until* character there we have what behaviorism defines as purpose. And upon further analysis, we discover that such a description appears whenever in order merely to *identify* the given behavior a reference to some 'end object' or 'situation' is found necessary" (Tolman, 1925a, pp. 37–38).

Tolman called attention to the persistent struggles of Thorndike's cats in the puzzle boxes as an example of how complete description of their actions requires some reference to the confinement *from which* the animal is struggling to escape or to the food *towards which* it struggles. For the struggling, as such, persists only until the end or goal is attained. Molar behavior is characteristically goal-seeking. This, for Tolman, was one of its major descriptive properties:

> "To sum up, then, whenever, in merely describing a behavior, it is found necessary to include a statement of something either *toward which* or *from which* the behavior is directed, there we have purpose" (Tolman, 1925a, p. 39).

Tolman distinguished this strictly behavioristic conception of purpose from that advanced by McDougall, for whom "purpose" seemed an introspectively defined, subjective entity much as it is for common sense. Tolman had been greatly influenced by the philosopher R. B. Perry (1918), who was the first to suggest the possibility of a completely objective, behavioristic definition of purpose, a term which had so many controversial philosophical and theological overtones. He made his position particularly clear in a talk once given to a group of philosophers who, in the days of the behavioristic revolution within psychology, must have been quite surprised to hear a psychologist who called himself a "behaviorist" even mention the word "purpose." Following a description of the Thorndike experiments (see p. 113) which he used to exemplify the purposive character of behavior, Tolman said:

> "But here a 'mentalist' may perhaps protest. 'Very true,' he may say, 'trial and error *do* exhibit purpose. But purpose is a mental phenomenon, and if you admit it, you are ceasing to be a behaviorist.' 'Not at all,' I must reply. 'The purposes we have here observed, these purposes which exhibit themselves in trial and error, these *persistences until*, are not mentalistically defined entities at all, but behavioristically defined ones.' To a mentalist, a purpose, if he sticks to his fundamental postulates, must be essentially an introspectively get-at-able affair. The purpose he means must be, in the last analysis, a 'content,' 'process,' or 'function' which is found introspectively within his or somebody else's *consciousness*. The purposes we have been pointing to, on the other hand, are different. They are discovered by looking *at* another organism. One observes that the latter *persists* through trials and errors *until* a given *end* is *got to* or *from*. Such a purpose is quite an objective and purely behavioristic affair. It is a descriptive feature immanent in the character of the behavior *qua* behavior. It is not a mentalistic entity supposed to exist parallel to, and to run along side of the

behavior. It is *out there in* the behavior; of its descriptive warp and woof" (Tolman, 1926, p. 355).

DOCILITY, THE DEFINING CHARACTERISTIC OF PURPOSIVE BEHAVIOR

By the time of his major work, *Purposive Behavior in Animals and Men* (1932), Tolman had come to recognize the full importance of another feature *out there* in the behavior of Thorndike's cats which provided the ultimate defining characteristic of purpose *in* behavior: the fact that on successive occasions in the problem situation the animal tended to *select* sooner and sooner the act which got it out of the box and to food most easily and quickly. Here again Tolman followed Perry (1918) in citing the *docility* of behavior as the primary justification for describing it as purposive or goal-seeking. By docility is meant the fact that behavior is teachable; it is tractible in relation to results or consequences. Tolman realized that continuation of variable behavior in some problem situation can be legitimately described as having the character of "persistence until" a goal is reached only because on future occasions the animal is observed to favor the actions which have led on most easily and quickly to that goal in the past:

> "It is only when such variations and such persistencies have implicit within them the further character of a resultant selection of the more efficient of the tries (i.e., *docility*) that they have their usual significance and are to be said to define purpose" (Tolman, 1932, p. 16 fn).

In summary, it is the observed tendency of behavior to persist through trials and errors until some goal is reached together with the subsequent selectivity of the most efficient of previous tries which gives the term "purpose" a completely objective meaning. When in everyday terms we say, "His purpose is to _____" or "His intention is to _____," we must mean that the person to whom we refer is in a state of readiness to persist in actions until some goal is attained and to select the most efficient means to that end. To avoid the traditional mentalistic connotations of these terms "purpose" and "intention," Tolman adopted one of the terms Woodworth had employed (see p. 125) to refer to an animal's state of readiness for activity directed towards some goal. He referred to this state of readiness as a "demand for the goal-object." He considered the demand for a goal-object to be one of the immediate determinants of an animal's behavior, a variable within the $O$, which intervened between the immediate environmental stimulus and the response.

## MOLAR BEHAVIOR IS ALSO COGNITIVE

Tolman argued that molar behavior has a second important descriptive property. It exhibits not only "purpose," but also "knowledge." It is both purposive *and* cognitive. Molar behavior imputes (or attributes) certain characteristics to the environment in which it occurs.

Consider again the behavior of Thorndike's cats struggling to get out of the problem box. Of what does the struggling consist? The animals exhibit specific patterns of biting, chewing, and clawing at various features of the box. The topography of this behavior is quite different from that of a rat observed running from the starting box to the end box of a maze. The latter confronts open pathways which call for running and choice points which call for a turn this way or that, instead of bars to be chewed and levers to be clawed at. Similarly, a man hurrying home from his place of business to dinner has the matter of locating his car in a parking lot and then of coping with the gadgets which make the car go, as well as the various stop signs and turns in the highway along the way. Molar behavior, argued Tolman, always involves a specific pattern of *commerce with environmental objects* which define the means to a goal. And when Thorndike's cats sooner and sooner perform the "correct" response instead of the many other responses they had made on earlier trials, this constitutes evidence of what everyday language might refer to as "knowledge" or "ideas" out there *in* the behavior itself. Molar behavior, Tolman asserted, *expresses* immanent cognitions as to the nature of the environment in which the getting on to some goal occurs.

His favorite illustration of what it means to say that an animal's behavior "imputes" certain characteristics to the environment or, as he was later to say, that an animal's behavior is in part determined by its cognitive "expectations" is this reference to an actual experimental observation:

"For example, consider a rat which has completely learned a maze, so that when put in at the entrance, he dashes through like a shot, turning here, there, and yonder, entering no blinds and arriving at the food box in only some four or five seconds from the start. Suppose, now, one of the alleys be considerably shortened between trials. What happens? On the trial after, the animal runs kerplunk into the new end of the alley. In short,

he acts as if the old length of alley were going to be still present. His behavior postulates, expects, makes a claim for that old length" (Tolman, 1926, p. 356).

It is clear that "ideas," "memory," "knowledge," "expectations"—all these mentalistic-sounding terms —were conceived by Tolman as purely empirical aspects of behavior:

"To say that an animal remembers 'such and such' is merely another way of saying that his present behavior can be shown to be causally dependent upon 'such and such.' The animal's going-to-or-from an object, not immediately present, does, to be sure, imply that his behavior is then and there a function of a now absent object. But this tempero-functional dependence of behavior is a purely objective fact and all that need be meant by memory. But such memory, like the 'purpose' itself, is but another objective aspect of the behavior.

"We conclude, then, that whenever in order to describe a behavior our description has to include that it is a function of an object toward or from which the animal is going, there we have *purpose*. And whenever, at the same time, this object is nonpresent to sense, there we also have memory" (Tolman, 1925a, p. 40).

These, then, were the two essential descriptive characteristics of molar behavior which, in Tolman's view, define the beginning point for experimental analysis: behavior expresses both purpose (goal-seeking) and possession by the animal of some kind of "knowledge" or "cognitive map" of its environment. Putting the matter pictorially, Tolman once likened the environment to a multidimensional spider's web radiating out from the behaving organism in many directions. The far ends of the threads terminated in to-be-sought goals or to-be-avoided disturbances. "Environmental objects and situations," he contended, "are responded to and cognized only in their character of providing bridges or routes along these threads" (Tolman, 1926, p. 358).

We can see already that Tolman's inclination was to view behavior much as Lewin did. And we can remind ourselves of the reason for this coincidence. Both men had begun their analyses with the everyday "mentalistic" language employed to explain behavior rather than with an initial presumption that their task was to translate all psychological problems into terms of neural connections between stimuli and responses. Where Lewin, concerned with human subjects, had immediately felt the need for a more systematic and coherent scheme of interrelated concepts than everyday language and intuition provide, Tolman, having to work from the outside in, so to speak, had to labor first to anchor outcast terms like "purpose" and "knowledge" in the external characteristics of an animal's behavior. Then, believing as most psychologists who analyze the behavior of animals do, that the same fundamental principles will one day explain the behavior of both man and lower animals, he could devote attention to experimentation with animals to discover the causes or antecedents of the "demands for goal objects" and "cognitive expectations" which seemed to be expressed in behavior. He once said:

"I believe that everything important in psychology (except perhaps such matters as the building up of a superego, that is everything save such matters as involve society and words) can be investigated in essence through the continued experimental and theoretical analysis of the determiners of rat behavior at a choice point in a maze" (Tolman, 1938, p. 34).

## ILLUSTRATIVE EXPERIMENTAL METHODS AND EVIDENCE

It is time we turned to the new kinds of experimental observations which Tolman considered in developing these ideas. It would be incorrect to assume, as the presentation of his views so far may have suggested, that he had only the observations of Thorndike and more general considerations to go on. Woodworth's distinction between the "problem of mechanism" and the "problem of drive" had set the stage for a decade of experimental interest (during the 1920's) in the effects of conditions like "hunger," "thirst," and "sexual arousal" on animal behavior. New methods of study were being introduced to study the influence of "physiological drives" *per se*. In addition, there were new explorations by Tolman and his co-workers of the effects of variations in hunger and in the type of reward offered in maze learning experiments with rats. The traditional speculative idea of purpose had finally worked its way from the sidelines into the mainstream of experimental research with animals. The dialogue between theoretical concepts and experimental facts was to begin. The new experimental problems which arose almost immediately attest the fruitfulness of Tolman's conceptual analysis. His work helped to move research on animal learning and behavior to a higher level of conceptual sophistication and paved the way for the construction and experimental test of more elaborate theories of animal behavior.

THE BEHAVIORAL EFFECTS OF INTERNAL "DRIVES"

Examples of the kind of research which began to reflect the impact of the arguments advanced by "purposivists" were investigations of the sort initiated by Richter (1922), which began to explore the relationship between the normal hunger cycle in an animal and the general level of its "spontaneous" activity. Richter first used cages mounted on tambours which enabled him to record every "spontaneous" movement an animal made, and later (1927) he employed revolving activity wheels for continuous measurement of the cycles of an animal's general activity over days at a time. He was interested in motility that could not be attributed to the action of some immediate external stimulus and the discovery of its internal physiological cause. He discovered that cyclical changes in hunger, thirst, and sexual arousal were reflected in cyclical changes in "spontaneous" activity. The cycle of activity in the case of hunger corresponded to the previously discovered temporal cycle of contractions in the stomach wall which was, presumably, the internal impetus to activity.

In 1924, Moss used Woodworth's term "drive" in reference to the strength of an animal's impulse to seek food. This impulse, he found, could be manipulated by starving the animal for a certain number of hours and measured in terms of the amount of resistance (electric shock) the animal would overcome to get to food. This usage of the term "drive" in reference to bodily states which could be experimentally controlled and which influenced activity level and/or the tendency to seek some type of goal-object, was adapted by Richter, Tolman, and others, including Warden and Jenkins, who perfected the Columbia Obstruction Method (see Figure 5.4) as a standard device for measuring "motivation" in animals. By 1930, Warden and his co-workers had accumulated a good deal of empirical information concerning an animal's willingness to cross an electric grid (the obstruction) to get to an "incentive" like food, water, or an animal of the opposite sex as a function of the number of hours it had been deprived of that type of incentive. Figure 5.5, taken from Warden's book, *Animal Motivation Studies* (1931), illustrates the kind of experimental evidence that animal psychologists had begun to accumulate during the 1920's in reference to what Woodworth had called the separate "problem of drive."

Usage of the term "drive" was not always con-

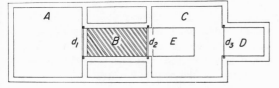

FIGURE 5.4   Diagram of floor plan of the obstruction box: A, entrance compartment; B, obstruction compartment; C, D, divided incentive compartment; E, release plate; $d_1$, manually operated door of entrance compartment; $d_2$, automatic door (operated by release plate) between two divisions of incentive compartment (From Warden, Animal Motivation, New York, Columbia University Press, 1931, p. 18)

sistent, nor has it been even in recent years. Nevertheless, this term did replace the older and vaguer one of "instinct" when psychologists made reference to changes in activity or goal-seeking tendencies that were brought about by depriving an animal of food, or of water, or by the estrus cycle in female animals. It came to be generally accepted that certain internal physiological conditions produced by deprivation would initiate general or exploratory activity (when the relevant goal object or "incentive" was absent) and strengthen the tendency to get to the goal object when it was present. Hanging on to one of the implications in the old doctrine of instinct, *Tolman (1922) had argued that these internal drives innately define the ends towards which an* animal's behavior is directed in the sense that each particular physiological disequilibrium—for example, the one produced by water privation—can only be "satisfied" by a certain type of goal object. Hence, when a particular physiological drive arose, behavior would persist until that particular kind of satisfying condition had been brought about through the appropriate type of consummatory activity. He argued that this scheme provided a better basis for naming drives in terms of the consummatory behaviors (goals) they required, and which could be observed, rather than in terms of internal physiological conditions which were then (and still are) matters calling for experimental research. Freud, we recall, had presented a similar argument in his 1917 paper on instinct (or need).

MOST RELEVANT MAZE EXPERIMENTS

We shall examine several studies of learning and performance of rats in mazes instead of the various empirical studies of animal drives which employed one or another of the newly introduced devices because behavior of a rat in the maze was the focal point of Tolman's theoretical interest. The details of a rat's activities in a maze in relation to its past experience, variations in the type of reward or incentive offered, and variations in drive conditions concretizes the relatedness of the purposive and cognitive characteristics of molar behavior more clearly than the studies with activity wheels and obstruction boxes. It was Tolman's conceptual analysis of maze behavior that showed how intertwined the problem of learning and the problem of motivation really are, so much so that the two problems had not been distinguished by those who had begun their work dominated by the ideas of association and reflex until new techniques were introduced by those with the "purposivist" orientation.

As an example of the type of maze employed in the studies which interested Tolman, we shall consider the one shown in Figure 5.6. This is a 14-unit T maze which was employed by Tolman and Honzik (1930) in several experiments which summarize the kinds of experimental findings which had appeared in a number of earlier studies by co-workers of Tolman. This maze is called a 14-unit T maze because each choice point, if considered separately, has the shape of the letter T. The animal approaches the choice point along the stem of the T and then turns either to the left or to the right into one of the arms of the T. Either turn may be "correct" in the sense of being part of the path which leads on

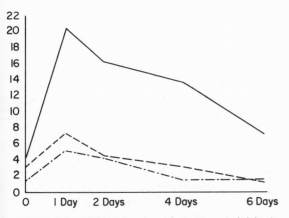

FIGURE 5.5   Average number of crossings (solid line), contacts (dot-dash line), and approaches (dash line) for each interval of water deprivation (From Warden, Animal Motivation, New York, Columbia University Press, 1931, p. 107)

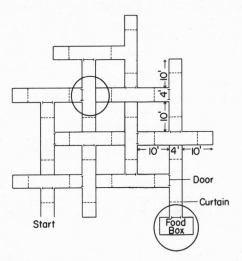

FIGURE 5.6   Plan of maze: 14-unit T-alley maze (*From Elliott, 1928, p. 20*)

to the next choice point (instead of into a blind alley) and eventually on to the goal box of the maze containing a "reward."

### GENERAL PROCEDURE

By prior arrangement of the animal's feeding schedule, the investigator may control how "hungry" it is when placed in the starting box to begin a trial. Getting through the maze to food in the end box is the problem to be solved. It corresponds to the problem faced by Thorndike's cats in the problem box except that food is not visible to the rat in the starting box of a maze as it was for Thorndike's cats. A trial ends when the animal has reached the end box from which it is taken and returned to its living cage. The time taken to get from start to end box on each trial may be plotted, giving a "time curve" similar to that obtained by Thorndike to show the course of learning over succeeding trials. In addition, the maze experiment enables the investigator to count the number of incorrect responses or "errors" made during each trial. An error is a turn into a blind alley instead of into the arm of the T which leads on to the end box. The "error curve" plotted over trials also shows a gradual decrease, indicating the increased selectivity of the correct path as learning progresses.

Two circles are superimposed on the maze shown in Figure 5.6 as an aid in relating the study of maze behavior to the kinds of incidents that had interested Thorndike and Pavlov. The circle drawn around one of the choice points in the maze, where the animal seems to make a particular response to the immediate stimuli at that point, identifies the issue of selective strengthening of the "correct" response that Thorndike had emphasized. The second circle, drawn in the vicinity of the goal box where certain environmental stimuli to which the animal is exposed are shortly followed by food in the animal's mouth on each rewarded trial, help us to place in this context the kind of incident which Pavlov had investigated when he sounded a metronome and then presented food. With these focal points in mind, let us turn to the new experimental facts which Tolman considered when developing his view that the molar behavior of animals is both purposive and cognitive in character.

Several experiments conducted in the University of California laboratories during the early and mid-1920's deserve special mention before we consider the summarizing experiments of Tolman and Honzik. They illustrate the kinds of experimental conditions which a "purposivist" would think to create.

### EFFECT OF DIFFERENT INCENTIVES ON PERFORMANCE

In 1924, Simmons compared the maze learning curves of hungry animals who were given different types of food in the goal box. She was concerned with the relative effectiveness of different "incentives." On each trial, she first placed the animal in the goal box and allowed it to nibble the food. Then she placed it in the starting box from which it began its run through the maze. When it finally got to the goal box, it was allowed another nibble of food before being removed from the maze. It did not receive its main daily ration of food until several hours later in a cage away from the maze. Both the time and error curves plotted over trials showed the gradual decrease noted by Thorndike, but the type of reward or incentive offered apparently influenced the speed of learning so defined. That is, the decrease in time taken to run the maze and the decrease in number of errors over the trials was noticeably faster when the animal was offered a nibble of bread and milk immediately before and at the end of a run than when it was offered a nibble of sunflower seed. And the latter incentive produced faster decrease of time and errors than when animals received no food reward at all, but were simply returned to their living cages after each run. This experiment concretizes what Tolman meant by *strength of demand for the goal object* as a variable in maze learning and performance. Holding physiological drive constant, *demand* is influenced by the type of "incentive."

In a study conducted in 1925, Blodgett (1929) showed that hungry rats which were rewarded with food on every trial showed the typical decrease in time and errors in succeeding trials, but other animals which ran the maze without any food reward for several trials showed very little decrease in errors until finally a food reward was introduced on a later trial. Then, *in the trial immediately after the first introduction of a reward, these animals showed a very substantial drop in errors.*

The curves showing average number of errors on each trial in a six-unit T maze for three experimental groups in Blodgett's experiment are shown in Figure 5.7. Group I consisted of 36 animals allowed

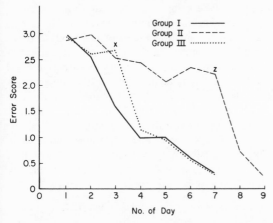

FIGURE 5.7   The latent learning phenomenon. Group I was given a food reward on every trial. In Group II, the food reward was not introduced until the seventh day (at point z). In Group III, the food reward was not introduced until the third day (at point x). Both Group II and Group III show a substantial decrease in errors after the first rewarded trial. (*From Blodgett, 1929, p. 120*)

to eat for three minutes in the goal box at the end of each run. Their performance is described by the typical Thorndikian learning curve. Group II consisted of 36 animals who found no food in the goal box and were kept in it *without reward* for two minutes on each of the first six trials, but on trial seven and thereafter, the food reward was given as in Group I. Group II shows a very substantial drop in errors on the trial immediately after the first re-

warded trial. Group III consisted of 25 animals who began with no reward on the first two trials but were given food reward on the third trial and thereafter. Group III shows a very substantial drop in errors on trial four, the trial immediately following the first rewarded trial.

The important question raised by Blodgett, and to which we shall return shortly is this:

"Do these sudden drops in errors which come after the introduction of reward indicate something to be called a *latent learning* developed during the non-reward period—a latent learning which made itself manifest after the reward had been presented?" (Blodgett, 1929, p. 22).

In 1928, Elliott conducted experiments which extended knowledge of the effect of different incentives on maze performance. A comparison of the learning curves of hungry rats rewarded on each daily trial for nine days with bran mash and equally hungry rats rewarded instead with sunflower seed showed superior performance by the group given bran mash (see Figure 5.8). Here, again, was evidence of differences in demand for the goal object when holding physiological drive constant. When on the tenth

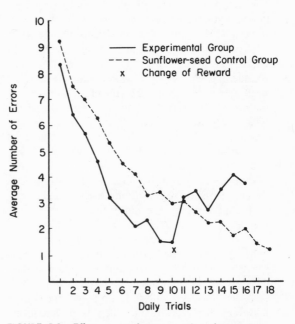

FIGURE 5.8   Effect on performance of a change from a more demanded reward to a less demanded reward (*From Elliott, 1928, p. 26*)

trial in this same experiment the reward was changed from the *more demanded* bran mash to the *less demanded* sunflower seed in the experimental group, the performance of this group deteriorated. Figure 5.8 shows an increase in average number of errors. The time curve showed a comparable change.

In still another experiment, Elliott (1929) produced a result much like that of Blodgett when a *slightly hungry* but *very thirsty* group of animals was rewarded with food (bran mash) for nine days and then the reward was shifted to water. The animals, who were only *slightly hungry* but *very thirsty*, performed somewhat poorly while they were receiving only food in the end box. But on the trial immediately after receiving water for the first time, they showed a decided improvement in both time score and errors. This experiment showed that "drive" and "incentive" were interrelated determinants of demand for the goal object.

ACQUIRED INCENTIVE VALUE
OF A NEUTRAL STIMULUS

Another experiment by Williams (1929) brought interest in the relative effectiveness of different rewards or incentives on maze performance into closer contact with Pavlov's observations. In preliminary training, Williams trained hungry animals to discriminate between a white box in which they were always fed and a black box in which they were never fed. Then, after their preference for the white box had been fully established, she ran three groups of hungry animals in the type of maze we have been considering. One group always found the familiar white box with food at the end of its daily run in the maze. Their time and error curves showed the typical decrease in subsequent trials. Another group found an unfamiliar box, empty and unpainted, at the end of each maze run. They showed much less improvement in time and errors in successive trials. A third group found this unpainted, empty box at the end of the maze run during the first eight daily trials, but then, on the ninth day and thereafter, they found *the familiar white box*, *though now with no food in it*, at the end of their maze run. Their performance began to improve immediately; by the thirteenth trial their time and error curves had dropped to the level attained by the group which had been rewarded with food on every trial. Later, however, their performance began to deteriorate and to resemble again that of the group running to the empty unpainted box.

Williams interpreted the *temporary* improvement

in performance as evidence that the white box, a stimulus which had become a "sign" for food in the preliminary training (that is, a conditioned stimulus for the salivary response in the Pavlovian sense), could function, at least temporarily, as a reward or incentive like food itself. In Tolman's terms, the stimuli defining the *place* where the animals were used to eating functioned like a subgoal; the demand for this subgoal apparently influenced performance, at least for a time, just like the demand for food itself. What Pavlov would call a conditioned stimulus (the white box), capable of eliciting a conditioned salivary response (because food had been presented in its presence in the past), was here conceived as a stimulus which had acquired the character of a subgoal or incentive for the animal.

Together, these studies illustrate the kinds of experimental procedures and observations which the guiding idea of "purpose" produced when the first attempts were being made to deal with "purpose" objectively in the learning experiment. It is certainly only a small jump from common sense to consider variations in "hunger" (time since last meal) and in the type of food "incentive" offered as factors which might influence the tendency of animals to get on quickly to the goal box. The fact that it took about 25 years of psychological research with animals before this set of interrelated experiments was even performed illustrates how remote from the mainstream of animal experimentation had been the speculative ideas about the ubiquity of goal-seeking behavior prior to Tolman.

SIGNIFICANCE OF THE BLODGETT EXPERIMENT

Of particular significance was the problem suggested to Blodgett. Could an animal learn something, that is, acquire some kind of "knowledge" about a maze, without obvious reward and without manifesting what it had learned in its performance? Up until this time, those interested in associative learning in animals had debated about whether or not reward was needed. Some took Pavlovian conditioning as their model and argued that frequency and recency of the association between stimulus and response was enough, but none had doubted that what learning amounted to was a strengthening of the connection between some stimulus and the impulse to respond. This meant that the correct response had to *occur* in order to be strengthened. Writing in 1925, Tolman called attention to the basic problem that was hidden in many learning experiments which had followed Thorndike's general procedure of offering a reward on each trial. He stated the problem in the language of common sense so there could be no mistake in his meaning:

> "Previous work . . . has made no distinction between an animal's mere *knowledge* of the behavior possibilities which will get him to food and his *desire* for those behavior possibilities. Whether an animal actually enters a given alley or not is probably a function, not merely of the growth of his *knowledge* about the nature of that alley but also of the state of his desires. . . . And experimental work must be done on tearing these two factors apart, before we can be certain to what extent the acquisition of mere knowledge, as such, is a function of mere frequency and recency (of experience) or how much it depends also upon the satisfactoriness or unsatisfactoriness of the result" (Tolman, 1925b, pp. 295–296).

EFFECT OF HUNGER DRIVE ON DEMAND
FOR GOAL OBJECT

We turn now to several experiments which summarize the findings in the separate explorations which preceded them. Tolman and Honzik (1930) examined the effects of both degree of hunger and reward versus non-reward on maze performance. They controlled the degree of hunger during the experiment by keeping some rats on short rations. The rats subjected to this treatment, and referred to as "Hungry," each lost anywhere from 5 to 26 grams of weight during the experiment. Rats not subjected to this experimental treatment designed to increase hunger, and referred to as "Less Hungry," gained anywhere from 5 to 38 grams of weight during the experiment. Half of each of these groups found a food reward in the goal box of the maze after each daily run. The other half did not; they had to wait for about two hours before receiving food in their living cages.

The summary of results presented in Figure 5.9 shows a typical learning curve for the group which, like Thorndike's cats, was both Hungry and Rewarded on every trial. Comparison of the curve for this group and the curve describing the behavior of the "Less Hungry-Reward" group clearly indicates that degree of "hunger" influences what Tolman referred to as strength of demand for the goal object. Rats who were made Hungry and Rewarded on every trial ran the maze faster and with fewer errors than any other group after the first few trials.

The effect of hunger on demand for the goal is most evident during the later trials in the comparison between the Hungry and Less Hungry group which was given Reward. Also evident in later trials is

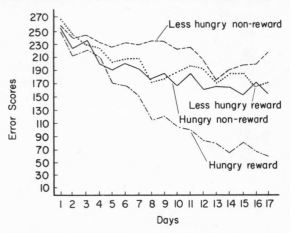

FIGURE 5.9    Effect of hunger, reward, and non-reward on maze learning in rats (*From Tolman and Honzik, 1930a, p. 246*)

evidence of the effect of differences in the incentive offered on demand for the goal. This can be read from the comparison between the curves for the two Hungry groups. One was immediately rewarded with food in the goal box; the other was not.

EFFECT OF SUBSTITUTING A LESS-DEMANDED
GOAL OBJECT

A result similar to that which Elliot had obtained by changing the reward from the *more demanded* bran mash to the *less demanded* sunflower seed was reproduced by Tolman and Honzik in another group of Hungry rats. This group was given a food reward in the goal box on each of the first 10 daily runs, but then on the eleventh trial and thereafter the reward was withdrawn. Here, instead of a shift from one type of food to another that is less preferred, the shift is from immediate food reward to no immediate food reward. The deterioration of performance was evident in both the error and time curves of this experiment.

EFFECT OF SUBSTITUTING A MORE-DEMANDED
GOAL OBJECT

The very important result of the Blodgett experiment was also reproduced with another group of Hungry animals who ran the first 10 daily trials *without* food reward in the goal box but then found food in the goal box for the first time on the eleventh trial, and thereafter. Curves in Figure 5.10 show that this hungry group behaves like the Hungry Non-Reward group until food is introduced. Then, in the twelfth trial, the one coming immediately after the

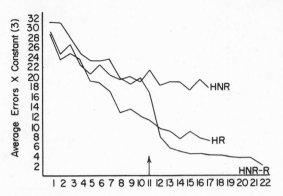

FIGURE 5.10   A replication of Blodgett's results. One group (HR) was rewarded on every trial. Another (HNR) was never given food reward in the goal box. The third group (HNR-R) was not rewarded until the 11th day (and thereafter); it displays a sudden improvement in performance. (From Tolman and Honzik, 1930b, p. 267)

first rewarded trial, this group shifts rapidly to the level of performance attained by the Hungry group that had been rewarded on every trial. Here again is evidence of what Blodgett had called a "*latent learning*" which is not manifested in performance until the animal is given some incentive to get on to the end box rapidly.

## THE FUNDAMENTAL DISTINCTION BETWEEN LEARNING AND PERFORMANCE

One of the first and most important contributions of research conducted with the presumption that the animal is an active goal-seeker is the "latent learning" phenomenon which concretizes the distinction between *what an animal learns* and *what an animal does*. Viewed from the orientation of Thorndike, variations in the degree of hunger and in the type of reward could be considered factors which influence the amount of "satisfaction" or amount of reward following each correct run of the maze. When reward is offered on each trial (as was conventional in the type of experiment designed by Thorndike), the more rapid drop in time and errors given one type of reward rather than another, or given more hunger rather than less hunger, could be explained by the Law of Effect as evidence that the degree of satisfaction influences the degree of strengthening of the connection between stimulus

and impulse to respond on each trial. The strengthening of connection between the correct response and the stimulus situation at each choice point would still be gradual, but the increment would be greater on each trial. Hence, the drop in time and error curves would be more pronounced when the reward offered is more substantial.

But how could the Law of Effect, as stated by Thorndike, explain the result obtained by Blodgett and reproduced by Tolman and Honzik? Here were animals whose performance after a series of trials *without* any obvious reward had suddenly taken a big jump to the level attained by animals which had been given a "strong" reward on every trial *immediately after the first "strong" reward had been introduced*. After one or two rewards, their performance was as good as that of the group which had been rewarded every time. Apparently, differential reward or "effect" had very little influence on learning *per se*, but was needed to provide *an incentive* for the animal to display in its performance what it had already learned without reward.

What and why the organism learns in successive trials is one thing. What it does and why it performs certain responses and not others on any given trial is another thing. The latent-learning experiments showed that the historical question (learning) and the ahistorical question (motivation of performance) needed to be distinguished. The laws of selective learning had been developed in terms of observed changes in an animal's *performance*, as if the changes *within* the animal corresponded exactly (in neural terms) with the observed changes in its performance. Now it seemed clear that laws of learning should have to do with changes *in* the animal, but changes which might or might not be immediately evident in subsequent observable performance, depending on other conditions. Laws of performance would have to be discovered to explain how the residue or imprint of past experience, whatever form it took, combined with other immediate influences to produce the actions that are observed and measured on any given trial in the learning experiment. This was the *broad problem of drive* as Woodworth had originally conceived it—the problem of selectivity and control of performance. And we may also recognize this problem of accounting for the animal's performance on each and every trial in the typical learning experiment—given sudden changes in the incentive or not—as the problem of bringing together into some coherent scheme a picture of all of the immediate effective influences on behavior which Lewin attempted to capture in his conception of the contemporaneous motivational state, the life space.

## THE LAW OF EFFECT CONSIDERED
## A PRINCIPLE OF PERFORMANCE

In Tolman's view, the Law of Effect was to be considered a principle of performance rather than a principle of learning:

"The latent learning experiments indicated very definitely that just as much learning *qua* learning goes on without differential effects, or, at the most, with only very minor degrees of such effects, as with strongly differential ones. The latent learning, which thus takes place without any strong differential effects, does not, to be sure, manifest itself until after such effects have been introduced. But, once these latter have been provided, then the sizes of the immediate drops in the performance curves which appear, indicate that the learning has been present throughout. Differential effects are, that is, necessary for *selective performance* but they are not necessary, or at the most in only a very minor degree, for the mere learning *qua* learning which underlies such performance" (Tolman, 1932, pp. 363–364).

Selectivity in performance relative to some goal is, we recall, what Tolman meant when he described behavior as purposive. And, recalling the earlier argument, this selectivity on a given trial implies some kind of knowledge of means-ends relations.

## WHAT DOES THE ANIMAL LEARN?

Tolman held that the animal develops cognitive expectations concerning what leads to what as a result of its experience in the maze and that neither the Law of Effect, which asserts that reward is essential for any associations to develop, nor the Law of Exercise, which emphasizes the importance of repeated performances of the correct sequence of responses, was an adequate principle:

". . . Our final criticism of the trial and error doctrine is that it is its fundamental notion of stimulus-response bonds, which is wrong. Stimuli do not, as such, call out responses willy nilly. Correct stimulus-response connections do not get 'stamped in,' and incorrect ones do not get 'stamped out.' Rather learning consists in the organisms' 'discovering' or 'refining' what all the respective alternative responses lead to. And then, if, under the appetite-aversion conditions of the moment, the consequences of one of these alternatives is more demanded than the others—or if it be 'demanded-for' and the others be 'demanded against'—then the organism will tend, after such learning, to select and to perform the response leading to the more 'demanded-for' consequences. But, if there be no such difference in demands there will be no such selection and performance of the one response, even though there has been learning" (Tolman, 1932, p. 364).

Trial and error learning, Tolman asserted, consists of building up differential cognitive expectations or "expectancies." The stimulus objects involved in the paths constituting the wrong responses become signs for the sorts of consequences to be reached by such wrong responses. The stimulus-objects involved in the path constituting the correct response become signs for the sorts of consequences to be expected as a result of this correct response. By virtue of trying out *both* correct and incorrect responses, the organism discovers their respective consequences. It builds up and refines the appropriately differentiated expectancies. Finally, it *performs* the one way or the other by virtue of these expectations *and* the demands for goal objects which are active at the moment.

## FACTORS INFLUENCING STRENGTH
## OF EXPECTANCY

Tolman held that the formation of any given expectancy would be favored insofar as the sequence of stimulus object (sign), means-end relation, and consequence involved in the given response had the advantage of *frequency*, *recency*, or *primacy*. In other words, it would be the earliest, most frequent or most recent experiences corresponding to the sign-object (stimulus), action, and signified consequence which favor the learning of expectations. Putting the idea in the language of stimulus and response, where Thorndike had held that the animal learned a connection between $S_1 \rightarrow R_1$, Tolman's concept of expectation referred to a whole sequence of $S_1$-$R_1$-$S_2$ and was later designated by him as $SR \rightarrow S$, indicating the greater importance he attached to the associative link between a response and its consequence.* According to Tolman, it was the strength of expectancy that a response, if performed, would lead on to an incentive, rather than the connection between stimulus situation and the impulse to respond, which changed in the usual learning experiment.

* MacCorquodale and Meehl (1953) were the first to translate Tolman's concept of *expectancy* clearly into the *S-R* language. Tolman subsequently employed *S-R* terms to convey his meaning.

## DEMANDS AND EXPECTATIONS AS "INTERVENING VARIABLES" DETERMINING PERFORMANCE

### EXPLANATION OF LATENT-LEARNING PHENOMENON

Here is how Tolman explained the latent-learning phenomenon. During the unrewarded trials, the animals develop cognitive expectations of the consequences of turning left or right at each of the various choice points. After several trials in the maze, these forward-pointing expectations constitute a kind of "cognitive map" of the maze that is "refined" during each run. In the very early trials, the animal's performance is presumably guided by very general expectations carried over from earlier occasions when it had demanded food goal-objects. The initial explorations of the maze are guided, in other words, by preliminary "cognitive hunches" or "hypotheses" as to what might lead to what in this unfamiliar situation. In Tolman's view, a hungry animal is always actively trying to find food. After developing a more refined set of expectations concerning what does lead to what in the maze, the animal comes upon food, a demanded goal-object, in the end box of the maze. The next day, as a result of this *recent* experience added to the cognitive expectations of what leads to what which had been built up without reward in earlier trials, the animal has both a demand for food and an expectation of a food object in the end box when placed in the starting box. The combination of these two determinants accounts for *the sudden change in selectivity of performance* at each choice point. The animal now selects the "correct" response, which is the one that it expects will lead on most quickly to the demanded goal-object.

### DETERMINANTS OF DEMAND FOR GOAL OBJECT

In Tolman's view, the strength of demand for the goal object depends upon both the strength of physiological drive (hunger) and the type of goal object (or incentive) that is expected. The deterioration of performance following substitution of a less-demanded goal object for a more-demanded goal object is explained in a similar manner. The most recent experience produces a change in the type of goal object that is expected. The demand for this expected goal object is weaker than the demand for the formerly expected goal object. Hence there is a deterioration in selectivity of performance relative to the goal object on subsequent trials.

### EXPLANATION OF THORNDIKE'S LEARNING CURVE

How is the typical learning curve explained when rats are rewarded on every trial, following Thorndike's procedure? Since drive and the type of incentive are held constant throughout, it may be assumed that the demand for the goal object is constant throughout. The gradual improvement in performance must, therefore, be attributed to the growth and refinement of the animal's cognitive expectations that certain responses will lead on to the goal object and others will not. The more rapid improvement in performance when the reward on every trial is a more demanded type of goal object is evidence of greater selectivity in performance on each trial, not evidence of faster learning of expectations.

## THE LOGIC OF INTERVENING VARIABLES IN PSYCHOLOGICAL THEORY

Tolman asserted that demands for goal objects, as inferred from the procedures employed to control physiological drive and the type of incentive employed on previous trials, and the strength of means-end expectations, inferred from past training, were two important variables which intervene between the stimulus and the response at any choice point. These intervening variables were, for Tolman, the *immediate* determinants of the animal's performance.

### THE PROBLEM FACED BY OBJECTIVE PSYCHOLOGY

One of Tolman's major contributions was to work out the logic for the development of a "psychological behaviorism" which would attempt to account for the hidden process within the organism which determines its behavior, but without explicit reference to the type of neurophysiological mechanisms that might be involved and without implying anything about private mental states. Let us examine his outline for the development of psychological theory in terms of objectively defined, inferred, intervening variables. Here, in general, is how he viewed the problem faced by an objective psychology:

"Organisms of given heredities, given kinds and amounts of previous training, and given maturities are immersed in environments and are driven by conditions of physiological disequilibrium. And because of these environments and these disequilibria, they behave. Mental processes are but intervening variables between the five independent variables of (1) environmental stimuli, (2) physiological drive, (3) heredity, (4) previous training, and (5) maturity, on the one hand, and the final dependent variable, behavior, on the other" (Tolman, [1936], 1951, p. 117).

Figure 5.11 presents a simplified version of what Tolman meant when he asserted that "mental processes are but intervening variables" between the observable and measurable antecedents on the one hand and observable features of behavior on the other. The variables which are the ultimate empirical antecedents or "causes" of behavior are listed at the left. Behavior, which is the determined consequence or "effect" of certain combinations of these empirical antecedents, is listed at the right. And in the middle, within a circle that reminds us that we are now speaking of what goes on within the behaving organism to determine its behavior at any given time, are listed the inferred intervening variables. From the diagram we can see that the *demands* and *expectations*, which Tolman first inferred from selectivity of performance in relation to some end and the persistence-until character of molar behavior, are themselves to be considered intermediate effects of the antecedents which, in turn, constitute the immediate determinants of the observed behavior.

OPERATIONAL DEFINITION OF INTERVENING VARIABLES

Tolman insisted that these inferred intervening variables could be defined objectively in terms of both antecedent conditions and their consequent effect on behavior. Let us take a simple example to see how he proposed to do this. We recall that he began with observations of behavior and the inference that a rat's selective performance of responses which lead on most readily to some goal express a demand for the goal object. Hence, the more selective the performance (that is, the fewer the errors and shorter the time taken to get through the maze), the stronger the inferred demand for the goal object. This anchors the intervening variable, strength of demand for goal object, in observations of behavior. Now we must examine how he proposed to define the strength of demand for the goal object in terms of observable antecedent conditions. He proposed a standard experiment in which all other relevant antecedent conditions except one would be held constant. Then the effect on behavior of variations in one antecedent condition would be observed.

Suppose that all factors (such as amount of previous training, and presence and type of reward) were held constant, but that the number of hours since the rat's last meal was varied systematically to produce different amounts of "hunger." If maze performance became more selective when hunger drive was increased in this way (as was, in fact, observed), this would show the effect of increase in drive as empirically defined on strength of demand for the goal object. It would tell that demand for food was an increasing function of hunger drive produced by food privation. In subsequent experiments, the relative strength of demand for food could then be inferred in advance from prior observations concerning the animal's feeding schedule.

In a similar way, he argued, the strength of an animal's expectation that some response would lead on to food could be defined objectively in terms of observations concerning its previous training. In a standard experiment, drive, incentive, and other factors could be held constant, and the type of training given the animal could be varied to discover what effects were produced on maze performance. To illustrate this we may consider one of Blodgett's subsidiary findings concerning latent learning which we

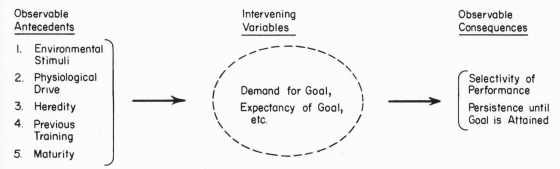

FIGURE 5.11   Tolman's conception of "mental processes" as variables which intervene between observable and measurable antecedent conditions and observable and measurable features of molar behavior.

have not, as yet, mentioned. Blodgett had one group of rats run through the maze *in reverse order* (i.e., from end box to starting box) a number of times before food was introduced in the end box and they were then run for the first time in the conventional direction. He found that prior experience running the maze in reverse order had little positive effect on subsequent performance when rats ran the maze in the forward direction. They did not, in other words, make as few errors and get through the maze as fast as rats who had run the maze in the normal direction but without reward. This could be taken to mean that the cognitive expectations inferred from selective performance when reward is finally introduced must be forward-pointing in character and their development must require forward-pointing past experiences.

### THE TASK OF THEORY CONSTRUCTION

*For Tolman, the task of constructing a theory to explain molar behavior was identified with the task of evolving the right kinds of intervening variables, of discovering their empirical antecedents, and finally of stating in a systematic way how the several kinds of intervening variables interacted with one another, or combined, to determine the observable performance in a given stimulus situation.* He felt, as we have already mentioned, that all of the important basic theoretical issues were to be confronted in the analysis of the behavior of a rat at a choice point. What kinds of hidden determining variables had to be inferred to explain what a rat would do? What were the historical or immediate empirical antecedents of these variables in terms of which they could be given objective definitions? How did strength of demand and strength of expectancy, and any other type of intervening variable which might be needed, *combine* to produce the performance that was observed? These, he felt, were questions that could be answered only by systematic experimentation guided by theoretical questions.

Tolman had worked up from observations of the characteristics of molar behavior in relation to experimental variations in a few relevant independent variables (drive, incentive, number of unrewarded trials in maze) to this very general conception of how a "psychological-," "operational-," "purposive" behaviorism might be constructed in terms of "intervening variables" that were objectively defined in terms of observable antecedents and consequences. This, in outline, was to be his substitute for the common-sense mentalism of the past and an alterna-tive to what he considered premature and inadequate attempts to explain behavior in terms of neurophysiological mechanisms.

### THE RELATION OF TOLMAN'S AND LEWIN'S IDEAS

By the mid-1930's, the striking similarities between the conceptions advanced by Tolman (working with animals) and by Lewin (working with humans) were quite generally recognized. We can identify the essential agreements and complementary nature of the two formulations by considering the way each would account for the performance of a rat at some choice point in a maze on any given trial. To provide a contrast, let us recall what the early Thorndike version of an *S-R* association theory would say: the stimulus provides the *impetus* to respond and whether the animal turns left or right depends upon the strength of $S-R_l$ versus $S-R_r$ developed as a result of differential reward in the past.

1. Both Tolman and Lewin recognized the need to make further inferences about the contemporary state of the animal as it confronted the choice point. Tolman's recognition of the need for intervening variables to account for the process that is hidden from the investigator's view corresponds to the Lewinian assertion that the psychologist's task is to account for the total situation (life space) as it exists for the behaving organism at the time.

2. The distinction between the problem of learning and the problem of performance which Tolman made in reference to the latent-learning phenomenon is the same distinction that Lewin made between the *historical* problem (Why does the situation have a particular structure for the organism at a given time?) and the *ahistorical* problem (How is the behavior of the organism to be explained in terms of the interaction of contemporaneous influences which comprise the present situation or life space?). Both men, in other words, wanted to identify the *immediate* determinants of behavior.

3. The two theorists agreed that a description of the contemporary state of the organism which immediately determines its behavior must include reference to its *goals*. Tolman referred to the strength of demand for some goal object which is influenced by physiological drive and the type of incentive (or reward) that is expected. Lewin referred to the same influence on behavior as the "valence" of the goal for the organism, its attractiveness resulting from the momentary state of need ($t_g$) and the character of the goal object (*G*). The "labels" are different,

but the concept is the same: the tendency to seek a goal is attributed by both to a combination of the temporary condition of the organism (its hunger) and the type of goal object that is expected at the time.

4. Both theorists also agreed that the tendency of the animal to perform one particular response rather than another at a choice point would depend also on its "knowledge" of means-end relations. Tolman referred to the animal's cognitive expectations, in a given stimulus situation, that one response would lead on to the demanded goal object and another would not. Lewin represented the organism's expectations as the perceived path connecting some immediate region in the life space (the first step) with a more distant goal region. The path between the immediate region, defining the first step, and the goal region corresponds to Tolman's conception of a means-end expectation. The link between a particular response and its respective consequence is a forward-pointing association developed and refined through prior explorations of the maze. The Lewinian concept of *Potency* (one of the determinants of *effective* force) is equivalent to Tolman's strength of *Expectancy*.

5. Finally, the conceptions of Tolman and Lewin agree on another fundamental point: *no single factor is to be considered the stimulus or impetus to perform a response*. Both a valent (or demanded) goal *and* knowledge of the path to it are needed to account for the impetus to respond. Neither factor by itself provides the stimulus (or cause) of the response. Together, in combination, these factors determine the tendency to respond which Lewin referred to as "force" and which Tolman a good deal later came to refer to as the "performance vector." In his early writings, Tolman had asserted the interdependence of demands and expectations as determinants of the response when he stated that selective performance always expresses *both* purpose and cognition.

In summary, both Tolman and Lewin conceived behavior in molar terms, as purposive or goal-seeking in character, and as occurring within an environment that would have to be described in terms of properties which the behaving organism *attributed* to its physical surroundings. While Tolman emphasized the need for objective, operational definitions of intervening variables, Lewin, paying less attention to this important matter, had evolved a coherent scheme which began to state how the several intervening variables *combined* to influence action.

# CHAPTER 6

# The Foundation

# of *S-R* Behavior

# Theory

*"It is believed that a clear formulation, even if later found incorrect, will ultimately lead more quickly and easily to a correct formulation than will a pussyfooting statement which might be more difficult to convict of falsity. The primary task of a science is the early and economical discovery of its basic laws. In the view of the scientifically sophisticated, to make an incorrect guess whose error is easily detected should be no disgrace; scientific discovery is in part a trial-and-error process, and such a process cannot occur without erroneous as well as successful trials. On the other hand, to employ a methodology by which it is impossible readily to detect a mistake once made, or deliberately to hide a possible mistake behind weasel words, philosophical fog, and anthropomorphic prejudice, slows the trial-and-error process, and so retards scientific progress"* (Hull, 1943, pp. 398–399).\*

By the late 1920's the viewpoint of the purposivists, which for a quarter of a century had been little more than a cry of criticism from the sidelines of experimental research with animals, had finally been brought into direct contact with experimental observations of animal behavior and had produced some innovations in the method of study. The claim that *molar* (as distinct from *molecular*) behavior was goal-seeking in character and in some way determined by "knowledge" of the means of attaining goals could no longer be completely ignored by scientifically-minded psychologists. For a long time, many of them had considered this assertion merely one last vestige of armchair teleology to be lived down by the new objective psychology. The empirical studies of animal drives and the type of experimental analysis of maze behavior that Tolman and his co-workers had undertaken gave a concrete meaning to the claim that an amimal's molar behavior expresses more than the mere strength of the connection between environmental stimulus and response. The new experimental facts had to be taken into account and some basic questions had to be answered, if they could be answered, by those who were convinced of the basic soundness of the *S-R* orientation.

Now, however, more was required than mere hopeful reiteration of the conjecture that all complex and patterned activities could be explained as mere chains composed of *S-R* links. This unsubstantiated argument, which had gained so much currency in the writings of Watsonian behaviorists, began to sound as hollow as the earlier chants of the purposivists before they had any concrete experimental facts to advance in support of their concepts.

The idea that molar behavior expresses both "purpose" and "knowledge" was in the air. It troubled psychologists of the *S-R* persuasion because, to their way of thinking, *S* (stimulus) had become equivalent to "cause" and *R* (response) to "effect" in the analysis of any psychological problem. "Purpose" still sounded mentalistic and teleological to them. And "knowledge," even when further specified as a type of association to be described as "cognitive expectation," sounded equally vaporous. How could one hope to give a scientifically respectable explanation of an organism's response except in terms of an eliciting stimulus which must precede it and provide the impetus, or push from behind? To some *S-R* psychologists like Edwin Guthrie, who, following Watson, viewed simple conditioning as the ultimate explanatory device, it seemed that Tolman's theorizing about "purposive" and "cognitive" characteristics of behavior "left the animal lost in thought at the choice point."

## PURPOSE AND KNOWLEDGE CONCEIVED IN TERMS OF STIMULUS AND RESPONSE

### THE CHALLENGE ACCEPTED BY CLARK L. HULL

The challenge presented by growing experimental interest in the "broad trend of behavior," to those who had been solely concerned with the details of *S-R* associations, was finally accepted by Clark L. Hull. Hull published a series of theoretical papers beginning in 1929, a few years after the full English translation of Pavlov's experiments had made the detailed properties of conditioned responses more widely known. In his analysis of "knowledge," "foresight," "purpose," "guiding ideas," and "goal attraction" as *habit* phenomena, Hull presented the kind of translation of these concepts into stimulus and response elements that James had attempted 40 years earlier in his speculations about the neural basis of "volition." But a lot had happened in those 40 years, and Hull's analysis differed from that of

James in several very important respects. He now had the experimental facts of Thorndike's selective learning experiments and, particularly, the reports of Pavlov's conditioning experiments to guide him as he attempted to identify the fundamental properties of associations between a stimulus and a response. In addition, Hull had behind him some of the more important transitions in orientation towards the subject matter of psychology which we have reviewed.

### CONDITIONING EXPERIMENTS AS THE SOURCE OF ASSUMPTIONS

*Hull used the experimental facts of conditioning* (summarized on pages 118–120) *as the source for certain basic assumptions about the properties of simple associations from which, he believed, the so-called purposive and cognitive characteristics of molar behavior could be derived as secondary phenomena.* He sought to construct a plausible picture of molar behavioral phenomena using stimulus, response, and the known properties of *S-R* associations (habits) as his basic elements of construction.

### RECOGNITION OF MOTIVATION AND LEARNING AS DISTINCT PROBLEMS

Hull clearly recognized "*striving*" for goals (Motivation) and "*strengthening*" of connections (Learning) as distinct problems; but he believed that the "striving," to which McDougall and later Tolman had called attention, could ultimately be derived from basic principles that had to do with "*strengthening*" of *S-R* connections. This meant that for Hull the problem of how "habits" develop and function was the matter ultimately to be given special attention. To lend credence to his belief, he had to accomplish what no associationist before had seriously attempted. He had to develop the implications of the viewpoint of *S-R* behaviorism in a systematic and detailed way to show that those characteristics of behavior which others (like Tolman) referred to as "purpose" and "knowledge," and earlier psychologists had called "foresight" and "guiding ideas," could be plausibly represented in terms of stimulus and response. Above all, in these early papers, Hull began to construct the foundation for an explicit and testable conceptual scheme in terms of principles having to do with the growth of associations between stimulus and response and the subsequent elicitation of responses by stimuli.

A PRELUDE TO HULL'S MAJOR WORK

Hull's analysis was presented in a series of theoretical papers published in *Psychological Review* from 1929 through the late 1930's. This analysis provided the prelude to the development of his systematic theory of behavior which was published as a book, *The Principles of Behavior*, in 1943. His formal theory will provide the major themes of the latter part of this chapter. We shall see that some of the ideas he developed in the essays of the early 1930's to take account of problems presented by Tolman's work were set aside when he formalized his theory in 1943, only to be slowly regained again some years later when it became obvious that his first statement of the formal theory was in need of overhaul. It turns out that systematic developments in science are much less orderly and systematic than many of us might naïvely have supposed.

A CLUE: THE ANTICIPATORY NATURE OF
A CONDITIONED RESPONSE

Perhaps the most significant thing to note as we consider Hull's first attempt to encompass "purpose" and "knowledge" with stimulus and response is the attention he gave to this basic question: *How can the goal or end of an action sequence become one of the most important determinants of the action sequence?* James, we recall, had wrestled with the same problem in his neural conception of volition. Psychologists who were convinced of the soundness of Watson's battle cry, that the task of psychology was "given the stimulus, to predict the response, and given the response, to infer the stimulus," had always been disdainful of arguments advanced by purposivists like McDougall and even Tolman because they seemed to be asserting that some *future* event (a goal) could determine *present* behavior. How could this possibly be? It does violence to the time sequence of natural events. In any scientific account of behavior, the "cause" of behavior must precede the "effect" which it is supposed to cause. That is what troubled them.

What Hull did was to show how the goal, or end, of an action sequence might itself be represented as a stimulus which precedes and provides impetus for responses that are instrumental in bringing about the goal. He saw that this could come about if an organism was capable of learning to make the appropriate response to some stimulus *before* the occurrence of the stimulus that was originally effective in eliciting that response. Wasn't this exactly

what Pavlov had discovered in his conditioning experiments? When a dog produced saliva in response to the sound of a metronome which in the past had preceded the presentation of food, the dog was making the response appropriate to food, but *before* the occurrence of the originally effective stimulus. The dog responded, in other words, *as if* the food stimulus were already present when in fact it was not. The *anticipatory* nature of conditioned responses provided Hull with the clue he needed to show how "knowledge" of future events might be represented in *S-R* terms.

THE IMPORTANCE OF RESPONSE-PRODUCED STIMULI

In these early writings (i.e., before his formal statement of theory in 1943), Hull assumed no more than a simple principle of association (or conditioning) to begin with: that is, he assumed only that any stimulus contiguous with the evocation of a response by some other stimulus would become associated with that response and subsequently capable of exciting it. He then showed how "foresight" (what Tolman referred to as "cognitive expectation") might be represented (Hull, 1930):

1. The temporal sequence of observable environmental stimuli to which an organism is exposed may be represented as follows:

$$S_1 \longrightarrow S_2 \longrightarrow S_3 \longrightarrow \text{etc.}$$

The numbers 1, 2, and 3 represent the normal time sequence.

2. If now we expose a reacting organism to this sequence of stimuli, the original *unconditioned* responses to each of the stimuli may be represented:

$$S_1 \longrightarrow S_2 \longrightarrow S_3$$
$$\searrow \quad\quad \searrow \quad\quad \searrow$$
$$R_1 \quad\quad R_2 \quad\quad R_3, \text{etc.}$$

Responses follow the stimuli that elicit them.

3. Now consider that whenever any kind of response occurs there are internal, kinaesthetic receptors which are stimulated by movements yielding an internal stimulus ($s$) which can function in the same manner as any external environmental stimulus:

$$S_1 \longrightarrow S_2 \longrightarrow S_3$$
$$\searrow \quad\quad \searrow \quad\quad \searrow$$
$$R_1 \longrightarrow s_1 \quad R_2 \longrightarrow s_2 \quad R_3 \quad \text{tc.}$$

4. This means that the internal stimulus ($s_1$), produced by the immediately prior response ($R_1$), will be present at the same time that some new environmental stimulus ($S_2$) is calling forth another response

($R_2$). Consequently, the stimulus ($s_1$) should become associated with the immediately subsequent response ($R_2$). Broken arrows refer to these newly acquired excitatory tendencies:

$$S_1 \longrightarrow S_2 \longrightarrow S_3$$
$$\searrow \qquad \searrow \qquad \searrow$$
$$R_1 \longrightarrow s_1\text{-}{\rightarrow}R_2 \longrightarrow s_2\text{-}{\rightarrow}R_3, \text{ etc.}$$

5. Now what should occur if the organism is later exposed *only* to $S_1$? The internal stimuli ($s_1$, $s_2$, $s_3$, etc.) should substitute for the sequence of environmental stimuli in exciting the sequence of previously conditioned responses (unless interrupted by more potent influences):

$$S_1$$
$$\searrow$$
$$R_1 \longrightarrow s_1\text{-}{\rightarrow}R_2 \longrightarrow s_2\text{-}{\rightarrow}R_3, \text{ etc.}$$

Here, Hull argued, is the way in which the world stamps its pattern of action upon the physical organism. After exposure to sequences of environmental stimuli of this kind, the organism should carry about *within it* a kind of replica of the world:

"Foresight may be defined for our present purpose *as the reaction to an event which may be impending, but which has not as yet taken place*. The difficulty seems largely to have been concerned with the problem of how an organism can react to an event not yet in existence. The reasoning runs: An event not yet in existence cannot be a stimulus; and how can an organism react to a stimulus which does not exist?" (Hull, 1930a, p. 514).

The importance of the clue in the conditioning experiments is now obvious. The conditioned reaction runs off at a higher speed than the world sequence which it parallels. The dog produces saliva in response to a metronome *before* the food is presented. The tempo of the acquired "subjective" parallel to the outer world sequence of stimulation is not limited to the latter. It may run ahead:

"Thus it comes about that, even when both series begin at the same instant, the end-reaction of the subjective series may actually antedate the stimulus in the world sequence which exclusively evoked it previous to the conditioning . . ." (Hull, 1930a, pp. 514–515).

In our illustration under (4) above, this means that $s_2$ might elicit $R_3$ before $S_3$ had occurred.

The organism can, in other words, display a kind of knowledge of events to come before they actually take place. This, Hull then believed, is the sense we must make out of defensive flight reactions which occur before the onset of an originally noxious stimulus:

"Thus the supposed impossibility of an organismic reaction to a situation before it exists as a stimulus is accomplished quite naturally through the medium of an internal substitute stimulus" (Hull, 1930a, p. 515).

A CONCEPTION OF RUDIMENTARY THOUGHT

Does this mean that an animal would have to run very quickly through the overt performance of all the intermediary steps in order to make the response to the last stimulus in an environmental series *before* the actual occurrence of that stimulus? Hull observed that, in the case of flight reactions, the animal which has previously approached and been burnt by the flame does not actually perform all the responses leading up and into the flame and then, once more, escape from the noxious event. Behavior, he pointed out, is more adaptive than that; "biological efficiency" demands the dropping out of all but what is necessary to perform some function.

He called attention to another example of "biological efficiency" in one of Thorndike's experiments. In the experiment, Thorndike had released the cat from the problem box as soon as it licked itself. Thorndike had, in other words, decided that a lick would constitute the "correct" response. He arranged for the door of the box to fly open so the cat could get out to the food reward as soon as the cat licked itself. He observed that as the series of learning trials progressed, the "lick" gradually became a short-circuited vestige of the original lick which had been followed by reward on earlier trials. As long as Thorndike continued to open the box as soon as a mere gesture of licking occurred, that was all the response the cat made. And so, Hull argued, we should also find in the case of a sequence of responses leading up to some noxious stimulus which originally elicits an escape reaction, that responses which perform no other function than to produce a stimulus for the escape reaction tend to become mere vestiges, a rudimentary form of thinking.

PURE STIMULUS ACTS

Hull referred to vestigial responses, or acts of this sort, as *"pure stimulus acts."* Their sole function is to serve as stimuli for other acts. Since they have no instrumental significance, they are reduced in magnitude to any degree consistent with delivery of a stimulus that *is* adequate to evoke the final instrumental or goal act. Hull acknowledged the possibility that in time nothing might be left of these responses but the "neural vestige" of the original act. That would mean that the responses and the internal stimuli they produced for the next step in the chain would occur only as some event in the central nervous system, that is, as thought. He acknowledged the possibility, but only in a footnote (Hull, 1930a, p. 517). Like other *S-R* theorists of his time, Hull favored the notion that some minimal muscular movement or glandular contraction must actually occur to mediate what common sense calls thought processes. Like Watson, who had considered thinking a form of subvocal talking involving the muscles of the throat, Hull was a "peripheralist" rather than a "centralist." He always expected to find some peripheral mechanism involved when the term "response" was used. Nevertheless, it is clear to us that these very minimal "pure stimulus acts," hidden as they are likely to be from any external observer, begin to take on the character of what Tolman called inferred, *intervening variables*. To represent the hidden process as one involving stimulus and response, as was also done in the earlier "wiring diagrams" advanced by William James, has always seemed to enhance the validity of an argument for many psychologists because they believe this is what central neural processes must be like. We must remind ourselves of what Hull was attempting to do. He wanted to show that whatever kind of process needed to be invented to account for what went on between an *observable* stimulus and an *observable* response to account for the properties of molar behavior, that process could be described in terms of association between *internal* stimuli and *internal* response. Concerning the importance of pure stimulus acts, he said:

"It is evident upon a little reflection that the advent of the pure stimulus act into biological economy marks a great advance. It makes available at once a new and enlarged range of behavior possibilities. The organism is no longer a passive reactor to stimuli from without, but becomes relatively free and dynamic. There is a transcendence of the limitations of habit as ordinarily understood, in that the organism can react to the not-here as well as the not-now. . . .

". . . Quite commonplace instrumental acts, by a natural reduction process, appear transformed into a kind of *thought*—rudimentary it is true, but of the most profound biological significance" (Hull, 1930a, pp. 516–517).

## ACTIONS CONCEIVED AS REACTIONS TO INTERNAL STIMULI

In this analysis there was no quarrel with McDougall's and Tolman's conception of an "active" organism already up and doing rather than merely waiting for some *external* stimulus to evoke a response. By implication, the apparently "spontaneous" actions of organisms would be conceived as the organism's *reactions* to its own internal stimuli. To the external observer who could see only the present environmental stimulus, responses of this sort would seem "actions" rather than "reactions."

## THE IMPORTANCE OF THE DRIVE STIMULUS ($S_d$) AND ANTICIPATORY GOAL REACTION ($r_g$)

In addition to the external stimulus and the proprioceptive (feedback) stimulus produced by action itself, there was another important stimulus to be taken into account. It was the persistent internal stimulus, like that resulting from hunger contractions, which was assumed to be associated with a particular physiological drive. (Recall now, Freud's conception of an instinct [or need] as a persistent internal stimulus.) This internal stimulus, called by Hull the drive stimulus, $S_d$, would be an unchanging component of the total stimulus complex through a sequence of actions until it was removed following the occurrence of what was called the consummatory or goal response of the sequence. This meant that while various external stimuli, $S_{e1,2,3}$, would each become associated with particular responses ($R_1$, $R_2$, $R_3$, etc.) in an instrumental action sequence, the $S_d$, which was present throughout the whole sequence, would be conditioned to each response in the series and particularly to the last response in the sequence, the goal response $R_g$. Thus, the $S_d$, like the sound of the metronome in the Pavlov conditioning experiment, would be present when the animal made its characteristic goal response to food.

The drive stimulus, $S_d$, should, in other words, have the power to elicit conditioned salivary responses as did the sound of the metronome whenever it occurred. Thus whenever the internal hunger cramps began ($S_d$ present), there should occur the goal response conditioned to it. But if the animal made a fullblown goal response, it would be prevented from making any other responses which might be needed to bring it into direct contact with food. Following Pavlov's observations, we should expect the goal response elicited by $S_d$ soon to *extinguish* because it was not followed by food in the mouth, the unconditioned stimulus which normally evokes eating responses and salivation. This is what happened in Pavlov's studies when the metronome elicited salivation but no food was presented *to reinforce* the conditioned response. However, the occurrence of only some fractional part of the total goal response of eating, such as salivation and mouth movements, would not interfere with normal locomotor responses that successfully lead on to the food. This *fractional anticipatory goal response* ($r_g$) could occur and should occur as a response to the internal drive stimulus $S_d$ at the very beginning of and throughout a behavior sequence. In this way, Hull could account for the animal's anticipation (expectation) of the goal while still in the starting box of a maze *before* the stimulus which normally produced the goal reaction (i.e., food in mouth) had occurred in the normal time sequence. In Hull's view, the anticipatory goal response, like any other response, would produce its own proprioceptive stimulus. This proprioceptive stimulus, called the *goal stimulus*, $s_g$, would be present whenever $r_g$ occurred. The combination $r_g \rightarrow s_g$ would occur whenever the $S_d$ was present. Hence, right from the beginning of a behavior sequence motivated by hunger, there should be two very important *internal* stimuli present throughout the whole sequence of behavior—$S_d$ and $s_g$. Both stimuli should become associated during training with every response in the series. Thus even without any appeal to the action of external stimuli, Hull could argue that the mere presence of $S_d$ and $s_g$ when an animal began to become "hungry" should excite a number of different competing responses that had been acquired in the past. The presence of an $S_e$ associated with any one of these responses would favor its performance, for Hull assumed that the combined strength of excitatory tendencies attributed to $S_d$, $s_g$, and $S_e$ at the time should be greater than any single component by itself.

EXPLANATION OF THE PURPOSIVE
CHARACTERISTICS OF MOLAR BEHAVIOR

With this more elaborate conception of the kinds of stimuli present at any time, the overt environmental stimulus ($S_e$), which had always been recognized, and the covert proprioceptive ($s_p$) and drive stimuli ($S_d$), Hull could ask and answer a number of basic questions about the characteristics of molar behavior displayed in Thorndikian trial and error learning experiments that required explanation. We

paraphrase the questions and answers as he stated them (Hull, 1930, 1931):

1. *Q.* Why does the organism persist in its trials or attempts even after repeated failures? (This, for Tolman, was one of the descriptive characteristics of purposive behavior.) *A.* Because of the persistent internal stimuli ($S_d$ and $s_g$) which, in the past, have been conditioned to a number of different responses.

2. *Q.* Why, in case success does not result from its first attempts, does the organism vary its reactions, often over a very wide range? *A.* Because the original response suffers experimental extinction, yielding its dominant place to the next response most strongly conditioned to the persistent inner stimuli.

3. *Q.* What principle or mechanism limits the range of variation of response which an organism will make to any problem situation? *A.* The nature of the persisting stimuli (i.e., whether they be the $S_d$ and $s_g$ of hunger or of thirst or of some other physiological drive) and the nature of past conditioning involving these stimuli.

4. *Q.* Why do organisms of the same general type differ so widely from each other in their reactions to the same (external) problem situation? (Here Hull addresses the problem of individual differences in behavior.) *A.* Because they have different life histories; viz. the conditioned responses elicited by $S_d$ and $s_g$ are different in animals who have had different past experiences.

5. *Q.* What principles determine the order of appearance of the several trial acts of a trial-and-error sequence? (Here Hull considers the problem of selectivity, another descriptive characteristic of purposive behavior.) *A.* The relative strengths of the conditioned responses which, in turn, depend upon past training.

6. *Q.* Why, in the series of trial acts preceding the first success, does the organism often stupidly commit the same erroneous reaction repeatedly? *A.* Because the extent of experimental extinction of a very strong, initially incorrect response on one or two trials may not weaken it sufficiently relative to the strength of the next strongest competing response.

7. *Q.* What constitutes success itself? *A.* Removal of the persistent stimulus which has provided motivation for the series of responses. (Again we are reminded of Freud's 1917 conception of instinct, or need, as an internal stimulus which persists until satisfied.)

8. *Q*. Why should the trial sequence come to an end as soon as success has been attained? Why should it not continue exactly as before? *A*. Because $S_d$, the persistent drive stimulus, is not present, and consequently neither is the $s_g$ produced by the $r_g$ elicited by $S_d$ any longer present. (Here we recall Tolman's assertion that physiological drives define the innate ends of behavior in that they define the state of affairs that must come about to terminate them.)

9. *Q*. Why, even after the successful reaction cycle has been performed one or more times, do reactions, repeatedly found to be unsuccessful, quite illogically continue sometimes to be made? *A*. One of the properties of conditioned responses is spontaneous recovery following their initial extinction.

10. *Q*. Why, in general, do these erroneous reactions become less and less frequent with each successful solution and why do they cease altogether? *A*. Spontaneous recovery is less after repeated occasions of experimental extinction. Furthermore, the correct or successful response is increasingly strengthened in subsequent correct trials.

11. *Q*. Why, for a particular organism, are certain trial and error problems so much more readily solved than others? Why, for certain organisms, is the same problem so much more difficult of solution than for other organisms, presumably of equally good natural endowment? *A*. The response which is destined to be successful in a given problem may already be relatively strong in one problem situation and not in another, or in one organism and not in another. This would depend upon the nature of earlier training.

12. *Q*. Why, on the whole, are the trial reactions in "blind" trial and error learning so much more likely to prove successful than would be a mere random sampling from the entire repertory of the organism's possible movements? Why is the organism so much more likely to try a successful act early in the trial and error sequence than pure random sampling might be expected to bring about? *A*. Because the responses made depend upon the nature of the internal stimuli ($S_d$ and $s_g$), which means they are more likely to be appropriate than responses based on $S_d$ and $s_g$ for some other drive. Furthermore, the strongest responses initially will be those strengthened in other situations that have similar environmental stimuli. It is the combined action of $S_e$, $S_d$, and $s_g$ which determines the initial response. (Here Hull considers the $S_d$ and $s_g$ as the kind of *selective agents* that Woodworth had suggested in

his early attempt to characterize the function of a drive or motive.)

Concluding this analysis of the descriptive characteristics of the behavior of Thorndike's animals, which the purposivists had marked as evidence of goal striving and central characteristics of *molar* behavior, Hull said:

"In conclusion it may be observed that the behavior deduced above, particularly the persistence of effort at solution by means of varied response, is one of the most commonly remarked differences between behavior, usually called psychic or mental, and that of ordinary automatic machines. Indeed it is common, by way of contrast, to call such behavior 'intelligent' and 'purposive.' It is the belief of the present author that these latter terms represent extremely important aspects of mammalian behavior, but that instead of being ultimate entities, all may be derived from certain combinations of more basic principles" (Hull, 1930b, p. 255).

Hull anticipated the possibility of the development of machines capable of the kind of behavior called "purposive":

"It is not inconceivable that 'psychic' machines may ultimately play an appreciable role in the life of industrialized communities. On the side of psychology it is possible that these mechanisms may dissolve the age-old problem of the opposition of mind to matter by practically demonstrating the characteristic mechanisms by means of which matter manifests the forms of behavior called psychic" (Hull, 1930b, pp. 255–256).

FUNCTIONAL PROPERTIES OF THE
ANTICIPATORY GOAL REACTION

As he continued to study the various implications of his analysis of the purposive characteristics of behavior, Hull gave increasing emphasis to the fractional anticipatory goal reaction ($r_g$) and the goal stimulus ($s_g$) which it produced. We must keep in mind what he meant by "fractional anticipatory goal reaction": viz., that portion of a goal reaction which could occur without limiting or interfering with the performance of other responses which were instrumental in bringing about the unconditioned stimulus for the goal or consummatory reaction. Implicit in this conception is the view that on the first occasions of "hunger" (or any other physiological need) in the life of an organism, there is no anticipation of the goal; but after the internal drive stimulus, $S_d$, has been associated with the consummatory or goal response a number of times (as it normally is during the first days and weeks of life), any subsequent arousal of that $S_d$ will immediately produce a conditioned $r_g$. The persistence of $r_g$ throughout any action sequence would then depend upon the persistence of the drive stimulus, $S_d$, which continuously evokes it. And the presence of $r_g$ necessarily implies the presence of an internal $s_g$, the *goal stimulus:*

> "Like all other movements, $r_g$ causes character-istic proprioceptive stimulations to arise from the muscles involved. This complex of stimulation flowing from $r_g$ may be represented conveniently by $s_g$ (see Figure 6.1). It is obvious that since $r_g$ persists throughout the behavior sequence, $s_g$ must also do so. It thus comes about that our dynamic situation is possessed of two persisting stimuli, $S_d$ and $s_g$." (Hull, 1931, pp. 495–496).

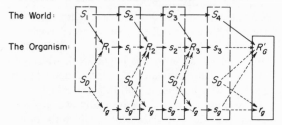

FIGURE 6.1 Hull's conception of the role of drive stimulus ($S_D$), anticipatory goal reaction ($r_g$), and goal stimulus ($s_g$) in the organization of a sequence of goal-directed activities. In later versions of this diagram (Hull, 1935), Hull also included broken arrows connect-ing the environmental stimuli ($S_1$, $S_2$, $S_3$, $S_4$) and re-sponse-produced stimuli ($s_1$, $s_2$, $s_3$) to the anticipatory goal reaction ($r_g$). *(After Hull, 1931)*

As shown in Figure 6.1, both $S_d$ and $s_g$ (the persistent core of internal stimulation) become as-sociated with all responses in the sequence, including the fullblown goal response ($R'_G$) and that fractional part of it which can be performed without interfering with other instrumental actions ($r_g$). In the case of the latter, $r_g$, Hull acknowledged that the association of $s_g$ to it was circular, since $r_g$ also produces $s_g$.

How do the two important internal stimuli, $S_d$ and $s_g$, differ? First, argued Hull, they differ in their source or origin. The $S_d$ of hunger, for example, has its origin in physico-chemical processes involved in nutrition, while $s_g$ depends in the main upon the existence of the $S_d$ and previous conditioning of $r_g$ to $S_d$. Thus, Hull argued, the drive stimulus ($S_d$) is not affected by the presence or absence of $s_g$, but anything which terminates $S_d$ will bring $s_g$ to an end. Hull emphasized the dependence of the $r_g$-$s_g$ mecha-nism (as it was soon to be called) on the presence of $S_d$, the drive stimulus; but he did entertain (in

reference to Figure 6.1) some other ideas which show how Tolman's concept of an expectancy that a particular response leads on to the goal might be represented in *S-R* terms. An important footnote to his comment that $s_g$ depends upon the presence of $S_d$ reads as follows:

> "This neglects the possibility that once $S_d$ has brought $r_g$ into the antecedent reaction sequence, stimuli there resident may acquire a tendency to evoke $r_g$ themselves and thus bring into existence $s_g$ independently of $S_d$. An example of such a pos-sibility would be the excitatory tendency repre-sented by $s_1 \dashrightarrow r_g$" (Hull, 1931, footnote p. 497).

This footnote merely acknowledges that once the physical basis of "the idea of the goal" is identified with a reaction ($r_g$) and the proprioceptive stimulus it invariably produces ($s_g$), what holds for responses in general must also hold for this particular response: viz., any stimulus, internal ($s_p$) or external ($S_e$), associated with that response can acquire the power of exciting it on subsequent occasions. Hull made little use of this important implication of his con-ception at the time.

There is a second difference between $S_d$ and $s_g$. From a single $S_d$ there may evolve many distinct goals. For example, organisms eat many different kinds of food:

> "The eating of each kind of food may become a different goal with the goal reaction in each case presumably in some sense distinct. Moreover, the same kind of food may constitute the goal in many different mazes. It is evident that this possibility of a multiplicity of goal stimuli for each drive stimulus has important dynamic potentialities, es-pecially in view of the small number of drives as contrasted with the immense variety of mammalian goals" (Hull, 1931, p. 497).

Hull went on to discuss the importance of the anticipatory goal reaction and the goal stimulus as the integrating elements in a sequence of goal-directed actions. He also considered how extinction of the anticipatory goal reaction, when the usual reward did not follow a sequence of instrumental actions, would account for the disruption (and hence extinction) of that particular action sequence because the important guiding and integrating goal stimulus $s_g$ no longer occurred. He then related his conception of the goal stimulus, $s_g$, in purposive behavior to earlier discussions of ideo-motor action. We recall James' insistence that if "the idea of the end" could once dominate consciousness then the whole habitual action sequence would run off automatically. (See page 25.)

A thorough discussion of these related topics would lead us far afield of our immediate objective, which is to see, in a general way, how Hull responded to the challenge of encompassing purposive behavior within the framework of stimulus and response. We conclude this discussion of the importance of the anticipatory goal reaction with his own summary:

". . . It has long been recognized that one of the prime functions of ideas is to guide and control instrumental acts in cases where the situation to which the acts really function is absent and, as a consequence, is unable to stimulate the organism directly. The capacity of anticipatory goal reactions as stimuli to control and direct other activity renders intelligible on a purely physical basis the dynamic guiding power of ideas. This, in turn, makes still more plausible the hypothesis that anticipatory goal reactions are the physical substance of purposive ideas.

"For the sake of definiteness and additional clarity the hypothesis elaborated above may be assembled in brief dogmatic form. Pure stimulus acts are the physical substance of ideas. Ideas, however, are of many varieties. Among them are goal or guiding ideas. The physical mechanism constituting these particular ideas is the anticipatory goal reaction. This appears to be substantially the same as ideo-motor action. The anticipatory goal reaction seems also to constitute the physical basis of the somewhat ill-defined but important concept of purpose, desire, or wish, rather than the drive stimulus as has sometimes been supposed. . . . This interpretation of purpose explains its dynamic nature and at the same time removes the paradox arising under the classical psychology where the future appeared to be operating causally in a backward direction upon the present. This hypothesis also renders intelligible the 'realization of an anticipation' by an organism. It is found where a fractional anticipatory goal reaction as a stimulus has motivated a behavior sequence which culminates in a full overt enactment of a goal-behavior complex of which it is a physical component" (Hull, 1931, pp. 505–506).

THE GOAL-GRADIENT HYPOTHESIS

With this analysis of purposive behavior as his foundation, Hull turned to the explanation of the details of maze learning experiments. He emphasized "that no mere chain-reaction hypothesis alone is adequate to account for various known facts" (Hull, 1932, p. 25). The increasing importance of the goal-reaction in his thinking is evident in the goal-gradient hypothesis, a new principle for the *S-R* account of learning which he then introduced:

"The mechanism which in the present paper will be mainly depended upon as an explanatory and integrating principle is that the goal reaction gets conditioned the most strongly to the stimuli preceding it, and the other reactions of the behavior sequence get conditioned to their stimuli progressively weaker as they are more remote (in time or space) from the goal reaction. This principle is clearly that of a gradient, and the gradient is evidently somehow related to the goal" (Hull, 1932, pp. 25–26).

## REINTERPRETATION OF THORNDIKE'S LAW OF EFFECT

This mounting concern with the goal reaction of a behavioral sequence, which was the upshot of answering the challenge of the purposivist's argument within the framework of stimulus-response psychology, culminated in Hull's reinterpretation of Thorndike's Law of Effect. In a special review of Thorndike's *Fundamentals of Learning* (1932), Hull (1935) set the stage for his major work which was to appear eight years later. He focused upon Thorndike's objective definition of a "satisfier" (see page 116) and argued that there are really two problems for investigation: (a) the extent to which the organism will strive to bring about the "state of affairs" (which Thorndike had pointed to as his objective evidence that a "state of affairs" was, in fact, a "satisfier"); and (b) the extent to which a connection (between *S* and *R*) will be strengthened by having the "state of affairs" occur.

"Which," he asked, "is primary": "*Does the motivation (striving) produce the learning (strengthening), or does the learning produce the motivation, or does some third and still more basic process produce both?*" (Hull, 1935, p. 821, italics added). Hull believed that strengthening, or conditioning, was the primary problem and that goal-directed striving could be derived from principles of learning as basic assumptions. We shall follow the line of his argument.

Which is the "causal variable" in the Thorndike Law of Effect, he asked, the "feeling of satisfaction" produced by a certain "state of affairs" or the "tendency to strive for it"? Which provides the scientific criterion that a "state of affairs" will function to produce learning? This was his answer:

". . . if objectively observable behavior is the real criterion, why complicate the situation with the entanglements of the subjective feelings of 'satisfyingness' at all? If the two are really equivalent why not substitute the former for the latter in the formulation of the law and thus avoid the ambiguity? In that event the law would read substantially as follows:

"When a modifiable connection between a situation and a response is made and is accompanied or followed by a state of affairs which the organism does more or less to attain or preserve, that connection's strength is increased" (Hull, 1935, p. 820).

In this form, argued Hull, the Law of Effect states a relationship between motivation (striving) and learning (strengthening). The investigator is forced to make two independent measurements and expects, if the law is correct, to find a correlation of 1.00 between those measurements. But the law can be further simplified as a principle of learning without the complication and possibly irrelevant hypothesis concerning a relationship between learning and motivation, as follows:

"When a modifiable connection between a situation and a response is made and is accompanied or followed by certain states of affairs, that connection's strength is increased" (Hull, 1935, p. 821).

Now, Hull believed, it would be possible to show that the fundamental problem was the problem of strengthening of connections (learning), and that striving (motivation) could be deduced from principles which refer essentially to the matter of strengthening of connections. Here is what he proposed:

"The deduction would probably set out from the assumption that there are originally certain *primary reinforcing 'states of affairs'* [italics added]. According to the hypothesis these 'states of affairs' (if positive) will tend to strengthen any stimulus-response combination which chances to occur in close temporal proximity. Now, *some* of these stimulus-response combinations will have no causal relationship to the 'state of affairs,' i.e. if they occur they will not be followed by the 'state of affairs'; if they are ever brought into operation the fact that they will not be followed by the reinforcing 'state of affairs' will cause them to suffer experimental extinction [or internal inhibition, following Pavlov] and they will therefore soon disappear. But in real life situations (as distinguished from the usual artificial laboratory situations) acts which precede the occurrence of any particular 'state of affairs' on any particular occasion are likely to be genuine causes of such 'states of affairs.' This is to say that unless over-ridden by opposing factors, such causal action sequences will always bring about the 'state of affairs' in question. It follows that whenever such causal stimulus-response combinations occur, the fact that they will tend strongly to be followed by the reinforcing 'state of affairs' will cause them to be strengthened more and more. But acts which invariably lead to certain 'states of affairs' unless over-ridden by opposing circumstances, constitute 'doing such things as attain,' i.e. striving for such

'states of affairs.' *Thus the organism through the mere process of conditioning will come to strive for states of affairs which are positively reinforcing*" (Hull, 1935, pp. 821–822).

This theoretical development, Hull believed, conformed to the principle of parsimony in that it reduced striving for goals to a secondary or derived principle, thereby reducing the number of primary assumptions needed in psychology by one. He continued:

"On this assumption states of affairs which organisms will strive to attain are reinforcing agents, not because they will evoke striving, but they evoke striving now because at some time in the past they were potent reinforcing agents, thereby joining stimuli and responses (or the habit-family equivalents of responses) which constitute the striving. Naturally, present effects of past reinforcing power should be excellent evidence of further powers of the same kind" (Hull, 1935, p. 822).

In this statement, Hull shifted from the position of accounting for learning in terms of Pavlovian concepts of conditioning to a general reinforcement theory based on the empirical Law of Effect. A year later, in his 1936 presidential address to the American Psychological Association, Hull specified what he *then* meant by a reinforcing state of affairs:

"A characteristic stimulus-reaction combination $(S_g \dashrightarrow R_g)$ always marks reinforcing states of affairs. . . . The particular stimulus-response combination marking the reinforcing state of affairs in the case of specific drives is determined empirically, *i.e.*, by observation and experiment" (Hull, 1937, p. 16).

Thus, as Spence (1956) has clearly pointed out, in the period immediately before the publication of his formal behavior theory (in which, as we shall see, he alters his position on this matter) Hull identified *reinforcing state of affairs* with the occurrence of the final, consummatory, or goal response of an action sequence. In the case of hunger, the combination Food-Eating Activity would define the reinforcing state of affaris from which, according to Hull's argument, the commonly observed striving for food and persistent food-seeking behavior to which the purposivists had called attention would be derived as a secondary phenomena.

But how, we might ask, except in the matter of the clarity of the analysis, does this position differ from the central argument of the purposivists that the *ends* of behavior are fundamental and innate while the *means* are learned?

## THE END OF THE TRANSITION
## FROM COMMON SENSE TO
## SCIENTIFIC VIEWPOINT

Hull's systematic analysis of the characteristics of purposive behavior during the 1930's brings to an end our discussion of the transition in orientation from common sense to scientific viewpoint in approach to the problem of motivation, which had begun nearly half a century earlier in James' introspective analysis of volition. What had Hull accomplished in this analysis of "purpose" and "knowledge" as habit phenomena?

First, he had exploited fully the implications of the *S-R* position to show the *plausibility* of accounting for the purposive characteristics of molar behavior in *S-R* terms. This indicated an acceptance of the broad behavioral problem of motivation as it had been conceived by those to whom we have referred as "purposivists."

In addition, he had answered the question that had led many "associationists" to consider "purpose" so much mentalistic and metaphysical nonsense. Hull showed how the goal or end of an action sequence, conceived as an anticipatory goal response, could become a scientifically respectable stimulus or *determinant* of actions leading to the goal without falling into an ambiguous mentalism of the sort apparent in McDougall's early conception.

Having showed this much, he then argued the plausibility of explaining current motivation (by this he meant *striving for goals*) in terms of principles which referred specifically to past strengthening of *S-R* connections (learning). One need not, in other words, assume that fullblown goal-directed tendencies were present at birth. One could work up from the notion of undirected behavior in the neonate to the directed (even consciously directed) behavior of the human adult given basic principles which explained learning and the excitation of responses by immediately present stimuli. The task, as he then saw it, was to get on with the job of systematic development of a *testable* theory of learning and behavior. This was the major countertheme of Hull's writings during the 1930's. He strove for clarity and specificity in the formulation of hypotheses derived from basic theoretical principles so that the self-corrective process of science could truly begin in the behavioral sciences. We catch something of the spirit which characterizes the modern era in psychology from one of Hull's papers in this period immediately preceding his major work:

"From the point of view of the longevity of hypotheses, it is extremely dangerous for them to become thoroughly definite and specific. The very definiteness of an hypothesis makes it possible to determine with relative ease whether its implications agree with known phenomena which it proposes to explain. In case of failure to conform, the unambiguous nature of the comparison is peculiarly fatal. Worse yet, an unambiguous hypothesis is likely to permit the deductive forecast of what should be observed under various experimental conditions which may as yet be untried. A single well-planned experiment may at any moment yield results quite different from the deductive forecast, and thus topple the entire hypothetical structure. This, of course, is all quite as it should be. The healthy development of a science demands that the implications of its hypotheses be deduced as promptly and unambiguously as possible. This will make it possible for them, if verified by experiment, to be incorporated into the structure or system of the science; or, if found to disagree with experimental findings, the hypotheses may be recast or simply discarded as errors in the long trial-and-error process of system construction. At the least, such hypotheses may be credited with the virtue of having stimulated experimental research. But if an hypothesis be so vague and indefinite, or so lacking in relevancy to the phenomena which it seeks to explain that the results neither of previous experiments nor those of experiments subsequently to be performed may be deduced from it, it will be difficult indeed to prove it false. And if, in addition, the hypothesis should appeal in some subtle fashion to the predilections of a culture in which it gains currency, it should enjoy a long and honored existence. Unfortunately, because of its very sterility and barrenness in the above deductive sense, such an hypothesis should have no status whatever in science. It savors more of metaphysics, religion, or theology" (Hull, 1930b, pp. 251–252).

THREADS FROM THE PAST: A DEFINITION
OF THE PROBLEM

The theory advanced by Hull in 1943 is evidence of the transition from common sense to scientific attitude which had been accomplished between 1890 and 1940, but it certainly did not resolve all the stubborn problems which had arisen in earlier analyses of motivation. Before plunging into Hull's formal theory, let us review some of the transitions in thought about the problem of motivation and how it should be studied.

Beginning in the late 19th century with James, we found the problem of motivation discussed in terms of the concepts of instinct, emotion, habit, and the introspective analysis of will or volition. Voluntary behavior was conceived as directed towards consciously apprehended ends, and from an *introspective analysis* of conscious thought during the act of willing it was concluded that acts occur when the idea of an act gains dominance over all other competing ideas. James advanced the view that an idea gains dominance over other ideas more easily when it represents an expression of instinctive impulse or is associated with pleasure or relief from pain. Here, in James, the problem of motivation was identified with *conscious volition*, essentially the traditional common-sense view of the problem.

In Freud we confront the great challenge to conventional wisdom: his cogent arguments and demonstrations of *unconscious motivation of behavior*. Again in Freud the discussion of what causes an impulse to act to be strong emphasized the instinctual origins of motives and the pleasure principle. Consciousness, however, was dethroned as the locus of the determinants of human action. The logic of *indirect methods* of inferring the presence of unconscious tendencies which function to impel and direct action towards the bringing about of certain effects was advanced.

Then, while Thorndike and Pavlov were making major breakthroughs in experimental methods of studying the behavior of animals and beginning the systematic analysis of the growth of association between a stimulus and a response, we find an evolution in the *definition of the problem of motivation in terms of objective behavior*. First in McDougall's arguments concerning the broad trend of goal-directed behavior, which he attributed to instinct, then in a recognition of the *separate problems of "mechanism" and "drive"* in the writings of Woodworth, and finally in Tolman's *identification of "purpose" with the "docility" of behavior (i.e., the selectivity of instrumental actions in relation to consequences) and the "persistence-until" character of behavior* we find the emergence of a behavioral definition of the problem of motivation. Purposive (i.e., goal-directed) behavior became a problem for experimental analysis as typified by the early studies of Tolman and his co-workers showing the effects of variations in strength of "drive," "incentive," and "expectancy of the goal" on the performance of rats in mazes.

In the writings of Lewin we confront the first systematic conceptual analysis of motivation and behavior, the beginnings of experimental study of human motivation, and the notion that the task for a psychology of motivation is to develop a useful conceptual scheme which explains thought and action in terms of immediate (contemporaneous) determinants. *Thus, the problem of motivation came to be defined both as an empirical problem*—that is, one that could be identified with the task of discovering factors which influence the purposive characteristics of observable behavior—*and as a theoretical or conceptual problem*—that is, one requiring the construction of a conceptual scheme which defines the functional properties of variables that influence performance and states coherently how those variables combine to determine the strength of a tendency to act in a certain way.

From the point of view of those early writers who emphasized the dynamics and goal-directedness of molar action, a particular *S-R* event, which was the matter of central interest among the early "associationists," had always to be considered merely an incident within the broad trend of the behavior of an organism conceived as an *active* goal-seeker rather than passively reactive to external influences.

Woodworth began to answer the challenge of the "purposivists' " argument for *S-R* psychology as far back as 1918 when he introduced the term "drive" as the name for a tendency within the organism that must be added to the environmental stimulus as a determinant of response. He urged that the simple *S-R* conception be replaced by a new paradigm, *S-O-R*.

Finally, around 1930, Hull accepted "striving for goals" (motivation) and "strengthening of connections" (learning) as separate problems. His main conclusion, in agreement with the contention of *S-R* behaviorism that *stimuli* are the causes of responses, was that striving for goals depended upon prior learning, that is, upon the elicitation by stimuli of previously acquired *S-R* connections (habits). He argued that the purposive characteristics of molar behavior, which others chose to view as spontaneous actions, could be conceived as reactions to certain critically important internal stimuli: the persistent stimulus associated with a particular condition of physiological drive ($S_d$) and the proprioceptive feedback from the anticipatory goal reaction ($r_g$-$s_g$) which was sustained throughout a sequence of actions by the continued presence of the drive stimulus. In general, Hull attempted to show how the persistence-until character of behavior could be attributed to the continued presence of an inner core of stimulation which persisted until a goal was reached and those inner stimuli were removed; how the variability of response in a trial and error sequence could be attributed to constantly changing environmental stimuli ($S_e$) and proprioceptive stimuli produced by previous responses ($s_p$); and how the integrative and guidance functions that once had been attributed to a mental entity called "purpose," (i.e., the idea of the end) could be performed by the anticipatory goal reaction ($r_g$-$s_g$) conceived as a *pure stimulus act* (i.e., as a vestigial response whose sole function was to produce a stimulus necessary for the elicitation of responses that were instrumental in bringing about a state of affairs that was commonly called the goal or consummatory reaction).

Certainly neither Tolman nor Lewin, whose views were quite similar, quarreled with the conclusion that the immediate determinants of present action depend upon the past experience of the organism and what has been learned. Tolman's concept of expectancy, as a determinant of performance, referred to the present influence on behavior of past experience. And Lewin clearly acknowledged the legitimacy of the question, "Why does the present life space of an organism (i.e., the conceptual representation of all immediate influences on his performance) have a certain structure and not some other?" He, like Tolman, admitted the dependence of the life space on past experience. But Lewin, more vigorously than any of his contemporaries, pointed out that it is the *present* structure of the life space—that is, the *combination* of various immediate and interrelated influences having certain functional properties—which determines present actions. In this connection, Tolman advanced the idea of representing the present effects of past experience and other immediate influences on performance as "intervening variables," as inferred behavioral dispositions which intervene between the observed stimulus and response in the determination of behavior. Both Tolman and Lewin took the view that hypothetical explanatory variables of this kind could be posited without specifying the nature of the underlying physiological structures and processes but by specifying their functional properties, that is, their implications for behavior.

Thus Hull's conclusion that striving for goals depended upon prior learning is a conclusion which opposed the earlier doctrine of instinct as inborn goal-directed tendency and not a disagreement with the conceptual analyses of Tolman and Lewin. Yet, as we have previously noted, in positing a *primary reinforcing state of affairs* (replacing Thorndike's concept of "satisfier") to explain learning, and in identifying this state of affairs with what had been called the goal or consummatory event ($S_G$-$R_G$), Hull's position was also in essential agreement with McDougall's central notion that the *ends* of behavior are given.

Hull had encompassed the characteristics of molar behavior described as the hallmarks of purpose by McDougall and Tolman in his essays of the 1930's. But his answer to the question, "What motivates a response?" did not differ in principle from that of Watson and other early *S-R* behaviorists. The response, as Hull then viewed the matter, was *excited* by the complex of $S_e$ (environmental stimulus), $s_p$ (proprioceptive feedback from immediately preceding response), $S_d$ (persistent internal stimulus associated with a condition of physiological deficit), and $s_g$ (the proprioceptive feedback from the anticipatory goal reaction, $r_g$, which was itself sustained by the presence of $S_d$ to which it had previously been conditioned). The only "principle" stated to explain how these various sources of stimulation combined, at a moment in time, to excite a response was the notion that their effects would be summative. The combined influence of $S_e$, $s_p$, $S_d$, and $s_g$, all favoring elicitation of the same response, would enhance its probability of occurrence.

Though Hull did not officially say so, his conception in the early 1930's posited the action of three types of intervening (i.e., non-observable) variables, all conceived as having the functional properties of stimuli: $S_d$, $s_p$, and $r_g$-$s_g$, the last of which also had the functional properties of a response. As we shall soon discover, Hull shortly thereafter explicitly adapted the intervening variable type of theory advocated by Tolman in his formal conception of the contemporaneous determinants of the strength of a response tendency. It is this particular aspect of Hull's formal behavior theory which explicitly deals with the problem of motivation (the immediate determinants of action) as it had evolved during the fifty-year period since James' analysis of volition.

A CONFUSION IN THE INITIAL STATEMENT
OF THE PRINCIPLES OF BEHAVIOR

Before beginning our survey of the evolution of the *S-R* theory since 1943, it will be helpful to consider one other matter. Having identified the separate problems of striving for goals (in reference to which he used the term "motivation") and strengthening of connections (in reference to which he used the term "learning"), Hull had argued that striving for goals could be derived from principles which explain learning, given the assumption that certain states of affairs (like eating when hungry) function to reinforce the connection between immediately preceding stimuli and responses. From this he concluded that the task of formulating principles which explain the growth and function of habits (the problem of "learning" as he conceived it) should take precedence if we are to have a theory which could work up from the simple, undirected activities of the neonate organism to the purposive pursuit of goals which is the hallmark of the behavior of more mature organisms, animal and human. This is a sound conclusion if one sets out to study the evolution of purposive behavior from birth in the life of an organism. But the experimental facts to which Hull turned in formulating his *Principles of Behavior* (1943) did not concern the primitive behaviors of neonate organisms but the molar activities of more mature organisms who, according to his own prior analysis, should have long since learned to anticipate eating ($r_{gh}$) whenever made hungry ($S_{dh}$), drinking ($r_{gt}$) whenever made thirsty ($S_{dt}$), etc. In other words, many or most of the details of animal behavior which he began to consider were already to be conceived as incidents in the purposive pursuit of goals. Yet the theory, as he initially stated it, seems explicitly aimed at explaining the growth of goal-directed behavior from the most primitive state of the organism. The animals whose experimental behavior he considered were too old to be relevant to that problem.

The inadequacy of Hull's initial formal statement, to which we now turn, became apparent almost immediately when he had to confront the criticism of Tolman, particularly, in reference to the "latent learning phenomena." The theory had to be revised to regain the important concept of anticipatory goal reaction which had been temporarily lost in the 1943 formulation. In the revision, Hull reintroduced anticipation of the goal as one of the fundamental variables in his conception of the immediate determinants of performance.

The conceptual similarity of *S-R* behavior theory and the views of Tolman and Lewin is much more apparent in later revisions of the theory than it was initially, and so we shall postpone further comparisons of viewpoints until later with this forewarning as to why Hull's initial formal conception of the determinants of instrumental action seems so different from the views, including his own, which had preceded it.

## HULL'S *PRINCIPLES OF BEHAVIOR* (1943)

A quotation taken from the concluding chapter of Hull's major work appears under the heading of this chapter. It conveys his tough-minded attitude as he attempted to elaborate an objective theory of the behavior of organisms. We cannot, of course, do full justice to this imposing theoretical structure in so short a space. We shall have to deal selectively with matters that are most related to the central thread of this introduction to motivation, eliminating many technical details and the specifics of Hull's mathematical treatment of the fundamental relationships specified in the theory. Hull's 1943 theory was both a mathematical formulation and an attempt to encourage the integration of molar behavior theory in psychology with physiology. He fully understood the dilemma faced by students of the social sciences:

"Students of the social sciences are presented with the dilemma of waiting until the physico-chemical problems of neurophysiology have been adequately solved before beginning the elaboration of behavior theory, or of proceeding in a provisional manner with certain reasonably stable principles of the coarse, macroscopic or molar action of the nervous system whereby movements are evoked by stimuli, particularly as related to the history of the individual organism.

"There can hardly be any doubt that a theory of molar behavior founded upon an adequate knowledge of both molecular and molar principles would in general be more satisfactory than one founded upon molar considerations alone. But here again the history of physical science is suggestive. Owing to the fact that Galileo and Newton carried out their molar investigations, the world has had the use of a theory which was in very close approximation to observations at the molar level for nearly three hundred years before the development of the molecular science of modern relativity and quantum theory. Moreover, it is to be remembered that science proceeds by a series of successive approximations; it may very well be that had Newton's system not been worked out when it was there would have been no Einstein and no Planck, no relativity and no quantum theory at all. It is conceivable that the elaboration of a systematic science of behavior at a molar level may aid in the development of an adequate neurophysiology and thus lead in the end to a truly molecular theory of behavior firmly based on physiology" (Hull, 1943, p. 20).

And so, acknowledging the limitations of knowledge but feeling the necessity of getting on with the task, Hull set out to develop the type of theory of molar behavior in terms of intervening variables which Tolman had advocated. But throughout his work, the types of variables considered and the descriptions offered of possible underlying neurophysiological mechanisms reveal Hull's conviction that the constructions of psychologists should always be guided by what seems best evidence or best guess as to the nature of the underlying physical process. The major hypothesis advanced by Hull in this molar behavior theory, and the one which for a good many years diverted attention from the traditional problem of motivation was his physiological hypothesis concerning the nature of reward or reinforcement.

THE BASIC PROBLEM FOR A THEORY OF BEHAVIOR

Hull saw his task within the framework of Darwin's theory of evolution. Living organisms, possessing receptors capable of being stimulated by both an internal and an external environment, and capable of motor response allowing movement through the external environment, are also so constituted that from time to time one or another of the commodities or conditions necessary for individual or species survival (like food or water) are lacking. Hull referred to such a deficiency as a "state of *primary need*" (Hull, 1943, p. 17). From these considerations, it follows that:

> ". . . *an organism will hardly survive unless the state of organismic need and the state of the environment in its relation to the organism are somehow jointly and simultaneously brought to bear upon the movement-producing mechanism of the organism*" (Hull, 1943, p. 18).

Unless the appropriate reaction is immediately elicited by the combined action of environmental stimulus ($S_e$) and organismic need, that is, unless behavior completely adequate to the problem of survival is innate and the need soon satisfied, the organism will perish. But, as a matter of fact, organisms do not perish, or at least sufficiently large numbers have not perished over millions of years. How, then, does this coordination of inner need and environmental stimulation to produce complicated sequences of adaptive behavior come about. It must be learned. But how is it learned? That, in brief, is the basic problem to which Hull directed his attention. He begins at the beginning.

INNATE ENDOWMENT

The first two postulates (basic assumptions) of Hull's theory assert an organism's sensitivity to stimulation and the interaction of neural traces of simultaneously present stimuli. (His critics have charged that he swallowed up the whole psychological problem of perception in these postulates, but that problem is off the mark of our present interest). In his third formal postulate, Hull assumed that organisms possess, at birth, unlearned tendencies to react to certain stimuli—in other words, reflexes:

> "Organisms at birth possess receptor effector connections ($_sU_R$) which, under combined stimulation ($S$) and drive ($D$), have the potentiality of evoking a hierarchy of responses that either individually or in combination are more likely to terminate the need than would be a random selection from the reaction potentials resulting from other stimulus and drive combinations" (Hull, 1943, Postulate 3, p. 66).

Hull assumed that when a condition of biological *need* arose, there would be produced what psychologists of the period had already taken to calling a *drive* which would activate the animal. Drive was to be considered an intervening variable which could be defined as a function of *antecedent* conditions. For example, the amount of food need increases with the number of hours elapsed since last feeding, and drive is a function of the need for food. Hull considered the demonstrations of increased activity in relation to number of hours of food privation, stage of estrous cycle in rats, etc., provided by Richter (1927) and others to be ample evidence of the activating or energizing function of *drive*. But in addition to assuming that need produces drive (i.e., activation of neural structures), Hull also assumed that different states of biological need produce qualitatively different patterns of internal stimulation, the now familiar drive stimulus ($S_d$). Thus, Hull's organism at birth possessed receptors which could be stimulated by external stimuli, the capacity for movement, the capacity to be activated (driven) by the presence of a biological need, internal receptors which were sensitive to particular need states ($S_d$), and also a hierarchy of innate response tendencies ($_sU_R$) which might be elicited by particular combinations of environmental stimulus ($S_e$) and drive stimulus ($S_d$). This joint elicitation of $_sU_R$ by $S_e$ and $S_d$ increased the probability that the responses originally elicited would be relevant in some way to the particular need which had arisen.

TWO IMMEDIATE CONSEQUENCES OF A
BIOLOGICAL NEED

Of particular importance is the assumption that a particular biological need has two immediate consequences: drive (activation) and $S_d$, as is shown schematically below:

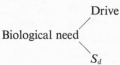

The function of a stimulus, whether external ($S_e$) or internal ($S_d$) is to elicit or evoke a response that is either innately associated with it ($_sU_R$) or connected to it as a consequence of learning. Thus, even in the first instance of behavior in the life of an organism we must, given this view, attribute selectivity of response, or direction of behavior, to the combined influence of $S_e + S_d$.

Drive, on the other hand, was conceived as a non-directional influence, as a *general exciter* of all responses that are elicited by the stimuli present at a given time. Thus it is the combination of stimulation ($S_e + S_d$) and drive together with the hierarchy of available unlearned dispositions ($_sU_R$) which constitutes the motivation of the very first response in the life of an organism.

Since both drive and an eliciting stimulus are required to initiate action, and drive is produced by biological needs, Hull's position was that biological needs are the ultimate springs of action:

> "The major primary needs or drives are so ubiquitous that they require little more than to be mentioned. They include the need for foods of various sorts (hunger), the need for water (thirst), the need for air, the need to avoid tissue injury (pain), the need to maintain an optimal temperature, the need to defecate, the need to micturate, the need for rest (after protracted exertion), the need for sleep (after protracted wakefulness), and the need for activity (after protracted inaction). The drives concerned with the maintenance of the species are those which lead to sexual intercourse and the need represented by nest building and care of the young" (Hull, 1943, pp. 59–60).

A MISLEADING RESTRICTION IN HULL'S
USE OF THE TERM "MOTIVATION"

Hull addressed the problem of motivation, as definition of this problem had evolved, in his search for the combination of factors which together determine the response of an organism. He clearly asserted his fundamental agreement with the principle of contemporaneity which Lewin had urged and acknowledged the plurality of causes of an event: "Now, it is assumed that *the immediate causes of an event must be active at the time the event begins to occur*" (Hull, 1943, p. 109).

A little later we shall confront the formal principle advanced by Hull in 1943 to account for the immediate strength of a tendency to respond in a certain way in terms of the combined influence of several different variables. Yet almost from the outset in his book *Principles of Behavior*, Hull began to use the term "motivation" as a synonym for *drive*, one of the immediate determinants of a response, rather than in reference to the combination of influences which together determined the response tendency. For example:

> "In the case of hunger, for example, there must be an equation expressing the degree of drive or motivation as a function of the number of hours' food privation, say, and there must be a second equation expressing the vigor of organismic action as a function of the degree of drive ($D$) or motivation, combined in some manner with habit strength" (Hull, 1943, notes, p. 66).

He had obviously begun to think of "motivation" as *one kind of determinant* of a response, that is, *drive*, and the connection between stimulus and response referred to as $_sU_R$ when it was innate and as *habit* ($_sH_R$) when it was learned, as *another kind of determinant* of response. His working assumption was:

> ". . . that motivation ($D$) as such, whether its origin be food privation, electric shock, or whatever, bears a certain constant relationship to action intensity in combination with other factors, such as habit strength" (Hull, 1943, notes, pp. 66–67).

This usage departs from his own earlier use of the term "motivation" in reference to one problem, "striving for goals" as distinct from another problem, "learning," or "strengthening of connections" (see pp. 156–157), and it certainly departs from traditional use of the term in reference to the problem of the immediate determinants of the direction, vigor, and persistence of action.

Much of the contemporary confusion concerning the meaning of the term "motivation" can be attributed to Hull's identification of the term with *one* of the important explanatory constructs in his own theory, *drive*. Advocates of the Hullian viewpoint have tended to follow Hull's usage, and so for many of them the psychology of "motivation" is now completely identified with the functional properties of the construct, drive (see for example, Brown, 1960). We shall ignore this restrictive use of the term "motivation," for it renders meaningless the question, "How do the theoretical conceptions of motivation advanced by Tolman, Lewin, and Hull differ?" Only in Hull, and, perhaps, in the Freudian concept of "libido" do we find systematic explanatory use of a general energizing concept as one of the immediate determinants of action. We shall refer to *drive* as *one* of the important motivational variables in Hull's 1943 theory. Now we turn to a discussion of another one, *habit*.

### THE PRINCIPLE OF PRIMARY REINFORCEMENT

Given the assumption of a hierarchy of innate stimulus-response connections ($_sU_R$), "the process of learning," in Hull's view, "consists in the strengthening of certain of these connections as contrasted with others, or in the setting up of quite new connections" (Hull, 1943, p. 69). The former is the phenomenon of *selective learning*, to which Thorndike had drawn attention; the latter is the phenomenon of *conditioning*, to which Pavlov had drawn attention. Hull considered both phenomena to be special cases of the operation of the same basic laws, the most important of which was the *principle of primary reinforcement*.

We recall Hull's earlier notion that purposive pursuit of goals could be derived from principles which explain learning, and his earlier assumption that what Thorndike had called a "satisfier" might be called "a reinforcing state of affairs." In 1935, he had identified "reinforcing state of affairs" with the stimulus-response event which normally terminates a behavioral sequence, the goal or consummatory reaction ($S_G \rightarrow R_G$). Now, however, in his formal theory he advocated the view that the "*primary*" reinforcing state of affairs was reduction of biological need. We paraphrase his statement of the principle or "law" of primary reinforcement, eliminating certain neurophysiological details in his statement:

> Whenever a reaction ($R$) takes place in temporal contiguity with a stimulus ($S$), and this conjunction is followed closely by the diminution in a need (and the associated diminution in the drive, $D$, and in the drive stimulus, $S_d$), there will be an increment in the tendency for that stimulus on subsequent occasions to evoke that reaction (based on Hull, 1943, p. 71).

The increment in tendency for the stimulus on subsequent occasions to evoke the reaction was referred to as an increment in habit strength, and habit strength, or more briefly, *habit*, was designated $_sH_R$.

This principle, when applied to Thorndikian trial and error learning, accounts for the selective strengthening of the correct response ($R$) to the stimulus situation ($S$). The correct response is followed by eating and ingestion of food which reduces the need for food. It also accounts for Pavlov's observation that a stimulus like the ticking of a metronome, which originally has no power to elicit salivation, acquires that power when consistently followed by presentation of food and its ingestion by the dog. In this case there is, to begin with, no connection between the metronome ($S$) and salivary reaction ($R$), but the new connection is formed when the novel $S$-$R$ event is closely followed by need reduction. Thus, Hull believed, he had embraced with one explanatory principle the two types of learning phenomena which had previously been treated as essentially different by learning theorists.

If we now imagine a neonate organism, as Hull conceived it, having only a family of reflexes ($_sU_R$) as innate equipment, we get this picture of what happens the very first time it becomes hungry. The first time the biological need for food occurs, the need produces *drive* and a distinctive internal pattern of stimuli, the drive stimulus, $S_d$. The momentary external stimulus situation ($S_e$), whatever it is, and the drive stimulus ($S_d$) jointly select one and then another unlearned response ($_sU_R$) according to the hierarchy of their initial (innate) strengths. The combined influence of *drive*, general exciter of responses, and the immediate stimulus situation $S_e + S_d$ accounts for the initiation and vigor of the various responses. If one of these—for example, a turn of the head, is quickly followed by the mother's breast in the mouth and reflexive sucking and swallowing, the connection between $S_e + S_d$ and that particular response ($R$) will be *selectively strengthened*. But so also will the primitive "consummatory" or "goal" reaction ($R_G$) of sucking and swallowing be *conditioned* to the $S_d$ produced by the need and removed when the need is reduced. In principle, then, the first instance of hunger is conceived as producing behavior that is in no sense influenced or guided by an anticipation of the goal, no matter how vague, unless it were to be assumed that the $S_d$ of hunger innately elicited some vestigial form of consummatory reaction, $r_g$. But by the repeated action of primary reinforcement (i.e., need-reduction) during the first days and weeks of life, the new habit defined by the connection between $S_d$ and $r_g (_{S_d}H_{r_g})$ should soon be greatly strengthened, allowing $r_g$-$s_g$ soon to begin to play the important guiding and integrative roles assigned to it by Hull in his earlier analysis of purposive behavior.

Hull did not discuss this particular problem in his 1943 statement of the theory. He put off until later a formal discussion of the important role of the anticipatory goal reaction. Had he dealt with this implication of his theory in 1943, he might have anticipated some of the difficulties that forced him later to revise his view of the immediate determinants of a response.

SECONDARY REINFORCEMENT

Hull was quick to recognize "that a great deal of behavior takes place in relatively protracted sequences in which primary reinforcement normally occurs only after the final act" (Hull, 1943, p. 84). Evidence had shown that reinforcement must follow soon after a particular *S-R* event to be effective. "Consequently," he asserted, "direct or primary reinforcement, as such, is inadequate to account for a very great deal of learning" (Hull, 1943, p. 84).

Consider how long it must take for food to be digested and thus repair the tissue deficit called hunger or need for food. Fortunately, experiments performed in Pavlov's laboratory had provided some evidence upon which could be based a principle to resolve this problem. Frolov had first presented food to a dog immediately after the sounding of a ticking metronome, producing the usual conditioned salivary response to the ticking metronome on subsequent occasions. Following this, the dog was presented with the stimulus of a black square in his line of vision. Initially, the black square had no effect on the dog's behavior, but then the black square was presented and followed, after an interval of 15 seconds, by the ticking of a metronome for 30 seconds, *no food being given*. On the tenth presentation of the black square by itself for 25 seconds, a total of 5.5 drops of saliva were secreted. This meant that the sound of the metronome, a stimulus which had earlier been associated with the ingestion of food, had acquired the capacity to act as a reinforcing agent itself. Hull referred to this as *secondary reinforcement*.

Hull cited other similar evidence that stimuli which have in the past been closely and consistently followed by primary reinforcement take on the capacity to serve as reinforcing states of affairs. Bugelski (1938) had trained two comparable groups of rats to press a bar which activated a mechanism that dropped a food pellet in a cup immediately before them in an apparatus invented by B. F. Skinner and often called "the Skinner Box." After the animals had learned to press the lever for food, this behavior was extinguished in both groups by adjusting the apparatus so that pressing the bar would no longer yield a food pellet. In one group, however, the bar press continued to produce the customary clicking noise of the food-release mechanism. In the other group, the mechanism was arranged so that a bar press would not produce a clicking noise during extinction trials. Bugelski found that the animals for whom the clicking noise followed a bar press, though no food was forthcoming, produced about 30 per cent more responses before reaching extinction of that response than the animals in the other group for whom a bar press produced neither the clicking noise nor the food. Hull considered this convincing evidence that a stimulus (the magazine click) which had been closely and consistently associated with receipt of food could contribute to the maintenance of another *S-R* connection, bar press.

Also cited by Hull were observations made by Cowles (1937) in studies of chimpanzees. Cowles had trained chimpanzees to insert colored discs into a slot machine which delivered a raisin for each disc and had observed that after this training the chimps would retain, hoard, and work for discs as if they had attained the status of subgoals. When given the task of learning which of five small boxes contained a token, Cowles found that performance compared favorably with performance when a food reward was employed. In one comparison, where the chance frequency of a correct response was 20 per cent, the average score of two chimps was 74 per cent for food tokens and 93 per cent for food reward.

In similar experiments, Wolfe (1936) had noted that both food and food tokens elicited anticipatory lip-smacking activity in chimpanzees, but a different kind of token that had not been associated with receipt of food did not. Hull was willing to leave open the question of the nature of secondary reinforcement in 1943. He considered the possibility that to reinforce another *S-R* connection a secondary reinforcing stimulus might have to elicit some component of the consummatory reaction or might itself have to be conditioned to the primary reinforcing state of affairs (i.e., diminution of need). But, as already stated, these matters which called for full discussion of the role of the anticipatory goal reaction were put aside for later treatment. Suffice to say that Hull broadened his principle of reinforcement to embrace the wider learning potentialities inherent in *secondary reinforcement*. Again, we paraphrase his statement:

Whenever a reaction (*R*) occurs in temporal contiguity with a stimulus (*S*) and this conjunction is closely followed in time with the diminution of need (and drive and drive stimulus, $S_d$) or with a stimulus situation which has been closely and consistently associated with such a need diminution, there will result an increment to the tendency for that stimulus to evoke that reaction (based on Hull, 1943, p. 98).

Experimental evidence shows that a stimulus loses its capacity to serve as a secondary reinforcement if not consistently followed by a primary reinforcing state of affairs. Grindley (1929) placed young chickens at the end of a runway and grains of boiled rice at the other end. He measured the speed of running on subsequent trials and found that chickens allowed to eat the rice showed a typical increase in speed of running on successive trials. However, chickens allowed only to look at the grains of rice through a glass plate showed an increase in speed on initial trials followed by a gradual reduction typical of extinction. From this experiment it appeared that the visual stimulus of the rice grains lost the power of secondary reinforcement as it lost the power of evoking the reaction (eating) conditioned to it at the time it had acquired its power of secondary reinforcement.

Hull considered the possibility that even the apparent reinforcing power of so-called goal or consummatory reactions should be conceived as instances of secondary reinforcement derived from frequent and consistent association of these particular reactions with the ultimate, primary reinforcing state of affairs:

"Since the various receptor discharges associated with the eating of food, its swallowing, digestion, and absorption, have throughout the entire life of each organism been associated in a uniform and practically invariable sequence with ultimate need reduction, it is to be expected that the stimuli associated with mastication would have acquired a profound degree of secondary reinforcing power" (Hull, 1943, note, p. 99).

Speculations of this sort, which agree in principle with earlier views of Freud (see page 58) and Tolman (see page 137) concerning the ultimate aims or ends of behavior, greatly stimulated research having to do with the underlying physiological nature of the process of reinforcement. But this question, while one of fundamental interest and importance to

physiological psychology, need not be answered to study systematically the functional properties and behavioral implications of objectively defined reinforcing states of affairs. The latter problem is of fundamental significance in contemporary efforts to develop an *ahistorical* and *aphysiological* mathematical conception of the motivation of behavior.

THE DETERMINANTS OF HABIT STRENGTH

Having developed his concept of drive, produced by biological need, as the general activator of response tendencies, Hull then identified four determinants of the strength of connection between a stimulus and response which he called *habit* ($_sH_R$). Strength of *habit* ($_sH_R$) was to be treated as a variable which together with *drive* intervenes between observable stimulus and observable response in the determination of present behavior.

On the observable response side, strength of habit could be indirectly measured in terms of the probability of response (given the appropriate stimulus), the speed or latency of the response (given the appropriate stimulus), and the resistance of the response to extinction when the normal reinforcing state of affairs was eliminated. That is to say, when both the stimulating circumstances and the strength of drive are held constant, an increase in the strength of habit can be inferred from an increase in probability of response, a decrease in the latency of response (i.e., the time between onset of stimulus and response), an increase in the magnitude of reaction, and increased resistance to extinction (i.e., trials to extinction) when reinforcement of that response is withheld.

Hull turned to experimental evidence which appeared, at the time, to justify the conclusion that the following four factors in the antecedent history of the organism determined the strength of habit:

1. The *contiguity of the stimulus and response during training;*
2. The closeness of the *S-R* event to a reinforcing state of affairs, which is referred to as *delay of reinforcement;*
3. The *number of reinforcements;* and
4. The *magnitude of reinforcement* during training.

In reference to the selective learning exhibited by Thorndike's dogs, Hull attributed the strength of habit of making the correct response to get out of the puzzle box to the degree of temporal contiguity between the stimuli of the box and the performance of the correct response, the relative absence of delay in attaining the food reward after performance of the correct response, the number of trials on which performance of that response in the presence of the stimuli of the box had been reinforced, and the magnitude of the reinforcement, which Hull identified with the magnitude of the reward offered the animals to reduce the need for food.

Hull's fourth basic postulate, which we paraphrase to avoid mathematical details, concerned the gradual growth of habit strength as a function of these four antecedents:

> Whenever a response $(R)$ and a stimulus $(S)$ occur in close temporal contiguity, and this conjunction is closely associated with the diminution of a need or with a stimulus which has been closely and consistently associated with the diminution of a need, there will result an increment to a tendency for that stimulus on later occasions to evoke that reaction. The increments from successive reinforcement summate in a manner which yields a combined habit strength $(_sH_R)$ which is a simple positive growth function of the number of reinforcements. The upper limit of this curve of learning is in turn a function of the magnitude of need reduction which is involved in primary, or which is associated with secondary, reinforcement; the delay of reinforcement; and the degree of contiguity between the stimulus and response (based on Hull, 1943, p. 178).

It was Hull's view that the amount of growth in habit strength on any single reinforced trial was a constant fraction of the growth potentiality still to be realized. Hence, variables which defined the upper limit of habit strength would influence the amount of increase in habit strength on any single reinforced trial.

In connection with amount of reward (or magnitude of reinforcement) as a determinant of habit strength, Hull presented evidence from a study by Gantt (1938), which is presented in Figure 6.2, showing that the amount of saliva produced by dogs in a salivary conditioning experiment depends upon the amount of reinforcing agent (food) used during training. Similar evidence of the positive effect of amount of reward on performance in a selective learning situation was presented. Grindley (1929–1930) had measured the speed with which chickens traversed a four-foot runway to food reward at the end of training when the number of grains of boiled rice present during each trial of training differed.

Hull was later to change his position regarding amount of reward and the problem with which we are already familiar in Tolman's work as the problem of incentive. In 1943, however, he had this to say about it:

"Motivation has two aspects, (1) that of drive $(D$, or $S_D)$ characteristic of primary needs, and (2) that of incentive. The amount-of-reinforcement hypothesis is closely related to the second of these aspects. The concept of incentive in behavior theory corresponds roughly to the common-sense notion of reward. More technically, the incentive is that substance or commodity in the environment which satisfies a need, i.e., which reduces a drive" (Hull, 1943, p. 131).

He then went on to argue that if amount of reward defines the magnitude of reinforcement of a habit, all other things equal, the visual stimulus arising from a large piece of food or a large number of pieces of food (i.e., a large reward) should become more strongly conditioned to the reaction of approach than the visual stimulus produced by a smaller piece of food or fewer pieces of food (i.e., a small reward). Thus, when a food reward of a certain magnitude is visibly present, as in the original Thorndike experiments,

> ". . . given a normal hunger drive, the organism will execute the correct one of several acts originally evoked by the situation more promptly, more vigorously, more certainly, and more per-

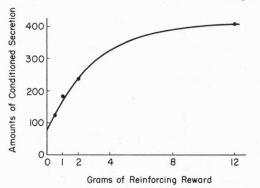

FIGURE 6.2 Graphic representation of the empirical functional relationship between the amount of the reinforcing agent (food) employed at each reinforcement of four conditioned reactions to as many different stimuli, and the final mean amount of salivary secretion evoked by each stimulus at the limit of training. *The appreciable secretional value of 75 units when the fitted curve is extrapolated to where the amount of reinforcing agent equals zero is presumably due to secretion evoked by static stimuli arising from the experimental environment. Plotted from unpublished data from the dog "Billy" kindly furnished by Gantt (1938) and published with his permission. The experimental work upon which this graph is based was performed prior to 1936.* (From Hull, *Principles of Behavior*, copyright 1943, Appleton-Century-Crofts, Inc., p. 125)

sistently when a large amount of food is stimulating its receptors than when they are stimulated by a small amount" (Hull, 1943, p. 132).

Hull summarized the view that his hypothesis concerning amount of reward encompassed one aspect of the problem of motivation as follows:

"From the amount-of-reinforcement hypothesis may be derived a special case of one phase of motivation, that of incentive or secondary motivation. This is the situation where the incentive (reinforcing agent) contributes a prominent, direct component of the stimulus complex which is conditioned to the act being reinforced. The stimulus component arising from a large amount of this substance will be different from that arising from a small amount, and will differ still more from a stimulus situation containing a zero amount. It follows from this and the amount-of-reinforcement hypothesis that in the course of reinforcement by differing amounts of the reinforcing agent, the organism will inevitably build up stronger reaction tendencies to the stimulus arising from large amounts than to that from small amounts, and no habit strength at all will be generated by zero amounts. It thus comes about, primary motivation (e.g., hunger) remaining constant, that large amounts of the agent will evoke more rapid, more vigorous, more persistent, and more certain reactions than will small or zero amounts. Thus a reinforcing agent as a stimulus becomes an incentive to action, and large amounts of the agent become more of an incentive than small amounts. This *a priori* expectation is well substantiated by quantitative experiment as well as by general observation" (Hull, 1943, p. 133).

## STIMULUS GENERALIZATION

A fifth basic assumption of Hull's theory takes account of the fact that very rarely, if ever, is exactly the same stimulus situation repeated in the life of an organism. It posits the functional equivalence of stimuli, which though not identical, are very similar. In brief, the assumption of *stimulus generalization* means that when a particular *S-R* is reinforced, the reaction becomes associated with a considerable range of stimuli which, in terms of one or another qualitative or quantitative dimension, are *similar* to the stimulus present when reinforcement occurred. Thus if one considers a response which has been conditioned to a white stimulus, it should be elicited on some subsequent occasion by a light gray stimulus and to a lesser extent by a darker shade of gray. Hull then introduced the concept of effective habit strength, $s\bar{H}_R$, to stand for the strength of habit elicited by a particular stimulus situation. Effective habit strength diminishes as the degree of

similarity between the stimulus at the time of reinforcement (i.e., during training) and the stimulus at the time of subsequent elicitation of response decreases.

If we consider Thorndike's dogs put into the same problem box on subsequent trials, the principle of stimulus generalization accounts for the tendency of the dogs to perform the correct response sooner in successive rewarded trials even though the visual stimulus of the interior of the box, to which the animal is responding, may vary slightly from trial to trial depending upon the animal's location, the brightness of the room, etc. The concept of stimulus generalization accounts for transfer of training from one learning situation to other similar situations. The phenomenon is illustrated in results obtained by Hovland (1937) to which Hull referred in stating the principle of stimulus generalization. (See Figure 6.3.)

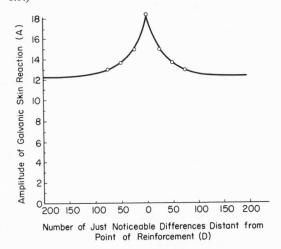

FIGURE 6.3  Empirical generalization gradient of conditioned galvanic skin reaction derived from data published by Hovland (1937). *Note that the gradient extends in both directions on the stimulus continuum (vibration rate) from the point originally conditioned. (From Hull, Principles of Behavior, copyright 1943, Appleton-Century-Crofts, Inc., p. 185)*

## DRIVE AND HABIT AS INTERVENING VARIABLES

It is apparent that Hull viewed *drive* and *habit* as variables which were hidden from the view of the external observer, within the organism, which together determined the impetus to respond in a given situation. The presence and strength of each of these variables was to be inferred from antecedent observations and their behavioral consequences. He sought to specify with great precision the relationship between observable antecedents and the strength of each of the intervening variables *drive* and *habit*. And he advanced a principle which states, explicitly, how they combine to influence jointly the strength of the tendency to act in a certain way at a particular time. This is the conceptual problem of motivation which Tolman and Lewin, in particular, had given so much emphasis and the problem which Hull, himself, had begun to consider in his own earlier treatment of the purposive characteristics of behavior in terms of the combined action of $S_e$, $S_d$, and $r_g$-$s_g$, the anticipatory goal reaction.

DRIVE AND HABIT AS DETERMINANTS
OF REACTION POTENTIAL

Hull began a chapter entitled "Primary Motivation and Reaction Potential" with these introductory remarks:

"It may be recalled that when the problem of primary reinforcement was under consideration . . . the matter of organic need played a critical part in that the reduction of the need constituted the essential element in the process whereby the reaction was conditioned to new stimuli. We must now note that the state of an organism's needs also plays an important role in the causal determination of which of the many habits possessed by an organism shall function at a given moment. It is a matter of common observation that, as a rule, when an organism is in need of food only those acts appropriate to the securing of food will be evoked, whereas when it is in need of water, only those acts appropriate to the securing of water will be evoked, when a sexual hormone is dominant only those acts appropriate to reproductive activity will be evoked, and so on. Moreover, the extent or intensity of the need determines in large measure the vigor and persistence of the activity in question.
"By common usage the initiation of learned, or habitual, patterns of movement or behavior is called *motivation*. The evocation of action in relation to secondary reinforcing stimuli or *incentives* will be called *secondary motivation;* a brief discussion of incentives was given above . . . in connection with the general subject of amount of reinforcement. The evocation of action in relation to primary needs will be called *primary motivation;* this is the subject of the present chapter" (Hull, 1943, p. 226).

Hull turned to empirical studies by Perin (1942) and Williams (1938) for evidence of "the functional dependence of the persistence of food-seeking behavior jointly on (1) the number of reinforcements of the habit in question, and (2) the number of hours

of food privation" (Hull, 1943, pp. 226–227). Holding constant the other factors which influence the strength of habit, these investigators had provided results which might be considered a demonstration of how habit (defined in terms of number of reinforcements) and drive (defined in terms of hours of food privation) combine to influence the strength of the impetus to respond in a certain way. They had trained animals to press a bar in the Skinner apparatus, giving separate groups of albino rats different numbers of reinforcements varying from 5 to 90 under 23 hours of food privation. Then, after this training, the food reward was eliminated, and the bar press response was subjected to experimental extinction with the amount of food privation during extinction trials varying from 3 to 22 hours in different groups of rats. The number of unreinforced reactions performed by each group of rats, until there came a five-minute pause between successive presses of the bar, was employed as the measure of resistance to extinction.

Figure 6.4 shows how "persistence of food-seeking behavior" was related to a number of hours of food privation (strength of drive) during extinction when the number of reinforced trials (habit) was held constant at 16 for all groups. (These data may be compared with those of Tolman *et al.* [see

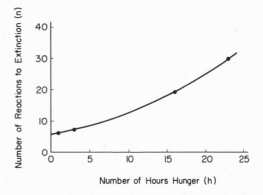

FIGURE 6.4 Graphic representation of the data showing the systematic relationship between the resistance to experimental extinction (circles) and the number of hours' food privation where the number of reinforcements is constant at 16. *The smooth curve drawn through the sequence of circles represents the slightly positively accelerated function fitted to them. This function is believed to hold only up to the number of hours of hunger employed in the original habit formation process: in the present case, 23. (From Hull, Principles of Behavior, copyright 1943, Appleton-Century-Crofts, Inc., p. 228; adapted from Perin, 1942, p. 104)*

p. 141] concerning effect of "drive" on selectivity and speed in maze performance.)

Even more instructive is the evidence obtained by Perin of the joint effect of *drive* and *habit* on "persistence of food-seeking." This is shown in Figure 6.5. When the number of reinforced trials is low,

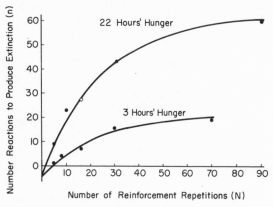

FIGURE 6.5 Combined effect of Drive and Habit (number of reinforcement repetitions) on performance (resistance to extinction) (*From Hull,* Principles of Behavior, *copyright 1943, Appleton-Century-Crofts, Inc., p. 228; adapted from Perin, 1942, p. 101*)

and hence inferred habit strength is weak, the level of performance during extinction trials is a little higher in the strong-drive group (22 hours' privation) than in the weak-drive group (3 hours' privation). However, when the number of reinforced trials is high, and hence inferred habit strength is strong, the performance level of the strong-drive group is substantially higher than that of the weak-drive group. Neither habit alone nor drive alone determines the strength of the "reaction tendency" which is expressed in the number of bar presses to extinction in this experiment. Instead it is possible to infer from Figure 6.5 that *drive and habit combine multiplicatively* to determine the strength of the "reaction tendency," which Hull then formally designated *reaction potential* and represented symbolically as $_sE_R$:

"This multiplicative relationship is one of the greatest importance, because it is upon $_sE_R$ that the amount of action in its various forms presumably depends. It is clear, for example, that it is quite impossible to predict the vigor or persistence of a given type of action from a knowledge of either habit strength or drive strength alone; this can be predicted only from a knowledge of the product of the particular functions of $_sH_R$ and $D$ respectively; in fact, this product constitutes the

value which we are representing by the symbol $_sE_R$" (Hull, 1943, pp. 239–240).

Thus, finally, we come to see how Hull conceived the immediate determinants of action in the form of a mathematical equation relating drive and habit to the impetus to respond, which he called reaction potential—$_sE_R = f(_sH_R) \times f(D)$.

It is instructive to consider his conjectures concerning the underlying physiological process described by this important equation. Although the mathematical statement which relates objectively defined drive and habit strength to reaction potential does not depend upon Hull's physiological interpretation, and should be evaluated as a conception of the process of motivation quite aside from the validity of his guesses as to the nature of the physiological process, we enhance our understanding of his viewpoint by considering the picture he had in mind of the underlying physiological process of motivation in his discussion of "primary motivation":

"Most, if not all, primary needs appear to generate and throw into the blood stream more or less characteristic chemical substances, or else to withdraw a characteristic substance. These substances (or their absence) have a selective physiological effect on more or less restricted and characteristic portions of the body (e.g., the so-called "hunger" contractions of the digestive tract) which serves to activate resident receptors. This receptor activation constitutes the drive stimulus, $S_D$. . . . In the case of tissue injury this sequence seems to be reversed; here the energy producing the injury is the drive stimulus, and its action causes the release into the blood of adrenal secretion which appears to be the physiological motivating substance.

"It seems likely, on the basis of various analogies, that, other things equal, the intensity of the drive stimulus would be some form of negatively accelerated increasing function of the concentration of the drive substance in the blood. However, for the sake of expository simplicity we shall assume in the present preliminary analysis that it is an increasing linear function.

"The afferent discharges arising from the drive stimulus ($S_D$) become conditioned to reactions just the same as any other elements in stimulus compounds, except that they may be somewhat more potent in acquiring habit loadings than most stimulus elements or aggregates. Thus the drive stimulus may play a role in a conditioned stimulus compound substantially the same as that of any other stimulus element or aggregate. . . . As a stimulus, $S_D$ naturally manifests both qualitative and intensity primary stimulus generalization in common with other stimulus elements or aggregates in conditioned stimulus compounds. . . .

"It appears probable that when blood which

contains certain chemical substances thrown into it as the result of states of need, or which lacks certain substances as the result of other states of need, bathes the neural structures which constitute the anatomical bases of habit ($_sH_R$), the conductivity of these structures is augmented through lowered resistance either in the central neural tissue or at the effector end of the connection, or both. The latter type of action is equivalent, of course, to a lowering of the reaction threshold and would presumably facilitate reaction to neural impulses reaching the effector from any source whatever. As Beach [1942] suggests, it is likely that the selective action of drives on particular effector organs in non-learned forms of behavior acts mainly in this manner. It must be noted at once, however, that sensitizing a habit structure does not mean that this alone is sufficient to evoke reaction, any more than that caffeine or benzedrine alone will evoke reaction. Sensitization merely gives the relevant neural tissue, upon the occurrence of an adequate set of receptor discharges, an augmented facility in routing these impulses to the reactions previously conditioned to them or connected by native (inherited) growth processes. This implies to a certain extent the undifferentiated nature of drive in general, contained in Freud's concept of the "libido." However, it definitely does not presuppose the special dominance of any one drive, such as sex, over the other drives.

"While all drives seem to be alike in their powers of sensitizing *acquired* receptor-effector connections, their capacity to call forth within the body of the organism characteristic and presumably distinctive drive stimuli gives each a considerable measure of distinctiveness and specificity in the determination of action which, in case of necessity, may be sharpened by the process of patterning . . . to almost any extent that the reaction situation requires for adequate and consistent reinforcement. In this respect, the action of drive substances differs sharply from that of a pseudo-drive substance such as caffeine, which appears to produce nothing corresponding to a drive stimulus.

"Little is known concerning the exact quantitative functional relationship of drive intensity to the conditions or circumstances which produce it, such as number of hours of hunger or the concentration of endocrine secretions in the blood. Judging from the work of Warden and associates [1934], the relationship of the hunger drive up to two or three days of food privation would be a negatively accelerated increasing function of time, though a study by Skinner [see Figure 6.6] suggests that it may be nearly linear up to about five days. For the sake of simplicity in the present explorational analysis we shall assume the latter as a first approximation.

"Physiological conditions of need, through their sensitizing action on the neural mediating structures lying between the receptors and the effectors ($_sH_R$), appear to combine with the latter to evoke reactions according to a multiplicative principle, i.e., reaction-evocation potentiality [or more simply, *reaction potential*] is the product of a function of habit strength multiplied by a function of the strength of drive:

$$_sE_R = f(_sH_R) \times f(D)"\quad \text{(Hull, 1943, pp. 240–242)}.$$

Hull stated the relationship of drive and drive stimulus formally in his sixth postulate, as follows:

"Associated with every drive ($D$) is a characteristic drive stimulus ($S_D$) whose intensity is an increasing monotonic function of the drive in question" (Hull, 1943, p. 253).

The principle of motivation was stated formally as the seventh postulate in Hull's 1943 theory:

"Any effective habit strength ($_s\bar{H}_R$) is sensitized into reaction potentiality ($_sE_R$) by all primary drives active within an organism at a given time, the magnitude of this potentiality being a product obtained by multiplying an increasing function of $_sH_R$ by an increasing function of $D$" (Hull, 1943, p. 253).

The major corollary of these two principles was that the strength of reaction potential ($_sE_R$) attributed to the effective habit strength ($S_e + S_D H_R$) and a particular condition of primary drive ($D$) would also be influenced by the presence of other "irrelevant" sources of drive. The aggregate strength of all sources of primary drive active at the time is what Hull intended to represent as the strength of drive ($D$) in his equation $_sE_R = f(_sH_R) \times f(D)$. Thus

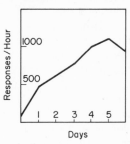

Days

FIGURE 6.6 Graph showing the relationship of the action potentiality as a function of the length of food privation following satiation. First note the fact that there is an appreciable amount of action potentiality at the beginning of this graph, where the amount of food privation is zero. Next, observe that the curve is relatively high at one day of food privation, which was the degree of drive under which the original training occurred. Finally, note that the rise in action potentiality is fairly continuous up to about five days, after which it falls rather sharply. This fall is evidently due to exhaustion, as the animals died soon after. (*From Heron and Skinner, 1937*)

hunger, thirst, and sexual need, all present at the same time, are expected—given this conception—to produce heightened excitability of whatever habits are evoked by the immediate stimulating circumstances, whether those habits are relevant or irrelevant to the ultimate satisfaction of any one of those primary need states.

While this certainly is the main implication of drive, conceived as a non-directive or non-selective activator, Hull believed that the drive stimulus ($S_D$), operating as part of the stimulus complex $S_e + S_D$ at any time, would account for the elicitation of habits likely to be instrumental in reducing the dominant need at the time. In this connection he reported the results of earlier experiments by himself (Hull, 1933) and Leeper (1935) which demonstrated that animals are capable of a discriminative reaction depending upon which of two drives, hunger or thirst, is dominant at the time.

In Hull's experiment, rats were run from the same starting box in a maze containing two paths, one to the left and the other to the right, both leading to the same goal box. On some days the animals were run when satiated for water but with 23 hours' food privation. On other days they would be satiated for food but under 23 hours' water privation. When the "hunger" condition prevailed, the reward was food and accessible only by taking the right entrance to the goal box; when the "thirst" condition prevailed, the reward was water and accessible only by taking the left entrance to the goalbox. The learning was slow, but the animals did learn to react discriminatively depending upon which drive stimulus, $S_H$ or $S_T$, was dominant at the time.

In the Leeper experiment, there were two distinct goal boxes, one always containing food and the other always containing water. Under these conditions, the animals learned to react discriminatively in terms of the dominant drive much more quickly. Both experiments seemed to Hull to substantiate the view that animals are capable of differential reactions to identical external environmental situations (the starting box) on the basis of distinct drives.

The main thing to understand about Hull's 1943 principle of motivation of action is that *it posits the joint multiplicative influence of a non-specific or non-directive variable called drive and a specific or directive, associative variable called habit*. The direction of behavior is attributed to the action of the stimulus aggregate, $S_e + S_D$. The probability, vigor, and persistence of a particular response is attributed

to the product of drive and habit and is called *reaction potential* ($_sE_R$). Reaction potential is the construct in Hull's theory which most nearly corresponds to what Lewin had conceived as a Psychological Force ($f_{P,G}$). Later, we shall compare in more detail various conceptions of the determinants of the strength of the tendency to act in a certain way.

### INHIBITION AND EFFECTIVE REACTIVE POTENTIAL

What happens during experimental extinction of a response? That is, what happens when the combination of drive and habit produces an impetus to respond ($_sE_R$) and the response occurs but is not followed by a reinforcing state of affairs? We know that after a number of extinction trials, the response no longer occurs. But why does the response extinguish? Is the habit strength reduced? Is the drive reduced in some way? These are the questions that lead Hull to essentially a motivational explanation of experimental extinction.

Hull's view was, in brief, "that each response evocation produces in the organism a certain increment of a fatigue-like substance or condition which constitutes a need for rest" (Hull, 1943, p. 391). The need for rest, called *reactive inhibition* ($I_R$) because it "has the capacity directly to inhibit the power of $S$ to evoke $R$" (*ibid.*, p. 391) is a function of the energy expenditure or amount of work involved in performance of the response. This fatigue-producing substance would be expected to accumulate during a series of non-reinforced trials and therefore produce experimental extinction. And rest would provide the condition needed for fatigue to dissipate, allowing subsequent *spontaneous recovery* of the response. (See page 119.) But since $I_R$ constitutes a need, the cessation of activity would initiate the need-reduction or reinforcing process, thus strengthening the habit of not responding, which Hull called *conditioned inhibition* and symbolized $_sI_R$. Thus, at any particular time, there would exist a *total inhibition* ($\dot{I}_R$) consisting of the summation of $I_R$ (temporary state of fatigue) and $_sI_R$ (the habit of not responding). Hull assumed that this total inhibition ($\dot{I}_R$) worked to reduce the effective strength of the reaction potential. He assumed, specifically,

". . . that the reaction potential actually available for reaction evocation, i.e., the *effective* [italics added] reaction potential ($_s\bar{E}_R, \ldots$), is what remains of the reaction potential ($_sE_R$) after the subtraction of the total inhibition, $\dot{I}_R$; i.e., $_s\bar{E}_R = {_sE_R} - \dot{I}_R$" (Hull, 1943, p. 392).

Among the important implications of these assumptions concerning the effect of a non-rewarded trial is the general hypothesis that:

". . . other things equal, organisms receiving the same reinforcement following two responses which require different energy expenditures will, as practice continues, gradually come to choose the less laborious response. This is the 'law of less work' " (Hull, 1943, p. 392).

Tolman had posited a "demand" for short paths and least effort in his attempt to take account of essentially the same behavioral phenomena which Hull considered under the topic of inhibition.

### THE OSCILLATION OF EFFECTIVE REACTION POTENTIAL

Several further assumptions were made by Hull concerning the link between *effective reaction potential* ($_s\bar{E}_R$) and observable measurements of the probability, latency, magnitude, and resistance to extinction of a response. He assumed that the full value of $_s\bar{E}_R$ was rarely realized in the evocation of action because of a little understood physiological process which had the power to neutralize reaction potentials more or less from moment to moment. He assumed that this *oscillatory process* worked in a random manner to depress reaction potentials more or less from moment to moment and that the magnitude of its action on different reaction potentials at a given instant was uncorrelated. Thus, at a given moment, the "*momentary reaction potential*" ($_s\dot{\bar{E}}_R$) of the weaker of two tendencies might actually exceed that of the stronger tendency, but this state of affairs would be less probable than the other way around.

### THE REACTION THRESHOLD AND RESPONSE EVOCATION

Hull also assumed that there was a *reaction threshold* which must be superseded by the momentary effective reaction potential ($_s\dot{\bar{E}}_R$) for action to occur. He conceived the reaction threshold as "the minimal amount of momentary effective reaction potential ($_s\dot{\bar{E}}_R$) which is necessary to mediate reaction evocation when the situation is uncomplicated by

competing reaction potentials . . ." (Hull, 1943, p. 394).

In the simple case of a single momentary reaction potential, Hull assumed that it must exceed the reaction threshold for the reaction to occur and that the extent to which the effective reaction potential exceeded the threshold would determine the probability, latency, magnitude, and resistance to extinction of a response.

When, however, tendencies to perform more than one response exceeded the threshold at the same time, the situation was more complicated. Hull's assumption, as stated in the final postulate of the 1943 theory was:

"When the reaction potentials ($_sE_R$) to two or more incompatible reactions ($R$) occur in an organism at the same time, only the reaction whose momentary effective reaction potential ($_s\dot{\bar{E}}_R$) is greatest will be evoked" (Hull, 1943, Postulate 16, p. 344).

These further assumptions concerning inhibition, oscillation of effective reaction potentials, the reaction threshold, and resolution of conflict among competing tendencies, which we have briefly reviewed, illustrate that there is more to a theoretical conception of the motivation of behavior than merely an articulate conception of the determinants of the tendency to act in a certain way.

Our discussion has emphasized Hull's conception of the determinants of *reaction potential* (i.e., $_sE_R = f(_sH_R) \times f(D)$) because, historically, one of the major conceptual issues in reference to the problem of motivation has been the question of whether or not anticipation of the goal of action is one of the immediate determinants of action. In Hull's essays of the 1930's, it appeared that he had taken the position that the guidance and integrative functions traditionally assigned to "the idea of the end" could be represented as an anticipatory goal reaction which functioned as a pure stimulus act in the determination of behavior. But, as we have now seen, that conception is missing in the initial formal statement of his theory which attributes the impetus to act to a multiplicative combination of a nonspecific excitement called *drive* and the specific associative variable called *habit*.

# CHAPTER 7

# The Evolution of *S-R* Behavior Theory

*"The success of the S-R language is partly due to the fact that it forces its user to think in terms of manipulable experimental variables and observable responses."* (Howard Kendler, 1959, p. 78).

The modern era in the psychology of motivation begins with the publication of Hull's *Principles of Behavior* in 1943. The various conceptions of motivation described in earlier chapters are still, however, of considerable contemporary significance. They continue to define the working viewpoints of various groups of psychologists who, in the absence of the generally useful and agreed-upon conception of motivation which psychology still seeks, must employ concepts that appear most germane to the particular problems they face. But the neobehavioristic orientation of Hull, his students, and the many researchers who have adopted his general viewpoint has provided the systematic central thread in the psychology of learning and motivation in relation to which the unique contributions and limitations of alternative views, both old and new, are actively discussed. Whether good or bad for the development of psychology, it is certainly true that the *S-R language* has come to dominate discussion of motivational problems. Why, we may ask? Perhaps, in addition to the spur given systematic research by Hull's 1943 theory, the answer is to be found in the assertion by Kendler quoted above.

In this chapter, we shall consider some of the most important developments of *S-R* theory that are pertinent to the problem of motivation, viz., the conceptual analysis of the contemporaneous determinants of action. The perspective gained from a survey of the transitions in thought about the problem since 1890 should help us to appreciate some of the inadequacies of Hull's initial formal statement of theory and to anticipate how it would have to be changed to accommodate the kind of phenomena given special emphasis earlier by Freud, Tolman, Lewin, and others. In particular, we shall consider how the general problems of anxiety and of approach-avoidance conflict have been encompassed by *S-R* theory and how critical evidence has forced re-evaluation of the adequacy of the drive-reduction theory of reinforcement. Of additional importance is the revision of the principle of motivation that Hull had advanced in 1943. It is subsequently revised to include the notion that the anticipated goal is one of the fundamental determinants of the impetus to action, a current development which is treated in the final section entitled "Incentive Motivation."

## FEAR AS AN ACQUIRABLE DRIVE

To illustrate the principle of primary reinforcement in selective learning, Hull often referred to a demonstration experiment in which a rat is placed in a box, the floor of which is a grid which can be charged with electricity to produce a sudden noxious stimulus. In the middle of the box, separating it into two compartments, is a barrier over which the animal can jump. The grid in the second compartment is not charged. Typically, an animal so placed and then exposed to the shock of the charged grill will become very active and finally jump over the barrier to safety. In repeated trials, the time taken to escape from the shocked grid decreases. The escape response, in other words, is learned.

Hull conceived the sudden onset of the noxious stimulus to the feet of the animal and consequent tissue injury (a need) as the source of drive and drive stimulus ($S_D$) which motivate the various actions culminating in "the correct response," escape over the barrier. This response is immediately reinforced by the diminution of need, drive, and $S_D$ because the grid of the compartment into which the rat jumps is not charged.

Hull also referred to this apparatus to demonstrate the learning of a new connection (conditioning). The procedure is the same except that a buzzer ($S_e$) is sounded continuously from a time two seconds before the shock is turned on the grid until the animal leaps over the barrier to safety. The course of learning to escape from the shock compartment is also evident given these arrangements. But after a number of trials, the animal will begin to leap over the barrier as soon as the buzzer ($S_e$) comes on *but before the grid has been charged*. The animal learns to *avoid* the shock by jumping in response to the buzzer ($S_e$) before the shock ($D$ and $S_D$), which originally motivated its escape, has come on.

Hull considered this phenomenon of avoidance an illustration of the *antedating* or *anticipatory* responses he had discussed in his essays of the 1930's. He treated the result as evidence that primary reinforcement (i.e., reduction of the tissue need, drive, and $S_D$ caused by the electrified grid and removed

when the animal leaped to safety) will produce new connections between a stimulus and a response, the phenomenon which Pavlov had called conditioning.

Many other investigators had observed the establishment of conditioned avoidance responses under similar training procedures, but had also observed that *avoidance responses, once acquired, are extraordinarily resistant to extinction*. That is, the animal will continue to perform an avoidance response many times following the onset of a stimulus, like the buzzer to which it has been conditioned, without ever again being shocked. Contemporary studies of avoidance by Solomon and associates (Solomon and Wynne, 1953; Solomon and Brush, 1956) have demonstrated that dogs trained in a similar manner will continue to show avoidance for hundreds of trials after a few very intense shocks. These investigators suggest that the process involved may be partially irreversible.

According to Hull's 1943 theory, there should be no continual reinforcement of the avoidance response if the animal does not get shocked, for there is no tissue need, drive, and $S_D$ to be reduced when it leaps to safety before the shock comes on. How, then, is the persistence or maintenance of successful avoidance responses to be explained? Why don't avoidance responses quickly extinguish when no longer followed by the reinforcing state of affairs, i.e., reduction of the drive produced by shock?

The phenomenon of avoidance was encompassed by the *S-R* Behavior Theory when the concept of fear (or anxiety) as an acquired drive, and fear-reduction as a reinforcing state of affairs, was introduced and clarified by O. Hobart Mowrer and Neal Miller. In 1939, Mowrer (1939) had seen the relevance of Freud's discussion of the problem of anxiety (1936). Freud's fundamental idea was that anxiety is a signal of forthcoming danger, itself an unpleasant state, which instigates defensive maneuvers, including repression. (See p. 60.) Mowrer introduced the idea that fear (the anticipation or expectancy of pain) should be conceived as the conditioned form of the pain reaction that is originally elicited by a strong, noxious stimulus, and that fear has the highly useful function of motivating, and fear-reduction of reinforcing behavior which tends to avoid or prevent the recurrence of the pain-producing (unconditioned) stimulus.

Thus, given Mowrer's view, the resistance to extinction of avoidance responses can be explained. After being immediately followed a number of times by a noxious stimulus such as shock, which causes pain, a buzzer ($S_e$) will elicit fear, the conditioned form of the original pain reaction to the noxious stimulus. Fear, a tension state, then functions like a drive to motivate behavior. Fear is reduced when the animal leaps over the barrier and the buzzer ($S_e$) causing the fear response goes off. The reduction of fear drive continues to reinforce the avoidance response. The habit of leaping over the barrier in this situation is thus strengthened. Hence, the avoidance response paradoxically continues long after the animal has ceased to receive painful shocks in the situation. It continues until first the fear response, which depends upon the shock for reinforcement, extinguishes, and then the avoidance response, which is no longer motivated by fear and reinforced by fear-reduction, also extinguishes.

An experiment by Miller (1948) clearly illustrates how fear may be conceived as a drive and fear-reduction as reinforcement in the learning of new responses. The apparatus employed is shown in Figure 7.1. The compartment on the left is white

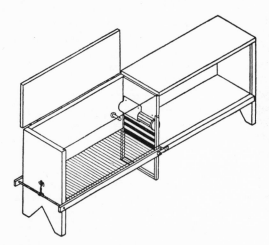

FIGURE 7.1    Acquired drive apparatus (From Miller, 1948, p. 90)

with a grid floor, and the one on the right is black with a smooth floor. At the bottom of the partition between the compartments is a door painted with horizontal black and white stripes. The door can be opened by the investigator pushing a button, by the rat moving a cylindrical wheel above the right side of the door, or by a bar projecting from the left side of the apparatus near the door.

First the animals were placed in the apparatus for about a minute with the door open to allow the investigator to observe their behavior before being

shocked. Then followed a series of ten trials in which animals were placed in the left side for a number of seconds without shock and then shock was applied with escape through the open door terminating a trial. On some trials, the shock was already on when the animals were placed in the left compartment. The procedure was carefully designed to attach the response of fear to as many cues of the white box as possible.

Then, after this training, the animals were dropped in the white compartment with the shock off to see if they would continue to run through the open door in the absence of the primary drive of pain.

Next, the animals were placed into the left compartment with the door closed to determine whether the acquired fear drive could motivate the learning of a *new* habit, moving the wheel a small fraction of a turn, to open the door.

Finally, to determine whether animals who had already learned to turn the wheel would extinguish that response and learn still another response to get out of the compartment, the situation was changed so that the wheel no longer opened the door, but pressing the bar did.

The animals displayed no tendency to avoid the left compartment at the beginning of the experiment before the shocks were administered. During the training trials, when shock was being administered and the door was opened by the investigator, all animals learned to run rapidly from the white (shocked) compartment.

What happened when the animals were then placed in the white compartment *without* shock and with the door closed but the apparatus rigged so that turning the wheel would open the door? We quote Miller's description:

"When the procedure of the non-shock trials was changed so that the $E$ no longer dropped the door and it could only be opened by moving the wheel, the animals displayed variable behavior which tended to be concentrated in the region of the door. They would stand up in front of it, place their paws upon it, sniff around the edges, bite the bars of the grid they were standing on, run back and forth, etc. They also tended to crouch, urinate, and defecate. In the course of this behavior some of the animals performed responses, such as poking their noses between the bars of the wheel or placing their paws upon it, which caused it to move a fraction of a turn and actuate a contact that caused the door to open. Most of them then ran through into the black compartment almost immediately. A few of them drew back with an exaggerated startle response and crouched. Some of these eventually learned to go through the door;

a few seemed to learn to avoid it. Other animals abandoned their trial-and-error behavior before they happened to strike the wheel and persisted in crouching so that they had to be lifted out of the white compartment at the end of the 100 sec. period. In general, the animals that had to be lifted out seemed to crouch sooner and sooner on successive trials" (Miller, 1948, p. 93).

The results are shown in Figure 7.2. Those animals that turned the wheel in at least four of their first eight trials learned to turn the wheel sooner and sooner after being placed in the compartment where they had *previously* been shocked. When

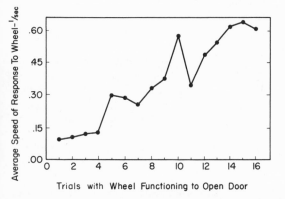

FIGURE 7.2 Learning the first new habit, turning the wheel, during trials without primary drive. With mild pain produced by an electric shock as a primary drive, the animals have learned to run from the white compartment, through the open door, into the black compartment. Then they were given trials without any electric shock during which the door was closed but could be opened by turning a little wheel. Under these conditions the 13 out of the 25 animals which turned the wheel enough to drop the door on four or more of the first eight trials learned to turn it. This figure shows the progressive increase in the average speed with which these 13 animals ran up to the wheel and turned it enough to drop the door during the 16 non-shock trials. (*From Miller, 1948, p. 94*)

the situation was changed so that the wheel no longer worked to open the door, the animals who had learned this response soon extinguished it and in the course of their movements struck the bar which opened the door through which they could again run to the black compartment. The learning curve for this second habit was comparable to that shown in Figure 7.2. Miller concluded:

"This trial-and-error learning of a new response demonstrated that the cues in the white compartment had acquired the functional properties of a drive and that escape from the white into the black compartment had acquired the functional properties of a reward. . . .

". . . Thus, this experiment confirms Mowrer's (1939) hypothesis that fear (or anxiety) can play a role in learning similar to that of a primary drive such as hunger" (Miller, 1948, pp. 96–97).

### DRIVE CONCEIVED AS A STRONG STIMULUS WHICH IMPELS ACTION

Miller's conception of the antecedents of drive differs from that of Hull. In later revisions of his theory, Hull tended to adopt Miller's conception. Rather than identifying drives with biological needs, Miller and Dollard (1941) had asserted "a drive is a strong stimulus which impels action. Any stimulus can become a drive if it is made strong enough. The stronger the stimulus the more drive function it possesses" (Miller and Dollard, 1941, p. 18). In reference to learned, acquired, or secondary drives, they argued: "Drive value is acquired by attaching to weak cues responses producing strong stimuli" (Miller and Dollard, 1941, p. 66).

### FEAR CONCEIVED AS A RESPONSE PRODUCING A STRONG INTERNAL STIMULUS

Miller clarifies what it means to refer to fear as an acquired drive in his interpretation of the results of the experiment we have just considered:

"In terms of the hypothesis put forward in Miller and Dollard (1941) the cues in the white compartment acquire their drive value by acquiring the capacity to elicit an internal response which produces a strong stimulus. Whether this strong stimulus is produced by peripheral responses, such as those involved in the blanching of the stomach and the tendency for hair to stand on end, or by central impulses which travel from the thalamus to sensory areas of the cortex is a matter of anatomical rather than functional significance. Fear may be called a stimulus-producing response if it shows the functional characteristics of such responses, in brief, obeys the laws of learning and serves as a cue to elicit learned responses such as the verbal report of fear.

"The general pattern of the fear response and its capacity to produce a strong stimulus is determined by the innate structure of the animal. The connection between the pain and the fear is also presumably innate. But the connection between the cues in the white compartment and the fear was learned. Therefore the fear of the white compartment may be called an acquired drive. Because fear can be learned, it may be called acquirable:

because it can motivate new learning, it may be called a drive.

"Running through the door and into the black compartment removed the animal from the cues in the white compartment which were eliciting the fear and thus produced a reduction in the strength of the fear response and the stimuli which it produced. This reduction in the strength of the intense fear stimuli is presumably what gave the black compartment its acquired reinforcing value.

"If the reduction in fear produced by running from the white into the black was the reinforcement for learning the new habit of wheel turning, we would expect this habit to show experimental extinction when that reinforcement was removed. This is exactly what happened. During the first trial on which turning the wheel no longer dropped the door, the animals gradually stopped performing this response and began to exhibit other responses. As would be expected, the one of these responses, pressing the bar, which caused the door to drop and allowed the animal to remove itself from the fear-producing cues in the white compartment, was gradually learned in a series of trials during which the wheel turning was progressively crowded out. Thus, it can be seen that the escape from the white compartment, which presumably produced a reduction in the strength of the fear, played a crucial role, similar to that of a primary reward, in the learning and maintenance of the new habits" (Miller, 1948, pp. 97–98).

The conception that fear (or anxiety) is an acquirable drive and fear-reduction is reinforcing suggests an hypothesis to bridge the vast gap between the fundamental biological urges of animals and the human infant and the purposive pursuit of more varied goals among human adults. Human striving for social approval, success, power, money, and more subtle goals can be meaningfully derived and interpreted as avoidance behavior—that is, as behavior driven by the fear of noxious consequences that early in life are associated with loss of parental love, failure, weakness, or lack of money. If one conceives every state of biological need as a noxious (i.e., painful) internal stimulus, it is possible to argue, as Mowrer has (Mowrer, 1950, 1952), that the anxiety produced in anticipation of deprivation of these biological needs should be sufficient to motivate the greatest variety of anxiety-reducing trends of behavior. This concept, more than any other, has encouraged the translation of psychoanalytic ideas into the conceptual framework of the S-R Behavior Theory (see particularly Mowrer, 1950; Dollard and Miller, 1950).

We must put aside the temptation to pursue a thorough analysis of the question of the origins and genesis of the observable goal-directed tendencies of animals and men, for this intrinsically interesting and important *historical* question, though intimately related, is not the fundamental problem in the psychology of motivation. The problem we pursue is that of identifying the various factors which, in combination at a particular moment, account for the direction, vigor, and persistence of action. The studies of fear as an acquirable drive tell us that in addition to the biological deficits produced by food and water privation, etc., and the pain produced by a strong, noxious stimulus, a previously neutral stimulus that has been followed by sudden onset of pain acquires the capacity of subsequently eliciting an anticipatory response, called fear, which has the *functional properties* of *drive* in the *S-R* Behavior Theory.

THE NON-SPECIFIC ACTIVATING FUNCTION OF FEAR

In his recent book, *The Motivation of Behavior*, J. S. Brown (1961) has systematically examined evidence concerning the non-specific activating function of drive, highlighting the results of two studies which demonstrate that fear systematically enhances the performance of an unrelated response.

In one study, Brown, Kalish, and Farber (1951) were able to measure the magnitude of a rat's startle reaction to a loud sound produced by shooting a toy pistol. They conditioned the fear response to a stimulus under their control by pairing the stimulus, which consisted of a buzzer and a light, with painful electric shocks administered to animals who were confined in a small box having a grid floor. The training continued for four days. On each day, three test trials with the pistol were interspersed among the shocked trials. On the test trials, the buzzer and light stimulus was presented, but then instead of shock, the toy pistol was shot off to produce a loud sound. The sharp sound of the pistol nearly always elicited a startle reaction, even prior to the training. And, as Figure 7.3 shows, the magnitude of the startle reaction increased in an orderly manner as the training designed to produce a fear response in the animals proceeded. The control group in this experiment was presented the buzzer and light stimulus and was also shocked during training, but the stimulus and the shock were temporally spaced (i.e., separated) to minimize the conditioning of a fear response to the stimulus.

These investigators also present curves of the magnitude of startle reaction during extinction of the fear response, which show an orderly decrease as fear produced by the stimulus decreases in strength. This

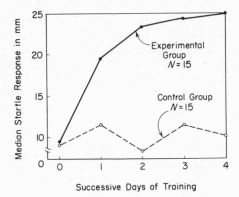

FIGURE 7.3 Curves showing the differential facilitative effect of fear conditioning upon magnitude of startle response to an explosive sound. The training procedure was designed to induce a state of fear in the experimental animals, but not the controls. The values plotted at the zero point on the abscissa were obtained from measurements of startle on the day prior to the initiation of training. (*From Brown, Kalish, and Farber, 1951, p. 321*)

evidence is interpreted as consistent with the view that drive, no matter what its source, should enhance the performance of responses elicited by immediately present stimuli—that is, $sE_R = f(D) \times f(sH_R)$.

In another experiment, Meryman (1952) sought to determine whether a primary source of drive, such as food deprivation, would have the same enhancing effect on the startle reaction produced by a loud sound and whether hunger and fear together would produce greater intensification of the startle reaction than either by itself. The procedure of this experiment was similar to that of the earlier experiment except that there were four groups of animals: one group was fearful and also deprived of food for 46 hours; another was fearful but deprived of food for only one hour; another was non-fearful but deprived of food for 46 hours; and the last was neither fearful nor hungry, having been deprived of food for only one hour. The combined influence of fear and hunger on the magnitude of the startle reaction is shown in Figure 7.4.

On the first day, before any of the animals had been shocked in the apparatus, all four groups were about equal in their reactions to the loud sound of the pistol shot. (We wonder why the expected enhancing effect of hunger is not immediately present?) However, as fear training proceeds, the two fearful groups show a marked increase in startle reaction, and in them the effect of hunger is clearly

apparent. Though the difference is less marked, the non-fearful but 46-hour-hungry group manifests greater magnitude of startle reaction than the non-fearful and non-hungry group of animals. This result is important because it shows that food deprivation can facilitate the performance of a response which seems remotely associated, if at all, with satisfaction of hunger.

Brown (1961) has suggested that the over-all pattern of results might be interpreted to mean that fear and hunger combine to increase the general level of drive which multiplies the unlearned startle reaction when it is elicited, or that hunger functions less directly, augmenting the fear reaction, which in turn enhances the startle reaction. In any case, these experimental results illustrate what is meant by the non-directive or non-specific effect of drive and furthermore show that an acquired fear reaction displays this functional property of drive.

IMPLICATION OF DEFINING DRIVE
AS A STRONG STIMULUS

Since we have introduced Miller's definition of drive as "a strong stimulus which impels action" and seen how it differs from Hull's early position that drives are produced by biological needs, it is worth noting that Miller's view concerning the influence of irrelevant drives on performance also differs from Hull's. Miller (1959) has called attention to the fact that his conception of a drive as a strong stimulus implies that "drive generalization should occur as a special case of stimulus generalization" (Miller, 1959, p. 253).

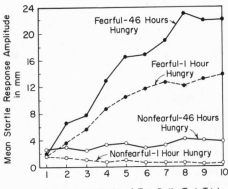

FIGURE 7.4 Startle-response amplitude as a function of fear, no fear, intense hunger, weak hunger, and their combination (*From Meryman, 1952 in The Motivation of Behavior by J. S. Brown, 1961, p. 153*)

Miller has summarized the results of some of his studies in the mid-1930's showing the effect of one drive on activation of habits learned in the service of another drive (Miller, 1937; 1948). Thirsty rats were trained to run down an alley for water and were then tested when not thirsty. They ran faster and drank more water (when not thirsty) if they were hungry than without this irrelevant drive. Other rats trained to take the correct arm in a T maze when hungry and rewarded with food and then tested without hunger but with the irrelevant drives of electric shock (pain) or fear ran faster and chose the correct path more frequently than non-hungry animals without these irrelevant drives. In reference to these studies and the non-specific influence of drives, Miller has said:

"Hull (1943), who was familiar with the results of the first experiments in this series, interpreted them in a different way. Instead of a gradient of drive-stimulus generalization, he assumed a completely general energizing effect, possibly mediated by substances in the blood. Aside from the fact that the blood-substance subhypothesis would be too slow to account for rapid response to pain, the chief difference between Hull's hypothesis and mine is that I would predict the type of relationships that would be expected from a gradient of stimulus generalization. For example, if irrelevant drive $A$ had more effect on a habit based on drive $B$ than drive $C$, then a habit based on drive $A$ should be more affected by $B$ as an irrelevant drive than by $C$. By contrast, Hull's 1943 postulate predicts completely equal effects, although his 1952 one is more guarded in this respect. The experiments required to decide between these two main alternatives have not yet been performed" (Miller, 1959, pp. 253-254).*

We shall return to this problem again when we compare various conceptions of motivation more thoroughly. Suffice to say that the 1943 Hullian formulation, in positing both non-directive drive and a drive stimulus ($S_D$) as immediate consequences of a biological need, contained two distinct mechanisms for the activation of habits by "irrelevant" drive conditions:

a) drive functioning as the non-specific multiplier of any and all habits elicited by the immediate stimulus complex; and

b) the drive stimulus ($S_D$), which is part of the eliciting complex $S_D + S_e$, functioning in terms of

* Excerpts from N. E. Miller, Liberalization of basic S-R concepts, in *Psychology: A Study of a Science*, Vol. 2, edited by S. Koch, copyright 1959, McGraw-Hill Book Company, are used by permission.

the principle of stimulus generalization to elicit responses (habits) that were connected during earlier training to other *similar* stimuli.

When hunger enhances the excitation of habits learned when the animal was driven by thirst and reinforced by drinking water, is it because all drives are functionally equivalent, general activators? Or is it because the internal stimulus which characterizes hunger ($S_H$) is in some degree similar to the internal stimulus which characterizes thirst ($S_T$) and therefore capable of eliciting (to a weaker degree than $S_H$, of course) habits learned when $S_T$ was present?

## APPROACH-AVOIDANCE CONFLICT THEORY

Another impressive addition to the conceptual framework of *S-R* behavior theory is the theory of approach-avoidance conflict advanced by Miller (1944; 1951; 1959) and the systematic program of experimental work associated with it. The conception is similar to that of Lewin, which was reviewed earlier, but the basic elements of construction are those of *S-R* theory. Miller's strategy is to attempt to work out in well-controlled experiments with animals the basic principles that may help us to understand neurotic behavior. Most of the problems which interested Freud have been systematically discussed by Dollard and Miller (1950) in terms of basic *S-R* principles, the conception of fear as an acquired drive, and the theory of conflict which we now consider.

### BASIC ASSUMPTIONS

The basic assumptions of Miller's theory of conflict are:

"(A) The tendency to approach a goal is stronger the nearer the subject is to it. This will be called the *gradient of approach*.

"(B) The tendency to avoid a feared stimulus is stronger the nearer the subject is to it. This will be called the *gradient of avoidance*.

"(C) The strength of avoidance increases more rapidly with nearness than does that of approach. In other words, the gradient of avoidance is *steeper* than that of approach.

"(D) The strength of tendencies to approach or avoid varies with the strength of the drive upon which they are based. In other words, an increase in drive raises the height of the entire gradient.

"(E) When two incompatible responses are in conflict, the stronger one will occur" (Miller, 1951, p. 90).

"[F] *Below the asymptote of learning, increasing*

*the number of reinforced trials will increase the strength of the response tendency that is reinforced"* (Miller, 1959, p. 206).

(This last assumption, not present in Miller's earliest statements of the theory, was added in 1959. Otherwise, the most recent statement is identical to earlier statements of it.)

In tests of the various implications of the theory, partial operational definitions of the key terms are given. For example, *nearness* is measured by spatial distance in an experimental runway; *approach* is identified with the tendency to run to food by hungry animals who have been given training; *avoid* is identified with the tendency to run away from the place where the animal has been shocked; food deprivation defines *hunger drive*, and strength of shock defines strength of *fear drive*.

Brown (1948) verified the basic hypotheses by placing animals in a little harness connected to a recording device which measured strength of pull when they were stopped at a particular place in the alley. One group of animals was trained to run to food when very hungry; another group when not hungry. Other groups of animals were trained to avoid the place in the alley where they had been given a very strong shock, or a weak shock. Then Brown measured the strength of pull near and far from the point of reinforcement. His results are shown in Figure 7.5.

### WHY THE AVOIDANCE GRADIENT IS STEEPER

Both Lewin and Miller assume that the gradient of avoidance is steeper than for approach. Why should this be? The answer, worked out by Miller and Brown, calls attention to the fact that the approach tendency is sustained by a drive stimulus which has its origin in the internal physiological condition of the animal. It does not change in strength as the animal moves about. But the avoidance tendency is motivated by fear, an acquired drive that is itself a response elicited by environmental cues. When the animal is right next to the place where it has been shocked, the fear is strongly aroused. However, when the animal is some distance away from the point of shock, the cues which arouse fear are similar but not identical to those present in training. Hence, according to the principle of stimulus generalization, the fear elicited some distance from the point of reinforcement is a weaker, generalized fear response. The habit of approach and the habit of avoidance are also elicited by environmental stimuli. So the effective habits are

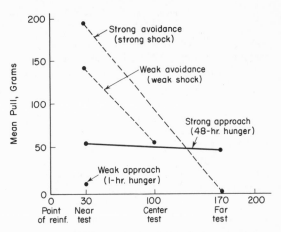

FIGURE 7.5 Effect of strength of drive upon height of gradient. The two avoidance gradients represent the strength of pull on near and far non-shock tests of two groups of rats that had received shocks of different strengths. The approach gradient represents the strength of pull at near and far points of animals tested after 48 hours of food deprivation; weak approach represents a single test at the near point of another group of animals with one hour of food deprivation. (From Brown, 1948, pp. 457–459)

weaker some distance from the point of reinforcement. *In the case of avoidance, both the drive and the habit depend upon external cues.* Hence avoidance suffers more weakening than approach as distance increases because both of the determinants of reaction potential are affected. In the case of approach motivated by hunger, only the habit variable is weakened by greater distance from the goal.

Miller's analysis of this problem illustrates how the basic assumption of one theory may itself be derived from even more basic principles. At the same time this analysis suggests that the condition might be reversed, that is, the approach gradient might be steeper than the avoidance gradient if the former depended primarily on external cues and the latter on internal factors. Miller has acknowledged this possibility (Miller, 1959).

### EXTENSION OF THE THEORY TO INCLUDE FREUDIAN DISPLACEMENT

Having seen that the characteristics of approach and avoidance gradients in spatial conflict depend upon the principle of stimulus generalization, Miller has extended the conception to embrace many other phenomena to which it is relevant. The definition of *nearness* has been extended "to apply to any situation in which the subject can be said to be coming nearer to a goal in space, time, or some dimension of qualitative or culturally defined similarity of cues" (Miller, 1951, p. 95).

Given this assumption, Miller and Murray (1952) tested the assumptions advanced to explain the greater steepness of the avoidance gradient. Animals were trained to run down an alley in order to escape from a strong electric shock. They were tested *without shock* in the original alley and in a different alley. The gradient of avoidance obtained from measurements of strength of pull in the two alleys was relatively steep. The animals pulled substantially harder to get out of the alley in which they had been shocked than in the different alley. Another group of animals were trained the same way but tested with *shock on* in both alleys. They displayed the expected flat gradient, for the change in the stimulus situation did not, in this case, influence the strength of drive affecting their behavior. Murray and Miller (1952) have used the same technique to show that generalized avoidance is weakened more than generalized approach.

Some of the more important implications of the theory can be read from the graphic presentation in Figure 7.6. One hypothesis, tested and confirmed by Miller and Kraeling (1952), is that when approach-avoidance conflict is established in one situation and then tested in another situation that is somewhat similar, the subjects should be more likely to approach the "dangerous" goal in the new situation than the original one. This is what Freud had called *displacement*. We need only be reminded that Freud's patients were severely anxious about expressing sexual or aggressive tendencies while the rats in the Miller-Kraeling experiment had developed a conflict concerning expression of hunger in a particular situation.

In their discussion of human conflict and psychotherapy, Dollard and Miller (1950) have extended the definition of *avoidance* to apply to responses producing inhibition and repression, and the definition of *approach* to include responses that are inhibited or repressed. Other studies have been undertaken to show the effects of various drugs on approach and avoidant tendencies. One of these, by Conger (1951), showed that alcohol produces a greater reduction of fear motivating avoidance than of hunger motivating approach. After receiving injections of alcohol, rats which had been both fed

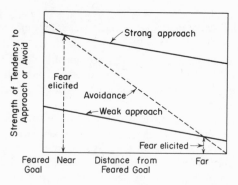

FIGURE 7.6 Graphic representation of an approach-avoidance conflict and of the effect of increasing the strength of motivation to approach. When the point at which the gradients intersect is between the subject and the goal, approach is stronger than avoidance. Therefore the subject moves toward the goal. When he passes the point of intersection, avoidance becomes stronger than approach; so he stops and turns back. Increasing the strength of the drive motivating approach raises the height of the entire gradient of approach. Since this causes the point of intersection to occur nearer the goal, the subject approaches nearer. Since this nearer point is higher on the gradient of avoidance, more fear is elicited.

These deductions hold only for the range within which the two gradients intersect. It is only for the sake of simplicity that the gradients are represented by straight lines in these diagrams. Similar deductions could be made on the basis of any curves that have a continuous negative slope which is steeper for avoidance than for approach at each point above the abscissa. (*From Miller, 1951, p. 92; adapted from Miller, 1944*)

and shocked at a certain place were more likely to go back to the food than before.

## CRITICAL ARGUMENTS AND EVIDENCE

The basic formulations of *S-R* behavior theory, including the concepts of secondary reward (or reinforcement), fear as acquired drive, and the conception of approach-avoidance conflict provided a tremendous spur to *systematic* experimental research with animals during the 1940's. The scheme seemed to embrace all the phenomena which together constitute the empirical or behavioral problem of motivation. Furthermore, it appeared testable, at least with animals. The firm anchoring of the intervening variables (drive and habit) in generalizations about empirical antecedents and the articulate statement of the functional properties of these variables, that is, their behavioral implications, made it possible to imagine what kinds of evidence would constitute disproof. Consequently, critical arguments and evidence could be advanced. The self-corrective process, which is one of the defining characteristics of science, could begin in earnest. And begin it did.

We shall consider two forms of criticism that are immediately pertinent to the problem of motivation:

(1) Arguments that question the adequacy of the *physiological* hypothesis which attributes activation of behavior to biological needs or a strong stimulus and primary reinforcement to reduction of need or of strong stimulus. This physiological hypothesis concerning the underlying nature of motivation and reward is virtually identical with Freud's 1917 conception of instinct or need. It implies that all goal-directed pursuits in animals and men are, in the last analysis, to be viewed as efforts to reduce stimulation. It is an hypothesis which identifies what common sense calls "pain" with any increase in stimulation and "pleasure" with any decrease in stimulation.

(2) Arguments and evidence that call into question the adequacy of Hull's formal conception of the immediate determinants of the impetus to respond, $sE_R = f(D) \times f(sH_R)$. This conception of what intervenes between observable stimulus and response, to comprise the immediate determinants of instrumental actions which constitute "striving for goals," clearly leaves out any explicit reference to the anticipated goal of action which Lewin, Tolman, and Hull himself in an earlier analysis of purposive behavior, had given special emphasis.

### IS BIOLOGICAL NEED THE ANTECEDENT OF DRIVE?

Does a biological need, defined as the absence of some commodity required for survival, always instigate action? The inadequacy of this conception was almost immediately apparent. In addition to the difficulty arising when one attempts to find a place for sexual motivation under the rubric "tissue deficit," this conception runs counter to evidence that certain important tissue deficits can occur and have no apparent effect on the behavior of an organism. McClelland has argued:

". . . some survival needs produce a motive and some do not. For example, it is now known that vitamin $B_{12}$ is necessary for the production of erythrocytes, and without $B_{12}$ the organism will suffer from pernicious anemia and die. Yet a person suffering from anemia or $B_{12}$ deficiency behaves in no way like a motivated person, at least as determined by any of the usual measures of motivation. Another example would be the

breathing of carbon monoxide which leads to sudden death and certainly to a tissue need, but which apparently produces no activity or behavior suggestive of a state of motivation. If anyone feels that these are merely isolated exceptions to the biological-need theory of motivation, a very brief perusal of medical literature should convince him of the great number of pathological organic conditions that by definition constitute tissue needs, but which do not give rise to any kind of "driving" stimulus or motive. Granted this fact, it follows that the presence of a biological need is not a reliable index of the existence of a motive" (McClelland *et al.*, 1953, p. 15).*

### COMPLICATIONS WHEN DRIVE IS DEFINED AS A STRONG STIMULUS

The difficulties with the biological-need hypothesis can be avoided by identifying drive with intensity of a stimulus, as Miller has. Accordingly, any increase in stimulation constitutes an increase in drive, and any decrease in stimulation constitutes a decrease in drive. Yet, as McClelland points out, some of the beautiful simplicity of this generalization is soon lost in the complications which arise:

"Often decreases in stimulation appear to cause an increase in motivation (e.g., a dark night), whereas an increase in stimulation may cause a decrease in motivation (e.g., a light on a dark night). Miller and Dollard recognize this possibility—in fact the 'dark night' example is their own (1941, p. 65)—but they argue that one must take into account the organism's past learning and the *total* amount of stimulation. Presumably the person who is alone on a dark night has a more active brain because of anxiety based on past negative experiences with absence of visual stimulation in the dark. 'The light may produce a moderate increase in the amount of stimulation reaching him through the eyes, but a marked decrease in the amount of stimulation from anxiety responses' (Miller and Dollard, 1941, p. 65). But this explanation only adds to our difficulties. For the theory has now lost some of its simplicity and becomes exceedingly hard to test crucially if we must always take into account past experience and total stimulation every time we try to decide whether a strong stimulus will be a drive or a reward. That is, the advantage of this type of theoretical model arises partly from the fact that one can presumably arouse a motive by increasing a particular peripheral stimulus intensity. But a good deal of the advantage is lost if we must take these other factors into account.

"Furthermore, there is other evidence which

* Excerpts from D. C. McClelland, J. W. Atkinson, R. W. Clark, and E. L. Lowell, *The Achievement Motive*, copyright 1953, Appleton-Century-Crofts, Inc., are reprinted by permission.

seems to cast doubt upon the adequacy of the stimulus intensity model. . . . Cattell and Hoagland (Morgan, 1943, p. 266) in an investigation, the intent of which was to determine if there was such a thing as a 'pure' pressure receptor, stimulated the skin of a frog with an interrupted air jet. They showed that the nerve fibres activated by this stimulation responded at their maximum rate (300 per second) but the frog showed no activity that would indicate the presence of a motive to avoid this stimulation which, in terms of intensity (frequency of firing), was as strong a stimulation (for the number of fibres involved) as the frog was capable of experiencing" (McClelland *et al.*, 1953, pp. 19–20).

Hebb (1949) has expanded the argument that degree of activation of behavior should not be conceived as related to amount of neural excitation in any simple manner, but rather as related to the *patterning* of central excitations and to the types of afferent fibers which are involved in transmission of an external stimulus to the central nervous system. Further pursuit of the underlying physiology of motivation and behavior, generated in part by these physiological hypotheses concerning the nature of drive, has become an important field in its own right within contemporary psychology as new techniques for investigation have been introduced.

### ACTIVITY NOT AN INEVITABLE CONSEQUENCE OF DRIVE

The conception of drive as activator of behavior had its origin in experimental demonstrations by Richter (1927) of the cyclical rise and fall of activity, as measured in activity wheels and tambour cages, in relation to the normal hunger cycle. But is increased level of activity an invariable consequence of increased drive? Could the level of activity be employed as an independent measure of drive if one were to set out to discover whether or not a particular antecedent condition—for example, an increase in peripheral stimulation as in the Cattell-Hoagland study cited above—produces drive? The answer to this question now appears to be *no*. In a study involving shock to generate the acquired drive of fear, Brown and Jacobs (1949) observed that anxious rats often "freeze." That is, sometimes an increase of drive produces a decrease in amount of activity. And so again we find a complication in the simple scheme which suggests that arousal of a biological need or a strong stimulus will activate the animal to begin the normal trial-and-error adjustive sequence.

The fact that an increase in drive may often produce a decrease in overt activity is not, however, inconsistent with the principle $_sE_R = f(D) \times f(_sH_R)$. If the habit of "freezing" is stronger than any other habit elicited by the stimulus complex at the moment, this particular response should be strongly excited. In fact, under such circumstances, the duration of immobility might provide an excellent index of the strength of the drive. The real difficulty lies in the fact that for years the concept of drive, in the thinking of many psychologists, has been equated with curves showing sheer amount of motility plotted in relation to hours of deprivation or some other controlled antecedent condition. The level of overt activity is more complexly determined than was earlier imagined; it is to be considered, at best, a fallible index of drive. Because of this complication it is often proposed that evidence of *learning when drive is reduced* should be taken as the major criterion for inferring the existence of drive.

### LEARNING WITHOUT EVIDENCE OF DRIVE-REDUCTION

The argument that has most shaken belief in the adequacy of the drive-reduction interpretation of what constitutes a reinforcing state of affairs is one based on the results of experiments which have demonstrated the fact of learning under conditions that either do not fit easily into a need-reduction or stimulus-reduction theory of reward or else quite dramatically refute it.

Sheffield and Roby (1950) demonstrated that thirsty rats learned to prefer to drink a saccharine solution to pure water. The reduction of thirst should be the same, but saccharine tastes sweet (to humans at least). Sheffield, Wulff, and Backer (1951) have shown that male rats will learn to run to copulate with a receptive female rat even though removed from the goal box before orgasm has occurred. When one considers the increase in peripheral stimulation involved in the act of copulation, it would appear that here is an instance of *increased* stimulation, rather than decreased stimulation, functioning to reinforce behavior. The animals in the experiment were sexually naïve, so an explanation of the result, shown in Figure 7.7, in terms of secondary reinforcement seems unwarranted.

Sheffield has taken the position that the elicitation of a consummatory response rather than need or drive reduction is what constitutes the critically important factor in reinforcement. Young (1949; 1961), who has advanced substantial evidence of taste preferences in animals that are not systematic-

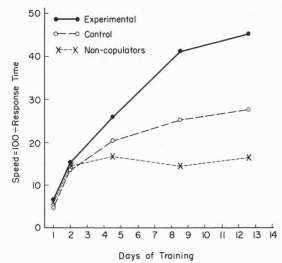

FIGURE 7.7   Reinforcing value of copulation without ejaculation. Experimental animals found a female in the goal box, control animals found a male, and non-copulators found one or the other but never attempted to copulate. (*From Sheffield, Wulff, and Backer, 1951, p. 5.*)

ally related to nutritional requirements, argues that "*affective arousal*," produced in these experiments by a sweet taste or by sexual stimulation, is the important factor in reinforcement.

These studies illustrate that states of affairs which common sense calls satisfying or pleasant, but which seem not to be embraced by the need-reduction or stimulus-reduction hypothesis concerning the physiological nature of reinforcement, do nevertheless constitute states of affairs in relation to which animals display "striving."

Another class of critical studies dramatizes the extent to which theoretical emphasis of visceral drives and pain as primary springs of action had tended to minimize interest in the motivating effects of external stimuli. Harlow (1953) reports experiments demonstrating that monkeys will learn to solve a three-device mechanical puzzle apparatus for no other reward than the activity itself. Other experiments with monkeys show an orderly increase in the number of correct responses in the learning of a six-device mechanical puzzle over a twelve-day period, though no reduction of hunger, thirst, pain, or sexual gratification has followed manipulation of the puzzle. In 10 hours of continuous testing, the frequency of total responses to puzzles decreased, showing some satiation of interest in them, but

Harlow reports that "the animals were still working enthusiastically on the puzzles during the last hour of testing" (Harlow, 1953, p. 32). He has observed that when food reward is introduced, monkeys tend to lose interest in the puzzles as soon as the food reward has been extracted. In contrast, monkeys who are not given the extrinsic food reward display a more continuous interest in manipulation of the puzzle devices throughout a test period.

Other investigators have focused attention upon exploratory behavior and curiosity. Butler (1953) has shown that monkeys will learn which of two differently colored windows to press when they are put into an opaque box, and the only reward following their response is the chance to look out of the window for a 30-second period. When animals were tested repeatedly for four hours a day, five days a week, or a total of 40 hours, this behavior, which is reinforced only by the opportunity to look out the window, was found to be remarkably persistent and stable. In reference to this, Harlow has said:

"On the basis of these data one can make out a strong case for the statement that the visual exploration drive is more persistent than any other known drive in the monkey—or any other primate. These monkeys received, day in and day out, over 200 visual rewards or reinforcements with no reduction in drive strength, a condition very different from hunger, where 200 swallows, with or without associated food, will put an end to any motivational spring" (Harlow, 1953, pp. 41–42).

Montgomery (1953), studying exploratory behavior in rats, found it present in satiated rats. And contrary to the belief that it would increase when animals were made hungry, Montgomery found that food privation *decreased* the amount of exploratory behavior. In another study, Montgomery (1954) ran animals in a Y maze in which one arm of the letter Y led to a large maze that they could explore and the other arm was a blind alley. The animals learned to enter the arm leading to the opportunity to explore, which here functioned to reinforce their instrumental response at the choice point. When the exploration maze was shifted to the other arm of the Y later in training, the animals reversed their choice of path in the Y maze. Montgomery (1953) found that exploratory drive is aroused by novel stimulation and satiates as a function of amount of exposure. Dember, Earl, and Paradise (1957) have found that the complexity of a stimulus situation defines its capacity as a reinforcing state of affairs.

Berlyne (1950), one of the first to assume that

novel stimuli would arouse a curiosity drive which would be diminished by continuous exposure of receptors to that stimulus, has reviewed the mounting evidence concerning this and related phenomena and has expanded his theoretical analysis of it in a recent book, *Conflict, Arousal, and Curiosity* (1960).

These recent studies of manipulation, exploration, and curiosity highlight the limitations of the drive-reduction theory of reinforcement. The activity of manipulating a puzzle and the activity of exposing the visual receptors to sufficiently complex and novel stimulation are, apparently, as capable of reinforcing antecedent actions as are the activities of eating when hungry and drinking when thirsty. It requires an excessively elaborate and complicated chain of theoretical reasoning to view these phenomena as derivatives, in some sense, of visceral drives or pain.

REINFORCING EFFECT OF ELECTRICAL
STIMULATION OF THE BRAIN

Finally, there is the dramatic discovery of Olds and Milner (1954) that direct electrical stimulation of certain areas of an animal's brain functions as a positive reinforcement. Utilizing a technique for direct implantation of an electrode into the brain, these investigators were interested in the reinforcing function of direct electrical stimulation. They implanted electrodes at various sites in the brain, leaving the animal "free to behave, intact and healthy, up and around" (Olds, 1955, p. 136). In the course of exploratory investigations, they found that stimulation at certain electrode sites had a positive-reinforcing effect on behavior. Systematic follow-up studies have employed a Skinner-box apparatus arranged so that a rat can stimulate his own brain electrically by pressing the bar. This sends a small charge of electricity to the wire connected to the electrode implanted in the animal's brain. Other studies have placed animals at the beginning of a complex maze in which the goal box contains a bar which the animal can press to stimulate its brain directly.

In both types of apparatus, the results are similar, obvious, and conclusive. In the Skinner box, the rate of bar pressing, when reinforced by direct electrical stimulation to certain areas of the brain, far exceeds what has been observed by the hungriest animals when rewarded by food. And clearly demonstrating that this behavior cannot be viewed as some form of compulsive and stereotyped response induced by the electrical stimulus are the results obtained when animals are given the opportunity to run a multiple unit maze for an opportunity to press a lever to stimulate their own brain. They display vigorous, purposive pursuit of an increase of stimulation. In these studies, animals are allowed to eat and drink regularly in their home cages and no food or water is present during experimentation.

Olds has employed percentages of time animals spend at lever pressing as a measure of the reward values of electrical stimuli at different places in the brain and for comparison with amount of pressing when the current is turned off so that no electrical "reward" is received. We quote his description of the results of one of the early studies:

> "For four animals with electrodes implanted in the septal area the acquisition percentage scores were 75%, 85%, 88%, and 92%. Corresponding extinction scores were 18%, 13%, 6%, and 12%. Thus, all septal animals spent more than three-quarters of their acquisition time responding regularly, and less than one-quarter of their extinction time. The 75% animal gave a total of more than 3000 responses in 12 hours of acquisition testing. Each response lasted for a little over one second. During acquisition he responded at a rate of 285 responses per hour. When the current was turned off, his rate fell to almost zero" (Olds, 1955, pp. 139–140).*

Since the initial demonstrations of the phenomena, systematic study of the effects of variations in amount of current, location of the electrode in the brain, effect of drive conditions in interaction with location of electrode, and amount of current have been undertaken by Olds and other investigators. This work has contributed to a generally revitalized neurophysiology of motivation in recent years. Developments are so rapid in this field that only the expert can digest and interpret their potential significance for the behavioral psychology of motivation. Here we shall be content to summarize Olds' conclusion concerning the import of the earliest of these studies for the theory of motivation:

> "Now we have to ask what the reward finding contributes to motivational psychology. In the first place it categorically answers the main questions which we asked at the outset. It *is* possible to reward an animal without either (a) satisfying some physiological need, or (b) explicitly withdrawing a drive stimulus. For, by no stretch of the imagination, could we suppose that our animals would perish without this electrical input to the septal

* Excerpts from James Olds, A physiological study of reward, in *Studies of Motivation*, edited by David C. McClelland, copyright 1955, Appleton-Century-Crofts, Inc., are reprinted by permission.

area of the brain. And, only by the introduction of a complex network of *ad hoc* hypotheses could we maintain that electrical *excitation* of the septal region has an effect which is the *opposite of excitation* on the input from some physiological drive stimulus. I do not mean to contend that the latter is impossible; septal excitation might somehow inhibit the input from a normal drive stimulus, and if such a possibility could be independently demonstrated, such an experiment might save the drive-reduction theory of reward. For the time being, however, we have categorical evidence that the *addition of a strong stimulus* can be reinforcing; and this certainly tends to infirm the drive-reduction theory which holds that, prior to learning, only the *reduction or withdrawal* of a strong stimulus should be reinforcing. Our reward stimulus is *not* a drive reduction, and it is also *not* a stimulus which has so far as we know any previous association with a drive reduction" (Olds, 1955, p. 141).

PHYSIOLOGICAL NATURE OF REINFORCEMENT:
AN OPEN QUESTION

Miller, who also has undertaken a program of physiological studies of motivation including direct electrical stimulation of the brain (Miller, 1957), recently summarized his own position with respect to the drive-reduction theory of reinforcement:

"It seems to be a fact that some stimulus situations are much more effective than others in determining whether or not the responses that lead to them will be learned and performed. Thus, all theorists are forced to assign the empirical law of effect some role in their theories. A consistent application of the empirical law of effect would result in a long list of stimulus situations that can serve as rewards and of those that are relatively neutral. In practice, most experimenters limit themselves to relatively few situations which are known to function as effective rewards.

". . . Since a catalogue of rewards is so cumbersome, some theorists have looked for a simple general principle, or principles, that will allow them to determine whether an event should be listed as a reward or not. One attempt at such a principle is the drive-reduction hypothesis of reinforcement.

". . . In its weak form, it states that the sudden reduction in the strength of any strong motivational stimulus always serves as a reward, or in other words, is a *sufficient* condition for reinforcement. In its strong form, it states that all reward is produced in this way, or in other words, that drive reduction is not only a sufficient but also the *necessary* condition for reinforcement.

"By defining drives as strong stimuli, I have sharpened the hypothesis into the assumption that it is the sudden reduction in the strength of intense stimulation that serves as a reinforcement.

". . . Although I believe that the foregoing hypothesis has a considerably less than 50 percent chance of being correct, especially in its strong form, I do believe it is better at the present moment than any other single hypothesis. Therefore, I feel that it is worthwhile to try out applying it consistently, if only to highlight the obstacles and infuriate others into devising superior hypotheses and the experimental programs to support them. . . .

". . . The stimulus-reduction hypothesis of reinforcement could be discarded without having an appreciable effect on the rest of my theoretical formulations. I take this occasion to urge attempts to formulate and rigorously test competing hypotheses, and time permitting, may even join in that activity myself. However unsatisfactory, the drive-reduction hypothesis is not likely to be abandoned as long as it is the best thing of its kind that we have. The decisive way to kill it is with a superior alternative" (Miller, 1959, pp. 256–257).

The underlying nature of reinforcing states of affairs is now generally considered an open question. The question first became an exciting directive for research when Hull proposed, in 1935, that Thorndike's Law of Effect could be restated in a way that might make it possible to derive present "striving for goals" from principles that had to do with past "strengthening of connections." At first Hull identified reinforcement with the occurrence of the terminal or consummatory event in a typical behavioral sequence, that is, $S_G \rightarrow R_G$. Then, in 1943, he proposed a physiological hypothesis concerning the nature of "primary reinforcement," the need-reduction hypothesis. Miller and Dollard (1941) had already identified drive with the strength of any stimulus rather than with biological need; so their hypothesis concerning the nature of reinforcement was reduction of stimulation. Hull soon adopted the Miller hypothesis when difficulties arising in attributing drive to biological needs became apparent. There then followed a period in which the implications of the drive-reduction hypothesis were exploited in speculative explanations of how the genesis of the great variety of human motives might be derived from the original visceral drives and pain. This type of speculation continues. But mounting experimental evidence with animals shows that the drive-reduction hypothesis of reinforcement is inadequate. Some new and interesting physiological hypotheses have been proposed, but none has yet produced the systematic program of research that is required to support its validity. Miller is right; the drive-reduction hypothesis, despite its acknowledged limitations, will not die until a new and more inclusive hypothesis is advanced to take its place.

While awaiting the new and better hypothesis,

many psychologists find it useful to define a reinforcing state of affairs *empirically* as one which increases the probability that an act which it follows will occur on a subsequent occasion when conditions are otherwise the same.

## INCENTIVE MOTIVATION

We turn now to another basic criticism of Hull's 1943 theory, one which asserts the inadequacy of the conception of the immediate determinants of the tendency to respond, $_sE_R = f(D) \times f(_sH_R)$. We have already noted the discrepancy between this conception of what excites a response and the more elaborate set of ideas Hull had advanced during the 1930's, which included the anticipatory goal reaction ($r_g$) as an effective determinant of action.

Two difficulties were almost immediately apparent. The principle $_sE_R = f(D) \times f(H)$ could not explain the latent-learning phenomenon which Tolman emphasized as evidence of the basic inadequacy of a theory which identifies learning with the strengthening of connections (see p. 143); and it could not explain the *immediate* effect on performance of a shift in the amount of reward or incentive.

Subsequent changes in this principle to accommodate matters which Tolman had emphasized, first in Hull's 1952 revision, and more recently in Kenneth Spence's elaboration of *S-R* behavior theory in *Behavior Theory and Conditioning* (1956), illustrate the gradual but final acceptance of the idea that anticipation (or expectancy) of the goal is one of the fundamental determinants of molar action.

In reference to the Blodgett experiment (see p. 139) and follow-up studies of the effect of changes in reward on maze performance, Tolman had argued that rewards do not function to cement *S-R* connections (habits) as Thorndike and then Hull had assumed in the Law of Effect and the Principle of Reinforcement. He asserted that previous rewards affect present performance because, after reward, the animal has acquired an expectancy that certain actions will be followed by reward. The expected reward provides an incentive to perform those responses which will lead on to the reward (or expected goal) most quickly and efficiently. The Law of Effect should be considered a principle of *performance*, not of learning. That was the gist of Tolman's argument.

As early as 1939 (the same year that Mowrer introduced the hypothesis that fear should be conceived as an acquired drive), Kenneth Spence had begun to wrestle with the problem of encompassing the phenomenon called "latent learning" within the *S-R* framework. There followed a decade of research by many different investigators on various facets of the "latent-learning controversy." The fruit of this research and further study of the effects of shifts in the amount of reward on performance was the concept of *incentive motivation* and some fundamental revisions of the principle within *S-R* theory which accounts for the immediate determinants of reaction potential.

### THE NATURE OF THE PROBLEM

What was the difficulty which the *S-R* theory faced? We shall simplify the problem in the interest of brevity.

Hull, like Thorndike before him, had assumed that frequency and amount of reward (and also delay of reward) influence the amount of growth in strength of habit on any given trial and that growth of habit strength is a gradual process. Furthermore, Hull assumed that *habit strength could not be erased or reversed*. When the reward was removed, experimental extinction of the response was thought to be a *gradual* process depending upon fatigue (reactive inhibition) and the gradual learning of a new habit of not responding (conditioned inhibition).

The main fact of the early studies of latent learning was the relatively sudden and substantial change in performance which occurs when food is introduced in the goal box of a maze for the first time after trials in which the animals have run the maze while hungry but without a food reward. (See Figure 5.7.) And comparable large and sudden shifts in performance were also observed in studies by Tolman and co-workers when the reward was changed from a "more-demanded" one to a "less-demanded" one or vice versa. (See Figures 5.8, 5.9, 5.10.) How are these abrupt changes in the level of performance to be explained if frequency and amount of reward are viewed as determinants of habit strength and growth of habit strength is a gradual, incremental process?

### REFINED STUDIES OF EFFECT OF CHANGE IN MAGNITUDE OF REWARD

More refined studies of the effect of changes in *amount* of food reward on speed of performance were conducted by Crespi (1942; 1944) and Zeaman (1949). Their results provided the impetus for a change in Hull's theory. Holding hunger constant, both investigators showed that rats given a large food reward ran faster than rats given a small reward during training. Then, after a number of trials, the amount of reward was shifted so that animals originally trained with large reward now got a small reward, and those originally trained under small reward now got a large reward. Both studies showed *abrupt* changes in the speed of running, as illustrated in Figure 7.8. The curves of

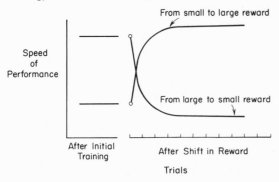

Speed of Performance

From small to large reward

From large to small reward

After Initial Training

After Shift in Reward

Trials

FIGURE 7.8   Idealized version of results obtained by Crespi (1942) and Zeaman (1949) showing effect of change in magnitude of reward on speed of perform- ance. Animals were pretrained for 19 or 20 trials with either a large or small reward and then the magnitude of reward was suddenly shifted.

the shifted groups actually went beyond the levels of performance attained by rats trained with large or small rewards to begin with. Crespi referred to these phenomena as an "elation effect" and a "depression effect" and advanced a motivational interpretation of the results.

Spence has spelled out the implications of these results for Hull's 1943 hypothesis that amount of reward influences *habit-strength:*

"With regard to the shift in the direction of a larger reinforcing object, the hypothesis had a clear-cut implication which Hull himself treated at some length in the *Principles*. According to it an increase in the incentive amount would be expected to lead to an increase in the limit to which the habit strength would grow with the consequence that if the asymptote had been at- tained with the smaller reward there would be a rise in the performance curve which would con- tinue until the new limit of habit growth was reached. While the results of all the studies are in agreement with this prediction as far as the direc- tion of the change is concerned, the abruptness of the performance shift was not to be expected. According to Hull's habit theory this change should have been a fairly gradual one resulting from the successive increments in habit strength. However, the shift to the new higher level occurred

fairly abruptly in all studies, reaching or surpass- ing the higher level of performance characteristic of subjects that had been trained on the large reward in a very few trials.

"The implication of Hull's theory with regard to reduction of incentive magnitude was never worked out in detail in the *Principles*. Hull merely stated that reduction of incentive size would be expected to lead on successive trials to a progres- sive lowering of performance level. Strictly speak- ing, Hull's hypothesis that the magnitude of *H* is a function of the magnitude of the reward, taken in conjunction with his assumption that habit (*H*) was a relatively permanent condition left by rein- forcement within the nervous system, implied, as far as the value of *H* itself is concerned, that a shift to a smaller reward should not lead to a decrement in performance. However, the well- known fact that reduction to zero reward (experi- mental extinction) results in response decrement apparently led Hull to believe that any reduction in reward size less than to zero was related in some manner to experimental extinction and thus would result in some response decrement. Apparently he intended to return to this topic in the later chapter on experimental extinction, but he did not do so" (Spence, 1956, pp. 132–133).*

HULL'S REVISION OF THEORY IN 1952

To accommodate these experimental facts and also to explain the findings of the closely related latent-learning studies of Blodgett and Tolman and Honzik, Hull (1952) revised his conception of the antecedents of habit strength and the determinants of reaction potential. He maintained the hypotheses that frequency of reinforcement and delay of rein- forcement influence the growth of habit, but he now introduced *amount of incentive* as a separate moti- vational variable (*K*) in the equation for reaction potential ($_sE_R$):

$$_sE_R = D \times K \times {_sH_R}.$$

Formerly, amount of reward had been considered one of the antecedents of habit strength. This change was consistent with an árgument that Spence had been developing in a series of studies related to the problem of latent learning. Spence and his co- workers had begun to make use of the fractional anticipatory goal reaction ($r_g$) and the proprioceptive stimulus produced by it ($s_g$) to explain various phenomena confronted in studies of unresolved problems inherent in the original studies of latent learning. For example, Kendler (1946) had run rats

* Excerpts from K. W. Spence, *Behavior Theory and Conditioning*, copyright 1956, Yale University Press, are reprinted by permission.

in a T maze containing food in one goal box and water in the other. The rats were *both* hungry and thirsty during training, but were then tested when only one of the drives, hunger *or* thirst, was operative. During training, responses to one side (leading to food) and to the other (leading to water) were equally reinforced. Hence the two habits should have been of comparable strength at the completion of training. But in the test, when only one of the drives was present, the animals responded correctly. That is, they made the response which led to food when hungry and to water when thirsty. Why?

The explanation proposed by Spence made effective use of ideas which Hull had proposed in his essays of the 1930's on purposive behavior but then had ignored in his 1943 theory:

". . . the stimulus cues in the water arm and end box become, during training, conditioned to fractional anticipatory drinking acts ($r_w$) and, in turn, the proprioceptive cues ($s_w$) resulting from these anticipatory acts become conditioned to the response of entering and continuing locomotion in this alley. In a like manner, conditioned, fractional anticipatory eating responses ($r_f$) develop in the food alley and these cues ($s_f$) become conditioned to the behavior of entering this alley. During the test series when only one drive is operative, the anticipatory act related to the goal for which the subject is motivated will, because of the greater strength of the particular drive stimulus . . . be much stronger (more vigorous) than the other and hence will produce stronger proprioceptive cues. Thus, if the S is thirsty, proprioceptive cues from anticipatory drinking responses will be stronger than those from anticipatory eating. As these cues ($s_w$) will be conditioned to the response of entering the alley leading to water, they will tend to give this response the greater excitatory strength. . . . When the animal is hungry, the proprioceptive cues ($s_f$) would be stronger and this would give the response of entering the food alley the greater excitatory strength. In other words, the relative excitatory strengths of the competing responses will be a function of the relative strengths of the two fractional anticipatory goal responses, and the latter will be dependent upon which drive is present and which is absent" (Spence *et al.*, 1950, p. 549).

In this development, Spence and others began to consider seriously the possibility that anticipatory goal reactions might become conditioned to environmental stimuli ($S_e$) and proprioceptive stimuli ($s_p$) in addition to the drive stimulus ($S_D$) which Hull had originally emphasized. It was the beginning of the idea of "incentive motivation" in S-R theory.

In his 1952 revision, Hull used the symbol K in reference to the anticipatory goal reaction, then conceived as a motivational factor like drive (D) which would combine multiplicatively with habit ($_sH_R$) to determine reaction potential ($_sE_R$), i.e., $_sE_R = D \times K \times _sH_R$. Sudden changes in level of performance when amount of reward (K) was shifted could be explained in terms of a sudden change in this motivational variable (K), which acted, like drive, to excite habits.

Hull used the same scheme to explain the original latent-learning results. In his view, the shift from no food reward to some food reward in the early studies by Blodgett and Tolman and Honzik was not to be conceived as a shift from *zero* incentive (K) to some larger incentive, but from a very small incentive to a much larger one. Hull assumed, in other words, that even an empty goal box must contain some minimal generalized secondary reinforcing properties for an animal during training. Hence habit, now no longer dependent upon the *amount* of reinforcement, could develop; but it would not be expressed in performance until the incentive (K) was increased.

There can be no question that Hull explicitly intended to take account of the phenomena to which Tolman referred with the term *expectation* or *expectancy*. Concluding his discussion of anticipatory goal reaction ($r_g$-$s_g$) and this new motivational variable (K), Hull wrote:

"When an organism begins to respond to a situation which does not yet exist but is impending, we say informally that the organism anticipates or expects the event to occur. Since time out of mind the ordinary man has used the words *expect, expectation, expectancy*, and *expectative* in a practically intelligent and intelligible manner. Around 1931, Tolman put forward the term *expectation* in a technical sense as 'an immanent cognitive determinant aroused by actually presented stimuli' (1932, p. 444). Moreover, Tolman insisted that none of his technical concepts should lend support to any sort of 'ultimately teleological and ultimately mentalistic interpretation of animal . . . behavior' (1932, p. xii). Were it not for the fact that his writings at the time and since appear to be strongly opposed to an approach resembling the one here presented, we might suppose that the $s_G$ cited above might be a concrete case of Tolman's immanent cognitive determining stimulus mediating the expectation, i.e., $r_G \rightarrow s_G$ as the covert expectancy, and $S_G \rightarrow R_G$ as the thing expected" (Hull, 1952, pp. 151–152).*

Hull suggested that it might help to avoid confusion in meanings if the term *anticipatory* were used

* Clark L. Hull, *A Behavior System*, copyright 1952, Yale University Press. Used by permission.

in reference to antedating reactions of which both animals and man are capable and the term *expectation* reserved for symbolic, verbalized reactions of which man alone is capable. But this distinction has never been widely applied.

SPENCE'S REVISION OF THEORY IN 1956

We may consider the reformulation advanced by Spence in *Behavior Theory and Conditioning* (1956) as an alternative to Hull's theory or as the most advanced formal statement of an *S-R* behavior theory which is in a continual process of evolution. We tend to view it as the latter. In many respects, it represents the convergence of *S-R* theory with some of the central ideas advanced by Tolman.

In the first place, Spence uses the terms *reinforcement*, *reinforcer*, and *reinforcing event* in reference to certain empirical events that may be designated on the basis of observation:

"Responses accompanied or followed by certain kinds of events (namely, reinforcers) are more likely to occur on subsequent occasions, whereas responses followed by certain other kinds of events (namely nonreinforcers) do not subsequently show a greater likelihood of occurrence" (Spence, 1956, p. 33).

This statement may be referred to as the *Empirical Law of Effect*. It is the point of departure for theorizing about such questions as the nature of reinforcement and whether reinforcement is required for learning to occur. In reference to the growth of an instrumental habit (e.g., learning the correct response to get out of a puzzle box, or the path to the goal box of a maze, or to press a bar in the Skinner box), Spence has taken the position that habit strength ($H$) is determined solely by *the number of times a response has occurred in the presence of a stimulus*:

"While acknowledging that this habit factor undoubtedly has some kind of physiological basis in the nervous system, we shall make no attempt to speculate as to its specific locus or detailed neurophysiological nature. Instead we shall limit our conception to the notion of a quantitatively changing capacity or property of the organism which, along with other factors, determines the strength of a response in any situation. More specifically, each time in one of these simple learning situations that a particular response occurs an increase will be assumed to occur in the capacity or habit strength of the contiguous stimulus to elicit the response.

"The effects of the presence or absence of a reinforcer and of other kinds of variation of it, such as delaying its occurrence or varying its magnitude, may be conceived to affect response strength through other intervening variables than $H$" (Spence, 1956, p. 94).

Restricting our attention to the portion of Spence's theory that refers to the immediate determinants of the impetus to respond, which Hull called *reaction potential* and which Spence now refers to as *excitatory potential* ($E$), we find *drive* ($D$), *incentive* ($K$), and *habit* ($H$) combined in this way:

$$E = (D + K) \times H.$$

As in Hull, time of deprivation is the assumed antecedent of strength of drive. But differing with Hull, Spence asserts that frequency of reward, amount of reward, and possibly also delay of reward are all to be considered antecedents of the "incentive motivational factor," $K$, which he identifies with the $r_g$-$s_g$ mechanism. Habit, which was so much the center of interest in 1943 when Hull formulated his principles for the first time, is now conceived by Spence to be dependent only upon the frequency of the conjunction $S$-$R$.

In light of evidence available in 1956, Spence proposed that the incentive motivational factor ($K$) and drive ($D$) combine *additively* (rather than multiplicatively as Hull stated in 1952) as non-specific exciters of habits.

Spence provides a foundation for understanding his conception of how factors related to "rewards" influence performance in a discussion of the Crespi-Zeaman studies, which showed "abrupt" changes in performance when the magnitude of reward was shifted:

"My own approach to these experimental phenomena has also always been a motivational one. Indeed, at the time that Hull was writing the chapter on magnitude of reinforcement for his *Principles of Behavior* our correspondence reveals a vigorous disagreement over his learning (habit) interpretation. The basis of my disagreement, in part, was the finding of Nissen and Elder (1935) and Cowles and Nissen (1937) with respect to variation of the magnitude of the goal object in delayed-response experiments with chimpanzees. After showing that the level of performance in this situation was a function of the magnitude of the incentive, these investigators further demonstrated that, after attaining a certain level of response with a given size of food, a drop in level of performance occurred if a smaller piece of food was used. Similarly, a shift to a larger piece of food was shown to lead to improvement in performance. These shifts up and down seemed to me to suggest changes in a motivational rather than a habit factor, and it is interesting to note that Cowles and Nissen interpreted their findings in terms of a mechanism which they described as reward expectancy.

"My preference for a motivational interpretation was also greatly influenced, as I have already indicated, by our theorizing concerning the role of the fractional anticipatory goal response in our latent learning experiments with the simple T maze (Spence, Bergmann, and Lippitt, 1950). This theory assumed, it will be recalled, that stimulus cues in the goal box and from the alley just preceding the goal box become conditioned to the goal response, $R_g$. Through generalization the stimulus cues at earlier points in the runway are also assumed to acquire the capacity to elicit $R_g$, or at least noncompetitional components of $R_g$ that can occur without the actual presence of the food (e.g., salivating and chewing movements). As a result this fractional conditioned response, which we shall designate as $r_g$, moves forward to the beginning of the instrumental sequence. Furthermore, the interoceptive stimulus cue ($s_g$) produced by this response also becomes a part of the stimulus complex in the alley and thus should become conditioned to the instrumental locomotor responses. *But more important, in addition to this associative function we have assumed that this $r_g$-$s_g$ mechanism also has motivational properties that vary with the magnitude or vigor with which it occurs* [italics added] (Spence, 1956, pp. 134–135).

We may pause, for a moment, to reflect on what Spence has said. Referring back to Figure 5.6, which identifies with circles the two different associative events which Pavlov and Thorndike had initially studied, we find in this conception by Spence the kind of influence of one mechanism on another that Woodworth had suggested in his early attempt to bring the phenomenon of purposive pursuit of goals into the orbit of an S-R psychology. (See p. 124.) For Spence, the $r_g$-$s_g$ mechanism is the classical conditioned form of the eating response which Pavlov had studied. This is the incentive motivational factor ($K$). And the instrumental locomotor response to which Spence refers is what Thorndike had considered in his studies of selective learning. The connection between S and R which Thorndike had discussed is represented as habit ($H$) in Spence's conception.

Through stimulus generalization, environmental cues at an early point in the runway leading to food, or even in the starting box of a maze, can elicit the anticipatory goal reaction ($r_g$-$s_g$). The aroused $r_g$-$s_g$ then functions to excite instrumental locomotor habits that are evoked by the complex of stimuli which are immediately present. That is the essential idea in Spence's theory of incentive motivation.

How does the $r_g$-$s_g$ mechanism operate to affect the level of motivation as Spence has suggested it does? Possibly, argues Spence, the occurrence of fractional goal responses produces a certain amount of conflict and a heightened tension of $s_g$ produced by a vigorous $r_g$ which functions like other intense stimuli in the motivation of performance. The question leads again to speculation about the underlying physiology of motivation and defines a direction for physiological research. But, as Spence and others (viz., Tolman, Lewin) have often argued, the task of developing a quantitative behavior theory in terms of objectively defined intervening variables can proceed without the answer to this and other similar neuro-physiological questions:

". . . my preference is merely to introduce an intervening variable, $K$, which is regarded as representing, quantitatively, the motivational property of the conditioned $r_g$-$s_g$ mechanism and which is defined in terms of the experimental variables that determine the vigor of the latter.

"From our assumption that the basic mechanism underlying this incentive motivational factor, $K$, is the classical conditioned $r_g$, we are necessarily committed to a number of assumptions as to the variables that determine its strength. Thus, being itself a conditioned response, $r_g$ will vary with the number of conditioning trials given in the goal box. Secondly we must assume that its intensity or vigor will be a negatively accelerated, exponential function of the number of these conditioning trials. Furthermore, on the basis of experimental studies of generalization of conditioning we will need to assume that its strength at any point in the alley distant from the goal box will be a function of the similarity of the environmental cues at that point and those in the goal box. If internal, proprioceptive cues from the running response play an important role, the differences in these cues at different distances from the goal box will have to be considered. Unfortunately we know very little, as yet, concerning either of these variables. Finally, any property of the goal object that produces unconditioned consummatory responses of different intensity or vigor will presumably determine the value of $K$, for there is some evidence to support the notion that the intensity or vigor of the response may be conditioned *as such* (Hull, 1943)" (Spence, 1956, pp. 135–136).

WHAT DETERMINES THE VIGOR OF
ANTICIPATORY GOAL REACTIONS?

With the introduction of incentive motivation, $K$, in the formal conception of the immediate determinants of the tendency to respond, the most striking difference between the early formulations of Tolman and Lewin, on the one hand, and S-R behavior theory, on the other, is greatly diminished. *There no longer is any disagreement with the assertion that the anticipated goal should be represented as one of the potent contemporaneous determinants of molar action.* In his essays during the 1930's, Hull had spelled out how "the idea of the end" might be represented using stimulus and response as basic elements of construction. The fruits of that analysis of purposive behavior were lost for a time, but finally are regained in the concept of incentive motivation.

Today, as Spence draws attention to the need for more information concerning the factors which influence the magnitude or vigor of the anticipatory goal reaction (incentive motivation), he directs interest to problems that are also suggested by the Lewinian concept of valence of the goal and Tolman's equivalent concept of demand for the goal. Tentatively, Spence supposes that "different experimental variations of reinforcing agents will determine $K$, either through the habit strength of $r_g$ or through the particular $r_g$, i.e., the particular vigor of $r_g$ being conditioned" (Spence, 1956, p. 137). We gain some appreciation of how amount of reward (e.g., amount of food) might influence incentive motivation from Spence's consideration of some possibilities:

"From the point of view of the hypothesis offered here a major problem is that of ascertaining the nature of the relations existing between the experimental manipulations of the reinforcing object and the two ways in which the vigor of the $r_g$ might conceivably be varied. Do, for example, two different magnitudes of the goal object in a goal box lead to the same amount of conditioning (i.e., same habit strength) of two $r_g$'s which differ in vigor? Or, does the fact that the subject spends more consummatory time in the goal box in the case of the larger reward mean that the difference in vigor results from a greater amount of conditioning of the $r_g$ to the cues in the goal box than in the case of the small reward? These questions have to do with the nature of the classical conditioning of the consummatory response in the goal box with variations in the magnitude of the reward object, the number of different pieces of the object, the time and vigor of the consummatory activity, and so on" (Spence, 1956, pp. 137–138).

Surprisingly little evidence bearing on these questions is available from classical reward conditioning studies of the sort performed by Pavlov. Yet the little that is known may provide a clue of great theoretical importance. Early salivary conditioning studies by Finch (1938) and Zener and McCurdy (1939) showed that, after a conditioned salivary response has been established, the magnitude of that response when the animal is satiated is very weak compared to the magnitude of conditioned salivation following a period of 24 hours' food privation. Lewin, it will be recalled, attributed the *valence* of a goal to the temporary state of need $(t_g)$ and characteristics of the object $(G)$; and Tolman's *demand* for the goal was conceived as jointly determined by the drive state and the incentive object. Spence's additive combination of the effects of deprivation $(D)$ and amount of incentive $(K)$ in the $S-R$ formulation implies the possibility that the vigor of the anticipatory goal reaction as it is influenced by the state of deprivation may be the sole mechanism of the general excitement represented in $(D + K)$. This possibility is suggested by Birch, Burnstein, and Clark (1958) and also in Sheffield's treatment of motivation which is reviewed in subsequent pages.

Some information concerning the questions Spence has raised may be gained from studies of instrumental performance. For example, Guttman (1954) varied the concentration of sucrose (which tastes sweet to humans) in a solution offered rats as the reward in a lever-pressing situation. He found the level of performance higher for the more concentrated of two solutions. Guttman also found that concentrations of sucrose produced higher levels of performance than equivalent concentrations of glucose. Again the difference favors the substance judged sweeter by humans. Spence's hypothesis would suppose that the sweetness of a substance may determine the vigor of the consummatory response.

Other pertinent evidence comes from studies by Sheffield and his co-workers which were explicitly designed to focus attention upon the consummatory reaction as the critical reinforcing event in studies of learning and performance. Using various combinations of rewarding substances, Sheffield, Roby, and Campbell (1954) related the speed of running in an alley to the strength of consummatory response in the goal box and found the striking relationship shown in Figure 7.9. Spence considers this evidence consistent with the hypothesis that the vigor of the anticipatory goal reaction—which depends, of course, upon the vigor of the goal reaction itself—should be reflected in the vigor of instrumental approach responses when habit $(H)$ is held constant.

Other studies by Sheffield and Roby (1950) and Sheffield, Wulff, and Backer (1951), described earlier (see p. 184), also present evidence that measures of the vigor of instrumental performance are related to

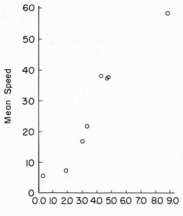

FIGURE 7.9 The relation between the strength of the consummatory response and the strength of the instrumental response with solutions varied independently in sweetness, nourishment, and prior opportunity to practice ingestion. Reading from left to right the groups are: water control, no pretraining; 20 gm. dextrose per liter, no pretraining; 20 gm. dextrose per liter, dextrose pretrained; 20 gm. dextrose per liter, water pretrained; 26 gm. dextrose per liter, water pretrained; 26 gm. dextrose per liter, dextrose pretrained; 1.30 gm. saccharin per liter, no pretraining; 20 gm. dextrose and 1.30 gm. saccharin per liter, no pretraining. (*From Sheffield, Roby, and Campbell, 1954, p. 352*)

the strength of consummatory reaction. According to the theory proposed by Spence, "these different strengths of consummatory activity reflect the strength of the conditioned fractional anticipatory goal response and thus provide an index of the value of $K$ in determining the reaction potential of the instrumental running response" (Spence, 1956, p. 147).

The design of experiments recommended for testing the incentive motivation hypothesis helps to provide a clearer understanding of Spence's conception:

"These studies make use of the implications of the theory that the strength of the $K$ factor, based as it is on the classical conditioned goal response, can be manipulated independently of the instrumental running response. Thus in one experiment now in progress two experimental groups of rats, $A$ and $B$, are being run in a straight alley four feet long to an empty goal box. A third control group ($C$) is being run to food. At the end of a given number of such trials, one of the experimental groups ($A$) is given a number of direct placements in the goal box, which is highly similar in its physical properties to the runway, and allowed to eat as much food as the control group ($C$) had in

its training trials. The second experimental group ($B$) is given a similar number of direct feedings in a box which is very different in its physical properties from those of the runway and goal box. According to our hypothesis the following predictions, among others, may be made concerning performance on the first test trials: (1) that the performance of experimental group $A$, that fed in the goal box, should significantly exceed its training level; (2) that the performance of this group should exceed that of experimental group $B$ which is fed in the box dissimilar from the goal box.

"The basis of these derivations is that through generalization the runway cues will evoke on the test trial the conditioned fractional anticipatory goal response in experimental group $A$, and hence the $K$ factor will be much greater for this group than in the training trials. Since generalization is greater in the case of group $A$ than group $B$, the $K$ factor should be greater in group $A$ and hence the subjects of this group should exhibit the greater speed of running on the test trials" (Spence, 1956, pp. 147–148).

From this plan of research, it is evident that the incentive motivational factor ($K$), which is coordinated with the magnitude of the classical conditioned anticipatory goal response, is assumed to act like a non-specific exciter of whatever instrumental locomotor habits are then and there elicited by environmental stimuli and other momentary cues. In this respect, $K$ functions just like drive ($D$) to excite, non-selectively, all habits that are presently elicited by momentary stimuli. If the alley in which the animals are first trained to run to an *empty* goal box is white, and then the animals are given a number of feeding trials in a different white box some five miles away from the experimental room, their subsequent running in the original white alley is expected to be enhanced because the whiteness of the alley will elicit a generalized conditioned anticipatory goal reaction which functions to excite the already established habit of running.

THE EFFECT OF DISTANCE FROM THE GOAL

Spence has called attention to two types of delay in reward in studies of instrumental approach behavior. The first type depends upon the length of the sequence of responses that must be performed to reach a goal. It is known, for example, that animals will learn to choose the shorter of two paths to the same goal (Grice, 1942) and to run faster in the first section of a short runway to a goal than in the first section of a long runway to a goal (Hull, 1934). Hull explained this in terms of the *gradient of reinforcement*. That is, Hull assumed there would be less growth of habit if the delay between a response and the reinforcing state of affairs was long than if it were short. Spence, however, explains the same phenomena in terms of variation in the strength of the incentive motivational factor ($K$):

> "That is, the longer the chain the less presumably is the similarity of the stimulus cues at the beginning and ends of the chain and hence the less strong will be the generalized $r_g$ at the beginning of the sequence. This theory implies, then, that differences in reaction potential ($E$) of responses at different distances from the reinforcement end of the behavior chain are due to differences in the $K$ factor rather than to differences in $H$" (Spence, 1956, p. 151).

Here, Spence is speaking to the problem that Tolman had attempted to resolve by positing a *demand for short paths and least effort*, and that Lewin treated in his concept of *psychological distance*. It will be recalled that Lewin assumed that *force* (the tendency to act) was jointly determined by *valence* of the goal and *psychological distance* from the goal. In the language of Spence's formulation of *S-R* behavior theory, Lewin's psychological distance depends upon the degree of similarity between environmental cues where the organism is presently located and the cues to which the consummatory or goal reaction is most strongly conditioned. The generalized anticipatory goal reaction ($K$) will be weaker than the one elicited by cues that have been immediately followed by eating, and weaker still as the cues eliciting the generalized reaction become less similar to the cues present at the time of eating. The gradient of reinforcement, which for so long had been treated as a fundamental phenomenon having to do with learning (i.e., habit) by Hull and others, is now viewed by Spence as a phenomenon in the motivation of performance.

The second type of delay of reward is fundamentally different. It is brought about by introducing a delay between the last instrumental response in a sequence of activities and presentation of the goal object, or reward. The problems arising are complicated and require attention to the question of what the animal does during the imposed delay period. Further discussion of this problem would lead away from our main interest and require a more complete presentation of Spence's scheme, particularly as it applies to inhibition.

Given our partial and simplified view of Spence's theory, it is possible to see that he conceives reward training much differently than Hull and other drive-reduction theorists do. A reward, or reinforcer (empirically defined), is assumed to determine the strength of the impetus to perform a response (excitatory potential) but is not conceived as affecting the learning of an instrumental *habit*. Like Tolman and Sheffield (whose views we shall consider in a moment), Spence concludes that the process of "reinforcement" is something having to do with the contemporaneous determination of instrumental performance and not the strengthening of associative connections. The anticipatory goal reaction ($K$), based on past rewards, *is aroused at the time of instrumental performance* and adds to the non-specific excitement of drive ($D$) in the immediate determination of the impetus to respond.

## SHEFFIELD'S "DRIVE-INDUCTION" THEORY OF REWARDS

The arguments and supportive evidence advanced by Fred Sheffield and his co-workers have had a very substantial effect on this evolution towards a motivational interpretation of reward within *S-R* behavior theory. Sheffield has consistently viewed the consummatory response, the terminal *behavioral event* in a sequence of actions, as the critical factor in reinforcement. Actions followed by consummatory reactions (such as ingesting sweet-tasting saccharin, or engaging in copulatory behavior) tend to be repeated on subsequent occasions *even though there is no apparent need-reduction or drive-reduction*. Why? His answer to this question goes even further than Spence's in reducing the relative importance of drive, as conceived by Hull or Miller, in the explanation.

First, Sheffield has questioned the notion that depriving an animal of food produces a *drive* and/or a *drive-stimulus* which goads the animal into spontaneous activity. Campbell and Sheffield (1953) showed that in a highly constant environment, food privation even up to 72 hours produces only a slight increase in "spontaneous" activity compared to the increase which occurs during 10-minute periods in which visual and auditory stimuli in the environment are altered. The change in level of activity *provoked by changes in environmental stimuli* are much more related to hours of food deprivation than are any so-called "spontaneous" activities. From this and other observations, Sheffield and Campbell (1954) propose that "hunger does not function as a stimulus to activity but instead is a state in which thresholds of normal activity responses to internal and particularly to external stimuli are lowered" (p. 97). These investigators found, further-more, that a five-minute daily change in external stimulation, imposed on an otherwise constant visual and auditory environment, produces a substantial rise in activity of animals when the stimulus change immediately precedes feeding. When the stimulus change is not immediately associated with eating, the amount of activity provoked by it decreases over a 12-day period. They view food as the uncondi-tioned stimulus for the consummatory response of eating and attribute the rise in restless activity, when stimulus change precedes feeding, to the conditioning of the consummatory response to external environ-mental cues. When the consummatory response is stimulated but prevented from occurring because food is not present (the rats obviously cannot consume the conditioned stimulus), "the excitement of delayed consummation is not manifested only in the vigor of restless movements, but rather in the vigor of any movements" (pp. 99–100) an animal makes. (Sheffield and Campbell suggest that the term "frustration" properly describes the state of affairs that exists when a consummatory response has been stimulated but prevented from occurring.)

The motivational significance of the "excitement" generated by conditioned arousal of a consumma-tory reaction is developed further by Sheffield *et al.* in a discussion of the results of another experiment which showed the striking relationship between strength of consummatory reaction and speed of instrumental approach to the goal box. (See Figure 7.9.) We can see, in their interpretation of what happens in the selective learning problem which Thorndike began to study in 1898, how markedly the views of some *S-R* theorists now converge on a conceptual scheme which emphasizes the motiva-tional significance of anticipated goals:

". . . in the case of instrumental learning with positive rewards the reward stimulus is at the out-set of training an "unconditioned" stimulus for the consummatory response in the sense that it will regularly elicit the response when presented. It would be expected that this terminal consum-matory response would become conditioned to immediate neutral cues, especially those which just precede the onset of the reward stimulus. On suc-cessive experiences after the first these cues will arouse the consummatory response *ahead* of the reward. Moreover, this arousal of the incomplete consummatory response will work its way from the goal backward over the instrumental sequence since *only the cues in this sequence invariably pre-cede reward. Thus performing the correct responses —and only the correct ones—becomes a cue-pro-*

*ducing situation that arouses the incomplete con-summatory response* [italics added].

"This inference can be made the basis for an explanatory mechanism if one assumes (a) that incomplete arousal of the consummatory response produces excitement if the animal is in the appro-priate drive state and (b) such excitement is channeled into whatever response is being per-formed at the moment. The first of these assump-tions is easy to accept—thus animals on a hunger regime, for example, are practically beside them-selves with excitement when exposed to the cues that just precede the arrival of their daily ration in their living cages. If the second assumption cor-responds with facts, correct responses would be-come prepotent over others because they alone would be performed with the added boost of excitement from anticipatory arousal of the con-summatory response. *And with several incipient response tendencies at a behavioral choice point, the one that arouses the consummatory response would be the most likely to carry through to com-pletion* [italics added]. With training the correct sequence gets the advantage of more rehearsal and more vigorous performance than incorrect se-quences.

"This alternative to the 'drive reduction' mech-anism might be called the 'drive induction' theory of rewards since it depends on arousal rather than reduction of excitement and treats rewards as in-centives rather than satisfiers. It also should be noted that the proposed mechanism requires only a contiguity principle of association" (Sheffield, Roby, and Campbell, 1954, pp. 353–354).

There appears to be no fundamental disagreement between Sheffield *et al.* and Spence in the treatment of incentive motivation, but there is an apparent difference in emphasis. Spence has emphasized that the arousal of the anticipatory goal reaction ($K$) by environmental stimuli ($S_e$) depends upon the degree to which they are similar to the stimuli of the goal box in which the consummatory reaction occurs. This highlights the non-directive exciting effect of anticipatory goal reactions and suggests that a rat's instrumental pursuit of a goal box containing only food could be strengthened merely by introducing some cues in the starting box that resemble, in some way, the stimuli closely associated with other con-summatory reactions, such as drinking or sexual activity. Mild arousal of these "irrelevant" anticipa-tory goal reactions should heighten the $K$ factor, which, together with *drive*, has a non-specific exciting effect on whatever instrumental locomotor habits are dominant in the immediate stimulus situation, the starting box. Since the animal would already have the habit of running out of the starting box to the goal box, the performance of this response should be enhanced.

Sheffield *et al.*, on the other hand, emphasize what the Spence formulation tends to minimize: the fact that every instrumental locomotor response produces both its own proprioceptive stimulus ($s_p$) and an immediate change in the external stimulus ($S_E$) and that the response-produced cues of the "correct" response will invariably be followed by the consummatory reaction, but response-produced cues of "incorrect" responses will not. Thus, Sheffield and his co-workers state, as quoted in the paragraph already cited: ". . . *with several incipient response tendencies at a behavioral choice point, the one that arouses the consummatory response would be the most likely to carry through to completion*" (italics added). This conception, which corresponds to one also advanced by McClelland *et al.* (1953, pp. 89–96), but phrased in terms of "positive affective arousal" rather than consummatory response, directs attention to the associative link between an act and its consequence, which Tolman called *expectancy of the goal*.

Stimulus-response theorists, from the time of James, have always assumed that muscular responses produce immediate proprioceptive stimuli. So any response an organism makes *always* indicates the presence of a response-produced stimulus with all the rights, privileges, and functional attributes normally accorded to a stimulus in the *S-R* scheme of thought. The associative link between response and its consequence ($R \rightarrow G$), which Tolman called *strength of expectancy*, is to be conceived as the conditioned arousal of the consummatory response (or anticipatory goal response ($K$)) by the response-produced cues. This is the associative link between immediate next step and valent goal in the Lewinian conception of the goal-directed path.

The Sheffield statement of how incentive motivation normally works suggests the polarizing effect on instrumental performance of the anticipated goal which Lewin captured in his conception of the field of forces generated by a positive valence. (See p. 80.) Given the *S-R* view, this would normally come about as a result of prior experience under natural conditions because instrumental responses which lead on most quickly to the consummatory reaction produce cues which are more strongly conditioned to the consummatory reaction than cues produced by responses which are not soon followed by the consummatory reaction.

The Spence emphasis, on the other hand, reminds us that there is nothing inherently directional about the motivational factor ($K$). The non-specific exciting function attributed to anticipatory goal reactions implies that under certain conditions the vigor of an apparent pursuit of a goal (as it might be described by an observer) might have relatively little to do with the "attractiveness" of the consequence of the instrumental actions. That is, the rat who has been trained to run in a maze to a small food reward should suddenly run considerably faster if other "irrelevant" anticipatory consummatory reactions can be made to occur by exposing the rat to appropriate conditioned stimuli but without, at the same time, evoking competing instrumental habits. This idea is not contained in the Lewinian conception of the determinants of force nor in Tolman's conception which attributes performance to expectancy that an act will lead on to a goal and demand for that goal. It is more suggestive of the kind of phenomena that interested Freud.

## IS A SEPARATE DRIVE CONSTRUCT STILL NEEDED IN *S-R* BEHAVIOR THEORY?

As implications of the guiding ideas advanced by Hull in the 1930's are being explored in the experimental analysis of animal motivation, the need for the concept of energizing drive, as specified by Hull in the 1943 *Principles*, is increasingly questioned. Postman (1953) was among the first to call attention to problems arising out of the operational confounding of *drive* and *drive stimulus* ($S_D$). That is, whenever food deprivation is employed to manipulate the strength of drive there is, simultaneously, a variation in the quality or intensity of the drive stimulus ($S_D$) associated with that condition of drive. And, as Miller has pointed out, defining drive as a stimulus (viz., the drive-stimulus) means that so-called general activating effects are to be expected as a special case of stimulus generalization. Estes (1958) has recently advanced a theoretical conception of most of the behavioral phenomena which seem to have demanded a concept of general activating drive employing only the concept of a drive-stimulus and principles of associative learning.

The recent development of the concept of incentive motivation further complicates the problem. We find that the vigor of the anticipatory goal reaction ($K$) is now also treated as a source of general excitement in the theoretical account of the contemporaneous determinants of a response. Bolles

(1958) has summarized the problem succinctly in a review of evidence pertinent to the functional properties of *drive:*

"The most crucial question here for the drive theorist is whether there is any possible way to distinguish between the energizing function of drives and a) the response-eliciting power of the stimuli that must be assumed to accompany drives and b) the energizing function of $r_G$" (Bolles, 1958, p. 23).

We may concretize the problem by considering the difficulties which arise whenever evidence is presented to show that some "irrelevant" drive has enhanced the performance of a response. (See p. 180.) Let us assume that a rat has been trained under hunger to run down an alley for food. The rat is now sated for food but made thirsty, and this rat runs down the alley faster than one which is also sated for water. The simplest explanation of this event is that the *drive* produced by thirst excites the dominant habit of running learned when the animal was hungry. But to be content with this explanation:

a. We must assume that the drive stimulus of thirst $(S_T)$ bears *zero* degree of similarity to the drive stimulus of hunger $(S_H)$, otherwise by the principle of stimulus generalization we expect $S_T$ to excite the habit of running learned when $S_H$ was present;

b. Even if we make assumption (a), we must further assume that the animal has never learned to run in a similar situation when thirsty—that is, that there is no similarity in past training connected with $S_H$ and $S_T$; otherwise the animal would manifest this training under $S_T$;

c. That there is no anticipatory drinking response $(r_g)$ elicited by $S_T$, otherwise the incentive motivation factor $(K)$ is present to do the normal work of $D$ anyway.

Sheffield *et al.* have proposed that conditioned arousal of the consummatory reaction, which is equivalent to the anticipatory goal reaction $(K)$ in the Spence formulation, performs the exciting function attributed to $D$ in Hull's 1943 theory and that the effect of deprivation is to lower response thresholds but not to activate.

Birch, Burnstein, and Clark (1958) have proposed another simplification of the theory. They suggest that the anticipatory goal reaction $(r_g)$ conditioned to the drive stimulus $(S_D)$ earlier in the life of an organism might be considered the physical mechanism of $D$. That is, they suggest that all the functional properties of drive $(D)$ be maintained in the theory but that $r_g$ be considered the underlying mechanism.

According to their argument, the $S_D$ produced by a given condition of need is assumed to vary discriminably along at least one dimension as a function of the time of deprivation. The $S_D$ can become associated with partial anticipatory goal reactions, $r_g$s, because $S_D$ is present whenever the animal eats. Thus, whenever an $S_D$ occurs (as when the animal is deprived of food for a time) it will elicit $r_g$ (incentive motivation), its strength depending upon how similar that $S_D$ is to the $S_D$ present when the animal habitually eats.

Birch *et al.* designed an interesting experiment to demonstrate the possibility. Their experiment calls attention to the fact that most researchers forget they are dealing with adult animals who have already learned a great deal during the first three months of their lives before the experiment ever begins. We paraphrase their argument:

Under a strictly controlled food-maintenance schedule in which eating occurs for a specified period of time every $t$ hours from early in life, the $S_D$ corresponding to $t$ hours may be expected to come to elicit $r_g$ related to eating. As a result of stimulus generalization, $S_D$s corresponding to other hours of deprivation will also come to elicit $r_g$ related to eating. But when $S_D$s corresponding to hours' deprivation *less* than $t$ elicit $r_g$, it is not followed by eating and so (following Pavlov) it tends to extinguish. The tendency *not* to produce $r_g$ in response to $S_D$s corresponding to hours of deprivation less than $t$ (where feeding normally occurs) will also tend to generalize.

The result of these two overlapping gradients of stimulus generalization (shown schematically in Figure 7.10) should be a gradient of the magnitude and/or probability of occurrence of $r_g$ over the range of the $S_D$ dimension. This gradient should rise to a maximum at or beyond the time of deprivation employed in the maintenance schedule and then fall with continued deprivation (based on Birch, Burnstein, and Clark, 1958, p. 350).

These writers employ the logic advanced by Spence (1937) to account for the phenomena of transposition in discrimination and by Logan (1954) in still another context. It is not essential to understand this logic fully to appreciate the point Birch and his colleagues seek to make. They seek to show how the curve of activity normally plotted in relation to time of deprivation to demonstrate the need for positing a separate drive construct can now be derived if one assumes a drive stimulus $S_D$ and acknowledges that the presence of this stimulus should imply a conditioned fractional anticipatory

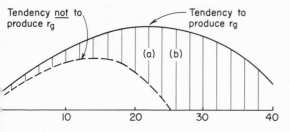

Hours Food Deprivation (the continuum of $S_D$)

FIGURE 7.10 Theoretical conception of the effect of a controlled food-maintenance schedule on the strength of anticipatory goal reaction ($r_g$) elicited by the drive stimulus ($S_D$) at a particular number of hours of food privation. It is assumed that animals have been fed every 22 hours from early in life and that $S_D$s produced by 0 to 40 hours' food deprivation constitute a stimulus continuum that varies in at least one dimension of similarity. Hence training to produce $r_g$ at 22 hours will generalize to other hours' food privation, but so also will the tendency not to perform $r_g$ which develops because $r_g$s produced at less than 22 hours are not followed by eating. The result of these hypothetical overlapping gradients of stimulus generalization is maximum strength of $r_g$ at point *b*, beyond the time of deprivation employed in the maintenance schedule, point *a*. (*Based on Birch, Burnstein, and Clark, 1958*)

goal reaction, at least after the initial eating experiences of early life.

Birch *et al.* took rat puppies from the mother three weeks after birth. After another week during which they had continuous access to food and milk, the animals were put on a maintenance schedule in which water was constantly present but food was available only for a three-hour period each day. That is, they were systematically fed after 22 hours' deprivation for the next 35 days.

After this substantial training in eating under 22 hours' deprivation, several tests were made. In one, the animals were divided into four different groups, and speed of running from start box to goal box in a three-foot alley was observed as a function of hours since last feeding at the time of the test. Two small food pellets were contained in the goal box and eaten by the animals on each trial. The time between trials was approximately 20 minutes for each animal. The results are shown in Figure 7.11.

On trial 1, their first experience in the box and before they had been rewarded for running, there is no significant difference between the four deprivation groups in speed even though there is some

indication of greater speed following 37 hours' deprivation. However, on trials 2, 3, and 4, speed reaches a maximum at 25 hours' deprivation and the differences between groups are significant.

Two things are striking about the results. First, there is little evidence of selective performance of the running response until the animal has had one trial followed by reward. Then, with habit presumably constant for all groups, the speed of performance on subsequent trials (taken as an index of magnitude of $r_g$ elicited by the $S_D$ corresponding to a particular time of deprivation) shows the trend expected, given the writers' assumption that habitual eating at 22 hours' deprivation would provide a foundation for generalized $r_g$ at other hours' deprivation. If the argument advanced by Birch *et al.* is correct, the shapes of activity and performance curves plotted in relation to time of deprivation since Richter's earliest experiments must depend heavily on the long-ignored life history of the animal from the time of birth. They propose that the sequence, time of deprivation $\rightarrow S_D \rightarrow r_g \rightarrow D$, com-

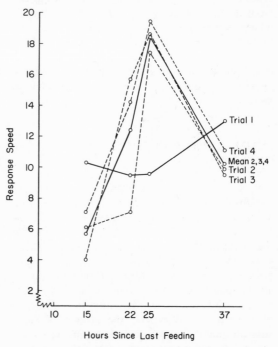

FIGURE 7.11 Response speed in enclosed runway as a function of hours since last feeding. After being fed at 22 hours' deprivation for 35 days, animals were tested in a runway with food reward at 15, 22, 25, and 37 hours' deprivation. (*From Birch, Burnstein, and Clark, 1958, p. 352*)

pletes a specification of $D$ as a function of time of deprivation. They would retain the term, *drive*, but use it in reference to the functional significance of anticipatory goal reactions.

The current questioning of the need for the separate drive concept, as Hull originally conceived it, is based mainly on a desire for parsimony. The *S-R* conceptual scheme contains a number of different interrelated variables all of which can produce general performance-enhancing effects. It is posited that drive $(D)$ and $r_g(K)$ are non-specific exciters. But, according to the principle of stimulus generalization (which no one suggests should be discarded), both $S_D$ and the usually ignored $s_g$ produced by $r_g$ are also capable of eliciting responses that were never immediately associated with them in training. The issues are perplexing and will require substantial future experimental and conceptual analysis.

Some writers, such as Hebb (1955), are encouraged to believe that recent discovery of the non-specific arousal function of the ascending reticular system of the brain by Moruzzi and Magoun (1949) provides anatomical support for a general drive concept. But given the plethora of possibilities for non-specific influences within *S-R* behavior theory, it is difficult to see how evidence of the spread of excitation from the reticular formation helps one to decide definitively between the several conceptual possibilities. Experimental analysis of behavior is more likely to do that.

## SUMMARY: THE CURRENT TREND OF *S-R* THEORY

It is obvious that experimental and conceptual analysis of the immediate determinants of performance, the problem of motivation, has taken the center of the stage. Hull's early (1930's) view that the problem of motivation ("striving for goals") could be explained in terms of principles which apply to the problem of learning ("strengthening of connections") has turned out to be only partly correct. He had in mind the notion that principles of learning would explain the growth of habit strength and this plus a knowledge of the stimuli present at a given time would explain the purposive pursuit of goals which characterizes molar behavior. But he soon discovered, as have others following in his footsteps, that *another kind of principle is required to explain the purposive pursuit of goals*. This must be a principle which explains how the various effects of prior learning experience and other contemporaneous influences on the organism are to be represented and combined in an equation which will account for the strength of the tendency to act in a certain way. The empirical problem of motivation ("striving for goals") presents its own conceptual problem, the one which Lewin emphasized in the principle of contemporaneity and in his attempt to conceptualize the life space, that is, all of the interrelated factors which influence the behavior of the individual at a moment in time.

Hull recognized the need of a principle of motivation when he advanced his formal, intervening-variable type of theory in 1943. He then advanced two principles which have since guided much research: a) his major principle of learning, the principle of primary reinforcement; b) his principle of motivation of performance, $sE_R = f(D) \times f(sH_R)$.

For a time, the main interest in research was the need-reduction, or drive-reduction, theory of reinforcement. And, as we have seen, the upshot of 20 years of research is the general view that something better is needed to embrace all of the different kinds of behavioral events that function empirically to reinforce actions. Currently, there is great interest in the neurophysiology of motivation and reward, which we have no more than touched upon in this introduction because sensible treatment of current research requires substantial background in physiology (see Hebb, 1949, 1955, 1958; Harlow and Woolsey, 1958; Miller, 1957; Olds, 1958; Pribram, 1960).

More recently, *S-R* theorists have tended to define a reinforcer or reward empirically or to focus attention upon the consummatory reaction as the critical factor in developing a theory of behavior. This position has been taken by those theorists who are more concerned with elaborating and refining Hull's second principle, the principle of motivation of performance. In the work of Spence and Sheffield we see the increasing importance attached to anticipatory goal reactions as a source of general excitement which, together with habit, motivates performance. This interest in incentive motivation $(K)$, the anticipation of reward, as a determinant of appetitional or approach behavior, parallels the earlier innovation by Mowrer and Miller in treating fear, the conditioned anticipatory reaction to a noxious stimulus, as a potent determinant of instrumental avoidance behavior. Thus the anticipation of both reward and punishment, which Lewin had captured in the concepts of positive and negative valence, are now embraced in the *S-R* conceptual scheme, and the convergence of fundamental ideas about motivation becomes increasingly apparent.

Another important consequence of the latest revision of the principle of motivation of performance by Spence, who asserts that $E = (D + K) \times H$, is the conclusion shared by Spence, Sheffield, and others that the Empirical Law of Effect is a principle of performance and not of learning. This is most clearly apparent in Sheffield's statement of the "drive induction" theory of reinforcement which asserts that so-called rewards or reinforcers exert their influence by providing incentives (anticipatory excitement) for subsequent performance rather than by "satisfying" a need or drive and cementing the bond between *S* and *R* in the instrumental habit. In this conception, we find essential agreement with the stand taken by Tolman in reference to the early studies of latent learning and other long-time critics of the drive-reduction scheme, such as McClelland (1951; 1953) and Young (1949; 1961).

As reliance upon drive and drive-reduction for an exhaustive framework in analysis of the problem of motivation diminishes, current attention is drawn to the question of whether or not the concept of deprivation-produced activating drive, which emerged from the activity-wheel studies of the 1920's, is needed at all. The number of different ways in which general performance-enhancing effects may be generated by the several variables which are linked to biological deficits suggests that *S-R* theory will soon evolve towards a more parsimonious account of the motivation of performance. Brown (1960) has considered experimental evidence related to this general problem in some detail.

As we now separate the problem of motivation and the principle of motivation from the problem of learning and the principle of learning, it is possible to argue that the problem of motivation has a kind of logical priority, at least when relatively mature adult organisms are employed in studies which seek to discover the laws of learning. Why is this so? If one considers a learning curve, plotted over trials, what does it represent? It represents some particular measure of the animal's *performance* plotted over trials and showing the change which has occurred as a function of practice under certain experimental arrangements. But performance on each trial is jointly determined by a number of interrelated factors, one or more of which has changed quantitatively during the sequence of trials. How can there be a systematic assessment of the influences responsible for the change we call learning until there is some clarity in the conception of the various factors to be considered and how they combine to determine the tendency to act on any single performance trial? The day of the simple belief that an observed change in response to a stimulus merely reflects a change in the strength of neural connection between *S* and *R* is past.

# CHAPTER 8

# Systematic Study

# of Human

# Motivation

*"Human motivation has always been a topic of key interest to psychologists, but the lack of adequate methods for measuring it has seriously hampered the development of systematic knowledge of the subject. . . . The difficulty is two-fold. On the one hand, 'tough minded' animal psychologists complain that clinical methods of assessing human motivation are not methods of measurement at all, but at best simply codified subjective impressions of doubtful reliability. On the other hand, 'tender-minded' clinical psychologists object that however tough-minded the experimental psychologists may be, they for the most part duck the problem of measuring motivation altogether or try to handle it by unchecked (and often uncheckable) extrapolations from studies of the white rat. Evidently if we are to make much headway, we need to focus our resources and energies on the measurement problem. Here, as elsewhere in science, real theoretical advance has to wait on methodological developments"* (David McClelland, 1958a, p. 7).\*

In this chapter we return to the problem of human motivation, which was the center of interest earlier in the book. From the wealth of contemporary research on human behavior that in one way or another relates to the problem of motivation, we shall consider three current developments that are directly relevant to the historical evolution of ideas we have traced. They are: experimental interest in human decision-making, systematic investigations of the effects of individual differences in anxiety, and the study of achievement motivation. In one way or another, these three areas of research address the problem of measuring individual differences in strength of motivational dispositions within the context of systematic experimental and conceptual analysis of the determinants of human performance.

Contemporary research on human decision-making has its conceptual origins in pre-Darwinian ideas about the nature of rational man. Research on effects of individual differences in anxiety and achievement motive, on the other hand, represent—at long last—an attempt to bring about an inte-

\* From *Motives in Fantasy, Action and Society*, edited by John W. Atkinson, copyright 1958, D. Van Nostrand Company, Inc.

gration of the study of individual differences in personality and experimental analysis of motivation.

### ISOLATED DISCIPLINES WITHIN PSYCHOLOGY

One of the major implications of Darwin's theory of evolution, which profoundly influenced psychologists late in the 19th century, was the importance he attached to individual variation within a species. This guiding idea spurred Galton and others to begin to develop tests of various mental abilities. By 1906, the first test of general intelligence was published by Binet. There soon followed the revision by Terman in 1916 and the development of the Army Alpha group intelligence test during World War I. This is generally considered the greatest practical achievement of psychology.

The practical problem-solving context within which the mental-test movement was born, together with its early success in the use of tests of intelligence and special skills as a basis for selection of personnel in the schools, the Army, and industry, has produced several generations of test-making specialists with little or no interest in the basic theoretical problems which arise in active experimental analysis of behavioral phenomena. Hence the traditional study of individual differences, even when it began to turn to the matter of differences in human preferences in the late 1920's, contributes virtually nothing to the evolution of a theoretical conception of motivation.

On the other side of the wall, the process orientation of experimental psychologists working with animals and humans alike produced much greater interest in the effects of *manipulable* antecedent conditions than of individual differences in motivating dispositions. Not until the late 1940's was the problem of measuring individual differences in human motivation faced in the context of systematic experimental and conceptual analysis of the problem of motivation. Since then, the work begun by McClelland and his co-workers, in studies of achievement motivation, and by *S-R* theorists, who have examined implications of the theory of anxiety drive using tests of individual differences, has provided a model of how the study of individual differences and experimental analysis of the process of motivation may be combined. Hopefully, these contemporary programs of research will serve to point the way towards an integration of the two historically isolated preoccupations of psychologists which Cronbach (1957) has aptly referred to as "the two disciplines of scientific psychology."

### THE CONTEMPORARY PSYCHOLOGY OF MOTIVATION

In earlier chapters, we have introduced the major trends and spokesmen whose varying viewpoints contributed to the transition from common sense to a scientific orientation towards the problem of motivation during the first half of this century. As we now attempt to bring our story of the study of motivation up to date, it may be helpful to have in mind a picture of these various trends which, projected into the present, constitute the contemporary psychology of motivation. They are shown schematically in Table 8.1.

Our discussion has barely touched on the renewed interest in the neurophysiological substratum of motivation and behavior which has accompanied the development of promising new methods of study in recent years. There are several reasons for this. The fund of new factual information is expanding so rapidly in this specialized field of study that all theoretical views are tentative, and fruitful treatment of them requires a sound fundamental background in neurophysiology. What is more, it has become increasingly evident that the *aphysiological* and *ahistorical* orientation espoused earlier in the writings of Lewin and Tolman is now shared by many more *S-R* theorists who turn to mathematical constructs, rather than to detailed knowledge or suppositions about the step-by-step intervening neurophysiological process, for conceptual clarification of the problems of *molar* behavior. The two orientations, *mathematical* and *neurophysiological*, are viewed as alternative foundations for the theoretical development of psychology. At present, the mathematical orientation provides a more useful approach to systematic analysis of the problem of *human* motivation and integrative discussion of studies of molar behavior in animals and humans than does the neurophysiological orientation. The two will one day be fused, but that day still seems a long way off.

Other recent contributions of a very specialized nature—for example, the factor-analytic approach of Cattell (1957) and Eysenck (1953)—have had to be ignored both because they require specialized knowledge and because they are of questionable direct relevance to the problem of central interest.

In this introduction to motivation, we have attempted to identify the behavioral problem of motivation and the basic concepts which have emerged in experimental analysis of that problem. This introduction provides a foundation for more advanced study of recent developments in special

TABLE 8.1

Major trends which influence contemporary conceptions of motivation and the method of study

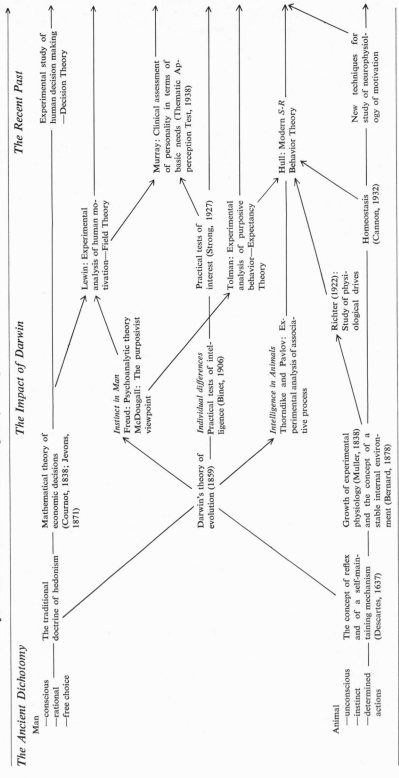

fields which in one way or another are related to that problem.

## BASIC CONCEPTS OF THE THEORY OF DECISION MAKING

Since the publication of *Theory of Games and Economic Behavior* by von Neumann and Morgenstern (1944), another conceptual scheme for analysis of the immediate determinants of action has excited the interest of mathematically oriented psychologists. It is the theory of decision making which had evolved in the field of economics. We shall consider the basic concepts of this scheme and some of the problems which have arisen in experimental analysis of human decision making in order to appreciate how this new field of interest is related to study of the traditional problem of motivation. Our intention is not to consider the complicated mathematical issues which mostly excite researchers on decision making, but to show how still another beginning, with one facet of the problem of motivation, has yielded a conceptual scheme very similar to that advanced by Tolman and Lewin in other contexts.

Current interest was spurred by the von Neumann-Morgenstern book, but the basic concepts of decision theory have a much longer history. Edwards (1954) has provided an outline of the genesis of the central ideas as they have evolved since the time of Jeremy Bentham (1748–1832). To begin with, let us have clearly in mind the problem which interests "decision theorists":

"The kind of decision making with which this body of theory deals is as follows: given two states, *A* and *B*, into either one of which an individual may put himself, the individual chooses *A* in preference to *B* (or vice versa). For instance, a child standing in front of a candy counter may be considering two states. In state *A* the child has $0.25 and no candy. In state *B* the child has $0.15 and a ten-cent candy bar. The economic theory of decision making is a theory about how to predict such decisions" (Edwards, 1954, p. 380).

This is the familiar problem of *selectivity* of response which we have already confronted in James' analysis of deliberate volition, in Thorndike's cats struggling to get out of the puzzle box, in the rats at a choice point in one of Tolman's mazes, and in human subjects trying to decide how difficult a task to undertake in the Lewinian level-of-aspiration experiment. Now we confront the same problem in the context of economic choices.

The early economic theory was really a formal statement of common-sense hedonism:

"The school of philosopher-economists, started by Jeremy Bentham and popularized by James Mill and others held that the goal of human action is to seek pleasure and avoid pain. Every object or action may be considered from the point of view of pleasure- or pain-giving properties. These properties are called the *utility* of the object, and pleasure is given by positive utility and pain by negative utility. The goal of action, then, is to seek the maximum utility. This simple hedonism of the future is easily translated into a theory of choice. People choose the alternative, from among those open to them, that leads to the greatest excess of positive over negative utility. This notion of utility maximization is the essence of the utility theory of choice. . . .

"This theory of choice was embodied in the formal economic analysis of all the early great names in economics. In the hands of Jevons, Walras, and Menger, it reached increasingly sophisticated mathematical expression and it was embodied in the thinking of Marshall, who published the first edition of his great *Principles of Economics* in 1890, and revised it at intervals for more than 30 years thereafter. . . .

"The use to which utility theory was put by these theorists was to establish the nature of the demand for various goods. On the assumption that the utility of any good is a monotonically increasing negatively accelerated function of the amount of that good, it is easy to show that the amounts of most goods which a consumer will buy are decreasing functions of price, functions which are precisely specified once the shapes of the utility curves are known" (Edwards, 1954, pp. 382–383).

Assumptions about man were made from the armchair by early economic theorists. Their theories attempted to specify how a *rational* man would, or should, act under certain conditions. Certain underlying assumptions were made about "economic man." For the theory to apply to the actual behavior of living men, man would have to be (a) completely informed, (b) infinitely sensitive, and (c) rational.

To assume that man is completely informed means to assume that he knows all the courses of action available to him in a given situation and also what the outcome of any action will be.

To assume that man is infinitely sensitive means to assume that he is capable of discriminating between alternatives on an infinitely divisible continuum of possible alternatives.

To assume that man is rational means two things. First, it means that he can always tell either that he prefers alternative $A$ to alternative $B$, or $B$ to $A$, or that he is indifferent between them, and that his preferences are transitive (i.e., if he prefers $A$ to $B$ and $B$ to $C$, then he prefers $A$ to $C$). Second, the assumption that man is rational means that he always makes choices so as to maximize something. In the early economic theory it was assumed that man always acted in such a manner as to maximize utility.

The notion of utility is obviously very similar to Lewin's concept of *valence* and to what Tolman called *demand for the goal*. Edwards (1954) has suggested that psychologists might consider experimental efforts to study and measure utility as an attempt to quantify that part of Lewin's theoretical scheme.

CURRENT THEORY: MAXIMIZATION OF
SUBJECTIVELY EXPECTED UTILITY $(SEU)$

Early economic theory dealt mainly with riskless choices, that is, preferential behavior when the outcome of action is never in doubt. A more general problem is that of decision making when there is something less than complete subjective certainty that a given outcome will come about as a consequence of action. This is the problem of risky choice, or choice under conditions of risk.

The traditional mathematical notion as to how risky decisions *should be* made is that choices should be made so as to maximize *expected value* $(EV)$. What this means can be made clear in a simple illustration. If you stand to win or lose a nickel on the toss of a coin, winning 5 cents if it is "heads" and losing 5 cents if it is "tails," the expected value $(EV)$ is 0 cents. It is assumed that the probability of the coin coming up "heads" is 0.5 and the probability of the coin coming up "tails" is 0.5:

"The expected value of a bet is found by multiplying the value of each possible outcome by its probability of occurrence and summing these products across all possible outcomes. In symbols:

$$EV = p_1\$_1 + p_2\$_2 + \ldots + p_n\$_n,$$

where $p$ stands for probability, $\$$ stands for the value of an outcome, and $p_1 + p_2 + \ldots + p_n = 1$" (Edwards, 1954, p. 391).

People obviously do not behave as this mathematical notion of expected value $(EV)$ proposes they should behave. They buy insurance even though the insurance company makes a profit; and they buy lottery tickets even though the sponsors of a lottery make a profit. In both cases, *the expected value* is negative. According to the theory of maximizing expected value, people should not be willing to buy insurance and lottery tickets, but they do.

Pondering these and related paradoxes way back in 1738, David Bernoulli proposed that the disturbing issues could be resolved if it were assumed that people act so as to maximize *expected utility* $(EU)$, rather than *expected value* $(EV)$. Utility is the *subjective* estimate of the worth of a thing. Value is the objective dollar value. The expected utility of an alternative, in symbolic form, is:

$$EU = p_1u_1 + p_2u_2 + \ldots + p_nu_n.$$

We have merely substituted the concept of utility (subjective value) for objective value.

In 1944, von Neumann and Morgenstern proposed a way to measure utility, a problem of long and great interest to economists, by utilizing the concept of *expected utility* $(EU)$. It could be done, they argued, if we add to the earlier assumptions about "economic man" that he is capable of arranging his preferences among alternatives in terms of their expected utilities:

"Thus, suppose that an economic man is indifferent between the certainty of $7.00 and a 50-50 chance of gaining $10.00 or nothing. We can assume that his indifference between these two prospects means that they have the same utility for him. We may define the utility of $0.00 as zero utiles (the usual name for the unit of utility . . .), and the utility of $10.00 as 10 utiles. . . . Then we may calculate the utility of $7.00 by using the concept of expected utility as follows:

$$U(\$7.00) = .5U(\$10.00) + .5U(\$0.00)$$
$$= .5(10) + .5(0) = 5"$$

(Edwards, 1954, p. 392).

Thus, in this example, we find that the utility (i.e., subjective value) of $7.00 is 5 utiles. By varying probabilities and using already found utilities, it should then be possible to discover the utility of any other amount of money for an individual. We might find, for example, that $10.00 is really not twice as attractive to an individual as $5.00.

If this kind of model is applied to actual choices, what can go wrong with it? Here is Edwards' answer:

"It might be that the probabilities by which the utilities are multiplied should not be the objective probabilities; in other words, a decider's estimate of the subjective importance of a probability may not be the same as the numerical value of that probability. It might be that the method of combination of probabilities and values should not be simple multiplication. It might be that the method of combination of the probability-value products should not be simple addition. It might be that the process of gambling has some positive or negative utility of its own. It might be that the whole approach is wrong, that people just do not behave as if they were trying to maximize expected utility." (Edwards, 1954, p. 393).

In other words, the same things can be wrong about the theory of decision making that can be wrong about any other theoretical conception of the determinants of action in terms of hypothetical variables which intervene between observable stimulus situation and observable action.

A burst of experimental interest in the concept of *expected utility* has revealed two problems connected with it (Edwards, 1962). First, people seem to make decisions in risky situations in terms of probabilities as they perceive them (i.e., in terms of *subjective* probabilities) rather than in terms of objective or stated probabilities. Second, it is difficult to apply the expected utility theory when objective probabilities are not meaningfully defined in a situation. So a new theory has been proposed. It asserts:

". . . that people choose among risky courses of action in such a way as to maximize what has come to be called *subjectively expected utility*. The subjectively expected utility of a course of action is defined as follows:

$$SEU = \psi_1 U_1 + \psi_2 U_2 + \ldots + \psi_n U_n,$$

where there are $n$ possible outcomes of the course of action, the first outcome has utility $U_1$, and

subjective probability $\psi_1$, and so on" (Edwards, 1962, p. 42).

*Illustrative example.* The following is typical of the kind of choice situation that is studied. The subject might be asked to imagine that he is participating in a dice game and stands to win or lose certain amounts of money on the throw of a single die. Since a die has six sides, he might have 1, 2, 3, 4, 5, or 6 out of 6 chances of winning depending upon what number(s) he rolls. He is then asked to make a choice between pairs of options. For example:

Option $A$:  1/6 chance to win $1.80
Option $B$:  5/6 chance to win $ .36

In this case, the expected value ($EV$) of each option is $.30. The act of choosing "Option $A$" or "Option $B$" is the behavior to be explained.

According to the theory, the strength of a tendency to point a finger at (i.e., to choose) "Option $A$" is determined by a multiplicative combination of a variable defined by the visual stimulus "1/6 chance to win" and another variable defined by the visual stimulus "$1.80." The strength of a tendency to point a finger at "Option $B$" is similarly determined by variables defined by the visual stimuli "5/6 chance to win" and "$.36." The two intervening variables are called *subjective probability* and *utility*, and their product is called *subjectively expected utility*. Whether the subject points at "Option $A$" or "Option $B$" depends upon the two values of *subjectively expected utility*, for the principle of action is maximization of subjectively expected utility. The general scheme is shown in Figure 8.1.

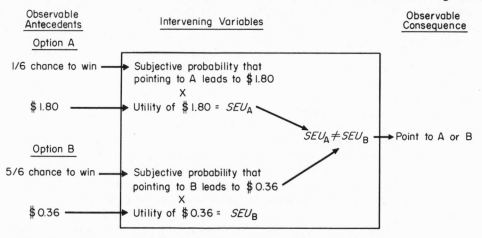

FIGURE 8.1  Subjective Probability, Utility, and Subjectively Expected Utility (SEU) conceived as intervening variables.

Decision theorists often tend to speak of choice between options, sometimes glossing over the fact that it is the performance of some particular act (in this case pointing a finger at *A* or *B*) which has subjectively expected utility for the person.

The significant questions that Edwards has raised can be concretized in terms of Figure 8.1. Is the variable which Tolman called *expectancy* and Lewin called *potency*, and which decision theorists call *subjective probability*, some simple function of the objectively stated probability of winning, or may other factors come in to influence subjective probability? Is the variable which Tolman called *demand for the goal* and Lewin called *valence*, and which decision theorists call *utility*, some simple function of the objectively stated amount of money to be won, or may other factors influence it?

Edwards has pointed out that in practice "utilities are ordinarily assumed to be functions only of the possible outcomes of the course of action, while subjective probabilities are ordinarily assumed to be functions only of the objective probabilities of those outcomes" (Edwards, 1962, p. 43).

Decision theorists acknowledge that it is difficult to see how the model can be applied without some such assumptions. That is to say, the intervening variables must be *operationally defined* if the implications of the theory are to be tested.

## TWO STUBBORN PROBLEMS

Edwards (1962) highlights two important problems which have arisen. Some writers have proposed that utility is determined by both objective probability and objective value. In this connection, we recall the assumption made by Lewin, Escalona, and Festinger in the resultant valence theory of level of aspiration (see Chapter 4) that the attractiveness of success increases the more difficult the task (i.e., the lower the probability of success). And some writers have proposed that subjective probability is also determined both by objective probability and by objective value. Irwin (1953), for example, has found that people consider an event more likely to occur when the consequences are favorable than when the consequences are unfavorable. The problem, in brief, is that of specifying ". . . some operations by which utilities and subjective probabilities can be measured independently of the decisions they are supposed to predict" (Edwards, 1962, p. 44).

The problem seems a particularly perplexing one to decision theorists because they have proceeded in their experimentation to treat utility of an outcome as if it should be influenced solely by the amounts of money to be won or lost and subjective probability as if it should be influenced solely by the stated odds. They have, in other words, proceeded as if these two aspects of the immediate stimulus situation provided an exhaustive account of what influences the human subject in these simple instances of preferential behavior. In many respects, the analysis of the behavior being studied has been as restricted as that of the early associationists who believed they would find the explanation of molar behavior in an exhaustive analysis of the details of the relationship between a stimulus and a response.

ATTRACTIVENESS OF OUTCOME INFLUENCED
BY PROBABILITY

Feather (1959) has called attention to the need for distinguishing the attractiveness (or utility) of an object and the "attractiveness of *attaining*" the object. He has urged that the *meaning* of the outcome of a decision depends upon situational factors which are normally ignored in decision research. Feather confronted Australian boys with a decision problem: which of two candies would they prefer? Five different candies were used, and pretesting showed that the attractiveness of the candies, as objects, was very similar. He sought to determine how the "attractiveness of *attaining*" a candy, as an outcome of a decision, would be influenced by the *ease* or *difficulty*, i.e., the probability, of attaining it. Subjects were shown a lottery box containing 15 red marbles and 5 blue marbles. One of the marbles could be rolled through a gate at the bottom of the box. The probability of attaining each of two candies presented to the subject for preferential choice was determined by implying that *attainment* of the candy would depend upon rolling one or another colored marble through the gate. The subjects were told, "If you decided to try for this one, you would get it only if you rolled a blue marble [or a red marble] out of the box . . ." (Feather, 1959, p. 158). Thus attainment of the candy could be seen by the subject as largely a matter of chance since there are obviously three times more red marbles than blue marbles in the box. Feather then presented the two candies and asked: "Now if you were to get one of these, which one would you feel most pleased about getting? Which one do you *wish* you could get the most?" (Feather, 1959, p. 158). The question, Feather points out, does not involve any commitment to act. The subject is not asked which one he will *try to get*, but merely which one he would "*feel most pleased about getting.*"

One group of boys was asked this question after the situation had been deliberately structured as a *test*. Another group of boys was asked this question after the situation had been structured as merely a *game*. Guided by the Lewinian assumption that feelings of success, on a test of skill, is greater the more difficult the task, Feather argued:

"It is assumed that the attainment attractiveness of a goal object may be related not only to its attractiveness *qua* object but also to the value which *S* places on its *achievement;* his wishes reflect both the attractiveness of the object for him and the extent to which he values achieving it" (Feather, 1959, p. 155).

The results shown in Table 8.2 strongly suggest that the attractiveness (utility) of the outcome, *attaining a candy*, is greater when that outcome

TABLE 8.2

Attractiveness of attaining a particular candy (*C*) in a lottery game, depending upon the difficulty of attaining it and whether or not the outcome was likely to be viewed as determined by chance or skill (Based on Feather, 1959, p. 159)

| | | % of choices in which candy *C* was selected as the one the subject "would feel most pleased about getting"* | |
| | *N* | Candy *C* difficult to attain ($P = .25$) | Candy *C* easy to attain ($P = .75$) |
|---|---|---|---|
| Task presented as a *game* | 24 | 56% | 52% |
| Task presented as a *test* | 24 | 65% | 19% |

* In each paired comparison, one of four other candies was presented as either easy or difficult to attain. Each percentage is based on 48 choices.

means, in addition to having a candy in hand, having a feeling of pride in one's accomplishment. When the task was structured in a relaxed way, as merely a game, the boys indicated that they would be equally pleased to get the candy that was highly probable or the one that was less probable. However, when they viewed the situation as a test, they more frequently indicated they would feel more pleased about getting the candy for which probability of success was low.

The utility of the outcome is, under one set of conditions, largely a function of the utility of the object. Under other conditions, there is added to the utility of the object the utility of achieving it, that is, the pride of accomplishment which is greater the more difficult the test of skill. The utility of the outcome is related to the probability of the outcome in a particular way in this instance because demonstrable skill on a *test* produces "the feeling of being pleased" in its own right, irrespective of any concrete object that is attained.

SUBJECTIVE PROBABILITY INFLUENCED
BY NATURE OF OUTCOME

Irwin (1953) and others (Crandall, Solomon, and Kellaway, 1955; Edwards, 1962; Marks, 1951) have shown that *positive outcomes seem more likely than negative outcomes*. Irwin (1953) asked college students to draw a card from a pack of ten cards containing 1, 3, 5, 7, or 9 marked cards. The subject was told in advance that there were 10 cards in the pack and also the number of cards in the pack that were marked. Before drawing a card, the subject was asked to state whether or not he expected to draw a marked card. Prior to half of the drawings, the subject was instructed that he would gain a point if he drew a marked card. This defined the outcome as positive or desirable. Prior to the other half of his drawings, the subject was told he would lose a point if he drew a marked card. This defined the outcome as negative or undesirable. Subjects in a "neutral" control group stated their expectation and drew a card with no prior information that they would gain or lose a point if the card they drew was marked.

Figure 8.2 shows the frequency of "yes" responses to the question: "Do you think you will draw a marked card?" This measure of subjective probability of the outcome is clearly influenced by both the stated or objective probability of drawing a marked card and the desirability of the outcome.

Since all subjects were tested twice with desirable outcomes and twice with undesirable outcomes at each level of objective probability, Irwin could show the over-all effect of desirability of outcome by comparing the average number of "yes" responses per subject when the outcome was desirable (6.1) with the average when the outcome was undesirable (4.8). The difference, while less pronounced than a similar effect obtained by Marks (1951) with 9- to 12-year-old children, is nevertheless statistically significant and of considerable theoretical import. For it means that verbally reported subjective prob-

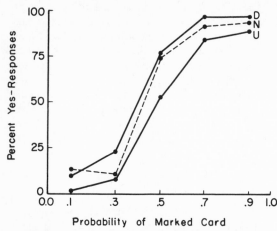

FIGURE 8.2   Per cent of "Yes" responses as function of probability of marked card. The curves for the Desirable, Neutral, and Undesirable conditions are labeled D, N, and U, respectively. (From Irwin, 1953, p. 331)

abilities (or expectancies), at least, are influenced by whether the utility of the outcome is positive or negative.

## PROBABILITY PREFERENCES AND VARIANCE PREFERENCES

In typical studies of gambling preferences, the subject is confronted with two options that have equal *expected value*. That is, the summation of stated probability times stated monetary value of all possible outcomes for one option (*EV*) equals that of the other option. The expected value of the two options may be positive (e.g., win 30 cents), negative (e.g., lose 30 cents), or zero.

Among the more interesting empirical results of such studies are those which are described as "probability preferences," first reported by Edwards (1953). Subjects were given choices between pairs of options having equal *expected values* but different probabilities of winning. Figure 8.3 shows that when the bets had *positive* expected value, there was an obvious peak of preference at the 50-50 bet where probability of winning is 4/8. Figure 8.4 shows that when the expected value of the bets was *negative*, the subjects clearly preferred a small probability of losing a large amount to higher probabilities of losing smaller amounts.

Other studies (e.g., Coombs and Pruitt, 1960) have shown that subjects also display what are called "variance preferences" when both the probability

of winning and the expected value are held constant in the two options. For example, consider the case of an individual confronted with choice between these two alternatives:

Option *A*:  1/6 chance to win $1.80
         and 5/6 chance to lose $0.36 (*EV* = 0)
Option *B*:  1/6 chance to win $3.60
         and 5/6 chance to lose $0.72 (*EV* = 0).

The expected value (*EV*) is zero for both options and the probability of winning is 1/6 for both options. The statistical quantity, *variance*, of a two-outcome bet is equal to $p(1-p)(A-B)^2$ where $p$ is the probability of winning amount $A$ and $1-p$ is the probability of winning amount $B$. In the example, the variance of Option $B$ is greater than the variance of Option $A$.

The intricacies of studies of "probability preferences" and "variance preferences" require more background than can be provided in an introduction to the topic. The interested reader can consult a recent review of behavioral decision theory and related empirical research by Edwards (1960) for further background.

RELEVANCE TO THE STUDY OF MOTIVATION

Active interest in the theory of decision making represents a revival of a conceptual scheme which

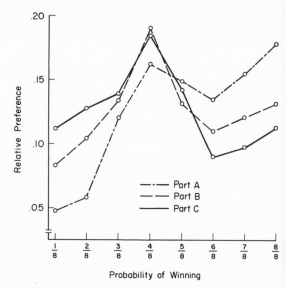

FIGURE 8.3   Preference as a function of probability for positive expected value bets (*From Edwards, "Probability-preferences in gambling,"* The American Journal of Psychology, *Vol. 66, 1953, p. 355*)

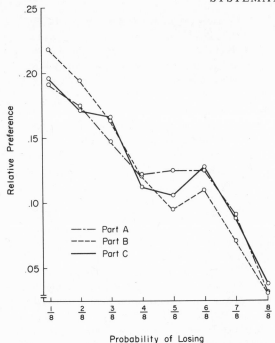

FIGURE 8.4   Preference as a function of probability for negative expected value bets (*From Edwards, "Probability-preferences in gambling," The American Journal of Psychology, Vol. 66, 1953, p. 355*)

had its origins in the pre-Darwinian conception of "rational man." Contemporary experimental research pertinent to this theory began with analysis of simple economic decisions of the sort it was first invented to explain. The similarity of basic concepts of decision theory and central concepts in the theories of Tolman and Lewin is now beginning to be generally recognized. Hence it is possible to view conscious, deliberate decision making as one aspect of the broad problem of motivation. It is to be hoped that recognition of this fact will enable workers in the field of human decision making to enlarge their conception of the variety of different kinds of influences and conditions that must be represented in the subjective probabilities and utilities of even the simplest instances of human choice. Perhaps, if the concept of utility is freed from its historical association with money and commodities in economics and an effort is made to embrace the "pleasure-giving" and "pain-giving" properties of other significant events like sexual activity, eating, pride of accomplishment, and rejection from the group, the more thorough-going conceptual analysis of motivation in terms of *valence*, provided by Lewin,

will provide the guide to a theory that combines mathematical elegance with empirical generality and fertility.

Contemporary decision theory represents a formal statement of the kind of theory of motivation of performance that Tolman and Lewin had proposed, using different terms to designate, on the one hand, the strength of expectancy that an act will lead on to some consequence and, on the other, the subjective value of the consequence. There is an essential difference between these "Expectancy × Value" theories of how the impetus to act is determined and the "Drive × Habit" conception of *S-R* behavior theory even though it is now fully appreciated that anticipatory goal reaction ($r_g$) and anticipatory emotional reaction ($r_e$), which roughly correspond to expectancy of a goal and expectancy of some noxious event, are immediate determinants of instrumental actions. We shall devote considerable attention to this question in the final chapter. But a preliminary discussion is useful now, as an introduction to contemporary research employing tests of individual differences in anxiety and tests of the strength of achievement motive. Why? Because these two programs of research have proceeded to study essentially the same behavioral problem, but one of them (the research on anxiety) has been guided by and interpreted in terms of the "Drive × Habit" theory, while empirical studies of achievement motivation have produced a theoretical conception of the "Expectancy × Value" type. The basic conceptual problems that were once debated solely or primarily in terms of studies of animal behavior are therefore becoming lively issues in the systematic experimental analysis of human motivation.

We can gain some appreciation of a fundamental difference between the two theories by constructing a decision problem for rats in a T maze and considering how the concepts of decision theory and contemporary behavior theory would apply. Suppose a hungry rat has gotten a large food reward and a small shock in a goal box after turning *left*, but a small food reward and no shock in a goal box after turning *right*. How are these *past* experiences represented as determinants of today's decision at the choice point of the T maze?

Decision theory, as an example of the type of theory which emphasizes the attractiveness and repulsiveness of expected consequences of actions, would represent the *magnitude* of food reward as an outcome having positive value (or utility) and the *magnitude* of the shock as an outcome having negative value (or disutility). The left-turning tendency would be influenced by the large positive utility of the large reward and the small negative utility of the mild shock. The right-turning tendency would be influenced by the small positive utility of the small reward. In other words, so-called "rewarding" and "punishing" events are conceived as having a *selective* or directive influence on performance according to an "Expectancy × Value" theory. *The value of an anticipated reward influences only the impetus to perform the act which is expected to lead to it. The value of an anticipated punishment influences only the impetus to perform the act which is expected to lead to it. The value of anticipated reward functions to enhance or strengthen the impulse to act; the value of anticipated punishment functions to weaken or reduce the impulse to act.* That is what "Expectancy × Value" theories of the type advanced by Tolman, Lewin, and decision theorists say.

In contrast, consider how the *magnitude* of anticipatory goal reaction ($r_g$) and *magnitude* of anticipatory emotional reaction ($r_e$) are supposed to influence performance at the choice point when both are conceived as sources of non-specific excitement (equivalent to drive) in the general equation $E = (D + K) \times H$. Clearly, both the magnitude of anticipatory goal reaction (which would correspond to what decision theorists mean to represent by positive utility) and the magnitude of anticipatory fear (which would correspond to what decision theorists mean to represent by negative utility) are assumed to have a similar *non-specific* or *non-directive exciting effect* on all habits elicited by the total complex of stimuli at the choice point.

The *S-R* behavior theory has other concepts which must be introduced as important determinants of what happens at the choice point—particularly the internal stimuli associated with hunger, anticipatory goal reaction, and anticipatory emotional reaction. Presently, we are not interested in developing fully the picture each theory gives us of what is happening, but in seeing how the magnitude *qua* magnitude of an anticipated goal or threat is represented in the two kinds of theory. One, the "Expectancy-Value" type of theory, whether phrased in terms of demand for the goal, valence of the goal, or utility of the consequence, has the magnitude of the anticipated event function *selectively* on actions which are expected to lead to it. The other, the "Drive × Habit" theory, views the magnitude of anticipated goals and "threats" as sources of general excitement—a nonselective influence on performance.

The "drive-induction" theory of reward proposed by Sheffield (see p. 195) may hold the clue as to how the two conceptions may be reconciled, at least in reference to the influence of anticipated rewards. We shall return to this and related issues in our discussion of the convergence of theoretical viewpoints in the final chapter. But now let us turn to research which employs tests of individual differences in the quest for a useful theory of motivation.

## STRATEGIES IN THE USE OF TESTS OF INDIVIDUAL DIFFERENCES

Before beginning the review of current research on anxiety and achievement motivation, we need to consider the various strategies or intentions that have accompanied the development and use of tests of individual differences in motivation. To appreciate why the study of individual differences and experimental analysis of motivation were so long isolated in psychology, one must grasp the fundamental difference between the *practical-problem orientation* and *basic-science orientation* which exists in all fields of scientific endeavor.

### PRACTICAL-PROBLEM ORIENTATION AND BASIC-SCIENCE ORIENTATION

The immediate intention of some research is the solution of a socially significant problem. Scientifically trained persons must often bring their specialized knowledge to the task of discovering, by trial and error, the solution of a practical problem. The improvement of automobile tires is an example that Conant (1951) has cited in his attempt to clarify the distinction between *technology* and *basic science* in the physical sciences. There is no basic theory which tells how to make a better tire. The practical problem will not wait for the development of the science. It must be solved today, and the measure of the success of the research effort lies in finding the solution. Naturally, when the *practical-problem orientation* prevails, the matters considered are always matters of obvious social significance. It is, in fact, the immediate social importance of a problem which defines the need for empirical, trial-and-check efforts to find the solution. As soon as one problem is solved, another arises in its place. The guiding intention of technological research on these matters is efficient solution of the immediate problem. If the science is relatively advanced, the basic theory already developed may encompass the particular problem and specify the nature of the solution without the need of a trial-and-check empirical approach to find out what works without knowing why it works. But if there is no useful theory to apply, common sense and technical wisdom directs the attack, and the problem is solved by a trial-and-check empirical approach. Solution of the practical problem is the goal of the whole endeavor.

The *basic-science orientation* is different. Here the intention is to contribute to the growth of a conceptual scheme which will account for some phenomenon more adequately than does the conventional wisdom (common sense) of the time. The conceptual analysis of a general problem leads to interest in some events that may appear very trivial when evaluated in terms of social importance. Imagine, for example, how surprised some of Galileo's contemporaries might have been to discover a grown man, reputedly a very intelligent one, rolling balls down an inclined plane. How similarly shocked are some students of psychology to find such a pervasive interest among psychologists in the behavior of a rat or in what appear to be very "trivial" instances of human behavior. What the layman misses is the fact that the intention of basic research is to contribute to the growth of a conceptual scheme and that the significance of solving some immediate empirical problem is to be evaluated *solely* in terms of the degree to which the solution does or does not contribute in some way to the enhancement of fundamental knowledge about the phenomena being studied. The immediate goal of basic research on motivation is *to find a more generally useful way of thinking about motivational problems* than the common sense which now must be applied to solve some critically important practical problems. One may solve practical problems without in any way effecting a change in the mode of thought about the problem. Within psychology, the study of individual differences has, for the most part, been dominated by a practical-problem orientation. Particularly has this been true, until very recently, in the use of the few tests of human motivation that had been developed.

THE USE OF VOCATIONAL-INTEREST TESTS

In the context of the important practical problem of vocational counseling and personnel selection, Edward Strong developed and published (in 1927) what is without question the most useful test of individual differences in motivation yet produced by psychology, the *Strong Vocational Interest Blank*. The intention in the development and use of the test is simple and straightforward: to provide some basis for knowing in advance whether young men and women will be interested and satisfied in the vocations they intend to follow. Some students choose occupations in terms of obvious characteristics of a job which may appear very attractive to them, but without knowing much about the particular kind of daily drudgery or isolation that a particular occupation may entail. A bad initial decision means subsequent unhappiness, drifting from one occupation to another, with the loss of time and money that may have been involved in special education. So Strong set out to do something about this problem, and he was eminently successful.

The test of interests he developed proceeds from a common-sense conception of motivation to ask the person to indicate whether he "likes," "dislikes," or is "indifferent" to several hundred different activities like "being an aviator" or "planning a sales campaign." This type of test which asks questions calling for self descriptions in a direct manner is usually called a "*self-report*" test.

Strong developed a method for scoring the test empirically. He sent out forms to over 23,000 persons in various age groups and occupations in order to discover how the interests of persons in particular occupations differed from the interests of men-in-general. If a particular activity was checked "like" much more frequently by persons in a particular occupational group than men-in-general, that particular response could be scored as evidence of interest in that occupation. For example, Strong found that psychologists responded "like" much more frequently than an unselected group of men to the item "Author of a technical book"! If a student should reply the same way, it would indicate he shared this particular interest with psychologists as a group.

Since there are several hundred items, the score a person obtains for interest in a particular occupation is based on many items. A high score means the person has a pattern of interests that is very comparable to the pattern of interests reported by men (or women) who are already successful and happy in a given occupation. A low score means he does not. Such scores may be obtained for a substantial number of male and female occupations.

Strong administered the interest test to college students when they were seniors and again 10 years later and found substantial stability in scores for particular occupations (correlations between .50 and .80) over this 10-year period. Other studies show somewhat less stability when the test is given to younger students. And Strong found that men who remain in an occupation have higher scores than men who try an occupation and then change. In other words, the empirical evidence supports the notion that a person's preferences (likes and dislikes) are relatively stable once he has reached college age and that if he has interests similar to those of people in the occupation he selects, he is more likely to be happy in it and to stay in it. The test works, and its use has provided much interesting factual information concerning "self-report" preferences (e.g., stability over time). It continues to be a very valuable tool whenever the practical problem of vocational counseling or selection of personnel arises. That was the goal in development of the test and, except for possible improvements in the test, that goal has been attained.

Many similar "self-report" tests of human preferences have been developed. The scores obtained from them are variously labeled measures of "interests," "motives," "needs," "values," or "attitudes." But the words used to describe what is measured have no particular technical or conceptual meanings. They are the descriptive words from the common-sense language of motivation which refer to human preference. Such tests have provided a fund of factual information about human preferences, but they have contributed nothing to enhance understanding of the basic process of motivation because their use has been isolated from the conceptual and experimental analysis of motivation. It is an unfortunate historical accident.

CLINICAL USE OF INDIRECT METHODS

Similarly, many *indirect* methods for assessment of human motivation that have evolved in clinical practice have contributed very little to advance understanding of motivation. Using the psychoanalytic conception of motivation as the framework for thought, some ingenious devices have been invented following the logic of Freud's indirect methods of analysis. But these devices have been employed mainly to gain information about the individual whom the psychologist is trying to help. The significance of the information obtained is interpreted and evaluated in terms of the conception of motivation advanced by Freud *to help the patient*. Helping the patient is the immediate practical problem that must be solved. Clinical psychologists attest the value of various indirect tests of motivation in their day-to-day efforts to understand and help those who are emotionally distressed. But here,

again, in meeting the socially significant problem presented by emotional distress, the psychoanalytic conception of motivation has merely replaced common sense as the basis for interpreting what the tests imply about the patient and what to do to help alleviate his problem.

In neither of these applied uses of tests of human motivation, given the *practical-problem orientation* which must prevail, has there been any notable contribution to advancement of the conception of the immediate determinants of human action, *for this has not been part of the intention in using the tests*.

In the sections which follow, we turn to the use of similar tests of individual differences in motivation, but in the context of systematic experimental-conceptual analysis of problems. Investigations are designed either to test some theory of motivation that has already been proposed (viz., research on anxiety as a source of drive) or to evolve a theory of *human* motivation in terms of experimental analysis of *human* behavior (viz., research on achievement motivation).

## INDIVIDUAL DIFFERENCES IN ANXIETY

Since the early 1950's a number of interrelated studies of effects of individual differences in anxiety have been undertaken to explore hypotheses derived from *S-R* behavior theory. The basic assumption in this work is that fear (or anxiety) should be conceived as an acquired drive. These studies examine, at the level of human performance, the kind of phenomena which Mowrer and Miller have considered in reference to avoidance learning in lower animals. More important, they make use of one or another device especially designed as a test of individual differences in disposition to be anxious. This shows how differences in personality are to be represented within the framework of basic *S-R* principles.

We shall consider first some of the more important results of studies conducted by Taylor, Spence, and others at Iowa which have employed the *Manifest Anxiety Scale* (MAS) developed by Taylor (1953). These studies have to do with the implications of considering the anticipatory emotional reaction $(r_e)$ called fear, or anxiety, as a source of non-specific *drive*. Then we shall consider studies undertaken by Mandler, Sarason, and their co-workers at Yale employing the *Test Anxiety Questionnaire* (TAQ), an instrument explicitly designed to tap the strength of fear or anxiety that is normally aroused in a person in achievement-test situations. It will be interesting to note how the different theoretical interpretations of the two groups highlight the confounding of drive and drive stimulus ($S_D$) in $S$-$R$ theory to which we have already called attention.

## STUDIES EMPLOYING MANIFEST ANXIETY SCALE (MAS)

Reviews of studies employing the MAS by Farber (1954), Taylor (1956), and Spence (1958) stress that the primary interest in the use of this test is to investigate the role of drive in certain human learning situations. Taylor, for example, has said "any other acceptable specification of drive (e.g., hunger) could be used in experimental tests of the hypotheses about the effect of drive level" (Taylor, 1956, p. 303). Characteristics other than a difference in assumed drive level, which might be associated with differences in scores that persons attain on the MAS, have not been matters of interest to proponents of drive theory.

Taylor developed the self-report scale of general anxiety (MAS) by having clinical psychologists select from a more comprehensive personality inventory those items which clearly indicated manifest symptoms of anxiety: e.g., I worry quite a bit over possible misfortunes; I sweat very easily even on cool days. Only items which four out of five clinical psychologists agreed were manifest symptoms of anxiety were included in the scale. It was assumed that such a test would differentiate subjects in terms of the degree to which they admitted frequently experiencing overt symptoms of emotionality. Follow-up studies have shown that expert clinical ratings of persons on anxiety correlate positively with the scores they attain on MAS. So the test may be considered a substitute for clinical judgment concerning the degree to which a person normally exhibits symptoms of anxiety. In conventional use of the test, persons whose scores fall into the top 20 per cent of scores are designated High in anxiety and those whose scores fall in the lowest 20 per cent of scores are designated Low in anxiety.

How should differences in level of anxiety affect human performance? Given the Hullian scheme, the probability, vigor, and persistence of a response should be a function of the excitatory potential, $E$, where $E = D \times H$. In a *simple* situation, when only one habit is elicited (or where one habit is substantially stronger than any other habits which are simultaneously elicited), a high level of drive should produce a higher level of performance than a low level of drive. Thus it was predicted that, in simple eyelid conditioning experiments, subjects having High scores on MAS would perform the conditioned eyeblink at a higher level than subjects having Low scores on MAS. This result has been produced a number of different times. Related studies of performance in a verbal learning task have shown a comparable result. When the paired-associates method is employed and items are constructed to control for the strength of prior association between the stimulus and response words, it is found that subjects who score High in MAS perform better than those who score Low in MAS when there is little associative strength between the stimulus and the correct response word to begin with, or when there is a relatively strong habit favoring the correct response to begin with (Spence, 1958). In other words, when the conditions are such that only a single habit is being elicited by the stimulus situation, and competition among alternative response tendencies is at a minimum, then the result expected on the assumption that MAS measures a difference in *drive* is found.

However, according to the theory that drive acts as a non-specific exciting influence on all habits elicited in a particular situation, the result expected in a more *complex* performance situation is different. By *complex* is meant a situation in which a number of competing habits are simultaneously elicited.

According to Taylor:

> "In situations in which a number of competing response tendencies are evoked, only one of which is correct, the relative performance of high and low drive groups will depend upon the number and comparative strengths of the various response tendencies. Predictions concerning the performance of the groups in such complex tasks involve the introduction of additional Hullian concepts: oscillatory inhibition [see p. 172] . . . and threshold [see p. 173] . . ." (Taylor, 1956, p. 304).

If habit strength of the "correct" response is *weaker* than habit strength of some other competing response, then the multiplicative effect of drive will enhance this difference in the strengths of the excitatory potentials for the two responses and performance will suffer more when drive is strong. Furthermore, Taylor has pointed out:

> ". . . the possibility exists that under a high-drive level new competing responses with very weak habit strengths may be brought over the

threshold value of $E$ with the consequence that the probability of occurrence of the correct response is lowered relative to that in a low-drive condition" (Taylor, 1956, p. 305).

Hence, it is generally to be expected that when the subject is presented a complex task, that is, one involving alternatives and competition among possibilities, that strong drive will produce a decrement in performance.

Taylor summarizes the general hypothesis as follows:

"It should be obvious, then, that maximum inferiority of high-drive $S$s would be expected when a large number of competing tendencies are present and the correct tendency is both relatively weak and low in the hierarchy. As the strength of the correct tendency increases relative to the incorrect, high-drive groups should become less inferior and eventually superior in performance to low-drive groups. The exact point of equality would be difficult to specify. Even when the correct response is highest (though not strongly dominant) in the hierarchy, high-drive $S$s could still conceivably be inferior in some instances since a greater number of suprathreshold tendencies could more than offset the advantage of the relatively higher $E$ value of the correct response for these individuals" (Taylor, 1956, p. 305).

This hypothesis has been tested in experiments which confront the human subject with the sort of complex problem a rat faces in learning to take the correct path through a multiple-unit maze. One may construct a serial verbal maze in which the correct response must be made to the stimulus word (the first choice point) before the second stimulus word is presented, and so on. The task is to "run" the serial verbal maze without making any errors. Or one may employ a stylus maze in which the subject actually has to learn to trace a path through a maze with a stylus as a rat runs through one. Studies by Taylor and Spence (1952) and Farber and Spence (1953) have shown that persons who score High in MAS perform less well than those who score Low in MAS in this type of situation where there is competition between different, simultaneously aroused habits at the choice points. Further analysis revealed that anxious subjects are more prone to make errors at the more difficult choice points, as expected. But there was no evidence that anxious subjects performed better than non-anxious subjects at the easiest choice points as predicted on the assumption that a stronger drive should enhance performance when the task is simple.

## IS ANXIETY CHRONIC OR SITUATIONALLY AROUSED?

The earliest studies employing the Manifest Anxiety Scale (MAS) to assess individual differences in anxiety proceeded on the implicit assumption that it was the normal chronic level of anxiety in a person that was being measured. But the results of some studies began to show that sizable differences between persons scoring High and Low on MAS were most apparent, or present at all, only when the situation at the time of performance contained some noxious stimulus or "threat." If fear is an anticipatory emotional reaction ($r_e$) conditioned to external cues, as shown in the early animal experiments by Mowrer and Miller, then the person who reports frequently experiencing symptoms of anxiety may be one who has learned to be afraid in such a great variety of situations that he is almost always anxious; or he may be one who has had more severely painful experiences in the same situations which others have lived through more fortunately; or he may be one whose training has been similar to others, but who was born with greater emotional sensitivity so that the magnitude of his fear reaction is stronger. The conception of a chronically anxious person derives mainly from the psychoanalytic conception of someone who has learned to fear his own inner impulses—which are with him all the time.

Taylor has stated the two major alternatives this way:

"One is that test scores reflect differences in a chronic emotional state so that individuals scoring high on the scale tend to bring a higher level of emotionality or anxiety 'in the door' with them than do $S$s scoring at lower levels (Taylor, 1951). A second alternative conception is that MAS scores reflect different potentialities for anxiety arousal, high scoring $S$s being those who tend to react more emotionally and adapt less readily to novel or threatening situations than do low scorers (Rosenbaum, 1950; Spence, Farber, and Taylor, 1954)" (Taylor, 1956, p. 306).

The question has not been definitively settled. Spence and Farber (1953) examined data from three eyelid-conditioning studies in which a strong, medium, or mild unconditioned stimulus was used to establish the conditioned eyelid response. They found that the magnitude of the difference between High and Low MAS groups remained relatively stable. But Spence *et al.* (1954) later found that when occasional electric shocks were given between conditioning trials, or there was the threat of a shock, the predicted performance differences between High and Low MAS groups were highly significant as compared with only a very slight difference in a control group conditioned without shock or threat of shock.

Bindra, Paterson, and Strzelecki (1955) conducted a salivary-conditioning experiment with human subjects and found no difference between High and Low MAS groups. At first this seemed to contradict the notion that the drive produced by anxiety was a non-specific influence. But the result is also consistent with the view that MAS measures disposition to be anxious in threatening situations but not chronic anxiety level.

While considering the question still open, Taylor has stated:

> "Speculating on this point, to many college sophomores psychology experiments *per se* may be seen as somewhat threatening, particularly when the task could be interpreted as reflecting on their personality or intelligence. It is perfectly possible that in experimental arrangements involving no noxious stimulation or stress-inducing instructions which call upon skills not particularly valued by college students, differences between groups might disappear" (Taylor, 1956, p. 312).

Lucas (1952) and Gordon and Berlyne (1954) were among the first to employ a "psychological" threat in studies employing MAS. Before the critical task, they had subjects perform another task and attempted to induce feelings of failure by telling subjects they had performed poorly on it. This method of inducing feelings of failure and/or threat of failure in subsequent performance had been worked out earlier by Sears (1937), who was the first to relate performance decrements to the Freudian concept of repression. Both of the above studies found a substantial decrement in performance of anxious subjects relative to that of non-anxious subjects following failure.

The results of the Lucas experiment are particularly instructive. He was concerned with the question: Under what conditions does lowered performance of anxious persons take place? Preliminary to the task from which he obtained his measure of performance, Lucas had subjects perform another similar task for six trials. He created four experimental groups, which varied in terms of the number of times they had been told they failed (i.e., had not achieved the expected standard on an important test). The test performance consisted of presenting subjects three lists each of 10 consonants. The subject was required to reproduce each list after

it had been presented. Figure 8.5 shows the mean performance scores of subjects having High MAS scores (anxious) and Low MAS scores (non-anxious) in relation to experimentally induced failure before the critical test.

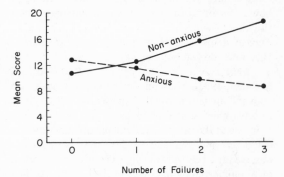

FIGURE 8.5 Mean scores on 30 consonants for each group of 12 Ss, classified on the basis of degree of anxiety and number of failures. (*From Lucas, "The interactive effects of anxiety, failure, and interserial duplication," The American Journal of Psychology, Vol. 65, 1952, p. 64*)

The performance of anxious subjects became increasingly worse following failure as a function of the number of failures. This result is consistent with an hypothesis that their anxiety was increasingly aroused. *But the performance of non-anxious subjects improved following failure as a function of the degree of failure.* Both trends were statistically significant.

Lucas had expected that failure would produce a decrement in the performance of both anxious and non-anxious groups, but less of a decrement in the non-anxious group because, presumably, the anxiety drive aroused would be weaker in them than in the anxious group. He concluded that the unanticipated improvement in performance of non-anxious subjects following failure "calls for some new theoretical assumptions regarding the properties of anxiety and failure" (Lucas, 1952, p. 65). We may recall, in this connection, a similar query raised by Cartwright (see p. 104), who had found both increases and decreases in *attractiveness* of a task following experimentally induced failure.

STUDIES EMPLOYING THE TEST
ANXIETY QUESTIONNAIRE (TAQ)

The development of the *Test Anxiety Questionnaire* (TAQ) grew out of Sarason's (1949) concern with the fact that both theoretical and practical approaches to intelligence testing have given insufficient attention to the nature and role of internal motivating states at the time of test performance. As distinct from the Manifest Anxiety Scale, which asks questions of a very general nature concerning symptoms of anxiety, the TAQ focuses attention upon how a person normally feels in an intelligence-test situation or when taking an examination in a course. Typical items ask: How do you feel *beforehand?* How often do you think of ways of avoiding the test? To what extent do you perspire? (Sarason and Mandler, 1952). Thus this self-report test has to do with the anxiety normally experienced by a person in achievement-test situations.

In one of the earliest experiments utilizing this test (Mandler and Sarason, 1952), the experimenter observed the behavior of subjects while they worked on a complex task and rated their behavior according to several criteria of overt manifestation of anxiety: perspiration, excessive movements, inappropriate laughter and exclamations, questioning of instructions, and hand movements. The ratings were found to correspond very well with scores the subjects had obtained on the Test Anxiety Questionnaire (phi = .59). So it can be assumed that persons who score High in Test Anxiety do, in fact, exhibit more symptoms of anxiety in test situations than those who score Low.

The theoretical analysis of how anxiety should influence performance on the *complex* tasks a person faces when taking an intelligence test or examination differs from that advanced by Taylor, Spence, and others who focus attention upon the non-specific exciting function of *drive* in the Hull and Spence formulations of *S-R* behavior theory. The position taken by Sarason, Mandler, and their co-workers is closer to that of Miller. They emphasize the drive stimulus ($S_D$). They conceive fear (or anxiety) as a response to situational cues which produces a strong internal stimulus. And they use the term *drive* in reference to that strong stimulus ($S_D$) as Miller does. Their analysis of the motivating factors which influence task performance includes:

". . . Learned drives which are a function of the nature of the task, test materials, and instructions. These include the need to achieve and to finish the task; in short, drives which evoke responses relative to satisfying the requirement set by the task or the experimenter. We shall refer to these as task drives ($S_T$). It is assumed that these drives are reduced by task responses ($R_T$), which are responses or response sequences which lead to completion of the task.

". . . A learned anxiety drive which is a function of anxiety reactions previously learned as responses to stimuli present in the testing situation. Anxiety is here considered as a response-produced strong stimulus with the functional characteristics of drives as discussed by Miller and Dollard (1941). Anxiety reactions are generalized from previous experiences to testing situations. The anxiety drive ($S_A$) primarily elicits responses that tend to reduce the drive. These responses are considered to be of two general types:

"(a) Anxiety responses which are not specifically connected with the nature of the task or materials. These responses (designated as $R_A$) may be manifested as feelings of inadequacy, helplessness, heightened somatic reaction, anticipations of punishment or loss of status and esteem, and *implicit attempts at leaving the test situation* [italics added]. . . .

"(b) Anxiety responses which are directly related to the completion of the task and which reduce anxiety by leading to completion of the task. These responses (designated $R_{AT}$) are functionally equivalent to $R_T$ responses . . ." (Mandler and Sarason, 1952, p. 166).

Mandler and Sarason assume the presence of certain learned *drives* which function to elicit *task-relevant* responses, but these are not measured. In addition, they assume the presence of *anxiety drive* which functions to elicit many different, previously acquired avoidant or *task-irrelevant* responses. *Anxiety drive* can also function to elicit responses which *are* directly related to completion of the task. This latter possibility is more likely after the person has had a chance to learn how to perform the task before him.

In further elaboration of these ideas, it is assumed that *task-relevant* and *task-irrelevant* responses are incompatible. So when both are present there is conflict. Persons with high test anxiety are assumed to possess a greater repertory of task-irrelevant (avoidant) habits than persons who are low in anxiety drive. So at the beginning of a test, that is, before the anxious person has learned to reduce anxiety through performance of specific task-relevant actions ($R_{AT}$ above), he experiences greater conflict between task-irrelevant tendencies and task-relevant tendencies than the person who is less anxious. Thus persons scoring High on TAQ are generally expected to perform less well on tests than those who score Low on TAQ, at least until they have learned to reduce anxiety through specific task-relevant actions. If the person has already had an opportunity to learn to reduce anxiety through successful performance of the task, then strong test anxiety should produce better learning and performance than weak test anxiety. In this case, both anxiety drive and the "learned drives" which normally elicit task-relevant actions should summate to motivate task-relevant actions. It is implicitly assumed that the "learned drives" which function to elicit task-relevant actions are equally strong in persons who otherwise differ in strength of anxiety drive as measured by TAQ.

Let us consider several of the experiments designed to explore the implications of this conception. Mandler and Sarason (1952) employed a block-design test adapted from the Wechsler-Bellevue Intelligence Test as a measure of performance. This task is one that is normally used to assess differences in "intelligence." The performances of subjects in the upper and lower 15 per cent of TAQ scores were compared under different experimental conditions.

At the beginning of the test session, the subject was told he was going to be given a series of intelligence tests. It was expected that subjects having Low TAQ scores would perform better than subjects having High TAQ scores, and this result was obtained as shown in Figure 8.6.

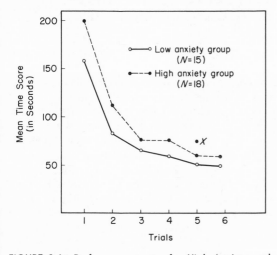

FIGURE 8.6   Performance curves for High Anxiety and Low Anxiety groups for six trials of first Kohs Block Design (X = mean score for High Anxiety group, including one extreme case) (*From Mandler and Sarason, 1952, p. 170*)

Then subjects were exposed to different experimental treatments. Some were given a false impression about how well or poorly they had performed. To induce feelings of success, the experimenter consulted a table of norms and told some subjects that they had done extremely well. They were then urged to see how well they would do on the second

part of the test. Other subjects were told they had failed, that they had done much worse than might have been expected from their aptitude scores. And they also were urged to see how well they could do on subsequent tests. Other subjects were told nothing. The experimenter merely indicated that it was time to move on to the second part of the testing. The three conditions were called "Failure," "Success," and "Neutral."

What were the effects on subsequent performance of "Success" and "Failure" in relation to the Neutral or control condition? Among subjects who were High in Test Anxiety, subsequent performance was much worse by those who had been told either that they had succeeded or failed than among those told nothing. This further emphasis of the achievement-test character of the situation apparently heightened their anxiety. However, just the reverse was true among subjects who had Low TAQ scores. When told they had succeeded or failed, they subsequently performed better than other subjects low in test anxiety who were told nothing. Following failure, the performance of subjects who were low in Test Anxiety was subsequently better than any other group. Table 8.3 shows the average time taken

TABLE 8.3

Mean time scores for experimental subgroups on first trial of new performance test following Success, Failure, or Neutral report concerning performance on earlier test (Based on Mandler and Sarason, 1952, p. 170)

| Experimental condition | High Anxiety Group Mean* | Low Anxiety Group Mean* | t | p |
|---|---|---|---|---|
| Neutral | 126.0 | 165.6 | 1.46 | .08 |
| Success | 163.6 | 138.0 | 0.94 | .17 |
| Failure | 162.2 | 108.6 | 1.98 | .03 |

* The S's scores on trial 1 of the first performance test were used as a statistical control for initial differences in performance on the second test. The mean time scores presented here are adjusted to eliminate initial differences between subgroups in level of performance. The test of statistical significance is based on analysis of covariance with 23 degrees of freedom for each t test.

to solve a new design problem on the very first trial following "Success," "Failure," and the Neutral (control) treatment.

Mandler and Sarason noted that following the Neutral interval between the first and second parts of the testing, the group having High TAQ scores performed better than the group having Low TAQ scores. In the six preceding trials the High Anxiety group had performed less well, as shown in Figure 8.6. This finding was interpreted to mean that after anxious subjects had had an opportunity to learn to reduce anxiety through task-relevant responses, the combined influence of *strong* anxiety drive and other "learned drives" motivating task-relevant responses produced better performance than when anxiety drive was relatively weak.

The most striking result of this study is the fact that "failure" produces diametrically opposite effects on subsequent performance in the High and Low anxiety groups, just as it did in the Lucas study. (See Figure 8.5.) This result is not very clearly explained, it seems, without some further specification about the action of those other "learned drives" which are assumed to produce task-relevant performance, but which are not measured in the experiment. What other learned drive but anxiety has been suggested in the research guided by *S-R* behavior theory?

In another experiment, Sarason *et al.* (1952) examined the effects of different instructions on performance of a digit-symbol substitution task adapted from a widely employed intelligence test. At the beginning of the testing session, subjects were told that they would be given some intelligence tests as part of a study relating to the aptitude tests given all college freshmen. One group of subjects was then told that "the test is designed so that it should be fairly easy for the average college student to complete the test within the time limit" (Sarason *et al.*, 1952, p. 561). Later during performance, they were reminded that they were *expected to finish* (ETF). Another *not-expected-to-finish* (NETF) group was told "that the test was constructed so that nobody could finish the test within the time limit" (Sarason *et al.*, 1952, p. 561). During their performance they were reminded not to worry about finishing because nobody could finish the task. In fact, nobody could or did finish the task in either condition in the time allowed.

The results of this experiment are shown in Figure 8.7. Though the major interest in designing the experiment was to discover how differences in instructions might influence the performance of anxious subjects, it is apparent in Figure 8.7 that the different instructions had more effect on those who were Low in Test Anxiety. Their performance was

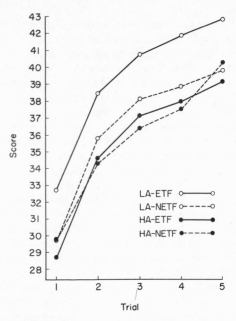

FIGURE 8.7   Performance curves of four experimental subgroups on Digit Symbol Test in Experiment I (*From Sarason, Mandler, and Craighill, 1952, p. 562*)

substantially better when given the instruction "you are expected to finish" (ETF) than when told "you are not expected to finish" (NETF). The High Test Anxiety groups performed relatively poorly in both conditions. The difference between High and Low anxiety groups is more marked when subjects are put under the stress of the instruction "you are expected to finish" than when they are told "you are not expected to finish." But again, the result is attributable to the *enhanced* performance of the least anxious subjects when put under greater pressure.

In another experiment, one group of subjects was given an ego-involving instruction (EI) which referred to the task as an "intelligence test," while another group was given the same tasks following a non-ego-involving instruction (NEI). The latter were *not* told the task was an intelligence test, but merely that the examiner wanted to standardize some tasks and that "your own performance is only of importance insofar as it contributes to the total performance of a group of students" (Sarason *et al.*, 1952, p. 563). The task was a stylus maze similar to that employed in some of the studies of manifest anxiety cited earlier. Figure 8.8 shows that subjects who are High in Test Anxiety make more errors when the task is presented as a test of intelligence (EI) than when it is not (NEI). Again, the result is diametrically

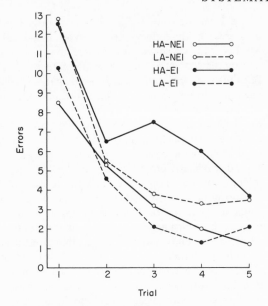

FIGURE 8.8 Error scores of four experimental subgroups on stylus maze in Experiment II (*From Sarason, Mandler, and Craighill, 1952, p. 564*)

opposite among subjects who are Low in Test Anxiety. They make the fewest number of errors when the importance of the task is stressed (*EI*). And, as is shown in most studies of both manifest anxiety and test anxiety, the difference between performance of High and Low anxiety groups is more marked when the situation is such as to arouse anxiety (in this case by ego-involving instructions) than when the situational "threat" is minimized.

THE PROBLEM IN INTERPRETATION
OF ANXIETY STUDIES

The two sets of anxiety studies, those conducted with Manifest Anxiety Scale and those conducted with Test Anxiety Scale, present the same problem of interpretation that arises in studies of drive in lower animals. One group of researchers emphasizes the non-specific activating function of *drive* posited in the Hullian theory. Another group of researchers emphasizes the drive stimulus ($S_D$) which is generally assumed to accompany and distinguish particular drives or particular sources of drive. If the studies of Test Anxiety are guided by the Miller hypothesis and drive is defined as a stimulus, then they need not take into account the non-specific exciting function assumed by Hull and Spence, for it is not a part of their theory. But certainly those who have employed

the Manifest Anxiety Scale must assume responsibility for distinguishing the effects of *drive* and the effects of *drive stimulus* as elicitor of the specific avoidant habits that are emphasized by Sarason and Mandler. Both theoretical interpretations of decrements in performance of complex tasks by persons scoring High on an anxiety test, particularly when the situation presents a threat, are consistent with the concept of fear as an acquired drive developed by Mowrer and Miller in research with animals. *But neither of these theoretical conceptions explains very adequately why persons who score Low on a test of anxiety should perform better under stress than when conditions are more relaxed.* Whether a low score on an anxiety test reflects a relatively weak component of non-specific drive attributable to fear (as Taylor, Spence *et al.* assume) or a relatively weak repertory of task-irrelevant habits (as Mandler and Sarason assume), certainly the stronger arousal of fear by ego-involving instructions or by the experience of failure, which implies the threat of future failure, should produce more non-specific drive or more task-irrelevant response tendencies than a relatively unstressful condition. Consequently, persons who are Low in anxiety should show some decrement in performance, although less than more anxious persons. Yet both sets of anxiety studies have shown that persons who score Low in anxiety *perform better* under "stress" than under "non-stress." To explain this result, we must turn to contemporary research on achievement motivation, which represents another fresh start in the search for a theory of motivation.

THE STUDY OF
ACHIEVEMENT MOTIVATION

Recognizing the need for a generally useful and valid method of measuring human motives, David McClelland and co-workers began, in 1948, to combine the clinical insight that human motivation is expressed in free-associative thought with experimental methods of manipulating and controlling the strength of motivation. They adapted the technique that had been invented by Henry A. Murray (1936) for eliciting imaginative stories (fantasies) from an individual in response to pictures, the *Thematic Apperception Test* (TAT), and were initially guided by the conceptual analysis of human personality which Murray had advanced in *Explorations in Personality* (1938).

MURRAY'S CONCEPTION OF PSYCHOGENIC NEED

At about the same time that Hull was initiating his effort to embrace purposive behavior within the framework of *S-R* principles, Murray was embroiled in a debate among personalogists as to the relative merits of describing personality in terms of traits (i.e., general habits) or more dynamically in terms of basic "psychogenic needs." The analysis of personality made by Murray and his co-workers in the Harvard Psychological Clinic during the 1930's reflects the same cross-currents of theoretical viewpoints (Freudian, Lewinian, Tolmanian, Thorndikian) that were at work on Hull. The core of Murray's conception of personality is the idea of a hierarchy or configuration of basic psychogenic needs or motives. Borrowing ideas from both Freud and McDougall, but without the instinctive overtones, Murray conceived a *need* as:

". . . a construct (a convenient fiction or hypothetical concept) which stands for a force (the physico-chemical nature of which is unknown) in the brain region, a force which organizes perception, apperception, intellection, conation and action in such a way as to transform in a certain direction an existing, unsatisfying situation" (Murray, 1938, pp. 123–124).*

It was Murray's view that a need (for dominance, affiliation, achievement, nurturance, autonomy, deference, aggression, abasement, etc.) could be aroused from within by internal visceral processes or from without by the effect on the person of the immediate situation (which he called *press*). A need would be overtly manifested in:

"1. A typical behavioural trend or effect (transformation of external-internal conditions).
"2. A typical mode [of action].
"3. The search for, avoidance or selection of, attention and response to one or a few types of press (cathected objects of a certain class).
"4. The exhibition of a characteristic emotion or feeling.
"5. The manifestation of satisfaction with the achievement of a certain effect (or with a gratuity), or the manifestation of dissatisfaction when there is failure to achieve a certain effect" (Murray, 1938, p. 124).

An acquired psychogenic need was assumed to have properties similar to those that McDougall had once attributed to an instinct.

* Excerpts from H. A. Murray, *Explorations in Personality*, copyright 1938, Oxford University Press, are reprinted by permission.

The Thematic Apperception Test was constructed to assess the underlying needs of an individual. Murray and his co-workers devised a system for scoring the content of thematic apperceptive stories. Both the test itself, and the method of analysis, have been widely employed in clinical practice and in studies of personality. The chief deficiency apparent to McClelland a decade later was the paucity of evidence to support the kinds of interpretations that were made of the content of thematic apperception and other related "projective" techniques that began to enjoy immense popularity as clinical tools.

Murray (1933) had studied the effect of fear on children's estimates of the maliciousness of pictures of faces cut from magazines. He had taken advantage of the opportunity provided by a child's birthday party to have children rate the faces both before and after a spooky game of murder with the lights out. He found that fear increased estimates of the "maliciousness" of the environment. (The major result of this pilot study with only eight cases would one day be sustained by Walker and Atkinson *et al.* (1958) when much later they were able to study the effects of an atomic explosion (the fear-inducing stimulus) on response to a modified thematic apperceptive test.)

And Sanford (1936; 1937), one of the group most actively involved in the early development of the TAT, had found that hunger had an effect on imaginal processes. He analyzed the content of associations suggested by an image under ground glass to relatively hungry and non-hungry subjects and found the frequency of food-related associations related to degree of hunger.

Both of these important pilot studies yielded suggestive evidence that motivation does have an effect on "projective" responses. But a firm foundation for use of thematic apperception or any other method for assessment of needs or motives was lacking when McClelland *et al.* began their systematic study of the effects of experimentally aroused motivational states on thematic apperception.

EFFECT OF EXPERIMENTALLY INDUCED
HUNGER ON THEMATIC APPERCEPTION

From our review of the study of motivation, we know that around 1948 there was no general consensus concerning theoretical conception of motivation, nor was there any generally agreed-upon measuring rod against which to test the validity of some new method of measurement except, perhaps, the traditional notion that food privation would, by whatever mechanism, produce an increase in strength of "hunger." So in order not to begin research with two unknowns (the method of measurement and definition of the strength of motivation), McClelland and co-workers began by investigating the effect of food privation on thematic apperceptive stories. It was generally agreed that food privation would produce hunger. If free-associative, imaginative stories told in response to pictures were, in fact, influenced by motivation as clinical psychologists from Freud to Murray had attested, then imaginative stories created by persons who had gone without food for 16 hours should contain more imagery related in one way or another to eating and food-seeking than stories created immediately after eating when hunger was satisfied. The intention of the research was to discover whether or not, and if so, *how* motivation was expressed in the content of imaginative stories.

The daily schedule of men at a submarine base was arranged so that some of them would report to a medical building for testing within 1 hour after the noon meal, but others would report late in the morning approximately 4 hours after breakfast, and still others would report late in the morning after missing breakfast (to sleep) and 16 hours' food privation. None of the men were given any reason to suspect that they were participating in an experiment dealing with effects of hunger. The chance to sleep through the morning call to "rise and shine," however it can be arranged, is a joyful experience for men in service.

In a preliminary experiment, McClelland and Atkinson (1948) asked men to record what they thought they saw when looking at a blank or smudged illuminated screen following an instruction and other realistic procedures which created the impression that it was a test of visual acuity. The results showed that the frequency of reports of *instrumental objects related to eating* (e.g., plates, knives, and forks) was positively related to degree of hunger, but frequency of reports of *goal objects* (apples, hamburgers) was not. This result seemed to challenge the accepted view that "fantasy" is necessarily wish-fulfilling in character. But too little information was obtained in this preliminary effort to study "projection" in the purest form, so attention turned to the thematic apperception technique of producing a rich sample of free-associative content to analyze for evidences of motivational effects.

The method established in a second study of hunger (Atkinson and McClelland, 1948) has been repeatedly employed, with very minor changes, in subsequent studies. The procedures developed by Murray for individual testing with the TAT were adapted so that pictures could be projected on a screen in a group situation and stories written instead of told to an examiner. A series of pictures which suggested food-seeking or eating in varying degree were selected from some of Murray's original set of TAT pictures and from ordinary magazines. Following a general instruction that the task was to construct interesting and imaginative stories, each picture was shown for 20 seconds and then withdrawn. The subjects were then given four minutes to write a story about the picture. The general questions that are normally given verbally in clinical use of thematic apperception were printed at equal intervals on otherwise blank story forms to guide subjects through the plot of a story. The guiding questions were:

1. What is happening? Who are the persons?
2. What has led up to this situation, that is, what has happened in the past?
3. What is being thought? What is wanted, by whom?
4. What will happen? What will be done?

As soon as the four minutes allotted for writing a story was up, another picture was shown. This procedure continued for 16 to 32 minutes, depending upon the number of pictures employed. It produced a substantial "thought sample," or sample of imaginative behavior, induced by certain picture cues under controlled motivating conditions.

Analysis of stories written under 1, 4, and 16 hours of food privation showed that food privation clearly influenced the frequency of certain categories of imaginative response. These categories were finally arrived at after exhaustive analysis and re-analysis of the data. The primary task was to evolve a useful system of analysis which summarized the kinds of changes in imaginative content that were readily apparent in reading the stories. The categories of response finally decided upon correspond to various features of the typical goal-directed sequence of actions which psychologists had already identified in studies of overt goal-seeking behavior. The authors of the stories had attributed needs, instrumental acts, anticipations of the goal or of frustration, positive and negative feelings in relation to progress towards a goal or not, etc., to the characters in the stories they had written. Many of these plots could be identified as clearly related to hunger and food-seeking. These plots were further analyzed for descriptive details which could be reliably identified as present or absent and then counted to yield a single numerical index which represented how saturated the stories were with imagery relating to the food-seeking sequence of behavior. After developing the scoring system, the experimenters scrambled the stories from different groups and recoded the stories without knowledge of the conditions under which they had been written to assure that results were unbiased and the method of analysis was objective. Refinement of the scoring system and tests of its objectivity were matters given considerable attention in subsequent studies.

The general result of this study encouraged the belief that thematic apperceptive content was, indeed, sensitive to motivational influence. The main conclusions were stated as follows:

"As hunger increased, there was no overall increase in the percentage of Ss showing food imagery or food themas, but there was a decided increase in the percentage showing food deprivation themas, characters expressing a need for food, and activity successful in overcoming deprivation, but not always instrumental in getting food. On the other hand, as hunger increased, there was a decided decrease in amount of goal activity (eating) and in friendly press favorable to eating.

"A composite need food score was devised by scoring $+2$, $+1$, or $-1$ for all instances in each record of categories which showed reliable increases or decrease for the groups as hunger increased. The mean need food score differentiated reliably the three deprivation groups with little overlap in score between the one and 16 hour deprivation groups . . .

". . . It is suggested . . . that the amount of need deprivation and of instrumental activity present in stories is a better index of the strength of a need than is the amount of goal activity. If the results are confirmed at more complex need levels, it should be possible to obtain a single score measuring need strength which would combine the shifts occurring in story content as the strength of the need increases.

"Consideration of the theoretical implications of these results indicates that it is desirable to treat apperceptive behavior as functioning like any other type of behavior rather than to attempt to fit it under the limited principles governing Freudian or defensive projection, which appears to be a special case" (Atkinson and McClelland, 1948, pp. 657-658).

EFFECT OF EXPERIMENTAL AROUSAL OF
ACHIEVEMENT MOTIVATION ON
THEMATIC APPERCEPTION

With this preliminary evidence that the thematic apperceptive method of measurement would work,

McClelland and co-workers initiated a program of research on "the need to achieve," which is fully described in *The Achievement Motive* (McClelland, Atkinson, Clark, and Lowell, 1953). More recent developments in the study of achievement motivation and extension of the method of measurement to the study of other psychogenic needs and societal problems are reported in *Motives in Fantasy, Action, and Society* (Atkinson, 1958) and *The Achieving Society* (McClelland, 1961).

Our present objective is to become familiar with the logic and procedures followed in experimental validation of a thematic apperceptive measure of individual differences in strength of the need to achieve. Then we shall review that phase of subsequent research which has been directed to conceptual analysis of what is being measured and to clarification of a principle of motivation, the topic of central interest throughout this book.

The programmatic intention of this research is clearly stated by McClelland *et al.* (1949) in the introduction to their first study of effect of need for achievement on thematic apperception:

". . . No one is particularly interested in diagnosing hunger from projective responses. The point is, do the same kinds of shifts occur for an experimentally controlled psychogenic need, or are the clues which have been discovered applicable only to some simple physiological tension like hunger?

"The present experiment was designed to answer this crucial question. It was decided to choose a psychogenic need which could be aroused experimentally and to see whether it produced perceptive and apperceptive changes similar to those already noted for hunger. The need chosen was 'need achievement' or 'need mastery,' the need which *presumably* is aroused by experimentally inducing ego-involvement, according to a technique which by now is fairly well standardized among psychologists experimenting in the field of personality (Alper, Thelma, 1946; Nowlis, 1941; Sears, 1942). The word 'presumably' is used advisedly. No one knows for certain that there is a unitary *n* Achievement which can be satisfied by success and aroused by failure in the same way that hunger is satisfied by food and aroused by deprivation of food. However, if manipulation of the conditions of ego-involvement produces the same kinds of effects on projection as manipulation on hours of food deprivation, there will be some basis for considering the psychogenic state aroused as a need, at least to the extent that it functions like a physiological one. It was to establish this kind of parallelism of function that work began in this series with a simple physiological tension which nearly everyone would accept as a need or drive. Consequently, if the results in this experiment are in substantial agreement with those obtained in earlier ones in the series, it will provide evidence for the existence of higher order psychogenic needs which at least function like those at a simpler physiological level.

"One of the crucial problems in this type of experiment is to find a scoring system for thematic stories which is objective enough to provide high observer agreement and sensitive enough to reflect changes in motivational states. So a further purpose of this experiment is to develop the scoring system further which was found useful for hunger . . . and to test its applicability to a more complex psychogenic need. The standardization of an objective scoring system for projective records should ultimately make possible some general principles for interpreting them. What is even more important, it should open up for experimentation the whole field of imagination, which has been more or less neglected, except by the clinicians, since introspection was discredited as a fruitful approach to arriving at psychological principles" (McClelland *et al.*, 1949, pp. 242–243).

The design of the original experiments on achievement motivation required the creation of experimental arrangements which would presumably raise or lower the intensity of inferred need for achievement immediately before male college students were asked to write imaginative stories in response to four pictures. These experimental conditions, as described by McClelland *et al.* (1953, Chapter 3) were:

*Relaxed condition:* Preceding the administration of a thematic apperception test, a college class was asked to work on some tasks that were described as in the developmental stage. The experimenter was introduced as a graduate student. He was informally dressed and attempted to minimize the importance of the tasks to the subjects by *not* asking them to sign their names. He conduced himself informally during the 25-minute period it took subjects to work on the tasks. This procedure was designed to minimize the arousal of need for achievement preceding administration of the "test of creative imagination" by suggesting that the experimenter was interested only in the characteristics of the tasks and not how well any particular person performed them.

*Neutral condition:* Nothing was done deliberately either to weaken or to strengthen achievement motivation before the administration of the thematic apperception measure to college students in a classroom. This condition attempted to assess the level of motivation that might normally be attributed to the everyday cues of a college classroom.

*Achievement-Oriented condition:* The same tasks employed in the Relaxed condition were presented to subjects, but now as tests of important abilities. Attention was drawn to the requirement that each subject put his name on all *test* forms and the importance of "doing one's best" was emphasized. The experimenter was formally dressed and conducted himself like someone proctoring a college examination. The "tests" continued for 25 minutes, and then a "test of creative imagination" (thematic apperception) was administered.

*Success condition:* The preliminary tasks were introduced as important tests (as in the Achievement-Oriented condition), but after the initial test was completed and then again at the end of the series of tests, subjects were led to believe that they had performed very well by allowing them to count or score their own tests and by comparing their scores with quoted norms which, by design, were sufficiently low so that every or nearly every subject would have the impression that he had achieved a good standing. Following the initial period of testing and "success," the thematic apperceptive measure was administered as in other conditions.

*Failure condition:* The tasks were presented as tests, as in the Achievement-Oriented condition, and subjects were allowed to score their own tests as in the Success condition. But this time the norms quoted were, by design, so high that all or most subjects would have the impression that they had done very poorly. Following this period of testing and "failure," the thematic apperceptive measure was administered.

*Success-Failure condition:* This condition differed from the Success and Failure conditions only in that norms quoted for the initial test in the battery were low, as in the Success condition, but norms quoted at the end of the series of tests were high, as in the Failure condition.

In the original analysis of results (McClelland *et al.*, 1949), the content of stories written under *Relaxed* and *Failure* conditions was carefully examined for imagery having to do with *concern over performing well in relation to a standard of excellence* (i.e., pride in skillful performance). It was assumed that these two conditions were probably most analogous to the weak and strong conditions of need that had been produced by 1 and 16 hours of food privation in the hunger study. The same kind of coding system developed in the hunger study was employed initially to assure that the fundamental nature of the changes in imaginative response accompanying heightened intensity of the motivational state were similar in the two studies. Later

(McClelland *et al.*, 1953), the coding system was revised, refined, and elaborated so as to summarize more fully the various kinds of differences observed when stories written under the *Relaxed condition* (weak achievement motivation inferred) and *Achievement-Oriented condition* (stronger achievement motivation inferred) were compared. This was done so that the scoring method would not be complicated by changes that might be considered specific reactions to failure rather than symptoms of greater arousal of motivation to achieve. In the Achievement-Oriented condition, subjects had been given instructions which emphasized the importance of doing well on important tests to heighten their motivation, but they had not been given systematic knowledge of results, either success (to reduce motivation) or failure (to heighten it further or produce specific reactions to failure), just before the thematic apperceptive measure was administered. *It was assumed that the state of motivation produced during the 20–30 minute initial test period before stories were written would persist through the period when subjects were asked to write imaginative stories.*

The results were not materially different in the two analyses. In comparison with the imaginative stories written in the Relaxed condition, those written immediately following Achievement Orientation significantly more often involved characters who were concerned over performing some task well in relation to an explicitly stated standard of excellence (e.g., getting a good grade on a test), or who were engaged in performance of some task which is socially defined as a unique accomplishment (e.g., an invention), or who were involved in pursuit of some long-term goal (e.g., a career), the attainment of which would represent a substantial accomplishment. In all cases, the characters of achievement-oriented stories were concerned about "success" in some enterprise. The particular categories of imaginative response which significantly differentiated Relaxed and Achievement-Oriented conditions in these various plots were accepted as *symptoms* of achievement motivation. A single score was then obtained for each subject in the various experimental conditions by counting the frequency of these symptomatic, achievement-related responses in all of the stories which the person had written. This over-all score for an individual has been called the "need for achievement score" or, following the form of abbreviation which Murray had earlier introduced, *the n Achievement score.*

The general result of these initial experiments is summarized in Table 8.4, which shows the mean or

TABLE 8.4

The effect of experimental conditions preceding the writing of thematic apperceptive stories on the mean *n* Achievement score (From McClelland, Atkinson, Clark, and Lowell, *The Achievement Motive*, copyright 1953, Appleton-Century-Crofts, Inc., p. 184)

| Condition | N | Mean | SD |
|---|---|---|---|
| Relaxed | 39 | 1.95 | 4.30 |
| Neutral | 39 | 7.33 | 5.49 |
| Achievement-Oriented | 39 | 8.77 | 5.31 |
| Success | 21 | 7.92 | 6.76 |
| Failure | 39 | 10.10 | 6.17 |
| Success-Failure | 39 | 10.36 | 5.67 |

average *n* Achievement score obtained by subjects in each of the experimental conditions. It is clear that the intensified state of motivation which is generally assumed to follow experimental procedures that are variously called "ego-involving" or "achievement-orienting" or "threat of failure" or "failure-stress," etc., produces significantly higher thematic apperceptive *n* Achievement scores than a Relaxed control condition. It is also evident that failure in achievement-oriented test performance produces higher average *n* Achievement scores than achievement-oriented test performance without explicit knowledge of results (Achievement Orientation) or achievement-oriented performance followed by success.

The major result, which shows that achievement-related imaginative responses provide a measure of the heightened state of motivation produced by achievement-orienting instructions, has been replicated in a number of other studies with male college students (e.g., Lowell, 1950; Martire, 1956; O'Connor, 1960; Haber and Alpert, 1958), with Air Force men using a somewhat different form of apperception test (French, 1955), with high school boys (Veroff, 1953; Ricciuti, Clark, and Sadacca, 1954), with 9th-grade Navaho boys (Lowell, 1950), with Brazilian men and women (Angelini, 1955), and with Japanese men and women (Hayashi and Habu, 1962).

Early studies with female college and high school students (Veroff *et al.*, 1953) did not show evidence of an experimentally produced increase in *n* Achievement score following Achievement Orientation using the coding system developed on men because the average score for female subjects was found to be already very high under Relaxed conditions. More recently, however, Lesser, Krawitz, and Packard (1963) and French and Lesser (1964) have begun to clarify the meaning of this result through experimental analysis guided in part by Margaret Mead's (1949) conception of special problems arising in connection with "striving for achievement" among American women. Because this special problem involved in use of the thematic apperceptive measure of *n* Achievement with women is still not completely resolved, most systematic studies of the effect of individual differences in strength of inferred achievement motive on performance, which we shall consider shortly, have employed male subjects.

SIMILAR STUDIES OF OTHER
MOTIVATIONAL TENDENCIES

The basic logic and design of the studies of hunger and achievement motivation have been applied to other kinds of motivation. Studies of the effects of experimental arousal of *n* Affiliation on thematic apperception (Shipley and Veroff, 1953; Atkinson, Heyns, and Veroff, 1954) have produced a scoring system which yields a *n Affiliation score*. In these studies, stories written under relaxed conditions were compared with stories written by college fraternity brothers immediately following a half-hour period in which they made sociometric ratings of one another in a group setting. This pretest period was explicitly designed to heighten their concern over how likable or acceptable they were to other persons. Compared to the control condition, the plots of stories in this experimentally-aroused condition significantly more often showed *concern over establishing, maintaining, and restoring positive relations with others*. Subjects whose thematic apperceptive *n* Affiliation scores were high were significantly more often described in ratings by the men who knew them well as *approval seekers* than were subjects whose *n* Affiliation scores were low. The tendency assessed through analysis of the imaginative content of stories they had written was obviously one that is apparent to others who had often observed their overt behavior.

Veroff (1957) has developed a scoring system for *n Power* which he defines as *concern over controlling the means of influencing the behavior of another person*. He found more imaginative responses of this kind in stories written by college students who were running for important student offices on the night of the election and at the place where ballots were being counted than in a relaxed control group. Veroff also found that students having high *n* Power scores were more frequently rated, by college instructors who had observed them in the classroom,

as *argumentative* and as displaying behavior described as *trying to convince others* than were students having low *n* Power scores.

Feshbach (1956) found that thematic apperceptive stories written immediately after a group of college students had been insulted (by design) contained significantly more aggressive content than stories written by a control group.

Walker and Atkinson et al. (1958) found that the strength of fear-related motivation expressed in thematic apperceptive stories by soldiers was related to their proximity to an atomic explosion, as might have been predicted from Miller's conception of how a fear gradient is related to distance from the noxious event. Different groups of soldiers were tested before they knew they would participate in an atomic maneuver at a place distant from the place of the bomb test; ten hours before the explosion at the locus of the bomb test after having participated in a rehearsal of the maneuver; approximately 15 minutes after the actual explosion of an atomic bomb while in trenches several thousand yards from the point of detonation with the atomic cloud boiling upward overhead; back at camp ten hours after the explosion; and two weeks later when they were back at their regular army post. The frequency of imaginative stories in which some external condition posed a threat to the physical welfare of a person, and elaborations of this central theme, were significantly more frequent when in close proximity to the explosion than either long before or long after the blast.

A STUDY OF SEXUAL MOTIVATION

One of the most interesting and significant set of experiments of the effects of experimentally aroused motivation on thematic apperception was conducted by Russell Clark (1952, 1955, 1956). He turned to the kind of motivation which Freud had treated most fully in laying the foundation for *indirect* methods, viz., sexual motivation. Clark aroused sexual motivation in a group of college men by presenting them with the task of evaluating the potentially attractive qualities in a series of pictures of nude females. His intention of provoking a mild sexual arousal was disguised by instructions which related the task to a theory concerning body type and certain physical and mental disorders. Immediately following this experience, another investigator had the men write stories in response to a set of pictures similar to those employed in other studies. Special measures were taken to encourage the view that the two tasks were parts of separate investigations. A control group in this experiment was asked to evaluate the aesthetic qualities of various landscape scenes in the period immediately preceding the writing of imaginative stories. Both groups were tested in a classroom setting.

Clark found that the sexually aroused group expressed significantly *less* manifest sexual content in their stories than the control group. This suggested that the aroused group was inhibiting sexuality because of anxiety or guilt. So a similar experiment was conducted in the context of a fraternity beer party, on the assumption that alcohol would reduce anxiety as Conger (1951) had demonstrated in studies of approach-avoidance conflict with animals. After the beer party was about an hour old, the pictures of nude females were exposed by a cohort of the experimenter who belonged to the fraternity. This was done to disassociate the experience and a "test of creative imagination" which was administered immediately afterward, presumably to determine effects of an informal environment and alcohol on imagination. Another fraternity beer party, but without prior exposure of any kind of pictures, was the control condition in this experiment. Clark found, as expected, that under the influence of alcohol the sexually aroused group produced *more* manifest content related to sexuality in their stories than did the control group.

A further analysis of the content of stories was made in terms of the categories of sexual symbolism which Freud had advanced in his classic work on interpretation of dreams. It was found that the group which had been sexually aroused in the classroom, but had apparently inhibited *manifest* expressions of sexuality produced significantly more sexual symbolism or *latent* sexual content than the control group which had viewed the landscape scenes. In other words, the arousal of sexual motivation *and* anxiety about its expression produced significantly less manifest sexual content but more latent sexual content than a control condition. But under the influence of alcohol, which apparently reduced anxiety and approach-avoidance conflict at the time of writing stories, the sexually aroused group produced more manifest sexual content in thematic apperceptive stories than a non-aroused group.

GENERAL IMPLICATIONS

Together, these initial studies of the effects on thematic apperception of experimentally induced motivation (Hunger, *n* Achievement, *n* Affiliation,

*n* Power, Aggression, Fear, and Sexual motivation), and similar studies which have since been undertaken, represent a substantial fund of experimental evidence that the content of imaginative behavior is sensitive to motivational influences. However, considerably more research of this kind, showing the specific effects of particular experimentally induced motivational states, is needed to sharpen and refine the inferences to be made about the strength of particular motivational dispositions from the content of imaginative behavior. Many of the unsettled problems arising in these and similar studies are discussed in *Motives in Fantasy, Action, and Society* (Atkinson, 1958), which reviews the progress made in the first decade of work in this experimental approach to human motivation.

As background for a review of studies concerned with how individual differences in strength of achievement motive affect performance, we consider conclusions reached by McClelland *et al.* (1949) in their first analysis of the effects of experimental arousal of achievement motivation on thematic apperception. These were general conclusions concerning the nature of motivation and the potentialities of this new method of study:

"*Nature of Motivation.* One of the most important implications of this experiment is suggested by a consideration of the categories which shifted in frequency when the need was presumably aroused. Most, if not all of them, appear to have a future reference—for instance, the stated wish for achievement, successful instrumental activity, anticipatory goal responses, and positive affect at the end of the story. On the other hand categories did not change which seemed to involve more of an objective description of the situation . . . without the striving or anticipatory dimension. This . . . suggests that it is one of the major characteristics of motivation—at least achievement motivation—to be anticipatory or forward looking. This might seem to be a somewhat radical departure from the usual conception of a motive as a persisting deficit stimulus, but oddly enough Hull (1931), working from entirely different data, has come to much the same conclusion—namely, that fractional anticipatory goal responses are the key to understanding purposeful and motivational phenomena. In fact, one can argue that the anticipatory goal responses observed in this experiment supply a kind of direct confirmation of Hull's view which has been very difficult to obtain with animals.

"*Methodological considerations.* Last but not least these results have an important bearing on the experimental methodology of handling verbal material. They report a method for scoring written thematic apperception stories which is sensitive enough to distinguish between the conditions under which the stories are written, which is objective enough to yield high agreement on a repeat scoring by two trained judges working together, and which is easy enough to apply quickly to an individual record. This in itself is of considerable importance in a field in which prior scoring systems have either been so complex or so dependent on clinical insight . . . that they are of little use to the experimental psychologist interested in studying imaginative processes.

"The potential value to psychological theory of an objective scoring method for free verbal behavior is illustrated by the fact that its application in this experiment clearly indicates that phantasy does not always serve the purpose of wish-fulfillment or substitute gratification for pleasures denied in reality, an assumption which has been rather frequently made. . . . Instead, a study of the variety of story characteristics which shifted in this experiment with an increase in need supports the parsimonious assumption that imaginative behavior is governed by the same general principles as govern any behavior. For example, a variety of experiments show the same increase in instrumental activity with increased drive at the gross motor level; others, as in the standard Pavlovian conditioning, show the same increase in anticipatory goal responses (salivation). If one grants that the principles governing imaginative behavior are no different from those governing performance when both are analyzed according to the same categories of response, then the method used here becomes a more subtle and flexible approach to the establishment and extension of those principles than the ordinary method of studying performance. Thus, for example, it would be difficult to get a performance response which would correspond to the anticipation of deprivation which follows drive arousal at the imaginative level. One might even go so far as to suggest that by the use of this method Tolman could study much more directly the 'cognitive maps' which the behavior of his rats has led him to infer are the important intervening variables in determining behavior . . ." (McClelland *et al.*, 1949, pp. 253–254).

USE OF THEMATIC APPERCEPTION TO ASSESS INDIVIDUAL DIFFERENCES IN MOTIVATION

Following these demonstrations of the sensitivity of thematic apperceptive content to experimentally induced motivation, many studies have been conducted employing the test of *n* Achievement and some employing the test of *n* Affiliation *to discover* how individual differences in these tendencies are related to other behavior. A good many of these studies seek to discover what kind of person is highly motivated to achieve or strongly motivated to affiliate. They contribute to the fund of empirical knowledge concerning the correlates of High versus Low *n* Achievement or *n* Affiliation scores and provide some basis for constructing a descriptive picture of the person who is strong in one or another of these tendencies. Other studies have attempted to employ the test of individual differences in *n* Achievement in the context of important practical problems like that of attempting to predict academic performance. Here, the strategy of research is much like that employed in the use of many other tests of interests and attitudes. But still other studies have employed thematic apperceptive measures of *n* Achievement and *n* Affiliation as tools in the effort to construct a workable conception of human motivation. They have been concerned with the problem of explaining the direction, vigor, and persistence of purposive behavior in particular situations. These studies share the basic theoretical orientation that is also apparent in much of the work using the Manifest Anxiety Scale and the Test Anxiety Scale, but the underlying strategy is different. Instead of using assessments of individual differences in human motivation in research that is designed to test specific hypotheses derived from a theory evolved in research with lower animals, these studies have employed the experimentally validated measures of *n* Achievement and *n* Affiliation as a new basis for constructing a theoretical conception of motivation. That is, the new measuring instrument has been systematically employed in combination with experimental procedures but without prior commitment to a particular conceptual scheme, as a means of providing a factual foundation for theoretical inferences about human motivation. *These studies constitute a fresh beginning in the task of clarifying the process of motivation in the human adult—broadly conceived as the invention of a useful conception of the variables to be taken into account and statement of a principle to show how they combine to influence purposive behavior*.

It is to these theoretically oriented studies of *n* Achievement, and the conception of motivation which has evolved in them, that we shall direct attention. Theoretical inferences have been based mainly on: (a) analysis of the various factors which influence the *n* Achievement score obtained from content analysis of imaginative stories; and (b) the relation of individual differences in thematic apperceptive *n* Achievement scores to performance under various experimental conditions. We shall review the two kinds of factual evidence and the concepts suggested. Then, in the next chapter, we shall turn to a formal statement of the theory of achievement motivation which currently guides research.

We have already reviewed evidence which shows that the average *n* Achievement score obtained from groups of subjects is systematically influenced by instructions, pressures, and other *cues of the immediate situation*. How is this situational effect on strength of motivation to achieve (as it is expressed in thematic apperceptive stories) to be conceptualized? That is the first question to hold in mind as we review the other factors which influence the magnitude of the *n* Achievement score.

Early investigations of the effects of particular pictures showed that those which contained obvious achievement-related cues (e.g., two men at work in a machine shop; a man at a desk in an office; etc.) elicited stories containing significantly more achievement-related imaginative responses than pictures without such obvious achievement-related cues (e.g., the heads of two men; two men standing in a well-furnished room gesturing, as if in conversation; etc.). Detailed analysis of the relationship between judgmental ratings of pictures and the *n* Achievement score obtained from imaginative stories about the pictures justifies the conclusion that seeing the pictorial situation as one in which "success" can be attained is one of the factors which influences the *n* Achievement score, but certainly not the only one (Haber-Alpert, 1958; Birney, 1958; Jacobs, 1958). How is this effect on the *n* Achievement score of the *cues contained in pictures* to be conceptualized?

Other factors like the location of the story in a sequence of stories, the length of the protocol, the sex of the subject, and the liberality or conservatism of judges who can otherwise agree .90 in rank-ordering subjects on *n* Achievement scores all have systematic effects on the magnitude of the *n* Achievement score (McClelland *et al.*, 1953; Atkinson, 1958). *But when all these factors are controlled, there remain individual differences that are more general than the specific effects of pictures and situations.*

Holding all other factors constant, persons who score High in *n* Achievement in response to one kind of picture or one set of pictures also score High in response to another kind of picture or another set of pictures. This is shown in Figure 8.9, taken from a study that was explicitly designed to investigate the effects of particular pictures while controlling for the effects of other factors. The figure shows that

persons who have High total *n* Achievement scores obtained from all the other pictures in a set tend, also, to have higher scores on specific pictures which vary greatly in the kinds of situations they portray. In other words, individual differences in total *n* Achievement score obtained from a set of pictures refer to something more general than reactions to specific picture cues.

A study by Winterbottom (1958; McClelland *et al.*, 1953, p. 297) showed that the mothers of 10-year-old boys who had High total *n* Achievement scores placed greater emphasis on early training in mastery and independent accomplishment and offered greater rewards for accomplishment than the mothers of boys who had Low *n* Achievement scores. This finding suggested that individual differences in *n* Achievement score (when all other factors are held constant) might represent differences in the strength of *a relatively general and stable disposition to achieve* that is acquired early in life. How can such a relatively general and stable disposition be conceptualized in a theory of motivation? What should it be called?

Other studies have held constant the pictures or equivalent stimuli employed to evoke imaginative stories on two separate occasions from the *same* subjects under relatively relaxed and achievement-oriented conditions. They have shown that persons who score High (above the median score) under relaxed conditions also score significantly higher under *achievement-oriented* conditions than persons who score Low (below the median) in the relaxed condition (Lowell in McClelland *et al.*, 1953, pp. 161, 191–194; French, 1955; Haber and Alpert, 1958). In other words, the average *n* Achievement score of a group of subjects may increase significantly, as it did in these and earlier studies, as the lifelike situation in which the person finds himself becomes more explicitly achievement-oriented, but those who tend to have High scores in one situation also tend to have High scores in another, significantly different, situation. Again we ask, how are relatively general and *stable* individual differences in disposition to achieve to be conceived in a theory of motivation which must, at the same time, take account of immediate and specific environmental influences on the strength of tendency to achieve that is aroused in a person at a particular time?

These and other studies of the measuring instrument itself are consistent with the guiding principle advanced earlier by Lewin, $B = f(P,E)$. That is, they suggest that the frequency of imaginative responses about achieving (*B*), which is called *n* Achievement score, is jointly determined by some relatively stable and general characteristic of the person (*P*) and by more immediate and specific environmental influences (*E*). When immediate environmental influences (*E*), viz., conditions at the time of the test and the set of pictures employed, are held constant, then variation in the magnitude of achievement response (*B*) allows the inference of individual differences in personality (*P*). On the other hand, when *P* is held constant, as when the same subjects or random samples from the same group of subjects are studied, then variation in the magnitude of average achievement response (*B*) allows inference concerning environmental influences (*E*).

THE ACHIEVEMENT MOTIVE AND PERFORMANCE

Studies of the effect of individual differences in the strength of the disposition to achieve, which has arbitrarily been called *the achievement motive*, on overt instrumental achievement-oriented performance yield the same general picture. The strength of

the tendency to achieve that is expressed in performance of a particular task in a particular situation appears to be jointly determined by the personality disposition (achievement motive) and by immediate environmental influences. We shall review some of the studies that have helped to clarify the nature of this interaction between personality and immediate environment in the determination of achievement-oriented performance.

Initial interest in studies of the effects of individual differences in strength of achievement motive on performance was directed to finding out whether or not the thematic apperceptive measuring instrument, which was demonstrably sensitive to situational influences on motivation, could be usefully employed to assess individual differences in the strength of the tendency that is expressed overtly in actual performance of achievement-oriented activities. The question of initial interest was: Would individual differences in *n* Achievement score obtained by individuals in the same situation and in response to the same set of pictures predict differ-

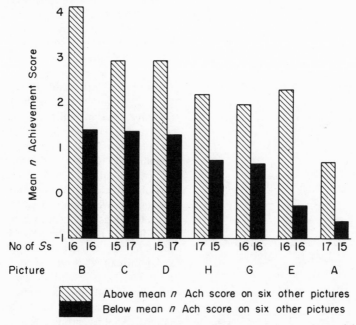

FIGURE 8.9  Graphic presentation of the average *n* Achievement scores obtained from stories to each of seven different pictures by persons who scored High (above the mean) or Low (below the mean) on six other pictures combined. The content of the pictures varied: A contained the heads of two men; B and C each showed two men working in a shop; D was a business office scene; E showed two men talking in a well-furnished room; G was a boy with a vague surgical mural in the background; H a boy seated at his desk in school. (Adapted from McClelland, Atkinson, Clark, and Lowell, The Achievement Motive, copyright 1953, Appleton-Century-Crofts, Inc., p. 190)

ences in the level of performance in another achievement-test situation?

The first study to present unambiguous evidence that the measure of *n* Achievement acted like a valid measure of individual differences in strength of motive to achieve was conducted by Lowell (1952). He found that persons having High *n* Achievement scores (above the median) showed a higher level of performance on both an arithmetic and a verbal task than persons having Low *n* Achievement scores. (See Figure 8.10.)

After several demonstrations of this kind, which

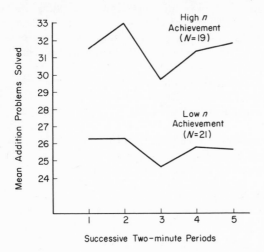

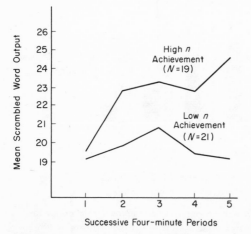

FIGURE 8.10   Mean output of addition problems solved in successive two-minute periods, and mean output of scrambled words in successive four-minute periods for subjects above and below the mean in *n* Achievement (*From a study by Lowell reported by McClelland, 1951, pp. 198–199*)

are reviewed in *The Achievement Motive* (McClelland *et al.*, 1953), questions of greater theoretical interest were raised. Did a High *n* Achievement score imply that a person was *chronically* motivated to perform well no matter what the task and situation at the time of performance? Or were *n* Achievement scores to be taken as measures of individual differences in a disposition which would be overtly expressed only under certain conditions? If so, what was the nature of the conditions which would activate or arouse the achievement motive? These questions called for an experimental design in which the performance of persons having High and Low *n* Achievement scores would be measured under various experimental conditions. The first of these, a study of the relation of *n* Achievement scores to the Zeigarnik effect (Atkinson, 1953), provided a set of guiding hypotheses for subsequent studies. We shall therefore consider the results of that experiment in some detail and then review findings of subsequent studies which provided additional clues needed to arrive at a more complete theory of achievement motivation.

According to Lewin, the magnitude of Zeigarnik effect following interruption of a task before it is completed should provide a sensitive measure of the strength of tendency to complete the task. (See pp. 83–87.) Zeigarnik had presented some evidence that persons who appeared "ambitious" recall interrupted tasks more readily than persons who display little interest in the tasks at the time of performance. So three experimental conditions were designed to vary the likelihood that subjects would perceive completion of tasks as evidence of personal accomplishment (or success) and incompletion as evidence of personal failure. This was accomplished by three sets of instructions. One group of subjects was given instructions which minimized the importance of the tasks by *not* asking them to sign their names and by referring to tasks as "in an early stage of development for use in later research." The experimenter was informally dressed and conducted himself in an informal manner, ending his instruction with a friendly appeal for cooperation so that he could learn something about the "tasks" (Relaxed Orientation). Another group of subjects was given no preliminary instructions which would either emphasize or de-emphasize the importance of the tasks. They were merely told how to perform them (Task Orientation). A third group of subjects was given a preliminary instruction which created the impression that the tasks were "tests" of highly valued attributes (e.g., intelligence) and that the scores achieved would be taken as the full measure of each person's ability (Achievement Orientation). In this condition, the experimenter was introduced formally, was dressed formally, and conducted himself like a person proctoring an examination. That is, he kept track of time and reminded the subjects to change tasks rapidly, etc., in order to reinforce the impression that the "tests" were important.

Following these different instructions, each subject was given a booklet containing 20 different tasks. He was given 75 seconds to complete each task. By prior arrangement, half the tasks in each booklet were too long to be finished in that amount of time. And the booklets were constructed and distributed so that each subject would find himself still working at certain tasks while others near him had already finished. This heightened the competitive atmosphere and accentuated success and failure in the Achievement-oriented condition.

In the analysis of results, subjects were divided into High (above the median) and Low (below the median) $n$ Achievement groups in terms of scores obtained from stories they wrote in the interval between performance on the last of the 20 tasks and an informal request for recall at the end of the experimental session.

There were no differences between High and Low $n$ Achievement groups in recall of completed tasks, but there were substantial differences in magnitude of Zeigarnik effect due entirely to differences in recall of interrupted tasks. Therefore we may consider the recall of interrupted tasks as an index of the strength of the tendency to complete the tasks that had been aroused in various groups of subjects.

Let us consider first the results for subjects classified High in $n$ Achievement as shown in Figure 8.11. There is a significant increase in recall of interrupted tasks (and Zeigarnik effect) as the instructions and other situational cues increase the likelihood that subjects will perceive completion as evidence of personal success and incompletion as evidence of personal failure. In other words, the strength of the tendency to achieve at these particular tasks was significantly greater among persons having comparably High $n$ Achievement scores when cues in the instructions and other features of the situation led them *to expect* that performance would be evaluated in terms of a standard of excellence than when situational cues made it patently clear that their performance would not be evaluated.

The behavior of subjects having High $n$ Achievement scores was comparable, in one respect, to the

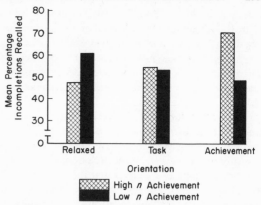

FIGURE 8.11   Mean percentage recall of interrupted tasks by subjects with high and low $n$ Achievement scores under three types of instructional orientation (*From McClelland, Atkinson, Clark, and Lowell, The Achievement Motive, copyright 1953, Appleton-Century-Crofts, Inc., p. 266*)

behavior of the animals in the classic studies of latent learning described on p. 139. We recall that hungry animals ran the maze slowly and made many errors until a food reward was introduced in the goal box. Then, on the next trial, when they had what Tolman called an *expectancy* that food was to be reached as a consequence of performing certain actions, they ran through the maze rapidly and with few errors. Similarly, persons having High $n$ Achievement scores displayed little evidence of having worked hard to complete the tasks when there was no expectancy that performance would lead to feelings of success (Relaxed Orientation). But when instructions did arouse an expectancy that performance would lead on to feelings of pride in accomplishment, which apparently is the goal of a person highly motivated to achieve, then they did work hard and were concerned about completing the tasks (Achievement Orientation). This, at least, is what we normally infer, following Lewin's arguments, from a substantial increase in recall of interrupted tasks.

It thus appeared that the arousal of a tendency to approach success should be conceived as jointly determined by a disposition called the *achievement motive* (as inferred from relatively High thematic apperceptive $n$ Achievement score in a given condition) and an *expectancy* that certain actions will lead to success (to be inferred from the nature of instructions and other situational cues at the time of performance).

The differences between High and Low $n$ Achievement groups in the Task-oriented and Achievement-oriented conditions (see Figure 8.11) were consistent with this theoretical interpretation. Given the ambiguity about possible consequences of performing the tasks that was inherent in the task-orienting instructions, which did no more than explain how the tasks were to be done, there is no evidence of a difference between groups assumed to differ in strength of achievement motive because the expectancy that performance will lead on to "feelings of success" has not been systematically aroused in all the subjects. However, in the Achievement-oriented condition it may be assumed that the expectancy of the goal (success) was systematically aroused in all subjects. Hence the group strong in achievement motive should be more strongly motivated to complete the tasks than the group weak in achievement motive. The significant difference in recall of interrupted tasks in the Achievement-oriented condition was consistent with these assumptions. But this budding theoretical conception failed to explain two other important details in Figure 8.11: (a) the trend in recall of interrupted tasks for the Low *n* Achievement group, from Relaxed Orientation to Achievement Orientation, implies a *decrease* in motivation to complete the tasks rather than a small increase, which the conception outlined above would predict; and (b) the Low *n* Achievement group recalled somewhat more interrupted tasks than the High *n* Achievement group under Relaxed Orientation. Why?

Two further hypotheses were advanced to account for these details. First, it was assumed that any situation which holds forth the promise of success must necessarily also present a threat of failure. Thus as instructions increase the likelihood that performance will be evaluated, there must be an increase in threat of failure, that is, an increase in expectancy of possible failure. If so, a decreasing tendency to recall interrupted tasks might mean, as Rosenzweig (1943) had suggested, increased repression of failures when there is sufficient anxiety about failing. The obtained result would make sense if persons having Low *n* Achievement scores were motivated by an *unmeasured* disposition to avoid failure, that is, a disposition to be anxious about failure. This possibility was first proposed by McClelland and Liberman (1949) in a study which showed evidence of perceptual defense in recognition of words connoting failure among persons having relatively Low *n* Achievement scores. And Brown (1952) had also found it plausible to interpret results which showed greater rigidity in problem-solving among persons

Low in *n* Achievement as evidence of their greater anxiety about failure.

But why did the Low *n* Achievement group recall more interrupted tasks than the High *n* Achievement group under Relaxed orientation? This result suggested that they were *then* more strongly motivated to complete the tasks than the High *n* Achievement group, but apparently not anxious about failure. That they should not be anxious about failure in a relaxed condition is plausible; but why should they appear to be more motivated to complete the tasks than subjects scoring High in *n* Achievement in this condition?

It is worthwhile, at this point, to call attention to one of the implicit assumptions in studies of the effects of individual differences in motivation. In this type of study, whether the test employed to provide an independent measure of individual differences measures Manifest Anxiety, Test Anxiety, *n* Achievement, or what not, it is quite generally assumed that groups which differ in the strength of the particular tendency which has been measured are alike in all other respects. Research is difficult without making some such assumption. But it is necessary to recognize that the assumption may not always be correct. Zeigarnik, for example, had proposed that in addition to personal ambition, a feeling of obligation to the experimenter and intrinsic interest in the tasks are often sufficient motives to complete experimental tasks. So in his initial discussion of the problem posed by greater recall of interrupted tasks under relaxed conditions by persons scoring Low in *n* Achievement, the writer (Atkinson, 1953) proposed that they might have been more motivated to comply with the experimenter's appeal for cooperation than persons who score High in *n* Achievement.

The question raised by this *post hoc* suggestion is more important than its possible validity as an interpretation of a trend in this particular experiment: *Why do human subjects perform experimental tasks at all when the investigator minimizes their importance and significance?* Subsequent experiments have shown that *n* Affiliation scores obtained from tests of imaginative behavior are positively correlated with measures of performance under "non-egoinvolving," relaxed conditions such as the one employed in this study of Zeigarnik effect (French, 1955; Atkinson and Raphelson, 1956). This strongly suggests that expectancy of social approval for complying with instructions is aroused by an appeal for cooperation in the kind of relaxed control conditions that are often employed in studies of human motivation. But no evidence obtained to date suggests that *n* Affiliation generally tends to be stronger among persons who are Low in *n* Achievement, although that might have been the case in the recall experiment. The suggestion advanced to explain greater recall of interrupted tasks by persons Low in *n* Achievement under relaxed conditions is more important as a reminder that the assumption of *all other things equal* may sometimes be incorrect than it is an adequate explanation of the result.

ADOPTION OF TOLMAN'S CONCEPT OF EXPECTANCY

The adoption of Tolman's concept of *expectancy of the goal* to represent the effect on the person of immediate situational cues seemed a fruitful step because it also allowed a meaningful interpretation of the influence of picture cues and situational cues on the imaginative behavior which provides the measure of achievement motive. Holding people (and hence *average* strength of motive) constant, the significant difference between average TAT *n* Achievement scores under Relaxed and Achievement-oriented conditions can be attributed to systematically stronger expectancy of the relevant goal under Achievement-oriented conditions. Similarly, the effects of picture cues on the *n* Achievement score can be meaningfully attributed to various strengths of expectancy, learned in life-like situations similar to those portrayed in the pictures, that performance will be evaluated (Atkinson, 1958, Chapter 42).

The guiding hypothesis, adapted from Tolman's principle of performance because it seemed to fit the data, was: "the goal-directed action tendency is a joint function of the strength of the motive and of the expectancy aroused by situation cues that performance is instrumental to attainment of the goal of the motive" (Atkinson and Reitman, 1956). The general design of experiments which tested this hypothesis required: (a) assessment of either *n* Achievement or *n* Affiliation by the thematic apperceptive method under Neutral conditions (i.e., when no experimental procedure is employed to heighten or weaken motivation prior to the writing of stories); and (b) measurement of performance under different kinds of experimental conditions on some other occasion. Often the two phases of an experiment are separated by a period of several months. Hence a positive relationship between *n* Achievement scores or *n* Affiliation scores and performance over this time period constitutes evi-

dence of the relative stability of the dispositions called achievement motive and affiliative motive.

A number of studies showed a positive relationship between performance and *n* Achievement scores when the cues of the performance situation were such that it could reasonably be inferred that the expectancy that performance would lead to a feeling of accomplishment had been aroused (Lowell, 1952; Atkinson, 1953; French, 1955; Atkinson and Raphelson, 1956; Wendt, 1955). On the other hand, when cues at the time of performance were deliberately manipulated so that subjects were given no reason to expect that they would experience pride in accomplishment, there was no positive relationship between performance and *n* Achievement scores (Atkinson, 1953; Atkinson and Raphelson, 1956; French, 1955). On two occasions (Atkinson and Raphelson, 1956; French, 1955), an explicit appeal for cooperation in situations not related to achievement had apparently served to produce an expectancy of social approval for working hard. In these studies, performance was unrelated to *n* Achievement, but positively related to *n* Affiliation. And French (1955) found that when an incentive unrelated to either *n* Achievement or *n* Affiliation was offered, no systematic relationship was found between performance and either of those two motives, assessed earlier under neutral conditions. The "unrelated" incentive was an opportunity offered to men in the armed service to go back to their barracks for an hour of rest as soon as they had completed the experimental task.

With this as background, Atkinson and Reitman (1956) tested another implication of the general conception of motivation of performance that was beginning to emerge. If more than one of an individual's motives are aroused by expectancies that the same act will lead to several different goals, the total strength of the tendency to perform a task should be equivalent to a summation of the different tendencies that have been aroused. In this case, the person who is weak in the motive the experimenter may have measured (e.g., *n* Achievement) may be strong in other unmeasured (ulterior) motives that are also engaged in performance of the same act. Since an action tendency that is influenced by several different motives is likely to be very strong, and since there is also likely to be an upper limit on the speed with which one can perform a task, the effect of arousing the expectancy of achievement but also of systematically arousing expectancies that other goals can be attained should be to reduce or to wash out completely the relationship between $n$ Achievement scores and performance.

These investigators followed a lead suggested in an earlier study by Wendt (1955). He had found a more substantial difference between the performance of High and Low $n$ Achievement groups when a group of subjects were left alone to work following achievement-oriented instructions than when the experimenter proctored the group test and also paced performance by keeping time, etc. So they attempted to create one experimental condition to arouse expectancy of achievement, but few if any other expectancies concerning immediate consequences of performance, and another experimental condition to arouse expectancy of achievement and also expectancies of attaining other goals through performance.

The first condition, Achievement Orientation, consisted of putting a subject into a small room all by himself following achievement-orienting instructions. The experimenter unobtrusively started a stopwatch in his pocket as he left the experimental room. Then he returned and stopped the subject exactly 14 minutes later.

The second condition, called a Multi-Incentive condition, included the same achievement-orienting instruction but it was given to subjects as a group in a classroom. Then added to the achievement-orienting instruction was the offer of a $5.00 prize for the best performance and some play-acting by the two investigators to convey the idea that they seriously disapproved any lack of attention to the tasks. They paced performance in this group test situation by calling out "skip" and having subjects skip the particular problem they were working on at the end of each minute. In addition, they walked about the room and looked directly at individual subjects, or over their shoulders, as if to show disapproval of any lack of serious effort to work at the task. The time allowed for performance, 14 minutes, was the same as for the other condition when subjects worked alone. The results are shown in Table 8.5.

Given achievement-orienting instructions and left alone to work, subjects who were High in $n$ Achievement performed significantly more arithmetic problems than subjects who were Low in $n$ Achievement. But in the Multi-Incentive condition, there was no difference between the High and Low $n$ Achievement groups. The fact that the pacing procedure forced subjects to skip about 13 problems they might have partially solved probably accounts for the decrement in performance of the High $n$ Achievement group in the Multi-Incentive condition. At least there was no way of ascertaining in this experiment whether this was responsible for the drop in performance or whether too intense motivation produces a decrement in problem-solving.

Other evidence obtained in this study showed that the biggest gain between the "working alone" and Multi-Incentive condition was made by subjects classified Low in $n$ Achievement but High in $n$ Affiliation. The affiliative motive did not by itself relate significantly to performance level in either

TABLE 8.5

Effect of individual differences in strength of achievement motive on arithmetic performance under Achievement Orientation and when there are additional incentives for performance (Multi-Incentive condition) (After Atkinson and Reitman, 1956, p. 363)

| Achievement Motive | Condition | | | | | |
|---|---|---|---|---|---|---|
| | Achievement Orientation | | | Multi-Incentive | | |
| | $N$ | Attempted solutions | Correct solutions | $N$ | Attempted solutions | Correct solutions |
| High | 21 | M 78.1 | 71.6 | 24 | M 67.1 | 60.3 |
| | | $\sigma$ 24.8 | 24.1 | | $\sigma$ 19.6 | 19.3 |
| Low | 30 | M 60.3 | 55.5 | 21 | M 69.1 | 60.1 |
| | | $\sigma$ 15.7 | 16.4 | | $\sigma$ 22.3 | 23.0 |
| Difference (H-L) | | 17.8 | 16.1 | | −2.0 | .2 |
| $\sigma$ difference | | 5.93* | 5.96 | | 6.23 | 6.26 |
| $t$ | | 3.00 | 2.70 | | n.s. | n.s. |
| $p$ | | .01 | .01 | | | |

* $\sigma$ diffs. derived from estimate of within group variance, $df = 92$.

condition, nor should it if the "ideal" condition for showing a positive relationship between strength of one particular motive and performance is a situation which arouses the expectancy that the goal of that motive, and no other, can be attained through performance of certain actions. But the trend of the relationship was negative when subjects worked alone under achievement orientation and positive in the Multi-Incentive condition.

INCONSISTENCIES IN STUDIES OF
ACHIEVEMENT-ORIENTED PERFORMANCE

The results obtained in some of these experiments of *n* Achievement and performance have not always been consistently replicated by other investigators who have tried to control expectancies regarding the consequences of performance by one means or another. The reasons for this are not yet fully understood. One of the inherent difficulties in studies of human motivation is to replicate the experimental conditions. Reitman (1960), for example, seriously attempted to get better control of situational cues which motivate a subject's performance by restricting the experimental manipulation to printed instructions which the subject read before performing a task. This procedure was only partially successful in producing the predicted relationship between *n* Achievement scores and performance under certain conditions and not others without play-acting on the part of the experimenter. More striking were results which did not correspond to predictions which suggest that more than printed instructions are needed to create lifelike experimental situations which effectively engage the basic motivating dispositions of a person.

Some investigators have paid less than the required amount of attention to certain problems which are inherent in the use of the sensitive thematic apperceptive method to assess differences in motivation, particularly the matter of always attaining expert proficiency in the method of content analysis of imaginative stories before proceeding to more elaborate experiments and tests. It took several years to clarify and refine the method of analysis so that persons unfamiliar with it could learn, with about 12 hours of practice using scoring manuals and precoded materials, to score stories and produce *n* Achievement and *n* Affiliation scores which correlate .90 or better with scores obtained from the same stories by those already well-trained in the method. Feld and Smith (1958), who designed and tested self-training manuals for analysis of the achievement-, affiliative-, and power-related content of thematic apperceptive stories, found that the median scoring reliability in published studies of *n* Achievement through 1958 was .89. This is an encouraging sign of the objectivity attained in the use of the method. Yet it suggests that the validity of *n* Achievement scores in some studies, when coding reliability slips into the .70's or is not even reported, is very questionable.

A recent study by Smith (1961) has suggested that the assumption that High and Low *n* Achievement groups are equivalent in strength of all other motives that might influence performance in a particular experimental condition may often be unjustified. He studied the relation of *n* Achievement scores obtained under neutral conditions to performance in a variety of experimental conditions. Then, after performance, he employed a self-report rating scale to assess the subjects' reasons for either working hard or not at the tasks. He found that the relative difference between performance of High and Low *n* Achievement groups in various experimental conditions was significantly related to the extent to which expectancy of achievement was the dominant "reason" reported by *S*s for working hard in the various experimental conditions. But the absolute difference between level of performance of High and Low *n* Achievement groups sometimes favored the Low *n* Achievement group. Given the assumptions that level of performance is determined by *total* strength of tendency to perform a task, and that total strength of tendency is a function of achievement motivation *plus* other extrinsic sources of motivation, Smith's result suggests that the other unmeasured sources of motivation for performance may sometimes be stronger among persons who score Low in *n* Achievement. Suppose, for example, that motive *X* is significantly stronger among persons scoring Low in *n* Achievement than among persons scoring High in *n* Achievement. In a test situation which arouses both the expectancy of achievement and the expectancy of satisfying motive *X* through the same performance, the level of performance would be very similar among High and Low *n* Achievement groups or even higher for the Low *n* Achievement group.

These are a few of the problems, sometimes ignored completely in studies of achievement motivation, which future research must resolve. Some other problems arising in the early studies of *n* Achievement and performance tend to be resolved when the ever-present influence of anxiety on performance is also taken into account systematically, as it is in current research guided by a more complete theory of achievement motivation which has evolved. (See Chapter 9.)

### THE INCENTIVE VARIABLE

As the conceptual problems came into better focus in successive studies of $n$ Achievement and performance guided by Tolman's concept of expectancy, it became increasingly apparent that another variable which Tolman had emphasized, the amount of *incentive*, needed to be taken into account. An important clue as to how strength of motivation to achieve might be conceived as a joint function of motive, expectancy, and incentive was provided in a study of the effects on the level of performance of variations in strength of expectancy of winning a monetary prize and in amount of the prize (Atkinson, 1958). The subjects in this experiment were female college students who were told they had been selected at random and assigned at random to various groups to compete for a monetary prize of $1.25 or $2.50. Each subject was told how many other persons she was competing with and the number of prizes that would be awarded. For example, some subjects were instructed that they were one of a group of four and that three prizes of $2.50 would be awarded to the three highest scorers in the group. Other subjects were instructed that they were one of a group of 20 and that only one prize would be awarded for the best performance. Still other subjects were instructed that they had been randomly paired with one other person and that whoever had the higher score would win the prize, etc. There were four stated probabilities of winning: 1/20, 1/3, 1/2, and 3/4. And there were two magnitudes of monetary incentive: $1.25 and $2.50. The subjects were asked to perform two 20-minute tasks. One involved no more than drawing X's inside small circles on page after page of circles. The other task consisted of a long series of three-step arithmetic problems. The results were so nearly alike for the two tasks that standard scores on the two tasks were combined and the average taken as the measure of performance level for each subject. Each subject was given exactly the same instructions regarding chance of winning and amount to be won on each of the tasks. Some subjects did, in fact, walk away from the experimental room with $5.00 for forty minutes of work.

The results of this experiment are shown in

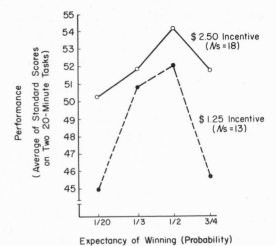

FIGURE 8.12   *Motivation directly expressed in performance as a function of monetary incentive and expectancy of winning (probability). (From Atkinson, Motives in Fantasy, Action and Society, Copyright 1958, D. Van Nostrand Company, Inc., Princeton, N. J., p. 294)*

Figure 8.12. Both the monetary incentive and the strength of expectancy of winning (probability) had a significant effect on the level of performance. Performance was higher when the amount to be won was $2.50 than $1.25. This much fits the common-sense prediction and is congruent with any theory that treats incentive (or amount of reward) as a determinant of performance. But what sense was to be made of the curvilinear relation between performance and strength of expectancy of winning a fixed monetary prize? If the strength of motivation is related to "subjectively-expected-utility," i.e., the product of probability of winning and amount to be won, then those offered 3 chances out of 4 of winning $2.50 should have performed at the highest level. But is the amount to be won the only source of attractiveness of the goal in this experiment? Or is the attractiveness of *attaining* it (to which Feather, p. 208, calls attention) also to be taken into account? These were the questions the investigator asked himself as he pondered the result and then suddenly saw the relationship between the result of this experiment and a discovery McClelland (1958b) had made in a study of "risk-taking" preferences of young children.

McClelland had advanced the hypothesis that economic development in a country depends upon entrepreneurial behavior which involves a willingness to take calculated risks in achievement-related activities where success and failure are the alternative outcomes. He examined the relationship of *n* Achievement to risk-taking behavior on the assumption that a strong motive to achieve, rather than money-seeking, is what spurs the calculated risk-taking behavior of the entrepreneurs who are chiefly responsible for the economic development of western nations. This hypothesis, which is fully developed in his recent book *The Achieving Society* (1961), led McClelland to repeat one of the earliest of level-of-aspiration experiments with young children in order to see whether or not a willingness to take risks was associated with a measure of strength of achievement motive in very young children. He had children toss a ring at a peg, allowing them to stand at whatever distance they chose. His result showed that children presumed to be strong in achievement motive did tend to take more shots from *intermediate* distances from the peg than children who were presumed weak in achievement motive.

The results of these two preliminary experiments—one showing higher level of performance when expectancy of winning is intermediate, the other showing that children highly motivated to achieve prefer intermediate risk in a ringtoss game—provided the clues needed to take account of *incentive* in a theory of achievement motivation proposed by Atkinson (1957). It is not surprising that the complete development of ideas initially influenced by Tolman's concept of expectancy would in time produce a theoretical conception having much in common with a theory advanced earlier by Lewin and co-workers in studies of level of aspiration. We shall consider it in the next chapter.

# CHAPTER 9

# A Theory of Achievement Motivation

*"Causes certainly are connected with effects; but that is because our theories connect them, not because the world is held together by cosmic glue"* (N. R. Hanson, 1958, p. 64).*

In this chapter, we shall consider the theory of achievement motivation which finally evolved in studies concerned with the relationship between performance and individual differences in strength of achievement motive as inferred from the thematic apperceptive measure of *n* Achievement developed by McClelland *et al.* As already suggested in the previous chapter, this theory has much in common with the earlier formulations of Tolman and Lewin, whose ideas soon began to provide the most useful guides in experimental and conceptual analysis of achievement-oriented behavior. The theory provides, it will be seen, a basis for conceptual integration of experiments on the effects of individual differences in *n* Achievement and some of the experiments reviewed in the previous chapter which deal with the relationship between performance on complex tasks and scores obtained by individuals on self-report tests of anxiety. The theory seems sufficiently well supported by factual evidence related to achievement-oriented behavior to justify an elaboration of some of the more general implications that pertain to the kinds of behavioral phenomena from which the conception of *S-R* Behavior Theory evolved. A comparison of the basic concepts in the two kinds of theory will be undertaken in the final chapter, which will also call attention to some fundamental deficiencies in these contemporary schemes and advance some proposals for further elaboration and development of the theory of motivation.

THE FACTS TO BE EXPLAINED

The theory of achievement motivation attempts to account for the determinants of the direction, magnitude, and persistence of behavior in a limited but very important domain of human activities. It applies only when an individual knows that his performance will be evaluated (by himself or by others) in terms of some standard of excellence and

* From N. R. Hanson, *Patterns of Discovery*, copyright 1958, Cambridge University Press. Reprinted by permission.

that the consequence of his actions will be either a favorable evaluation (success) or an unfavorable evaluation (failure). It is, in other words, a theory of *achievement-oriented* performance.

In addition to the clues provided in the study of how expectancy of winning a monetary prize influences the level of performance and in McClelland's exploration of risk-taking in children, there were a number of other significant facts from earlier studies which began to fall into place like pieces of a puzzle. Winterbottom (1958), for example, had found that boys who scored High in *n* Achievement were rated by their teachers as showing *more pleasure in success* than boys who scored Low in *n* Achievement. This suggested that the disposition called achievement motive might be conceived as *a capacity for taking pride in accomplishment* when success at one or another activity is achieved. Other studies had suggested that persons who score Low in *n* Achievement act as if they were more motivated by a fear of failure than a tendency to seek and enjoy success. Raphelson (1957) had found that thematic apperceptive *n* Achievement scores obtained under achievement-oriented conditions correlated −.43 with Test Anxiety scores on the same subjects. This study showed that Test Anxiety scores were positively related to psychogalvanic skin reaction (sweating) in an achievement-test situation, but that *n* Achievement scores were negatively correlated with this physiological symptom of "anxiety." Furthermore, other studies of the effects of individual differences in *n* Achievement on behavior under relaxed versus achievement-oriented conditions (Atkinson, 1953; Moulton *et al.*, 1958) produced results that looked like the results being obtained in studies of the effects of Manifest Anxiety or Test Anxiety under comparable conditions—*but upside down*. That is, increasing the test-like nature of the situation produced enhancement of performance among persons scoring High in *n* Achievement, but it produced decrements in the performance of persons scoring Low in *n* Achievement. Studies of anxiety were showing that those who score High in anxiety suffer a decrement in performance of complex tasks under similar circumstances, while those scoring Low in anxiety show an increment that is not clearly explained by the *S-R* formulation. How are all these facts related to one another?

## IMPORTANT SITUATIONAL DETERMINANTS

Following the outline of the theoretical conception developed by Tolman, it is assumed that the impact of important situational factors should be conceived in terms of two variables. First, to what extent does the individual, in sizing up the task before him, *expect* that his performance will lead on to the goal, success. Second, how attractive does success at this particular activity appear to the individual, that is, how much of an *incentive* does it present? McClelland (1961) has emphasized that for the motive to achieve to be aroused in performance of some activity, the individual must consider himself *responsible for the outcome* (success or failure), there must be *explicit knowledge of results* so that the individual knows when he has succeeded, and there must be *some degree of risk* concerning the possibility of success.

It is assumed that as a consequence of past experience in situations similar to the one he now confronts, an individual's expectancy of success may be very strong, moderately strong, or very weak. It is helpful to think of the strength of expectancy of success as the individual's subjective probability of success ($P_s$). This at least provides numbers ranging from 0 to 1.00 in terms of which variations in the degree of expectancy of success can be specified. When an individual is almost certain of success, the subjective probability of success ($P_s$) is very high—for example, .90. When expectancy of success is very weak, we may think of $P_s$ as having a much lower value, such as .10. And when he is uncertain as to whether or not he will succeed, the $P_s$ may be represented as near .50.

Obviously, if success and failure are alternative outcomes when performance is evaluated in relation to some criterion of skill, the expectancy of failure ($P_f$) must be weak when expectancy of success ($P_s$) is strong and vice versa. Tentatively, it is assumed that $P_s$ and $P_f$ add to 1.00.

Let us turn now to the matter of the value of the incentive. In sizing up the task, how much pride of accomplishment does the individual anticipate if he achieves his goal? Certainly there is much less of a sense of accomplishment in completion of certain tasks than others. As a consequence of past experience in which success has been acclaimed and pride actually experienced, the individual should be able to assess the potential value of certain accomplishments in relation to others, just as he is able to anticipate greater satisfaction from eating a big turkey dinner than from eating a liverwurst sandwich when he is hungry. This suggests that a third variable, the incentive value of success at a particular task, must be considered as one of the immediate determinants of strength of motivation to achieve at that task.

## THE TENDENCY TO ACHIEVE SUCCESS

The general principle of motivation proposed is a simple one. It is assumed that the motive to achieve success ($M_S$), which the individual carries about with him from one situation to another, combines multiplicatively with the two specific situational influences, the strength of expectancy or probability of success ($P_s$) and incentive value of success at a particular activity ($I_s$), to produce the tendency to approach success that is overtly expressed in the direction, magnitude, and persistence of achievement-oriented performance. In other words, the strength of motivation to achieve, or tendency to approach success ($T_s$) *through performance of certain actions*, may be represented: $T_s = M_S \times P_s \times I_s$.

The first variable, $M_S$, is a relatively general and stable characteristic of the person which is present in any behavior situation. But the values of the other two variables, $P_s$ and $I_s$, depend upon the individual's past experience in specific situations that are similar to the one he now confronts. These variables change as the individual moves about from one life situation to another and so are treated as characteristics of particular situations or particular tasks.

A SPECIAL ASSUMPTION: $I_s = 1 - P_s$

A very important and special assumption based on a proposal first suggested in the early work of Escalona, Festinger, and Lewin on level of aspiration turns this scheme into a theoretical model of achievement activities having specific and testable implications. Escalona and Festinger had noted that accomplishment of a difficult task is normally more attractive to an individual than accomplishment of some trivial or easy task. In other words, persons take greater pride in accomplishment when the task has been difficult than when it has been easy. In the theory of achievement motivation, this idea is given further specification. The difficulty of a task as it appears to a person may be represented in terms of the strength of his expectancy of success, $P_s$. When a task appears difficult, the $P_s$ is very low. When it appears easy, the $P_s$ is very high. In other words, the difficulty of a task as it appears to an individual equals $1 - P_s$. So the idea that incentive value of success is greater the more difficult a task can now be stated more precisely as a relationship between $I_s$ and $P_s$. A simple assumption, to begin with, is that the incentive value of success at a task ($I_s$) is equal to the apparent difficulty of the task, that is, $I_s =$

$1 - P_s$. If so, then when a task is very easy, as when $P_s$ equals .90, the incentive value of success ($I_s$) is very low, .10. However, when a task appears very difficult, as when $P_s$ equals .10, then $I_s$ is very high, .90. The ultimate value of this assumption is to be judged in terms of its testable implications. What are they?

IMPLICATIONS OF $T_s = M_s \times P_s \times I_s$

In Table 9.1 the most important implications of this conception of the determinants of the tendency

### TABLE 9.1

Tendency to achieve success ($T_s$) as a joint function of Motive to achieve ($M_S$), Expectancy of success ($P_s$), and Incentive value of success ($I_s$) for individuals in whom $M_S = 1$ and $M_S = 8$. *It is assumed that $I_s = 1 - P_s$.*

| Task | $P_s$ | $I_s$ | $(T_s = M_S \times P_s \times I_s)$ When $M_S = 1$ | When $M_S = 8$ |
|---|---|---|---|---|
| A | .90 | .10 | .09 | .72 |
| B | .70 | .30 | .21 | 1.68 |
| C | .50 | .50 | .25 | 2.00 |
| D | .30 | .70 | .21 | 1.68 |
| E | .10 | .90 | .09 | .72 |

to achieve success are spelled out. If the strength of the tendency to achieve success through performance of certain actions ($T_s$) is assumed equal to $M_S \times P_s \times I_s$, and $I_s$ is assumed equal to $1 - P_s$, then:

1. The tendency to approach success ($T_s$) should be strongest when a task appears to be one of intermediate difficulty, for the product of $P_s \times I_s$ is greatest when $P_s$ equals .50. But a substantially stronger tendency to approach success ($T_s$) when $P_s$ is .50 than when $P_s$ is either very high or very low is only to be expected when $M_S$ is relatively strong.

2. When the apparent difficulty of a task ($P_s$) is held constant for a group of persons, the tendency to achieve success ($T_s$) is stronger when $M_S$ is strong than when $M_S$ is weak. But the difference in strength of tendency to approach success ($T_s$) that is attributable to a difference in strength of achievement motive ($M_S$) should be substantial only when the task is one of intermediate difficulty, that is, when $P_s$ is near .50. When $P_s$ is very high (an easy task) or very low (a very difficult task), the difference in strength of tendency to approach success attributable to a difference in strength of $M_S$ is very small.

This means—ignoring all other factors for a

moment—that when an individual is confronted with a series of tasks which differ in apparent difficulty ($P_s$) and is asked to choose the one he wishes to perform, the preference for tasks of intermediate difficulty (or intermediate risk) should be more apparent when the achievement motive is very strong than when it is very weak. Given the hypothetical persons described in Table 9.1, we see that when $M_S$ is relatively strong ($M_S = 8$), the tendency to approach success through performance of the task where $P_s$ is .50 has a value of 2.00 compared to values of .72 for very easy or very difficult tasks. However, when $M_S$ is relatively weak ($M_S = 1$), the difference in strength of tendency to approach success where $P_s$ is .50 versus either very high or very low is greatly reduced. The comparable values of $T_s$ are then .25 and .09. It is generally assumed that when the strength of tendencies to perform one or another act are nearly equal in strength, no clearcut preference will be observed. When, on the other hand, one tendency is substantially stronger than competing tendencies, a clearcut preference is predicted.

This, of course, is what McClelland had already observed in the risk-taking preferences of young children: those who were High in $n$ Achievement showed a greater preference for "intermediate risk" than those who were Low in $n$ Achievement. And earlier experiments which have dealt with verbally stated levels of aspiration have shown that the "typical" or most frequent result among students in western societies is to select an intermediate level of aspiration falling somewhere between what is obviously so easy that success is assured and obviously so difficult that success is impossible. This frequently reported result in early studies which did not assess individual differences in strength of achievement motive suggests the hypothesis that college students, who were the most frequent source of subjects, must be relatively strong in achievement motive. A recent national survey study by Veroff et al. (1960), which included a thematic apperceptive measure of $n$ Achievement, showed that $n$ Achievement is significantly higher among men and women who have attended college than among the rest of the population. Thus the "typical" result in studies of level of aspiration is explained. But early experiments on level of aspiration always report a minority of "atypical" cases who set either very high or very low levels of aspiration. We shall consider them a little later.

In addition to explaining the risk-taking prefer-

ences that McClelland had observed, this conception of the determinants of the tendency to approach success also explains why the level of performance was greatest when probability of winning a monetary prize was 1/2. The curve of performance level in relation to probability of winning shown earlier in Figure 8.12 is the shape expected if in addition to the incentive value of money *qua* money there is an incentive to achieve inherent in the competitive nature of the task. If so, holding average strength of $M_S$ constant in the several groups of randomly selected subjects, the tendency to achieve success should be strongest when $P_s$ is .50.

Consider now the implication that tendency to approach success ($T_s$) should always be stronger when $M_S$ is strong than when $M_S$ is weak, no matter what the $P_s$ at the task. It is supported by all results which show achievement-oriented performance (or some indicator of strength of motivation like recall of interrupted tasks) to be greater when $n$ Achievement scores are High than when $n$ Achievement scores are Low. The further implication that the difference in $T_s$ attributable to High versus Low $n$ Achievement will be slight when tasks are very easy or very difficult, coupled with the lack of specification of degree of difficulty of tasks in many early experiments on $n$ Achievement, may account for some instances of failure to find a substantial relationship between $n$ Achievement and performance.

When there is no expectancy that performance will lead to pride of accomplishment, that is, when $P_s = 0$ because instructions or other cues rule out the possibility of expecting evaluation of performance and "feelings of success" as in "relaxed" conditions, there is, according to the theory, no incentive to achieve. Hence there is no basis for predicting that performance of persons scoring High and Low in $n$ Achievement will differ under "relaxed" conditions.

Considering only the determinants of motivation to achieve, that is, the tendency to approach success, this conceptual scheme summarizes very well the main results of the early studies of $n$ Achievement and performance. But until now we have proceeded as if no other factors needed to be considered in the analysis of achievement-oriented performance, as if the behaving individual had no other motive that might influence his aspirations, effort, and persistence in achievement activities. How does this kind of conceptual scheme embrace the well-documented fact that the threat of failure has a detrimental effect on the performance of some persons, notably those who score High on one or another of the self-report tests of anxiety? And how does this theory explain "atypical" levels of aspiration?

## THE TENDENCY TO AVOID FAILURE

It is assumed that in addition to a general disposition to seek success, called the achievement motive, there is also a general disposition to avoid failure, called *motive to avoid failure*. Where the motive to achieve might be characterized as a capacity for reacting with pride in accomplishment, the motive to avoid failure can be conceived as a capacity for reacting with shame and embarrassment when the outcome of performance is failure. When this disposition is aroused within a person, as it is aroused whenever it is clear to a person that his performance will be evaluated and failure is a distinct possibility, the result is anxiety and a tendency to withdraw from the situation.

A SPECIAL ASSUMPTION: $I_f = -P_s$

Whenever there is some probability of attaining success through performance of a task there is also, inextricably bound up with the promise of success, the threat of failure. The expectancy of failure ($P_f$) is strong when the expectancy of success ($P_s$) is weak, and vice versa. As stated earlier, it is tentatively assumed that $P_s$ and $P_f$ add up to 1.00. Following another proposal advanced earlier by Escalona, Festinger, and Lewin, it is assumed that the shame and embarrassment of failure is normally greater when the task failed appeared easy than when it appeared very difficult. Normally little or no stigma is attached to an inability to perform the nearly impossible. In parallel with the treatment of incentive value of success, it is assumed that the repulsiveness of failure is related to the difficulty of a task, but in a manner just opposite to the attractiveness of success. It is assumed that the incentive value of failure, $I_f$, has a value equal to $-P_s$. The minus sign implies a noxious event, something to be avoided like the shock grid employed in studies of fear in animals. In other words, when a task is very easy and $P_s$ is high, .90, then the *negative* incentive value of failure at the task is also very high, $-.90$. When, however, the task appears very difficult and $P_s$ is very low, .10, then the *negative* incentive value of failure is also very low, $-.10$.

IMPLICATIONS OF $T_{-f} = M_{AF} \times P_f \times I_f$

Table 9.2 spells out the implications of conceiving the strength of motivation to avoid failure—that is,

TABLE 9.2

Tendency to avoid failure ($T_{-f}$) as a joint function of Motive to avoid failure ($M_{AF}$), Expectancy of failure ($P_f$), and negative Incentive value of failure ($I_f$) for individuals in whom $M_{AF} = 1$ and $M_{AF} = 8$. *It is assumed that $I_f = -P_s$.*

| Task | $P_f$ | $I_f$ | ($T_{-f} = M_{AF} \times P_f \times I_f$) When $M_{AF} = 1$ | When $M_{AF} = 8$ |
|------|-------|-------|------|------|
| A | .10 | $-.90$ | $-.09$ | $-.72$ |
| B | .30 | $-.70$ | $-.21$ | $-1.68$ |
| C | .50 | $-.50$ | $-.25$ | $-2.00$ |
| D | .70 | $-.30$ | $-.21$ | $-1.68$ |
| E | .90 | $-.10$ | $-.09$ | $-.72$ |

the tendency to avoid failure ($T_{-f}$)—as jointly determined by motive, expectancy, and incentive: $T_{-f} = M_{AF} \times P_f \times I_f$.

The implications concerning the arousal of the tendency to avoid failure are the same as those already reviewed for the tendency to approach success, *but the behavioral implications are just the opposite:*

1. The tendency to avoid failure, or anxiety about failure ($T_{-f}$), should be strongest when a task appears to be one of intermediate difficulty, for the product of $P_f \times I_f$ yields the greatest *negative* tendency when $P_f$ equals .50. But the tendency to avoid failure ($T_{-f}$) will be substantially stronger when $P_f$ is .50 than when $P_f$ is either very high or very low *only* when $M_{AF}$ is relatively strong.

2. When the apparent difficulty of a task is held constant for a group of persons, the tendency to avoid failure ($T_{-f}$) is stronger when $M_{AF}$ is strong than when it is weak. But the difference in strength of tendency to avoid failure ($T_{-f}$) that is attributable to a difference in strength of $M_{AF}$ should be substantial only when the task is one of intermediate difficulty, that is, when $P_f$ is near .50. When $P_f$ is very low (an easy task) or very high (a very difficult task) the difference in strength of tendency to avoid failure that is attributable to a difference in strength of $M_{AF}$ is very small.

THE TENDENCY TO AVOID FAILURE CONCEIVED AS AN INHIBITORY TENDENCY

There are several important things to notice about this conception of how "anxiety about failure" is influenced by individual differences in disposition to be anxious in achievement-oriented situations and how "anxiety" is related to performance. The theoretical conception is markedly different from those proposed in studies employing the Manifest Anxiety Scale and the Test Anxiety Questionnaire. First, it is assumed that a disposition to be anxious about failure tends to make all activities in which performance is evaluated threatening to an individual; and actions which might lead to a potential threat are actions to be avoided whenever that is possible. That is precisely what the minus sign on the strength of tendency to avoid failure $(T_{-f})$ implies: the person is *negatively* motivated, or motivated *not to perform* an act which might have, as a consequence, failure. In other words, the theory of achievement motivation asserts that the achievement motive and expectancy of success produce positive interest and active pursuit of success, but the motive to avoid failure and expectancy of failure function to steer an individual away from achievement-related activities because they produce a tendency to avoid or inhibit actions which might lead to failure. This avoidant or inhibitory tendency $(T_{-f})$ is strongest when the activity appears to be a realistic challenge, that is, when the expectancy of success and failure are near equal in strength, as they are in tasks of intermediate difficulty.

Viewed this way, a disposition to be anxious provides no motor for performance of an activity but is conceived as the source of inhibition of activity. With no positive "inducement" to choose between one and another activity which differ in apparent difficulty, a hypothetical person who has *only* a strong disposition to avoid failure should, according to what is stated in the theory, not act at all. But when he is constrained by other inducements to act, which must, given this type of theoretical conception, be conceived as other sources of *positive* motivation to act, then it is expected that the very anxious person will set his aspiration either very high or very low. This comes about because the strength of the tendency to avoid failure, which *opposes* the tendency to perform an act, is strongest when the probability of success is .50 and weakest when the probability of success is either very high or very low. Whatever the source of positive motivation to undertake the activity at all, there is a weaker avoidant or inhibitory tendency to be overcome when the task appears either very easy or very difficult. Hence, one of these rather than a task of intermediate risk, where avoidance is strongest, will be a more likely choice in an anxious person.

Both of these "unrealistic" strategies in setting an aspiration or taking an achievement risk are pro-tective. They minimize the arousal of anxiety about failure. In one case, the individual is protected from the pain of failure by seeming to attempt the impossible. Who can blame him if he should fail? In the other case, when setting a very low level of aspiration by choosing a very easy task, he is protected from the pain of failure because failure at the task is such a remote possibility.

## EFFECT OF TENDENCY TO AVOID FAILURE ON PERFORMANCE

When we consider how "anxiety about failure" should affect the over-all efficiency of an individual's performance of a task, given this theoretical conception, we are forced to predict that the tendency to avoid performing actions which could possibly lead to an unfavorable evaluation should consistently interfere with or *dampen* positive motivation to perform the task. The vigor and level of performance of achievement-related activities should depend upon the strength of factors which determine the positive tendency to act and which overcome the tendency to avoid failure, thus holding the person in an achievement situation which he would otherwise much prefer to leave.

In the initial statement of the theory of achievement motivation (Atkinson, 1957; 1958, Chapter 22), this interpretation of the meaning of the *negative* tendency $(T_{-f})$ generated by $M_{AF} \times P_f \times I_f$ was fully appreciated in reference to risk-taking preferences, but not in reference to how the tendency to avoid failure should influence the level of performance at a specific task, which was then given less systematic discussion. At that time, the writer allowed his own intuitions to intervene and take precedence over what the theory, as stated, implied. For example, he then asserted:

"How does the more fearful person behave when offered only a specific task to perform? He can either perform the task or leave the field. If he chooses to leave the field, there is no problem. But if he is constrained, as he must be to remain in any competitive achievement situation, he will stay at the task and presumably work at it. But how hard will he work at it? He is motivated to avoid failure, and when constrained, there is only one path open to him to avoid failure—success at the task he is presented. So we expect him to manifest the strength of his motivation to avoid failure in performance of the task. He too, in other words, should *try hardest\** when $P_s$ is .50 and less hard when the chance of winning is either greater or less. The 50-50 alternative is the last he would choose if allowed to set his own goal, but once constrained he must try hard to avoid the failure which threatens him. Not working at all will guarantee failure of the task. Hence, the thought of not working at all should produce even stronger avoidant motivation than that aroused by the task itself." (Atkinson, 1957, p. 364).

A footnote to this passage, inserted at the asterisk (*) above, stated:

"I do not mean to exclude the possibility that the very anxious person may suffer a performance decrement due to the arousal of some 'task-irrelevant' avoidant responses, as proposed in the interpretation of research which has employed the Mandler-Sarason Measure of Test Anxiety. . . ."

These initial common-sense conjectures were misleading in that they missed what is clearly implied when failure is conceived as having a *negative* incentive value. If a particular act is expected to lead to a *negative* incentive, then the product of motive, expectancy, and incentive will be *negative* and the tendency ($T_{-f}$) must be conceived as a tendency *not* to perform the act—that is, as an inhibitory tendency. Thus, given this conception, the threat of failure does not directly *excite* avoidant actions *or* "task-relevant" actions. Instead, the threat of failure is conceived as producing a tendency to *inhibit* the performance of actions which are expected to produce failure. This inhibitory tendency, called the tendency to avoid failure, opposes and dampens the positive tendency to approach success which does *excite* actions that are expected to lead to the goal, success.

## APPROACH-AVOIDANCE CONFLICT IN ACHIEVEMENT SITUATIONS

The theory of achievement motivation assumes that all individuals have both a motive to achieve success ($M_S$) and a motive to avoid failure ($M_{AF}$), so there is inevitably aroused in the person at the time of performance an approach-avoidance or excitation-inhibition conflict. Following the earlier views of Lewin, Escalona, and Festinger in the treatment of level of aspiration, it is assumed that the conflict between positive interest in achievement (the tendency to approach success) and anxiety about failure (the tendency to avoid failure) is resolved algebraically. That is, the resultant tendency equals $T_s + T_{-f}$. Since $T_{-f}$ is always a negative quantity implying avoidance, the resultant tendency to approach success is always weakened by the avoidant tendency associated with anxiety about failure.

Table 9.3 shows the major implications of the theory of achievement motivation in reference to four hypothetical persons. One is assumed to have a

### TABLE 9.3

Resultant achievement motivation ($T_s + T_{-f}$) in four hypothetical persons who differ in strength of Motive to achieve ($M_S$) and Motive to avoid failure ($M_{AF}$)

| | When $M_S = 3$ and $M_{AF} = 1$ | | | | | | |
|------|-------|-------|-------|-------|-------|--------|-----------|
| Task | $P_s$ | $I_s$ | $T_s$ | $P_f$ | $I_f$ | $T_{-f}$ | $T_s + T_{-f}$ |
| A | .90 | .10 | .27 | .10 | −.90 | −.09 | .18 |
| B | .70 | .30 | .63 | .30 | −.70 | −.21 | .42 |
| C | .50 | .50 | .75 | .50 | −.50 | −.25 | .50 |
| D | .30 | .70 | .63 | .70 | −.30 | −.21 | .42 |
| E | .10 | .90 | .27 | .90 | −.10 | −.09 | .18 |

| | When $M_S = 3$ and $M_{AF} = 2$ | | | | | | |
|------|-------|-------|-------|-------|-------|--------|-----------|
| Task | $P_s$ | $I_s$ | $T_s$ | $P_f$ | $I_f$ | $T_{-f}$ | $T_s + T_{-f}$ |
| A | .90 | .10 | .27 | .10 | −.90 | −.18 | .09 |
| B | .70 | .30 | .63 | .30 | −.70 | −.42 | .21 |
| C | .50 | .50 | .75 | .50 | −.50 | −.50 | .25 |
| D | .30 | .70 | .63 | .70 | −.30 | −.42 | .21 |
| E | .10 | .90 | .27 | .90 | −.10 | −.18 | .09 |

| | When $M_S = 3$ and $M_{AF} = 3$ | | | | | | |
|------|-------|-------|-------|-------|-------|--------|-----------|
| Task | $P_s$ | $I_s$ | $T_s$ | $P_f$ | $I_f$ | $T_{-f}$ | $T_s + T_{-f}$ |
| A | .90 | .10 | .27 | .10 | −.90 | −.27 | 0 |
| B | .70 | .30 | .63 | .30 | −.70 | −.63 | 0 |
| C | .50 | .50 | .75 | .50 | −.50 | −.75 | 0 |
| D | .30 | .70 | .63 | .70 | −.30 | −.63 | 0 |
| E | .10 | .90 | .27 | .90 | −.10 | −.27 | 0 |

| | When $M_S = 1$ and $M_{AF} = 3$ | | | | | | |
|------|-------|-------|-------|-------|-------|--------|-----------|
| Task | $P_s$ | $I_s$ | $T_s$ | $P_f$ | $I_f$ | $T_{-f}$ | $T_s + T_{-f}$ |
| A | .90 | .10 | .09 | .10 | −.90 | −.27 | −.18 |
| B | .70 | .30 | .21 | .30 | −.70 | −.63 | −.42 |
| C | .50 | .50 | .25 | .50 | −.50 | −.75 | −.50 |
| D | .30 | .70 | .21 | .70 | −.30 | −.63 | −.42 |
| E | .10 | .90 | .09 | .90 | −.10 | −.27 | −.18 |

very strong motive to achieve and a weak motive to avoid failure. Another is assumed to have a very strong motive to achieve and a motive to avoid failure that is almost as strong. A third is assumed to have equally strong motives to achieve success and to avoid failure. A fourth is assumed to have a substantially stronger motive to avoid failure than to achieve success.

Figure 9.1 is a graphic presentation of the strength of tendency to approach success, tendency to avoid failure, and *resultant tendency* for each of these four hypothetical persons. It is clear from both Table 9.3 and Figure 9.1 that when the person's motive to achieve success is stronger than the motive to avoid failure ($M_S > M_{AF}$), the resultant tendency is positive and strongest when $P_s$ is .50. When the two motives are equal in strength ($M_S = M_{AF}$), the resultant tendency is zero at all levels of difficulty. Hence there is no basis for predicting a risk preference, level of aspiration, or even performance of an achievement-related task without appealing to other motives and expectations which excite tendencies to perform the very same actions. And when the motive to avoid failure is stronger than the motive to achieve success ($M_{AF} > M_S$), the resultant is negative and strongest when $P_s$ is .50. This implies avoidance or

inhibition of achievement-related activities. Here, again, the prediction of a risk-preference, level of aspiration, or performance of an achievement-related task demands assumptions about or knowledge of the strength of other *extrinsic sources of positive motivation to perform the same actions.*

In tests of this theory of achievement motivation, it is assumed that performance is a function of the total strength of tendency to perform an act and that the total strength of tendency equals achievement-related motivation ($T_s + T_{-f}$) plus extrinsic motivation. *By extrinsic motivation is meant the strength of the tendency to act that is attributable to the influence of other motives and incentives that are not intrinsically related to the evaluation of performance as are the two achievement-related motives.*

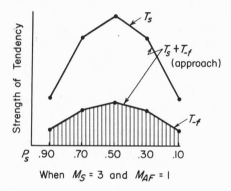
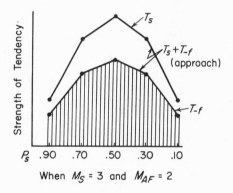
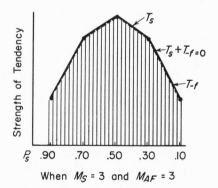
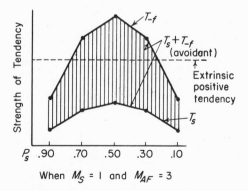

FIGURE 9.1  Graphic presentation of the strength of Tendency to approach success ($T_s$), Tendency to avoid failure ($T_{-f}$), and Resultant Tendency ($T_s + T_{-f}$) for individuals who differ in strength of $M_S$ and $M_{AF}$ as shown in Table 9-3. The assumed effect of extrinsic positive motivation to undertake an activity is shown in the case where $M_S = 1$ and $M_{AF} = 3$.

## EVIDENCE RELATED TO THEORY OF ACHIEVEMENT MOTIVATION

Since the initial statement of the theory of achievement motivation, which attempted to summarize what had already been learned in studies employing the TAT measure of $n$ Achievement and to provide guidelines for subsequent research, some studies have employed both the test of $n$ Achievement (on the assumption that it measures strength of $M_S$) and the Test Anxiety Questionnaire (on the assumption that it measures the strength of $M_{AF}$). These studies have been designed to test implications of the theory and to search out its weak points so that the self-corrective process can begin in earnest in the context of systematic study of human achievement-oriented behavior as it has already in studies of fear and food-seeking in animals.

### RISK PREFERENCE, PERFORMANCE, AND PERSISTENCE

Atkinson and Litwin (1960) employed measures of individual differences in $n$ Achievement and Test Anxiety in a study designed to reproduce the kinds of relationships that other studies had already shown between $n$ Achievement and risk-preference, level of performance, and persistence in achievement-oriented activity in separate investigations of each. In addition, they wanted to investigate the effects of individual differences in Test Anxiety on these same performance variables and then to see how simultaneous classification of persons in terms of their scores on both tests would influence the pattern of results. Given the assumptions of the theory, and the further assumption that $n$ Achievement score provides a measure of $M_S$ and that Test Anxiety score provides a measure of $M_{AF}$ in the subjects, it was predicted that $n$ Achievement would be positively related and Test Anxiety negatively related to preference for intermediate risk, level of achievement-oriented test performance, and persistence in achievement-oriented activity before clear knowledge of results had been attained. Furthermore, it was predicted that when subjects were simultaneously classified High (above the median) and Low (below the median) on both tests, the greatest differences should be evident when the group classified High in $n$ Achievement but Low in Test Anxiety was compared with the group classified Low in $n$ Achievement but High in Test Anxiety. According to the theory, the former group should have the strongest resultant tendency to approach success $(T_s + T_{-f})$,

and the latter group should have either the weakest tendency to approach success or a resultant avoidance tendency. Subjects who were classified High on both motives or Low on both motives should, according to the theory, fall between these two extreme groups in strength of resultant tendency to approach success $(T_s + T_{-f})$. Consequently they should also fall between the extreme groups in degree of preference for intermediate risk, level of achievement-oriented performance, and persistence in achievement-oriented activity.

Atkinson and Litwin found an insignificant negative correlation, $-.15$ ($N = 47$), between $n$ Achievement scores and Test Anxiety scores when both tests were administered under *Neutral* conditions. Other recent studies have tended to confirm the belief that there is no significant relationship between $n$ Achievement and Test Anxiety among male college students when both tests are administered under Neutral conditions, e.g., Mahone (1960); O'Connor (1960); Feather (1961). This, together with other evidence (Martire (1956); Scott, (1956)) suggests that the negative correlation which Raphelson (1956) had reported (see p. 241) can probably be attributed to the fact that he had assessed $n$ Achievement under relatively stressful *achievement-oriented* conditions— at a time, in other words, when anxiety about failure was also strongly aroused in some subjects and capable of inhibiting the expression of achievement-oriented responses in thematic apperceptive stories that might otherwise have been expressed under Neutral conditions. Recall, in this connection, Clark's findings (see p. 227) concerning the inhibition of manifest sexual responses in imaginative stories when anxiety was also aroused at the time of writing the stories.

The absence of a correlation between scores on the two tests, at least within samples of male college students tested under Neutral conditions, means that about one fourth of the subjects are classified High $n$ Achievement-Low Test Anxiety and Low $n$ Achievement-High Test Anxiety when the criterion is the median of the distribution of scores.

In the experiment, risk-taking preference was measured by having the male college students play a ringtoss game (like that employed earlier by McClelland (1958) with young children) in a realistic game-like atmosphere. Each subject was given an opportunity to take 10 shots from any distance he chose between 1 and 15 feet from the peg. The subjects, standing around watching each other shoot, were goaded on by the instruction "to see how good you are at this." The measure of level of achievement-oriented performance was the score each subject obtained on the final examination in the same college course a few months later. And the measure of persistence in achievement-oriented activity was the amount of time spent working on the exam before turning it in. It was a three-hour exam period, but very few subjects worked for the full three hours. The investigators noted the time of each subject's departure from the examination room without other subjects knowing that this was being done. French and Thomas (1958) had earlier shown a striking positive relationship between *n* Achievement in Air Force personnel and their persistence in attempting to solve a complex problem when they were free to leave whenever they so desired.

Figure 9.2 shows the predicted result in the ring-toss game. Significantly more shots were taken from an intermediate distance by men who were High in *n* Achievement and Low in Test Anxiety than by men who were Low in *n* Achievement and High in Test Anxiety. And the two subgroups in which the two competing tendencies were either both High or both Low fall between the extreme groups, as predicted.

Table 9.4 shows how the use of either the measure of *n* Achievement by itself or the measure of Test

Anxiety by itself produces the diametrically opposite results predicted by the theory on all three performance variables. And Table 9.4 also shows how simultaneous use of both tests—by which one takes account of the strength of both $M_S$ and $M_{AF}$ within a subject—improves the discrimination between groups on all three dependent performance variables.

This demonstration of the relationship between studies of *n* Achievement and studies of Test Anxiety provides a reasonably firm basis for interpreting the meaning of some of the unexplained trends in earlier studies which have employed only a measure of *n* Achievement or only a measure of anxiety. If it can be assumed that *n* Achievement and Test Anxiety are normally uncorrelated among male college students, certain further assumptions can be made. When a group is High (above the median) in *n* Achievement, one can assume that the achievement motive ($M_S$) is relatively strong in relation to the average strength of the unmeasured motive to avoid failure ($M_{AF}$) in such a group. When a group is Low (below the median) in *n* Achievement, one can assume that the achievement motive ($M_S$) is relatively weak in relation to the average strength of motive to avoid failure ($M_{AF}$) in such a group. The absence of correlation between *n* Achievement scores and Test Anxiety scores means that the average

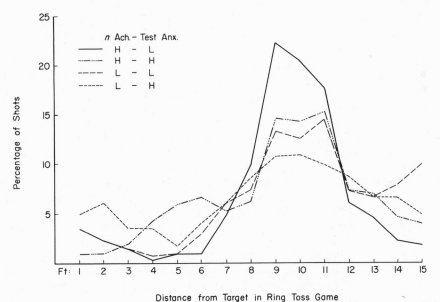

FIGURE 9.2   Percentage of shots taken from each distance by college men in a ringtoss game. Graph is smoothed according to the method of running averages, for Ss classified as High or Low simultaneously in *n* Achievement and Test Anxiety, H-L (N = 13), H-H (N = 10), L-L (N = 9), L-H (N = 13). (*From Atkinson and Litwin, 1960, p. 55*)

TABLE 9.4

Effect of individual differences in *n* Achievement and Test Anxiety on risk-taking preference, persistence in an examination, and performance on examination. *Subjects are classified in terms of each motive separately and simultaneously in terms of both motives.* (After Atkinson and Litwin, 1960)

| | | % Above combined group median | | | | |
|---|---|---|---|---|---|---|
| *n* Achievement | *N* | Prefer intermediate risk | *N* | Persistence on exam | *N* | Performance on exam |
| High | (23) | 61% | (25) | 60% | (25) | 64% |
| Low | (22) | 36% | (19) | 32% | (19) | 32% |
| | | *p* < .04 | | *p* < .03 | | *p* < .02 |
| **Test Anxiety** | | | | | | |
| High | (23) | 35% | (22) | 32% | (22) | 41% |
| Low | (22) | 64% | (22) | 64% | (22) | 59% |
| | | *p* < .04 | | *p* < .06 | | *p* < .06 |
| ***n* Achievement    Test Anxiety** | | | | | | |
| High    —    Low | (13) | 77% | (15) | 73% | (15) | 67% |
| High    —    High | (10) | 40% | (10) | 40% | (10) | 60% |
| Low    —    Low | (9) | 44% | (7) | 43% | (7) | 43% |
| Low    —    High | (13) | 31% | (12) | 25% | (12) | 25% |
| | | *p* < .025 | | *p* < .01 | | *p* < .025 |

NOTE: Tests of significance are one-tailed Mann-Whitney U Tests of predicted differences between extreme groups. One subject missed the final examination.

Test Anxiety score is the same among High and Low *n* Achievement groups. Hence, relative to the strength of *n* Achievement (which has been measured), Test Anxiety is a more potent influence on the behavior of persons scoring Low than High in *n* Achievement.

The same logic can be applied, but in reverse, when Test Anxiety has been measured but *n* Achievement has not. Most anxiety studies deal with more extreme groups than those defined by splitting the distribution of scores at the median as in the experiment described above. If *n* Achievement and Test Anxiety are uncorrelated, a group of persons who score in the top 20 per cent on Test Anxiety will have the same average *n* Achievement score as a group which scores in the bottom 20 per cent on Test Anxiety. This means that the disposition to be anxious is virtually absent in the Low anxiety group, which is otherwise as highly motivated to achieve as the High anxiety group. Subjects classified Low in anxiety, in most of the anxiety studies, are persons in whom the resultant tendency to approach success should be relatively strong. Subjects classified High in anxiety are persons in whom resultant tendency

to approach success is either very weak or, what is more likely since only those with the highest 20 per cent of anxiety scores are normally employed, the resultant tendency is avoidant.

This is the key to understanding why persons scoring Low in *n* Achievement recall fewer interrupted tasks under Achievement-oriented conditions than under Relaxed conditions (see p. 233) and why subjects classified Low on either Test Anxiety or Manifest Anxiety (the two tests are normally correlated about .50) show the previously unexplained increment in level of performance of complex tasks when the test situation becomes more "threatening," "stressful," or "ego involving" (see pp. 217 and 221). Their behavior is to be understood as an expression of a strong tendency to achieve success which is aroused when the situation is structured as an important test but is not aroused in the usual relaxed, control condition which minimizes "ego-involvement" in the task.

In addition to those already mentioned, studies by Clark, Teevan, and Ricciuti (1956), Litwin (1958), Vitz (1957), Atkinson, Bastian, Earl, and Litwin (1960), and Mahone (1960) show that risk preference or level of aspiration in achievement-oriented activities is related to *n* Achievement and/or Test Anxiety as described above. In one of these studies (Atkinson *et al.*, 1960), there was also some evidence of probability preferences in gambling of the sort reported earlier by Edwards. (See p. 210.) When subjects High and Low in *n* Achievement were confronted with options having the same expected value, 30¢, but different probabilities of winning (e.g., 1/6 chance to win $1.80 versus 3/6 chance to win $0.60) in an imaginary dice game, subjects scoring High in *n* Achievement showed a significantly greater preference for intermediate probabilities of winning (2/6, 3/6, 4/6) versus extreme probabilities (5/6 and 1/6) than subjects scoring Low in *n* Achievement. But this difference between High and Low *n* Achievement groups in preference for intermediate probabilities of winning in gambling was the result of significant avoidance of intermediate probabilities by subjects Low in *n* Achievement. Men High in *n* Achievement did not prefer intermediate gambles to extreme gambles any more than would be expected by chance.

A further study by Littig (1959), which involved 12 hours of testing gambling preferences in a dice poker game, showed very clearly that when persons clearly recognize that the outcome is determined by chance, as in rolling dice, and not by their own skill, as in achievement-oriented tests, the assumptions of the theory of achievement motivation do not apply. Littig found that subjects who were strong in *n* Achievement and weak in Test Anxiety developed a significant preference for the option having the *highest* probability of winning in the game of chance. He argued that when it is realized that the outcome is determined by chance, there is no differential incentive value of success ($I_s$) attributable to the "difficulty" of the task because the task does not require skill. There is no basis for pride in accomplishment to begin with. So the assumption $I_s = 1 - P_s$ does not hold. The incentive value of "success" in *gambling* is constant across all probabilities of winning. But persons who score High in *n* Achievement "like to win," so when you multiply $M_S \times P_s \times I_s$ (and $I_s$ is the same for all values of $P_s$), the tendency to approach success ($T_s$) is stronger the higher the probability of success ($P_s$). Thus persons who are High in *n* Achievement prefer the highest probability of winning when the expected monetary values of the options presented to them are equal.

The research on risk-taking in achievement-ori-ented situations has raised some important questions for decision theorists who have been concerned with choices between options entailing the possibility of winning or losing certain amounts of money. The issue of greatest importance is the need for decision theorists to begin to consider the possibility that there are other sources of utility present in studies of human choice involving amounts of money than merely the *amount* of money to be won or lost.

REALISTIC AND UNREALISTIC
VOCATIONAL ASPIRATION

Mahone (1960) tested the theory of achievement motivation in a study of the vocational aspirations of college men who differed in strength of *n* Achievement and Test Anxiety. His work provides the key to extending the logic of the theory to studies of aspiration and achievement in society. His measure of the degree of realism of a subject's vocational aspiration was the discrepancy between the subject's estimate of his own general ability and the amount of general ability the subject himself felt was required to be successful in the vocation he aspired to.

Mahone presented his subjects with a long list of occupations and asked them to indicate how many, out of 100 typical students at the college, had the general ability required to attain each occupational goal. The average of these estimates produced an ordering of occupations in terms of their perceived difficulty, or probability of success ($P_s$), as viewed by college students. Mahone's data showed that the correlation between this average obtained measure of $P_s$ at different occupations correlated −.85 with the rank-ordering of these occupations in terms of prestige normally accorded persons in them which sociologists have obtained in national surveys. What is more, the correlation was −.90 when only the estimates made by persons scoring High in *n* Achievement and Low in Test Anxiety were employed. Mahone's data show, for example, that college students felt that only 7 out of 100 students ($P_s = .07$) had sufficient general ability to become medical specialists (who are normally accorded much prestige), but that 72 out of 100 ($P_s = .72$) had enough ability to be successful clerks (who are normally accorded much less prestige).

What does this mean? It means that the ordering of occupations, which sociologists use to define social status, and which has been found highly similar and stable in all modern industrialized societies (Inkeles and Rossi, 1956), may be viewed as a hierarchy of tasks which differ in apparent difficulty having the same conceptual properties as a ringtoss game in which shots may be taken from different distances. That is, the lower the probability of success ($P_s$), the higher the incentive value of success ($I_s$). The assumption in the theory of achievement motivation that $I_s = 1 - P_s$ leads to the prediction that the correlation between an ordering of occupations in terms of their generally recognized standing (prestige), and estimates of probability of success (apparent ease of attaining the goal) should be $-1.00$. The correlation obtained by Mahone is sufficiently close to $-1.00$ to justify the assumption that the occupational hierarchy can be viewed as a series of achievement tasks which differ in difficulty. If so, the theory of achievement motivation should apply directly to the problem of explaining vocational aspirations.

Mahone also asked each subject to indicate where he would stand among 100 college students in general ability. So for each subject he had an estimate of own ability, the stated vocational aspiration, and an estimate by that subject of the ability required to succeed at that particular occupation. He computed the *subjective goal discrepancy* between estimate of own ability (past performance) and estimate of ability required to be successful in the chosen occupation (level of aspiration). A very large positive goal discrepancy implied that the subject was aspiring to an occupation that demanded so much more ability than he said he had that it was comparable to choice of a very difficult task, that is, one having a very low probability of success *for him*. A negative goal discrepancy implied just the opposite; the subject was setting his aspiration low—choosing what was an easy task *for him*. This distribution of "goal discrepancy scores" (see p. 98) was divided into thirds, yielding the results shown in Table 9.5 which confirm the prediction that men strong in achievement motive but weak in motive to avoid failure would have "realistic" (intermediate) levels of vocational aspiration while the most anxious group (Low $n$ Achievement-High Test Anxiety) would be unrealistic in vocational aspiration.

Mahone also had three clinical psychologists consider each student's vocational aspiration in reference to ability test scores, past performance in school, and other pertinent data and to rate the aspiration as "realistic" or "unrealistic." The clinical psychologists were also asked to indicate how confident they felt of their ratings in each case. Table 9.6 shows the results obtained when only those ratings

TABLE 9.5

Effect of individual differences in $n$ Achievement and Anxiety on subjective Goal Discrepancy of vocational aspirations of male college students. *The distribution of goal discrepancy scores was divided into thirds.* (Based on Mahone, 1960)

| | | | Absolute Goal Discrepancy score | |
|---|---|---|---|---|
| $n$ Achievement | Anxiety | N | Mid-third | Highest or Lowest third |
| High | — | Low | 36 | 50 %* | 50 % |
| High | — | High | 30 | 30 % | 70 % |
| Low | — | Low | 40 | 38 % | 62 % |
| Low | — | High | 28 | 18 %* | 82 % |

*$p < .01$

in which the clinicians were very confident are considered: a striking confirmation of the result obtained using an index of level of aspiration derived from the theory of achievement motivation. It is of interest to note that most of the "unrealism" in aspiration in the Mahone study took the form of overaspiration. This is the most socially acceptable way of protecting oneself from the anxiety about failure which accompanies realistic achievement-oriented action. The major findings of this study have recently been confirmed in a study of vocational aspiration in high-school boys (Atkinson and O'Connor, 1963).

TABLE 9.6

$n$ Achievement and Anxiety related to confident clinical judgements of realistic-unrealistic vocational choice in male college students (Based on Mahone, 1960)

| | | | Clinical judgements of stated aspirations | |
|---|---|---|---|---|
| $n$ Achievement | Anxiety | N | Realistic | Un-realistic |
| High | — | Low | 18 | 94 %* | 6 % |
| High | — | High | 9 | 56 % | 44 % |
| Low | — | Low | 19 | 74 % | 26 % |
| Low | — | High | 12 | 17 %* | 83 % |

*$p < .001$

NOTE: Only cases on which two clinical psychologists not only agreed in the judgement but also indicated they were "Very confident" or "Moderately confident" are included in this table.

## SOCIAL MOBILITY

Mahone's study provides encouraging evidence of the potential generality of the theory of achievement motivation which has evolved through experimental analysis of the effects of differences in $n$ Achievement and anxiety on risk-preference (aspiration) and performance of simple tasks. Crockett (1962) has reviewed other evidence obtained by sociologists which substantiates what the data obtained by Mahone implies: occupations which are perceived as more difficult to attain are accorded higher prestige, that is, $I_s = 1 - P_s$. Crockett employed the theory of achievement motivation to derive the hypothesis that men who are strong in $n$ Achievement should be more upwardly mobile in society than men who are weak in $n$ Achievement. Since the hierarchy of occupations has the conceptual properties of a series of achievement tasks which differ in difficulty, the greater realism, effort, and persistence in achievement-oriented activity found to characterize the behavior of persons scoring High in $n$ Achievement in simple laboratory experiments should also be expected in day-to-day activities on the job. Consequently they should advance rapidly and be promoted to positions that rank higher on the status ordering of occupations. Crockett tested this hypothesis in a secondary analysis of data obtained by Veroff *et al.* (1960) in a national survey study which included thematic apperceptive measures of $n$ Achievement, $n$ Affiliation, and $n$ Power. He classified the male respondents in this survey study according to the occupational prestige category of their fathers and then compared the occupational prestige category of each respondent (i.e., his present occupation) with that of his father. The results, shown in Table 9.7, represent the first empirical evidence, employing an experimentally validated measure of human motivation, that strength of motive to achieve is a significant factor in social mobility. The result is of course consistent with the common-sense presumption that "ambitious" people move ahead faster. The significance of the result lies not in its novelty as a fact, but in the demonstration it provides of the apparent validity of the measuring instrument and of a more general application of the theoretical scheme which led to its use in such a study.

## BROAD SOCIETAL IMPLICATIONS

Considerably more is known about the social origins and consequences of the achievement motive as assessed through content analysis of samples of imaginative behavior. Much of this work is reviewed in *Talent and Society* (McClelland, Baldwin, Bronfenbrenner, and Strodtbeck, 1958), *Motives in Fantasy, Action, and Society* (Atkinson, 1958), and in studies by Rosen *et al.* (1956, 1959a, 1959b), Strodtbeck *et al.* (1957, 1958a, 1958b), and Veroff (1960, 1961). The most comprehensive and thought-provoking integration of all this material is presented by McClelland (1961) in *The Achieving Society*. This book presents evidence of the relationship of $n$ Achievement, as assessed through content analysis of

TABLE 9.7

Strength of Achievement Motive and occupational mobility. (Based on Crockett, 1962)

| Occupational prestige category of father | Strength of Achievement Motive | $N$ (368) | Occupational prestige category of Respondent in relation to that of father | | | | | |
|---|---|---|---|---|---|---|---|---|
| | | | Below | Difference | Same | Difference | Above | Difference |
| High (78–93) | High | 20 | 55% | | 45% | 0 | .. | |
| | Low | 11 | 55% | | 45% | | .. | |
| Upper middle (69–77) | High | 50 | 42% | 0 | 32% | | 26% | +3% |
| | Low | 43 | 42% | | 35% | | 23% | n.s. |
| Lower middle (61–68) | High | 67 | 16% | −12% | 41% | | 43% | +18% |
| | Low | 52 | 28% | $p < .16$ | 47% | | 25% | $p < .06$ |
| Low (33–60) | High | 60 | .. | | 33% | | 67% | +21% |
| | Low | 65 | .. | | 54% | | 46% | $p < .04$ |

NOTE: The numbers within parentheses represent the occupational prestige index of the father's occupation. Statistical tests of significance are one-tailed tests of directional predictions.

historical literary documents and through other means, to indices of economic development and the rise and fall of whole societies, and the results of similar behavioral studies conducted in several different contemporary societies. We must put aside the temptation to go farther in our review of the societal implications of this work in order to direct attention to some implications of the theory of achievement motivation for integration of studies of *n* Achievement and Anxiety and for the general theory of motivation. This we shall attempt to do in the remaining sections of the present chapter and in the final chapter.

## EXPECTANCY OF SUCCESS: AN IMPORTANT MOTIVATIONAL VARIABLE

### ABILITY AS AN INDEX OF PROBABILITY OF SUCCESS

A recent study by Spielberger (1959) of the effects of Manifest Anxiety on academic performance in college students who differed in general ability provides an occasion for seeing the importance of "expectancy of success" as a motivational variable. Spielberger hypothesized that anxious students would obtain poorer grades and would be more likely to drop out of school due to academic failure than non-anxious students. The Manifest Anxiety Scale was administered to all introductory psychology students at a large university at the beginning of six consecutive semesters. The American Council of Education Examination for college freshmen provided a measure of scholastic ability. And the grade-point average (GPA) obtained by each student for the single semester during which he took the MAS served as the criterion of academic performance. The GPA at the particular school was a weighted average of grades assigned, where 4 points were credited for each hour of A, 3 points for each hour of B, and so on to 0 points for each hour of F. Male students who scored in the upper and lower 20 per cent of MAS scores were designated High and Low in manifest anxiety.

The students were subdivided into five levels of scholastic ability so that each level represented about one fifth of the total sample. The lowest level of ability was designated I and the highest level of ability was designated V. The average GPA (performance) of the High and Low anxiety groups were then compared at each level of ability.

The results, shown in Figure 9.3, indicate that in

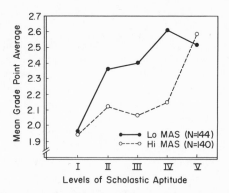

FIGURE 9.3    Mean grade point average for college students at five levels of scholastic ability who are High and Low in Anxiety. (*From Spielberger, 1962, p. 423*)

the broad middle range of ability, students who were High in MAS obtained poorer grades than students who were Low in MAS. The effects of both anxiety and ability on academic performance were statistically significant.

Further analysis of the results, including all subjects tested rather than just extreme groups, showed what is suggested in Figure 9.3. The correlation between MAS scores and GPA was insignificant among students in the lowest ability group ($r = -.04$) and the highest ability group ($r = -.05$), but was statistically significant ($r = -.18$) among students in the three middle levels of ability combined, which represent the middle 60 per cent of intellectual ability.

These results are consistent with the theory of achievement motivation if it can be assumed (a) that the Manifest Anxiety Scale provides a measure of the motive to avoid failure ($M_{AF}$) that is normally aroused in achievement-oriented academic performance; and (b) that a student's knowledge of his own relative ability is one of the most important determinants of his expectancy of success, or subjective probability of success ($P_s$), in schoolwork. The increase in grade-point average associated with an increase in the measured level of ability can obviously be attributed to ability. But the difference between High and Low anxiety groups at each level of ability is the sort of motivational effect on performance which is normally studied in achievement-oriented experimental conditions. According to the theory of achievement motivation, the effects of individual differences in strength of disposition to be anxious about failure should be most pronounced when the task is one of intermediate difficulty. When the task appears either extremely difficult or very easy to the person, that is, when the $P_s$ is either very high or very low, neither positive motivation to achieve nor anxiety about failure is strongly aroused. But when strength of expectancy of success is intermediate, as presumably it would be among students in the middle range of ability, then both achievement-related motives are strongly aroused and differences in strength of motivation that are attributable to differences in strength of motives are maximized.

Further evidence presented by Spielberger concerning subsequent rates of dropping out of college among High and Low anxiety groups may be considered in reference to results in studies of persistence. Considering only the relatively able students (those in Levels II, III, IV, and V on ability), he found that the percentage of students High in anxiety who dropped out due to academic failure was nearly four times as great as the percentage of students Low in anxiety who dropped out for that reason.

Interpretation of these findings in terms of the theory of achievement motivation suggests that similar studies, employing measures of both $n$ Achievement and of Test Anxiety (which focuses more directly on anxiety experienced in academic situations) should find trends similar to those reported by Spielberger, but exaggerated when the subgroup High in $n$ Achievement and Low in Anxiety is compared with the subgroup Low in $n$ Achievement and High in Anxiety.

MOTIVATIONAL EFFECT OF ABILITY
GROUPING IN SCHOOLS

The assumption that an individual's knowledge of his own ability (past performance) influences his expectancy of success ($P_s$) in an academic situation has further interesting implications for understanding motivation in the schools. When the full range of abilities is represented among the students in a classroom, only the students of average ability should be very strongly motivated to achieve and/or to avoid failure, depending upon the relative strengths of their $M_S$ and $M_{AF}$, the two personality dispositions which they "bring in the door." Neither the very bright nor very dull student should have his achievement-related dispositions aroused, for the competitive achievement situation will seem either "too easy" or "too difficult." What, then, should happen if classes are organized in terms of ability level? The bright student, surrounded by other equally bright students, and the less endowed student, surrounded by peers of comparable ability, should find themselves in an altogether different achievement-oriented situation. If the theory is correct, and the assumption that knowledge of one's own general ability influences the subjective probability of success at any task, there should be an intensification of both interest in achieving and anxiety about failing (depending upon the relative strength of the achievement-related dispositions of personality) when students of nearly equal ability sit in the same classroom.

Atkinson and O'Connor (1963) have investigated some of the motivational implications of ability grouping among sixth-grade children. It was assumed that success in the classroom is largely a matter of comparing one's own day-to-day performance with the observed performance of peers. If so, the very bright child should normally have a very high $P_s$ and the very dull child a very low $P_s$ in the traditional classroom in which ability is heterogeneous. This means that the achievement-related motivation of quite a number of students is likely to be less strongly aroused than if students were placed into classes that were homogeneous in ability. These investigators compared the reported interest of sixth-grade students in their schoolwork and the amount of growth in achievement between 5th and 6th grades as measured by the standard tests of school achievement hat are administered each year in the school system of a midwestern city. The results shown in Table 9.8 for students of different levels of ability, according to whether they were in traditional "heterogeneous classes" (the control group) or classes that were "homogeneous" in ability (the experimental group), are generally consistent with the theory of achievement motivation. There was a substantially higher level of performance among students who were strong in $n$ Achievement and weak in Test Anxiety ($M_S > M_{AF}$) when in homogeneous classes than when in heterogeneous classes, and the growth of this group exceeded that of students who were weak in $n$ Achievement and strong in Test Anxiety ($M_{AF} > M_S$) in the homogeneous classes. There was, however, no evidence that students of average ability were more highly motivated than other students in the traditional, heterogeneous class.

Degree of interest and satisfaction in schoolwork was assessed in a smaller number of the classes by asking students to rate their interest in a number of school activities in sixth grade as compared to their interest and satisfaction when in fifth grade. Accord-

TABLE 9.8

Motivational effects of ability grouping in sixth grade: the percentage of students showing above-median growth for their intelligence level in Reading and Arithmetic on California Achievement Test (Based on Atkinson and O'Connor, 1963)

| Resultant Achievement motivation (n Achievement-Test Anxiety) | Homogeneous Classes | | Heterogeneous Classes | |
|---|---|---|---|---|
| | N | % Above Median | N | % Above Median |
| | IQ 125 AND ABOVE | | | |
| | Both Areas | | Both Areas | |
| High | (24) | 71% | (37) | 46% |
| Low | (10) | 50% | (27) | 37% |
| | IQ 113–124 | | | |
| | Both or One Area | | Both or One Area | |
| High | (11) | 90% | (17) | 41% |
| Low | (17) | 65% | (19) | 58% |
| | IQ 112 AND BELOW | | | |
| High | (8) | 88% | (8) | 38% |
| Low | (23) | 52% | (14) | 36% |

NOTE: When all levels of intelligence are combined, the difference between motivation groups within the homogeneous classes and the difference between classes for the high motivation group are statistically significant.

ing to the theory, students in whom $M_S > M_{AF}$ should indicate increased interest when placed in homogeneous classes, but students in whom $M_{AF} > M_S$ should be more threatened, and hence less satisfied, by the more competitive atmosphere in a class that is homogeneous in ability. The results shown in Table 9.9 are consistent with these hypotheses, all based on the assumption that it is a change in the expectancy of success which mediates the change in motivation that is expressed in both school performance and reported interest in schoolwork.

## A THEORY OF VALENCE (OR UTILITY)

An important implication of the theory of achievement motivation is the theory of valence (or utility)

TABLE 9.9

Effect of ability grouping and motivational disposition of student on interest in schoolwork: percentage of students who reported above-median interest in sixth as compared with fifth grade (From Atkinson and O'Connor, 1963)

| Resultant Achievement motivation (n Achievement-Test Anxiety) | Homogeneous Classes | | Heterogeneous Classes | |
|---|---|---|---|---|
| | N | % Above Median | N | % Above Median |
| High | 18 | 78 | 78 | 56 |
| Moderate | 22 | 41 | 82 | 43 |
| Low | 22 | 36 | 73 | 52 |

| | $\chi^2$ | p (one-tail) |
|---|---|---|
| Homogeneous: High vs. Low Motivation | 6.86 | <.005 |
| High Motivation: Between classes | 2.79 | <.05 |
| Low Motivation: Between classes | 1.67 | <.10 |

which is implicit in the statement $T_s = M_S \times P_s \times I_s$. The terms in this equation are normally stated in the order given to draw attention to the fact that the theory represents an attempt to specify the nature of the interaction implied by Lewin's programmatic equation $B = f(P,E)$. The motive to achieve ($M_S$) is conceived as a relatively general and stable personality disposition ($P$), and the environmental influence on motivation to achieve at a given task ($E$) is represented as the product of $P_s$, expectancy that performance will lead to success, and $I_s$, the value of success at that particular task. But the terms may be arranged another way to show how similar this conception is to the "Expectancy × Value" principles advanced by Tolman, Lewin, and decision theorists: $T_s = P_s \times (M_S \times I_s)$. Now it is apparent that the subjective value of success—what Tolman referred to as "demand for success," what Lewin referred to as "valence of success," and what decision theory refers to as "utility of success"—is considered a multiplicative function of $M_S$ and $I_s$.

Preliminary evidence supporting this supposition is presented in an experiment conducted by Litwin (1958). In the course of investigating risk-preferences in a variety of different games, Litwin obtained evidence bearing directly on the assumption that $I_s = 1 - P_s$ and the supposition that the subjective attractiveness of success at a given task could be conceived as equivalent to $M_S \times I_s$. He had one group of college students stand on each line drawn on a floor at one foot intervals from 1 to 18 feet from a peg employed in a ringtoss game and est mate how many times in 10 shots they would expect to throw a "ringer." This was done before they played the game. Another group of subjects was given a different task at the end of a long session in which they had played a variety of games including the ringtoss game. They were given the following instruction: "We are thinking of running the Ring Toss game again at a later date, but paying money for each hit. I would like you to designate on these sheets how much it should be worth in money to hit from each one of these lines. These values can run anywhere from 0 to $1.00" (Litwin, 1958).

Figure 9.4 shows that as the average estimated $P_s$ decreases with distance from the peg, the average

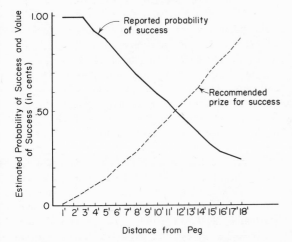

FIGURE 9.4 Average reported probability of throwing a ringer from various distances in a ringtoss game ($N = 20$) and average estimate of what would constitute a suitable monetary prize for success at each distance ($N = 20$). (*After Litwin, 1958*)

estimate of what would constitute an equitable "prize" for hitting ($I_s$) increases almost exactly as the assumption $I_s = 1 - P_s$ states that it should. It is, of course, assumed that the estimates of what would constitute a suitable prize are directly proportionate to anticipated pride in accomplishment at each distance.

Now consider what should be expected if the valence of success (or utility of success) for a particular person equals $M_S \times I_s$: *the gradient of attractiveness of success ($Va_s$) plotted in relation to the difficulty of a task should be steeper when $M_S$ is strong than when $M_S$ is weak.* This hypothesis was

tested by plotting separately the curves for average prize suggested by students who had High $n$ Achievement scores and Low $n$ Achievement scores. The result obtained is shown in Figure 9.5. The slope of the curve for the High $n$ Achievement group is

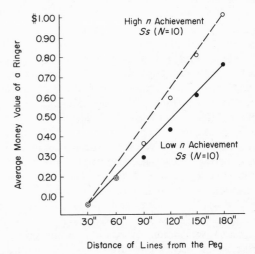

FIGURE 9.5 Average estimate of what would constitute a suitable monetary prize for success at each distance in a ringtoss game by subjects with High and Low $n$ Achievement. (*From a study by Litwin reported in McClelland, 1961, p. 236*)

significantly steeper than the slope of the curve for the Low $n$ Achievement group. That is, the difference between High and Low $n$ Achievement in attractiveness of success ($Va_s$) is larger when $I_s$ is large (a very difficult task) than when $I_s$ is small (a very easy task). That is exactly what the supposition that $Va_s = M_S \times I_s$ means. It is a specification of what is meant when one asserts that the motive to achieve might be conceived as a capacity for reacting with pride in accomplishment. Presumably, the person who is strong in achievement motive swells more with pride (like a peacock) when he succeeds at a given task than a person who is weak in achievement motive. We recall, in this connection, the important clue provided by Winterbottom (1958; also in McClelland *et al.*, 1953), who had found that teachers rated boys having high $n$ Achievement scores as expressing greater pleasure in success than boys having low $n$ Achievement scores. Anticipation of pride in accomplishment ($M_S \times I_s$) is what constitutes the subjective attractiveness or valence of success for a particular person at a particular task.

A result directly analogous to that provided in

Litwin's study had been reported even earlier by Strodtbeck *et al.* (1957), who had asked a similar question of high school boys concerning the attractiveness of various occupations. Strodtbeck *et al.* had selected 12 different occupations for ratings, two at each of six different levels in the prestige hierarchy of occupations. We have already noted (see p. 251) that the rank-order correlation between the prestige standing of occupations and the average of college students' estimates of probability of success in those occupations is −.85. Among high school students, the correlation is −.90 (Atkinson and O'Connor, 1963). We might therefore expect that the slope of attractiveness ratings in relation to the prestige ordering of occupations would provide some information concerning the strength of achievement motive among those who made the ratings.

Strodtbeck *et al.* asked approximately 1000 high school students to indicate if they would be *pleased* or *displeased* should they end up in each of the 12 occupations. The slope of percentage of *pleased* responses was plotted in relation to the prestige ordering of occupations for boys belonging to various socio-economic subgroups in the society. It was found that the slope of the curve was steeper among middle-class boys than among working-class boys and steeper among Jewish boys than among Italian boys. These results are of particular theoretical interest because other studies which have employed thematic apperception to assess *n* Achievement in various social groups have found *n* Achievement stronger in the middle class than in the working class (Douvan, 1956; Milstein, 1956; Rosen, 1955; Veroff *et al.*, 1960) and relatively stronger among Jews than among most other religious and ethnic groups (Rosen, 1959; Veroff *et al.*, 1960). In other words, the very same social groups which produced steeper slopes of attractiveness of success in relation to increasing prestige of occupations are groups known to score higher on an independent measure of strength of achievement motive.

The correspondence of results obtained in the laboratory and in societal studies of attractiveness of success at tasks which differ in difficulty, suggesting that $Va_s = M_S \times I_s$, means that the steepness of the slope of $Va_s$ as difficulty of task increases might be employed as a measure of individual differences in strength of achievement motive ($M_S$). This possibility has already been explored by Morgan *et al.* (1962, 1964) with some promising results in a survey study of economic behavior. And McClelland (1961, pp. 233–257) considers the pos-

sibility in the context of some cross-cultural results. In the next chapter, we shall discuss the possibility that the valence or utility of any goal, $Va_g$, might be conceived as equal to $M_G$ (strength of motive for a particular class of goals) $\times I_g$ (incentive value of a particular goal relative to that of others of the same class) and consider the general method for assessment of the strength of any motive that is suggested.

## EFFECTS OF SUCCESS AND FAILURE ON SUBSEQUENT MOTIVATION

So far, we have considered the theory of achievement motivation as a conception of the immediate determinants of the strength of the tendency to act in a certain way in *achievement-oriented* situations. The theory proposes that the strength of the tendency to approach success through performance of some particular act ($T_s$) is a multiplicative function of $M_S \times P_s \times I_s$ in the simplest case. This turns out to be one particular phrasing of an "Expectancy $\times$ Value" theory. It is designed to account for the same behavioral phenomena that are discussed in terms of the $_sE_R = D \times {_sH_R}$ principle of *S-R* behavior theory. In empirical studies, it has been assumed that the *n* Achievement score obtained from thematic apperceptive stories provides a measure of $M_S$ and that cues in the environment at the time of performance define the strength of expectancy of success ($P_s$) at a particular task. But virtually nothing has been said concerning the antecedents of $P_s$. Why, when a particular person confronts a particular task, does he have a strong, moderately strong, or weak expectancy of success at the task? What kind of theory of learning is implied in the use of Tolman's concept of expectancy of the goal to represent the motivational effect of immediate cues in the environment?

The use of the expectancy concept implies that the relative frequency of success and failure following previous performance in similar activities determines the present strength of expectancies of success and failure at a particular task. If a person has previously taken 100 shots two feet from the target and has hit the target 95 times and missed it five times, on the next trial his expectancy of success should be very strong and his expectancy of failure should be very weak. We might assume, tentatively, that the strength of expectancy of success ($P_s$) is a function of the number of times the act has been followed by success divided by the number of times the act has been performed. Then the strength of expectancy of failure ($P_f$) will be a function of the number of times the act has been followed by failure divided by the number of times the act has been performed. This means that the effect of success is assumed to be an increase in the strength of expectancy of success at that task on a future occasion and a decrease in the strength of expectancy of failure a that task on a future occasion. In a similar manner, failure at a task is assumed to strengthen the subsequent expectancy of failure and weaken the subsequent expectancy of success.

## CHANGE IN ASPIRATION WHEN ACHIEVEMENT MOTIVE IS DOMINANT

Given these assumptions, let us consider the effects of success and failure on subsequent motivation to perform a task. We shall do this first in reference to the behavior of a person in whom $M_S > M_{AF}$ who is playing a ringtoss game. Table 9.1 (p. 242) provides a useful graphic reference for our discussion.

If the person in whom $M_S > M_{AF}$ is given a choice among tasks which differ in difficulty, he should select the task where $P_s$ equals .50—that is, Task C in Table 9.1. This constitutes what has been called "a preference for intermediate risk" and "a realistic level of aspiration." If he now undertakes this task (Task C) and succeeds one or more times, the $P_s$ at the task should increase so that on some subsequent trial the $P_s$ will exceed .50. And, assuming that the effects of success and failure generalize to other similar tasks, the $P_s$ at Task D, which was initially only .30, should increase towards .50. Thus, after one or more successes, the $P_s$ at the originally chosen task (Task C) will be greater than .50, and the $P_s$ at what initially appeared a more difficult task (Task D) will be near or at .50. The result of this change in $P_s$, given the assumption $I_s = 1 - P_s$, is diminished motivation to achieve at the initially chosen task (Task C) and increased motivation to achieve at what had initially appeared a more difficult task (Task D). The person should now choose to perform Task D. To the external observer, this constitutes a rise in the level of aspiration following success at a task.

One can appreciate more fully how success produces a change in the strength of subsequent motivation to achieve at the same task by considering what would happen if the person in whom $M_S > M_{AF}$ had been given a single, very difficult task to perform instead of a choice among alternatives which differ in difficulty:

". . . given a single, very difficult task (e.g., $P_s = .10$), the effect of continued success in repeated trials is first a gradual increase in motivation as $P_s$ increases to .50, followed by a gradual decrease in motivation as $P_s$ increases further to the point of certainty ($P_s = 1.00$). Ultimately, as $P_s$ approaches 1.00, satiation or loss of interest should occur. The task no longer arouses any motivation at all. Why? Because the subjective probability of success is so high that the incentive value is virtually zero. Here is the clue to understanding how the achievement motive can remain insatiable while satiation can occur for a particular line of activity. The strength of motive can remain unchanged, but interest in a particular task can diminish completely. Hence, when free to choose, the person who is stronger in achievement motive should always look for new and more difficult tasks as he masters old problems. If constrained, the person with a strong achievement motive should experience a gradual loss of interest in his work. If the task is of intermediate difficulty to start with ($P_s = .50$), or is definitely easy ($P_s > .50$), his interest should begin to wane after the initial experience of success" (Atkinson, 1957, p. 368).

The effect of failure on the subsequent behavior of a person in whom $M_S > M_{AF}$ is to be explained in terms of the effect of failure on subsequent strength of expectancy of success ($P_s$). If the person has initially chosen the task at which $P_s = .50$ and then he fails, the $P_s$ is reduced. Again assuming that the effects of success and failure generalize to similar activities, the $P_s$ at the task which initially appeared close in order of difficulty—that is, Task B in Table 9.1—wil also be reduced. After one or more failures, the $P_s$ at the initial task (Task C) will have dropped below .50, and the $P_s$ of the task that had initially appeared easier (Task B) will have dropped to near .50. The person should then shift to this task, which is objectively less difficult in the ordering of tasks. This change in behavior constitutes what an external observer would call a lowering of the level of aspiration. It is explained in terms of the change in strength of motivation to achieve at the task initially chosen and similar tasks that is brought about by a decrease in $P_s$ following failure.

We gain a clearer understanding of the process assumed by again considering what happens to the strength of motivation to achieve at a task when the person in whom $M_S > M_{AF}$ is given only a single task to perform rather than a choice between tasks which differ in difficulty:

"What is the effect of continued failure at a single task? If the initial task is one that appeared relatively easy to the subject (e.g., $P_s = .80$) and he fails, his motivation should increase! The $P_s$ will drop toward .70, but the incentive value or attractiveness of the task will increase. Another failure should increase his motivation even more. This will continue until the $P_s$ has dropped to .50. Further failure should then lead to a gradual weakening of motivation as $P_s$ decreases further. In other words, the tendency of persons who are relatively strong in achievement motive to persist at a task in the face of failure is probably attributable to the relatively high subjective probability of success, initially. Hence, failure has the effect of increasing the strength of their motivation, at least for a time. Ultimately, however, interest in the task will diminish if there is continued failure. If the initial task is perceived by the person as very difficult to start with ($P_s < .50$), motivation should begin to diminish with the first failure" (Atkinson, 1957, pp. 368–369).

The assumption that success increases subsequent expectancy of success and failure decreases subsequent expectancy of success, coupled with the basic assumption that $I_s = 1 - P_s$, explains the "typical" shift in aspiration following success and failure observed in many earlier studies of level of aspiration. This is the "typical" or most frequently appearing result in studies which have employed college students because most college students are more highly motivated to achieve than to avoid failure.

CHANGE IN ASPIRATION WHEN "ANXIETY" IS DOMINANT

Let us now see how the same assumptions concerning effects of success and failure on expectancy of success and failure work out when we consider the case of an individual in whom $M_{AF} > M_S$. This would be the so-called "very anxious" person, assuming that he is one in whom the tendency to avoid failure is always stronger than the tendency to approach success. He is the fellow whose resultant tendency is to avoid intermediate risk, that is, activities where $P_s = .50$.

It must be recalled that when $M_{AF} > M_S$, the resultant tendency $(T_s + T_{-f})$ in achievement-oriented situations is always negative or avoidant no matter what the level of difficulty of the task. This means that the individual is not positively motivated to undertake achievement-oriented activities at all. His tendency to avoid (or inhibit) the performance of actions which are expected to lead to failure must be overcome by other "extrinsic" sources of positive motivation. One source of extrinsic positive motivation is the need for social approval and the

expectancy that performing one of the achievement-related tasks presented to him will lead to approval. It is always assumed that total strength of the tendency to perform an achievement-oriented task equals resultant achievement motivation $(T_s + T_{-f})$ plus extrinsic motivation to perform the task. When the resultant of the two achievement-related tendencies is negative, implying avoidance or inhibition, there would be no action if extrinsic motivation to perform an activity did not overcome the avoidance or inhibition. With this in mind, we may consider the effects of success and failure on the motivation and behavior of someone in whom $M_{AF} > M_S$, as stated in the initial formulation of the theory. Table 9.3 (p. 246) provides a useful graphic reference:

"Let us turn now to the effect of success and failure on the motivation of the person who is more strongly disposed to be fearful of failure. If the person in whom the motive to avoid failure is stronger has chosen a very difficult task in setting his level of aspiration (. . . where $P_s = .10$) and succeeds, $P_s$ increases and his motivation *to avoid* the task is paradoxically increased! . . . Fortunately for this person, his strategy (determined by the nature of his motivation) in choosing a very difficult task to start with protects him from this possibility, because $P_s$ is so small that he will seldom face the paradoxical problem just described. If he fails at the most difficult task, as is likely, $P_s$ decreases further, $P_f$ increases further, and the aroused motivation to avoid failure is reduced. By continued failure he further reduces the amount of anxiety about failure that is aroused by this most difficult task. Hence, he should continue to set his level at this point. If he plays the game long enough and fails continuously, the probability of failure increases for all levels of difficulty. Sooner or later the minimal motivation to avoid failure at the most difficult task may be indistinguishable from the motivation to avoid failure at the next most difficult task. This may ultimately allow him to change his level of aspiration to a somewhat less difficult task without acting in gross contradiction to the proposed principle of motivation" (Atkinson, 1957, p. 369).

Unstated in the initial formulation, but certainly implied by the theory, is the hypothesis that if the person in whom $M_{AF} > M_S$ were to succeed at a very difficult task consistently enough to raise the $P_s$ sufficiently in the direction of .50, he would then lower his level of aspiration very substantially. That is, he should then switch to some very easy task— where $P_s$ is, for example, near .90. Why? Because the tendency to avoid failure is weaker at this task than at one where $P_s$ begins to approach .50. But if he has initially selected a task where the objective probability of success is, in fact, very low, the possibility of his having consistent enough success to produce this apparently irrational shift in aspiration is very slim indeed.

Consider now what happens if the person in whom $M_{AF} > M_S$ has been given a choice and has chosen a very easy task to perform:

> "If our fearful subject has initially chosen the easiest task (. . . where $P_s = .90$) and if he fails, $P_s$ decreases toward .80, and his motivation to avoid the task also increases. If there is no easier task, the most difficult task should now appear least *unattractive* to him, and he should jump from the easiest to the most difficult task. In other words, continued failure at a very easy task decreases $P_s$ toward .50; and, . . . [as Table 9.3 shows], a change of this sort is accompanied by increased arousal of avoidant motivation. A wild and apparently irrational jump in level of aspiration from very easy to very difficult tasks, as a consequence of failure, might be mistakenly interpreted as a possible effort on the part of the subject to gain social approval by seeming to set high goals. The present model predicts this kind of activity without appealing to some extrinsic motive. It is part of the strategy of minimizing expected pain of failure after one has failed at the easiest task.
>
> "If our fear-disposed subject is successful at the most simple task, his $P_s$ increases, his $P_f$ decreases, and his motivation to avoid this task decreases. The task becomes less and less unpleasant. He should continue playing the game with less anxiety" (Atkinson, 1957, p. 369).

The main point of what the theory of achievement motivation has to say about the person in whom the disposition to be anxious about failure is stronger than the disposition to achieve success is simply this: *his behavior in achievement-oriented situations is to be understood in terms of what he is trying not to do.* What previously were called "atypical" levels of aspirations and "atypical" changes in aspiration following success and failure are represented as lawful instances of motivated behavior in a person who would not even undertake achievement-related activities unless there were some extrinsic incentive to do so. When extrinsic positive motivation to undertake achievement activities is sufficiently strong to overcome the resistance that is attributable to his having a stronger motive to avoid failure than motive to achieve success, his behavior is characteristically defensive. That is, it is more strongly influenced by the tendency to avoid failure by avoiding realistic achievement risks than by the tendency to achieve

success. In contrast, the behavior of the person in whom $M_S > M_{AF}$ might be called an "offensive" achievement-oriented strategy. It is determined primarily by the strength of the tendency to approach success, that is, by the excitation of action tendencies which are expected to lead to success.

A number of early studies of level of aspiration conducted by Sears, Rotter, and others (reviewed in Lewin *et al.*, 1944; and Rotter, 1954) show that there is much greater variability in level of aspiration among anxious than among non-anxious groups. Eysenck and Himmelweit (1946), Himmelweit (1947), and Miller (1951), have shown that persons with affective disorders (neurasthenia or dysthymia) typically set extremely high levels of aspiration while hysterics, on the other hand, typically display very low levels of aspiration, often setting their future goals even below the level of their past performance. In these and other studies reviewed by Rotter (1954) which tend to show that "atypical" changes in aspiration following success and failure are associated with "atypical" levels of aspiration, we confront the pathology of achievement-oriented behavior. The theory of achievement motivation suggests that the pathological extremes in achievement-oriented behavior may represent merely going through the motions of achievement activity, for which there are many extrinsic pressures in modern societies, by persons who have relatively little positive interest in achieving but a potentially overwhelming disposition to be anxious about failure. Setting a very low level of aspiration, where success is virtually guaranteed, is quite obviously a protective strategy; but so, also, is the setting of extremely high goals which common sense often mistakenly takes to be the measure of a man's ambition. Excessively high level of aspiration is also to be viewed as an avoidance of more realistic achievement-oriented activities.

To date, very little work has been done to follow up the implications of the theory of achievement motivation concerning effects of success and failure in conventional studies of changes in level of aspiration. In one preliminary experiment, Vitz (1957) found that college students who were High in Test Anxiety more frequently showed "atypical" changes in aspiration following success and failure than students who were Low in Test Anxiety, as predicted. More recently Moulton (1963) has shown that "atypical" shifts in aspiration occur more frequently when $n$ Achievement is Low and Test Anxiety is High than when the two motives are nearly equal in strength or $n$ Achievement is dominant.

## PERSISTENCE IN ACHIEVEMENT-ORIENTED ACTIVITY

The most instructive application of the theory of achievement motivation is provided by Norman Feather (1960, 1961, 1962) in a study of the relationship of persistence at a task to expectation of success and the strength of achievement-related motives. This study goes beyond earlier studies of persistence in achievement-oriented activity by French and Thomas (1958) and Atkinson and Litwin (1960), in its theoretical conception of persistence, by explicitly dealing with expectancy of success ($P_s$) and achievement-related motives ($M_S$ and $M_{AF}$) as joint determinants of the resultant tendency that is expressed in persistent problem-solving activity in the face of failure. Furthermore, Feather begins to sharpen assumptions concerning the effect of failure on subsequent $P_s$, and he provides a very explicit analysis of why a subject stops performing a task before he has attained his goal. The study asks this general question: *How is persistence at a task affected by both the initial subjective probability of success (i.e., its apparent difficulty) and the personality ($M_S$ and $M_{AF}$) of the subject?*

Since Feather's work represents the most sophisticated use of ideas which have evolved in studies of *n* Achievement, his analysis of the problem and derivation of hypotheses will serve as an excellent review. We shall follow the line of his argument in some detail, but first it will help to have very clearly in mind a concrete picture of the experiment itself.

Feather first obtained thematic apperceptive *n* Achievement scores and Mandler-Sarason Test Anxiety scores for 89 college men under neutral conditions. Another investigator classified subjects High *n* Achievement-Low Test Anxiety and Low *n* Achievement-High Test Anxiety in terms of their standing above or below the median scores. Only these two extreme subgroups, one in which Feather assumed $M_S > M_{AF}$ and the other in which he assumed $M_{AF} > M_S$, were later tested for persistence. On a later occasion, each subject was tested individually by the experimenter, who did not know to which motivation group the subject belonged. Each subject was given an achievement-oriented instruction concerning a new kind of "perceptual reasoning test" he was asked to perform. It consisted of four items. Each item was a type of line puzzle which the subject was asked to solve without retracing any lines or lifting his pencil once he had started. The puzzle was printed on a white card, and there were a stack of cards for each puzzle so the subject could simply take another of the same kind if he felt he had made a false start and wanted to start over on the same item. Unknown to the subject, the first "item" he was given was insoluble. So all subjects had the experience of trying the first card, not getting the solution, picking up another identical card to start over on it, and so on. Since all cards in the stack for the first item were identical, each new card represented another trial at the original puzzle following a failure. Feather kept track of both the number of trials and the amount of time spent on the first puzzle. When the subject decided to give up on the first "item" of the test, he was free to move on to the second item. Subjects were not allowed to spend more than 40 seconds on any single card, but they could have as many identical cards (trials) as they desired before moving on to the next "item" of the test.

In the instructions to the subjects, the examiner made it clear that the test consisted of *four items which varied in difficulty*. He said: "Some are harder than others, and you're not expected to be able to solve all of them, but do the best you can" (Feather, 1961, p. 556). Then, to give subjects some idea of the difficulty of the first item (and thus to control the probability of success at the first item), the examiner referred to a table of norms which supposedly showed how others in the same age group had done on that item in earlier tests. The norms quoted to subjects were fictitious and designed to create the impression that the first task was either rather easy or very difficult. Half the subjects were told that approximately 70 per cent of college students are able to get the solution (an easy task). The other half of the subjects were told that only about 5 per cent of college students were able to get the solution (a very difficult task). Thus Feather was in a position to study persistence in achievement-oriented activity by persons in whom $M_S > M_{AF}$ and persons in whom $M_{AF} > M_S$ as a function of the apparent difficulty of the task (when $P_s = .05$ and when $P_s = .70$).

Now let us consider his conceptualization of the problem and his derivation of hypotheses from the theory of achievement motivation. Feather made a very important discovery in designing the experiment. *He realized that he could not derive a very specific hypothesis about how long anyone would continue to persist in the attempt to solve the first puzzle without knowing something about the alternative to which the individual might turn when he decided to give up the initial activity.* Earlier studies by French and Thomas (1958) and Atkinson and Litwin (1960) had merely observed time spent in an achievement activity before the subject left the situation to do something else. But Feather realized it was necessary to begin his study with the assumption that *once a person has initiated a task "he will continue to persist at this task as long as total motivation to perform it is stronger than total motivation to perform the alternative available to him"* (Feather, 1961, p. 552, italics added). The full significance of this assumption for the general theory of motivation will be discussed in the final chapter. The need for such an assumption is what led Feather to study persistence at an initial item in a larger achievement test consisting of four different items. This provided some basis for assumptions about the strength of motivation to undertake the alternative activity.

THE COMPONENTS OF THE TENDENCY
TO PERFORM A TASK

Given this basic assumption, the next step was to analyze the components of the total strength of motivation to perform the initial task and the alternative to which the individual might turn. Following the arguments developed in earlier work, Feather considered the total strength of the tendency to perform a task to be the summation of the *resultant* of tendency to approach success and tendency to avoid failure (the achievement-related component) and extrinsic motivation to perform the task, that is, the strength of the tendency to perform the task that must be accounted for in terms of other motives and incentives than those intrinsically related to achievement and failure. His argument concerning extrinsic motivation is worth noting to reinforce the conception advanced in earlier pages:

"If achievement related motivation were the only motivation elicited in the situation it is apparent that a subject with stronger motive to avoid failure should not even undertake performance of an achievement task. Instead he should avoid the task and choose activities which do not arouse anxiety about failure. In contrast, a subject with stronger motive to achieve success should show some positive interest in performing an achievement task.

"The concept of extrinsic motivation to perform a task is introduced to account for the fact that the subject is in a social situation in which he has the role of a subject in an experiment and knows he is expected to make some attempt at the task.

In any test situation there are certain extrinsic constraints that influence the subject to perform the task irrespective of the nature of his achievement related motivation. Studies by French (1955), and by Atkinson and Raphelson (1956) have shown, for example, that other motives like *n* Affiliation are sometimes systematically related to task performance in a situation where no achievement orientation is given but cooperation is requested. The usual social constraints (i.e., desire for approval, fear of disapproval) provide an important source of motivation for subjects in whom $M_{AF} > M_S$. If these subjects are to perform the task at all, some positive motivation must exist to oppose their tendency to avoid an achievement task. For subjects in whom $M_S > M_{AF}$, the extrinsic motivation to perform an assigned task enhances their normally positive motivation to perform achievement related tasks. In both cases, task performance may be considered overdetermined, that is, the result of two or more different kinds of motivation to perform or not to perform the task (cf. Atkinson and Reitman, 1956)" (Feather, 1961, p. 553).

In light of this analysis of the components of the total strength of the tendency to perform a task, Feather assumed that the basic condition for performance of the initial task rather than the alternative task was:

*Initial Task*
Achievement-related Motivation
  + Extrinsic Motivation

*Alternative Task*
  > Achievement-related Motivation
    + Extrinsic Motivation

Feather assumed that the subject would turn to the alternative achievement task (the second item on the test) when:

*Initial Task*
Achievement-related Motivation
  + Extrinsic Motivation

*Alternative Task*
  < Achievement-related Motivation
    + Extrinsic Motivation

The reader is reminded that in studies of *n* Achievement the term *motivation* is often used in reference to the aroused state of a person to strive for some goal. It refers to the strength of the tendency to act in a certain way in order to get on to the goal. The term *motive* is used in reference to a relatively general and stable personality disposition which is assumed to be one of the determinants of *motivation*, the tendency to strive for the goal. We may avoid confusion by substituting the term tendency for motivation in Feather's conception.

Thus it is assumed that the basic condition for performance of the initial task rather than the alternative task is:

Initial Task (A)

$$T_A = (T_{s_A} + T_{-f_A}) + T_{ext_A}$$

Alternative Task (B)

$$> T_B = (T_{s_B} + T_{-f_B}) + T_{ext_B}$$

This may be read, the strength of the tendency to perform the initial activity ($T_A$) is greater than the strength of the tendency to perform the alternative activity ($T_B$), given that the strength of $T_A$ is determined by the resultant achievement-related tendency ($T_{s_A} + T_{-f_A}$) plus the tendency to perform that activity which is attributable to other extrinsic motives and incentives ($T_{ext_A}$) and assuming that the strength of the tendency to perform the alternative activity ($T_B$) represents a similar summation of resultant achievement-related tendency ($T_{s_B} + T_{-f_B}$) and extrinsic tendency ($T_{ext_B}$).

It is assumed, then, that the subject will turn to the alternative activity when:

Initial Task (A)

$$T_A = (T_{s_A} + T_{-f_A}) + T_{ext_A}$$

Alternative Task (B)

$$< T_B = (T_{s_B} + T_{-f_B}) + T_{ext_B}$$

## DERIVATION OF HYPOTHESES

How does the strength of the tendency to perform the initial task ($T_A$) become weaker than the strength of the tendency to perform the alternative ($T_B$) so that the subject gives up the initial task and undertakes the alternative instead? This was the question Feather posed, and these are the additional assumptions he introduced in order to derive specific hypotheses for persons in whom $M_S > M_{AF}$ and in whom $M_{AF} > M_S$:

1. The strength of extrinsic tendency to perform the initial activity ($T_{ext_A}$) and extrinsic tendency to perform the alternative activity ($T_{ext_B}$) were assumed to be equal (constant) across experimental conditions. (This assumes that whatever the extrinsic sources of positive motivation for undertaking the tasks, the net effect is equal when the initial task is

presented as easy ($P_s = .70$) and very difficult ($P_s = .05$).)

2. The extrinsic tendency to perform the initial task ($T_{ext_A}$) is somewhat stronger than the extrinsic tendency to perform the alternative activity ($T_{ext_B}$). (This assumption acknowledges that the subject is asked by the experimenter to begin the initial task first.)

3. Subjective probability of success ($P_s$) for the alternative task is assumed constant across experimental conditions. Hence the resultant tendency to achieve success at the alternative task ($T_{s_B} + T_{-f_B}$) has a constant positive value for subjects in whom $M_S > M_{AF}$ and a constant negative value for subjects in whom $M_{AF} > M_S$, whether they start with an initial task that is very difficult or relatively easy.

Any or all of these assumptions may be incorrect. The point of importance is to note that some such assumptions must be made in order to specify clearly how the strength of achievement-related motives and the apparent difficulty of a task will influence persistence at that task. Research on achievement motivation has come a long way from the earliest studies which proceeded to explore the simple hypothesis that TAT *n* Achievement scores should be positively related to achievement-oriented behavior.

Given this set of assumptions, Feather points out that any decrease in the tendency to perform the initial task must come about as a result of some change in the strength of the resultant achievement-related tendency ($T_{s_A} + T_{-f_A}$). Since the general motives to achieve ($M_S$) and to avoid failure ($M_{AF}$) are considered relatively stable personality dispositions, the change must be mediated by a change in the strength of the subject's expectancy of success ($P_s$) as he works unsuccessfully at the initial task.

Following the initial statement of the theory (Atkinson, 1957), Feather assumed that repeated unsuccessful attempts at the initial task would produce successive decreases in the subjective probability of success at the task ($P_s$). In addition, he advanced two specific assumptions about the decrease in $P_s$ following failure:

"1. When the task is presented as a test of skill, reduction in $P_s$ to a particular value is assumed to require more unsuccessful attempts at the task when $P_s$ is initially high than when $P_s$ is initially low.
"2. The rate at which decrease in $P_s$ occurs is assumed not to be systematically related to the strength of either the motive to achieve success

$(M_S)$ or the motive to avoid failure $(M_{AF})$" (Feather, 1961, p. 554).

Given this full analysis of the factors to be taken into consideration, and plausible assumptions to fill the gaps where knowledge is lacking, Feather derived the following hypotheses:

1. When $M_S > M_{AF}$ (i.e., when the motive to achieve success is dominant within the person), persistence at the initial task should be greater when initial $P_s$ is high (i.e., $P_s = .70$) than when initial $P_s$ is low (i.e., $P_s = .05$). When the resultant tendency is to approach success and the person begins a task that appears relatively easy (e.g., $P_s = .70$) and then fails, the magnitude of the resultant tendency to achieve success should initially increase as $P_s$ drops to .50 and only then begin to decrease. Hence the tendency to perform the initial task will initially become stronger, and only after $P_s$ has dropped to .50 will it begin to decrease. Finally, some low level of $P_s$ is reached at which point the tendency to perform the initial task will be weaker than the tendency to perform the alternative. In contrast, when the initial task appears very difficult ($P_s = .05$) to begin with, the resultant tendency to achieve success will begin to diminish immediately as the subject fails. So it should take fewer failures to weaken the tendency to perform that task sufficiently so that the tendency to perform the alternative task is the stronger tendency.

2. When $M_{AF} > M_S$ (i.e., when the disposition to avoid failure is dominant), persistence at the initial task should be greater when the initial $P_s$ is low (i.e., $P_s = .05$) than when the initial $P_s$ is high (i.e., $P_s = .70$). Here, we must recall, the resultant achievement-oriented tendency $(T_s + T_{-f})$ is negative, implying avoidance and inhibition. When the task initially appears easy ($P_s = .70$) and then the subject fails, the $P_s$ begins to drop immediately towards .50, where the strength of the avoidance tendency is greatest. At this point the tendency to perform the initial activity should be at its minimum. And, as Feather has asserted:

"It follows that, if the subject is to quit the task at all, he should do so as his $P_s$ at the task falls to .50 since it is during this stage of task performance that total motivation to perform the task is decreasing.

"In contrast, if the initial task were presented to this subject as very difficult (i.e., some $P_s < .50$), there would be an immediate decrease in negative achievement related motivation as his $P_s$ drops with repeated failure. Hence, total motivation to perform the initial task would increase immedi-

ately, and the subject should continue to perform the task indefinitely. We would therefore expect a subject in whom $M_{AF} > M_S$ to persist longer at the initial achievement task when $P_s$ is initially low than when his $P_s$ is initially high" (Feather, 1961, p. 555).

The arguments presented above justify two further hypotheses:

3. When the initial $P_s$ is high (i.e., $P_s = .70$), subjects in whom $M_S > M_{AF}$ should persist longer at the initial task than subjects in whom $M_{AF} > M_S$.

4. When the initial $P_s$ is low (i.e., $P_s = .05$), subjects in whom $M_{AF} > M_S$ should persist longer at the initial task than subjects in whom $M_S > M_{AF}$.

In other words, the theory of achievement motivation produces the hypothesis that *under certain circumstances persistence in achievement-oriented activity will be greater among more anxious individuals than among individuals who are strongly motivated to achieve.* This should occur when the alternative to which the individual might turn represents an even greater threat than the activity in which he is currently engaging. This, presumably, is why some persons maintain an unrealistically high level of aspiration in the face of consistent failure.

INTERACTION OF PERSONALITY AND
ENVIRONMENTAL FACTORS

The major results of Feather's study are shown in Table 9.10. He found that the amount of time spent in attempting to solve the initial puzzle was perfectly correlated with the number of trials taken, which ranged from 2 to 41 among all his subjects. The median number of trials taken before leaving the first puzzle was 20, so Feather tested his hypotheses in terms of the number of subjects in a particular group who were high in persistence (above the median) and low in persistence (below the median).

The results shown in Table 9.10 confirm all of the hypotheses. Subjects who were High in $n$ Achievement but Low in Test Anxiety were more persistent when the initial task appeared easy ($P_s = .70$) than when it appeared very difficult ($P_s = .05$). Subjects who were Low in $n$ Achievement but High in Test Anxiety were more persistent when the initial task appeared very difficult ($P_s = .05$) than when it appeared relatively easy ($P_s = .70$). When the task appeared relatively easy, the group in which the motive to achieve was dominant were more persistent in the face of failure than the group in whom the disposition to be anxious about failure was dominant. When, however, the task appeared very

TABLE 9.10

Persistence following failure related to initial expectancy of success and motivational disposition of the individual: number of subjects who were high and low in persistence in relation to stated difficulty of the initial task and the nature of their motivation (From Feather, 1961)

| | | | Persistence trials | |
|---|---|---|---|---|
| $n$ Achievement | Test Anxiety | Stated difficulty of task | High (above median) | Low (below median) |
| High — Low | | $P_s = .70$ (easy) | 6 | 2 |
| | | $P_s = .05$ (difficult) | 2 | 7 |
| Low — High | | $P_s = .70$ (easy) | 3 | 6 |
| | | $P_s = .05$ (difficult) | 6 | 2 |

Partition of $\chi^2$

| Source | Value | $df$ | $p$ |
|---|---|---|---|
| Motivation $\times$ Persistence | .12 | 1 | ns |
| Expectation $\times$ Persistence | .12 | 1 | ns |
| Motivation $\times$ Expectation $\times$ Persistence | 7.65 | 1 | <.01 |
| Total | 7.89 | 3 | <.05 |

difficult to begin with, the group in whom the achievement motive was dominant were *less* persistent than the group in whom the motive to avoid failure was dominant. Those more highly motivated to achieve success spent very little time trying to solve a puzzle which they had been told that only 5 out of 100 college students were able to solve. They moved on to the next item, which, in light of the experimenter's instruction that the four items differed in difficulty, probably represented a more realistic risk. The group disposed to be anxious about failure, however, were very persistent in their attention to this task. Some of them finally had to be interrupted by the experimenter after 41 trials without success.

Feather's results illustrate the motivational effect of the expectancy that a given activity will lead to *success*. Furthermore, they show how the same change in expectancy of success following failure produces diametrically opposite effects in different persons when individual differences in the nature of their achievement-related motives is taken into ac-

count. Perhaps more clearly than any other study, Feather's results give meaning to Lewin's programmatic equation $B = f(P,E)$.

## A CRITICAL PROBLEM: MEASURING THE EXPECTANCY OF SUCCESS

The most critical problem in contemporary research on achievement-related motivation is that of defining the strength of expectancy of success ($P_s$) for particular individuals. The theory of achievement motivation leans heavily on the assumption that $I_s = 1 - P_s$ and $T_s = M_S \times P_s \times I_s$, where $P_s$ is the measure of expectancy of success for a particular person. A number of studies of level of aspiration, or risk preference, have been undertaken on the assumption that given a sufficient range of tasks which differ in apparent difficulty, the point at which $P_s$ equals .50 for all subjects will fall somewhere in the intermediate range of difficulty. Other studies, like Feather's, have assumed that there would be enough correspondence between stated probabilities and subjective probabilities of success aroused by them to conduct meaningful research guided by the theory. These techniques are useful first approximations, but the need for greater precision in defining the strength of expectancy of success for particular individuals at particular tasks is an imperative one.

Consider what might occur if an experimenter wanted to conduct a study of risk preference involving putting golf balls into a cup from various distances and, unknown to him, several professional golfers were among the subjects in his experiment. The experiment might be arranged so that subjects could putt anywhere from 1 foot to 10 feet from the cup on the assumption that $P_s$ would be near 1.00 for everyone at 1 foot and near 0 at 10 feet from the cup, with $P_s = .50$ falling somewhere in between. But in this case, the professional golfers (who would undoubtedly score High in $n$ Achievement and Low in Test Anxiety) would probably take most of their shots from around 8, 9, or 10 feet from the cup *because* their subjective probability of success ($P_s$) was near .50 at those distances and very much higher at shorter distances. Their actions would be consistent with the theory, but would represent evidence contrary to the theory if the experimenter had blandly assumed $P_s = .50$ for all subjects in the region 4, 5, or 6 feet from the cup. The professional golfers would appear to be setting their aspiration unrealistically high. It would appear to an observer that they were avoiding intermediate risks when, in fact, they were taking what *for them* was an intermediate or realistic risk.

The problem is complicated by the fact that there is some evidence that persons who are strongly motivated to achieve normally have a higher subjective probability of success than persons who are weak in achievement motive or anxious about failure when the task is held constant. McClelland *et al.* (1953) report that when students are asked what score they *expect* to make on a final exam, those who are High in *n* Achievement report a higher grade than those who are Low in *n* Achievement. Pottharst (1955) asked high school boys what score they *expected* to make on a novel task and also found that those having high *n* Achievement scores reported a higher score than those having low *n* Achievement scores. Atkinson *et al.* (1960) report a similar result when subjects were asked how many students in the class they *expected* to beat in a ringtoss game. All these results suggest that $P_s$ may normally be somewhat higher at a given task among those subjects in whom $M_S$ is strong than among those in whom $M_S$ is weak. If so, this would appear to be a special case of the relationship between the subjective value (or utility) of an outcome and subjective probability of that outcome to which Irwin has directed attention. (See p. 209.) When the determinants of the tendency to approach success ($T_s$) are formulated $T_s = P_s \times (M_S \times I_s)$, it is clear that $M_S \times I_s$ corresponds to what decision theorists call *utility* and what Lewin called *valence*. In the case of achievement motivation, $M_S$ is one of the determinants of the valence or utility of success. So results which show that persons having high *n* Achievement scores report higher expectancy of success than persons having low scores (holding the task constant) mean essentially the same thing as Irwin's results which show that reported expectancy of attaining a goal is higher when the incentive value of the goal is higher.

It appears to be congruent with another important implication of the theory that subjective probability of success at a given task should be somewhat higher among persons in whom $M_S > M_{AF}$ than persons in whom $M_{AF} > M_S$. Why? Because if previous success and failure at similar activities is what really determines the expectancy of success at a given activity, it is to be expected that persons in whom $M_S > M_{AF}$ will have had more past successes than persons in whom $M_{AF} > M_S$. That is what most experiments on the effects of *n* Achievement or Test Anxiety on achievement-oriented performance have shown. One group performs at a higher level than the other. An accumulation of such experiences would show that one group has, in fact, had greater frequency of success in the past than the other group.

It is this kind of argument which suggests that some independent measure of a subject's general ability may provide a useful indicator of his probability of success in academic work or at tasks which appear to be intelligence-type tests, as pointed out in reference to the Spielberger study of anxiety and academic performance (see p. 254) and the study of effects of ability grouping (see p. 255). The problem of measuring expectancy of success for a particular individual at a particular task remains a critical one in current research guided by the theory of achievement motivation. The general problem of measuring expectancies has been advanced in the work of Rotter and co-workers (1954) and is taken up in reference to research on achievement motivation by McClelland (1961).

## SUMMARY: THE STUDY OF ACHIEVEMENT MOTIVATION

We have traced the evolution of a conception of the immediate determinants of performance in research employing the thematic apperceptive measure of individual differences in *n* Achievement. The research began with a demonstration that college students in an experimentally heightened state of motivation to perform well on certain tests produced more future-oriented imaginative responses having to do with achievement in thematic apperceptive stories than students who were in a relaxed state at the time of writing thematic apperceptive stories. Then followed a number of exploratory studies guided by the general hypothesis that persons who obtain high thematic apperceptive *n* Achievement scores under neutral conditions are normally more highly motivated to achieve than persons who obtain low *n* Achievement scores under the same conditions. These exploratory studies examined the relationship between TAT *n* Achievement scores and performance under a variety of conditions and gave birth to the notion that the strength of motivation to achieve at a particular task in a particular situation must be viewed as jointly determined by a general disposition to achieve (called achievement motive) and an expectancy concerning the consequences of action that is defined by situational cues at the time of performance. Studies guided by this general hypothesis finally led to an interest in the effects of strength of expectancy that action will lead to success and incentive value of success at a particular task. In 1957, the initial statement of a theory of the determinants of achievement-oriented performance in terms of two equally important achievement-related motives, $M_S$ and $M_{AF}$, appeared. The theory, which is an extension and elaboration of ideas originally advanced by Lewin, Escalona, and Festinger in the resultant-valence theory of level of aspiration, provides a conceptual framework within which results from studies of individual differences in n Achievement and/or disposition to be anxious may be integrated and compared.

In the initial statement of the theory (Atkinson, 1957), the diametrically opposite behavioral implications of a tendency to approach success and a tendency to avoid failure were spelled out fully in reference to risk-taking preferences and level of aspiration, but the interpretation of how a tendency to avoid failure would influence the level of performance when a subject was given a single task to perform was muddled by intuition and common-sense conjecture. At that time, it was assumed that the tendency to avoid failure was equivalent to anxiety as conceived by Mandler, Sarason, and co-workers in studies of Test Anxiety. That is, it was assumed that "anxiety about failure" would *excite* both task-relevant responses and task-irrelevant responses. As a result, anxious persons would suffer some performance decrement when anxiety about failure was strongly aroused. But this deficiency of the initial statement was soon recognized when subsequent studies were designed to test implications of the theory and the meaning of a *negative* tendency ($T_{-f} = M_{AF} \times P_f \times I_f$) as distinct from a *positive* tendency ($T_s = M_S \times P_s \times I_s$) became fully apparent.

If the tendency having a *positive* sign that is generated by the product of $M_S$, $P_s$, and $I_s$ implies excitement or activation of a response which is expected to lead to success, then the tendency having a *negative* sign that is generated by the product of $M_{AF}$, $P_f$, and $I_f$ must imply just the opposite of excitement or activation. It must represent a tendency to *inhibit* (i.e., to avoid the performance of) an act which is expected to lead to failure. This was the interpretation of the tendency to avoid failure in the initial discussion of how it would influence selection of an activity among a set of activities which differed in apparent difficulty. In reference to the level of performance of a single task, the tendency to avoid failure—*conceived as an inhibitory tendency*—functions to oppose and dampen the tendency to perform the task. This, rather than too much general excitement of responses (Taylor, Spence, *et al.*) or competing avoidant responses (Mandler-Sarason *et al.*), is the explanation of the performance decrements suffered by "anxious" people in achievement-oriented tests derived from the theory of achievement motivation.

In the final chapter, we shall discuss more fully the implications of this and other differences between an "Expectancy-Value" type of theory of motivation and the "Drive-Habit" conception of *S-R* behavior theory.

# CHAPTER 10

# A Speculative Review and Prospectus

"I had the same idea, once, but I just didn't stick to it long enough." (By permission of Ed Fisher and Saturday Review)

This introduction to motivation has been far from exhaustive in its coverage. It was not meant to be. A number of important developments have been ignored in order to give special emphasis to the main transitions in thought about motivation which characterize the first half century of empirical study of the problem, to identification of two different conceptions of the process of motivation which have evolved in experimental study of purposive behavior, and to the beginning of an attempt to bring about an integration of the study of individual differences in personality and experimental analysis of the process of motivation, which is a significant feature of current developments in the study of human motivation.

While hardly a comprehensive treatment of all the interesting facets of motivation that are being studied by psychologists today, these three themes serve to introduce the basic problems and concepts and to focus attention upon the central issues in terms of which other approaches and theoretical schemes can be considered and evaluated. Most of the important current developments are represented in the annual volumes of the *Nebraska Symposium on Motivation*, which was instituted in 1953 to keep workers abreast of innovations that in one way or another touch upon the broad problem of motivation. To confront the integrative task presented by the vast array of contemporary studies which pertain to motivation, one must be able to define the behavioral problem of motivation and understand the nature of the conceptual problem it poses. These have been focal points of interest in this introduction.

In this final chapter, we shall look back and we shall attempt to look ahead. We shall briefly review the major transitions in thought presented in earlier chapters. Then we shall examine some of the general implications of "Expectancy × Value" and "Drive × Habit" conceptions of motivation in order both to appreciate the degree of convergence of basic concepts in these two schemes which has come about in recent years and also to identify some important differences between them which define unresolved problems for future study. Our purpose is to consider some issues which must be further clarified so that subsequent research can perform the self-corrective function of scientific inquiry more efficiently. A scientific theory, we must remember, is a policy—a guide to future action—and not a settled creed (Conant, 1952). So we shall undertake an appraisal of the two conceptions of motivation which provide the present guides. When we do this, we shall see that still another transition in thought is required if the principle of motivation is to encompass some fundamental characteristics of behavior which the current conceptions overlook. We shall end by noting certain deficiencies in the contemporary mode of thought about motivation and considering some proposals designed to overcome them.

## TRANSITIONS IN THOUGHT ABOUT MOTIVATION

### CONSCIOUS VOLITION

From the writings of William James, we get a good picture of how psychologists of the late 19th century approached what has since come to be defined as the problem of motivation. The experimental method, which had begun to encompass the problem of perception and memory by that time, had not yet been applied to matters which were related to the psychology of the will (volition). Speculation was mainly concerned with the basic springs of action (instinct), the effect of past experience (habit), and the relation of pleasure, pain, and other strong feelings (emotions) to action. Of particular interest, at that time, was the task of describing the contents of consciousness during the process of volition. Conventional thought viewed consciousness as the

locus of the reasons for acting in a certain way, as the seat of conflict and decision-making. Analysis of the contents of consciousness in the act of willing yielded by introspection, the primary method of study, convinced James that action occurs when the idea of a given act gains dominance over all others. He realized the importance of trying to explain how certain ideas do, in fact, gain dominance over others, but made very little headway in the analysis of this question. Another central issue in the late 19th century was the relation of mind (consciousness) to body (brain). Guided by the belief that conscious ideas and feelings must correspond to certain neural conditions which account for the excitation and integration of behavior, James speculated about the kinds of neural arrangements that would be required to explain what introspection revealed about the process of volition. In this we see an anticipation of the neurophysiological orientation of the early "behaviorists" who would later confront the behavioral problem of motivation and attempt to work out a coherent neural "wiring diagram" to account for purposive actions.

### THE IMPACT OF FREUD

In the work of Freud we confront the first significant transition in thought about motivation: the dethronement of consciousness as the locus of the determinants of human action. Freud's clinical observations produced a convincing number of demonstrations that an individual's actions are often determined by influences of which he is, at the time, completely unaware. This notion of unconscious motivation means, in simplest terms, that an individual cannot employ the method of introspection and hope to identify fully the determinants of his own behavior. The general conception of the nature of the task in studying motivation and the method of study were greatly influenced by Freud. The scientific task, as he came to view it, was to construct a plausible conception of the unconscious determinants of both conscious thought and action. The method of study which he developed had of necessity to become more indirect. His theoretical analysis of mental conflict and of the origin and genesis of motives emphasized the dynamic, striving character of behavior at a time, early in this century, when it seemed to many that the explanation of behavior was merely a matter of connections between stimuli and responses. Freud's conception of instinct, or need, as a persistent internal stimulus gave added impetus to the arguments of men like McDougall who called attention to the goal-striving character of behavior. The theory of drive and drive-reduction which later evolved owes much to Freud.

## THE EMPIRICAL PROBLEM OF MOTIVATION

The next development of consequence for scientific study of motivation was Tolman's clarification of the *behavioral* problem of motivation. When psychology gave up introspection and began to evolve an objective methodology which focuses on the observable behavior of some other organism as the subject matter, it was initially spurred by the belief that the concept of reflex, *S-R*, borrowed from physiology provided the essential clue as to what went on in the brain of the behaving organism to determine its action. Experimental interest became riveted on the details of the relationship between the observable stimulus and response and factors which seemed to account for changes in the strength of "connection" between stimulus and response.

Guided by the intuitions and arguments of early "purposivists," but not their mentalistic orientation, Tolman bucked this tide and identified *the purposive characteristics of molar behavior* which define the empirical problem of motivation for an objective psychology: the selectivity of behavior in relation to objectively defined ends and the tendency of behavior to persist until the end is reached. These characteristics of molar behavior define the empirical problem of "striving for goals," to which Hull later referred as the separate problem of motivation in distinguishing it from the problem of "strengthening of connections," or learning, which had been emphasized in the work of Thorndike and Pavlov.

## CONCEPTUAL ANALYSIS OF MOTIVATION

Equally important was the transition in thought encouraged by Lewin's arguments that psychology must get on with the task of developing a more coherent and useful conceptual scheme for thought about the contemporaneous determinants of action than is provided by either the intuitive categories of the common-sense language or the physiological concept of reflex. The first thorough conceptual analysis of the problem of motivation and attempt to formulate a principle to account for action in terms of the combined influence of a number of contemporaneous determinants was provided by Lewin (1938).

The need for some principle other than a learning principle to explain the initiation and persistence of an activity was finally acknowledged within the *S-R*

tradition by Hull in 1943. Until then, *S-R* "learning theorists" had proceeded on the assumption that knowledge of the present stimulus and knowledge of past learning in relation to that stimulus would provide a full explanation of those purposive characteristics of molar behavior which Tolman had emphasized. They had concentrated on the search for basic principles of *learning*. Since 1943, however, the story is different. The initial statement of a principle of motivation within *S-R* behavior theory (i.e., $sE_R = f(D) \times f(sH_R)$) has undergone several revisions, bringing it much closer to the earlier formulations of Tolman and Lewin which emphasized the motivational significance of anticipated goals and anticipated threats. And, in recent years, there has been a rebirth of interest in the kind of Expectancy $\times$ Value theory of motivation proposed by both Tolman and Lewin. This appears in contemporary research on decision-making and in the experimental analysis of achievement-oriented behavior.

## THEORETICAL ORIENTATION IN STUDY OF INDIVIDUAL DIFFERENCES

A most encouraging development in recent experimental analysis of motivation guided by these two theoretical conceptions of the process is the use of tests to assess individual differences in the strength of theoretically-relevant motivational dispositions of humans. Here again, the broad implication of Lewinian ideas is apparent. The guiding hypothesis, $B = f(P,E)$, is now represented in a methodological development that may provide a means of bridging the gap between the study of individual differences in personality and the search for basic explanatory principles which has so far seriously handicapped both enterprises in psychology's relatively short history.

The most disturbing thing about so much contemporary research in the field of individual differences in personality is the use of one or another *ad hoc* test device to assess some motivational characteristic which is called a need, a value, or what not. Test scores given these motivational names are then shown to be related in some way to behavior, and an interpretation of the result is advanced. But the research is neither systematically related to one or another of the basic conceptions of motivation, nor is it part of another systematic program of research designed to evolve a conception of motivation, nor is it immediately addressed to the solution of some practically important question.

Many studies of this sort are neither fish nor fowl. They produce isolated facts which, after taxing the memory of students for a short time, are soon forgotten because they lack any relatedness to the central task of the science. It is to be hoped that contemporary research on *n* Achievement, within the context of an Expectancy × Value theory, and contemporary research on individual differences in anxiety, within the context of Drive × Habit theory, will point the way towards more fruitful systematic use of personality tests in future research on human motivation.

THE PURPOSE OF A CONCEPTUAL SCHEME

Over the years, the transition in thought about motivation has been mainly one of clarifying the nature of the empirical problem to be studied and of developing suitable methods of study—methods that encompass the behavioral problem of motivation. In addition, as the scientific training of psychologists has improved, there has been increased understanding of the relationship between theory and experiment in science. Theories, that is, conceptual schemes, are introduced both to summarize what is already known about the phenomena in question and to serve as a guide to future study by suggesting the experiments that need to be performed to test the adequacy of present concepts and to extend knowledge. Science is more than the accumulation of great numbers of isolated facts which serve merely to tax one's memory. At the core of basic scientific inquiry is the intention to provide a conceptual integration of what would otherwise appear to be a mere bundle of discrete facts.

Psychologists have learned that the criteria for evaluating the usefulness of a conceptual scheme depend wholly on what you want to do with it. This raises a very important question: What do psychologists want to do with the conceptual schemes they have been inventing in experimental studies of motivation? It is quite apparent that they are constantly torn between using their tentative schemes only in reference to the particular kinds of experimental facts which suggested them in the first place and the tendency to apply their concepts more generally as a basis for better understanding of human behavior under natural, social conditions.

It is the ultimate or programmatic goal of all basic research on motivation to evolve a conceptual scheme that will provide a better understanding of human behavior. This intention is explicit in the writings of scientists who study the molar behavior of lower animals and then discuss implications for understanding human behavior or who study relatively simple instances of human behavior and then deal with the more general implications of the concepts which emerge. So when we refer to a scientific conceptual scheme as a guide to action, we must mean more than a guide to specific next experiments to be undertaken in the hope of testing, refining, extending, or elaborating the scheme. We must also include the guide to practical actions in the social world which a conceptual scheme suggests to those whose professional interest it is to apply what is known in their attempt to solve socially significant motivational problems of the time. That is why it means something to say that the *ultimate* task of science is to improve common sense, that is, to provide a more useful way of thinking about the phenomena in question than the conventional intuitive wisdom of the time.

The student may wonder why all scientists with this ultimate aim do not attack the practical problems of motivation as they arise in everyday life. By now, it is hoped, the reasons for concentrating on simpler instances of behavior are better understood. The ancient Aristotelian qualitative dichotomies, "animal" versus "human," "normal" versus "pathological," have broken down. The subject matter of psychology has been homogenized. Instances of the behavior of living organisms may differ greatly in the simplicity or complexity of the conditions to be taken into account, but it is believed that the fundamental conception of motivation should apply to all instances of molar behavior. If this were not the viewpoint of contemporary psychology, there would be little justification for treating the conceptions of motivation which have arisen in studies of purposive behavior in animals and men within the covers of one book.

Psychologists who seek to clarify the basic conception of motivation study simple instances, to begin with, because they have learned how difficult it is to attain conceptual clarity and to conduct theoretically relevant experiments even in the simplest instances of purposive behavior. They do the equivalent in psychology of rolling balls down an inclined plane with the conviction that "lower" and "higher" forms of motion are to be interpreted and explained in terms of the same basic principles. It is a dream that has paid off in the physical sciences. Is it merely a dream among behavioral scientists? "The basic researcher," George Selye has written, "must be able to dream and have faith in his dreams. To make a great dream come true, the first requirement is a great capacity to dream; the second is persistence—a faith in the dream" (1958, p. 155).

## THE MEANING OF THE TERM "MOTIVATION"

### VARIOUS USES OF THE TERM

The introductory chapter sidestepped the task of defining the term "motivation" very precisely until we had completed a survey of transitions in thought about the problem. Now, perhaps, the reasons for doing this have been made apparent. The term has no fixed technical meaning in contemporary psychology. It is often used in reference to the conscious feeling of desire and the whole complex of ideas and feelings which together seem to constitute the conscious antecedents of behavior according to traditional wisdom. Just as often, "motivation" is used to refer to the unconscious determinants of behavior which Freud emphasized, to the purposive characteristics of overt behavior which Tolman identified as an empirical problem in its own right, to a coherent theoretical account of the contemporaneous determinants of action like the Lewinian scheme or Hull's principle of performance, or to some particular variable in a particular theoretical conception of the contemporaneous determinants of the impulse to action—for example, as a synonym for *drive* in *S-R* behavior theory.

### EMPHASIS ON CONTEMPORANEOUS DETERMINANTS OF BEHAVIOR

To trace the evolution of thought about motivation, we have had to pay close attention to the confounding of ideas about learning and motivation in research with animals during the first half of this century. The most significant result of this work was clarification of the separate problems of motivation and learning and, finally, a realization that separate explanatory principles are needed in reference to each of these fundamental behavioral problems.

Lewin, who had begun his conceptual analysis of motivation in reference to experiments conducted with human subjects, was the first to understand what is now generally recognized: present behavior must be explained in terms of some coherent conception of its immediate, contemporaneous determinants and not by mere extrapolation of what has frequently been observed in the past. That was the

central point of his argument about the need to adopt a Galilean mode of thought in psychology and his criticism of the traditional doctrine of association (or "adhesion") between $S$ and $R$ as the basic explanatory principle for psychology. He called attention to the Aristotelian character of the argument of early "associationists" who believed that the present stimulus and assertions about the strength of connection between that stimulus and a particular response, *which was inferred from observations of what had frequently occurred in the past*, would provide a sufficient explanation of present behavior. We can see the shift from an Aristotelian to a Galilean mode of thought within *S-R* psychology by comparing this early view of how behavior is motivated with the more complicated conception of the immediate determinants of a response provided in Spence's current theory of the factors which intervene between observable stimulus and observable response. The effect of past frequency of *S-R* (Habit) is now viewed as but one of several factors whose present *functional properties* must be included in the principle which accounts for the strength of an impetus to act in a certain way in a particular situation at a particular moment in time.

### CONFUSION OF "DRIVE" AND "MOTIVATION"

Psychologists in the *S-R* tradition, for whom the central problem for many years was "learning," must assume a share of the responsibility for contemporary confusion about the meaning of the term "motivation" in the psychological literature. In the early days of this century the term was employed in reference to the question: *What causes a response?* The evolution of ideas about motivation has involved clarifications in reference to "response" and clarifications in reference to "what causes" it. Tolman is chiefly responsible for urging acceptance of the idea that what psychologists mean by "response" is molar action. His arguments helped to identify the several characteristics of molar action—selectivity (direction), vigor, and persistence—which require explanation. Lewin is chiefly responsible for urging acceptance of the idea that "what causes" molar actions is a much more complicated question than early *S-R* psychologists ever believed it to be. It is a question which requires the invention of a conceptual scheme that will adequately represent the various contemporaneous influences which together, in combination, account for the tendency to act. Thus, the problem of motivation was defined as a behavioral problem (by Tolman) and as a theoretical problem (by Lewin). When psychologists in the *S-R* tradition finally acknowledged the existence of the empirical problem of motivation (which Hull described as "striving for goals") and the need for a theoretical principle distinct from a learning principle to explain selectivity, vigor, and persistence of action, they then quite arbitrarily began to use the term "motivation" in reference to *one* of the explanatory constructs introduced into their scheme to account for the occurrence of a response: the theoretical construct, *drive*. But, as Littman (1958) has cogently pointed out, the implication that "drive" is the *activator* or cause of response while "habit" is a passive, inert variable that has little or nothing to do with motivating a response is meaningless when both drive and habit strength are posited as necessary determinants of the impetus to respond in the famous equation, $sE_R = f(D) \times f(sH_R)$. These two variables, and any other variables that are needed in a theoretical representation of the immediate influences which combine to determine the strength of a tendency to act in a certain way, are to be considered *motivational* variables—that is, factors to be taken into account in answering the traditional question, "What causes a response?"

Some psychologists whose conceptual orientation is that of the *S-R* tradition now ask, "Is the concept of motivation still needed in psychology?" When they do this they do *not* mean, "Is there any longer a need for a conception of the immediate determinants of action?" They mean, "Can we do without the concept of drive as a non-specific exciter of response tendencies?" This restricted use of the term "motivation" (i.e., motivation = drive) began in 1943. It reflects how little attention has been given the historical evolution of ideas about motivation in the past.

RECOMMENDED USE OF THE TERM "MOTIVATION"

The view urged throughout this book is that the term "motivation" *should* be used in reference to:

(a) the behavioral problem identified by the early "purposivists," viz., the tendency for the direction or selectivity of behavior to be governed in some way by its relation to objectively definable consequences, and the tendency of behavior to persist until the end or goal is attained; and

(b) a theoretical conception of the contemporaneous determinants of these purposive characteristics of behavior.

Thus one may speak of the empirical or behavioral problem of motivation and mean the problem of accounting for the direction, vigor, and persistence of behavior. And one may speak of a theory of motivation and mean a coherent conception of the contemporaneous determinants of direction, vigor, and persistence of action.

Enough work has been done to show that there are two different basic conceptions of motivation. We have labeled these "Drive × Habit" and "Expectancy × Value." It would be surprising, indeed, if either one in its present form should turn out to be anywhere near the generally useful conceptual scheme psychologists hope to produce. So we turn to a comparison of these schemes with a future orientation to discover and to clarify their implications. We shall look for critical issues in search for directives for further study that may help to refine, clarify, improve, choose between, or reconcile the two conceptions.

## EXPECTANCY × VALUE THEORY

Beginning with Lewin, we have considered four different theoretical statements which employ essentially the same concepts but use different terms in reference to those concepts. They are: Lewin's conception of the determinants of effective force; Tolman's conception of the determinants of performance; the conception of subjectively expected utility of an option provided in contemporary Decision Theory; and the conception of the determinants of the strength of the tendency to act arising in recent studies of achievement motivation. Table 10.1 shows the equivalence of the concepts in these Expectancy × Value theories of motivation and, for the sake of completeness, also includes the equivalent concepts employed by Julian Rotter (1954, 1955), who has applied them to analysis of problems in social learning and clinical psychology.

DETERMINANTS OF IMPULSE TO ACTION

Common to all is the notion that the strength of the tendency to act in a certain way depends upon the strength of expectancy that the act will be followed by a given consequence (or goal) and the value of that consequence (or goal) to the individual. What Lewin called the *Valence of the goal* $(Va_g)$—that is, its attractiveness to a particular individual in a particular situation—is called *Demand for the goal* by Tolman, *Utility of the consequence* in Decision Theory, and would be represented as *the product of Motive and Incentive* $(M_G \times I_g)$ in a general statement of the theory suggested in studies of

TABLE 10.1

The equivalence of concepts in various statements of an Expectancy × Value theory of motivation
(After Feather, 1959)

| Theorist | Context | Determinants of impulse to action | The impulse to action |
|---|---|---|---|
| Tolman | Maze behavior | Expectancy of goal, Demand for goal | Performance vector |
| Lewin, et al. | Level of aspiration, decision making | Potency × Valence | Force |
| Edwards | Economic decisions | Subjective Probability × Utility | Subjectively-Expected Utility |
| Atkinson | Achievement-oriented behavior | Expectancy × (Motive × Incentive) | Tendency (or motivation) |
| Rotter | Social learning and behavior | Expectancy, Reinforcement Value | Behavior Potential |

achievement motivation. All of these statements refer to the value of an anticipated event *to a particular person*. They all imply that a particular anticipated event, like eating a candy bar, or being handed $5.00, or seeing the thrown ring slip over the peg in a ringtoss game, or getting an A− on a final exam, may have different values for different individuals. Both Lewin and Tolman asserted that attractiveness of the goal, *valence*, or *demand*, was determined by some characteristic of the individual and some characteristic of the goal object. Lewin stated that $Va_g = (t_g, G)$, where $t_g$, a system in tension, represented the momentary strength of "need" of the individual for that type of goal object and $G$ represented the incentive characteristics of the object itself. Tolman, thinking mainly of experiments involving hungry rats with food rewards, asserted that demand for the goal was a function of both drive (food privation) and incentive (kind and amount of food). The general conception suggested in research on achievement motivation is that the valence or utility of a goal is equal to $M_G \times I_g$, where $M_G$ represents the strength of a relatively general and stable disposition in the person which refers to a particular class of goals ($G$) and $I_g$ represents the value of the particular goal ($g$) relative to the value of other goals of that class.

What Tolman originally called the *expectancy of the goal* and conceived as a forward-pointing cognition based on prior experience is represented as the subjective probability of attaining the goal by both Lewin (who called it *potency*) and decision theorists. The two terms *expectancy* and *subjective probability* have been used interchangeably in the theory of achievement motivation which, guided by the clarifications of expectancy theory presented by Mac-Corquodale and Meehl (1953, 1954), calls attention

to the fact that the concept of expectancy refers to a particular act; it serves to represent the associative link between performance of an act and attainment of the goal ($R \to G$).

THE IMPULSE TO ACTION

In his later years, Tolman referred to the impulse to act produced by demand for the goal and expectancy of the goal as the *performance vector*. He followed, rather closely, Lewin's conception of a force on the person having an immediate direction towards the next act in a path leading to a goal. Decision theorists call the product of subjective probability and utility the *subjectively expected utility* but are not often explicit in acknowledging that *SEU* refers to some particular act or path of action.

In early studies of achievement motivation, the aroused tendency to strive for a particular goal was referred to as *strength of motivation*. To avoid confusion, the neutral term *tendency* has been introduced with subscripts referring to a particular act and the expected consequence (goal) of that act ($T_{r,g}$). The intention, following Lewin, is to convey the idea that the tendency to perform a given act is, at the same time, an expression of a tendency directed towards a particular goal which is the expected consequence of the act. When a particular act ($r$) is expected to lead to a consequence having negative incentive value ($-g$), the tendency has a negative sign. It is conceived as an inhibitory tendency, a tendency not to perform the act. It is a tendency to avoid the expected negative consequence and is represented by $T_{r,-g}$.

In comparing the Expectancy × Value theory and the Drive × Habit theory, we shall focus attention upon the general implications of the conception which has arisen in research on achievement-oriented performance because it spells out more explicitly than other formulations how individual differences in personality are to be represented in a principle of motivation. One of the long-term objectives of basic research on motivation is to provide a principle which will specify the behavioral implications of scores obtained when personality tests are employed in the context of solving important practical problems. But even more important than this practical objective is the general need of psychology to bring about an integration of the study of individual differences and basic behavioral processes. This has been an explicit aim of research on achievement motivation, which has employed one set of operations to assess individual differences in behavioral dispositions and another set of experimental operations to produce the kinds of environmental influences on behavior that are normally studied in experimental psychology.

APHYSIOLOGICAL CHARACTER OF THEORY

One striking characteristic of the several programs of research which have produced Expectancy $\times$ Value conceptions of the motivation of behavior is the extent to which the task of explaining purposive characteristics of molar behavior is divorced from the *physiological language* of motivation. Neither Tolman nor Lewin were explicitly guided by any preconceptions concerning neurophysiology, and this is equally true of contemporary work on human decision making and research on achievement motivation. In each case, the task of explanation is conceived as one calling for conceptualization of the process which intervenes between observable stimulus situation and observable behavior in terms of variables whose functional properties are defined in a mathematical principle which states how they combine to influence the strength of a tendency to act in a certain way. Thus, in the general conception $T_{r,g} = M_G \times E_{r,g} \times I_g$ suggested by studies of achievement motivation, there is explicitly stated the idea that strength of the tendency to act in a certain way to attain a particular goal in a particular situation is influenced by a relatively non-specific variable called motive ($M_G$), which is tentatively assumed to be a relatively stable characteristic of a person carried about from one life situation to another, and two relatively specific influences which refer to the particular act in question and which are defined by cues in the immediate environment: the strength of expectancy that the act will be followed by a particular consequence ($E_{r,g}$) and the incentive value of that particular consequence ($I_g$).

UNANSWERED QUESTIONS AND
GUIDES FOR RESEARCH

This kind of conception raises, but does not answer, certain very important questions: e.g., What are the antecedents of the expectancy that a particular act will lead to the goal? Why does the particular goal have a certain incentive value and not another? What are the antecedents of the strength of motive which is currently assessed by the thematic apperceptive method? It provides a guide for re-examination of experimental evidence in studies concerning frequency of reward of a particular response, for the concept of expectancy directs attention to the associative link between performance of a particular response and attainment of the goal ($R \rightarrow G$). It suggests that individual differences in the strength of motive to eat, for example, might be measured in rats by some index of the vigor of the consummatory reaction given a standard food incentive ($S_G \rightarrow R_G$). And, since the theory explicitly states that $M_G$ and $I_g$ combine multiplicatively, it suggests that rats who normally eat more vigorously than other rats should display substantially higher level of instrumental performance than other rats when given a large food incentive, but only slightly higher level of instrumental performance when the incentive is very small. This comparison would provide a test of the hypothesis that $Va_g = M_G \times I_g$ in the context of the kind of animal studies which have provided the basis for the Drive $\times$ Habit conception.

In other words, the Expectancy $\times$ Value theories provide suggestive guides for re-examination of much of the evidence obtained in animal research and for new kinds of experiments, but they are still subject to the criticism directed at Lewin's original formulation: the operational definition of the explanatory constructs is not sharp and specific. We have witnessed the difficulties which have arisen in experiments on decision making which suggest that utility and stated value of money are not necessarily equal and in studies which show that subjective probability of attaining a goal is influenced by factors other than the visual stimulus of the stated odds in a game of chance. Clarification of the empirical definitions of constructs in terms of objectively defined antecedents remains the central problem for those who propose the Expectancy $\times$ Value theory of motivation.

## THE EVOLUTION OF
## DRIVE × HABIT THEORY

Perhaps the most striking thing about contemporary research in the *S-R* tradition which is concerned with the purposive characteristics of molar behavior is its emancipation from the program that was conceived by *S-R* theorists earlier in this century. The mind-body issue which James discussed in terms of plausible neural mechanisms for "ideas" was soon translated into a behavior-body issue in the work of Thorndike, Pavlov, and others whose work encouraged the neurophysiological orientation of *S-R* behaviorism. As we have seen, the physiological concept of neural reflex provided the standard terms for cause (stimulus) and effect (response) in the analysis of behavior.

This orientation began to change when the soundness of Tolman's analysis of molar versus molecular behavior was recognized. (*Response* is no longer conceived as a Watsonian muscle twitch, but as an effect on the immediate environment.) It changed more when striving for goals was finally identified as a problem separate from strengthening of connections. It changed even more when Hull finally realized that he needed a new kind of principle to account for motivation, something other than a principle to explain how *S-R* connections were strengthened, and when he decided to construct the kind of intervening-variable theory which Tolman had advocated. In 1943, Hull proposed a mathematical theory of motivation ($_sE_R = D \times _sH_R$), but he also retained a neurophysiological orientation, particularly when he formulated the famous physiological hypothesis about the nature of reinforcement, his fundamental principle of *learning*.

What happened subsequently is very interesting. Those *S-R* psychologists who maintain the neurophysiological orientation have devoted a great deal of attention to experiments bearing on the question of whether or not all reinforcing states of affairs involve need-reduction or stimulus-reduction. Is the consummatory reaction important? Or can food be introduced directly into the stomach and have the same rewarding effect? Neal Miller (1957) has pursued a systematic program of research on these very important questions and other related issues. And it is in the context of research on these questions that Olds' (1958) investigations of the positive reinforcing effects of direct electrical stimulation of certain brain centers presents evidence against the need-reduction and stimulus-reduction hypotheses concerning the nature of reinforcement.

But while these very important neurophysiological problems are being pursued, systematic experimental analysis of purposive behavior guided by the mathematical principle $_sE_R = D \times _sH_R$ has brought about a fundamental change in the *S-R* theory, one which no longer views "reinforcement" as even involved in the *learning* of instrumental habits. The separate status of a mathematical conception of the determinants of action and hypotheses about possible underlying neurophysiological mechanisms is now fully appreciated, at least by theorists like Spence who no longer attempt to incorporate neurophysiological arguments or evidence in the theoretical analysis of behavior.

Thus we see a clearcut separation of fundamental interests within the *S-R* tradition: one directed towards further development of a physiological psychology, which, with the aid of new techniques of investigation, is making rapid strides in filling the gaps in empirical knowledge concerning the relation of brain functions to behavior; the other now directed towards elaboration of a systematic and mathematically stated theory of behavior in terms of relations between antecedents, which may be observed without the use of special instruments which get under the skin of the organism being studied, and observable characteristics of molar behavior. This is the kind of theory of molar behavior envisioned in the early writings of Lewin, and Tolman, who once asserted: "A psychology cannot be explained by a physiology until one has a psychology to explain."

## A COMPARISON OF THE THEORIES

Today, we can begin to examine the implications of both Expectancy × Value and Drive × Habit theories in reference to experimental evidence concerning achievement-oriented behavior of human subjects. We have already done this in the preceding chapter. But we might also try to conceptualize a typical instance of food-seeking behavior of a rat in a maze in terms of motive, expectancy, and incentive to see how the conception compares with the drive, habit, incentive formulation of Spence. Let us suppose that 30 rats have been deprived of food for 10 hours and then put in a T maze containing one food pellet in the left hand goal box and nothing in the right hand goal box. The rats are given 30 trials under these conditions. The situation is shown schematically in Figure 10.1. How do the two theories account for performance on the 31st trial?

On each trial, when the animal turns left at the choice point and finds food in the goal box and eats it, the temporal sequence of observed events is summarized in Figure 10.1 as $S_e\text{-}R_l\text{-}S_g\text{-}R_g$. On each

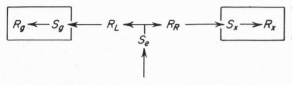

FIGURE 10.1 Schematic analysis of the sequence of events in a T maze when animal always finds and eats food after turning left and confronts an empty goal box after turning right at the choice point.

trial when the animal has turned right and found an empty goal box the temporal sequence of observed events is summarized $S_e\text{-}R_r\text{-}S_x\text{-}R_x$. In this case, $S_x$ represents the stimulus situation of an empty end box and $R_x$ represents whatever the rat does in the empty box on the non-rewarded trials.

According to Spence's statement

$$E = (D + K) \times H$$

and his specification of the determinants of $D$, $K$, and $H$, the situation at the choice point on the 31st trial is one in which $S_e$ elicits two competing loco-motor habits, $_{S_e}H_{R_l}$ and $_{S_e}H_{R_r}$. Both habits are affected by the non-specific excitement of drive ($D$) attributable to 10 hours' food deprivation plus the non-specific excitement attributable to the food incentive ($K$). This latter source of non-specific excitement is produced by the vigor of the animal's fractional anticipatory goal reaction ($r_g\text{-}s_g$), which is also elicited by the stimulus situation ($S_e$) at the choice point. The vigor of the anticipatory goal reaction depends in part upon the vigor of the goal reaction ($R_G$) on earlier trials. And this in turn depends upon the character and amount of the food reward ($S_g$) and how hungry the rat is ($D$). But the vigor of the anticipatory goal reaction which pro-duces incentive motivation ($K$) also depends upon the strength of the habit $_{S_e}H_{R_g}$. The strength of this classically conditioned habit depends upon the num-ber of times $S_e$ has been followed by $S_g - R_g$. Since the food stimulus $S_g$ has always been presented after the animal turned left, but not when it turned right, the habit $_{S_e}H_{R_g}$ has substantial strength after 30 trials. According to Spence, $S_e$ at the choice point

should elicit $r_g$ to the extent that $S_e$ at the choice point is similar to the stimulus situation in the goal box. The elicitation of $r_g$ (incentive motivation) at the choice point is conceived as an instance of stim-ulus generalization.

So far, we are led to predict that the animal will turn left on the 31st trial if he has turned left more often than right during the 30 preceding training trials. The non-specific excitement of ($D + K$) will affect both $_{S_e}H_{R_l}$ and $_{S_e}H_{R_r}$. So turning left on the 31st trial should occur because the number of previous $S_e\text{-}R_l$ events exceeds the number of previous $S_e\text{-}R_r$ events which define the strength of the two competing habits. The only question which remains is: Why did the animal turn left more than right during the 30 training trials?

The Sheffield drive-induction theory of reward (see p. 195), which also employs $S\text{-}R$ concepts con-sistently, provides help in answering this question. Sheffield has proposed that when the animal gets to a choice point like the one we are describing and begins to make incipient responses (e.g., turning the head) in one direction or the other, it will receive a bigger boost from the conditioned consum-matory reaction (incentive motivation) when it is beginning to make the "correct" response because it will then be exposed to cues (environmental stimuli and/or proprioceptive stimuli from its own incipient responses) which are more strongly conditioned to the goal reaction than when it begins to make the "incorrect" response. We wish to note the special emphasis given response-produced cues by Sheffield in light of what an Expectancy $\times$ Value theory has to say about this behavior situation.

If we apply the $T_{r,g} = M_G \times E_{r,g} \times I_g$ conception to this situation, we must note, to begin with, that there is no assumption that the incentive value of the goal ($I_g$), eating food, is related to the strength of expectancy of attaining food through some action ($E_{r,g}$). They are considered independent. The as-sumption that $I_s = 1 - P_s$ is a special assumption, supported by experimental evidence, that is employed only when ego-involved achievement-oriented per-formance is conceptualized in terms of Expect-ancy $\times$ Value theory.

Next we must note that we have no information pertinent to the question of individual differences in strength of motive to eat ($M_G$) because there has been no independent assessment of something like the vigor of eating reactions in each of the 30 ani-mals in this typical animal experiment to allow classification of them into High and Low $M_G$ groups.

The critical incidents from the viewpoint of Expectancy × Value theory are $R_l$-$(S_g$-$R_g)$ and $R_r$-$(S_x$-$R_x)$. Whenever the animal has turned left, this response has been followed by food ($S_g$) and eating ($R_g$). Whenever the animal has turned right, this response has been followed by an empty box ($S_x$) and non-eating activities ($R_x$). The incentive value of eating in this situation ($I_g$) is defined by the one food pellet used as reward. For simplicity, we shall have to assume that the incentive value of the non-eating activities ($R_x$) that the animal engaged in whenever he turned right and ended in the empty goal box ($S_x$) is zero. But we must bear in mind the possibility that mere exploration of an empty box ($R_x$) might, under certain circumstances, have greater incentive value than eating one food pellet ($R_g$). According to this theory, $T_{l,g}$ should be stronger than $T_{r,x}$ on the 31st trial because ($E_{r,g} × I_g$) exceeds ($E_{r,x} × I_x$). On the 31st trial the animal is more strongly motivated to turn left than to turn right because the anticipated goal functions *selectively* to excite performance of responses which are expected to lead to it. That is the essential difference between a theory which conceives anticipation of a goal as one source of general excitement having the functional properties of drive and the main implication of Expectancy × Value theory.

A DEFICIENCY OF EXPECTANCY × VALUE THEORY

We now take note of one of the general deficiencies of Expectancy × Value theories. In putting so much emphasis upon the expected consequence of a particular response, they fail to explain how it is that an organism even "thinks" of performing that response in a given situation. That is, there is no reference to the events $S_e$-$R_l$ and $S_e$-$R_r$. Do Expectancy × Value theories assume that the organism will "consider" both turning left and turning right irrespective of the number of times it may have turned left or right in this situation in the past? The answer is yes in that the principle which accounts for the strength of a tendency to respond in a given way completely ignores *Habit*, the associative link between a particular stimulus situation and a response.

This point was made dramatically clear to the writer by one of his colleagues in reference to use of the theory of achievement motivation to explain the behavior of college students playing a ringtoss game. The theory, as spelled out in Chapter 9, formulates the choice problem as one involving conflict among tendencies to throw a ring from each of several lines that are marked on the floor before the subjects. In

other words, it is assumed that the presence of these environmental stimuli will suggest to the subject the responses of throwing a ring from each of the several lines. But why doesn't a person who is strong in *n* Achievement stand backwards on a line up close to the peg and throw the ring over his head? That would be a moderately difficult task, an intermediate risk. He doesn't do this because *it never occurs to him to do this*. And in giving this answer to an important question, we see that habit strength must be included to represent the mere tendency of the subject to "consider" performing a response in a given situation. The concept of Habit defines what responses are entertained as possibilities in a given stimulus situation. This problem has been systematically ignored in Expectancy × Value formulations.

Perhaps the point is most clearly made in reference to one of the most obvious deficiencies of the early economic theory of decision making. It was assumed that the individual was always completely informed concerning the nature of actions which could be undertaken in a given situation and all possible consequences of each of those potential actions. This meant, specifically, that it was assumed an individual would think of *all possible actions* he might undertake in a given situation and then consider all possible outcomes of all those actions before arriving at a decision. We must now recognize that leaving out habit strength, which defines the set of possible actions elicited (or entertained as possibilities) in a given situation, is a major deficiency of current statements of Expectancy × Value theories of motivation.

Acknowledging this, suppose we repair the deficiency by putting Habit (as Spence conceives it) into the equation which accounts for the strength of the tendency to perform a particular response in order to continue our discussion of the two theories of motivation: i.e., $T_{r,g} = {_sH_r} × E_{r,g} × I_g × M_G$. Now, it is clear, the theory implies that an individual might perform an action out of "force of habit" even though the variables (Expectancy, Incentive, Motive) which refer to the motivational significance of expected consequences of an act might tend to favor performance of some other act. This more fully elaborated version of an Expectancy × Value theory would now direct attention to the number of times the act in question has occurred in the present stimulus situation or situations similar to it ($_sH_r$), relative frequency of reward (goal-attainment), or what is often called the reinforcement history *of that particular act* ($E_{r,g}$), amount of reward ($I_g$), and individual differences in motive ($M_G$)—a disposition which refers to a particular class of rewards (or incentives).

## TRANSLATION OF EXPECTANCY × VALUE THEORY INTO S-R LANGUAGE

What differences, if any, remain between Expectancy × Value and Drive × Habit theory? We can sharpen our comparison even more by attempting to complete the translation of the Expectancy × Value theory into *S-R* language. The concept of expectancy refers to the associative link between a particular response and its consequence. The consequence is called a "goal" when it has positive incentive value and a "threat" when it has negative incentive value. Let us first consider the case of a consequence that has positive incentive value, the situation of a rat running a T maze for food, as depicted in Figure 10.1. The associative link between the instrumental response and its consequence can be conceived as the connection between the response-produced cues, including the proprioceptive stimulus produced by the response itself ($s_p$), and the consummatory reaction $R_G$. In other words, the arousal of a fractional anticipatory goal reaction ($r_g$-$s_g$) by $s_p$ (see Figure 6.1, p. 155) would provide a physical mechanism representing the functional properties of expectancy as it is defined in Expectancy-Value formulations. Then the difference in vigor of anticipatory goal reaction ($r_g$-$s_g$) that is usually attributed to a difference in the magnitude of the incentive (e.g., amount of food) would provide the physical mechanism for incentive value ($I_g$). Finally, the concept of motive ($M_G$) refers to *individual differences in vigor of anticipatory goal reaction when the food incentive is held constant*. This is a variable which has not been systematically explored in animal studies of hunger and food reward, though it is suggested in the work of Sheffield *et al.* which has shown a correlation between measures of the vigor of consummatory reaction and speed of instrumental approach to the goal.

The hypothesis that $Va_g = M_G \times I_g$, which is normally read "the attractiveness of a particular goal to the subject ($Va_g$) is a multiplicative function of his capacity for enjoyment of that class of goals ($M_G$) and the value of the particular goal relative to others of that class ($I_g$)," can very easily be translated into *S-R* terms and tested. Holding hours of food deprivation constant, animals having a strong motive to eat should perform the consummatory reaction more vigorously (i.e., with greater lip-smacking

enjoyment) than rats having a weak motive to eat when the incentive (kind or amount of food) is held constant. What is more, if some index of vigor of consummatory reaction is obtained for animals using food incentives of small, medium, and high values, the result predicted in Figure 10.2 should be

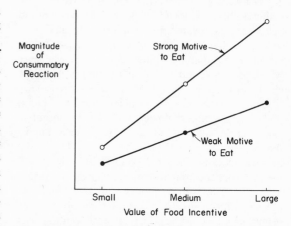

FIGURE 10.2 Implication of the assumption that $Va_g = M_G \times I_g$ for study of magnitude of consummatory reaction to food incentives in rats. Rats would be classified High (above median) and Low (below median) in motive to eat in terms of vigor of consummatory reaction to one value of food incentive. Then the vigor of reaction to food incentives of higher and lower values would be observed. The curve describing magnitude of consummatory reaction (attractiveness) in relation to increasing value of the incentive should be steeper for those rats classified High in motive to eat.

obtained. Vigor of consummatory reaction to one of the food incentives could be used as a basis for classifying animals as High (above the median) and Low (below the median) in strength of motive to eat. Then when vigor of consummatory reaction to each of the incentives is plotted separately for the groups High and Low in motive to eat, the slope of "attractiveness" should be steeper in relation to increasing incentive value of the foods for animals who are classified High in motive to eat. That is what is implied by $Va_g = M_G \times I_g$, and the assumption that the vigor of anticipatory goal reaction in a particular rat is the physical equivalent of Lewinian *valence*. This type of study would present evidence analogous to that already obtained with human subjects in reference to the attractiveness of success at tasks which differ in difficulty and hence in incentive value of success.

## SELECTIVE VERSUS NON-SPECIFIC INFLUENCE OF THE ANTICIPATED GOAL

/Now that we have translated the basic ideas of Expectancy-Value theory into *S-R* terms, we can see the difference between theories in reference to the motivational significance of an anticipated reward or goal. The Expectancy-Value type of theory, from the time of Tolman and Lewin's earliest formulations, states (now to use the *S-R* language) that the excitement of an anticipatory goal reaction is transmitted *only* to responses whose response-produced cues are conditioned to it. The magnitude of anticipatory goal reaction is assumed to have a *selective* or *directive* influence on instrumental behavior. This is the fundamental idea developed in Lewin's conception of the field of forces generated by a positive valence. (See p. 80.) In contrast, Spence's conception of incentive motivation (*K*) states that the excitement of an anticipatory goal reaction is transmitted to all responses (habits) that are elicited in a given stimulus situation. He has emphasized the arousal of fractional anticipatory goal response by external environmental cues, $S_e$, and has argued that this should occur as an instance of stimulus generalization to the extent that cues at the beginning or choice point of a maze are similar to cues in the goal box which are most strongly conditioned to the goal reaction. But Sheffield has attached special importance to the cues produced by instrumental responses in his drive-induction theory of reward. Sheffield's interpretation comes closer than any other *S-R* statement to Tolman's original conception of how expectancy of the goal directs performance.

It is extremely difficult to state precisely what the two kinds of formally stated principles of motivation of performance imply because even if the excitement of an anticipatory goal reaction (*K*) is completely non-specific, as Spence asserts, there are ways of explaining why the most frequently rewarded response in a choice situation will tend to profit most from this excitement. Sheffield's conception of why the organism selects the "correct" response in a Thorndikian selective learning situation is entirely consistent with the notion that the excitement is non-specific. He merely asserts that the excitement (although non-specific) will always be a little stronger when the animal is beginning to perform the "correct" response because the cues which are immediately produced by even an incipient response in the right direction (i.e., the stimulus conditions at that particular moment) will elicit a somewhat stronger $r_g$ and this heightened excitement will "boost" the impetus to keep on with that response. This conception thus turns out to yield a picture similar to the Lewinian concept of a field of forces, but it is still consistent with the non-specific influence attributed to the anticipated goal in Spence's equation $E = (D + K) \times H$. Thus the concept of a field of forces all directed towards an activity that has positive valence yields a clear picture of the usual effect of "rewarding" the correct response in a typical learning experiment of the sort first explored by Thorndike even though the *S-R* analysis may eventually turn out to be essentially correct in saying that an anticipatory goal reaction produces *non-specific* excitement.

Perhaps the point can be made clear with a lifelike example. Suppose a young male college student is working on his final examination in a course when the odor of perfume from an attractive girl in the seat behind him begins to tickle his nostrils and produce, ever so slightly, the arousal of the kind of anticipatory consummatory reaction we might imagine appropriate under these circumstances. If this slight anticipatory sexual arousal is all that happens, and the stimulus does not become so strong that a head-turning habit is also elicited, the young man should begin to work more vigorously at his examination according to the theory which says anticipatory goal reactions produce non-specific excitement; but there should be no change in the level of his performance (working on the examination) if the Expectancy × Value conception is correct. That is the moot point under discussion.

## THE S-R EQUIVALENT OF ACHIEVEMENT MOTIVATION

We can translate the Motive × Expectancy × Incentive conception of achievement motivation into *S-R* terms, following leads that R. Sears (1936, 1937, 1942) provided in some of the earliest experimental studies of effects of failure within the *S-R* framework. But the reasons for wanting to do this are much less compelling in the human case than in reference to food-seeking and eating in animals because the consummatory reaction and anticipatory reaction are much more covert than the lip-smacking inhalation of a piece of meat by a hungry dog and the visible froth of saliva that Pavlov studied, which yields a concrete and measurable anticipatory goal reaction. For the sake of completeness, however, we may consider a line drawn on the floor four feet from a peg in a ringtoss game and the response to it. In reference to the situation depicted in Figure 10.1, the visual stimulus of the line on the floor is comparable to $S_e$; walking to the line and throwing the ring at the peg is comparable to the instrumental response, $R_1$; the visual stimulus of the ring slipping over the peg like a ringer is $S_g$; and the immediate reaction of the subject who has thrown the ring over the peg to this stimulus, $S_g$, is $R_g$, the goal reaction. The stimulus produced when the ring misses the peg is comparable to $S_x$, the empty goal-box stimulus in our earlier example. And the subject's reaction to this stimulus is comparable to $R_x$ in the earlier example. We shall not pursue the fact that $S_x$ defines failure and that $R_x$ is the immediate reaction to failure in an achievement-oriented situation.

We may treat the anticipatory goal reaction in this situation just as we do in the case of food and eating. Pride in accomplishment is merely the name for the goal reaction, just as eating is the name for the goal reaction when hunger is under scrutiny. The concept of *expectancy of success* may be translated as *anticipatory pride of accomplishment* if one is clear that pride is the name of the usually covert reaction to success. Yet sometimes it is quite overt, as when a baseball player hits the winning home run in a World Series game and then literally leaps into the air as he begins to run around the bases. This is his gross reaction to seeing the ball disappear over the distant fence. It is the kind of reaction which most people have learned to make covertly to success out of modesty under more ordinary circumstances. When we refer to the achievement motive as a capacity for pride in accomplishment or as a capacity for enjoyment of success, we mean to say no more than what we should mean if we said the same thing about a rat's motive to eat. Some rats get greater enjoyment out of eating. They are like people who eat with great lip-smacking enjoyment and vigor. Sometimes people are described as "swelling with pride." This refers to their reaction when they have performed a task well.

The *S-R* type of analysis is useful in that it suggests that all so-called goals might be conceived as reactions to some stimulus situation. This was acknowledged by Lewin, who sought to represent various *activities*, whether instrumental or consummatory, as regions in the life space of an individual. But if many or most goal reactions in people are covert, and if the events described by stimulus and response are usually central neural events rather than peripheral ones in the human case, the argu-

ment for analysis in terms of stimulus and response ceases to be a very compelling one.

## AN ALTERNATIVE CONCEPTION OF THE EFFECT OF FOOD PRIVATION

One question remains: How is the effect of hours of food privation which is treated as drive (*D*) in *S-R* behavior theory to be conceived within the framework of the Motive × Expectancy × Incentive theory? A tentative answer to this question, following what has already been suggested in criticisms of the separate concept of drive (see p. 197), is consistent with Spence's view that the effect of time of deprivation (*D*) and the effect of amount of reward (*K*) are additive. Birch *et al.* (see p. 198) have already proposed, that $r_g$-$s_g$ elicited by the drive stimulus ($S_d$) may be the physical mechanism of drive. In other words, all effects attributed to *D* may be attributable to the vigor of anticipatory goal reactions. This line of argument might be taken one step farther. The additive relationship $(D + K)$ could be accounted for if the real effect of hours' food privation was to control the threshold of the consummatory eating response. When an organism is satiated, the threshold would be so high that no food stimulus would elicit an eating reaction *even if the food were placed in the animal's mouth*. However, as time of deprivation increases, the threshold for the consummatory reaction would drop, as depicted in Figure 10.3. After a substantial number of hours' food privation, the threshold of consummatory reaction would be so low that even a food stimulus that was normally ineffective in eliciting an eating reaction might do so. A starving man will attempt to eat his shoes. Notice, in Figure 10.3, that a change in the threshold for consummatory reaction associated with hours' food privation would produce the additive effect of time of deprivation and amount of incentive which Spence has summarized $(D + K)$.

Given the Motive × Expectancy × Incentive conception of motivation, both amount of reward and time of deprivation are conceived as antecedents of the incentive value of a food object. This is essentially what Lewin proposed in his conception of valence ($Va_g$) as jointly determined by degree of hunger ($t_g$) and characteristics of the goal object (*G*). Given this conception, food has zero incentive value to a completely sated organism. It does not perform the consummatory reaction when sated, and it is equally incapable of performing an anticipatory consummatory reaction. Thus food holds no "attraction" for the sated organism, and the expectancy

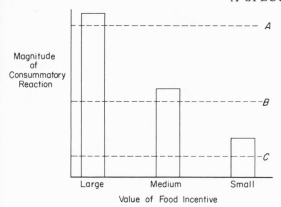

Magnitude
of
Consummatory
Reaction

Large     Medium     Small

Value of Food Incentive

FIGURE 10.3 Schematic presentation of the hypothesis that time of deprivation $(T_D)$ may control the threshold for consummatory reaction and thus influence the magnitude of anticipatory goal reaction. The changing threshold is represented by lines A, B, and C. Line A represents the threshold when an animal is nearly sated; B, after some time without food; and C, after a very substantial number of hours without food. It is assumed that the magnitude of reaction is a function of the strength of suprathreshold tendency.

that food can be attained as a consequence of performing a particular response has little effect on strength of the tendency to perform that response because under the condition of satiation the incentive value of food $(I_g)$ in the equation $T_{r,g} = M_G \times E_{R,G} \times I_g$ is zero.

This view presupposes that chemical changes produced by food privation function to lower the threshold for the consummatory reaction, that particular magnitudes of food reward which are described by the concept of incentive value $(I_g)$ differ in the degree to which they are capable of exciting the consummatory reaction, and that the concept of Motive refers to the individual organism's capacity for excitement of the consummatory reaction. Thus, holding hours of food privation and amount of food constant, the consummatory reaction is greater the stronger the motive. Holding motive and amount of food constant, the consummatory reaction is greater the greater the number of hours of food privation (because the threshold of reaction is lower). Holding motive and hours of food privation constant, the consummatory reaction is greater given a large incentive than a small one (because the large incentive is capable of exciting a greater reaction than the small incentive). A similar conceptual analysis is suggested for all other consummatory reactions which are known to be influenced

by metabolic conditions associated with time, such as sexual activity and thirst.

This alternative conception, though obviously not very clearly worked out, is nevertheless generally consistent with some evidence obtained by Olds (1958) concerning the effect of food privation and chemical changes which control sexual behavior on rate of response produced by electrical stimulation of the brain in certain areas. Hours of food privation was found to influence the rate at which a rat would press a lever for self-stimulation of its brain when the electrodes were located in one area but not when electrodes were placed in another area which was, however, sensitive to the chemical changes which normally influence sexual behavior. The chemical changes which normally control sexual behavior had no influence on the rate of bar pressing when electrodes were located in the area which was sensitive to the effects of food privation. There is, in other words, some neurophysiological evidence to suggest that particular areas of the brain may control particular consummatory reactions. This is the kind of neurophysiological substratum suggested when it is proposed that the effect of a particular kind of deprivation be conceived as controlling the threshold for a particular kind of consummatory reaction.

## METHOD FOR ASSESSMENT OF MOTIVATIONAL DISPOSITIONS IN ANIMALS

From time to time, psychologists concerned with experimental analysis of the determinants of animal behavior have attempted to employ various tests of individual differences, but without much success. The integration of the study of individual differences and experimental analysis of basic processes has lagged behind in animal research. But now, it appears, there is real reason for optimism in the results of a study by Allison (1963). He has developed a test of individual differences in the strength of preference for food using a hexagon maze recently designed by David Birch (see Figure 10.4) to allow accurate assessment of the amount of time a rat will spend having commerce with one or another incentive object when in a choice situation which permits it to move back and forth between places where various incentive objects are located.

Allison's method was to present hungry rats with successive pairs of incentive objects, 10 minutes for each pair, and to measure the amount of time a rat spent in the presence of each incentive object. The three incentive objects were: food (*F*); another rat (*R*), which could be seen, heard, and smelled through a wire screen window as shown in Figure 10.4; and

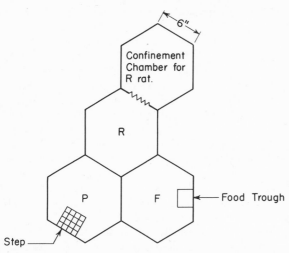

FIGURE 10.4    Floor plan of hexagon assessment maze. (*From Allison, 1963*)

a plaything (*P*) that consisted of a bent wire screen which formed a little step in one of the chambers on which the rat could sit or stand or under which he could crawl. The measure of preference for food was the proportion of total time (*T*) the rat spent in commerce with food (*F*) rather than with *R* or *P*— that is, *F/T*. Food preference was assessed at 22 hours' food deprivation. The assessment consisted of three 10-minute observation periods spaced at intervals of 11–12 minutes. During each observation period, a rat was presented with one pair of incentives, the other object being blocked off by a wall inserted where the door to that chamber normally would be found. An observation period began when the experimenter placed an animal in one or the other of the two chambers available to him in that period.

Allison found substantial individual differences among 44 rats in the proportion of time spent with food under 22 hours of food deprivation. The magnitude of *F/T* ranged from .12 to .85 with a mean of .63. Analysis of each observation period into odd and even minutes (a split-half test) provided encouraging estimates of the reliability of various measurements ranging from .97 to .57.

Even more encouraging are the results obtained when the *F/T* measure of individual differences in

preference for food is related to other performance variables. Allison measured the latency of eating (i.e., the time between being placed in the assessment maze the first time and the first eating response) and found it correlated $-.73$ ($N = 44$) with the *F/T* measure. This means that rats which were strong in preference for food in terms of *F/T* measure initiated eating sooner in this strange environment than rats which were weak in preference for food. The same rats were later trained in a T maze with food reward and in a straight alley leading to food reward. Rats who had scored high in food preference (*F/T*) made significantly fewer errors in learning the T maze and ran significantly faster in both the maze and straight alley than rats who scored low in food preference. The results, in other words, were similar to those obtained when the *n* Achievement scores of human subjects are related to measures of instrumental performance in an achievement-oriented situation.

In a second experiment, Allison employed the same procedure to assess individual differences in food preference and speed of running in a straight alley under 22 hours' food deprivation, but with different amounts of food incentive (1 pellet versus 10 pellets) in the alley test. His range of *F/T* scores was similar to that of the first experiment. This time he divided a group of 46 rats into high (*F/T* 1), middle (*F/T* 2), and low (*F/T* 3) thirds in order to study the joint influence of individual differences in food preference, number of training trials, and amount of incentive on instrumental performance in the straight alley. Figure 10.5 shows that response speed in the straight alley, with food deprivation held constant at 22 hours, is significantly greater when preference for food is strong (*F/T* 1) and when the magnitude of food incentive is large (10 pellets). An over-all test of the way in which food preference and food incentive combine to influence the speed of running suggests that they combine *additively*. In other words, the measure of food preference relates to instrumental performance in a manner comparable to drive, that is, hours of food privation.

There is no obvious support for the hypothesis that $Va_g = M_G \times I_g$ (as elaborated in Figure 10.2) were we to proceed on the premise that the *F/T* measure should be conceived as a measure of a motive to eat having functional properties comparable to those attributed to a motive in the theory of achievement motivation. The fundamental contribution of Allison's work lies in the methodological innovation. It should begin to promote an integra-

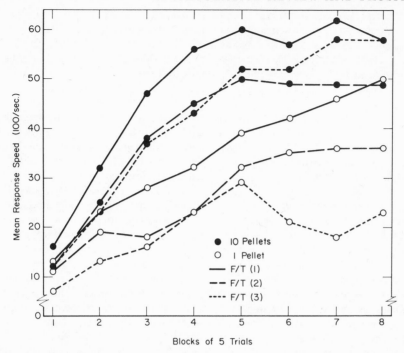

FIGURE 10.5   Speed of response in a straight alley as a function of number of trials, magnitude of reward, and strength of preference for food [F/T (1) is strongest and F/T (3) is weakest.] (*Based on Allison, 1963*)

tion of the study of individual differences and experimental analysis of the process of motivation in animal research which will answer this kind of theoretical question definitively. This new method of study brings the logic of assessment of personality into contact with theory of motivation in animal research.

## A DIFFERENT CONCEPTION OF "FEAR" AND "AVOIDANCE"

The convergence of Expectancy × Value and Drive × Habit theories of motivation of performance is readily apparent when the motivational significance of a reward or positive incentive is considered. But the two theories still differ substantially in the conception of the motivational significance of "punishments," or noxious events. We have discussed this difference in a preliminary way in reference to how "anxiety" influences achievement-oriented performance. The Drive × Habit conception emphasizes the non-specific exciting effect (*D*) of the anticipatory emotional reaction ($r_e$) called fear and/or the specific avoidant habits elicited by

the internal stimulus ($S_D$) produced by the fear response. But given an Expectancy × Value theory, which accounts for the strength of the tendency to perform a response in terms of expected consequences of that response, we have seen that a noxious consequence—that is, one having negative incentive value ($I_{-g}$)—generates a tendency to inhibit or to avoid subsequent performance of that response.

INITIAL BEHAVIOR BEFORE SHOCK IS APPLIED

We can clarify the difference between the theories in reference to the type of experiment performed in studies of avoidance conditioning which have yielded the concept of "fear as an acquired drive." Let us consider a simple situation in which an animal is placed in one side of a box having a grid floor with a small barrier over which the animal can jump to another side of the box not having a grid floor. Typically, animals are placed in the box on the side having the grid floor and their behavior is observed before any shock is administered. The animals move about, sit, sniff, preen, put their paws up on the barrier, even cross the barrier to the other side. They are motivated to perform many different responses *even before the first shock is applied.* These initial responses to the stimulus situation are attributed to generalized habits elicited by cues in the box, habits acquired earlier in similar situations. The fact that the animals perform them at all implies the presence of some minimal amount of drive ($D$) and/or incentive motivation ($K$). If there were no generalized habits elicited by cues in the box, or if there were no minimal amount of ($D + K$) already present, the animals would presumably fall asleep as soon as they were placed in the box. That is what is implied by $E = (D + K) \times H$.

An Expectancy $\times$ Value theory must make similar assumptions to explain the behavior of the animal in the box before the first shock is ever applied. We have already acknowledged the need for the concept of habit in an Expectancy $\times$ Value formulation to define the set of responses which are "entertained as possibilities" in a stimulus situation. In addition, Expectancy $\times$ Value theory leads one to speak of generalized expectancies and the assumption that some minimal positive incentive values are also transferred to this situation from earlier experience in similar situations. For all that anyone knows, the animals may be moving around looking for food, or for water, or for a mate, or merely exploring the complex features of this novel stimulus situation. The important point is that both theories must account for the fact that animals do perform a variety of responses when placed in the box *before* any shock is applied. Both theories assume that the particular response which occurs at any particular moment does occur because at that moment it is the dominant or strongest tendency in the animal's repertoire or hierarchy of activated tendencies.

### EFFECT OF SHOCK FOLLOWING
### A PARTICULAR RESPONSE

Now what happens when the experimenter begins to administer shocks to the animal in the side of the box having the grid floor? The animal is "punished" either while it is performing some response (like sniffing in a corner) or immediately after it has performed such a response. This event, particular response followed by shock ($R \rightarrow -G$), is the temporal sequence which should strengthen an expectancy that performance of that particular response is followed by shock ($E_{r,-g}$). The intensity and/or duration of shock is represented as the magnitude of negative incentive ($I_{-g}$). According to the principle $T_{r,-g} = M_G \times E_{r,-g} \times I_{-g}$, the animal should subsequently be more strongly motivated to

inhibit (i.e., to avoid) performance of that particular response after it is "punished" than before the shock was applied. If shock is repeatedly applied so that most or all of the responses which the animal was initially motivated to perform in the box are punished one or more times, the subsequent strength of tendencies to inhibit these responses will increase and begin to oppose and dampen the excitatory tendencies *that were present even before shocks were applied.* Soon some tendency to perform a response that was relatively low in the initial hierarchy of tendencies aroused in the box will be relatively stronger because the resultant tendencies to perform responses that were initially dominant have been weakened. This follows from the assumption that the resultant tendency to perform a response equals $T_{r,g} + T_{r,-g}$, the same assumption employed in the discussion of how the conflict between tendency to seek success and tendency to avoid failure is resolved in achievement-oriented performance. One of these resultant tendencies to respond, which though initially weaker than others is now stronger because the other responses have been followed by "punishment," may be the tendency to perform the response of climbing over the barrier. This is the response which the experimenter calls "the avoidance response" because it gets the animal away from the place where shock has been administered. And this particular response is the only response that never will be followed by shock. Any other response the animal makes in the side of the box containing the grid will sooner or later be followed by shock and the subsequent resultant tendency to perform it weakened.

### SIGNIFICANCE OF THE INITIAL
### AVOIDANCE RESPONSE

In discussing the results of his experiment demonstrating "fear as an acquired drive and fear-reduction as reinforcement," Miller correctly pointed out that the "correct" response must occur for the first time before it can ever be reinforced. We recall, in this connection, that only about half of the animals in his experiment ever did perform the correct response (turning the wheel which opened the escape door and running out), so only half the animals showed improvement in performance of this response in subsequent unshocked trials in a manner consistent with the notion that fear motivates and fear-reduction reinforces habit strength.

From the viewpoint of Expectancy $\times$ Value theory, the initial occurrence of the successful "avoidance response" is particularly significant. It suggests that the animal would have gotten out of the place where shock is applied, sooner or later, even if the shock had never been introduced. The tendency to perform this response is already present in the initial hierarchy of tendencies aroused by the stimulus situation even before the first shock is administered. The Expectancy × Value theory implies that performance of the so-called avoidance response is speeded up because other initially more dominant response tendencies have been weakened by punishment. That is, they have been performed and followed by shock. Subsequently there is, in each case, an expectancy that performance of the response will lead to shock and an increase in the strength of the inhibitory tendency which opposes or dampens excitation to perform that response again. This process, repeated for a number of different responses, finally leaves the tendency to climb over the barrier as the strongest excitatory tendency even though absolutely nothing has happened to change its initial strength. It is now *relatively* stronger because all the competing excitatory tendencies are opposed, dampened, or weakened by an inhibitory tendency.

## THE CHANGE OF INITIAL HIERARCHY OF RESPONSE TENDENCIES

Figure 10.6 shows how the competitive position of the weakest of four tendencies can be improved by weakening the three competing tendencies. All theories agree that the response which occurs is the dominant tendency at the time and that the latency of a response (the speed with which it occurs in a stimulus situation) depends upon its strength *relative* to the strength of competing tendencies. The Expectancy × Value theory accounts for short latency "avoidance" responses primarily in terms of the weakening of competing tendencies by punishment rather than in terms of the strengthening by fear-reduction of the response which takes the animal out of a threatening situation. In fact, we have so far had to say nothing at all about the arousal of fear in the animal.

Since we have already acknowledged the need for the concept of habit in Expectancy × Value theory, we may complete the explanation of avoidance behavior by assuming, as Spence now does, that sheer frequency of performance of a response in a stimulus situation (*S-R*) strengthens habit. If so, then the strength of the tendency to climb over the barrier should grow stronger as a function of repetition. This would explain why the latency of so-called

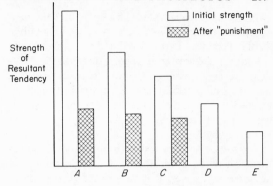

FIGURE 10.6   The assumed change in the initial hierarchy of resultant action tendencies brought about by "punishment" following overt expression of the initially dominant tendencies, A, B, and C. The expectancy that A, B, and C will be followed by "punishment" introduces tendencies to avoid performance of those activities which are in conflict with the initial tendencies to undertake those activities. As a consequence, the tendency to undertake activity D, which has not been followed by punishment, becomes the dominant member of the hierarchy and is expressed in behavior.

avoidance responses decreases on subsequent trials when the animal is no longer being shocked. This explanation states, in brief, that the animal performs the so-called avoidance response the first time because the tendency to perform that response was contained in the hierarchy of generalized tendencies called forth by the stimulus situation even before shocks were administered. The shocks tend to weaken the resultant tendency to perform all other responses but the one which gets the animal out of the place where shocks are administered. So sooner or later the so-called avoidance response is performed for the first time (unless, of course, it is not contained in the original hierarchy of activated tendencies). This event, *S-R*, strengthens the habit somewhat so that on the next trial everything is the same as at the instant of the initial performance of the avoidance response except that the tendency to perform it is a little stronger because habit has been strengthened—not by fear-reduction, but by mere occurrence on the previous trial.

The picture to have in mind when applying Expectancy × Value theory to experiments on avoidance behavior is similar to what would happen if both the President and Vice President of the United States were to die on the same day. Within the hour, the Speaker of the House of Representatives would be sworn in as President, and the newspapers the next day would make him as visible to the general public as the President had been the day before. Some would wonder how he happened to get to be President overnight, having forgotten that there exists a hierarchy of potential presidents for just such an emergency. The only thing that has happened is the removal of those above him in the hierarchy that already existed.

The same condition exists in any behavior situation. There is, from the outset, a hierarchy of activated tendencies. If it happens to be a selective learning experiment of the Thorndikian type, one of those tendencies is destined to produce a response that will be followed by "reward." If it is an avoidance conditioning experiment, one of those tendencies is destined to produce the only response that will not be followed by "punishment." In such a situation, the initially dominant tendencies are weakened by punishment. This produces the kind of change in hierarchy of resultant strength of tendencies shown in Figure 10.6.

### OBSERVATIONS IN STUDIES OF TRAUMATIC AVOIDANCE CONDITIONING

Some of the observations made by Solomon et al. (1953a, 1953b, 1954, 1956) concerning the effects of traumatic intensities of shock in avoidance conditioning of dogs seem consistent with this conception of avoidant behavior. They provide some basis for considering particular implications of the Drive $\times$ Habit conception of avoidance behavior in relation to implications of the Expectancy $\times$ Value conception which has just been presented. Solomon and his co-workers have shown that after a few very intense shocks applied 10 seconds after a buzzer signal begins to sound, dogs will successfully avoid further shock by jumping over a barrier to "safety" when the signal of forthcoming shock is presented on subsequent occasions. They will do this for *hundreds of trials* without ever again being shocked and without showing any signs whatever of extinguishing the avoidance response. What is more, the latency of the avoidance response to the signal (i.e., the time between signal and jumping response) continues to decrease long after the animal has ceased exposing himself to shock. Even more significant, the latency of the avoidance response is so short that the animal has already performed it before having time to be afraid. Solomon and Wynne (1953) argued from available evidence that the latency of the conditioned emotional reaction called fear or anxiety should be

about 1.5 to 2.5 seconds. The autonomic reaction called fear, in other words, takes that long to occur in response to a stimulus. But in their studies of avoidance behavior in dogs, the latency of the entire jumping response approximately 100 trials after the last shocked trial is found to decrease to about 1.7 seconds; and at the end of 200 trials the latency of jumping had dropped to about 1.6 seconds. The problem for the Drive $\times$ Habit theory, which emphasizes the role of fear as drive and fear-reduction as reinforcement to explain an avoidance response, is put by Solomon et al. as follows:

"The instrumental jumping response *itself* usually has a latency of from 1.0 to 1.5 seconds at its asymptote. (Some individual animals produced latencies as short as 0.9 seconds, though very rarely.) Thus, if the animals' jumps were responses to their own emotional reactions, or if they were responding to drive arousal, the asymptote for the latency of the jumping response in the presence of the CS should have been approximately 2.4 to 3.4 seconds, i.e., the sum of the latencies for drive arousal and for jumping. But the animals were jumping faster than this within 10 to 20 trials after meeting the acquisition criterion. . . . Obviously, the animals at this point *could not* have been responding to their own emotional reactions. The assumption that autonomic arousal serves as the stimulus for the jumping response is contradicted by the facts. The latency data indicate that, at this point, the jumping response has an extremely high habit strength and is activated by minimal drive. In any event, it cannot be argued that the jumping is energized by a *full-blown anxiety reaction to the CS.*

"It is clear that either something was fundamentally wrong with our interpretation of acquisition [Solomon and Wynne, 1953], or that additional principles have been overlooked. For, once the animals are jumping in a period of time shorter than that required for the emotional reaction to take place in the presence of the CS, we can no longer argue that jumping continues to be reinforced by anxiety reduction. Then, since no further reinforcement occurs, the jumping response ought gradually to extinguish" (Solomon, Kamin, and Wynne, 1953, p. 298).

In our earlier discussion of how the tendency to avoid failure operates to influence behavior in achievement-oriented situations (see p. 244), the importance of a complete conceptual analysis of the sources of motivation to perform particular responses was stressed. The concept of "extrinsic motivation" was introduced to explain why persons whose achievement-related motivation is negative (i.e., inhibitory) perform an achievement-oriented task at all. Now, in our analysis of avoidance behavior as it has been studied in lower animals, we make essentially the same point: the instrumental responses which an animal does perform in the shock-box experiments are to be explained in terms of sources of positive motivation to perform those actions. What they are, no one knows. But from the time of Thorndike's very first study of selective learning in animals, the occurrence of the first "correct" response has always been attributed to innate or previously acquired tendencies which the stimulus situation was said to elicit on the very first trial. As S-R theory developed, these initial reactions were viewed as instances of stimulus generalization, that is, the elicitation of habits previously acquired in similar situations and excited by minimal drive. They are now generally taken for granted.

## FEAR CONCEIVED AS A SYMPTOM
## RATHER THAN AS A CAUSE

The main point of the interpretation of avoidance behavior guided by the implications of Expectancy × Value theory is that "fear" should not be conceived as the exciter of avoidance responses, but as a symptom that an animal is already performing a response with an expectancy of a negative consequence. Animals show visible signs of being afraid (squealing, defecating, urinating, etc.) while performing responses in the box in which they have been shocked because these particular responses have, in the past, been followed by shock. When they begin to perform the avoidant response which has never been followed by shock, visible signs of a fear reaction tend to disappear. And, as Solomon et al. have shown, the performance of the avoidant response in repeated trials soon occurs so quickly that the animals do not even have time to be afraid.

Several other observations from these studies of traumatic avoidance conditioning are consistent with this interpretation. Solomon et al. have noted that the visible manifestations of fear reaction become less and less evident after the animals have begun to perform the avoidance response as soon as the signal of forthcoming shock is presented. For several hundred trials, virtually no visible manifestations of anxiety are present. But then, several hundred trials later when a glass barrier is introduced to prevent the animal from leaving the place where it was once shocked, all the visible symptoms of a very intense fear reaction immediately return. In other words, when the dogs are physically constrained and made to perform some response which is expected to be followed by shock, whether it be standing still or crouching in the box, the fear reaction returns. These are responses which the animal would not otherwise have performed if given the opportunity to perform the so-called avoidance response, the net excitatory tendency for which is strongest.

Under what other conditions might an organism be constrained to perform a response that is expected to have a negative consequence? This is equivalent to asking: In what other conditions is an inhibitory tendency likely to be overcome? We have already discussed this problem in connection with achievement-oriented performance in calling attention to the usually ignored sources of extrinsic positive motivation to perform laboratory tasks which constrain a person who is strongly disposed to be anxious about failure. And the conception of a person who is more strongly motivated to achieve success than to avoid failure provides another illustration of an instance in which the inhibitory tendency is overcome by an even stronger positive, excitatory tendency. One of the paradoxes of this viewpoint was noted in the initial statement of the theory of achievement motivation:

> "In summary, the person in whom the achievement motive is stronger [than the motive to avoid failure] should set his level of aspiration in the intermediate zone where there is moderate risk. To the extent that he has any motive to avoid failure, this means he will voluntarily choose activities that *maximize* his own anxiety about failure! On the other hand, the person in whom the motive to avoid failure is stronger should select either the easiest of the alternatives or should be extremely speculative and set his goal where there is virtually no chance for success. These are activities which *minimize* his anxiety about failure" (Atkinson, 1957, p. 364).

Solomon et al. maximized the arousal of anxiety in their dogs by imposing a physical barrier to performance of the one response for which there was no expectancy of shock as the consequence. The full-blown return of the fear reaction, as conceived from the viewpoint of Expectancy × Value theory, was *caused* by forcing the animal to perform one or another response with a strong expectancy of the noxious consequence last associated with performance of that response in the stimulus situation.

This conception of the autonomic physiological reaction called fear or anxiety and the conscious experience it produces explains why persons who report that they have experienced a great deal of anxiety in achievement-test situations normally suffer inhibition of performance of actions which might eventuate in failure. They do, in fact, attend classes in school and also undertake examinations because they are constrained by all the other positive incentives and motives which determine academic performance. But what they "feel" in test situations and report on anxiety questionnaires is symptomatic of the strength of inhibitory tendency which has been overcome. When given a choice between undertaking a competitive achievement activity or not, they should voluntarily avoid the competitive activity. When forced to choose between achievement-related activities which differ in difficulty, they avoid the activity where the product of expectancy of failure and negative incentive value of failure is greatest in the same sense that animals in avoidance conditioning studies avoid the expected shock by performing the response which has never been shocked. In both cases, the excitatory tendency to perform the so-called "avoidance response" is attributed to extrinsic sources of *positive* motivation and not to "anxiety."

## EXTINCTION OF SO-CALLED AVOIDANCE RESPONSE

Other writers who have employed Tolman's concept of expectancy in reference to avoidance conditioning (e.g., Ritchie, 1951) have called attention to the fact that the so-called avoidance response will not extinguish until the animal stays in the place where it has been shocked long enough and often enough to find out that the shock is no longer applied. Specifically, this means *the animal must perform responses that are expected to be followed by shock, but without shock as the consequence, so that the expectancy that the response is followed by shock can be weakened.* As the expectancy of shock is weakened, the tendency not to perform the response (the inhibitory tendency) will also be weakened and the visible symptoms of fear reaction will be weakened. In time, performance of the so-called avoidance response which got the animal out of the threatening place should finally extinguish because the excitatory tendencies to perform other responses in the box will no longer be dampened, but will again compete successfully with the so-called avoidant response. But how is the animal to change its expectancy of the consequences of responses performed in the box unless it stays in the box and performs them?

Solomon *et al.* found that the glass-barrier technique was moderately effective as a form of "reality testing." It produced some extinction of the avoidance response. Another technique employed consisted of shocking the dogs for jumping over the barrier. This also was moderately effective in producing extinction of the avoidance response. In terms of Expectancy × Value theory, what this procedure accomplished was inhibition of the one response not previously followed by shock. In time, some of the dogs stayed in the place where they had been shocked because now even the jumping response was expected to be followed by shock and so was inhibited. The animals were placed in the box by the experimenter and so if now all responses are inhibited, they would remain frozen in the place where shock had initially been administered and begin to undergo a change of expectancy concerning the consequences of doing what they were doing. The best procedure for producing extinction of the avoidance response, according to Solomon *et al.*, combined the "reality testing" (glass barrier) and shock for jumping over the barrier with reality-testing preceding the punishment of the jumping response.

## DIFFERENCE BETWEEN THEORIES IN REFERENCE TO ANTICIPATED THREATS

Whether or not Expectancy × Value can handle all details of avoidance conditioning and "fear" studies is an open question. The concept of *a tendency to avoid performance of a particular response which is expected to have a negative consequence* seems clearly implied by theories which multiply a variable called expectancy (which refers to a particular response) by a negative incentive value. This does not tell what the organism will do, but what it will not do. In this respect, the treatment of anticipated threats differs substantially from the view that the anticipatory emotional reaction ($r_e$) has the same functional properties as anticipatory goal reactions ($r_g$), as stated in the Drive × Habit conception of the motivation of performance. The functional significance of anticipated threats in Expectancy × Value theories is to generate a tendency which opposes or dampens the tendency to perform a response. Inhibition of action is the observable consequence. The reaction called fear ($r_e$) must have time to occur if it is to influence subsequent behavior. And it seems, from the account given by Solomon *et al.*, that avoidance responses occur too rapidly to be explained by the concept of fear as an acquired drive. Thus there is some factual basis for an open mind concerning the possibility that the interpretation suggested by Expectancy × Value theory which has developed in other contexts may produce the clue needed to unravel some of the persistent dilemmas in studies of avoidance conditioning.

## EXTREME AVOIDANCE CONDITIONING WITHOUT TRAUMATIC SHOCK

A simple experimental situation for use with human subjects has been devised by the writer and Stuart Karabenick to concretize some of the points made in this discussion of the determinants of avoidance behavior. Subjects are seated at a table on which before them are five colored cards—white, yellow, red, blue, green. They are instructed that at each click of a timing device they may place their hand on one of the cards or none of them. They are also instructed that the amount of money (up to $5.00) which they will be paid at the end of the period will depend upon the number of points they accumulate relative to the total number of points it is possible to accumulate during the period. When the timing device clicks for the first time, the subject places his hand on one of the colors. The experimenter immediately reports "Win 25" or some "rewarding" or "punishing" consequence that has been predetermined. This procedure continues for more than an hour with the interval between responses set at approximately four seconds. If the subject passes, that is, does not touch one of the cards when the timing device clicks, the experimenter immediately reports the consequence of that particular act to the subject.

This situation is designed to provide an exhaustive account of what the subject is doing throughout the experimental period. At every click of the timing device, he has his hand on one of the colors or not. And each of the six alternatives (including "Pass") is considered a particular act having some immediate consequence to the subject, that is, a number of points won or lost.

In advance of the experiment, the investigators predetermined what the consequence of each response would be on each occasion when the timing device clicked. In one condition, it was decided to mold a hierarchy of responses by rewarding the subject for any response during the first 90 clicks of the timing device but varying the average amount of reward for the different colored cards and the pass response.

During the next 70 clicks, a signal light came on and remained on for a number of clicks of the timing device on several occasions but without producing any change in the amount of reward following each of the responses. This light did not produce much change in the hierarchy of response tendencies which had been established by differential reward as shown in Figure 10.7.

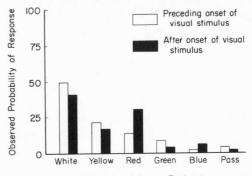

FIGURE 10.7    Initial hierarchy of action tendencies produced by different positive incentives before beginning of avoidance training. The frequency of various responses on the trial immediately preceding the onset of the visual stimulus which was later to become the conditioned stimulus for avoidance, and on the first trial after its onset during five adaptation trials, is not remarkably different. The results, based on data from 10 subjects, show that "Blue," which was destined to become the "avoidance response," was very low in the initial hierarchy of action tendencies. (*From unpublished data collected by Atkinson and Karabenick, 1963*)

After the hierarchy of responses in this situation had been established, "avoidance conditioning" was begun. During avoidance training, the signal light (CS) came on and stayed on until the subject placed his hand on "Blue," which was the second weakest response in the initial hierarchy. The rewards following any response were the same as usual for the first six clicks after the light (CS) came on, but on the seventh click and thereafter until the response "Blue" occurred, the consequence of any response other than "Blue" was "Lose 1000." When the subject placed his hand on "Blue," he both turned off the light and received the usual weak reward for the "Blue" response.

The investigators view this situation as analogous to the usual avoidance training situation with animals. There are a number of different responses an animal can make in the context in which he will later be shocked, including the response that the experimenter will later call the avoidance response. It is assumed that each of these responses is expected to have some rewarding consequence by the animal, or else it would not be performed. It is established that the stimulus which later will be the conditioned stimulus for the avoidance response (the light) has no effect on the behavior of the subject before avoidance training is begun. Then avoidance training is begun with a seven-click interval between the onset of the light (*CS*) and the onset of the report "Lose 1000," which is considered analogous to the extremely negative consequence, the shock, normally employed in animal studies.

The results for 10 subjects show that the so-called avoidance response, in this case putting the hand on "Blue," is learned within 11 to 55 trials by all subjects to a criterion of 10 successive "Blue" responses within six clicks following the onset of the light. After this criterion of learning has been met, the extinction trials begin, and the subject is never again punished for any response when the light comes on. Hand on "Blue," however, continues to turn off the light. Other responses are rewarded, as during the pre-training period, but do not turn off the light.

In this preliminary experiment, 4 out of 10 subjects continued to perform the so-called avoidance response within six clicks whenever the light came on until interruption of the experiment by the end of the planned experimental period (an hour and a half). Two subjects reached an extinction criterion of five successive trials with light on without putting their hand on "Blue" within 15 clicks of the timing device. These subjects took 18 and 21 trials to extinguish the "Blue" response. Four subjects were taking somewhat more than six clicks to put their hand on "Blue" by the end of the period, but had not yet reached the arbitrary extinction criterion.

Figure 10.8 shows the results obtained for the subject who had the most trials with the light on after training. It is obvious that his behavior begins to resemble the behavior of the dogs in the Solomon experiment which had been exposed to a traumatic shock during training. He had shown no signs of extinction after 204 trials.

According to Expectancy × Value theory, this subject continues to perform a weakly but positively motivated response because nothing has happened to change his expectancy that performance of one of the other responses, which normally produces more points when the light is off, will be followed by a great loss of points when the light is on. When the light was off, this subject showed the same preference for "White" and the other more highly rewarded responses that he had displayed before the avoidance training was instituted.

It seems very doubtful, in this instance, that the

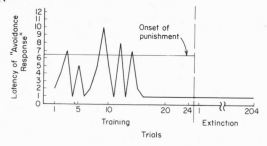

FIGURE 10.8   Avoidance training and extinction series for one subject (6A) under conditions described in text. This subject took 24 trials to meet the arbitrary criterion of learning (10 consecutive trials on which the "avoidance response," Blue, occurred within six clicks following onset of the visual stimulus). He then continued to make this response immediately after the onset of the light for 204 trials with no sign of extinction. At this point the experiment was concluded. (*From unpublished data collected by Atkinson and Karabenick, 1963*)

extreme resistance to extinction is to be explained in terms of an intense fear that is being aroused every time the light goes on and reduced every time the light goes off.

## THE LAW OF EFFECT: A MISLEADING GUIDE

Since the time of Thorndike's earliest experiments on selective learning, most psychologists have assumed that the Law of Effect, which states that rewards strengthen behavior, provides a common beginning point for the development of theory. In contemporary psychology, it is now common to refer to a "rewarding" state of affairs which increases the subsequent probability of a response as a *reinforcement*. This gives a technical ring to the old idea and leaves open the question of why certain states of affairs function to increase the subsequent probability of the responses they have followed.

We have seen that the old Thorndikian view that reward (or reinforcement) serves to strengthen the subsequent tendency to respond by somehow cementing the connection between a stimulus and a response (habit) has gradually given way to the view, which Tolman was the first to emphasize, that anticipated rewards function as incentives at the time of subsequent performance. This view is now shared by Drive × Habit theory and Expectancy × Value theory, even though they differ in specifying exactly how an anticipated reward influences subsequent performance of a response. Thorndike's earliest view that punishment serves to weaken the tendency to respond, as if by dissolving the connection between a stimulus and a response, has similarly given way to explanations of the effect of punishment and "annoying states of affairs" in terms of the influence of anticipated noxious events on subsequent performance. The Drive × Habit and Expectancy × Value theories provide fundamentally different conceptions of how anticipation of a noxious (punishing) event influences subsequent performance, but both are motivational explanations. That is, both tend to emphasize that it is the anticipation of punishment at the time of subsequent performance which explains why punished responses are less likely to be repeated.

## ALLPORT'S CRITICISM

The most serious deficiency of the Law of Effect as a "guiding idea" was stressed by Gordon Allport (1943) in the very year that many psychologists greeted Hull's physiological explanation of the Law of Effect (need or drive-reduction) as, perhaps, the basic building block for a theory of behavior. Allport, considering the implications of the Law of Effect in reference to the phenomena of "ego-involvement" in research on human personality, called attention to the fact that the Law of Effect simply does not apply to "ego-involved" human behavior. He cited evidence from the early studies of level of aspiration which showed that "success" at a task does not typically increase the likelihood of a repetition of the very same activity (the same responses). When, for example, a person throws a ringer from a certain distance in a ringtoss game, the event defining "success" does not reinforce the particular actions it followed. The subsequent probability of the "rewarded" responses (viz., throwing a ring from exactly the same distance) is not typically increased, but decreased. Typically, following "success," the subsequent response is a different one, one commonly described as a change in the level of aspiration. Concretely, this change is defined by a change in behavior following success. And, as we have seen in the review of studies of achievement-oriented performance (see Chapter 9), neither does "failure" uniformly produce a decrease in the subsequent probability of the responses it has followed. How is the apparent inadequacy of the Law of Effect in the domain of achievement-oriented (or "ego-involved") behavior to be reconciled with its continued popularity as a fundamental guiding idea in research on learning and the motivation of performance?

## AS VIEWED BY EXPECTANCY × VALUE THEORY

One of the strong points of the Expectancy × Value theory of motivation of performance is that it can derive the behavior which gave rise to the Law of Effect in the first place and still explain changes in response following success and failure in achievement-oriented activity where the Law of Effect does not hold. When a hungry rat turns left in a maze and finds food, the subsequent increase in tendency to turn left is explained in terms of an increase in the strength of expectancy that turning left leads to food. Each rewarded trial produces a further increase in the strength of expectancy. Given the assumption that the strength of the tendency to act is a multiplicative function of expectancy and the incentive value of the expected consequence, the tendency to perform the rewarded response should become stronger as the expectancy of reward becomes stronger *as long as the incentive value of an expected consequence is unrelated to the strength of the expectancy of attaining it*. This condition prevails in the animal experiments that are neatly summarized by the Law of Effect. Similarly, if the rat is punished by shock after every left turn, its tendency to do something else instead of turning left on subsequent occasions is also explained in terms of Expectancy × Value *as long as the value of the negative incentive is unrelated to the strength of the expectancy of attaining it*. But consider now the variety of different observed effects of success and failure in achievement-oriented activities which depend, as we have seen, upon the personality of the subject and the difficulty of the task. There is no general and systematic strengthening of a response by success, which common-sense extrapolation from the Law of Effect would lead us to consider a reward or positive reinforcement, or weakening of response by failure, which we are likely to consider a punishment. Sometimes "success" will increase the subsequent probability of the same response; just as often it will do the reverse. Sometimes "failure" will decrease the subsequent probability of the same response; just as often it will do the reverse.

The variety of possible changes in behavior produced by "success" and "failure" are integrated by Expectancy × Value theory when it is acknowledged that sometimes the incentive value of an anticipated consequence of action is systematically related to the strength of the expectancy of attaining it. The special assumptions of the theory of achievement motivation (viz., $I_s = 1 - P_s$ and $I_f = -P_s$) are introduced *to describe the conditions which exist in instances of achievement-oriented human behavior.* These assumptions, which are supported by other evidence independent of changes in behavior following success and failure, do not explain *why* the incentive value of success and failure are related in this way to an individual's expectations. They merely acknwledge *that* incentive values of the anticipated consequences in achievement-oriented actions are related to strength of expectancy and, in so doing, explain why the Law of Effect as it is generally understood does not apply to this domain of behavior. The Law of Effect does not apply simply because the value of the so-called rewarding event is not, in this instance, independent of the past frequency of attaining it, and both are determinants of the strength of a subsequent tendency to perform the same activity.

### HISTORICAL PERSPECTIVE

The *empirical law of effect*, as a guiding idea, is the last misleading vestige of Thorndike's early attempt to encompass the basic idea of the commonsense hedonistic theory of behavior in a more objective theory which would explain behavior solely in terms of associative changes. It was maintained as the important guiding principle by Hull, who substituted "reinforcing state of affairs" for Thorndike's "satisfier" and proposed a physiological explanation of reinforcement, conceiving it as a process that strengthened connections, which he called habits. We recall that in the 1930's, before the first formal statement of his theory of behavior, Hull still believed that "striving for goals" would be explained by principles which account for "strengthening of connections," given the assumption that the present stimulus is what motivates the response.

Events since 1943 have forced *S-R* psychologists to distinguish the *empirical law of effect* from theoretical interpretations of the law which attempt to state how reinforcement operates to bring about the changes in subsequent behavior which the law summarizes. Two very important things have happened. First, the two general physiological hypotheses (need-reduction and stimulus-reduction), which were advanced to explain the nature of reinforcement conceived as a process which affected learning of habits, have been shown to be grossly inadequate summaries of the kinds of events which function as reinforcers of behavior. Second, the idea that reinforcement refers to the learning of habits has given way to the idea that reinforcement refers to the motivation of perform-

ance. This was the position that Tolman had taken in the early debate over the meaning of the classic latent-learning studies. The earliest ideas within *S-R* behavior theory about the Law of Effect had missed on both counts. This is perhaps most clearly apparent in Sheffield's statement of a drive-induction theory of reward. (See p. 195.) This contemporary theory asserts, as does Spence's theory of incentive motivation, that "reinforcement" refers to something happening at the time of the motivation of performance (and not to learning) and what is more, that it should be conceived as an increase of excitation and not a decrease as presumed in the need-reduction and stimulus-reduction theories of reinforcement which view the process as fundamental in the learning of habits!

Within the framework of contemporary research on animal behavior in terms of *S* and *R*, the *empirical law of effect* is still considered a useful summary statement and guide to research. Spence, for example, has recently stated:

"... in ... simple selective learning situations the psychologist has observed that when certain types of environmental events accompany or follow a particular response, the response is more likely to occur on subsequent occasions. Omissions of such events following a response, moreover, may be observed to lead subsequently to a lessened likelihood of its occurrence. Environmental events exhibiting this property of increasing the probability of occurrence of responses they accompany constitute a class of events known as *reinforcers* or *reinforcing events*. All environmental events not exhibiting this property fall into a different class that may be designated as *non-reinforcers*. By means of these two classes of events it becomes possible to formulate the following law: Responses accompanied or followed by certain kinds of events (namely, reinforcers) are more likely to occur on subsequent occasions, whereas responses followed by certain other events (namely, non-reinforcers) do not subsequently show a greater likelihood of occurrence. This statement, which we shall refer to as the *empirical law of effect*, summarizes an observed relationship between the subsequent strength or likelihood of occurrence of a response and two different classes of effects or outcomes. It does not imply, it should be noted, any theory as to how the effects operate to bring about the change in response probability. As far as I can see, all psychologists, whether they support or oppose some form of reinforcement theory of learning, would agree to this empirical law of effect" (Spence, 1956, pp. 32–33).

Spence is probably correct in asserting that all (or at least many) psychologists agree to this *empirical law of effect*—despite the fact that it is a useful memory aid only in reference to a restricted set of instances of instrumental behavior. The law is misleading simply because it is not qualified by some statement which identifies the conditions under which it holds. Thus it is often mistakenly believed to be a much more general "law," or memory aid, than it is. As a misunderstood guide to action, it can suggest to teachers in the schools, for example, that repeated success is the best way to encourage interest in learning in the schools. But is it? As a misunderstood guide to action, the *empirical law of effect* suggests that if throwing a ringer in a ringtoss game is observed to increase the likelihood that a person will throw another ring from the same distance (i.e., a repetition of the response), subsequent ringers will have a similar effect for that person, or ringers thrown by other persons will have a similar effect on their behavior. In fact, this is not true. Nor is it likely to be true under other achievement-oriented circumstances where the incentive value of success changes as the expectancy of success changes.

Considered from the point of view of an Expectancy $\times$ Value theory of motivation, the Law of Effect is a secondary principle to be derived from a more general principle which accounts for changes in expectations concerning the consequences of actions and from a principle of motivation which states that the strength of a tendency to act in a certain way is determined by the product of expectancy that an act will have a certain consequence and the value of that consequence to the individual. The Law of Effect is a *limited* secondary principle in that it is a useful memory aid only in reference to conditions where the value of the consequence is independent of the strength of expectancy of attaining that consequence or where the value of the consequence increases as the expectancy of attaining it increases. When, however, the value of the expected consequence decreases as the strength of expectancy of attaining it increases—for whatever reason—then the empirical law of effect as traditionally understood does not apply. Human achievement-oriented performance in which "success" and "failure" are the most important consequences of action is one domain in which the Law of Effect is a hindrance to understanding rather than a help. There are undoubtedly other domains of behavior in which similar conditions prevail. These will be more fully understood when psychologists can break through the conceptual barrier imposed by the Law of Effect which they have implicitly accepted as a generally useful guiding idea.

## OVER-EMPHASIS OF THE IMMEDIATE STIMULUS SITUATION

There is another and even more important conceptual obstacle to be surmounted in future study of motivation. It becomes apparent when we consider how the conceptual spectacles of either the Drive $\times$ Habit or Expectancy $\times$ Value theories make us view the instigation of purposive action. They are both *stimulus-bound* theories of motivation. They encourage us to think of the immediate stimulus situation as the *cause* of the arousal of a tendency to act in a certain way. Without a stimulus to set things in motion by eliciting a particular habit, there can be no excitatory tendency, according to the principle $E = (D + K) \times H$ which has evolved in the *S-R* analysis of behavior. The same implication is present when we change conceptual spectacles and view the instigation of action in terms of the other scheme. Although it seems closer to the views of early "purposivists" in emphasizing the determinative role of expected consequences of an act, there is still no way of accounting for the apparently spontaneous actions of an *active*, goal-seeking organism, which was also given special emphasis in the early viewpoint. The immediate stimulus situation is what accounts for the arousal of a cognitive expectation, and without this stimulus-aroused expectancy of a goal, there would be no tendency to act. That is what the principle $T_{r,g} = M_G \times E_{r,g} \times I_g$ implies. It captures the general idea of a hierarchy of goal-directed dispositions, as once advocated by McDougall (instincts) and later by Murray and McClelland (psychogenic needs), in the conception of personality, but a goal-directed disposition is viewed as *latent* until aroused by cues in the immediate stimulus situation which define an expectancy that some relevant goal can be attained as a consequence of certain actions. Only then, according to what is explicitly stated in the principle, will there be an activated tendency to strive for the goal.

### THE DOMINANCE OF THE *S-R* MODE OF THOUGHT

The priority given the immediate stimulus situation in both conceptions of how action is motivated attests the dominance of the *S-R* mode of thought in contemporary psychology, even among those whose ideas are not explicitly linked to the underlying neurophysiological orientation which produced the *S-R* psychology. Looking back, we can see that the commonly understood meanings of *S* (stimulus) and *R* (response) have changed a good deal from the time that the concept of reflex-arc spurred the work of the early "associationists." Nevertheless, the basic concept of a *reactive* organism still persists. The assumption of sensory dominance in the determination of behavior, which rests on the belief that the brain must be stimulated into activity, has had a pervasive influence on the development of psychological theory. It still prevails as an implicit assumption in the principles which guide experimental analysis of the problem of motivation.

In earlier chapters, we have seen how arguments and evidence presented by psychologists who did not share the early *S-R* viewpoint affected the evolution of *S-R* behavior theory. It is equally important to recognize the impact of the *S-R* orientation on the subsequent development of ideas that were initially advanced by McDougall and Tolman, and to note the relative lack of further systematic development of the Lewinian psychology of individual motivation, which originally looked more to physics than to physiology for its basic concepts. This must be attributed to the dominance of the *S-R* orientation in the past 25 years.

Psychologists who thought mainly in terms of connections between stimulus and response were finally compelled to attempt to embrace the purposive characteristics of molar behavior and to view particular *S-R* events, of the sort that Thorndike had originally studied, as incidents within the broader context of the behavioral trend toward an objectively definable end or goal. Hull's essays of the 1930's represent this transition from the "old" to the "modern" *S-R* viewpoint. Hull exploited the full power of stimulus and response, as basic elements of construction, to show how rudimentary thought processes and the so-called "actions" emphasized by "purposivists" might be conceived as reactions to internal stimuli that were hidden from the view of the external observer. Hull did all this without departing from the conception of the brain as at rest unless stimulated into activity, the idea that later became the basis for the theory of drive and drive-reduction.

On the other hand, Tolman and others who shared the general orientation of the early "purposivists" were also compelled to accept the fundamental argument of the *S-R* psychology: any scientific theory worth its salt must specify with some degree of precision what the subject of study will do in a particular stimulus situation. As a consequence, the kind of theory evolved on both sides of the traditional debate came to focus attention on the problem of describing the process which intervenes between the stimulus situation, as defined by an external observer, and the reaction of the subject to that stimulus situation. This behavioral incident, which has its roots in the methodological innovations of Thorndike and Pavlov, emphasizes the need for stating theories so that they are testable—which is good. But the priority now given the immediate stimulus situation in the two conceptions of motivation has directed attention away from some fundamentally important insights about behavior that were advanced in earlier discussions of the problem of motivation.

McDougall, for example, stressed the apparent "spontaneity of behavior" and the persistence of the goal-directed trend long after the initiating stimulus has ceased to exist. This, he believed, called for a theory of an *active* organism rather than one which is merely reactive to immediately present stimuli.

Freud emphasized the importance of the persistence of the tendency to bring about a certain effect, the unfulfilled wish, in his theory of dreams and in his analysis of the determinants of subsequent slips, errors, neurotic symptoms, and the initiation of substitute activities (displacement).

Lewin, not at all constrained by the assumptions underlying an associative psychology, focused attention upon the persistence of the tendency to complete an interrupted task which was subsequently manifested in recall or resumption of the interrupted activity or the "spontaneous" initiation of a substitute activity.

And Woodworth, having considered and understood the merit of the early arguments of the purposivists, had called attention to incidents like that of the hunting dog who has lost the scent and whose continued search for the lost trail does not fit the notion of reaction to a stimulus, for here the stimulus is absent; and the tendency of a dog already on the trail of a prey and completely absorbed in the hunt to ignore other stimuli, like another dog with whom it would normally stop to pass the time of day. All of these are phenomena that de-emphasize the importance of the immediate stimulus situation which is given priority in today's explicitly stated conceptions of the immediate determinants of action.

THE TRADITIONAL ASSUMPTION
OF AN ORGANISM AT REST

What is not sufficiently appreciated is the extent to which contemporary conceptions of the determinants of an action tendency lull us into the habit of thinking of the subject of study, whether it be animal or human, as if it were at rest until the critical stimulus in which the experimenter is interested occurs. We implicitly think of the brain of the organism as merely passively reactive to the changing pattern of sensory stimulation to which it is exposed from moment to moment. Carried out of the laboratory to life in general, this mode of thought pictures the flux of behavior which defines the life of an organism as a series of discrete incidents, each having a well-defined beginning—like a series of separate 100-yard dashes each of which begins with the shot of a starter's gun.

Two things are wrong with conceiving the sequence of activities which comprise the life of an organism as a series of reactions to an ever-changing pattern of sensory stimulation. In addition to encouraging us to ignore some of the most fundamental ideas about the motivation of behavior that were suggested in the early writings of the "purposivists" or explicitly stated by Freud and Lewin (who, we must remember, were the ones who began to define the problem of motivation in the first place), *this traditional conception is now known to be inconsistent with current knowledge of how the brain functions.* It is an anachronism in light of evidence obtained in recent years by neurophysiologists who, exploiting the power of new techniques of study, have finally discovered the existence and importance of *relatively autonomous central processes* in the determination of behavior.

Writing in 1949, D. O. Hebb called attention to the fundamental inadequacy of the traditional underlying assumption of psychological theory:

> "It is the idea that behavior is a series of *reactions* (instead of actions), each of which is determined by the immediately preceding events in the sensory systems. . . .
> "It may be noted in passing that the assumption of a sensory dominance of behavior is not the property of any particular theory. Theories differ as to how a sensory event has its effect, but not as to its all-important role" (Hebb, 1949, p. 3).*

Hebb identified two main reasons for the prevalence of this mistaken assumption among psychologists in the face of considerable behavioral evidence that organisms do not merely passively respond to stimulus situations but, on the contrary, *actively attend* to certain features of a stimulus complex and not others (Gibson, 1941). First, psychologists have persistently

* Excerpts from D. O. Hebb, *The Organization of Behavior*, copyright 1949, John Wiley & Sons, Inc., are reprinted by permission.

attempted to overcome animistic thinking by reducing psychological phenomena to a pattern of cause and effect. Traditionally, this flight from animism has taken the form of ". . . a search for the property of the stimulus which by itself determines the ensuing response, at a given stage of learning" (Hebb, 1949, p. 4). Second, this effort received its initial impetus from "antiquated physiological conceptions." As we have learned from the review of the work of James, Thorndike, Pavlov, and later the Hullians, the only means at hand seemed to be "a physiology of the nervous system in which knowledge of sense organs and peripheral nerve was the main content" (Hebb, 1949, fn p. 4). Any departure from the stimulus-response mode of thought has always seemed to run the risk of regressing back into the animistic mode of thought of the earlier, prescientific period.

### THE CONTEMPORARY CONCEPTION OF THE BRAIN

We need only return to Woodworth's early discussion of the need to take into account the problem of *the internal determining tendency* (see Chapter 5) or to Lewin's attempt to divorce the theory of motivation from the underlying assumptions of the doctrine of association (see Chapter 4) to appreciate how long the general problem which Hebb and others again emphasize has been recognized. The development of psychological theories in terms of variables which intervene between environmental stimulus and response was directed to the general problem. But, as we have seen in examining how the principles evolved are now phrased, there is no departure from the implicit notion that the brain is otherwise passive unless there is some sensory input, a stimulus, to arouse a tendency to act. Psychological theory has lagged behind what observations of behavior had suggested, apparently because there never had seemed any neurophysiological rationale for nonsensory influences on behavior. But now, as Hebb has pointed out, the situation is different:

> "Modern electrophysiology has more than caught up with psychology and now provides abundant evidence to support the same idea. When detailed evidence of neurophysiology and histology is considered, the conclusion becomes inevitable that the nonsensory factor in cerebral action must be more consistently present and of more dominating importance than reluctant psychological theory has ever recognized. Instead of a joker to occasionally confuse the student of behavior, nonsensory activities appear in every fall of the cards and must make up a large share of the deck.

Neurophysiologically, it may even become a problem to account for *any* consistent effect of a specific stimulus. . . .

"Electrophysiology of the central nervous system indicates in brief that the brain is continuously active, in all its parts, and an afferent excitation must be superimposed on an already existent excitation. It is therefore impossible that the consequence of a sensory event should often be uninfluenced by the pre-existent activity. . . .

"So there really is a rational basis for postulating a central neural factor that modifies the action of a stimulus. The theoretical problem now is to discover the rules by which it operates. At first glance this is a problem for the neurophysiologist only. But look closer; much of the evidence, from which these rules must be worked out, is psychological, or behavioral. The problem is after all the problem of attention, and seen best in the activity of the whole animal. . . .

"Our problem, then, is to find valid 'molar' conceptions of neural action (conceptions, *i.e.*, that can be applied to large scale cortical organizations). Bishop (1946, p. 370) has made the point, in another context, that this is an essential problem for neurophysiology also. But psychologists can hardly sit around with hands folded, waiting for the physiologist to solve it. In its essence the problem is psychological and requires a knowledge of the psychological as well as the physiological evidence for its solution" (Hebb, 1949, pp. 6–11).

Here, then, is a clear directive for psychologists to get on with the task of developing the theory of motivation in terms of what their observations of behavior require, unconstrained by the pervasive assumptions of the antiquated physiological conception which has tended to dominate discussion of the problem of motivation since the time of William James.

What are the major implications of these recent developments within neurophysiology for the development of psychological theory? We find an up-to-date summary of them in a review of recent theoretical developments in physiological psychology by Pribram:

"The shift is from the notion that an organism is a relatively passive protoplasmic mass whose responses are controlled by the arrangement of environmental stimuli to a conception of an organism that has considerable control over what will constitute stimulation" (Pribram, 1960, p. 4).

The new conception of the brain arising from contemporary neurophysiological research

". . . places emphasis on an active organism that controls the stimuli to which it is sensitive and upon which it acts. This conception differs from an *S-R* reflex-arc concept in which a passive organism is completely subject to the exigencies of its environment.

". . . This view of an active organism gains support from the fact that the central nervous system, in conjunction with its receptors, is intrinsically and spontaneously active. Electrical activity is recorded in the total absence of environmental input. Even brief stimulation has long-lasting aftereffects that alter the intrinsic rhythms for hours and days and thus change the response of the organism to subsequent stimulation" (Pribram, 1960, p. 32).

There can be little doubt that the directive for the psychology of motivation now coming from neurophysiology echoes the arguments of early writers who had urged the development of a theory of an *active* organism in terms of their observations of the descriptive characteristics of purposive action.

## A NEW PREMISE FOR THE STUDY OF MOTIVATION

In the pages remaining, we shall consider some conceptual developments growing out of the most recent studies of achievement-oriented behavior which represent steps towards a theory of an active organism. As outlined by Atkinson and Cartwright (1964)*, these proposals constitute an explicit attempt to recapture some of the fundamental insights of earlier theorists that are neglected in contemporary, stimulus-bound conceptions of the determinants of decision and action.

### A CLUE IN THE STUDY OF PERSISTENCE

Our discussion begins with an important clue which suggests the need for still another transition in thought about the problem of motivation. It is contained in Feather's analysis of the persistence of achievement-oriented activity presented in the previous chapter. The clue in Feather's study suggests a new and better way of phrasing a principle of motivation. It leads us back to the analogy between the motion of a physical object and behavior which, instead of the concept of reflex, provided the guiding idea in Lewin's conceptual analysis of the problem of motivation. It provides a foundation for the statement of a new premise—really an explicit statement of an old premise—for the study of motivation.

Feather's conceptual analysis of the determinants of persistence of a goal-directed activity went beyond

* The sections which follow quote freely from this earlier statement by permission of my colleague Professor Dorwin Cartwright, and the editors of *Psychological Reports*, 1964. © Southern Universities Press.

the traditional view that, other things equal, persistence should be greater the stronger the tendency to perform an activity. He employed the theory of achievement motivation to show how the strength of the tendency to solve a particular puzzle would be either directly weakened or initially strengthened and then weakened as a consequence of repeated failure, depending upon the personality of the subject and the difficulty of the task. This, of course, should affect persistence at the activity. But more important, he realized that an attempt to explain persistence of an activity only in terms of the strength of the tendency to engage in that activity was incomplete. He found it impossible to predict, with any precision, when a person would cease work at the initial task he had been given without knowing something about the strength of his tendency to do something else instead of continuing to work at the initial task. He found it necessary to assume that an initial activity would persist as long as the strength of the tendency sustaining that activity $(T_A)$ exceeded the strength of the tendency to initiate some alternative activity $(T_B)$. The individual should persist in the initial activity as long as $T_A > T_B$. But the initial activity should cease when the strength of the tendency to perform an alternative activity exceeded the strength of the tendency sustaining the initial activity, that is, when $T_B > T_A$. It seems a fairly obvious point, but the further implications are not immediately as obvious and they are of fundamental theoretical importance.

As an aid to seeing what is implied in this analysis of persistence, let us consider a more commonplace example. This will also help us to appreciate how the basic idea applies to everyday action outside the controlled stimulus-situation of the laboratory. Let us suppose that some children are playing in the living room of their home when their mother calls from the kitchen, "Dinner is ready!" Observing the children, we would notice that their mother's call has a very significant effect on the persistence (that is, the duration) of their play activity. If the children are typical, she will probably have to call them several times before one and then another of them gives up the play activity and goes to the evening meal. Without the stronger competing tendency resulting from mother's repeated calls, the children would continue to play for a longer time. Eventually one and then another might stop playing and turn to something else. But even then, the fact that they do stop playing and turn to something else must mean that at the time they do stop, the strength of the tendency to do that something else, whatever it

is, exceeds the strength of the tendency to play—either because the tendency to play has become weaker or because some other stimulus has caught their eye and aroused a new and stronger tendency. The children do not stop behaving when they stop playing. There are no behavioral vacuums in the life of an individual. They merely stop playing and initiate some other activity instead. Even if it be standing still and looking bored, this is still to be considered *an activity*. If their muscles went flabby (no activity), they would fall in a crumpled heap the way an individual falls when he is killed by a bullet. And so we see that in this commonplace instance the idea that the initial activity will persist as long as the tendency sustaining it exceeds the tendency to engage in some other activity, $T_A > T_B$, applies.

Now let us shift attention to the children's response to their mother's call, "Dinner is ready!" Suppose we take the traditional view that the *latency* of a response to a stimulus, that is, the time between the onset of a particular stimulus and the initiation of the response to it, provides a measure of the strength of the tendency to respond. After mother's call, "Dinner is ready!" first one and then another of the children appear at the table. It is generally assumed that the shorter the latency of response to a stimulus (i.e., the greater the speed of initiating the response), the stronger the tendency. But is this assumption correct? In the present case, it is obvious that one of the children might be very slow to come to the table to eat, not because he is less hungry than the others, or less certain of the path to the kitchen, but because his interest in the play activity is much stronger than that of the other children.

The further implication of recognizing that to explain persistence of an activity adequately one must know both the strength of the tendency sustaining that activity $(T_A)$ *and* the strength of the tendency to undertake some alternative activity $(T_B)$, which replaces the initial activity, is now perfectly obvious. One similarly cannot adequately explain the initiation of a response to a particular stimulus without knowing the strength of the tendency sustaining the activity that is already in progress $(T_A)$ when the stimulus for the new activity is presented *in addition* to knowing the strength of the tendency to engage in that new activity $(T_B)$, *unless one assumes to begin with that there is no activity in progress*. And this assumption of an organism at rest is precisely the mistaken one implied by our contemporary formulations, despite universal recognition of the fact that living organisms are constantly behaving, that is, doing something that a comprehensive theory of behavior must represent as the expression of an action tendency.

## THE INTERRELATEDNESS OF PERSISTENCE AND LATENCY OF RESPONSE

Persistence of activity and speed of initiation of an activity are thus seen to be two sides of one problem. A clock is used to measure the duration of an activity in progress (persistence). A clock is also used to measure the duration between presentation of a stimulus and initiation of some activity (latency of response). This means that the very same time measurement is called persistence when duration of the activity already in progress is the matter of central interest and latency of response when the initiation of some new activity happens to be the matter of central interest.

To appreciate more fully the limitation of our contemporary conceptions of behavioral incidents, we need only refer again to the example of the children playing when mother calls and suppose that there is a very intent but *deaf* psychologist in the living room studying the persistence of the children's play activity and an equally intent but *blind* psychologist with a timing device in the kitchen to study the initiation (latency) of the response to mother's call to dinner. The deaf psychologist will see the children playing but will not hear mother's call to dinner, and so he will attempt to attribute variations in observed persistence of play, as measured by his clock, to variables which he supposes determine the strength of the tendency to play (all other things assumed equal). The blind psychologist in the kitchen will not see that the children are engrossed in play activity at the time he hears the mother call, "Dinner is ready!" At this point (the onset of the stimulus of interest to him) he will start his clock. He will stop his clock when he hears the children arrive in the kitchen, and then he will attempt to attribute variations in the measured latency of response to variables which he considers determinants of the tendency to eat (all other things assumed equal).

Why do these two hypothetical psychologists, and their colleagues more generally, make this kind of obvious mistake? They do so because the context of events embraced by the conventional schemes of thought—or at least the traditional use of these schemes that is fostered by the way they are phrased—is restricted to the immediate effect of a particular stimulus situation and the response in which the experimenter is interested.

Contemporary conceptions of motivation do not make us think of behavior as a continuous stream with one kind of activity giving way to another and then another until the organism dies. They do not make it apparent to us that *accounting for change of activity is the fundamental problem*. Instead they lead us to think of life as a series of discrete track meets, each having a well-defined beginning (the starter's gun), a middle, and an end, and to think of each episode as if it were separated from others by a period of inactivity in which the subject of study is at rest, passively awaiting the sound of the next gun.

## TRADITIONAL AVOIDANCE OF THE PROBLEM

Psychologists attempt to make the conditions of their experiments correspond to this conception of the single, goal-directed episode. They either implicitly assume that the subject is at rest to begin with or try to arrange conditions so that it will appear that the subject is at rest because the contemporary mode of thought, the general conception of the problem of motivation, is not phrased to make them think of doing anything else. The animal experimenter, for example, typically waits until the rat placed in the starting box of a maze settles down and is oriented directly towards the door leading out before it is opened to provide the stimulus to run, at which time the clock which will yield the measure of latency (or speed) is started. And in the human case, the experimenter waits until the conversation between the eager young men and attractive young woman in the back row has ceased (if it be a group experiment) or until the individual subject looks at rest and "ready" before presenting the critical stimulus for some activity. The principles which attempt to account for motivation have not been formulated in a way which systematically takes into account the initial activity, that is, *the activity already in progress*, when the episode of interest to the experimenter is supposed to begin. Hence, he implicitly thinks of the subject as at rest when he is not, or he tries to arrange it so that the subject will appear to be at rest before the critical stimulus is presented.

## THE NEED FOR A BROADENED CONCEPTION

What is required is another transition in thought about the factors to be taken into account systematically in theoretical conceptions of the immediate determinants of a particular action. The context of behavioral events embraced in the principle of motivation must again be broadened. The early view that the immediate environmental stimulus was the cause of the response was recognized as inadequate. It became necessary to view the particular *S-R* event as an incident within the goal-directed trend of behavior, the episode having a beginning (a state of motivation), a middle (instrumental goal-striving activity), and an end (attainment of the goal, consummatory activity, a cessation of striving); and to include the anticipated goal as one of the determinants of the response. But now we can see the limitations of this, the contemporary view. It implicitly assumes that what the subject is doing before the critical stimulus which defines the beginning of the episode has no systematic influence on the initiation of activity in response to that stimulus, and it also implicitly assumes that what the subject does immediately after the episode of interest has no systematic influence on the characteristics of behavior during that episode. The difficulty clearly lies in a failure to appreciate what it means to acknowledge that a living organism is constantly active—that is, always doing something that must be conceptualized in a theory of behavior as an expression of the then dominant tendency—even when it is asleep or resting and when it superficially appears that "activity" has ceased. (We might recall, in this connection, that Freud treated sleep as a "motivated" activity, and so did Hull treat resting, inhibition of a response, as a "motivated" activity in his theory of extinction.)

INITIAL PREMISE: A CONSTANTLY ACTIVE ORGANISM

Given the initial premise of a constantly active organism, it is apparent that the simplest and most fundamental decision problem is not the one that is normally studied at the choice point of a maze or when the human subject is presented a stimulus situation defining possible choice between two options in a simple decision-making experiment. The more fundamental and simpler problem of decision, and the one that has been ignored as such, is that which occurs when there is the option of continuing an activity already in progress or of undertaking some other activity instead. It is this problem of *change* from one activity to another activity that is inadequately treated in contemporary conceptions of the determinants of initiation of a particular activity and of persistence of a particular activity, which, we have seen, are two inseparable aspects of a single problem. The important issue is not adequately identified by the separate questions of what causes the initiation of activity and what causes the cessation of activity,

but by the single question: *What causes a change in activity?* The psychology of motivation should be primarily concerned with the problem of change in ongoing activity.

A NEW PHRASING OF THE PRINCIPLE OF ACTION

Now let us consider how a new conception of the determinants of a particular activity might be phrased, once we have explicitly recognized that the initiation of that activity represents a change in behavior and not initiation of behavior from the state of rest (inactivity). We shall continue to employ the traditional symbols *S* and *R* to stand for the environmental stimulus situation (as defined by the external observer) and molar action (which is observed and measured by the external observer). The activity already in progress when the stimulus for some new activity occurs is designated $R_1$, the initial activity; and the new activity, the one which replaces it, is designated $R_2$. We may have in mind, for example, a rat that has been placed in the starting box of a maze who is engaged in exploring one of the corners of the box ($R_1$) when the door to the alley leading away from the starting box, accompanied by an auditory signal of some sort, is raised. This is traditionally viewed as the stimulus ($S_2$) for the activity of running down the alley ($R_2$). Our conception might begin with an assertion in this form:

$$R_2 \text{ will occur when } T_{r_2} > T_{r_1}.$$

This states that the response of running out of the starting box and into the alley ($R_2$) will be initiated when the strength of the tendency to engage in that activity ($T_{r_2}$) exceeds the strength of the tendency sustaining the exploratory activity that is already in progress ($T_{r_1}$). This simple principle to describe the change in activity is in the same form as Feather's representation of the condition that must exist to produce cessation of the initial activity when persistence of it is the matter of central interest. Now, however, we focus attention upon the initiation of an activity, a problem traditionally emphasized in the study of motivation since the question, "What is the cause of the response?" was first raised.

Our basic assertion agrees with the general assumption of all theories that the strongest of two incompatible tendencies will win out and be expressed in overt behavior. But it differs from the traditional conceptions in its explicit recognition of the fact that the organism is already engaging in some activity rather than merely waiting for the stimulus with a blank mind and inactive brain *by including the strength of the tendency sustaining the initial activity as one of the determinants of any subsequent activity.*

### ACTIVITY IN PROGRESS AS A DETERMINANT OF SUBSEQUENT ACTIVITY

The next step is to substitute for $T_{r_1}$ and $T_{r_2}$ a theoretical conception of the determinants of each of these two competing tendencies. If we tend to think in terms of the concepts of S-R behavior theory, we will introduce values of $D$, $K$, and a particular $H$ in place of $T_{r_1}$ and $T_{r_2}$. If, on the other hand, we tend to think in terms of the Expectancy × Value theory, we might substitute the appropriate $M_G$, $E_{r,g}$, and $I_g$ for $T_{r_1}$ and $T_{r_2}$. For the moment, let us stay on neutral ground and consider hypothetical variables, $A$, $B$, and $C$, as the determinants of the strength of a particular tendency. When we make the substitution our conception looks like this:

$R_2$ will occur when

$$(A_2 \times B_2 \times C_2) > (A_1 \times B_1 \times C_1).$$

The variables $A_2$, $B_2$, and $C_2$ are the determinants of $T_{r_2}$; the variables $A_1$, $B_1$, and $C_1$ are the determinants of $T_{r_1}$, the initial activity. Now, in this simple case, we are in a position to state two sets of hypotheses concerning the initiation of $R_2$. The first set of hypotheses are familiar ones. They attribute variations in the speed of initiating $R_2$ to the strength of such factors as $A_2$, $B_2$, and $C_2$, which are known to affect the strength of $T_{r_2}$. But the second set of hypotheses is novel. They refer to the effect on initiation of $R_2$ of variables $A_1$, $B_1$, and $C_1$, which are known to influence the strength of $T_{r_1}$, the activity already in progress when the stimulus $S_2$ is presented.

When the tendency sustaining the initial activity is very weak, as would occur whenever $A_1$, $B_1$, and/or $C_1$ are weak, this conception would lead us to expect that variations in the performance (latency) of $R_2$ would be mainly a function of variables which influence the strength of $T_{r_2}$. This is what our conventional theories presume. They lead us to assume, implicitly, that the organism is at rest when $S_2$ is presented. The new conception is more general. It would include as a special case the condition implicitly assumed in our conventional way of thinking about the problem, which ignores activity already in progress as a systematic determinant of subsequent performance.

The two sets of hypotheses concerning the initiation of $R_2$ are, at the very same time, hypotheses about the determinants of persistence of $R_1$, the

activity in progress when the stimulus for the new activity is presented. Here, then, is a conception that can begin to embrace one of the phenomena to which the early purposivists called attention—that exemplified by the hunting dog on the trail of a prey who ignores the stimulus of another dog which might normally elicit the pattern of behavior which Woodworth described as "passing the time of day." When the tendency sustaining the activity in progress ($T_{r_1}$) is very strong, it will take a very strong external inducement to interrupt the ongoing trend of behavior. We say the dog is so thoroughly engrossed in the hunt that it does not even attend to the stimulus of the other dog. This may mean one of two things. It may mean that the pattern of neural activity already in progress effectively blocks reception of the stimulus of the other dog. This possibility is supported by recent neurophysiological evidence (Pribram, 1960). Or it may mean that the stimulus of the other dog is noticed, but that the tendency produced by it ($T_{r_2}$) is so weak *relative* to the tendency sustaining the hunt ($T_{r_1}$) that it has no noticeable effect on the overt behavior of the dog. It does not even produce the usual orienting responses, viz., turning the head and looking, which represent a behavioral expression of attention to the stimulus.

The same two possibilities exist in our earlier example of the children at play when mother calls. They may be so thoroughly engrossed that they literally do not hear the call until their mother does what mothers so often have to do under these circumstances: she raises her voice in order to get through to them. Or it may be that the children do hear her call, but ignore it because the tendency to eat cannot, at that time, compete effectively with the very strong tendency to continue at play, a tendency which is sustained, we should note, by the immediately present environmental stimulus of the toys they are playing with.

Before moving on, we may recall several observations that were treated casually by Pavlov in the classical studies of salivary conditioning, but which seem very much related to the problem under discussion (see p. 120). One was the failure of the conditioned stimulus to elicit a salivary reaction from a particular dog until it was allowed to get off the stand on which it was harnessed to urinate, after which the conditioned stimulus was again effective. Another was the difficulty encountered in eliciting conditioned salivary reactions in response to the signal when the tests were conducted while the female dogs in the laboratory were in heat. The dogs were physically constrained, we recall, and could not express overtly what would appear, in light of the present analysis, to be the dominant behavioral tendency when the conditioned stimulus for salivation was being presented. Without constraints, we expect that the one dog would have jumped from the table to urinate and the others would have undertaken a pursuit of the females.

## EFFECT OF INDIVIDUAL DIFFERENCES IN STRENGTH OF MOTIVES

Consider how the basic conception of action (or more accurately, change of activity) that is proposed might apply in contemporary research which employs thematic apperception to assess individual differences in the strength of basic social motives. We might imagine an experimental situation similar to that designed by Feather, but one which would bring into conflict two different motives of an individual, the need for achievement and the need for affiliation. The experimental situation would be a controlled experimental analog of the following type of lifelike situation:

A college professor is at work at his desk on a difficult paper. To simplify matters, we shall assume that this is strictly an achievement-oriented activity for him. No other motives are engaged in the activity. Suddenly there is a call from a colleague and friend announcing that coffee is ready in an adjoining room with an invitation to take a break. Let us further assume that the professor's past experiences in the coffee room have amounted mainly to good fellowship, informal chit-chat with friends—in other words, affiliative activity.

We shall let $R_2$ represent the activity of walking to the coffee room and $R_1$ represent the initial achievement-oriented activity that is already in progress. We begin our analysis with the statement:

$$R_2 \text{ will occur when } T_{r_2,aff} > T_{r_1,s}.$$

This means that the activity of walking to the coffee room ($R_2$) will occur when the strength of the tendency to engage in affiliative activity exceeds the strength of the tendency sustaining work at the desk which is expected to lead to success, the goal of the achievement motive. Our conception leaves open the question of whether this will come about because there is random fluctuation in the strengths of the two tendencies about a mean value (as some previous theories have supposed) or *possibly because the affiliative tendency grows in strength in the period of time*

*following exposure to the friend's initial call as a function of duration of exposure to that stimulus.*

Next, we substitute for $T_{r_2,aff}$ and $T_{r_1,s}$ the determinants of each of these separate tendencies as presently conceived. Again, to simplify the presentation, we shall assume that the tendency to avoid failure is so weak in the professor that it has no significant effect on the resultant tendency to achieve success. It should be clear, however, that a complete conceptual analysis of the problem would include any other determinants of the two tendencies under discussion. When we make the substitution, we have:

$R_2$ will occur when
$$(M_{Aff} \times E_{r_2,aff} \times I_{aff}) > (M_S \times E_{r_1,s} \times I_s).$$

In this instance, the functional significance of $S_2$, the environmental stimulus (or cue) provided by the friend's call, is represented by the cognitive expectancy it produces that walking to the coffee room will lead to affiliation with friends ($E_{r_2,aff}$) and the incentive value of this anticipated consequence ($I_{aff}$). The task at which the professor works is the stimulus situation ($S_1$) which sustains an expectancy that work at the task will lead to success ($E_{r_1,s}$) and the incentive value of this goal ($I_s$). These are the environmental determinants of the tendency sustaining the activity in progress at the time of the friend's call.

Now, in order to have clearly before us a descriptive picture of the initial condition of the subject (the professor) before the stimulus of interest (the call to coffee break) is presented, we must bring to the right side of the expression all the variables which refer to characteristics of the person in the interaction between person ($P$) and environment ($E$) at the moment that $S_2$, the environmental influence of interest, occurs. The variable on the left side of the expression which must be moved over is the motive to affiliate ($M_{Aff}$). This is conceived as a relatively general and stable property of the professor's personality. We accomplish this change algebraically by dividing each side of the expression by $M_{Aff}$ without changing its implication. Now we have before us the idea that the traditional notion $B = f(P,E)$ should be conceived as an environmental influence ($E$) imposed on a particular personality already actively engaged in some activity ($P$):

$R_2$ will occur when $(E_{r_2,aff} \times I_{aff})$
$$> \frac{(M_S \times E_{r_1,s} \times I_s)}{(M_{Aff})}.$$

From this statement, we begin to see the kinds of systematic hypotheses that might be formulated concerning the kind of person (or personality) who will be slow to leave work for a coffee break with friends and the kind of person who might be expected to dash off at the first opportunity. Both $M_S$ and $M_{Aff}$ are conceived as stable characteristics of personality. So we now begin to have a somewhat more complete notion of how personality (conceived as a hierarchy of motives within a person) will influence action.

In this situation, the latency of $R_2$ (i.e., the length of time before the professor gets up to go to the coffee room if he does, in fact, get up to go at all) should be proportionate to the strength of the achievement motive ($M_S$) and inversely proportionate to the strength of affiliative motive ($M_{Aff}$). Just the opposite would be expected should we reformulate the expression to fit the situation of the professor leaving the coffee room to return to his desk. In other words, we begin to see that persistence is not likely to be a very general trait of personality (as some earlier conceptions of personality had supposed), but a characteristic of behavior that depends entirely upon the nature of the personality-environment interaction at a particular time, as argued by Feather (1961).

AN INSTRUCTIVE PHYSICAL ANALOGY

If we tentatively adopt the Lewinian term, *psychological force*, in reference to the effect on the person of the environmental inducement to act that is produced by $S_2$, the call of a friend, we can phrase a very interesting question: How much *external* psychological force (or inducement) is required to move a particular person from working at his desk to the coffee room? The answer implied in the expression above is: the *external* psychological force that is required is proportionate to the strength of motive sustaining the initial activity (in this case, $M_S$) and inversely proportionate to the strength of motive which, so to speak, answers the call of the incentive signified by an environmental stimulus for a new activity (in this case, $M_{Aff}$). This is the kind of question that is asked and answered in classical mechanics concerning the amount of external force required to move a physical object. It draws attention to an interesting correspondence between motive, conceived as a relatively stable disposition or property of an individual's personality, and the concept of the mass of an object in physics. In asserting that the *external* psychological force, or inducement, required to provoke $R_2$ is proportionate to the strength of motive which sustains activity in prog-

ress, we have said—in effect—that the motive sustaining an initial activity functions like *inertial mass*, resistance to change, in the laws of motion. When we study persistence of an activity, we are studying something comparable to the resistance of a piano or chair to change. Both objects are caught up in the earth's gravitational attraction and, as a result, are difficult to move. But the piano requires more external force to move because its inertial mass, that is, its resistance to change, as inferred from the measure called weight, is greater. Similarly, a professor with a very strong motive to achieve (as now inferred from the thematic apperceptive *n* Achievement score) should require more *external* psychological force to move from an achievement-oriented activity, that is, he should be more resistant to change of activity, than one who has a weaker motive to achieve.

On the other hand, when we assert that the *external* psychological force, or environmental inducement, required to provoke $R_2$ is *inversely* proportionate to the strength of motive which answers the call of the incentive signified by the environmental stimulus (the call to affiliation), the analogy with the physical concept of *gravitational mass* is striking. We assume that strength of motive, conceived like the mass of an object as a stable property of the person, combines multiplicatively with a property of the expected goal which is at a distance from the subject. We call this property of the anticipated goal its incentive value. In Newton's famous gravitational principle, gravitational force equals the product of the masses of two objects divided by the square of the distance between them. Earlier (see p. 82), we especially noted the similarity between Lewin's conception of the determinants of psychological force and Newton's principle of gravitational force. Now it is apparent that motive, conceived as a stable property of personality, provides an even closer analogy to the concept of gravitational mass than does the transient tension system ($t_g$) which Lewin employed to represent what is commonly called a "need."

In Newtonian physics, there is only one kind of mass, so the ratio of inertial mass to gravitational mass is always equal to 1. Because of this, a heavy and a light object beginning their fall to earth from a state of rest will fall equally fast. That is, the greater gravitational attraction produced by the larger mass is canceled out by its greater resistance to change (inertial mass). In psychology, we suppose that there is more than one kind of motive, and so the ratio of "inertial motive" to "gravitational motive" will not always equal 1. But a somewhat similar situation arises in psychology (given the assumptions of the present scheme) when the initial activity, that is, the activity already in progress, and the tendency produced by some subsequent stimulus *are both directed to the same kind of goal.* In our present example, this would occur if the second tendency were also an achievement-oriented tendency. Then the achievement motive ($M_S$) would appear both as the "inertial motive" in the numerator and as the "gravitational motive" in the denominator of the right side of the expression. This means that the two motives cancel out algebraically, and the occurrence of $R_2$, the second activity, depends only upon the relative strengths of the environmental influences, the product of Expectancy × Incentive for each of the two tendencies. That is,

$R_2$ will occur when $(E_{r_2,s} \times I_s) > \dfrac{(M_S \times E_{r_1,s} \times I_s)}{M_S}$.

We recognize this situation as the special case that was initially considered by Norman Feather in the study of persistence of achievement-oriented activities (see Chapter 9) which provided the clue needed for consideration of the more general problems now under discussion.

It is worth noting the extent to which certain concepts and theoretical issues which have arisen in the psychology of motivation are in some respects analogous to those which arose much earlier in the attempt to explain the motions of physical objects. For it may be that Lewin's belief that physics provides a useful guide for conceptual analysis of the problem of motivation will in the end turn out to be more correct than the alternative belief that psychology should look to physiology for its guiding concepts. Physics made great strides with molar principles which described *how* motion occurs long before there was an adequate molecular conception of the underlying nature of the cause of motion. The attempt to accomplish both tasks at the same time has so far not been eminently successful in psychology. Grossly inadequate neurophysiological preconceptions have implicitly been given priority over behavioral observations in the attempt to develop a workable conceptual scheme. Only recently has it become apparent how fundamentally inadequate they are and the extent to which they have influenced the mode of thought. We shall find it useful, in the pages ahead, to turn again to the conceptual analysis

of motion as a guide in the attempt to overcome the deficiencies of the traditional mode of thought about motivation.

## SOME IMPLICATIONS OF THE NEW CONCEPTION

The present conception handles the matters of initiation of an activity, cessation of an activity, persistence of an activity, and interruption of an activity all in a single breath. It does this by: (a) acknowledging that from the viewpoint of a psychologist, the behavioral life of an organism must be considered a succession of molar activities; and (b) by viewing change of activity as the most fundamental problem. Initiation of one activity always corresponds to cessation of another. Interruption of an activity always corresponds to initiation of another. Persistence of an activity always corresponds to failure to initiate some other, etc. Traditionally, these have been viewed as separate problems. Now we view their interrelatedness. And as we do, we must finally acknowledge a weakness in the argument of the early purposivists. A dog on the hunt will not *always* ignore another passing stimulus. If the dog has been running a long time and the scent of the prey has grown weak, the strength of the effective tendency sustaining the hunt may be sufficiently weak so that a passing stimulus like a tree or another dog may provide a sufficiently strong inducement to interrupt the hunt. The dog will stop and tarry a while.

It is apparent that the early purposivists chose their examples well in order to score points for their basic idea that *behavior* persists until the goal is attained. Accepted uncritically, this idea seems to rule out the possibility of natural interruptions of a goal-seeking trend. But *interruption of activity in progress is just as common as persistence until the goal is attained.* The child engrossed in rushing home from school to play is often diverted from his goal-directed path by the tinkling of the ice cream vendor's bell on another street. A normally hungry boy who has just sat down to supper will often run outside to play at the call of a friend if he is not detained by his parents. The scientist at work on an important paper will often interrupt his work to have coffee with a friend, etc.

Tolman made a great point of the continued striving of Thorndike's dogs to get out of the puzzle box to the food a few feet away and of the cessation of goal-striving when the food had been obtained. It served to draw attention to the molar, goal-directed trend of behavior and the special problems this posed for an oversimplified *S-R* view of the motivation of behavior. But with our new conceptual spectacles in place, we can appreciate how little else the animals had to do in that relatively barren environment, which explains their singleness of purpose. What might have happened, we now think to ask, if a cat had appeared on the scene after the dog's struggle to get out to the food had been going on for a while and it had just opened the door to the box? Would the pursuit of the food have continued? Or would this behavior have been interrupted by attention to the cat and the initiation of a qualitatively different kind of goal-directed pursuit? It would depend, we can see, upon the strength of the tendency sustaining the activity already in progress relative to the strength of the freshly aroused tendency. And this in turn would depend upon the strengths of the several variables which together determine each of the competing tendencies at the given time.

The new conception, which focuses on the problem of change of activity, can tolerate the idea that *sometimes* behavior will express the kind of persistent, directed quality that gave rise to the purposivist's emphasis of the end, objective, or goal. This will always occur when the tendency sustaining an activity in progress is very strong relative to other competing tendencies which arise along the way to the original objective. But the new conception can equally well accommodate interruption of goal-directed behavior and periods of listlessness or sporadic, variable behavior. The latter should occur when no particular goal-directed tendency is dominant relative to all others which arise from moment to moment, either because the environment is barren of possibilities or for other reasons.

THE INFERRED EFFECT OF ATTAINING THE GOAL

If we stick to the basic idea that an initial activity will persist so long as the tendency sustaining it exceeds the strength of some alternative tendency and will cease when an alternative tendency is stronger, there is another important implication. When we consider the dramatic change in the quality of behavior which so often occurs immediately after certain kinds of events like eating a substantial amount of food, drinking a substantial amount of water, children's playing with particular toys for a prolonged period—even when there is no obvious change in the stimulus properties of the immediate environment to suggest that some other behavioral

tendency might suddenly have been strengthened— we must infer that *these so-called goal activities must function to reduce the strength of the tendency that produced them.* The inference requires no specific hypothesis about the underlying neurophysiological mechanism of this change. It is based solely on the fact, given so much emphasis by the early purposivists, that behavior does undergo a qualitative change when the goal of a sequence of activities is attained. Whatever the nature of the behavior immediately after the animal has eaten which replaces what is described as food-seeking, this must be considered an instance in which the tendency sustaining the initial activity (food-seeking) has been reduced or weakened relative to some other tendency by the very activity of eating *unless* there is some basis for supposing that another behavioral tendency has suddenly become stronger relative to an undiminished food-seeking tendency. And often there is no obvious change in the properties of the environment to justify the latter inference. Hence we are led to suppose that the tendency to eat, which is expressed in actions which have in common the fact that they are instrumental in bringing about the activity of eating, must be reduced when finally expressed in the activity of eating. If reduced in strength, the tendency to eat cannot compete effectively with tendencies to engage in other kinds of activities *immediately following* the activity of eating. How long it will be before the organism again expresses the tendency to eat will depend on the initial strength of the tendency to eat, how much eating activity has occurred, the relative strengths of other behavioral tendencies which begin to be expressed once the tendency to eat is no longer dominant, and the stimuli to which the organism is exposed during this period of time.

In other words, we are led to assume that certain behavioral events, those referred to as consummatory reactions, when they can be identified as such, or as attainment of a goal, when they cannot as easily be described as activities, must function to reduce the strength of the tendency to bring about that kind of event. This idea, it bears repeating, is not based on any kind of neurophysiological preconception. It is an inference based entirely on the observation that behavior typically undergoes a noticeable qualitative change after one of these so-called goal events. *The cessation of striving for a particular kind of goal following attainment of a goal must mean that the strength of the tendency directed towards that kind of goal has been weakened relative to other tendencies which now, as a result, attain dominance.*

## INTERRUPTION OF BOTH INSTRUMENTAL AND GOAL ACTIVITIES

Nothing in what we have just said implies that the strength of the tendency must necessarily be reduced to zero when it is expressed in the goal activity for a noticeable change in the quality of activity to occur. The strength of a tendency need only be reduced sufficiently so that some other tendency will be stronger relative to it for the nature of activity to change. That is all the basic conception requires.

The activity of eating can be interrupted before the tendency to eat is fully expressed and satisfied. This is apparent to any parent who has attempted to keep his children at the table when a friend outside begins to emit the call to play or when an attractive toy is spotted on the dining-room floor midway through the meal. Even the so-called goal activity (what Lewin called activity in the goal region) has a limited compelling quality. It is, however, very difficult to document this fact from examination of experimental evidence concerning amount eaten or drunk by hungry and thirsty rats because these activities are traditionally studied under very barren environmental conditions. Nevertheless, Richter (1927) did observe on one occasion that the amount eaten by animals during the normal hunger cycle was substantially reduced when opportunities for engaging in other kinds of "interesting" activities were made constantly available. And everyday observation forces us to appreciate the fact that interruption of intrinsically enjoyable (goal) activities, as well as instrumental goal-seeking activities, is as common under natural conditions as the persistence-until quality of behavior that was so strongly emphasized by the early purposivists—perhaps even more common.

## THE EFFECT OF INTERRUPTION OF AN ACTIVITY

So now, finally, we come to some critical questions: What do our contemporary stimulus-bound conceptions of motivation have to say about the strength of a goal-directed tendency that is sustaining an activity when there is an interruption of that activity and the goal is not attained—when, in other words, the tendency has not been fully consummated? What happens when the new activity, which constitutes the interruption, takes the subject away from the stimulus situation that was sustaining the initial goal-directed tendency? What happens, in other words, when the stimulus responsible for the expectancy of attaining some goal through performance of some particular act is withdrawn? Under these circumstances, does the strength of the initial goal-directed tendency immediately drop back to zero?

Let us consider carefully what these questions ask in reference to the examples we have discussed. In the case of the children who have been interrupted at play by mother's call to dinner, the question is: Does the tendency to play immediately subside as soon as the children have left the living room and the toys are out of sight? In the case of the professor who has left his desk to join friends in the coffee room, the question is: Does the strength of the tendency to achieve, which had been sustained by the immediate stimulus of his work, drop to zero as soon as the professor has left his office to engage in affiliative activity in the coffee room?

The contemporary conceptions of motivation, which require an immediately present stimulus to elicit or cause or sustain a goal-directed action tendency, imply that the tendency is gone when the stimulus supporting it is gone. But both Freud, in his assumption that the wish persists until it is satisfied, and Lewin, in his treatment of the "spontaneous" recall and resumption of an activity or the initiation of a substitute following interruption of an activity, have asserted something different: *a goal-directed tendency, once aroused, will persist until it is satisfied.* Their views acknowledge that *overt goal-directed behavior* might not persist until the goal is attained, but they assert that a *covert tendency towards the goal* will nevertheless persist even though it is no longer being directly expressed in overt behavior. This is the fundamental idea in Freud's interpretation of dreams as the expression of a previously aroused but unfulfilled wish and the more general emphasis given the persistent influence of unsatisfied needs in the psychoanalytic view of the dynamics of behavior, which, if anything, tends to *under*-emphasize the determinative role of the immediate environment.

To account in a general way for the persistent internal impetus, Freud introduced the concept of instinct or need as a *persistent internal stimulus*. The same idea was later developed more systematically in the concept of drive stimulus and the theory of drive and drive-reduction. But this conception, we must remind ourselves, is the very one that rests on the assumption that the brain is reactive, not active, a machine designed to turn off stimulation. It is the assumption that has yielded the presently inadequate conception of a reactive organism.

Lewin, not bound by the notion that there must be a *stimulus* to cause every tendency to act, attempted to represent the persistence of a tendency towards a goal in his concept of a subsystem within the person which would persist in a state of tension ($t_g$) until the tension was discharged when the goal was attained. His conception of the internal dynamics of motivation, which was never fully developed, was designed to show how tension might flow from one subsystem to another functionally related subsystem to account for the spontaneous initiation of substitute activities and how reduction of tension in one activity might thereby be a substitute for attainment of the goal of some other activity that had been interrupted. Lewin, in other words, emphasized the idea that a particular "need" or "intention" ($t_g$) will persist in the absence of direct stimulus support, and he attempted to work out a representation of the internal dynamics of motivation to account for all the coordinate phenomena related to this idea which he and his colleagues had begun to explore experimentally. But, as Heider (1960) has recently pointed out, the relationship between Lewin's internal model of motivation (tension systems) and environmental model of motivation (force as a function of valence, psychological distance, potency) is not completely coherent, and it has not been systematically developed. Since it is Lewin's external or environmental model of motivation which is expressed in current versions of Expectancy $\times$ Value theory, our present task will be to see how the idea of the persistence of an unsatisfied goal-directed tendency might be recaptured and explicitly represented in the principle which purports to account for the determinants of a tendency to act in a certain way in a given situation.

THE PERSISTENCE OF A GOAL-DIRECTED TENDENCY

The need to recapture the idea of the persistence of a goal-directed *tendency* is evident when we take the general conception of the determinants of a tendency that has evolved in analysis of individual differences in achievement-oriented behavior, viz., $T_{r,g} = M_G \times E_{r,g} \times I_g$, and attempt to employ it to explain the imaginative behavior (thematic apperception test response) which currently provides the measure of strength of achievement motive. It has been assumed that the pictures employed to stimulate imagination function just like any environmental stimulus situation to produce cognitive expec-

tations concerning potential consequences of actions in the type of situation that is portrayed in the picture (Atkinson, 1958, Chapter 42). Hence when a standard set of pictures is employed, and it is assumed that the effect of pictures ($E_{r,g} \times I_g$) is constant for all subjects, individual differences in frequency of achievement-oriented responses in the stories produced by subjects ($T_{r,g}$) imply individual differences in strength of motive ($M_G$). This analysis of the determinants of the imaginative response raises the important question of whether or not it can always be assumed that the picture stimuli produce equivalent effects ($E_{r,g} \times I_g$) in all subjects. This matter has been given considerable attention (Atkinson, 1958). Otherwise, it seems to provide a fairly adequate justification for assuming that individual differences in the imaginative $n$ Achievement score obtained in a standard, neutral condition do imply individual differences in strength of achievement motive.

But consider now the experimental findings in those initial studies by McClelland *et al.* which provided the foundation for subsequent studies of effects of individual differences in $n$ Achievement. These were experiments which showed that the content of thematic apperception is significantly influenced by experimental arousal of a particular kind of motivation *immediately before* subjects are asked to write imaginative stories in response to a standard set of picture stimuli. When these experiments were initially designed and their results interpreted, it was implicitly assumed that motivation to achieve aroused in connection with a particular set of tasks that were undertaken immediately before the thematic apperception test was administered *would persist* long enough to influence the content of imaginative stories produced immediately thereafter. And the results from the various experimental conditions (described on pp. 224–226) show quite clearly that subjects in whom the tendency to achieve was aroused in the period before writing stories produced significantly more achievement-oriented responses to the standard set of pictures than those in a deliberately relaxed control group or in a neutral condition in which nothing was done either to heighten motivation or to relax the subjects before they were asked to write stories.

Most relevant to the present discussion are those results which show that the frequency of achievement-oriented imaginative responses was highest when the tendency to achieve had been aroused and then subjects had been given false norms to create the impression that they had failed (i.e., had not attained their goal). The frequency of achievement-oriented responses was significantly lower (i.e., comparable to a neutral condition) when the tendency to achieve had been aroused but then subjects had been given false norms to create the impression that they had been successful (i.e., had attained their goal). The stimulus-bound conception, $T_{r,g} = M_G \times E_{r,g} \times I_g$, cannot explain these results. There is nothing to represent the effect of previously aroused and unsatisfied motivation to achieve on $T_{r,g}$, the strength of tendency expressed in a particular imaginative story. According to this principle, the tendency to achieve in subjects in all the experimental conditions is implicitly viewed as "at rest" until the picture stimulus for the first story, which arouses an $E_{r,g}$, is presented.

The results of these initial investigations of the effects of experimentally aroused motivation to achieve certainly suggest that when a tendency to strive for a particular kind of goal has been aroused in reference to one activity it will persist, if not satisfied, and subsequently influence the strength of other tendencies directed towards that kind of goal which are aroused by other stimuli for other types of activity. A closer look at some results from the experiments by McClelland *et al.* (1953, p. 204) will concretize the point. The results presented in Figure 10.9 show that the effect of prior arousal of motivation to achieve at a task defined as an intelligence test is to increase, by a constant amount, the frequency of achievement-oriented responses normally elicited by different picture stimuli in a relaxed control condition. This means that the strength of the tendency to achieve at one particular activity, the intelligence test, persists and has a *general* effect on subsequent achievement-oriented activities, viz., response to pictures which portray very different kinds of life situations in which striving for achievement might, or might not, occur. *How is this relatively general effect of the persistent (unsatisfied) goal-directed tendency to be represented in the conception of the immediate determinants of a tendency to engage in a particular activity?*

## FURTHER CONSIDERATION OF THE PHYSICAL ANALOGY

To answer the question, we shall find it helpful to consider an analogous conceptual problem which arose much earlier in the attempt to explain the motion of a physical object. The ancient Aristotelian view of the matter was that an external force is required to cause and sustain the motion of an object. Objects, considered inherently at rest by Aristotle, could only be moved, he believed, by the direct action of an external force. It is apparent that our traditional stimulus-bound mode of thought about the determination of a *tendency* to act implies essentially the same thing concerning the observed behavior of a living organism: viz., an external influence, a stimulus, is required to cause and sustain a tendency to act. The Aristotelian view of the determinants of motion never did explain why a ball given a kick with the foot would continue to roll for a while after the impact of foot and ball, that is, after the direct action of the external force had ceased. This fact tended to be conveniently ignored or weakly explained by the conjecture that it would take a short time for the motion imparted to the ball to die out.

The whole mode of thought about the problem of motion was changed by Galileo, who deduced that the kicked ball would roll farther if the surface were smoother and would continue to roll indefinitely if the surface were perfectly smooth. Galileo appreciated, in other words, that under ideal conditions the motion imparted to a physical object by an external force would persist indefinitely, that it is an inherent property of physical objects to persist in their present state of motion or rest unless this state is changed by an external force acting on the object.

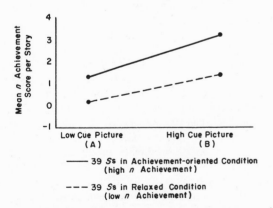

FIGURE 10.9  Mean *n* Achievement score per story as a function of number of cues in the picture and differences in motivation produced by experimental manipulation of cues in the situation preceding the TAT. (*From McClelland, Atkinson, Clark, and Lowell,* The Achievement Motive, *copyright 1953, Appleton-Century Crofts, Inc., p. 204*)

The idea of inertia, resistance to change of present state, was later explicitly formulated by Newton as the first law of motion. It was explicitly recognized that an external force does not cause motion, but a *change of motion*, in an object that may already have momentum attributable to the action of earlier, but not immediately present, external influences. We have a familiar illustration of what this means in the matter of getting a space vehicle into orbit. A certain amount of external force is needed to produce acceleration (change) to the final velocity required to project a vehicle into orbit. Once this velocity has been attained it persists, unchanged, in frictionless space though no longer sustained by any external force.

The seed of the same general idea for a psychology of motivation is contained in Freud's assumption that the wish persists until it is expressed or satisfied and in Lewin's attempt to account for the persistence of the *tendency* to complete a task when activity has been interrupted. It is *the idea that the immediate stimulus situation (conceived as an influence that is external to the relatively autonomous process of the brain) does not cause a tendency to act*—that is, does not elicit a certain response tendency from a state of rest—*but operates on already active tendencies to produce a change in their strength.*

Most psychologists would willingly concede that the subject they study is at least as active as a rolling ball. Yet the conceptual schemes which have arisen in objective study of behavior (except for Lewin's) still correspond to an Aristotelian conception of motion, that is, the stimulus (external influence) is viewed as the *cause* of the tendency to act. What would follow if we were to assume, as a *first principle of motivation*, that *a goal-directed tendency, once aroused, persists until it is satisfied?*

Under natural conditions near the surface of the earth, physical objects do slow down and stop eventually after the push that got them started is withdrawn because there are frictions (i.e., external forces) which oppose the momentum that has been established. An external force, conceived as the cause of change of motion, can reduce as well as increase the momentum of an object. We might anticipate the existence of similar "frictions" in the natural domain of behavior which would account for gradual dissipation of a goal-directed tendency once the stimulus responsible for its initial arousal had been removed. We are even led to the notion that attainment of the goal, which apparently functions to reduce the strength of the goal-directed tendency,

would have to be conceived as analogous to an external force which opposes the psychological momentum that has been established. We would certainly be compelled to rethink many old problems.

The initial assumption that a goal-directed tendency persists would begin to yield a picture of an active organism for whom the immediate stimulus situation does not function to arouse certain tendencies from a state of rest, but rather functions to enhance, selectively, the strength of some already activated tendencies to behave and not others. The traditional "Aristotelian" conception of the stimulus would give way to a "Galilean" conception of the stimulus. The traditional "Aristotelian" conception of an organism inherently at rest (the assumption of an inactive brain and reactive organism that is anchored in the concept of reflex) would give way to a "Galilean" conception of an inherently active organism (the assumption of relatively autonomous central neural processes that have a *selective* influence on subsequent behavior, which current evidence about the brain seems to support).

In an attempt to incorporate the idea of the persistence of a goal-directed tendency into the conception of motivation which has evolved in recent studies of achievement-oriented behavior, we are guided in part by some behavioral observations in these studies which require such a concept and in part by the analogy provided in the conceptual analysis of motion in classical mechanics. After positing inertia as the first law of motion, Newton then accounted for change of motion in his second law:

$$mv_f = \text{Force} + mv_i.$$

This law asserts that the final momentum of an object at a particular time ($mv_f$) is equal to the external force that is applied plus the initial momentum of the object ($mv_i$) at the time the force is applied. When the object is at rest, the initial momentum ($mv_i$) is zero. Hence the final momentum ($mv_f$) is then proportionate to the external force applied. This was the condition that Aristotle had assumed to exist generally, and it is the condition which our contemporary conceptions of behavior implicitly assume to exist generally when they view the strength of a tendency to act as completely dependent upon the immediate stimulus situation as, for example, in the principle $T_{r,g} = M_G \times E_{r,g} \times I_g$. For, as already emphasized, without an external stimulus situation to account for an expectancy of the goal ($E_{r,g}$), the product of the three determinants of $T_{r,g}$, which is analogous to $mv_f$, is zero.

A REFORMULATED CONCEPTION OF THE
DETERMINANTS OF AN ACTION TENDENCY

Given the assumption that a previously aroused but unsatisfied tendency to attain a goal will persist, we can restate the conception of the immediate determinants of a particular goal-directed tendency at a given time as follows:

$$T_{r,g_f} = (M_G \times E_{r,g} \times I_g) + T_{G_i}.$$

In this assertion, $T_{G_i}$ is introduced to represent the persistent unsatisfied tendency. It might appropriately be called "*the inertial tendency*" to remind us of the physical analogy. By employing the capital $G$ as the subscript on the inertial tendency we mean to imply, for example, that when the tendency to achieve has been aroused in some particular activity and the particular goal is not attained, what persists is the *general* tendency to achieve success. The persistent tendency towards success ($T_{S_i}$) should enhance the final strength of any particular tendency to achieve ($T_{r,s_f}$) that is subsequently aroused. The inertial tendency, $T_{G_i}$, should, in other words, have a relatively non-specific effect on a whole class of subsequent activities that is comparable, in this respect, to the relatively non-specific effect of a motive, $M_G$. This means that the persistent tendency to achieve will influence the strength of any subsequent tendency to undertake an activity that is expected to lead to success, but will not influence specific tendencies to undertake activities which are expected to lead to other kinds of consequences (e.g., eating, sexual activity, affiliation, etc.). Applied to another kind of motivation—for example, sexual motivation—the concept $T_{G_i}$ implies that sexual motivation aroused in reference to one particular activity or one particular goal object will, if unsatisfied, persist and influence any other subsequent instance of sexual activity regardless of the activity or goal object. The idea is that what persists when the particular goal ($g$) of a particular activity ($r$) is not attained is a general tendency towards *that kind of goal* ($G$).

The notion that the inertial tendency ($T_{G_i}$) adds to the strength of *any other tendency to attain the same general goal* that is subsequently aroused by an environmental stimulus, according to the principle $T_{r,g_f} = (M_G \times E_{r,g} \times I_g) + T_{G_i}$, is offered as a tentative guiding hypothesis. This is a first approximation suggested by evidence of the sort shown in Figure 10.9 that prior arousal of a tendency to achieve at one particular task does influence the subsequent expression of a tendency to achieve in other, different achievement-oriented activities. It is the central idea in Freud's development of the concept of displacement and is also suggested by experimental evidence concerning the phenomenon of substitution presented in some of the early experiments by Lewin and co-workers. The need for such a concept has been consistently pointed out by psychoanalytically oriented psychologists, like Lazarus (1961), who have emphasized this factor in theoretical discussions of the inferences to be made from content analysis of thematic apperception and other projective tests.

Translated into the terms of *S-R* theory, the concept of inertial tendency, $T_{G_i}$, implies that the anticipatory goal reaction ($r_g$-$s_g$), once aroused by some stimulus (internal or external), will persist *in the absence of direct stimulus support* and enhance the strength of any tendency towards that goal that is subsequently aroused by some other stimulus. One might go so far as to suggest that the persistence of $r_g$-$s_g$ would mean that a whole family of particular response tendencies associated with $s_g$ are already activated *before* the occurrence of some environmental stimulus which is normally effective in arousing one or more of them. This general idea was presented earlier by the writer (Atkinson, 1954, p. 87) in an argument based in part on Hull's concept of habit family hierarchy (Hull, 1934) and in part on arguments presented by Hebb (1949) concerning the functional significance of relatively autonomous central processes. Perhaps the assumed effect of interruption of either instrumental or goal activity before full consummation (i.e., reduction) of the tendency has occurred would be more adequately represented by the notation $T_{any\,r,G_i}$. This states somewhat more explicitly the idea that the inertial tendency will influence (add to) the strength of the subsequent tendency to engage in any act that is expected to produce the same kind of goal. The reader may assume that $T_{G_i} = T_{any\,r,G_i}$. The concept redirects attention to the whole problem of initiation of substitute activities and substitute value of different activities, topics which have been given substantially less systematic experimental attention than they deserve.

IMPLICATIONS OF THE ASSUMED
INERTIAL TENDENCY ($T_{G_i}$)

The main implication of the assumption that a goal-directed tendency will persist when activity directed towards a goal is interrupted can be fully appreciated by turning our discussion back to the general problem of change of activity which brought us to the question: What happens to the strength of the goal-directed tendency when the stimulus sustaining that tendency is removed? We now have in mind the notion that the children called from play to supper *are still actively motivated to play* even though they have left their toys and are seated at the table eating. And the professor who was called from his work for a coffee break is still conceived as *actively motivated to achieve* even though he has left his desk and is chatting in the coffee room. This suggests that both the children and the professor should be likely to resume the interrupted activity at the first opportunity. How long these unsatisfied goal-directed tendencies will persist is the kind of question for future research that arises when we recover, for the experimental psychology of motivation, the important insights of Freud and Lewin.

Let us again consider the example of the college professor at work at his desk when a friend calls him to coffee and include the concept of inertial motivation in our analysis of the determinants of a change of activity. We begin again with the assertion that the professor will initiate the activity of walking to the coffee room ($R_2$) when the tendency to affiliate is stronger than the tendency to achieve which is sustaining the activity of working at his desk already in progress when his friend calls. But now we include the subscript $f$ on both tendencies to remind us that we are talking about the *final* strengths of particular action tendencies at the instant a decision is made:

$$R_2 \text{ will occur when } T_{r_2,aff_f} > T_{r_1,s_f}.$$

Next, in our conception of the determinants of the *final* strengths of the two competing tendencies, we must include the inertial component of motivation. We no longer think of the strengths of the two tendencies as if they were completely bound to the immediate stimulus situation as implied before in the principle $T_{r,g} = M_G \times E_{r,g} \times I_g$. For simplicity, we shall take it one step at a time. First, let us focus on the determinants of the tendency to engage in the affiliative activity:

$R_2$ will occur when

$$(M_{Aff} \times E_{r_2,aff} \times I_{aff}) + T_{Aff_i} > T_{r_1,s_f}.$$

Our conception now includes the idea that the professor may already be actively motivated to affiliate ($T_{Aff_i}$) even before the call of a friend ($S_2$)

occurs. To have a clear picture of the initial condition of the professor immediately before $S_2$ occurs, we must now move to the right-hand side of the expression all those variables which are descriptive of his condition at that time. First, we move the inertial tendency to affiliate ($T_{Aff_i}$) by subtracting $T_{Aff_i}$ from both sides of the expression without changing its implications:

$R_2$ will occur when

$$(M_{Aff} \times E_{r_2,aff} \times I_{aff}) > T_{r_1,s_f} - T_{Aff_i}.$$

This immediately tells us that it will not take much of a psychological force ($M_{Aff} \times E_{r_2,aff} \times I_{aff}$) to get the professor away from his desk for a visit with his friends if his persistent, unsatisfied tendency to affiliate ($T_{Aff_i}$) is already almost as strong as the tendency to achieve ($T_{r_1,s_f}$) which is sustaining the activity in progress. In fact, we are led to the hypothesis that he might "spontaneously" initiate the search for a friend if the tendency to achieve were to be reduced somewhat, as it might be by partial success at the task, even without such an obvious change in environmental stimulation as $S_2$. In other words, when $T_{Aff_i}$ is very strong relative to $T_{r_1,s_f}$, the dominant tendency which is being expressed in the activity in progress, the professor should be ready to initiate affiliative activity with very minimal environmental inducement. The vaguest sound of activity in the coffee room, for example, might provoke the change of activity even though the professor might be very uncertain that there was anyone there to talk to (i.e., he might have a weak $E_{r_2,aff}$).

We must remember, at this point, that $T_{Aff_i}$ represents the strength of a persistent, unsatisfied tendency to affiliate that is attributable to prior arousals of the tendency to affiliate which have not been adequately expressed or satisfied in affiliative activity. The magnitude of $T_{Aff_i}$ represents the degree to which the professor is already actively motivated to affiliate, even though he is in the presence of environmental stimuli which sustain his tendency to achieve and he is overtly expressing this dominant tendency in achievement-oriented activity at his desk, and even though the call from a friend ($S_2$) has not yet occurred. When $S_2$ occurs, it will have the effect of increasing the momentary strength of the tendency to affiliate and of specifying the particular action that should be undertaken to produce the affiliative goal.

If we apply the same line of reasoning to the

situation of the professor in the coffee room immediately following interruption of his work, or the situation of the children seated at the dinner table immediately following the interruption of their play activity, we realize that the persistent tendency towards the goal of the earlier activity that has been interrupted will increase the likelihood of an early resumption of those activities. The professor should spend less time chatting with his friends, and the children should spend less time eating, than if they had not been engrossed in activity directed towards other goals immediately beforehand. As soon as the professor's affiliative tendency has been reduced somewhat by his affiliative activity, and as soon as the children's tendency to eat is reduced somewhat by the activity of eating, the persistent unsatisfied tendency is likely to become dominant again, particularly since the cues of the immediate environment define the path back to the previously interrupted activities. If the second activity had taken the professor or the children far away from environmental cues defining the path back to the initial, interrupted activities, then we might suppose that our subjects would be likely to initiate functionally equivalent substitute activities shortly thereafter. For example, the children taken to the home of a friend for dinner would quickly initiate play activity with the friend's toys as soon as they could escape from the table. We can begin to appreciate, from this kind of analysis, how *infrequently* goal-directed tendencies are likely to be reduced to zero strength before some new activity is initiated under natural conditions and, therefore, how pervasive the role of inertial tendencies is likely to be in producing the pattern of change of activities which is characteristic of the daily stream of behavior in the life of an individual.

To complete our descriptive picture of the professor's initial condition before $S_2$ (the friend's call) occurs, we must also move the motive to affiliate to the right side by dividing both sides of the expression by the quantity $M_{Aff}$, as before:

$$R_2 \text{ will occur when } (E_{r_2,aff} \times I_{aff}) > \frac{T_{r_1,s_f} - T_{Aff,i}}{M_{Aff}}.$$

What we have added to our earlier analysis of the problem (see p. 303), by virtue of assuming the persistence of an unsatisfied goal-directed tendency, is the general implication that, other things equal, the external force or inducement required to move the professor from his desk to the coffee room will be less, the greater the magnitude of $T_{Aff,i}$, the inertial

tendency to affiliate. Other things equal, the professor should be slower to leave his work on some days than others. If he has had a "satisfying" chat with some friends within the past hour, he should be less likely to go to coffee or slower to leave his work than if he has recently experienced social rejection. In the latter case, the inertial tendency—the unsatisfied "need" for affiliation—would be stronger.

Until now we have focused on the way that an inertial tendency would function to enhance or strengthen the tendency to initiate a new activity. Let us not neglect the other possibility: viz., a strong inertial component in the tendency sustaining an activity already in progress should produce what might appear to the external observer as an unusual amount of persistence in the initial activity, a "disproportionate" resistance to change of activity, given the observer's assessment of the external environmental conditions at the time. In our example, this might come about if the professor had recently experienced some failures in achievement-oriented activities, that is, if the tendency to achieve had been previously aroused but the professor had not attained his goal (as in the experiments by McClelland *et al.* which showed the effect of recent "failure" on subsequent TAT response).

This possibility comes into focus when we complete our specification of the determinants of the tendency to achieve that is sustaining the activity in progress ($T_{r_1,s_f}$) at the time of the friend's call to coffee ($S_2$):

$$R_2 \text{ will occur when } T_{r_2,aff} > (M_S \times E_{r_1,s} \times I_s) + T_{S_i}.$$

Now we have separated that component of the final strength of the tendency to achieve which is attributable to the immediate stimulus situation ($S_1$) defined by the cues of the professor's office and the work before him at the very moment that $S_2$ occurs (viz., $M_S \times E_{r,s} \times I_s$), from the already active tendency to achieve ($T_{S_i}$) which the professor may have brought into the office with him that morning, or which may have accumulated in a long series of unsuccessful efforts to solve the particular problem before him. To the list of hypotheses concerning factors which influence the change of activity that already have been identified, we must add still another one: the external force, or inducement, required to produce a change of activity will be greater the stronger the inertial component of the tendency sustaining the activity in progress.

A complete conceptualization of the determinants

of the change of activity in this hypothetical instance would look like this:

$R_2$ will occur when $(E_{r_2,aff} \times I_{aff})$

$$> \frac{[(M_S \times E_{r_1,s} \times I_s) + T_{S_i}] - T_{Aff_i}}{M_{Aff}}.$$

It must be remembered that we have deliberately simplified matters by assuming that no other motives or other inertial tendencies have any influence on either the initial activity or the activity which replaces it at this particular moment in the life of our hypothetical subject. The general logic of the analysis can be applied when two or more different kinds of motive and inertial tendency influence the final strength of a particular action tendency, but then, as the reader can well imagine, the mathematical expression of the basic ideas becomes more complicated.

TWO MEANINGS OF THE ASSUMPTION
OF AN ACTIVE ORGANISM

Our discussion has drawn attention to the fact that the contemporary mode of thought about motivation, as it is expressed in the Drive × Habit and Expectancy × Value theories which now guide research, is stimulus bound—although the intuitions of most psychologists are not. This has come about because an antiquated neurophysiological conception has provided the underlying premise of the mainstream of thought about motivation for many years. Recognizing this, we have looked again at some important insights and assumptions based on behavioral observations. These were advanced in theoretical discussions of motivation before the systematic attempt by Hull and others to explain the purposive characteristics of behavior using stimulus and response as the basic elements of construction. The new working premise for study of motivation, which is suggested by recent developments in neurophysiology and also by an effort to profit from the conceptual analysis of motion which once changed the traditional mode of thought in physics, turns out to be not a "new" premise at all, but a very old and

neglected one: *the assumption of an active organism.*

The proposals advanced in the preceding pages are these: *activity already in progress, and the persistence of previously aroused but unsatisfied goal-directed tendencies should be taken into account systematically in the theory of motivation.* The subject of study, in other words, should be conceived as already active in two senses when exposed to some environmental influence. The subject is already doing something and is already actively motivated to do a number of other things when the stimulus, of traditional interest to experimental psychology, is presented.

THE INTEGRATIVE TASK
FOR THE FUTURE

Conceptual analysis of the contemporaneous determinants of a change of activity helps to define the integrative task which still lies ahead for the psychology of motivation. It must bring together into a single, coherent conceptual scheme *the impact on behavior of the immediate environment*, which has traditionally dominated the interest of experimental psychologists; *the effect of stable individual differences in personality*, which is an interest of the mental test movement in psychology; and *the constant influence on behavior of the persistent undercurrent of active tendencies to bring about particular effects which can be attributed to previous inhibition or inadequate expression of certain impulses in the past*, the factor which clinical psychologists from Freud onward have emphasized in their discussions of the dynamics of behavior.

An adequate psychology of motivation will one day provide an integration of the two disciplines of scientific psychology, the one concerned with basic process and the other with individual differences in personality. It will yield a picture of the subject of study in psychology as at least as active as a rolling ball. Perhaps a renewal of interest in the conceptual analysis of the motion of a rolling ball will help to provide a model of how to proceed towards this objective.

# References

ALLISON, J. (1963) Preference for food, magnitude of food reward, and instrumental conditioning. Unpublished doctoral thesis, University of Michigan.

ALLPORT, G. W. (1943) The ego in contemporary psychology. *Psychol. Rev.*, **50**, 451–478.

ANGELINA, A. L. (1955) Un novo método par avaliar a motivação humana. Unpublished doctoral dissertation, Universidade de São Paulo, Brazil.

ATKINSON, J. W. (1953) The achievement motive and recall of interrupted and completed tasks. *J. exp. Psychol.*, **46**, 381–390. Also in D. C. MCCLELLAND, editor (1955) *Studies in motivation.* New York: Appleton-Century-Crofts.

ATKINSON, J. W. (1954) Explorations using imaginative thought to assess the strength of human motives. In M. R. JONES, editor. *Nebraska symposium on motivation, 1954.* Lincoln: University of Nebraska Press.

ATKINSON, J. W. (1957) Motivational determinants of risk-taking behavior. *Psychol. Rev.*, **64**, 359–372.

ATKINSON, J. W. (1958) *Motives in fantasy, action, and society.* Princeton: D. Van Nostrand Company, Inc.

ATKINSON, J. W., BASTIAN, J. R., EARL, R. W., & LITWIN, G. H. (1960) The achievement motive, goal setting, and probability preferences. *J. abnorm. soc. Psychol.*, **60**, 27–36.

ATKINSON, J. W., & CARTWRIGHT, D. (1962) Some neglected variables in contemporary conceptions of decision and performance. Predecisional processes symposium, Wright-Patterson Air Force Base.

ATKINSON, J. W., & CARTWRIGHT, D. (1964) Some neglected variables in contemporary conceptions of decision and performance. *Psychol. Rep.*, **14**, 575–590.

ATKINSON, J. W., HEYNS, R. W., & VEROFF, J. (1954) The effect of experimental arousal of the affiliation motive on thematic apperception. *J. abnorm. soc. Psychol.*, **49**, 405–410.

ATKINSON, J. W., & LITWIN, G. H. (1960) Achievement motive and test anxiety conceived as motive to approach success and motive to avoid failure. *J. abnorm. soc. Psychol.*, **60**, 52–63.

ATKINSON, J. W., & MCCLELLAND, D. C. (1948) The projective expression of needs. II. The effect of different intensities of the hunger drive on thematic apperception. *J. exp. Psychol.*, **38**, 643–658.

ATKINSON, J. W., & O'CONNOR, PATRICIA (1963) Effects of ability grouping in schools related to individual differences in achievement-related motivation. Final report, Office of Education Cooperative Research Program, Project 1283. Available in microfilm from Photoduplication Center, Library of Congress, Washington, D. C.

ATKINSON, J. W., & RAPHELSON, A. C. (1956) Individual differences in motivation and behavior in particular situations. *J. Pers.*, **24**, 349–363.

ATKINSON, J. W., & REITMAN, W. R. (1956) Performance as a function of motive strength and expectancy of goal attainment. *J. abnorm. soc. Psychol.*, **53**, 361–366.

BEACH, F. A. (1942) Analysis of the stimuli adequate to elicit mating behavior in the sexually-inexperienced male rat. *J. comp. Psychol.*, **33**, 163–207.

BERLYNE, D. E. (1950) Novelty and curiosity as determinants of exploratory behavior. *Brit. J. Psychol.*, **41**, 68–80.

BERLYNE, D. E. (1960) *Conflict, arousal and curiosity.* New York: McGraw-Hill.

BERNARD, C. (1859) *Lecons sur les proprit'es physiologiques et les alterations pathologiques des liquides de l'organisme.* Vols. I & II. Paris: Balli'ere.

BERNARD, C. (1865) *Introduction a l'étude de la médecin expérimentale* (English translation by H. C. Greene, 1940). Ann Arbor: Edwards Bros.

BERNOULLI, D. (1738) Speciment theorial novae de mensura sortis. *Comentarii Academiae Scientiarum Imperiales Petropolitanae*, **5**, 175–192.

BINDRA, D., PATTERSON, A. L., & STRZELECKI, J. (1955) On the relation between anxiety and conditioning. *Canad. J. Psychol.*, **9**, 1–6.

BIRCH, D., BURNSTEIN, E., & CLARK, R. (1958) Response strength as a function of hours of food deprivation under a controlled maintenance schedule. *J. comp. physiol. Psychol.*, **51**, 350–354.

BIRNEY, R. (1958) Thematic content and the cue characteristics of pictures. In J. W. ATKINSON, editor. *Motives in fantasy, action, and society.* Princeton: D. Van Nostrand Company, Inc.

BISHOP, R. L. (1946) Professor Knight and the theory of demand. *J. polit. Econ.*, **54**, 141–169.

BLODGETT, H. C. (1929) The effect of the introduction of reward upon the maze performance of rats.

Berkeley: *University of California Publ. in Psychol.*, **4**, #8, 113–134.

BOLLES, R. C. (1958) The usefulness of the drive concept. In M. R. JONES, editor. *Nebraska symposium on motivation, 1958.* Lincoln: University of Nebraska Press.

BORING, E. C. (1929) *The history of experimental psychology.* New York: Century Co.

BROWN, J. S. (1948) Gradients of approach and avoidance responses and their relation to level of motivation. *J. comp. physiol. Psychol.*, **41**, 450–465.

BROWN, J. S. (1961) *The motivation of behavior.* New York: McGraw-Hill.

BROWN, J. S., & JACOBS, A. (1949) The role of fear in the motivation and acquisition of response. *J. exp. Psychol.*, **39**, 747–759.

BROWN, J. S., KALISH, H. I., & FARBER, I. E. (1951) Conditioned fear as revealed by magnitude of startle response to an auditory stimulus. *J. exp. Psychol.*, **41**, 317–328.

BROWN, R. W. (1952) Some determinants of the relationship between rigidity and authoritarianism. Unpublished Ph.D. thesis, University of Michigan.

BUGELSKI, R. (1938) Extinction with and without subgoal reinforcement. *J. comp. physiol. Psychol.*, **26**, 121–134.

BUTLER, R. A. (1953) Discrimination learning by rhesus monkeys to visual-exploration motivation. *J. comp. physiol. Psychol.*, **46**, 95–98.

CAMPBELL, B. A., & SHEFFIELD, F. D. (1953) Relation of random activity to food deprivation. *J. comp. physiol. Psychol.*, **46**, 320–322.

CARMICHAEL, L., editor (1946) *Manual of child psychology.* New York: Wiley.

CARTWRIGHT, D. (1941) Decision-time in relation to the differentiation of the phenomenal field. *Psychol. Rev.*, **48**, 425–442.

CARTWRIGHT, D. (1942) The effect of interruption, completion and failure upon the attractiveness of activities. *J. exp. Psychol.*, **31**, 1–16.

CARTWRIGHT, D. (1951) Achieving change in people: some applications of group dynamics theory. *Hum. Relat.*, **4**, 381–392.

CARTWRIGHT, D. (1959) Lewinian theory as a contemporary systematic framework. In S. KOCH, editor. *Psychology: A study of a science.* Vol. 2. New York: McGraw-Hill.

CARTWRIGHT, D., & FESTINGER, L. (1943) A quantitative theory of decision. *Psychol. Rev.*, **50**, 595.

CATTELL, R. B. (1957) *Personality and motivation: Structure and measurement.* New York: World Book Co.

CLARK, R. A. (1952) The projective measurement of experimentally induced levels of sexual motivation. *J. exp. Psychol.*, **44**, 391–399.

CLARK, R. A. (1955) The effects of sexual motivation on phantasy. In D. C. MCCLELLAND, editor. *Studies in motivation.* New York: Appleton-Century-Crofts.

CLARK, R. A., & SENSIBAR, MINDA R. (1956) The relationships between symbolic and manifest projections of sexuality with some incidental correlates. *J. abnorm. soc. Psychol.*, **50**, 327–334.

CLARK, R. A., TEEVAN, R., & RICCIUTI, H. (1956) Hope of success and fear of failure as aspects of need for achievement. *J. abnorm. soc. Psychol.*, **53**, 182–186.

CONANT, J. B. (1951) *Science and common sense.* New Haven: Yale University Press.

CONANT, J. B. (1952) *Modern science and modern man.* New York: Columbia University Press.

CONGER, J. J. (1951) The effects of alcohol on conflict behavior in the albino rat. *Quart. J. Stud. Alcohol.*, **12**, 1–29.

COOMBS, C. H., & PRUITT, D. G. (1960) Components of risk in decision-making: probability and variance preferences. *J. exp. Psychol.*, **60**, 265–277.

COWLES, J. T. (1937) Food tokens as incentives for learning by chimpanzees. *Comp. Psychol. Monogr.*, **14**, #71, 96 pp.

COWLES, J. T., & NISSEN, H. W. (1937) Reward-expectancy in delayed responses of chimpanzees. *J. comp. physiol. Psychol.*, **24**, 345–358.

CRANDALL, V. J., SOLOMON, D., & KELLAWAY, R. (1955) Expectancy statements and decision times as functions of objective probabilities and reinforcement values. *J. Pers.*, **24**, 192–203.

CRESPI, L. P. (1942) Quantitative variation of incentive and performance in the white rat. *Amer. J. Psychol.*, **55**, 467–517.

CRESPI, L. P. (1944) Amount of reinforcement and level of performance. *Psychol. Rev.*, **51**, 341–357.

CROCKETT, H. J. (1962) The achievement motive and differential occupational mobility in the United States. *Am. soc. Rev.*, **27**, 191–204.

CRONBACH, L. J. (1957) The two disciplines of scientific psychology. *Amer. Psych.*, **12**, 671–684.

DEMBER, W., EARL, R., & PARADISE, N. (1957) Response by rats to differential stimulus complexity. *J. comp. physiol. Psychol.*, **50**, 514–518.

DEMBO, T. (1931) Der arger als dynamisches problem. *Psychol. Forsch.*, **15**, 1–44.

DESCARTES, R. (1637) *The discourse on method* (English translation by J. VEITCH, 1935). Chicago: Open Court Publishing Co.

DOLLARD, J., & MILLER, N. E. (1950) *Personality and psychotherapy.* New York: McGraw-Hill.

DOUVAN, ELIZABETH (1956) Social status and success strivings. *J. abnorm. soc. Psychol.*, **52**, 219–223.

EDWARDS, W. (1953) Probability-preferences in gambling. *Amer. J. Psychol.*, **66**, 349–364.

EDWARDS, W. (1954) The theory of decision making. *Psychol. Bull.*, **51**, 380–417.

EDWARDS, W. (1960) Measurement of utility and subjective probability. In H. GULLIKSEN and S. MESSICK, editors. *Psychological scaling: Theory and applications.* New York: Wiley.

EDWARDS, W. (1962) Utility, subjective probability, their interaction, and variance preferences. *J. conf. res.*, **6**, 42–51.

EINSTEIN, A., & INFELD, L. (1951) *The evolution of physics.* New York: Simon and Schuster.

ELLIOTT, M. H. (1928) The effect of change of reward on the maze performance of rats. Berkeley: *University of California Publ. Psychol.*, **4**, #2, 19–30.

ELLIOTT, M. H. (1929) The effect of appropriateness of reward and of complex incentives on maze performance. Berkeley: *University of California Publ. Psychol.*, **4**, 91–98.

ESCALONA, SYBILLE K. (1940) The effect of success and failure upon the level of aspiration and behavior in manic-depressive psychoses. *University of Iowa Stud. Child Welf.*, **16**, 199–302.

ESTES, W. K. (1954) Kurt Lewin. In W. K. ESTES *et al. Modern learning theory.* New York: Appleton-Century-Crofts.

ESTES, W. K. (1954) Individual behavior in uncertainty situations: an interpretation in terms of statistical association theory. In R. M. THRALL, C. H. COOMBS, & R. L. DAVIS, editors. *Decision processes.* New York: Wiley.

ESTES, W. K. (1958) Stimulus-response theory of drive. In M. R. JONES, editor. *Nebraska symposium on motivation, 1958.* Lincoln: University of Nebraska Press.

ESTES, W. K., KOCH, S., MACCORQUODALE, K., MEEHL, P., MUELLER, C., SCHOENFELD, W., & VERPLANCK, W. S. (1954) *Modern learning theory.* New York: Appleton-Century-Crofts.

EYSENCK, H. J. (1953) *The structure of human personality.* London: Methuen & Co.

EYSENCK, H. J., & HIMMELWEIT, H. T. (1946) An experimental study of the reactions of neurotics to experiences of success and failure. *J. gen. Psychol.*, **35**, 59–75.

FARBER, I. E. (1954) Anxiety as a drive state. In M. R. JONES, editor. *Nebraska symposium on motivation, 1954.* Lincoln: University of Nebraska Press.

FARBER, I. E., & SPENCE, K. W. (1953) Complex learning and conditioning as a function of anxiety. *J. exp. Psychol.*, **45**, 120–125.

FEATHER, N. T. (1959) Subjective probability and decision under uncertainty. *Psychol. Rev.*, **66**, 150–164.

FEATHER, N. T. (1960) Persistence in relation to achievement motivation, anxiety about failure, and task difficulty. Unpublished doctoral dissertation, University of Michigan.

FEATHER, N. T. (1961) The relationship of persistence at a task to expectation of success and achievement related motives. *J. abnorm. soc. Psychol.*, **63**, 552–561.

FEATHER, N. T. (1962) The study of persistence. *Psychol. Bull.*, **59**, 94–114.

FELD, SHEILA, & SMITH, C. P. (1958) An evaluation of the objectivity of the method of content analysis. In J. W. ATKINSON, editor. *Motives in fantasy, action, and society.* Princeton: D. Van Nostrand Company, Inc.

FESHBACH, S. (1955) The drive-reducing function of fantasy behavior. *J. abnorm. soc. Psychol.*, **50**, 3–11.

FESTINGER, L. (1942) A theoretical interpretation of shifts in level of aspiration. *Psychol. Rev.*, **49**, 235–250.

FINCH, G. (1938) Hunger as a determinant of conditional and unconditional salivary response magnitude. *Amer. J. Psychol.*, **123**, 379–382.

FRANK, J. D. (1935) Individual differences in certain aspects of the level of aspiration. *Amer. J. Psychol.*, **47**, 119–128.

FRENCH, ELIZABETH G. (1955) Some characteristics of achievement motivation. *J. exp. Psychol.*, **50**, 232–236.

FRENCH, ELIZABETH G., & LESSER, G. S. (1964) Some characteristics of the achievement motive in women. *J. abnorm. soc. Psychol.*, **68**, 119–128.

FRENCH, ELIZABETH G., & THOMAS, F. H. (1958) The relation of achievement motivation to problem solving effectiveness. *J. abnorm. soc. Psychol.*, **56**, 46–48.

FREUD, S. (1922) *Beyond the pleasure principle* (English translation by C. J. M. HUBBACK). London and Vienna: Internationale Psychoanalytic Press.

FREUD, S. (1935) *Autobiography.* New York: Norton.

FREUD, S. (1936) *The problem of anxiety.* New York: Psychoanalytic Quarterly Press.

FREUD, S. (1943) *A general introduction to psychoanalysis.* New York: Garden City. Excerpts reprinted with permission of George Allen & Union Ltd., and the Liveright Publishing Corp.

FREUD, S. (1949) *Collected papers.* London: The Hogarth Press and the Institute of Psychoanalysis; New York: Basic Books.

FREUD, S. (1958) *Standard edition of the complete psychological works. Vols. XII and XIV* (James Strachey, editor). London: The Hogarth Press and the Institute of Psycho-analysis; New York: Basic Books.

GANTT, W. H. (1938) The nervous secretion of saliva: the relation of the conditioned reflex to the intensity of the unconditioned stimulus. Proceedings of the American Physiology Society. *Amer. J. Physiol.*, **123**, 74.

GIBSON, J. J. (1941) A critical review of the concept

of set in contemporary experimental psychology. *Psychol. Bull.*, **38**, 781–817.

GORDON, W. M., & BERLYNE, D. E. (1954) Drive-level and flexibility in paired associate nonsense-syllable learning. *Quart. J. exp. Psychol.*, **6**, 181–185.

GRICE, G. E. (1942) An experimental study of the gradient of reinforcement in maze learning. *J. exp. Psychol.*, **30**, 475–489.

GRINDLEY, G. C. (1929) Experiments on the influence of the amount of reward in learning of young chickens. *Brit. J. Psychol.*, **20**, 173–180.

GUETZKOW, H., editor (1951) *Groups, leadership, and men.* Pittsburgh: Carnegie Press.

GUTTMAN, N. (1954) Equal-reinforcement values for sucrose and glucose solutions compared with equal sweetness values. *J. comp. physiol. Psychol.*, **47**, 453–463.

HABER, R. N., & ALPERT, R. (1958) The role of situation and picture cues in projective measurement of the achievement motive. In J. W. ATKINSON, editor. *Motives in fantasy, action, and society.* Princeton: D. Van Nostrand Company, Inc.

HANSON, N. R. (1958) *Patterns of discovery.* Cambridge, England: Cambridge University Press.

HARLOW, H. F. (1953) Motivation as a factor in the acquisition of new responses. In *Current theory and research in motivation: a symposium.* Lincoln: University of Nebraska Press.

HARLOW, H. F., & WOOLSEY, C. N., editors (1958) *Biological and biochemical bases of behavior.* Madison: University of Wisconsin Press.

HAYASHI, T., & HABU, K. (1962) A research on achievement motive: an experimental test of the "thought sampling" method by using Japanese students. *Japanese Psychol. Research*, **4**, 30–42.

HEBB, D. O. (1949) *The organization of behavior.* New York: Wiley.

HEBB, D. O. (1955) Drives and the C. N. S. (conceptual nervous system). *Psychol. Rev.*, **62**, 243–254.

HEBB, D. O. (1958) Alice in wonderland or psychology among the biological sciences. In H. F. HARLOW & C. N. WOOLSEY, editors. *Biological and biochemical bases of behavior.* Madison: University of Wisconsin Press.

HEIDER, F. (1960) The Gestalt theory of motivation. In M. R. JONES, editor. *Nebraska symposium on motivation, 1960.* Lincoln: University of Nebraska Press.

HERON, W. T., & SKINNER, B. F. (1937) Changes in hunger during starvation. *Psychological Record*, **1**, 51–60.

HIMMELWEIT, H. T. (1947) A comparative study of the level of aspiration of normal and neurotic persons. *Brit. J. Psychol.*, **37**, 41–59.

HOLT, E. B. (1915) *The Freudian wish and its place in ethics.* New York: Holt.

HOPPE, F. (1930) Untersuchungen zur Handlungs— und affeckt—psychologie. IX. Erfolg und Musserfolg. (Investigations in the psychology of action and emotion. IX. Success and failure). *Psychol. Forsch.*, **14**, 1–63.

HOVLAND, C. I. (1937) The generalization of conditioned responses. IV. The effects of varying amounts of reinforcements upon the degree of generalization of conditioned responses. *J. exp. Psychol.*, **21**, 261–276.

HULL, C. L. (1930a) Knowledge and purpose as habit mechanisms. *Psychol. Rev.*, **37**, 511–525.

HULL, C. L. (1930b) Simple trial-and-error learning: a study in psychological theory. *Psychol. Rev.*, **37**, 241–256.

HULL, C. L. (1931) Goal attraction and directing ideas conceived as habit phenomena. *Psychol. Rev.*, **38**, 487–506.

HULL, C. L. (1932) The goal gradient and maze learning. *Psychol. Rev.*, **39**, 25–43.

HULL, C. L. (1933) Differential habituation to internal stimuli in the albino rat. *J. comp. Psychol.*, **16**, 255–274.

HULL, C. L. (1934) The concept of the habit-family hierarchy and maze learning. I. *Psychol. Rev.*, **41**, 33–54.

HULL, C. L. (1934) The rat's speed of locomotion gradient in the approach to food. *J. comp. Psychol.*, **17**, 393–422.

HULL, C. L. (1935) Special Review: Thorndike's fundamentals of learning. *Psych. Bull.*, **32**, 807–823.

HULL, C. L. (1937) Mind, mechanism, and adaptive behavior. *Psychol. Rev.*, **44**, 1–32.

HULL, C. L. (1943) *Principles of behavior.* New York: Appleton-Century-Crofts.

HULL, C. L. (1952) *A behavior system.* New Haven: Yale University Press.

HUNT, J. McV. (1944) *Personality and the behavior disorders.* New York: Ronald.

INKELES, A., & ROSSIE, P. H. (1956) National comparisons of occupational prestige. *Amer. J. Soc.*, **61**, 329–339.

IRWIN, F. W. (1953) Stated expectations as functions of probability and desirability of outcomes. *J. Pers.*, **21**, 329–335.

JACOBS, B. J. (1958) A method for investigating the cue characteristics of pictures. In J. W. ATKINSON, editor. *Motives in fantasy, action, and society.* Princeton: D. Van Nostrand Company, Inc.

JAMES, W. (1890) *The principles of psychology.* Vols. I and II. New York: Henry Holt.

JAMES, W. (1892) *Text-book of psychology: Briefer course.* New York: Henry Holt.

JAMES, W. (1902) *The principles of psychology.* Vol. I. New York: Holt.

JONES, M. R., editor (1953–1963) *Nebraska symposium on motivation.* Vols. I–XI. Lincoln: Nebraska University Press.

JONES, M. R., editor. (1955) *Nebraska symposium on motivation.* Lincoln: University of Nebraska Press.

JUCKNAT, M. (1937) Performance, level of aspiration and self consciousness. *Psychol. Forsch.,* **22,** 89–179.

KENDLER, H. H. (1946) The influence of simultaneous hunger and thirst drives upon the learning of two opposed special responses of the white rat. *J. exp. Psychol.,* **36,** 212–220.

KENDLER, H. H. (1959) Learning. In P. R. FARNSWORTH & Q. MCNEMAR, editors. *Annual Review of Psychology,* Vol. 10. Palo Alto: Annual Reviews, Inc.

KOCH, S. (1959) *Psychology: A study of a science.* Vol. 2. New York: McGraw-Hill.

LAZARUS, R. S. (1961) A substitutive-defensive conception of apperceptive fantasy. In J. KAGAN & G. S. LESSER, editors. *Contemporary issues in thematic apperceptive methods.* Springfield, Illinois: Charles C. Thomas.

LEEPER, R. (1935) The role of motivation in learning: a study of the phenomenon of differential motivational control of the utilization of habits. *J. genet. Psychol.,* **46,** 3–40.

LESSER, G. S., KRAWITZ, RHODA N., & PACKARD, RITA (1963) Experimental arousal of achievement motivation in adolescent girls. *J. abnorm. soc. Psychol.,* **66,** 59–66.

LEWIN, K. (1935) *A dynamic theory of personality.* New York: McGraw-Hill.

LEWIN, K. (1938) *The conceptual representation and the measurement of psychological forces.* Durham, North Carolina: Duke University Press.

LEWIN, K., DEMBO, TAMARA, FESTINGER, L., & SEARS, PAULINE S. (1944) Level of aspiration. In J. McV. HUNT, editor. *Personality and the behavior disorders.* New York: Ronald.

LEWIN, K. (1946) Behavior and development as a function of the total situation. In L. CARMICHAEL, editor. *Manual of child psychology.* New York: Wiley.

LEWIN, K. (1948) *Resolving social conflicts.* New York: Harper & Row, Publishers, Inc.

LEWIN, K. (1951) *Field theory in social science* (D. CARTWRIGHT, editor). New York: Harper & Row.

LISSNER, K. (1933) Die entspanning von be durfnissen durch ersatzhandlungen. *Psychol. Forsch.,* **18,** 218–250.

LITTIG, L. W. (1959) The effect of motivation on probability preferences and subjective probability. Unpublished doctoral thesis, University of Michigan.

LITTMAN, R. A. (1958) Motives, history and causes. In M. R. JONES, editor. *Nebraska symposium on motivation, 1958.* Lincoln: University of Nebraska Press.

LITWIN, G. H. (1958) Motives and expectancies as determinants of preference for degrees of risk. Unpublished honors thesis, University of Michigan.

LOGAN, F. A. (1954) A note on stimulus intensity dynamism. V. *Psychol. Rev.,* **61,** 77–80.

LOWELL, E. L. (1950) A methodological study of projectively measured achievement motivation. Unpublished master's thesis, Wesleyan University.

LOWELL, E. L. (1952) The effect of need for achievement on learning and speed of performance. *J. Psychol.,* **33,** 31–40.

LUCAS, J. D. (1952) The interactive effects of anxiety failure and interserial duplication. *Amer. J. Psychol.,* **65,** 59–66.

MACCORQUODALE, K., & MEEHL, P. E. (1953) Preliminary suggestions as to a formalization of expectancy theory. *Psychol. Rev.,* **60,** 55–63.

MACCORQUODALE, K., & MEEHL, P. E. (1954) Edward C. Tolman (Chap. 2). In W. K. ESTES *et al. Modern learning theory.* New York: Appleton-Century-Crofts.

MAHLER, V. (1933) Ersatzhandlungen verschiedenen realitatsgrades. *Psychol. Forsch.,* **18,** 26–89.

MAHONE, C. H. (1960) Fear of failure and unrealistic vocational aspiration. *J. abnorm. soc. Psychol.,* **60,** 253–261.

MANDLER, G., & SARASON, S. B. (1952) A study of anxiety and learning. *J. abnorm. soc. Psychol.,* **47,** 166–173.

MARKS, ROSE W. (1951) The effect of probability, desirability, and privilege on the stated expectations of children. *J. Pers.,* **19,** 332–351.

MARROW, A. J. (1938) Goal tension and recall. I. *J. gen. Psychol.,* **19,** 3–25. II. *J. gen. Psychol.,* **19,** 37–64.

MARTIRE, J. G. (1956) Relationships between the self concept and differences in the strength and generality of achievement motivation. *J. Pers.,* **24,** 364–375.

MCCLELLAND, D. C. (1951) Measuring motivation in phantasy: The achievement motive. In H. GUETZKOW, editor. *Groups, leadership, and men.* Pittsburgh: Carnegie Press.

MCCLELLAND, D. C. (1951) *Personality.* New York: William Sloane.

MCCLELLAND, D. C., editor (1955) *Studies in motivation.* New York: Appleton-Century-Crofts.

MCCLELLAND, D. C. (1958a) Methods of measuring human motivation. In J. W. ATKINSON, editor. *Motives in fantasy, action, and society.* Princeton: D. Van Nostrand Company, Inc.

MCCLELLAND, D. C. (1958b) Risk taking in children with high and low need for achievement. In J. W.

ATKINSON, editor. *Motives in fantasy, action, and society*. Princeton: D. Van Nostrand Company, Inc.

MCCLELLAND, D. C. (1961) *The achieving society*. Princeton: D. Van Nostrand Company, Inc.

MCCLELLAND, D. C., & ATKINSON, J. W. (1948) The projective expression of needs. I. The effects of different intensities of the hunger drive on perception. *J. Psychol.*, **25**, 205–222.

MCCLELLAND, D. C., ATKINSON, J. W., CLARK, R. W., & LOWELL, E. L. (1953) *The achievement motive*. New York: Appleton-Century-Crofts.

MCCLELLAND, D. C., BALDWIN, A. L., BRONFEN-BRENNER, U., & STRODTBECK, F. L. (1958) *Talent and society*. Princeton: D. Van Nostrand Company, Inc.

MCCLELLAND, D. C., CLARK, R. A., ROBY, T. B., & ATKINSON, J. W. (1949) The projective expression of needs. IV. The effect of the need for achievement on thematic apperception. *J. exp. Psychol.*, **39**, 242–255.

MCCLELLAND, D. C., & LIBERMAN, A. M. (1949) The effect of need for achievement on recognition of need-related words. *J. Pers.*, **18**, 236–251.

MCDOUGALL, W. (1908) *An introduction to social psychology*. London: Methuen & Co.

MCDOUGALL, W. (1923) *Outline of psychology*. New York: Scribner.

MEAD, MARGARET (1949) *Male and female*. New York: William Morrow.

MEEHL, P. E., & MACCORQUODALE, K. (1951a) A failure to find the Blodgett effect, and some secondary observations on drive conditioning. *J. comp. physiol. Psychol.*, **44**, 178–183.

MEEHL, P. E., & MACCORQUODALE, K. (1951b) Some methodological comments concerning expectancy theory. *Psychol. Rev.*, **58**, 230–233.

MERYMAN, J. J. (1952) Magnitude of startle responses as a function of hunger and fear. Unpublished master's thesis, State University of Iowa.

MILLER, D. R. (1951) Responses of psychiatric patients to threat of failure. *J. abnorm. soc. Psychol.*, **46**, 378–387.

MILLER, N. E. (1937) Reaction formation in rats: An experimental analog for a Freudian phenomenon. Film presented before the American Psychological Association at Minneapolis.

MILLER, N. E. (1944) Experimental studies of conflict. In J. McV. HUNT, editor. *Personality and the behavior disorders*. New York: Ronald.

MILLER, N. E. (1948) Studies of fear as an acquirable drive. I. Fear as motivation and fear-reduction as reinforcement in the learning of new responses. *J. exp. Psychol.*, **38**, 89–101.

MILLER, N. E. (1951) Comments on theoretical models illustrated by the development of a theory of conflict. *J. Pers.*, **20**, 82–100.

MILLER, N. E. (1957) Experiments on motivation: Studies combining psychological, physiological and pharmacological techniques. *Science*, **126**, 1271–1278.

MILLER, N. E. (1959) Liberalization of basic *S-R* concepts. In S. KOCH, editor. *Psychology: A study of science*. Vol. 2. New York: McGraw-Hill.

MILLER, N. E., & DOLLARD, J. (1941) *Social learning and imitation*. New Haven: Yale University Press.

MILLER, N. E., & KRAELING, DORIS (1952) Displacement: greater generalization of approach than avoidance in a generalized approach-avoidance. *J. exp. Psychol.*, **43**, 217–221.

MILLER, N. E., & MURRAY, E. J. (1952) Displacement and conflict: learnable drive as a basis for the steeper gradient of avoidance than of approach. *J. exp. Psychol.*, **43**, 227–231.

MILSTEIN, A. FREDA (1956) Ambition and defense against threat of failure. Unpublished doctoral dissertation, University of Michigan.

MONTGOMERY, K. C. (1953) Exploratory behavior as a function of "similarity" of stimulus situations. *J. comp. physiol. Psychol.*, **46**, 129–133.

MORGAN, C. T., & MURRAY, H. A. (1935) A method for investigating fantasies. *Arch. Neur. and Psychiat.*, **34**, 289–306.

MORGAN, C. T. (1943) *Physiological psychology*. New York: McGraw-Hill.

MORGAN, J. N. (1964) The achievement motive and economic behavior. *Econ. develop. and Cult. change*, **XII**, 243–267.

MORGAN, J. N., DAVID, M. H., COHEN, W. J., & BRAZER, H. E. (1962) *Income and welfare in the United States*. New York: McGraw-Hill.

MORUZZI, G., & MAGOUN, H. W. (1949) Brain stem reticular formation and activation of the EEG. *EEG clin. Neurophysiol.*, **1**, 455–473.

MOSS, F. A. (1924) Study of animal drives. *J. exp. Psychol.*, **7**, 165–185.

MOULTON, R. W. (1963) Effects of success and failure on level of aspiration: A test of Atkinson's risk-taking model. Prepublication manuscript, University of California, Berkeley.

MOULTON, R. W., RAPHELSON, A. C., KRISTOFFERSON, A. B., & ATKINSON, J. W. (1958) The achievement motive and perceptual sensitivity under two conditions of motive-arousal. In J. W. ATKINSON, editor. *Motives in fantasy, action, and society*. Princeton: D. Van Nostrand Company, Inc.

MOWRER, O. H. (1939) A stimulus-response analysis of anxiety and its role as a reinforcing agent. *Psychol. Rev.*, **46**, 553–565.

MOWRER, O. H. (1950) *Learning theory and personality dynamics*. New York: Ronald.

MOWRER, O. H. (1952) Motivation. In C. P. STONE & D. W. TAYLOR, editors. *Annual Review of Psychology*. Vol. 3. Stanford: Annual Reviews, Inc.

MURRAY, E. J., & MILLER, N. E. (1952) Displacement: Steeper gradient of generalization of avoidance than of approach with age of habit controlled. *J. exp. Psychol.*, **43**, 222–226.

MURRAY, H. A. (1933) The effect of fear upon estimates of the maliciousness of other personalities. *J. soc. Psychol.*, **4**, 310–329.

MURRAY, H. A. (1936) Techniques for a systematic investigation of fantasy. *J. Psychol.*, **3**, 115–143.

MURRAY, H. A. (1938) *Explorations in personality.* New York: Oxford University Press.

NISSEN, H. W., & ELDER, J. H. (1935) The influence of amount of incentive on delayed response performance of chimpanzees. *J. genet. Psychol.*, **47**, 49–72.

NOWLIS, H. H. (1941) The influence of success and failure on the resumption of an interrupted task. *J. exp. Psychol.*, **23**, 304–325.

O'CONNOR, PATRICIA (1960) The representation of the motive to avoid failure in thematic apperception. Unpublished doctoral thesis, University of Michigan.

OLDS, J. (1955) A physiological study of reward. In D. C. MCCLELLAND, editor. *Studies in motivation.* New York: Appleton-Century-Crofts.

OLDS, J. (1958) Self stimulation of the brain: Its use to study local effects of hunger, sex, and drugs. *Science*, **127**, 315–324.

OLDS, J., & MILNER, P. (1954) Positive reinforcement produced by electrical stimulation of septal area and other regions of rat brain. *J. comp. physiol. Psychol.*, **47**, 419–427.

OVSIANKINA, M. (1928) Die wiederaufnahme unterbrochener handlungen. *Psychol. Forsch.*, **11**, 302–379.

PAVLOV, I. P. (1927) *Conditioned reflexes.* Oxford, England: Clarendon Press.

PEIRCE, C. S. (1877) Illustrations of the logic of science. First paper—The fixation of belief. *The Popular Science Monthly*, **12**, 1–15.

PERIN, C. T. (1942) Behavior potentially as a joint function of the amount of training and the degree of hunger at the time of extinction. *J. exp. Psychol.*, **30**, 93–113.

POSTMAN, L. (1953) Comments on papers by Professors Brown and Harlow. In *Current theory and research in motivation: A symposium.* Lincoln: University of Nebraska Press.

POTTHARST, B. C. (1955) The achievement motive and level of aspiration after experimentally induced success and failure. Unpublished doctoral dissertation, University of Michigan.

PRIBRAM, K. H. (1960) A review of theory in physiological psychology. In P. R. FARNSWORTH & Q. MCNEMAR, editors. *Annual Review of Psychology*, **11**. Palo Alto: Annual Reviews, Inc.

RAPHELSON, A. C. (1956) Imaginative and direct verbal measures of anxiety related to physiological reactions in the competitive achievement situation. Unpublished doctoral dissertation, University of Michigan.

RAPHELSON, A. C. (1957) The relationship between imaginative, direct, verbal, and physiological measures of anxiety in an achievement situation. *J. abnorm. soc. Psychol.*, **54**, 13–18.

REITMAN, W. R. (1960) Motivational induction and the behavioral correlates of the achievement and affiliation motives. *J. abnorm. soc. Psychol.*, **60**, 8–13.

RICCIUTI, H. N., & CLARK, R. A. (1954) A comparison of need-achievement stories written by experimentally "relaxed" and "achievement-oriented" subjects: Effects obtained with new pictures and revised scoring categories. Princeton: Educational Testing Service.

RICHTER, C. P. (1922) A behavioristic study of the activity of the rat. *Comp. Psychol. Monog.*, **1**, #2.

RICHTER, C. P. (1927) Animal behavior and internal drives. *Quart. rev. Biol.*, **2**, 307–343.

RITCHIE, B. F. (1951) Can reinforcement theory account for avoidance? *Psychol. Rev.*, **58**, 382–386.

ROSEN, B. (1955) The achievement syndrome. *Amer. soc. Rev.*, **21**, 203–211.

ROSEN, B., & D'ANDRADE, R. C. (1959) The psychosocial origins of achievement motivation. *Sociometry*, **22**, 185–218.

ROSEN, B. C. (1959a) Race, ethnicity and the achievement syndrome. *Amer. Sociol. Rev.*, **24**, 47–60.

ROSENBAUM, G. (1950) Stimulus generalization as a function of clinical and experimentally induced anxiety. Unpublished doctoral dissertation, State University of Iowa.

ROSENZWEIG, S. (1943) An experimental study of "repression" with special reference to need-persistive and ego-defensive reactions to frustration. *J. exp. Psychol.*, **32**, 64–74.

ROTTER, J. B. (1943) Level of aspiration as a method of studying personality. III. Group validity studies. *Charact. and Pers.*, **11**, 254–274.

ROTTER, J. B. (1954) *Social learning and clinical psychology.* New York: Prentice-Hall.

ROTTER, J. B. (1955) The role of the psychological situation in determining the direction of human behavior. In M. R. JONES, editor. *Nebraska symposium on motivation, 1955.* Lincoln: University of Nebraska Press.

SANFORD, R. N. (1936) The effects of abstinence from food upon imaginal processes: A preliminary experiment. *J. Psychol.*, **2**, 129–136.

SANFORD, R. N. (1937) The effects of abstinence from food upon imaginal processes: A further experiment. *J. Psychol.*, **3**, 145–159.

SARASON, S. (1949) *Psychological problems in mental deficiency.* New York: Harper & Row.

SARASON, S. B., & MANDLER, G. (1952) Some correlates of test anxiety. *J. abnorm. soc. Psychol.*, **47**, 810–817.

SARASON, S. B., MANDLER, G., & CRAIGHILL, P. G. (1952) The effect of differential instructions on anxiety and learning. *J. abnorm. soc. Psychol.*, **47**, 561–565.

SCOTT, W. A. (1956) The avoidance of threatening material in imaginative behavior. *J. abnorm. soc. Psychol.*, **52**, 338–346.

SEARS, PAULINE S. (1940) Level of aspiration in academically successful and unsuccessful children. *J. abnorm. soc. Psychol.*, **35**, 498–536.

SEARS, R. R. (1936) Experimental studies of projection. I. Attribution of traits. *J. soc. Psychol.*, **7**, 151–163.

SEARS, R. R. (1937) Initiation of the repression sequence by experienced failure. *J. exp. Psychol.*, **20**, 570–580.

SEARS, R. R. (1942) *Success and failure: A study of motility.* New York: McGraw-Hill.

SELYE, H. (1958) What makes basic research basic? *Adventures of the mind, #19. Saturday Evening Post*, **231:30**, pp. 30, 78–80.

SHEFFIELD, F. D., & CAMPBELL, B. A. (1954) The role of experience in the "spontaneous" activity of hungry rats. *J. comp. physiol. Psychol.*, **47**, 97–100.

SHEFFIELD, F. D., & ROBY, T. B. (1950) Reward value of a non nutritive sweet taste. *J. comp. physiol. Psychol.*, **43**, 471–481.

SHEFFIELD, F. D., ROBY, T. B., & CAMPBELL, B. A. (1954) Drive reduction versus consummatory behavior as determinants of reinforcement. *J. comp. physiol. Psychol.*, **47**, 349–354.

SHEFFIELD, F. D., WULFF, J. J., & BACKER, R. (1951) Reward value of copulation without sex drive reduction. *J. comp. physiol. Psychol.*, **44**, 3–8.

SHIPLEY, T. E., & VEROFF, J. (1952) A projective measure of need affiliation. *J. exp. Psychol.*, **43**, 349–356.

SIMMONS, R. (1924) The relative effectiveness of certain incentives in animal learning. *Comp. Psychol. Monog.*, **2**, 1–79.

SKINNER, B. F. (1938) *The behavior of organisms.* New York: Appleton-Century-Crofts.

SMITH, C. P. (1961) Situational determinants of the expression of achievement motivation in thematic apperception. Unpublished doctoral thesis, University of Michigan.

SOLOMON, R. L., & BRUSH, E. S. (1956) Experimentally derived conceptions of anxiety and aversion. In M. R. JONES, editor. *Nebraska symposium on motivation, 1956.* Lincoln: University of Nebraska Press.

SOLOMON, R. L., KAMIN, L. J., & WYNNE, L. C. (1953) Traumatic avoidance learning: The outcomes of several extinction procedures with dogs. *J. abnorm. soc. Psychol.*, **48**, 291–302.

SOLOMON, R. L., & WYNNE, L. C. (1953) Traumatic avoidance learning: Acquisition in normal dogs. *Psychol. Monog.*, **67**, #4.

SOLOMON, R. L., & WYNNE, L. C. (1954) Traumatic avoidance learning: The principles of anxiety conservation and partial irreversibility. *Psychol. Rev.*, **61**, 353–385.

SPENCE, K. W. (1937) The differential response in animals to stimuli varying within a single dimension. *Psychol. Rev.*, **44**, 430–444.

SPENCE, K. W. (1956) *Behavior theory and conditioning.* New Haven: Yale University Press.

SPENCE, K. W. (1958) A theory of emotionally based drive (*D*) and its relation to performance in simple learning situations. *Am. Psychologist*, **13**, 131–141.

SPENCE, K. W., BERGMANN, G., & LIPPITT, R. (1950) A study of simple learning under irrelevant motivational-reward conditions. *J. exp. Psychol.*, **40**, 539–551.

SPENCE, K. W., FARBER, I. E., & TAYLOR, ELAINE (1954) The relation of electric shock and anxiety to level of performance in eyelid conditioning. *J. exp. Psychol.*, **48**, 404–408.

SPIELBERGER, C. D. (1962) The effects of manifest anxiety on the academic achievement of college students. *Mental Hygiene*, **46**, 420–426.

SPIELBERGER, C. D., & KATZENMEYER, W. C. (1959) Manifest anxiety, intelligence, and college grades. *J. consult. Psychol.*, **23**, 278.

STRODTBECK, F. L. (1958a) Family interaction, values and achievement. In D. C. MCCLELLAND *et al. Talent and society.* Princeton: D. Van Nostrand Company, Inc.

STRODTBECK, F. L. (1958b) Jewish and Italian immigration and subsequent status mobility. In D. C. MCCLELLAND *et al. Talent and society.* Princeton: D. Van Nostrand Company, Inc.

STRODTBECK, F. L., MCDONALD, M. R., & ROSEN, B. (1957) Evaluation of occupations: A reflection of Jewish and Italian mobility differences. *Amer. soc. Rev.*, **22**, 546–553.

TAYLOR, JANET A. (1951) The relationship of anxiety to the conditioned eyelid response. *J. exp. Psychol.*, **41**, 81–92.

TAYLOR, JANET A. (1953) A personality scale of manifest anxiety. *J. abnorm. soc. Psychol.*, **48**, 285–290.

TAYLOR, JANET A. (1956) Drive theory and manifest anxiety. *Psychol. Bull.*, **53**, #4, 303–320.

TAYLOR, JANET A., & SPENCE, K. W. (1952) The relationship of anxiety level to performance in serial learning. *J. exp. Psychol.*, **44**, 61–64.

THORNDIKE, E. L. (1911) *Animal intelligence*. New York: Macmillan.

THORNDIKE, E. L. (1932) *The fundamentals of learning*. New York: Teachers College, Columbia University.

THRALL, R. M., COOMBS, C. H., & DAVIS, R. L. (1954) *Decision processes*. New York: Wiley.

TOLMAN, E. C. (1922) Can instincts be given up in psychology? *J. abnorm. soc. Psychol.*, **17**, 139–152.

TOLMAN, E. C. (1923) A behavioristic account of the emotions. *Psychol. Rev.*, **30**, 217–227.

TOLMAN, E. C. (1925a) Behaviorism and purpose. *J. Phil.*, **22**, 36–41.

TOLMAN, E. C. (1925b) Purpose and cognition: The determiners of animal learning. *Psychol. Rev.*, **32**, 285–297.

TOLMAN, E. C. (1926) A behavioristic theory of ideas. *Psychol. Rev.*, **33**, 352–369.

TOLMAN, E. C. (1932) *Purposive behavior in animals and men*. New York: Century Co. By permission of the University of California Press.

TOLMAN, E. C. (1936) Operational behaviorism and current trends in psychology. Proc. 25th Anniv. Inauguration Graduate Studies, Los Angeles: University of Southern California, 89–103.

TOLMAN, E. C. (1938) The determiners of behavior at a choice point. *Psychol. Rev.*, **45**, 1–41.

TOLMAN, E. C. (1951) *Behavior and psychological man*. Berkeley: University of California Press.

TOLMAN, E. C. (1951) *Collected papers in psychology*. Berkeley: University of California Press.

TOLMAN, E. C. (1959) Principles of purposive behavior. In S. KOCH, editor. *Psychology: A study of a science*. Vol. 2. New York: McGraw-Hill.

TOLMAN, E. C., & HONZIK, C. H. (1930a) Degrees of hunger, reward and non-reward, and maze learning in rats. Berkeley: *University of California Publ. Psychol.*, **4**, #16, 246.

TOLMAN, E. C., & HONZIK, C. H. (1930b) Introduction and removal of reward, and maze performance in rats. Berkeley: *University of California Publ. Psychol.*, **4**, #19, 267.

VEROFF, J. (1957) Development and validation of a projective measure of power motivation. *J. abnorm. soc. Psychol.*, **54**, 1–8.

VEROFF, J. (1960) Relationships of demographic variables to strength of *n* Achievement. Unpublished results. Survey Research Center, University of Michigan.

VEROFF, J. (1961) Thematic apperception in a nationwide sample survey. In J. KAGAN and G. S. LESSER, editors. *Contemporary issues in thematic apperceptive methods*. Springfield: Charles C. Thomas.

VEROFF, J., ATKINSON, J., FELD, SHEILA, & GURIN, G. (1960) The use of thematic appercep-

tion to assess motivation in a nationwide interview study. *Psychol. Monog.*, **74**, Whole No. 499.

VEROFF, J., WILCOX, SUE, & ATKINSON, J. W. (1953) The achievement motive in high school and college age women. *J. abnorm. soc. Psychol.*, **48**, 108–119.

VITZ, P. C. (1957) The relation of levels of aspiration to *n* Achievement, fear of failure, incentives and expectancies. Unpublished honors thesis, University of Michigan.

VON NEUMANN, J., & MORGENSTERN, O. (1944) *Theory of games and economic behavior*. Princeton: Princeton University Press.

WALKER, E. L., & ATKINSON, J. W., with the collaboration of VEROFF, J., BIRNEY, R., DEMBER, W., & MOULTON, R. (1958) In J. W. ATKINSON, editor. *Motives in fantasy, action, and society*. Princeton: D. Van Nostrand Company, Inc.

WARDEN, C. J. (1931) *Animal motivation*. New York: Columbia University Press.

WATSON, J. B. (1919) *Psychology, from the standpoint of a behaviorist*. Philadelphia: Lippincott.

*Webster's Seventh New Collegiate Dictionary*. (1963) Springfield, Mass: Merriam.

WENDT, H. W. (1955) Motivation, effort, and performance. In D. C. MCCLELLAND, editor. *Studies in motivation*. New York: Appleton-Century-Crofts.

WILLIAMS, S. B. (1938) Resistance to extinction as a function of the number of reinforcements. *J. exp. Psychol.*, **23**, 506–522.

WILLIAMS, K. A. (1929) The reward value of a conditioned stimulus. *Univ. Calif. Publ. Psychol.*, **4**, 31–55.

WINTERBOTTOM, MARIAN R. (1953) The relation of childhood training in independence to achievement motivation. Unpublished doctoral dissertation, University of Michigan.

WINTERBOTTOM, MARIAN R. (1958) The relation of need for achievement to learning experiences in independence and mastery. In J. W. ATKINSON, editor. *Motives in fantasy, action, and society*. Princeton: D. Van Nostrand Company, Inc.

WOLFE, J. B. (1936) Effectiveness of token-rewards for chimpanzees. *Comp. Psychol. Monog.*, **12**, #5.

WOODWORTH, R. S. (1918) *Dynamic psychology*. New York: Columbia University Press.

WOODWORTH, R. S. (1921) *Psychology: A study of mental life*. New York: Holt, Rinehart and Winston.

WOODWORTH, R. S. *Adjustment and mastery*. New York: Century Co.

YOUNG, P. T. (1949) Food-seeking drive, affective process, and learning. *Psychol. Rev.*, **56**, 98–121.

YOUNG, P. T. (1961) *Motivation and emotion: A survey of the determinants of human and animal activity*. New York: Wiley.

ZEAMAN, D. (1949) Response latency as a function of the amount of reinforcement. *J. exp. Psychol.*, **39**, 466–483.

ZEIGARNIK, B. (1927) Das Behalten erledigter und unerledigter Handlungen. *Psychol. Forsch.*, **9**, 1–85. Translated and condensed as "On finished and unfinished tasks" in W. D. ELLIS (1938) *A source book of gestalt psychology.* New York: Harcourt, Brace and World, 300–314.

ZENER, K., & McCURDY, H. G. (1939) Analysis of motivational factors in conditioned behavior. I. The differential effect of changes in hunger upon conditioned, unconditioned, and spontaneous salivary secretion. *J. Psychol.*, **8**, 321–350.

# Name Index

# Subject Index

Ability, as index of expectancy of success, 267
Ability grouping in schools, 255–256
Academic performance, as function of ability grouping and personality, 255–256
Achievement motivation, anticipatory character of, 228–229
  assumed persistence of, 308–309
  effect on thematic apperception, 224–227
  evidence related to theory, 248–266
  in various social groups, 258
  in women, 226–227
  produced by ability grouping, 255–256
  resultant, 246–247
  review of, 267–268
  situational determinants of, 241
  social origins and consequences of, 253–254
  symptoms of, 226
  theory of, 242 ff
  translated into S-R language, 281–282
  unexplained trends in studies of, 249–250
Achievement motive (n Achievement), 230, 233
  and ability grouping in schools, 255–256
  and examination performance, 248–250
  and expectancy of success, 267
  and performance level, 231–238
  and persistence, 248–250, 262–266
  and probability preferences in gambling, 251
  and recall of interrupted tasks, 232–233
  and risk-preference, 248–252
  and social mobility, 253
  and Test Anxiety, 241
  and vocational aspiration, 251–252
  conception of, 241
  insatiability of, 259
Achievement Orientation, effect on thematic apperception, 225–226
  and Zeigarnik effect, 232–235
Achievement-oriented behavior, defined, 240–241
  inconsistencies in studies of, 237
  pathology of, 260–266
Action, conceived as reaction, 152
  Hull's conception of neonate, 164
  James' "springs of," 30
  resultant of conflict, 28
Action tendency, reformulated conception of, 311 ff
Active organism, assumption of, 298, 314
  initial premise of, 301
Activity, cyclical changes in, 184
  studies of, 136
Activity in goal region, interruption of, 307
Activity in progress, 299 ff
  as determinant of subsequent activity, 302–303
Activity level, determinants of, 195–196
  theoretical interpretation of Birch et al., 198–200

Activity wheel, 136
Affective arousal, 185, 197
Affiliative motivation, effect on performance of, 235–237
  effect on thematic apperception, 227
Ahistorical problem, 146–147
Alcohol, effect on anxiety, 182
  effect on thematic apperception, 228
American Council of Education Examination, 254
Anamnesis, 105
Anger, effect on thematic apperception, 227
  Tolman's definition, 130–131
*Animal Intelligence*, 112, 116
*Animal Motivation Studies*, 136
Annoying state of affairs, Thorndike definition of, 116
Anthropomorphism, 108
Anticipatory emotional reaction (re), in Expectancy × Value theory, 285–292
Anticipatory goal reaction (see also Incentive motivation), 152–153, 156, 158, 161, 189, 190, 192
  as physical mechanism of drive, 193, 198–200, 282–283
  functional properties of, 154–156
  in achievement-oriented activity, 281–282
  in latent learning studies, 189–192
  in TAT stories, 228–229
  individual differences in vigor of, 280–283
  motivational property of, 192
  persistence of, 311
  related to Pavlovian conditioning, 192
  related to valence and utility, 280–283
  vigor of, 192–197
Anticipated threats, theoretical treatment of, 290–291
Anxiety, about failure, 234, 244–247, 260–261, 268, 289
  conceived as symptom, 289–290
  conceived as source of inhibition, 244–246
  early and later conception of Freud, 60–61
  effect on persistence, 262–266
  in Expectancy × Value theory, 285–292
  in achievement-oriented situation, 241
  in traumatic avoidance training, 288–290
  Mowrer's (1939) hypothesis, 175–176
  study of individual differences in, 214–220
Anxiety-produced decrement in performance, 241
  Atkinson's views, 244–247, 268
  Mandler-Sarason's view, 218–219
  Taylor-Spence's view, 215–217
Anxiety studies, interpretation of, 221
Aphysiological orientation, 276
Approach-Avoidance conflict, 180 ff
  basic assumptions by Miller, 180
  displacement, 181–182
  effect of alcohol on, 182
  experimental evidence, 181–182
  in achievement situations, 246–247
  repression, 182

38852